ORGANISATIONAL BEHAVIOUR

(Text and Cases)

For the Students of MBA, PGDBM, M. Com. & Other Management Courses

S S KHANKA

MCom (Gold Medallist), PhD

Professor (HR)

University School of Management & Entrepreneurship

Delhi Technological University (Formerly Delhi College of Engineering)

East Delhi Campus, Delhi

and

National Trainer on Ethics and Values in Public Governance

Recognised by the Department of Personnel and Training, Government of India

in Collaboration with the United Nations Development Programme (UNDP)

S Chand And Company Limited

(ISO 9001 Certified Company)

S Chand And Company Limited

(ISO 9001 Certified Company)

Head Office: D-92, Sector–2, Noida – 201301, U.P. (India), Ph. 91-120-4682700

Registered Office: A-27, 2nd Floor, Mohan Co-operative Industrial Estate, New Delhi – 110 044, Phone: 011-49731800

www.schandpublishing.com; e-mail: info@schandpublishing.com

Marketing Offices:

Chennai	:	Ph: 23632120; chennai@schandpublishing.com
Guwahati	:	Ph: 2738811, 2735640; guwahati@schandpublishing.com
Hyderabad	:	Ph: 40186018; hyderabad@schandpublishing.com
Jalandhar	:	Ph: 4645630; jalandhar@schandpublishing.com
Kolkata	:	Ph: 23357458, 23353914; kolkata@schandpublishing.com
Lucknow	:	Ph: 4003633; lucknow@schandpublishing.com
Mumbai	:	Ph: 25000297; mumbai@schandpublishing.com
Patna	:	Ph: 2260011; patna@schandpublishing.com

First Edition 2002
Subsequent Editions and Reprints 2002, 2004, 2005, 2006, 2007
Revised Edition 2009
Reprints 2010, 2011, 2012, 2013, 2014, 2015, 2016, 2018, 2019, 2020 (Twice), 2021 (Twice), 2022 (Thrice)

Reprint 2023

ISBN: 978-81-219-2014-8 **Product Code:** H8ORB60BMGT10ENAD09O

PRINTED IN INDIA

By Vikas Publishing House Private Limited, Plot 20/4, Site-IV, Industrial Area Sahibabad, Ghaziabad – 201 010 and Published by S Chand And Company Limited, A-27, 2nd Floor, Mohan Co-operative Industrial Estate, New Delhi – 110 044.

PREFACE TO THE FOURTH EDITION

Change in organisational context is ephemeral and, in turn, the subject matter of organisational behaviour. Since the publication of the last edition (Third Edition) of my book "Organisational Behaviour (OB).", in 2004, the emergence of some new topics in the subject of organisational behaviour alongwith constructive feedback received from the discernible readers, and my own learning and teaching experience of organisational behaviour over the period have necessitated the revision of the book. Accordingly, while some new chapters have been added to the present edition, a number of existing chapters have been enlarged, revised, and rehashed. The following six new chapters have been added to the present edition:

- **Organicational Citizenship Behaviour (Chapter 9)**
- **Emotions and Moods (Chapter 10)**
- **Transactional Analysis (Chapter 11)**
- **Morale (Chapter 14)**
- **Team Building (Chapter 16)**
- **Organisational Climate (Chapter 26)**

The major additions and revisions made in different chapters include attitude change, developing values, determinants, and theories of job satisfaction, and organisational commitment in the chapter 7: 'Attitudes, Values, and Job Satisfaction' and negotiations in the chapter 17: 'Organisational Conflict'. A number of experiential activities have also been added at the end of some chapters to make the learning more and more practice-oriented. Besides, an OB quotation is given at the beginning of the each chapter to introduce the theme of the chapter. The chapter-end summary is also restructured in the light of learning objectives given in the beginning of the chapter. The important key terms used in the additions made in the text have also been incorporated in the Glossary given at the end of the book.

The above additions and enlargements make the book more comprehensive and contemporaneous. It is hoped that the discernible readers - students, teachers, and management practitioners - will find this revised edition more rewarding and useful. No book of this nature is complete and perfect once for all times. Hence, constructive suggestions from the readers will be highly appreciated and acknowledged for the further improvement of the book in its subsequent editions.

Faridabad

Dated 10-10-2008 **Vijaya Dashmi** **S. S. Khanka**

PREFACE TO THE FIRST EDITION

Organisations are made of the people, by the people and for the people. Therefore, organisational effectiveness depends on the behaviour and performance of the people constituting organisations. That is why human behaviour at work, popularly known as **'organisational behaviour'** has become a subject of much interest and concern. Every individual is unique and his/her behaviour is highly unpredictable and complex. Nonetheless, knowing why people behave as they behave at work sharpens the mind, increases vision, and offers an array of tools and techniques to choose from when faced with the problem of resolving a difficult situation. Moreover, how others resolved the problem serves as a doubling guidance and help.

The books on Organisational Behaviour are so far written mainly by the foreign authors in the foreign context. As these books lack the Indian flavour, the students find it difficult to comprehend the concepts of Organisational Behaviour without real-life examples from the Indian organisations. It is against this background, I have made a modest attempt to remedy this situation by providing real-life examples from the Indian context. I do not claim any originality of ideas presented on the subject. At best, I have endeavoured to interpret the vast knowledge generated by others in my own sense, style, and easy to understand language. In long and short, I have tried to combine theory and experiential vignettes to rehash the existing knowledge on the subject.

There is a presumptuousness in trying to cover all aspects of organisational behaviour in three-hundred odd pages. This book is divided into four parts consisting of 31 chapters. Part I, in its 3 chapters, provides a background for the study of organisational behaviour. Knowing that organisations are run by individuals, Part II spreading over 11 chapters, is devoted to discuss the individual perspective like personality, perception, learning attitude, values, and job satisfaction. That the behaviour of a person as an individual varies from his or her behaviour as a member of a group serves as a background for Part III that focuses on aspects of group dynamics such as group conflict, job frustration, job stress, communication, leadership, and power and politics. As organisation itself also is affected by the human behaviour at work, the last Part–IV consisting of 9 chapters deals with dynamics of organisation. The aspects covered are, organisational structure, theory, climate, culture, change and development, effectiveness, quality of work life (QWL).

I must confess that this is not my solitary activity but a rehash of the existing knowledge on organisational behaviour generated by several organisational theorists and behavioural scientists whose works I have read, learnt from and drawn upon for more than two decades. I do not know how much I owe to them. I could do no more than to express my sincere indebtedness to them.

I am ever beholden to my erudite supervisor-teacher Prof. T.S. Papola, Ex- Head, Mountain Enterprise and Infrastructure Division, International Centre for

Integrated Mountain Development (ICIMOD), Kathmandu, Nepal, who switched on the lightbulb in my head to keep on working. Whatever little academic work I could do so far is but due to his teachings and goadings.

Thanking one's own family members seems a ritualistic, but it is not so for my family where all three members agreed to compromise their interests by granting me station leave to stay away from them with the fetch hope that I shall do some good work which fetch a psychic reward for them. Now, this is the time when, as a mark of my appreciation to my beloved wife **Geetu,** and loving sons **Abhineet** and **Abhinav,** I dedicate this work to them.

Last but not the least my special thanks are due to Shri Ravindra Kumar Gupta, Managing Director, S. Chand & Company Ltd., whose sincere efforts have brought this book in such an excellent getup.

I hope this book would serve as a useful text for the students of MBA, M. Com., and other diploma courses in management. It would also be useful to practising managers who want to effectively manage human behaviour at work.

Feedback for further improvement in the book are most welcome and will be gratefully acknowledged.

Tezpur **S.S. KHANKA**
July 11, 2003

CONTENTS

PART ONE
FOUNDATION FOR ORGANISATIONAL BEHAVIOUR (OB)

PART TWO
INDIVIDUAL PERSPECTIVE

PART THREE
GROUP DYNAMICS

PART FOUR
DYNAMICS OF ORGANISATION

PART ONE

FOUNDATION FOR ORGANISATIONAL BEHAVIOUR

- **Introduction to Organisational Behaviour**
- **Organisational Behaviour in Historical Perspective**
- **Research in Organisational Behaviour**

1

INTRODUCTION TO ORGANISATIONAL BEHAVIOUR

"There is no animal more difficult to understand than man".

– Leonardo Salviati

"I am not smart. I try to observe. Millions saw the apple fall, Newton was the one who asked why".

– B. Baruch

Learning Objectives

After studying this chapter, you should be able to:

- **Define** organisational behaviour.
- **Identify** the key elements, nature and scope of organisational behaviour.
- **Describe** why managers require a knowledge of organisational behaviour.
- **List** the discipline that contribute the understanding of O.B.
- **Provide** an overview of the major challenges faced by today's management.
- **Delineate** the process organisational behaviour follows.
- **Present** models of organisational behaviour in use.

All organisations, be these business, educational or government, are social systems. These are run by people. Take a business/industrial organisation, for example. It is a combination of men, money, machinery, material and management, commonly known as five Ms. In fact, it is management, *i.e.* people who actually take care of other four Ms. Then, it means that the functioning of an organisation depends upon how people work or behave in the organisation.

Human behaviour is caused and is highly unpredictable also. Why people behave as they behave has, therefore, been a subject of much interest and concern since our earliest years. Therefore, understanding human behaviour has assumed great significance for the managers for managing people effectively. In other words, knowledge about why people behave as they behave helps managers extract maximum results from people's efforts for accomplishing organisational goals in an effective manner. For this, managers need to seek answers mainly to these two questions : (*i*) Why people behave as they behave or why people do what they do at work in organisations? and (*ii*) What influences people's behaviour at work? The same constitute the subject matter of **organisational behaviour** (often abbreviated as OB). This chapter being the first one, accordingly, presents an introduction to organisational behaviour *i.e.* OB.

We shall begin with the definition of OB.

1.1 DEFINITIONS

OB is concerned with the study of human behaviour at work. In other words, OB is the study and application of knowledge about how people as individuals and as groups behave or act in organisations. Different behavioural scientists have defined OB differently. A few important definitions on OB are given here.

According to **Luthans**[1] "OB is directly concerned with the understanding, prediction, and control of human behaviour in organisations."

Davis and **Newstrom**[2] have defined OB as "the study and application of knowledge how people act or behave within organisation. It is a human tool for human benefit. It applies broadly to the behaviour of people in all types of organisations such as business, government, schools and service organisations."

In the opinion of **Robbins**[3], "OB is a field of study that investigates the impact that individuals, groups, and structure have on behaviour within organisations for the purpose of applying such knowledge towards improving an organisation's effectiveness."

The above definitions are comprehensive ones as these contain all characteristics of OB. In brief, what OB studies is three determinants of behaviour in organisations : **individuals**, **groups**, and **structure**.

To sum up, OB is concerned with the study of how and what people act in organisations and also how their acts affect the performance of the organisation. It also applies the knowledge gained about individuals, groups and the effect of structure on human behaviour in order to make organisations work more effectively.

1.2 KEY ELEMENTS OF OB

Like all other disciplines/subjects, OB is also based on certain key elements also called '*fundamental concepts* or *assumptions*'. There are four key elements in OB. These are: people, structure, technology, and the environment. Each of these four elements of OB are now discussed briefly.

People

As mentioned earlier, organisations are run by people. People consist of individuals and groups. Though people have much in common (they become happy by having gains and sad by losing something valuable), yet they differ from each other. One can find glaring differences in people's trait, intelligence, personality or any such trait. It is, in fact, individual differences the manager cannot adopt one formula or standard across the board for dealing with employees. Instead, manager has to treat employees with individual differences differently. It is because of individual differences, the subject matter of OB begins with individual.

An individual joins organisation alongwith his/her social background, likes and dislikes, pride and prejudices. What is to say is that an individual's family life cannot be separated from organisational life. Therefore, OB studies an individual as a whole person.

Human behaviour is always caused. Behaviour is directed towards some goals. There is always a cause behind every human behaviour or act. For example, when a worker is absent from work, there is a cause behind. The manager must know the cause to solve the problem. People are living, thinking, feeling beings. The manager, therefore, needs to treat them with human dignity, not just like an economic tool.

Structure

Organisations are social systems. There are two types of social systems that exist side by side in an organisation. One is the **formal** and other is the **informal** social system. The formal relationship of people in organisations is called structure. Different jobs are required to accomplish the organisational goals and objectives. For example, there are managers and employees, accountants and assemblers. These all people performing different jobs at different levels have to be related in some structural way so that their work can be effectively coordinated.

That people need organisations and organisations also need people also comes under the purview of OB. It means that OB is based on mutuality of interest. It is mutual interest that unites people and organisation to go side by side for accomplishing individual and organisational goals.

Technology

Technology provides the resources with which people work and also affects the tasks that they perform. The great benefit of technology is that it allows people to do more and better work. But, it also restricts people from doing things in various ways. In fact, it has costs as well as benefits.

Environment

All organisations operate within a given internal and external environment.[4] In fact, no organisation exists alone. An organisation is a part of a larger system that contains other factors or elements, such as a government, the family, and other organisations. All of these mutually influence one another in a complex way. Thus, organisations are influenced by the external environment. Environment, thus, affects people by influencing their attitudes, working conditions, etc. It will not be less than correct to mention that an organisation is the effect for which environment is the cause. Hence, environment also becomes a key element in the study of OB.

1.3 NATURE AND SCOPE

Organisational behaviour has emerged as a separate field of study. The nature it has acquired by now is identified as follows:

1. **A Separate Field of Study and Not a Discipline only**: By definition, a discipline is an accepted science that is based on a theoretical foundation. But, OB has a multi-interdisciplinary orientation and is, thus, not based on a specific theoretical background. Therefore, it is better reasonable to call OB as a separate field of study rather than a discipline only.

2. **An Interdisciplinary Approach:** OB is essentially an interdisciplinary approach to study human behaviour at work. It tries to integrate the relevant knowledge drawn

from related disciplines like psychology, sociology, and anthropology to make them applicable for studying and analysing organisational behaviour.

3. **An Applied Science:** The very nature of OB is applied. What OB basically does is the application of various researches to solve the organisational problems related to human behaviour. The basic line of difference between pure science and OB is that while the former concentrates on fundamental researches, the latter concentrates on applied researches. As OB involves both applied research and its application in organisational analysis, hence, OB can be called both science as well as art.

4. **A Normative Science:** OB is a normative science also. While the positive science discusses only cause effect relationship, OB prescribes how the findings of applied researches can be applied to socially accepted organisational goals. Thus, OB deals with what is accepted by individuals and society engaged in an organisation. Yes, it is not that OB is not normative at all. In fact, OB is normative as well that is well underscored by the proliferation of management theories.

5. **A Humanistic and Optimistic Approach:** OB applies humanistic approach towards people working in the organisation. It treats people as thinking, feeling human beings. OB is based on the belief that people have an innate desire to be independent, creative, and productive. It also realizes that people working in the organisation can and will actualise these potentials if they are given proper conditions and environment. As stated earlier, environment affects performance of workers working in an organisation.

6. **A Total System Approach:** The systems approach is one that integrates all the variables affecting organisational functioning. The systems approach has been developed by the behavioural scientists to analyse human behaviour in view of his/her socio-psychological framework. Man's socio-psychological framework makes him a complex one and the systems approach tries to study his/her complexity and find solution to it.

Scope of OB

As mentioned earlier, OB is the study of human behaviour at work in organisations. Accordingly, the scope of OB includes the study of individuals, groups and organisation/structure. Let us briefly reflect on what aspects each of these three cover.

Individuals: Organisations are the associations of individuals. Individuals differ in many respects. The study of individuals, therefore, includes aspects such as personality, perception, attitudes, values, job satisfaction, learning and motivation.

Groups of Individuals: Groups include aspects such as group dynamics, group conflicts, communication, leadership, power and politics, and the like.

Organisation/Structure: The study of organisation/structure includes aspects such as formation of organisational structure, culture and change and development.

In nutshell, OB studies how organisations influence people or how people influence organisations.

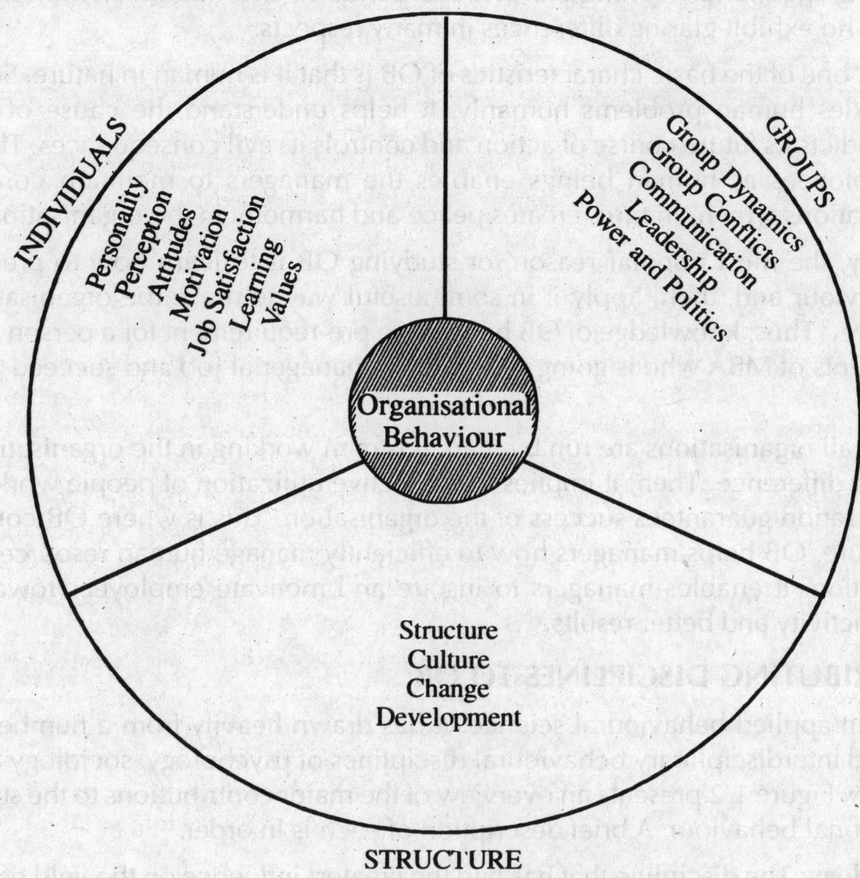

Figure 1.1. Scope of OB

The scope of OB is depicted in the following Figure 1.1.

1.4 NEED FOR STUDYING ORGANISATIONAL BEHAVIOUR

As mentioned earlier also, organisational behaviour is the study of people at work in organisations. And we study organisations because we spend our lives interacting with them. If all the world is a stage, it is a stage filled with organisations. Regardless of the part we play as a student, employee, manager or customer, we play our roles/parts on an organisational stage. By acting our parts, we influence organisations and organisations also influence us. The same underlines the need for studying OB.

The study of OB benefits us in several ways.

Firstly, the study of OB helps us understand ourselves and others in a better way. This helps greatly in improving our inter-personal relations in the organisations. Friendly and cordial relations between employees and management and also among the employees create a congenial work environment in organisations.

Secondly, the knowledge of OB helps the managers know individual employees better and motivate employees to work for better results. It helps managers apply appropriate motivational techniques in accordance to the nature of individual employees who exhibit glaring differences in many respects.

Thirdly, one of the basic characteristics of OB is that it is human in nature. So to say, OB tackles human problems humanly. It helps understand the cause of the problem, predicts its future course of action and controls its evil consequences. Thus, treating employees as human beings enables the managers to maintain cordial industrial relations which, in turn, creates peace and harmony in the organisations.

Fourthly, the most popular reason for studying OB is to learn how to predict human behaviour and, then, apply it in some useful way to make the organisation more effective.[5] Thus, knowledge of OB becomes a pre-requirement for a person like you the students of MBA who is going to assume a managerial job and succeed as a manager.

Finally, all organisations are run by man. It is man working in the organisations makes all the difference. Then, it implies that effective utilization of people working in the organisation guarantees success of the organisation. This is where OB comes into the picture. OB helps managers how to efficiently manage human resources in the organisation. It enables managers to inspire and motivate employees towards higher productivity and better results.

1.5 CONTRIBUTING DISCIPLINES TO OB

OB is an applied behavioural science. It has drawn heavily from a number of other applied interdisciplinary behavioural disciplines of psychology, sociology and anthropology. Figure 1.2 presents an overview of the major contributions to the study of organisational behaviour. A brief description of each is in order.

Psychology: The discipline that has had the greatest influence on the field of OB is psychology. It is a science that focuses directly on understanding and predicting individual behaviour. It has greatly contributed to the intra-personal dynamics of human behaviour. Topics such as personality, perception, attitude, opinion, learning and motivation describe intra-personal aspects of OB.

Sociology: Auguste Compte[6], a French philosopher of the nineteenth century, is generally credited with coining the term **sociology** as part of his attempt to reclassify and rearrange the field of science. Sociology is the study of people in relation to their fellow human beings. Whereas psychologists focus on the individuals, sociologists study groups of individuals. The field of sociology has made valuable contributions to our understanding of group dynamics within organisations. The topics derived from sociology include group dynamics, formation of groups, communication, formal and informal organisations and the like.

Anthropology: Anthropology is the study of societies to learn about human beings and their activities. Anthropology helps us understand differences in fundamental values, attitudes, and behaviour between people in different regions and organisations. In sum and substance, anthropology studies culture. Culture dictates what people learn and how they behave. Organisations create a unique culture that influences the way organisational members think about the organisation and how they should behave.

Some important insights about organisational culture are derived from the field of anthropology. Organisation culture is studied, in detail, later in chapter 21.

Other Social Sciences: Besides psychology, sociology and anthropology, three other disciplines also contributed to our understanding of OB are economics, political science, and history. Several economic models describe the behaviour of individuals when they are confronted with a choice, and these economic models have made valuable contributions to our understanding of both individual and organisational decision-making processes. Power, politics, and authority are popular topics derived from the field of political science. They help explain certain influence processes in OB. History has also greatly contributed to our understanding of OB by describing the lives of great leaders and the successes and failures of organisations they managed.

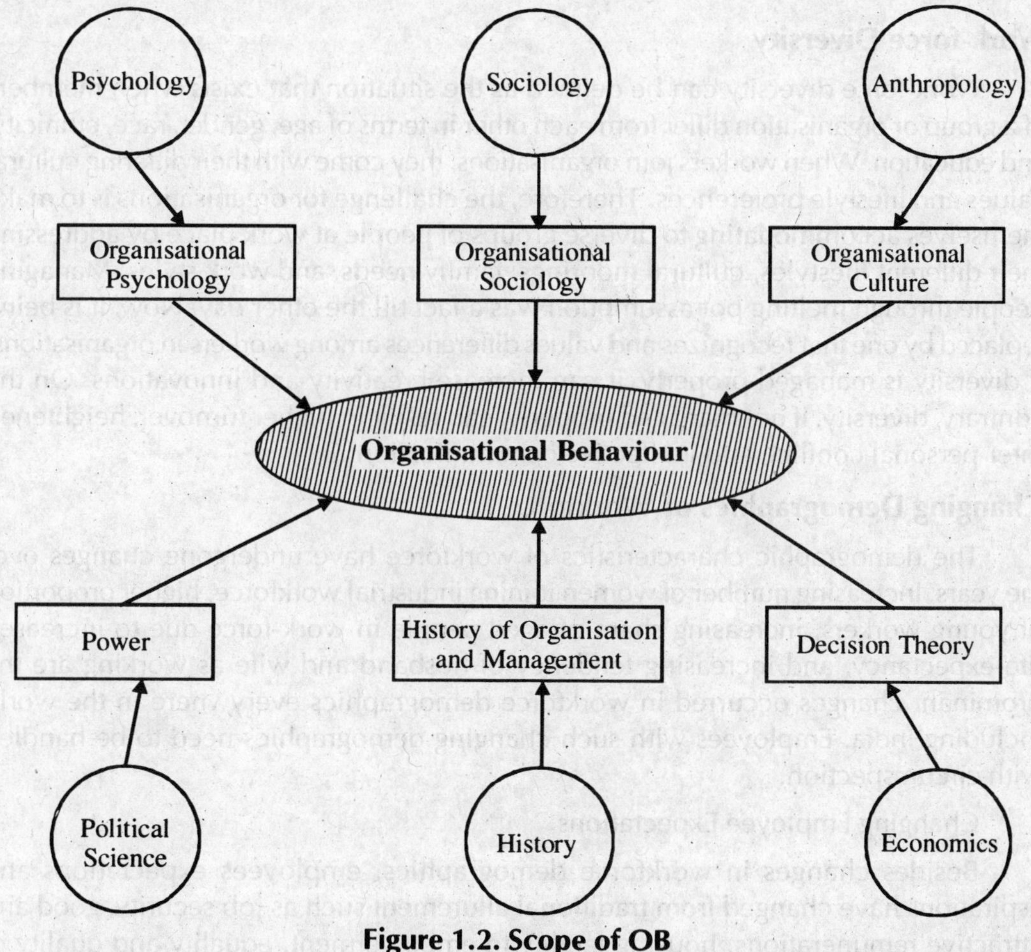

Figure 1.2. Scope of OB

The, case studies from history have helped in clarifying the roles played by decision-makers in particular circumstances and situations.

1.6 THE CHALLENGES FACED BY MANAGEMENT

Although the field of OB has been around the past three decades, there are a few dramatic challenges taking place as we have entered the twenty-first century. For example, the typical employee is becoming older, his/her expectations are fast changing, loyalties to the organisations have become a feature of the other day, more and more women and nonwhites are joining the work force, and the ever increasing global competition of business is requiring employees to become more flexible and to learn to cope with rapid changes posing challenges. In sum, there are a lot of challenges for OB to face in the twenty-first century. In fact, a time has come to understand OB better and more than before. Here, we are discussing some of the more critical issues/challenges confronting managers for which OB offers solutions or atleast some meaningful insights towards solutions.

Work-force Diversity

Work-force diversity can be defined as the situation that exists when members of a group or organisation differ from each other in terms of age, gender, race, ethnicity, and education. When workers join organisations, they come with their differing cultural values and lifestyle preferences. Therefore, the challenge for organisations is to make themselves accommodating to diverse groups of people at work place by addressing their different lifestyles, cultural moorings, family needs, and work styles. Managing people through melting pot assumption was a fact till the other day. Now, it is being replaced by one that recognizes and values differences among workers in organisations. If diversity is managed properly, it can increase creativity and innovations. On the contrary, diversity, if not managed properly, can result in higher turnover, heightened inter-personal conflict, and ineffective communication[7].

Changing Demographics of Workforce

The demographic characteristics of workforce have undergone changes over the years. Increasing number of women joining industrial workforce, higher proportion of young workers, increasing share of aged people in work-force due to increased life-expectancy, and increasing tendency of husband and wife as working are the prominant changes occurred in workforce demographics everywhere in the world including India. Employees with such changing demographics need to be handled with circumspection.

Changing Employee Expectations

Besides changes in workforce demographics, employees expectations and aspirations have changed from traditional allurement such as job security, good and attractive remunerations, housing facility to empowerment, equality and quality of work life (QWL). Employee expect equality with management. They emphasise on leading by example.

That a new change in employees' expectation has been shifting them from factory-place to the home is illustrated by a Bangalore-based Veri-Fone[8].

In this organisation, all the 100 employees used to work with computers at home. They were linked to the office and customers. Thus, employees' homes turned into surrogate offices. In the recent years, such paradigm shift has undergone even in educational field. Under open/distance education system, the student does not go to the educational institution for learning his/her subject. Instead, the teacher in such case goes to the student's place through the study material, tele conferencing, radio broadcast,etc.

That the average worker's expectations have now changed to better treatment, challenging jobs and career advancements is well evidenced by the voices raised for these by the workers' unions of Hindustan Lever, Tomco, Blue Star, and Central Bank in the recent years. That is why monetary incentives alone are not found sufficient to motivate workers all the times, as is discussed later in Chapter 10. The manager has, then, to redraw new methods of motivation such as job design, for example, to motivate workers to contribute toward accomplishment of organisational goals.

Ever Expanding Globalisation

By now, the whole world has become a global village. Business has crossed the national boundaries and, thus, has become global, popularly known as 'multi-national business'. This has made managing men more complex. Globalisation of business poses at least two major challanges for managers:

First, in case of multi-national companies, the managers are frequently transferred to another countries. In a new country, the managers have to manage a workforce that is very different in needs, aspirations, and attitudes from the ones they were used to back in the former country.

Second, even in their own country, the managers have to work with superiors, subordinates, and peers who were born and brought up in a different culture. The managers' problem, then, is what motivates them may not motivate others, i.e., superiors, subordinates, and peers. For example, the manager may like to adopt an open and straightforward communication style, but the subordinates may find the same style as threatening and uncomfortable. In order to manage these people effectively, the managers need to understand their varying culture acurately and know how it has shaped as such and then learn to adapt the management styles accordingly. In sum, the managers need to modify their practices to face the challenges before them.

Towards Improving Quality

Yet another major challenge before today's managers have to face is offering of quality products and services to the customers. This is because the delivery of quality products and services to the customers has a direct impact on the success of organisations. The ever increasing concern for quality products and services has given genesis to today's buzzword **'Total Quality Management'.** (TQM). TQM is different things to different people and has been both "cussed" and discussed in the management literature and the actual practice of management. TQM is a philosophy of modern management that is driven by the constant attainment of customer satisfaction through the continuous improvement of all organisational processes. There is no denying of the fact that price, brand loyalty, attractive design, and technical innovations are still important to consumers in developing and developed countries, yet the quality of product has surged ahead in relative importance. Similarly, the delivery of quality services in the ever exploding service sector has become very critical[9]. The challenge for managers across the world is, therefore, have human resources to deliver quality to products and services to the customers and clients.

1.7 ORGANISATIONAL BEHAVIOUR PROCESS

As mentioned earlier, OB studies human behaviour at work. Thus, OB can be the behaviour of the members of the organisation toward each other, toward the organisation, toward the customers or clients, and toward the society at large. Human behaviour is often caused. Psychologists have taken it as axiomatic that a cause must precede its effect[10]. For example, a Professor, who enters the classroom after having a hot exchange and quarrel with his colleagues, may reveal bitterness to his students in the class. Similarly when a manager comes to office after quarrelling with his wife in the morning, may possibly exhibit unpleasant behaviour like rebuking for pretty things to his subordinates. In sum and substance, OB is the behaviour of people with each other in an organisational framework. It follows cause-effect process and affects both inter-personal relations and managerial effectiveness in the organisation.

OB process is now illustrated with an imaginery cause-effect model as shown in Figure 1.3.

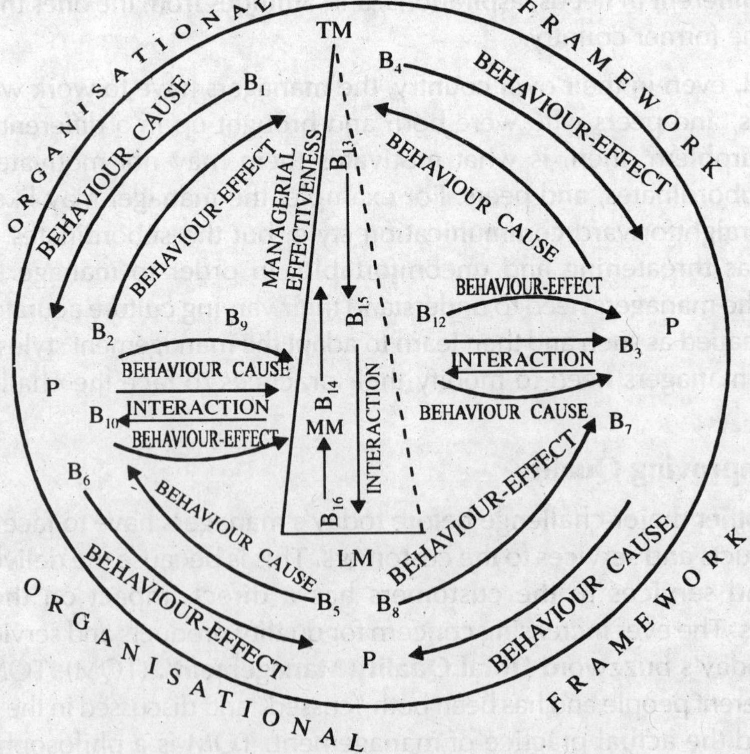

Figure 1.3. Cause-Effect Process of OB

In Figure 1.3, circle represents organisational framework. It contains three levels of managers, viz., Top Level Managers (TM), Middle Level Managers (MM), and Lower Level Managers (LM) and people denoted by P. The hierarchy of managers is indicated by the triangle within the overall organisational framework. The bold line and dotted line of triangale represent managerial effectiveness and human relations respectively.

The diagram exhibits that behaviour is caused, or say, behaviour has a cause-effect relationship. In other words, the behaviour of one individual serves as cause for another's behaviour. The behaviour of another individual, thus, becomes effect. For example, B_1 behaviour of top level management (TM) toward its people (P) becomes cause for B_3 behaviour (*i.e.* effect) of the people. Similarly, B_2 is the cause of B_4 effect. This goes on and on in the whole organisational framework. Finally, the diagram shows a positive relationship between behaviour, human relations, and managerial effectiveness in the organisation. To be precise, better the human relations maintained among the people, greater would be the positive behaviour, and in turn, greater would be the managerial effectiveness and vice versa. Thus, it becomes clear that OB follows a cause-effect process.

1.8 MODELS OF ORGANISATIONAL BEHAVIOUR

Models are frameworks or possible explanations why do people behave as they behave at work. There are so many models as many are organisations. Varying results across the organisations are substantially caused by differences in the models of organisational behaviour. All the models of organisational behaviour are broadly classified into four types: autocratic, custodial, supportive, and collegial. We now discuss these four models beginning with the autocratic.

The Autocratic Model

In case of an autocratic model, the managerial orientation is dictorial. The managers exercise their commands over employees. The managers give orders and the employees have to obey the orders. Thus, the employees' orientation towards the managers/bosses is obedience. Under autocratic conditions, employees usually give minimum performance and, in turn, get minimum wages. Some employees give higher performance either because of their achievement drive or their personal liking to the boss or because of some other factor.

Evidences such as the industrial civilization of the United States and organisational crises[11] do suggest that the autocratic model produced results. However, its principal weakness is its high human cost.[12] The combination of emerging knowledge about the needs of the employees and ever changing societal values and norms suggested managers to adopt alternative and better ways to manage people at work. This gave genesis to the second type of models of organisational behaviour.

The Custodial Model

While studying the employees, the managers realized and recognized that although the employees managed under autocratic style do not talk back to their boss, they certainly think bad about the system. Such employees filled with frustration and aggression vent them on their co-workers, families and neighbours. This made the managers think how to develop better employee satisfaction and security. It was realized that this can be done by dispelling employees' insecurities, frustration, and aggression. This called for introduction of welfare programmes to satisfy security needs of employees. Such provision for an on-site day–care centre for quality child care is an example of such welfare programme meant for employees. **Welfare programmes lead to employee dependence on the organisation**. Stating more accurately, employees having dependence on organisation may not afford to quit even there seem greener pastures around. Here is a case of IGNOU in point.

The welfare programmes for employees started by the Indira Gandhi National Open University (IGNOU), New Delhi are worth citing in this context. IGNOU, in the beginning provided its employees facilities like house-lease facility, subsidized transport facility, day-time child care centre in the campus, etc. These made employees dependent on IGNOU which, in turn, became custodian of its employees.

Although the custodian approach brings security and satisfaction, it suffers from certain flows also. Employees produce anywhere near their capacities. They are also not motivated to increase their capacities of which they are capable. Though the employees are satisfied, still they do not feel motivated or fulfillled in their work they do. This is in confirmity with the research.findings that **"the happy employee is not necessarily the most productive employee.**[13] Consequently, managers and researchers started to address yet another question, "**Is there better approach/way to manage people?"** The quest for a better way provided a foundation for evolvement to the next type of model of organisational behaviour.

The Supportive Model

The supportive model is founded on leadership, not on money or authority. In fact, it is the managerial leadership style that provides an atmosphere to help employees grow and accomplish their tasks successfully. The managers recognize that the workers are not by nature passive and disinterested to organisational needs, but they are made so by an unappropriate leadership style. The managers believe that given due and appropriate chances, the workers become ready to share responsibility, develop a drive to contribute their mite, and improve themselves. Thus, under supportive approach, the management's orientation is to support the employee's job performance for meeting both organisational and individual goals.

However, the supportive model of organisational behaviour is found more useful and effective in developed nations and less effective in developing nations like ours because of employees' more awakening in the former and less one in the latter nations.

The Collegial Model

The collegial model is an extension of the supportive model. As the literal meaning of the word 'college' means a group of persons having the common purpose, the collegial model relates to a team work/concept. The basic foundation of the collegial model lies on management's building a feeling of partnership with employees. Under collegial approach, employees feel needed and useful. They consider managers as joint contributors to organisational success rather than as bosses.

Its greatest benefit is that the employee becomes self-discipline. Feeling responsible backed by self-descipline creates a feeling of tearn work just like what the members of a football team feel. The research studies report that compared to traditional management model, the more open, participative, colllegial managerial approach produced improved results in situations where it is appropriate.

Now, the sum and substances of these four models of organisational behaviour are summarized in Figure 1.4.

	Authocratic	**Custodial**	**Supportive**	**Collegial**
Basis of model	Power	Economic sources	Leadership	Partnership
Managerial orientation	Authority	Money	Support	Teamwork
Employee orientation	Obedience	Security and benefits	Job performance	Responsible behaviour
Employee psychological result	Dependence on boss	Dependence on organization	Participation	Self-discipline
Employee needs met	Subsistence	Security	Status and recognition	Self-actualization
Performance result	Minimum	Passive cooperation	Awakened drives	Moderate enthusiasm

Figure 1.4 : Four Models of OB

SUMMARY

This summary is organized by the 'learning objectives^given on page no. 3

- *OB is the study and application of knowledge about how people - as individuals and groups - behave at work places.*
- *There are four key elements in OB : people, structure, technology, and environment. OB has emerged as an interdisciplinary discipline, an applied science, a normative science, and a humanistic approach.*
- *The main objective of OB is to make managers more accurate and effective at describing, understanding, predicting, and controlling human behaviour at work.*
- *OB, being an interdisciplinary discipline, draws heavily from other behavioural sciences as psychology, sociology, and anthropology*
- *Changing demography, work - force diversity, ever increasing expectations, of work force, ever expanding globalization of business, and increasing concern for improving quality in offering quality products and services pose challenges for managers to deal with human behaviour at work.*
- *OB being often caused follows a cause - effect process.*
- *Autocratic, custodial, supportive, and collegial are the major models of OB.*

REVIEW QUESTIONS

1. Define organisational behaviour. What is its scope?
2. What is organisational behaviour? What is the need for studying OB?
3. Consider your Department of Business Administration where you at present are studying. What model of OB does your Head of the Department follow?
4. What are some of the major challanges facing to-day's organisations and management? Briefly describe these developments.
5. Discuss similarities and dissimilarities among the models of OB.
6. "The supportive and collegial models of OB are especially appropriate for use in the more affluent nations." Do you agree or disagree? Discuss.
7. Describe how OB is an inter-disciplinary subject.
8. "Human behaviour is generally caused and predictable." Explain.

REFERENCES

1. Fred Luthans: **Organisational Behaviour**, McGraw Hill, New York, 1995 (Seventh Edition), p.15
2. J.W. Newstrom and Keith Davis: **Organisational Behaviour:** Human Behaviour at Work, Tata McGraw-Hill Publishing Company Limited, New Delhi, 1995 (Ninth Edition), pp. 4–5.
3. Stephen P. Robbins: **Organisational Behaviour**: Concepts, Controversies and Applications, Printice-Hall of India Private Limited, New Delh, (Eighth Edition) 1998, p.7.
4. William C. Frederick, James E. Post and Keith Davis : **Business and Society**, McGraw-Hill Book Company, New York, 1992 (Seventh Edition).
5. Stephen P. Robbins: **Op. cit.,** 1998, p.8.
6. Auguste, Compte: **The Positive Philosophy**, trans. and ed. Harriet Martineau, London, Ball, 1915.
7. R.R. ThomasJt: From Affirmative Action to Affirming Diversity, **Harvard Business Review**, March–April 1990, pp. 107-117.
8. K. Aswathappa: **Organisational Behaviour,** Himalaya Publishing House, Bombay (Third Edition), 1996, p. 19.
9. George S. Easton: The 1993 State of U.S. Total Quality Management, **California Management Review**, Spring, 1993, pp. 32-52.
10. James C. Coleman: **Psychology and Effective Behaviour,** Foreman & Co., Scott, U.S.A., 1969, p. 23.
11. W. Stevens: The Alaskan Oil Spill: Lessons in Crisis Management, **Management Review,** April 1990, p. 20.
12. J.W. Newstrom and Keith Davis: **Op. Cit.,** 1995 (Ninth Edition), p.32.
13. Daniel Katz, Nathan Maccoby and Nancy C. Morse: **Productivity, Supervision, and Morale in an Office Situation, Part I,** Institute of Social Research, University of Machigan, 1950.

CASE – 1.1 : Maharashtra Association of Resident Doctors (MARD)*

MARD (Maharashtra Association of Resident Doctors) has called on a strike demanding an increase in their remuneration in March 1987. There can be difference

* V.P. Michael: **Organisational Behaviour and Managerial Effectiveness,** S. Chand & Company Limited, New Delhi, 1989.

of opinion regarding the humanitarian aspect of life-saving physicians' strike-work approach, though there cannot be much controversy regarding their right to demand a remuneration sufficient enough to meet both ends of their own life.

Dr. Rajan Shelatkar has been one of the striking resident doctors, who was working in the general medicine ward of the KEM Hospital of Bombay. He did not take the routine rounds of the ward on March 3, since he was an activist of the strike. It has been alleged that he left the duty place without the permission of his superior Dr. G.H. Tilve, who has reported it to Dr. (Mrs) S.R. Satoskar, Asst. Dean of the hospital. Dr. Tilve's misunderstanding against Rajan has resulted in his behaviour of levelling a complaint against Dr. Rajan, while Dr. Satoskar has called for his explanation on March 7.

Though the resident doctors were striking the normal work, they held an out-patient department on the pavement outside the hospital for helping the outpatients. A junior lady doctor has collected some 'Antistine' tablets carrying the MCGB mark (Municipal Corporation of Greater Bombay) for the pavement OPD from ward 13 of the hospital on the 2nd of March. Though it was an improper act on the part of the junior lady doctor to carry away the municipal medicine out of the municipal hospital according to municipal rules, the purpose and situation behind her action could have been reckoned with, before any disciplinary action was taken against her. Dr. Satoskar, who caught the junior doctor red handed, however, has taken disciplinary action against the junior lady doctor, without giving much thought to the consequences and reactions. The concerted behaviour of the striking resident doctors has been stimulated for direct action against Dr. (Mrs.) Satoskar. Of course, group behaviour is different from individual behaviour.

As already mentioned in this chapter, behaviour has a cause-effect relation. Rajan Shelatkar's behaviour to his boss Dr. Tilve has resulted in Tilve's retaliation by calling for explanation and harbouring Dr. Satoskar's displeasure. Similarly, junior lady doctor's behaviour, and the act of carrying away medicine in support of the pavement OPD programme of the striking resident doctors, have invited the wrath of Asst. Dean. Satoskar's behaviour towards the striking doctors has resulted in her gherao by the strikers. When the gherao has become a collective affair, its proceedings have gone beyond the control of even its organisers.

The striking doctors have proved to be unruly, violent and indecent. They removed calendars from Dr. Satoskar's office, stuck their own posters on the walls, threw telephone receivers on the floor, squatted menacingly close to her, climbed on to the window sills and blew cigarette smoke into her face. The doctors under the leadership of Dr. Karmarkar have abused Mrs. Satoskar, Dr. G.H. Tilve, Dr. C.V. Patel, and Dr. Satoskar's son (a resident doctor). The gherao continued for 3½ hours, and the victim was denied even a glass of water during the whole gherao period, while the strikers had snacks and tea. The ordeal was beyond tolerable limits for a lady, since she was subjected to a great deal of obnoxious behaviour. Many of the junior doctors, who abused the Asst. Dean Dr. Mrs. Satoskar, were junior lady doctors and her own students. Curiously enough, the junior doctors have not gheraoed the Dean Dr. G.B Parulkar, but their target was the Asst. Dean Mrs. Satoskar. Another striking fact was that all these junior doctors have been top rankers and Post-graduate doctors, who behaved as ruffians. They have been guided by militant trade union leader Dr. Dutta Samant, who himself was a medical practitioner. Dr. Parulkar, the dean of the hospital, has remarked "That is the kind of doctors you have been turning out all allong".

The whole episode did not end there. The services of the two leaders of the action Dr. Santosh Karmarkar and Dr. V. Murlidhar have been terminated, while a lot of tension and strife prevailed in the KEM hospital. [The actual sufferers and victims of the whole incident have been the public and the patients, while these doctors (both juniors and seniors) fight tooth and nail for maintaining their *status quo*]. The dismissed doctors have approached the High Court, which has restrained the Bombay Municipal Corporation from dismissing the two leaders. Further, the administration has initiated action to take departmental and criminal proceedings against the 33 junior doctors, irrespective of the apology tendered by MARD. Junior doctors of other hospitals have also joined the stir, and the whole situation has become tense. Much complication prevailed in the various hospital circles. The whole array of incidents indicates the cause-effect relation of organisational behaviour, and its impact on the whole organisational effectiveness.

An analysis of this case would enable the student of organisational behaviour to establish an array of cause-effect relationships throughout the case. Dr. Satoskar's behaviour to the junior doctors, not only during the strike but also in the past, deserves a detailed examination, especiallly because the junior doctors' gherao was only directed towards her (Asst. Dean), while they have not acted against the Dean (Dr. Parulkar). (It cannot be ignored that most of the junior doctors were her students).

QUESTIONS

1. What would have been the real nature of individual behaviour of the junior doctors in the context of their personal background (top rankers, the cream of the society, or people belonging to good families, *i.e.*, good heredity and environment)?
2. How far their good behaviour, as revealed in the gherao, differed from the expected individual behaviour?
3. For a better behaviour from the juniors, what would have been the approach of both the seniors and the administrators?

2

ORGANISATIONAL BEHAVIOUR IN HISTORICAL PERSEPECTIVE

"When I want to understand what is happening to-day or try to decide what will happen tomorrow, I will look back." **– *Oliver Wendell Helmes***

Learning Objectives

After studying this chapter, you should be able to:

- **Define** organisational behaviour.
- **Trace out** the evolution of OB.
- **Present** the hitherto developments in OB over the period in a sequential order.
- **Describe** the Hawthorne experiments in the field of human relations in organisations.

The present state of an area or field or subject cannot be fully understood without some awareness of the events that have preceded it. The reason being the past serves to illuminate the present and predict the future. Keeping this fact in mind, an attempt has been made in this chapter to delineat OB in its historical persepective. More precisely, the chapter outlines the evolution and development of OB in a sequential manner.

2.1 EVOLUTION OF OB

It will not be less than correct to mention that beginning dates in any complex historical study are not only hard to come by but often are impossible to establish also. History bears no evidence for sequence of human behaviour and thinking ever has had one point where it clearly can be said to have started. At the same time, it is also true that attempts to understand or explain the human behaviour at individual and group levels undoubtedly have been made as long back as man itself has been in existence on this planet. What we usuallly do is we make our educated guesses about the human relations among people from the artifacts they left behind. We can say much about human behaviour and relations inferring from plans of our oldest cities, carving and paintings in our historical monuments and caves and alike.

Thus, the fact remains that the human relationships have existed since the beginning of time and some concern for human (as workers) has also been in existence since ages. In the early ages, people worked either alone or in such small groups that their work relationships were easily handled. Then, it has been popular to assume that under these conditions people worked in a Utopia of happiness and fulfilment. That is why the early examples of written records on human behaviour at work did not amount to a full philosophical system encompassing most aspects of human behaviour. They mainly provided human behaviour description of either actualities or normative guides. However, the actual work condition were brutal and backbreaking. Workers worked from dawn until dusk and that too under intolerable conditions of disease, filth, danger, and scarcity of necessary resources. Too little concern and effort were devoted to their job satisfaction in the early ages[1]. There is no gainsaying the fact that the life of workers in the early ages was miserable to say the least.

Although there are traces to the effect that behavioural approaches had existed in the ancient Egypt as early as in BC 1700, its actual origin could not be traced beyond doubt. Human behaviour has often been caused. In this regard, Kolasa[2] opines that cause and effect are, as always, hard to separate and identify. Suffice it to say that an interrelationship exists. However, the behavioural scientists actually tried to chronicle the growth of the subject *i.e.*, OB only from the beginning of the nineteenth century. The hitherto development in behavioural thought can be presented under various stages for the sake of convenience of analysis: viz. (1) industrial revolution, (2) scientific management, (3) human relations movement, and (4) Hawthorne Studies. These are discussed one by one.

2.1.1 INDUSTRIAL REVOLUTION

The industrial revolution (1776) visited in the beginning of the last quarter of the eighteenth century. It brought about materialism, discipline, monotony, boredom, job displacement, impersonality, work interdependence, and other related behavioural phenomena[3]. Though in the beginning the condition of people did not improve perceptibly, nonetheless at least the seed was planted for potential improvement. The industrial revolution led to increase in production that eventually gave workers increased wages followed by increased job satisfaction and decreasing work hours. In this new but positive environment, Robert Owen, a young Welsh Factory owner, about the year 1800, was one of the first to emphasize the human needs of his employees. He refused to employ the young children, on the one hand, and educated his adult workers about proper cleanliness and temperance, on the other. Of course, this could hardly be called organisational behaviour in the modern context, but it was certainly a beginning towards modern organisational behaviour. That is why he was called the **'father of personnel administration'** by an early writer Frank Podmore[4].

In 1835, Andrew Ure, a pioneering behavioural scientist, published his work on The Philosophy of Manufacturers[5]. Besides, the mechanical and commercial parts of manufacturing, Ure recognized a third factor, *i.e.*, human factor. He provided workers with hot tea, medical treatment, a fan apparatus for ventilation, and sickness payments.

Our own land India did not remain untouched with human recognition of workers. Around this time, J.N. Tata took a special interest in the welfare of his workers. The welfare schemes included were installing humudifiers and fire sprinklers, installation of pension fund, payment for accident compensation. His these experiments done in the Express Mill showed that not only profits but people/workers also mattered to him[6].

2.1.2 SCIENTIFIC MANAGEMENT

Then came there of scientific management. The interest in the behavioural aspects of management was recognized. It was Frederick W. Taylor who inaugurated the interest in people's behaviour at work in the United States in the early 1900s. For introducing the scientific thought in management, Taylor is often called **'the father of scientific management.'** What actually Taylor did is he converted broad generalisations into practical and scientific manners which paved the way for later development of organisational behaviour. Taylor advocated the selection of right worker for right jobs, imparting them adequately, and remunerating them handsomely. His work, thus, eventually tend to improved recognition and productivity for industrial workers. He emphasized that as there was a best machine for a job, so were there best ways for workers to do their work. There is no denying of the fact that Taylor's main goal was technical efficiency, yet at least he awakened the management to the importance of human resources which was so far neglected. His major work was published in 1911.

Though Taylor laid down a scientific foundation in management thinking, his thought was criticised on several counts. The important among the comments were its anti-social, anti-democratic and psychologically unfair nature. He was much criticised for his belief in rationalising everything and assuming human behaviour based on **rabble hypothesis**.

2.1.3 HUMAN RELATIONS MOVEMENT

Failure of scientific management gave birth to the human relations movement. It was founded on more emphasis on workers cooperation and morale. In other words, under the human relations approach, workers were distinguished from non-human factors such as capital, machine, building, etc. That workers have feelings, sentiments, retionality, and ambitions were duly recognized. As a result, workers were involved in decision-making process. Historically speaking, three factors contributed to the recognition of human as a distinct factor amongst others in an organisation. These were: the Great Depression, the labour movement, and the Hawthorne Studies[8].

The Great Depression is traced back to 1929 when the stock exchange in America crashed. Wide-spread unemployment, declining purchase power, market collapse, and lowering standards of living of people were some of the major consequences witnessed world-wide. It is important to mention that the Great Depression was accompanied by some positive consequences also. One of the positive outcome of the Depression was that the management began to recognize the importance of functional areas like finance, marketing, and personnel to keep a business survive and grow. In sum, human relations received increasing significance as an indirect effect of the Depression.

Though human relations got recognition in business, production still continued to claim dominating place in business operation. Speaking truthfully, production still preceded workers in order of its importance in business organisation. Human aspects of work such as decent hours of work, fair wages, and good working conditions were next to production. However, such a situation did not last for long.

The continued exploitation of workers made them realize that their protection against exploitation rests in their own hands. Such realisation led to the formation of trade unions. This, in turn, made the realisation down side up. So to say, people now preceded production in order of importance in organisations. In other words, management started to accord primary emphasis on employee relations and wages, work hours and work conditions were assigned the secondary place in the organisations.

2.1.4 HAWTHORNE STUDIES

We have stated earlier that F.W. Taylor through his experiments increased production by rationalizing it. Elton Mayo and followers sought to increase production by humanizing it through behavioural experiments popularly known as **Hawthorne Experiments/Studies.** The fact remains that an exposure to the study of organisational behaviour will remain incomplete without a mention of Hawthorne studies/experiments. Hence, what follows next is the same.

In November 1924, a team of researcher-professors from the renowned Harward Business School of U.S.A began investigating into the human aspects of work and working conditions at the Hawthorne plant of Western Electric Company, Chicago. The company was producing bells and other electric equipments for telephone industry. Prominent Professors included in the research team were Elton Mayo (Psychologist), Roethlisberger and Whilehead (Sociologists), and William Dickson (company representative). The team conducted four separate experimental and behavioural studies over a seven-year period.[9] These were :

1. **Illumination Experiments** (1924-27) to find out the effect of illumination on workers' productivity.
2. **Relay Assembly Test Room Experiments** (1927-28) to find out the effects of changes in number of work hours and related working conditions on worker productivity.
3. **Experiments in Interviewing Workers** (1928-30) to find out workers attitudes and sentiments toward work, and
4. **Bank Wiring Room Experiments** (1931-32) to find out social system of an organisation.

The important details on each of these four experiments are given hereunder:

Illumination Experiments: The experiments in illumination were a direct extension of Elton Mayo's earlier illumination experiments[10] done in the textile industry in 1923 and 1924. This experiment began in 1924. It consisted of a series of studies of test groups in which the levels of illumination varied but the conditions were held constant. The purpose behind it was to examine the relation of the quality and quantity of illlumination to the efficiency of workers. It was found that the productivity increased to almost the same rate in both test and control groups selected for the experiments. In the final experiment, it was discovered that output decreased with the decreased illumination level *i.e.* moonlight intensity. As the researchers did not find a positive and linear relationship between illumination and efficiency of workers, they concluded that the results were **'screwy'** in the absence of simple and direct cause and effect relationship.

One of the significant facts disclosed by the study was that people behave differently when they are being studied than they might otherwise behave. It is from this the term **Hawthorne Effect** was coined.

Relay Assembly Test Room Experiments: The researchers undertook the next experiment to study the workers segregated on the basis of a definite range of working condition variables. The selected variables included work room temperature and humidity, work schedule, rest breaks, and their food consumption. Five women were chosen in the relay assembly test room and kept careful records of the prediction variables as well as output. The amount of time each woman took to assemble a telephone relay of about forty parts was measured.

Like their experiments in illumination, the researchers were surprised to discover that relationship between the predictor variables and industrial efficiency was simply not found. But, these experiments of relay assembly test room made the researchers to suspect that employee attitude and sentiments were critically important variables not previously accounted for. The researchers, in turn, underwent a radical change of their thought.

Experiments in Interviewing Workers: In 1928, a number of researchers began to go directly to workers, keep the variables of previous experiments aside, to talk about what was, in their opinion, important to them. For this, around 20,000 workers were interviewed over a period of two years. Unlike previous experiments in which interviewer had a set of preconceptions, the interviewers set out to skillfully listen what the worker was saying all about himself/herself and job.

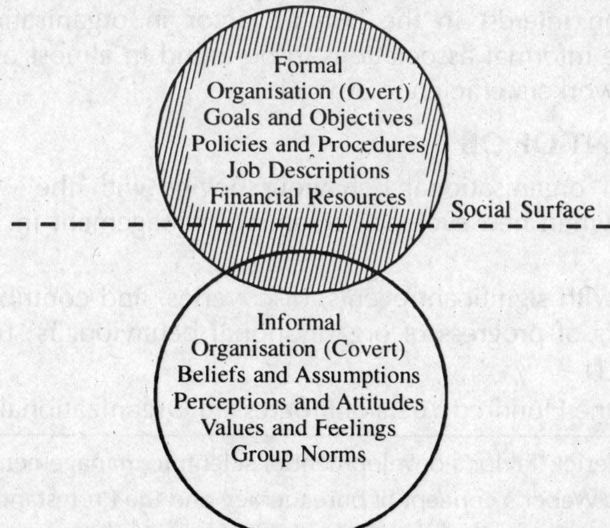

Figure 2.1 : Formal and Informal Elements of Organisations.

With the progress in interviewing the workers, the researchers discovered that the workers would open up and talk freely about what was the most important, and at times problematic, issues in their minds. The interviewing experiments enabled the researchers to discover a rich and intriguing world previously remained undiscovered and unexamined within the Howthorne Works undertaken so far. The discovery of the informal organisation and its relationship to the formal organisation, as shown in the Figure 2.1, was a landmark of experiments in interviewing workers. These experiments led to a richer understanding of the social, interpersonal dynamics of people at work.

Bank Wiring Room Experiments: The researchers did their last experiment on workers in the bank wiring room. Through this experiment, the workers found that the behavioural norms set by the work group had a powerful influence over the productivity of the group. In sum and substance, the higher the norms, the greater the productivity and vice versa. The bank wiring room experiments well confirmed the effect of the power of the peer group and importance of group influence on workers' behaviour and productivity.

The finest contribution of the Hawthorne Studies is that it laid a foundation of understanding people's social and psychological behaviour at the work place. It opened new vistas and frontiers to the study of managing men which has been folllowed by many behavioural scientists since then. That it has paved the way for further researches in human management as Landsberger[11] puts it, "A most spectacular academic battle has raged since then or perhaps it would be more accurate to say that a limited number of gunners has kept up a steady barrage, reusing the same ammunition. The beleaguered Mayo garrison, however, has continued its existence behind the solid protection of factory walls." However, the Hawthorne Experiments are not free from criticism. These experiments have been severely criticised by the Australian and English researchers as being inadequately controlled and interpreted. However, what is the most important in the Hawthorne Studies that these stimulated an interest in the human factor in organisations. The studies discovered that the informal associations to be found in almost every organisation profoundly affect workers efficiency at work.

2.2 DEVELOPMENT OF OB

The history of organisational behaviour begins with the work of Frederick Winslow Taylor[12] when he developed scientific management in 1890 at Midwale Steel Company.

It progressed with significant events, discoveries, and contributions over time. One hundred years of progress of organisational behaviour is summarized in the following Table 2.1:

Table 2.1 One Hundred Years of Progress in Organizational Behaviour

1890s	• Frederick Taylor's development of scientific management
1900s	• Max Weber's concept of bureaucracy and the Protestant Ethic
1910s	• Walter Cannon's discovery of the "emergency (stress) response"
1920s	• Elton Mayo's illumination studies in the textile industry
	• The Hawthorne Studies at Western Electric Company
1930s	• Kurt Lewin's, Ronald Lippitt's, and Ralph White's early leadership studies
1940s	• Abraham Maslow's need hierarchy motivation theory
	• B.F. Skineer's formulation of the behavioural approach
	• Charles Walker's and Robert Guest's studies of routine work
1950s	• Ralph Stogdill's Ohio State leadership studies

	• Douglas McGregor's examination of the human side of enterprise
	• Frederick Herzberg's two-factor theory of motivation and job enrichment
1960s	• Arthur Turner's and Paul Lawrence's studies of diverse industrial jobs
	• Robert Blake's and Jane Mouton's managerial grid
	• Patricia Cain Smith's studies of satisfaction in work and retirement
	• Fred Fiedler's contingency theory of leadership
1970s	• J.Richard Hackman's and Greg Oldham's job characteristics theory
	• Robert House's path-goal and charismatic theories of leadership
1980s	• Peter Block's political skills for empowered managers
	• Larry Hurschhorn's teamwork approach
	• Charles Manz's approach to self-managed work teams
	• Edgar Schein's approach to leadership and organizational culture

SUMMARY

This summary is organized by the 'learning objectives' given on page no. 19 :

- *Although the interest in the welfare of workers is age old, the origin and development of discipline of organisational behaviour is traced back to the beginning of the nineteenth century.*
- *The industrial revolution benefited workers in more than one way. It increased wages, on the one hand, and decreased working hours, on the other. At the same time, two scientists–Robert Owen and Andrew Ure–pleaded for facilities to be given to the workers.*
- *F.W. Taylor inaugurated and revived interest in human resources at work. He advocated for increase in production by rationalising it.*
- *The significant events like the Great Depression and the labour movement and contributions like Hawthorne studies gave genesis to human relations movement. The continued developments in human relations approach by 1950s gave birth to the modern organisational behaviour.*

REVIEW QUESTIONS

1. Give origin and development of organisational behaviour in historical perspective.
2. Give an account of Hawthorne Studies. Also mention its implications, if any.
3. Mention the major milestones in the history of organisational behaviour.

REFERENCES

1. John W. Newstrom and Keith Davis: ***Op. cit.*** 1996, p.7.
2. Blair J. Kolasa: **Introduction to Behavioural Sciences for Business**, Wiley Eastern Limited, New Delhi, 1991, p.26.
3. M.M. Perline and L.T. Kurtis: Automation: Its Impact on Organised Labour, **Personnel Journal**, Vol. 48, No. 5, 1969, p. 340.
4. Frank Podmore: **Robert Owen,** Augustus M. Kelly, New York, 1968.

5. Andrew Ure: **The Philosophy of Manufacturers**, Charles Knight, London, 1835.
6. R.M. Lala: **The Creation of Wealth**, IBH Publishing Company, Bombay, 1981, p. 13.
7. Frederick W. Taylor: **The Principles of Scientific Management**, Harper & Brothers, New York, 1911.
8. Fred Luthans: **Op. cit**., 1995, p.9.
9. F.J. Roethlisberger: **Management and Morale,** Harvard University Press, Cambridge, Mass, 1941.
10. Elton Mayo: **The Human Problems of an Industrial Civilization**, Harvard University Press, Cambridge, Mass, 1933.
11. Henry A. Landsberger: **Hawthorne Revisited**, Cornelll University, Ithaca, 1951, pp. 1–2.
12. F.W. Taylor: ***Op. cit***., 1911.

3

RESEARCH IN ORGANISATIONAL BEHAVIOUR

"Research is a movement from the known to the unknown to gain new knowledge for solving a problem."
– Anonymous

Learning Objectives

After studying this chapter, you should be able to:

- **State** the purpose of research.
- **Explain** the key terms used in research in organisational behaviour.
- **Describe** the various types of researches in organisational behaviour.
- **Delineate** the process involved in research in organisational behaviour.
- **List** the salient characteristics of a good research.

In the first two chapters, you have learnt what organisational behaviour is and has been in its historical perspective. Given the fast and euphemeral changes in the business world, human behaviour at work has been becoming more and more complex and highly unpredictable. Knowing human, at the same time, in a better way and more orderly manner, has become the necessity of the time for managers to effectively manage men in organisations. Studying human behaviour in a scientific manner also called **behavioural research** helps managers understand human behaviour more accurately.

Behavioural research contributes to our knowledge of organisational behaviour by enabling us to make observations, formulate theories to explain our observations and then test the application of theories. Hence, now managers need to understand research in organisational behaviour. So much so, the students like you (who are the budding managers of tomorrow) who are studying organisational behaviour also need to understand how research is used in organisational behaviour. In fact, **research in organisational behaviour is as important for managers as biological research is for medical students.** Hence this chapter is imperative in a book on organisational behaviour.

3.1 PURPOSE OF RESEARCH

Let us first understand what research is. The word **research** is derived from the French word **Rechercher'** which means to search back. In common partance, research means search for new knowledge. Advanced Learner's Dictionary of Current English defines research as a careful investigation or enquiry especially through search for new facts in any branch of knowledge[1]. Thus, research can be defined as an organised and systematized effort to gain new knowledge for solving a problem[2].

Human beings possess the vital instinct of inquisitiveness for when the unknown confronts us, we wonder and our inquisitiveness makes us probe and attain fuller understanding of the unknown. In fact, this inquisitiveness is the mother of all knowledge. The method employed for obtaining the knowledge of unknown is called **research**. As such, research is a movement from the known to the unknown. It is actually a voyage of discovery.

As regards the purpose of research, it is to discover answers to questions through the application of systematic and scientific investigation. The main purpose of research is to discover the truth which is, however, hidden and has not been discovered as yet. Though each research study has its own specific purpose, the various purposes of research studies can be listed into the following broad ones:

1. To gain familiarity with a phenomenon or to achieve new insights into it.
2. To portray accurately the characteristics of an individual, situation or a group, whichever be the case.
3. To determine frequency with which something occurs or with which it is associated with something else.
4. To test a hypothesis of a casual relationship between variables.

3.2 RESEARCH TERMINOLOGY

In order to make research more scientific and to effectively communicate its results with others, certain vocabulary is used by the researchers. The folllowing is the commonly used vocabulary in behavioural researches.

Hypothesis

Hypothesis ordinarily means a mere assumption or some supposition to be proved or disproved. But, in a research study, hypothesis is a formal question that is intended to be resolved. Thus, a hypothesis may be defined as a proposition or a set of propositions set forth as an explanations for the occurance of some specified group of phenomena either asserted merely as a provisional conjucture to guide some investigation or accepted as highly probable in the light of established facts. In other words, a research hypothesis is a tentative explanation about the relationship between two or more variables. Hence, hypothesis needs to be tested by scientific methods otherwise it remains only a predictive statement or tentative explanation.

Following statements are the examples of hypothesis:

1. Students who receive counselling will show a greater increase in creativity than students not receiving counselling.

2. Increase in salary leads to higher job satisfaction.

Methodology

Research methodology is a way to systematicallly solve the research problem. It may be termed as a science of studying how research is done scientifically. In methodology, we study not only methods or techniques in studying research problems, but also the logic behind them. A researcher not only needs to know how to develop certain indices or tests, how to calculate the mean, the mode and the median, but also he/she also needs to know which of the method/technique is relevant and which are not, and what would they mean and indicate and why. The researcher has to specify very clearly and precisely what decisions he selects and why he selects them so that they can be evaluated by others also.

There is a difference between research method and methodology. While research method refers to those methods/techniques that are used for conduction of research, research methodology includes the logic behind the methods used in studying the research problem. Methodology explains why a particular method/technique is used and why others are not used so that research results are capable of being evaluated either by the researcher himself or by others.

Variable

A variable refers to any quantity or characteristic which may possess different numerical values or categories. Job satisfaction, job stress, attitude, values, personality, etc. are some examples of variables in organisational behaviour. These are discussed, in detail, later in the book.

Variables can be classified into three types:

(*i*) **Dependent Variable:** The response of a variable as an effect of another variable (independent) is called dependent variable. In turms of hypothesis, it is the variable that the researcher intends to answer or explain. The most popular dependent variables in organisational behaviour are productivity, absenteeism, job satisfaction and remuneration/compensation.

(*ii*) **Independent Variable**: It is a variable that is a presumed cause of change in dependent variable. Motivation, leadership styles, selection method and organisational design are some examples of independent variable in organisational behaviour researches.

A variable may be both dependent and independent variable depending upon its place in research hypothesis. Consider a variable, namely job satisfaction. In the statement of hypothesis "**Increase in job satisfaction leads to increased commitment",** job satisfaction is an independent variable. But, in another statement of hypothesis "**Increase in salary leads to higher job satisfaction**" job satisfaction becomes a dependent variable.

(*iii*) **Moderating Variable:** Simply stating, a variable that abates the effect of the independent variable on the dependent variable, is called the moderating variable. For example, the effect of increase in the amount of direct supervision (independent variable) on change in the workers' productivity (dependent variable) will depend on or moderated by the complexity of the tasks performed (moderating variable)[3].

Model/Theory

A model or theory describes all interrelated concepts in a systematic manner to explain a phenomena. In organisational behaviour, theories and models are used interchangeably. Theories of motivation and leadership are the popular examples of theories/models in organisational behaviour.

3.3 TYPES OF RESEARCH

The main types of research are as follows :

1. **Applied vs Fundamental**: Research can either be applied research or fundamental. Research done to generate a body of knowledge about some phenomena of interest to the researcher, is called fundamental research. It is also known as *basic research* or *pure research*. The most University Professor are engaged in fundamental research. When research is conducted to find out solution to a specific real life problem, it is called applied research. Finding solution for why there are frequent strikes in Hindustan Paper corporation is an example of applied research. Most business/ industrial organisational consultants conduct applied research.

2. **Descriptive vs Analytical:** Descriptive research is also known as ***Ex post facto research***. In descriptive research, the researcher presents a description of the state of affairs as it exists at present. The researcher can present only what has happened or what is happening[4]. The variables remain beyond his/her control. The most commonly used method for conducting descriptive research is survey methods of all kinds, including comparative and correlational. On the other hand, in analytical research, the researcher only makes analysis of facts and information already available to make a critical evaluation of the material.

3. **Conceptual vs Empirical:** In conceptual research, the researcher tries to develop new concepts or to reinterpret the existing ones. Thus, it is related to some theory. It is generally used by the philosophers and the thinkers. As regards empirical research, it relies on experience or observation of the researcher. It is a research based on first-hand data and facts. Thus, in empirical research, the researcher has control over variables. Empirical research enables the researcher to seek proof that certain variables affect other variables in one way or other. Hence, empirical researches are considered to be the most powerful support for a given hypothesis.

4. **Quantitative vs Qualitative:** Quantitative research is based on the measurement of quantity and, hence, is applicable to phenomena that can be expressed in terms of quantity. On the contrary, qualitative research is concerned with qualitative phenomena relating to some quality or kind. For example, if we are interested to know why people behave as they behave, then we often talk of qualitative phenomenon, *i.e.*, motivation. Qualitative research is especially important in the behavioural sciences where the objective of research is to discover underlying motives of human behaviour. Through such research, the researcher can analyse the various factors which motivate people to behave in a particular manner or which make people like or dislike a particular thing.

Some other types of research are (*i*) one-time research or longitudinal research, (*ii*) field-setting research or laboratory research, (*iii*) clinical or diagnostic research, and (*iv*) historical or conclusion-oriented research. However, these are least in use in behavioural sciences research. Hence not discussed in detail.

3.4 PROCESS OF RESEARCH

Research, be it applied or fundamental, descriptive or analytical, conceptual or empirical, qualitative or qualitative, needs to be conducted following a scientific process. This ensures meaningful research results. A scientific research usually involves the following steps in its process:

1. Identification and selection of a research problem
2. Review of literature to identify the gaps in the existing knowledge.
3. Concept clarification.
4. Preparation of research design consisting of objectives, hypotheses, coverage of study, and time schedule for the study.
5. Selection of research methodology. Research methodology includes components such as data sources, preparation of interview schedule and questionnaire, and the like.
6. Collection of data.
7. Processing of data involving coding, tabulation, and preparation of tables, diagrams and charts.
8. Analysis of data
9. Drafting of report.

Since all steps mentioned above are quite self explanatory, hence these are not explained in details.

3.5 RESEARCH METHODS

Though there are several research methods in use, the following five methods are the commonly used ones in behavioural sciences research:

1. Case Studies
2. Laboratory Experiments
3. Field Experiments
4. Survey Research, and
5. Simulation

A brief description of these follows:

Case Studies

What is a case? In brief, a case is a description of a situation or a problem actually faced by a person or an organisation. Case is not just an example. It is not, on the other extreme, simply a straight out photographic slice of life. It is somewhere between these two things. An example is used to illustrate a situation. On the other hand, case, rather being an example, has a structure or a series of structures that present sequence of events over the period[5].

The use of case study method in organisational behaviour research is on increasing. It has proved the excellent method of describing a situation or a problem in its exactness. Case studies have become a useful tool for gathering initial information about various aspects of a problem or system. It serves as seed-bed for more and more knowledge acquisition about the problem or system. However, case studies method also suffers from some shortcomings. **First,** there are some variables, in which the researcher is interested, beyond the control of the researcher. This affects the cause-and-effect relationship of the variables. **Second,** the researcher's potential bias also affect the real presentation of the situation. As we shall see in chapter 6, perception is an important variable that intervenes between reality and behaviour. Therefore, in a case study researcher's perception of events is likely to alter the description significantly. That is why it is sometimes opined that case studies at times reveal more the case researcher/writer than they reveal about the problem or situation studied. Hence, the organisational behaviour researchers need to keep in mind these two shortcomings while doing case studies.

Laboratory Experiments

The laboratory experiment method is used to identity a cause-effect relationship between two variables. Experiments are made to measure the impact of independent variable on the dependent variables by controlling the contaminating factors. The independent variable is manipulated and dependent variables are controlled in order to identify the cause-effect relationship between two types of variables.

Let it be exemplified with an imaginary example.

> Suppose, a researcher is interested in identifying cause-effect relationship between increase in pay (independent variable)of workers and their performance (dependent variable). Simply speaking, the researcher has to be certain that increase in workers' pay will increase their performance. For this, the researcher needs to control other relevant factors (contaminating variables) such as workers' greater experience, better background knowledge, superior strength, etc. that also increase performance. How the contaminating factors will be controlled is done by doing laboratory experiments. Laboratory experiments are now used to study the cause-effect between various variables on human behaviour. One such popular behavioural laboratory experiment was done by Ivan Pavlov[6] to identify the impact of ringing a bell on dog's behaviour in exhibiting salivalion.

However, laboratory experiments are not free from criticism. The main criticism is that laboratory experiments are conducted in an artificially created environment by manipulating dependent variable and controlling independent variables. As such, the results may not be generalisable because they may not carry over to the real organisational setting where more complex and varied tasks are performed.[7]

Field Studies

Research studies conducted in real organisational settings where the events actually occur, are called "field studies". In field studies, information is collected from individuals or available records in the organisation on the variables of interest to the researcher. The researcher first identifies and selects the important variables relevant to his/her investigation and, then, studies them very closely.

Survey Research

Survey research is the most popular method in organisational behaviour research. A questionnaire consisting of a series of questions is formulated to supply it to the respondents to collect required information from them. Data so collected is tabulated, analysed and interpreted to reach to some conclusions. Like other methods, survey method also suffers from certain problems. The important ones are: (*i*) respondents' bias to answer the questions, and (*ii*) different interpretation by different respondents to the same question. However, the problem of misinterpretation of questions by the respondents can be minimized by pretesting questionnaires before the research study is actually conducted.

Simulations

In simulation method, real-life situation is approximated by developing a model composed of the significant variable in the phenomena or situation. This helps the researcher understand how the real situation happens. Simulations are used in a variety of situations for both teaching and research purposes. The experience and results derived from simulations suggest the researcher to apply it in the real situations of the world. In order to accrue advantages of simulation, the simulation model needs to be accurate, to the extent possible. The simulation method becomes the most valuable when it behaves like a real-world counterpart. As regards the use of simulation in organisational behavioural research, it is least used method. The reason being the typical and highly unpredict.able human behaviour does not lend itself to a precise model building.

3.6 CHARACTERISTICS OF A GOOD RESEARCH

Research, to be considered good, must have characteristics like purposiveness, methodological rigour and generalisability. A brief description of these follows:

Purposiveness

Purposiveness is the first hallmark of a good research. Good research is always conducted after determining the purpose for which the study is undertaken. It is the purpose of the study that determines the complexity of the research questions to be addressed.

Methodological Rigour

Methodological rigour refers to (*i*) choosing the appropriate sample of the universe (total), (*ii*) using appropriate measures that ensure reliability and validity, (*iii*) using multiple data collection techniques that minimise biases, and (*iv*) using the appropriate statistical techniques in data analysis. These are not discussed in more detail as these are self explanatory.

Generalisability

Generalisability is yet another characteristics of a good research. The results of the research should be generalisable to groups of individuals other than those who were studied in sample. In other words, the characteristics of the sample described in the study should be representative of the characteristics of workers working in the organisation. The researcher cannot generalise the findings drawn from a sample of workers who are different than the one you have in your organisation and that too, to your situation. For example, if the study has a sample of young, predominantly male workers, and your organisation has predominantly older male workers, then the findings of the study may not be generalisable to your organisation. Infact, the strength of a research depends upon its generalisability.

SUMMARY

This summary is organized by the 'learning objectives' given on page no. 27.

- *Research is an organised and systematized effort to gain new knowledge for solving a problem. Research, thus, helps managers understand human behaviour more accurately and, in turn, facilitates them to effectively deal with human beings in the organisation*
- *The unique terms used in research are hypothesis, methodology, variable, and model or theory.*
- *Research may be applied or fundamental, descriptive or analytical, conceptual or empirical.*
- *A systematic research follows a process involving certain steps in it. The common methods of research include case studies, laboratory experiments, field experiments, survey research, and simulations.*
- *Purposiveness, methodological rigour, and generalisability make a research good or ideal.*

Now that we have exposed you to the perspectives of OB in chapters 1 to 3, we are in a good position to take a closer and orderly look at the aspects of individual behaviour at work place. Accordingly, in the next section II, we shall examine the behavioural aspects of an individual like behavioural foundation, personality, perception, attitudes, values, job satsifaction, learning, and motivation.

REVIEW QUESTIONS

1. What is research? Why is it conducted?
2. Describe the types of research. Which one, in your opinion, is most appropriate for organisational behaviour research and why?
3. Describe the different research methods. Which method do you consider the most appropriate for studying human behaviour at work? Justify.
4. What makes a research an ideal or good one.
5. Write short notes on the following:
   (*a*) Hypothesis (*b*) Variable (*c*) Case Studies
   (*d*) Simulations (*e*) Applied Research

REFERENCES

1. **The Advanced Learner's Dictionary of Current English,** Oxford Univeristy Press, 1952, p. 1069.
2. William C. Emory: **Business Research Methods**, Illinois Richard D. Irwin, Homewood, 1976, p.8.
3. Stephen P. Robbins: ***op. cit.,*** 1998, p. 26.
4. F.N. Kerlinger: **Foundations of Behavioural Research**, Surjeet Publications, Delhi, 1978, p.379.
5. Nand Dhameja (Ed.): **Case Studies in Administrative Environment and Decision Making,** Indian Institute of Public Administration, New Delhi, 1995, p.2.
6. I.P. Pavlov: **The Work of the Digestive Glands**, trans. W.H. Thompson, Charles Griffin, London, 1902.
7. Uma Sekaran: **Organisational Behaviour: Text and Cases,** Tata McGraw–Hill Publishing Company Limited, New Delhi, 7th Edition, 1998, p. 20.

PART TWO

INDIVIDUAL PERSPECTIVE

- Foundation of Individual Behaviour
- Personality
- Perception
- Attitudes, Values and Job Satisfaction
- Learning
- Organisational Citizenship Behaviour (OCB)
- Emotions and Moods
- Transactional Analysis (TA)
- Motivation : Concepts
- Motivation : Application
- Morale

4

FOUNDATIONS OF INDIVIDUAL BEHAVIOUR

"Business organizations are made or broken in the long-run not by markets or capital, patents, or equipments, but by men." **– *L.F. Urwick***

"Man, of all the resources available to man, can grow and develop."

– *Peter Drucker*

Learning Objectives

After studying this chapter, you should be able to:

- **Appreciate** the need for understanding human behaviour at work in organisations
- **Understand** individual differences.
- **Explain** how the human behaviour is caused.
- **Know** the various models of man found in organisations.

4.1 INTRODUCTION

All organisations are composed of individuals. No organisation can exist without individuals. The organisational performance is largely affected by the way individuals behave at work. That individuals with different characteristics behave differently in the similar and different situations underlines the need for managers to understand individual/human behaviour at work so as to extract the best and maximum contribution from them. This chapter is, therefore, devoted to dislcuss the foundations of individual behaviour at work in organisations.

4.2 THE INDIVIDUAL AND INDIVIDUAL DIFFERENCES

Like other fields of social sciences, behavioural sciences have also a philosophical foundation of basic concepts that guide and govern its development. Take "**double-accounting**", for example, which is based on the basic concept that "**for every debit, there will be an equal credit.**" Even in physical sciences, the law of gravity, for example, operates uniformly in Delhi and London. But the same cannot be said of people/ individuals. The behaviour of individuals is determined by the characteristics of individuals and environment they live in.

Individuals differ from each other owing to their varying characteristics that form an individual's individuality. This is the reason why each individual is considered as an island in himself/herself. All individuals are different. This is a fact supported by science[1] too. Each one is different from all others just as each of their fingerprints is different, as far as we commonly know.

As regards individual differences at work, the important ones are outlined here:

1. Depending upon different psychological make-ups, people differ in attaching importance to **rewards vis-a-vis kinds of jobs**. For example, while some people will prefer to assume challanging jobs for expressing their abilities, others may like to prefer jobs offering job security.
2. People also differ in the **type of compensation plan** they want. Some may prefer to have compensation under time-wage system, while others may like piece-wage system as their compensation plan.
3. People differ in **the style of leadership** they want to work under. While some may like to work under autocratic leadership style, others may prefer to be under democratic or **laissez-faire** style.
4. People also differ in their **stemina to bear with job stress.** While some may prefer to flight from stress, others may like fight with and work more effectively under stress.
5. People may also differ in **expression to their grievances**. Some may be extrovert in expressing their grievances, while others may be introvert in doing so.
6. Last but not the least, people also differ in their **personal characteristics** like sex, age, race, education, abilities, perception, personality, values, attitudes, etc.

These individual differences cause differences in human behaviour.

4.3 HUMAN BEHAVIOUR AND ITS CAUSATION

Before we proceed to understand the causation of human behaviour, it seems pertinent to know first what the term **behaviour** actually means. Though different behavioural scientists have defined 'behaviour' differently, it simply means as a response to certain stimuli which is observable directly and indirectly. Behaviour is observed directly by studying the responses of people to their work environment. Indirect observation refers to how people describe decision making processes and attitudes verbally.

The human behaviour is caused by certain reasons. Behaviour is the result of interaction between individual characteristics and the characteristics of the environment in which the behaviour occurs. In other words, behaviour is a function of both the person and the environment.

As stated earlier, each person with a unique combination of characteristics is different from all others. Some of these characteristics are **inherited** from birth while others are **learned** over time. Personal characteristics remain inside the person whereas environmental ones outside the person. These personal and environmental characteristics serve as the foundations of individual behaviour.

What includes in the person and the environment in the context of human behaviour is shown in Table 4.1.

Table 4.1: Foundations of Individual/Human Behaviour

The Person	The Environment
I. Personal Biographical Factors	**Environmental Factors**
1. Sex 2. Age 3. Education 4. Abilities 5. Marital Status	1. Economic Conditions 2. Political Situations 3. Cultural Values 4. Social Norms
II. Psychological Factors	**Organisational Factors**
1. Personality 2. Perception 3. Attitudes 4. Values 5. Learning	1. Physical Facilities 2. Organisational Structure 3. Organisational Design 4. Leadership Styles 5. Reward System

The person and the environment can also be termed as the internal perspective and external perspective respectively of human behaviour at work.

Sometimes the person and the environment are so closely related to behaviour that it becomes difficult to clearly state whether the behaviour is caused by the person or by the environment. They offer alternative explanations for human behaviour. For example, the personal persepective might say Mr. Kottey is an outstanding Professor because he has a high need for achievement, whereas environmental perspective might say that Mr. Kotler is an outstanding Professor because he is paid extremely well for his work. Given such situation, Kurt Lewin[2] captured both perspectives and opined that **behaviour is a function of both the person and the environment.**

Now, let us understand how the characteristics of the person and the environment affect his/her behaviour at work.

Personal Biographical Factors

Sex: Sex has a profound impact on behaviour at work. It affects one's turnover and absenteeism. Research has proved beyond doubt that the tendency to change job and abstain from work is higher among female employees than their male counterparts. The reason is not difficult to seek. Historically, our society has placed home and family responsibility on the females. When a child is ill or some one needs to await the electrician or plumber, it is often woman who has to abstain from work. Added to these is our so far less appreciated and encouraged women as employees in organisations.

Age: Age also has an important impact on performance, turnover, absenteeism and job satisfaction. With advances in age, employee's performance tends to decline. The older one grows, less likely he/she becomes to quit the job due to decreasing propensity to move from one job to another and from one place to another. The absenteeism rate among the older/aged is likely to be higher mainly due to poor health associated with old age. Older age also results in reduced productivity because of the individual's skill tends to decline with advancement in age. An employee's age and job satisfaction are found positively associated as propensity to change job and place tends to reduce with one's becoming older and older.

Education: Both the level and type of education also affect individual behaviour. Higher the educational level, higher will be one's expectation for reward and, in turn, increased will be job satisfaction. The opposite is true when level of education is lower. However, job-dissatisfaction may occur when rewards do not match expectation.

The type of education an individual has received also affects his/her behaviour. Education can be either 'general including areas like arts, humanities and social sciences or 'special' covering disciplines such as engineering, medicine, management, computer science and the like. The individuals having these two types of education are likely to exhibit distinct behaviour at their work places as evince the graduates in arts and management in a University Campus, for example:

Abilities: Simply stating, ability means an individual's skill and capacity to perform a job. Ability is made up of two types of skills—intellectual and physical.

Abilities needed to perform mental activities are called **intellectual abilities**. Nowadays, the popular management admission tests like MAT, GMAT and CAT are designed to ascertain candidate's intellectual abilities to pursue management course are examples of intellectual abilities. Robbins[3] has listed the following four relevant dimensions that make up an individual's intellectual abilities:

Table 4.2 : Four Dimensions of Intellectual Abilities

Dimension	Job Example
Number Aptitude	**Accountant**—Completing sales tax on a set of items
Verbal Comprehension	**Plant Manager**— Following corporate policies
Perceptual Speed	**Fire Investigator**— Identifying clues to support a charge of arson.
Inductive Reasoning	**Market Researcher**—Forecasting demand for a product in the next time.

Physical abilities refer to one's stamina, manual dexterity, leg strength and the like. Physical abilities gain importance for successfully doing less skilled jobs. One researcher[4] has identified nine basic abilities involved in successful performance of physical jobs or tasks. These are described in Table 4.3.

Table 4.3 : Nine Basic Physical Abilities

Ability	Description
Strength Factors	
1. **Dynamic Strength**	Ability to exert muscular force repeatedly over time.
2. **Trunk Strength**	Ability to exert muscular strength using the trunk muscles.
3. **Static Strength**	Ability to exert force against external objects.
4. **Explosive Strength**	Ability to expand a maximum of energy in one or a series of explosive acts.

Flexibility Factors	
5. **External Flexibility**	Ability to move the trunk and back muscles as far as possible.
6. **Dynamic Flexibility**	Ability to make rapid, repeated flexing movements.
Other Factors	
7. **Body Coordination**	Ability to co-ordinate the simultaneous actions of different parts of the body.
8. **Balance**	Ability to maintain equilibrium despite forces pulling off balance.
9. **Stamina**	Ability to continue maximum effort requiring prolonged efforts over time.

Marital Status: Though there are not enough studies to establish any concrete relationship between an employee's marital status and his/her behaviour at work, it is believed that married employees have fewer absences, undergo less turnover and are more satisfied with their jobs than their unmarried co-workers. Very possibly, the need for a steady job and regular income experienced by the married employees to meet their increased responsbilities explains the case.

Psychological Factors

Psychological factors refer to an individual's mental characteristics and attributes that are not always observable. But these too affect human behaviour in a considerable way. Among the several psychological factors, the important ones having their profound impact on behaviour are perception, personality, attitudes, values and learning. These have been discussed in detail in the subsequent chapters later in the book.

Environmental Factors

Economic Conditions : Though economic factors include several ones, the prominent among them are employment level, wage rates, economic outlook, and technological change. These greatly affect human behaviour at work.

Level of employment opportunities available in the country bear strong influence on the behaviour of individuals. For example, fewer job opportunities reduce turnover and absenteeism of employees due to the fear of losing the present job. On the contrary, when job opportunities are available in plenty, tendency on the part of employees for job-hopping increases and, in turn, employees' turnover and absenteeism do also increase. As such, one's loyalty to an organisation also gets adversely affected.

Employees work to earn wages that satisfy their needs. It is widely accepted that higher the wages, more attraction for employees to be attracted to join an organisation and vice versa. Accordingly, higher wages offer greater job satisfaction and more stability and regularity in an employee's job. Reverse is also true in case of lower rates of wages.

The general economic outlook prevalent in an economy also affects employees' expectations and, in turn, their behaviour at work. For example, the employees who experience frequent lay-offs due to economic cycles, are more likely to be motivated by such factors that provide job security. But, the employees who attach less importance to job security are likely to be affected or motivated by other factors[5].

Technological change in the form of automation, robotics, computerisation, and sophisticated production, technologies affects job opportunities and, in turn, employees' behaviour as well. Technological change reduces skill required for employees to perform a job and pushes wage-rates down-ward. Thus, requirements for employees with reduced skill, on the one hand, and perceived lack of advancement opportunities, on the other, adversely affect the employees' job satisfaction.

Political Situations: The political climate hovering in a country in which an individual lives affects the individual behaviour in one way or other. Enough evidence is available from our own homeland to argue that the stability or otherwise of the Government affects the employment opportunities, both in quantity and quality. For example, in a politically unstable country like ours during the nineties, neither the new entrepreneurs were attracted to establish their industries, nor they were interested in making huge investments in the expansion and diversification of their industrial units. As such, employment opportunities got adversely affected, both in quantity and quality.

Cultural Values: People living in different regions imbibe different cultural values. Culture is made up of the factors like basic beliefs, values, work-ethic, need for achievement that have behavioural implications. Let us briefly see how these factors affect behaviour.

Value is tinged with one's moral that guides an individual to judge what is right and what is wrong. Such value-based judgement influences one's perception, attitudes, etc. These, in turn, affect one's behaviour.

The work ethic is also tinged with moral. An employee's hard work and commitment to his/her work is called work ethic. While strong work ethic motivates employees to behave positively, the weak one does just opposite.

Need for achievement motivates an individual to work more and hard. This improves employees' stability on jobs and, in turn, have less turnovers and absenteeism. In fact, both the work ethic and the need for achievement affect the employee's behaviour at work in a similar way.

Organisational Factors

Besides individual characteristics, the characteristics of an organisation, also called organisational factors, affect human behaviour at work. The prominent among organisational factors are physical facilities, organisational structure and design, leadership styles and reward system. These have been discussed, in detail, in later chapters of this book.

Causation of Human Behaviour

We stated earlier that the human behaviour is caused. Here, we shall explain how it is actually caused.

The best way to understand causation of human behaviour is the systems concept. A system consists of the four definite parts, viz., input, thruput, output and feedback. How the human behaviour is caused following this system concept is diagramatically presented below in Figure 4.1.

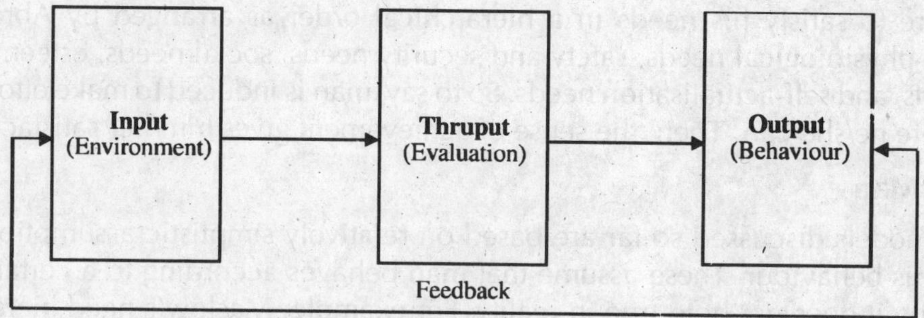

Figure 4.1: Behaviour Follows System

Whatever enters in the system from the environment in the form of information serves as raw material or 'input'. Thruput is the evaluation or transformation of input received. Finally, employee's overt behaviour based on input and thruput is the 'output'. Feedback serves the system with alternatives for changes in the sequence or time period of the systems operations. Even a change in one small factor can bring about relatively large changes in behaviour.

4.4 MODELS OF MAN

Study of human behaviour is both rewarding and necessary for management. It is doubtful whether the management can perform its functions successfully without having understanding why people behave as they do. The fact remains that individual differences among people cause differences in their behaviour. Based on individual differences, individuals are classified into certain models or types. The following are the important models of man observed in organisations:

1. Rational Economic Man
2. Self-Actualising Man
3. Complex Man
4. Social Man
5. Organisation Man

A brief description of these models follows :

Rational-Economic Man

This is the oldest model of man. The basic doctrine of this model is that man strives for earning more money in a rational manner. Thus, this model assumes that man can be motivated to produce more by providing more economic incentives as is done in case of piece-rate system of reward. But, it is important to mention that man works following the marginal utility theory. Similarly, the organisation also continues to give employees incentives till it is receiving matching contribution from them. Beyond that, organisation will not because it will incur losses to it.

Self-Actualising Man

This model is based on the assumptions that man is self-motivated and controlled. These assumptions are mostly based on McGregor's Theory[6] (discussed in Chapter 9). Economic incentives have their limitations in inducing man to work more. Man works more to satisfy his needs in a hierarchical order as arranged by Abrahim Maslow[7]—physiological needs, safety and security needs, social needs, esteem and status needs, and self-actualisation needs. So to say, man is induced to make efforts to reach where he/she can. Then, the sense of achievement gives him/her satisfaction.

Complex Man

The models discussed so far are based on relatively simplistic assumptions of man and his behaviour. These assume that man behaves according to a certain set pattern. But, it does not hold true in reality. For example, Maslow's need hierarchy cannot be uniform for all individuals, but there can be overlapping in needs. As we stated earlier, behaviour of individuals is caused and individual differences make it unpredictable. Given the two persons having the same needs, still they may behave differently because the variable that determine human behaviour are themselves unpredictable. Thus, human being is quite complex and so his/her behaviour also. Therefore, managers need to take clues for their managerial actions realising that no single action can be utilized successfully in all situations but depending upon complexities of variables affecting human behaviour.

Social Man

Social man concept is based on the assumption that man being a part of society is influenced and motivated by social variables. According to this model, man is induced more by his desire to maintain his social relationships and ties than economic motives. Added to this is man's more responsiveness to his group pressure and sanction. In fact, the human relations approach in management beginning from the famous Hawthorne Experiments discussed in Chapter 2, is also based on the concept of social man. Therefore, while dealing with individuals in organisations, managers need to be concerned mainly with people's feelings about their belongingness to their groups and society.

Organisation Man

The concept of 'organisation man' is given by Whyte[8]. In fact, the organisation man is an extension of social man. Organisation man model assumes that man attaches high importance to the loyalty to his organisation and cordial relationship with his co-workers. Thus, this concept sacrifices individuality for the sake of the organisation. The reason being organisation itself takes care of individual interest. Its implication for management is that management should design its various functions suitable to satisfy the organisational needs.

The following caselet of a Taxi Company will exemplify how human relations matter in good human dealings more especially in business.

Good Human Relations for Good Business

It's 7 am in Kyoto, Japan, and the taxi company has just called a second time to say they can't find my house. Once again I spell out directions even a blind cabby could follow, glance impatiently at my watch, and wait. Only two hours remain until my flight leves and it's an-hour-and-a-half trip to Osaka airport.

Outside, torrential rains are threatening to sweep my little house off the mountain slope on which it teeters, so far north in Kyoto that city buses lurch past only three times a day.

The telephone rings again. "Terribly sorry," begins the dispatcher. then I realise what's happened. flooded with calls, the company is maximising profits by handling only in-city runs. I'd heard this happens when the weather gets bad and inclement. I shout into the phone that I have a flight to catch-I must be in Seoul by noon-and I'll meet the taxi a few hundred meters away on a bridge over the Kamo River.

Standing above the gale-swelled torrent, horisontal wind-driven rain drenching my overcoat, I gaze up and down the road. No taxi. Finally, struggling staring at the lunatic, well-dressed foreigner walking backwards and holding his thumb out in the downpour.

From the other direction a white Nissan approaches, then jams on its brakes. A young man throws open the door, gesturing for me to get in. Shaking with cold anger, I climb inside.

In the most humble Japanese, the main identifies himself as the dispatcher with whom I have spoken three times this morning. to get me to my plane, he has abandoned his post and raced from the company in his personal car. He apologizes profusely, but does not explain why a taxi could not pick me up, except to say they are "very, very busy" this morning. Delivering me and with more apologies implores me to patronize his company in the future also.

A few hours later settling back into my seat as the storm-delayed 727 takes off, I open the newspaper. On the second page my eyes wander to the headline of a short article : "**Taxi Strike begins This Morning] in Kyoto**."

SUMMARY

This summary is organised by the 'learning objectives' given on page no. 37 :

- *Organisations are made of the people, by the people, and for the people. The need for and significance of understanding people / human behaviour lies in better utilization of them for effective achievement of organisational goals.*
- *Almost all human behaviour is caused by following the system of 'Input → Throughput, and → Output.*
- *Individuals differ in various respects such as personality, perception, attitude, values, emotions, learning, motivation, etc. Hence, no two individuals are alike.*
- *Based on individual differences, people in organisations are classified into various models such as economic - rationale man, self - actualizing man, complex man, social man, and organisation man.*

REVIEW QUESTIONS

1. Why should managers give importance in understanding human behaviour?
2. "Human behaviour is caused". Examine this statement.
3. What are the foundation factors that determine human behaviour in organisations?
4. Bring out the impact of personal factors in determining individual behaviour.
5. Discuss the nature of individual differences found in organisations. Reflect on the managerial implications of individual differences.
6. Discuss the major models of man noticed in organisations.

REFERENCES

1. John W. Newstron and Keith Davis : **Organisational Behaviour** (Human Behaviour at Work), Tata McGraw-Hill Publishing Company Limited, New Delhi, Third Reprint 1996, p.11.
2. Kurt Lewin : Field Theory in Social Science, In : Dorin Cartwright (Ed.) : **Selected Theoretical Papers**, Harper, New York, 1951.
3. Stephen P. Robbins : **Organisational Behaviour**, Printice Hall of India Private Limited, New Delhi, Seventh Edition 1996, p. 89.
4. E.A. Fleishman: Evaluating Physical Abilities Required by Jobs, **Personnel Administrator**, June 1979, pp. 82-92.
5. Gray and Starke : **Organisational Behaviour - Concepts and Applications**, Merrill, 1988, p.64.
6. Douglas McGregor : **The Human Side of Enterprise**, McGraw-Hill, New York, 1976.
7. Abrahim H. Maslow : **Motivation and Personality**, Harper & Row, New York, 1954.
8. William H. Whyte : **The Organisation Man**, Doubleday, New York, 1956.

Case 4. 1 : The Audit Objection*

One morning, the Director of Ramanlal Institute of Research. Dhanbad, received a telephone call from the government requesting the Institute to participate in the exhibition which was being organised at Durgapur to coincide with the All-India Congress Committee session. The exhibition was scheduled to open in about a week's time.

The Director called the administrative officer, the engineer, and the information officer for an urgent meeting. Because of the urgency of the work, it was decided at the meeting to make immediate arrangements for the erection of a stall at the exhibition site. All the three officers were advised to proceed to Durgapur by the afternoon train and asked to contact the local parties engaged in the erection of stalls, invite quotations, and award work so that the stall would be ready within the next four days.

The officers reached Durgapur the same day. They completed their work by 8.30 p.m. and reached Durgapur Railway Station to return to Dhanbad. At the booking window, they learnt that a mail train was due at 10.00 p.m. but as the distance between Durgapur and Dhanbad was only 130 kms they could not be issued first class tickets. They could either buy first class tickets for a station beyond 300 kms or A.C. tickets

* Adapted from **Behavioural Processes in Organisations** by Udai Pareek, T.V. Rao and D.M.Pestonjee, Oxford and IBH Publishing Co. Pvt. Ltd., New Delhi, 1996(Sixth Printing), pp. 317-318.

from Durgapur to Dhanbad. The third possible alternative was to travel the next day but this would involve additional cost to the Institute in terms of D.A. and personal inconveniences as none of them had carried any baggage.

The officers finally decided to buy A.C. tickets which are cheaper than the first class tickets for beyond 300 kms. But when boarding the train, they could not get into the A.C. coach and had to travel by first class.

At the time of preferring the T.A. claims the actual circumstance of the case was explained. The Audit Officer while admitting the claim, reduced it to the standard first class fare between Durgapur and Dhanbad.

QUESTIONS

1. What caused the behaviour of three officers to act as they acted?
2. Which one models of men applies to the three officers?
3. Do you think that the audit officer's objection was not right? Justify.

5

PERSONALITY

"Personality is like a tree and reputation like its shadow. The shadow is what we think of it. The tree is the real thing." – ***Abraham Lincoln***

"We boil at different degrees." – ***Ralph Waldo Emerson***

Learning Objectives

After studying this chapter, you should be able to:

- **Define** personality and state what determines personality.
- **Discuss** the theories of personality.
- **State** how personality develops from its infancy to maturity.
- **Explain** the ways personality influences individuals' behaviour in organisations.
- **Scan** the personality traits the Indian managers exhibit.

Personality of an individual also affects human behaviour. Personality is the sum total of an individual's psycho-physical systems that determine his/her behaviour in a given environment/situation. Personality differs from person to person depending on their varying psycho-physical aspects. For example, we find in our day-to-day life that some people are quiet and passive, while others are loud and aggressive in their behaviours. Therefore, understanding human/employees behaviour in organisations in a better way underlines the need to understand personality in its various aspects. What exactly personality is? What do determine an individual's personality? How do the theories of personality help us understand and predict human behaviour in a given situation? The aim of this chapter is to attempt to answer these questions.

5.1 CONCEPT OF PERSONALITY

There may be so many personalities as many persons. Hence, there is no consensus what personality is. Personality means different things to different people. To some, it means one's charm, dress and attractiveness, to others, it means a unitary mode of response to life situations.

The English word 'personality' has been derived from the Latin word per sonare. It means 'to **speak through'.** Originally, the term denoted the masks worn by the actors in the ancient Greek dramas. In this way, personality is used in terms of physical attractiveness. However, perceiving personality in terms of external appearance is in narrow sense. Personality includes something more. Let us go through some definitions on personality that will help us understand personality in a proper and better sense.

According to Hilgard et at[1], "Personality may be understood as the characteristic patterns of behaviour and modes of thinking that determine a person's adjustment to the environment."

In the opinion of Ruch[2], "Personality can be described as how he understands and views himself, and his pattern of inner and outer measurable traits".

Allport[3] has defined personality as : " the dynamic organisation within the individual of those psycho-physical systems that determine his unique adjustment to his environment."

Thus, it reflects from above definitions that personality includes both internal and external aspects of a person. Here, external aspects relate to one's height, weight, facial features, colour and other physical aspects and traits. One's attitude, values, learning etc. are the examples of internal aspects of personality. Of more importance to organisational behaviour are internal aspects of personality.

Now, personality can be defined as the sum total of ways in which an individual reacts and interacts with others and environment. In other words, personality is an organised behaviour of an individual to react to a given stimulus in a set manner. This is most often in the form of consistent response to environmental stimuli.

An individual's personality is influenced by the personal life and where he/she is working. We now, therefore, turn our attention to this aspect of personality.

5.2 DETERMINANTS OF PERSONALITY

In this section, we shall try to probe into what determines an individual's personality. Is the personality predetermined at birth itself? or is it the result of individual's interaction with one's environment? Strictly speaking, there is no clear-cut answer to this question. Different thinkers have listed different determinants of personality. For example, McClelland[4] has categorised them into four fundamental theories – (*i*) Traits, (*ii*) Schema, (*iii*) Motives, and (*iv*) Self Schema. There are others—Scott and Mitchell[5], who have classified personality determinants into heredity groups and cultural factors. However, the various determinants of personality are broadly classified into three groups, namely, (*i*) Heredity, (*ii*) Environment, and (*iii*) Situation. These are now discussed in seriatim.

Heredity

Heredity refers to those factors that were determined at conception. Thus, heredity refers to biological factors. Heredity is the transmission of the qualities from the parents to the children through a biological mechanism lying in the chromosomes of the germ cells. Physical stature, facial attractiveness, temperament, sex, muscle composition and biological rhythms are the examples of heredity characteristics that are generally influenced by who one's parents are[6].

Besides, studies on job satisfaction[7] also lend credibility to the argument that heredity surely plays a role in determining one's personality. Research has proved that individual job satisfaction remains remarkably stable over time. Not only that, job satisfaction tends to remain stable even when employers or occupations change.

Environment

The environment, *i.e.*, one's early conditioning, the family norms, friends and social groups exerts pressures on one's personality formation. Culture establishes the norms, attitudes and values that are passed along from generation to generation. Thus, a cultural consistency is created over time. Evidences are available to believe that the cultural environment in which people are raised plays a major role in shaping personality. For example, in India, children learn from an early age the values of hard work, frugality and family closeness. The Indian culture expects different behaviours from males and females.

Home environment generated to a child also exerts important influence in shaping his/her personality. For example, children reared in orphans or in unstimulating homes are much more likely to socially and emotionally maladjusted than their counterparts raised by parents in a warm, loving and stimulating environment[8]. Research studies[9] have also revealed that parents have more effect on the personality development of their children as compared to other members of the family. Besides parents, siblings (brothers and sisters) also influence shaping of personality. Elders serve as models for youngers.

The contineous impact of different social groups called, **socialisation process,** on an individual also affects his/her personality development. The socialisation process starts with the initial contact between a mother and her new infant. They, infact, gradually come into contact with the social groups outside home/family such as peers, school friends, and the members of the work group. The socialisation process is, thus, not confined to early childhood, rather it takes place throughout one's life. Organisation itself also contributes much to socialisation. On the whole, this socialisation process influences one's personality development.

Situation

No doubt, both heredity and environment are the primary determinants of personality. But, there is a third factor also, i.e., the situation, that influences the effects of heredity and environment on personality. In practice, an individual's personality does change depending on the situation. This is because the different demands of the different situations call forth different aspects of one's personality. As an example, the same person while facing an employment interview and while enjoying picnic with his/her friends in a public park behaves quite differently depending on two different situations.

Situation, in fact, exerts an important pressure on the individual to behave in a particular manner. In certain cases, how one will behave is not determined by what kind of person one is, but by in which kind of situation one is placed. There may be, for example, a worker whose personality history suggests that he had need for power and achievement. But, when the same worker is placed in a highly bureaucratised work situation, may feel frustrated and behave apathetically or aggressively. This clearly indicates that his personality changed under changed situation.

However, it is difficult, if not impossible, to state the exact impact of various types of situations exert on one's personality. Nonetheless, it can safely be mentioned that certain situations are more relevant than others in influencing personality.[10] Hence, personality needs to be looked at situational context, not in isolation.

5.3 TYPES OF PERSONALITIES

As stated earlier, there are so many personalities as many are persons. Personalities differ in traits. A trait is any distinguishable, relatively enduring way in which one individual differs from another. Though behavioural researchers have attempted to identify the personality traits, the 16 traits reported by Cattell[11] are generally accepted ones. These are listed in the following Table 5.1

Table 5.1: Sixteen Primary Traits of Personality

1.	Reserved	vs	Outgoing
2.	Less Intelligent	vs	More Intelligent
3.	Affected by Feeling	vs	Emotionally Stable
4.	Submissive	vs	Dominant
5.	Serious	vs	Happy-Go-Lucky
6.	Expedient	vs	Conscientious
7.	Timid	vs	Venturesome
8.	Tough-Minded	vs	Sensitive
9.	Trusting	vs	Suspicious
10.	Practical	vs	Imaginative
11.	Forthright	vs	Shrewd
12.	Self-assured	vs	Apprehensive
13.	Conservative	vs	Experimenting
14.	Group-Dependent	vs	Self-Sufficient
15.	Uncontrolled	vs	Controlled
16.	Relaxed	vs	Tense

Groups of above traits serve as basis for classifying personalities into types. Based on these groups, following are the main types of personalities:

1. Introvert and Extrovert Personalities
2. Type A and Type B Personalities
3. Judging and Perceptive Personalities

Let us discuss what each of these types means.

Introvert Personalities: Introvert is one of the two basic orientations of people have. Persons with introvert orientation are primarily oriented to the subjective world. Such people look inward and experience and process their thoughts and ideas within themselves. They also avoid social contacts and initiating interaction with other group mates, withdrawn, quiet and enjoy solitude. People with introvert personality are found more inclined to excel at tasks that require thought and analytical skill.

Extrovert Personalities: Simply speaking, extroverts are just contrary to introverts. Extroverts are friendly, sociable, lively, gregarious, aggressive and expressing their feelings and ideas openly. Accordingly, they are more suitable and successful for the positions that require considerable interaction with others. Sales activities, publicity departments, personal relations unit, etc. are the examples of activities suitable for extroverts.

Look at following Table 5.2 and see how introverts differ from extroverts.

Table 5.2 : Introverts vs Extroverts

Introverts	Extroverts
Like quiet for concentration	Like variety and action.
Tend to be careful with details, dislike sweeping statements	Tend to work faster, dislike complicated procedure.
Have trouble remembering names and faces.	Are often good at greeting people.
Like to think a lot before they act, sometimes without acting	Often act quickly, sometimes without thinking.
Work contentedly alone.	Like to have people around.
Have some problems communicating	Usually communicate freely.
Tend not to mind working on one project for a long time uninterruptedly.	Are often impatient with long slow jobs.
Dislike telephone intrusions and interruptions.	Often do not mind interruptions of answering the telephone.

Validity of results have showed that introvert/extrovert is applicable to only the rare extremes. The fact remains that most of the people really tend to be neither introverts nor extroverts, but ambiverts. That is, they are in between introversion and extroversion.

Type A Personality: Type A people are characterised by hard-working, highly achievement-oriented, impatient, have sense of time urgency, aggressive, with competitive drive, etc. Such people tend to be very productive and work very hard. In fact, they are workholics. Being impatient and aggressive, such people are more prone to heart attack.

Type B Personalities: Easy-going, sociable, free from urgency of time, laid-back and non-competitive are the characteristics of Type B personalities. Such people do better on tasks involving judgements, accuracy rather than speed and team work.

Judging Personalities: People with judging personality types like to follow a plan, make decisions and need only that what is essential for their work.

Perceptive Personalities: These are the people who adapt well to change, want to know all about a job and at times may get overcommitted. Go through the folllowing Table 5.3, will help you understand better about the two types of personalities.

Table 5.3: Judging vs. Perceptive Personalities

Judging Type	Perceptive Type
Work best when they can plan work and follow the plan.	Adapt well to changing situations.
Like to get things settled.	Do not mind leaving things open for alterations.
May decide things too quickly.	May have trouble making decisions.
May not notice new things that need to be done	May start too many projects and have difficulty in finishing them.
Want only essential things needed to begin their work	Want to know all about their work.
Tend to be satisfied once they reach a judgement on a thing or situation or person	Tend to be curious and welcome new information on a thing or a situation or a person.

5.4 THEORIES OF PERSONALITY

As there are so many definitions of personality, so are theories of personality as well. As such, there is no consensus among the theorists about the theories of personality. Among several theories, the more prominent are: type, trait, psycho-analytic, social learning and self theory. A brief discussion of each follows.

Type Theory

Like other sciences, the first students of human nature also endeavoured to study human personality by classifying them into certain types. Personality classification was made on two bases: (*i*) Body Build, and (*ii*) Psychological Factors. In case of body build basis, personalities were classified into types by establishing relationship between one's body build/features and personality. Accordingly, persons having a short or plumb body build were characterised as sociable and relaxed, tall and thin persons as restrained, self-conscious and fond of solitude and those with heavy set mascular body build as noisy, callous and fond of physical activity. Admittedly, an individual's body build/physique may exert some influence on his/her personality, yet the relationship between the two seems much subtle than what such classification implies.

Personality types on the basis of psychological factors are based on the assumption that personality is the totality of a person's interacting sub-systems. Then, personalities are, accordingly, classified into two types: (*i*) introverts, and (*ii*) extroverts. As already mentioned while discussing types of personalities, introverts are those who primarily look inward at themselves, avoid social contacts and interaction with others, quiet and enjoy solitude. On the contrary, extroverts are sociable, friendly, gregarious, aggressive, etc. No doubt, typing personalities into introverts and extroverts looks simple and interesting, but it does not serve much of its purpose in understanding personalities in more detail and depth. The reason is that, as stated earlier also, most of the people tend to be neither introverts nor extroverts but ambiverts, that is, they are in between the two extremes of introverts and extroverts.

Trait Theory

Some psychologists have tried to understand personality on the basis of individual's traits. Trait is an enduring characteristic of a person in which he/she differs from another. Popular human characteristics include shy, aggressive, submissive, lazy, ambitious, loyal and timid. In practice, the more consistent the characteristics and more frequently these occur in diverse situations, the more important traits become in describing a person. Thus, traits can be described as individual variables or dimensions.

Trait theory is based on the folllowing three assumptions:

1. Traits are common to many individuals but vary in absolute amounts between the individuals.
2. Traits are relatively stable. Their consistent occurance influences the human behaviour.
3. One's trait can be inferred by measuring his/her behavioural indicators.

Allport and Cattell have been among the early psychologists who made efforts to isolate individual traits. Allport[12], in his study, identified as many as 17,953 traits. Obviously, predicting human behaviour based on such a large number becomes virtually impossible. Realising the need for reducing such large number to a manageable one, Cattell[13] first isolated 171 traits and, then, the same reduced to 16 traits, which he termed as **source or primary traits**. These 16 traits have already been listed in Table 5.1 while describing the types of personalities on page 41.

Thus, trait theory of personality attempts to understand how a set of personality variables exerts on one's behaviour. However, this theory suffers from one lacuna is that it is very descriptive rather than analytical. In fact, no hard evidence supports trait theory as a valid measure of personality.

In recent years, John[14] has propounded a personality model called **The Big 5 Model**. In this model, he advocates that the following **five** basic personality variables/ dimensions underly all other variables:

1. **Extraversion**: Who is sociable, talkative, and assertive.
2. **Agreeableness:** One who is goodnatured, co-operative and trusting.
3. **Conscientiousness**: A person who is responsible, dependable, persistent and achievement oriented.
4. **Emotional Stability**: Someone characterised by calm, nervous, enthusiastic, depressed and insecure.
5. **Openness to Experience:** A person who is imaginative, artistically sensitive, and intellectual.

Psychoanalytical Theory

Psychoanalytical theory is yet another type of personality. The basic notion on which psychoanalytical theory is based on is that human behaviour is influenced more by unseen forces than conscious and rational thoughts. Sigmund Fraud developed psychoanalytical theory based on his 40 years of writings and clinical practice. Fraud's clinical experiments on his patients' behaviour led him to conclude that behaviour is mainly influenced by unconscious framework. This unconscious framework is composed of three elements—**id, ego** and **super ego**. Fraud himself considers the division as hypothetical one rather than specific structures of one's personality. The reason being the failure of neuroanatomy in properly locating them within the central nervous system.

A brief description of these three elements *i.e.*, id, ego and super ego, follows:

(*i*) **The Id:** The id is innate and the source of psychic energy. It seeks immediate gratification for biological or instinctual needs. It is like raw and, thus, remains basic to the individual throughout life. The id follows the basic principal of all human life *i.e.*, the immediate discharge of psychic energy (libido) produced by animal drives such as sex and aggression which if pent up, causes tension in the personality system. The id, by immediately reducing tension, thus, obeys the **pleasure principle**. As id knows and obeys no laws and rules, it may result in, as Fraud himself felt, danger for the person concern and for society as well.

(*ii*) **The Ego:** The id is unconscious part while the ego is conscious part of human personality. The ego is associated with reality. It checks the id through logic and intellect. The ego can best be described as controlling id through realities. A starving man cannot control or satisfy his hunger simply by eating images, but by really having food. Thus, here lies the role of ego *i.e.* reality in satisfying hunger or reducing tension created by hunger.

(*iii*) **The Super Ego:** The super ego represents system of values, norms, and ethic that guide and govern a person to behave properly in the society. In one sense, the super ego can be described as conscience. It provides norms and values to ego to determine what is wrong or right at a given time in given situation/society. In other words, the super ego judges whether an action/behaviour is right or wrong as per the set norms and standards of the society.

In total, it can be concluded that the **id seeks pleasure, the ego verifies reality and the super ego strives for perfection.**

As mentioned earlier, Fraud's psychoanalytical theory is hypothetical based on theoretical conception. However, it does not provide any measure for its scientific verification and validity. That is why this theory is not found very relevant and appropriate in predicting human behaviour. Nonetheless, it provides the idea of unconscious motivation which adds to the understanding of human behaviour in a better manner.

Social Learning Theory

In fact, human behaviour is generally either learnt or modified by way of learning. Though learning is discussed, in detail, in Chapter 8, here you are mainly exposed to how learning affects one's behaviour or personality.

Learning can simply be defined as any change in one's behaviour that occurs as a result of experience. In other words, learning occurs when an individual behaves as a result of experience in a manner different from the way he/she formerly behaved.

Learning occurs through two ways : (*i*) Reinforcement, and (*ii*) Observing Others. Learning by observing others is also called **'vicarious learning'**. The social learning theory emphasises on how an individual behaves or acts in a given situation. This theory holds the view that the specific characteristics of a situation determine how an individual will behave in such situation. His/her understanding of the situation and behaviour evinced in past in similar situations may also influence how he/she will behave in given situation. Admittedly, situation evokes an individual's behavioural pattern. At the same time, it is also true that an individual's behaviour also at times influences the situational conditions. Individual, by selectively attending to what is happening, can prevent certain conditions from impinging on him/her. Thus, the relationship between the situation and the individual is of reciprocal pattern.

Self Theory

Carl Rogers[15] is credited with self theory of presonality. This theory is also described as 'phenomenological' which studies individual's subjective experience, feelings and his concepts of world and self. Rogers self theory is composed of perceptions of the 'I' or 'me'. The following four factors are included in self theory:

(*i*) **Self-Image:** By nature, every person has certain beliefs about what or who he/she is. In other words, self-image is one's image of oneself. This is how one sees oneself.

(*ii*) **Ideal-Self:** The ideal-self refers to what one would like to look like. The basic line of difference between self-image and ideal-self is that the former indicates the reality of a person whereas the latter implies the ideality of the person. The latter one, *i.e.*, ideal self stands more important to motivate an individual to behave in a particular manner.

(*iii*) **Looking Glass-Self:** This refers to how others are perceiving the individual. In other words, this means the way an individual thinks people perceive about him and not the way people actually see him. This indicates that one's belief about self is a reflection of others' perception about the person.

(*iv*) **Real-Self:** The real-self is what one actually is. The first three self-concepts relate to an individual's perception about himself/herself. They may be the same or differ from the real-self.

People perceive the same situation differently depending upon their conception of the situation. This, in turn, influences them to behave differently. Thus, in any attempt of analysing and understanding organisational behaviour, the self-concept plays a significant role in reacting/behaving in a particular manner.

5.5 HOW PERSONALITY DEVELOPS ?

Personality develops with advancement in an individual's age passing through certain stages in a sequential order. Different psychologists and behavioural scientists have come out with different stages explaining how an individual's personality develops or shapes. The more important of them have been discussed here.

Fraud's Four Stages of Personality

Sigmund Fraud is considered one of the pioneers among the stage theorists. Fraud's personality stages are based on the belief that events occurred in one's childhood has their bearings on adulthood and, in turn, behaviour in adulthood. According to Fraud, there are four stages of psychological development that shape one's personality and its development. These are: (*i*) oral, (*ii*) anal, (*iii*) phallic, and (*iv*) genital. These names refer to the regions of body which stimulate the discharge of sexual energy. These are now briefly discussed one by one.

The Oral Stage: The *oral stage* lasts for the first year of one's life. This can also be called the infancy stage of personality development. The infants are totally dependents upon others for their survival and growth. For an infant, mouth becomes the first body zone through which biological drives are sought to be met or reduced. Thumb sucking by an infant gratifies his/her sex drive. Later on when teeth erupt, biting satisfies the drive for seeking pleasure. That mouth remains an important zone of body throughout one's life, as believed by Fraud also, is indicated by one's adulthood oral behaviour in the forms of gum chewing, nail biting, smoking, kissing, over eating, etc.

Fraud postulates that the stimulation given to the infant both in excessive and inadequate amounts, makes the infant optimistic about the world. He/she also has a tendency to exploit or dominate others to satisfy the needs.

The Anal Stage: The *anal stage* extends throughout the second and third year of a child. In this age, the anal becomes the body zone for sexual gratification. How the parents give toilet training to the child gets its reflection in adulthood behaviour. For example, in case a mother becomes harsh in toilet matters, the child tends to withhold faces. When faces become excessive, the child develops personality traits like orderliness, punctuality and cleanliness. On the other hand, if mother advises her child for having regular bowel movements, its reflection on the personality is in the form of cruelty, destructiveness, disorderliness and hostility.

The Phallic Stage: The *phallic stage* develops at the age of four years. Now, the focus of body zone for sexual gratification shifts from anals to sexual organs. This stage is also characterised as the stage of psychosexual development. The children in this age can be observed examining and fondling their genitalia, masturbating and enjoying in discussing matters of birth and sex.

The Latency Stage: The *latency period* takes place between ages of six and seven years. This period is characterised by children's disinterest in matters related to sex. They are interested in seeking gratification of the libido from the external sources, knowledge and alike. The latency period also refers to the elementary school age. Hence, this period has long lasting effects in one's personality and its shaping in a definite pattern or type.

The Genital Stage: During adolescence and adulthood occurs the *genital stage*. The sexual drive and interest are revived in this stage. One takes interest in opposite sex. In other words, one tends to seek sexual gratification through hetrosexual love and attraction.

Erikson's Eight Life Stages

Erikson extended Fraud's psychosexual development in a more systematic manner and identified eight stages of human life. Erikson asserted that each stage is plagued by conflicts that need to be resolved successfully before an individual moves to the next stage. Movement from one stage to next one is developmental. At times, movement can even involve regression *i.e.* from next stage to earlier stage when events are of traumatic nature. A brief description of these eight stages follows:

1. **Infancy:** The first year of life of a person is characterised by **trust vs mistrust.** The infants raised in loving and affectionate atmosphere learn to trust others. Lack of love and affection, on the contrary, leads to mistrust. This bears long lasting impact on one's personality and the reluctant behaviour.

2. **Early Childhood**: This stage spreads between two and three years of a child. During this period, the child starts to acquire independence. When the child is allowed to it, he/she feels autonomy. If disallowed, a sense of **shame and doubt** develops in the child.

3. **Play Age:** In the age of four and five years, the child seeks to discover what can be done. If the child is allowed and encouraged to do what he/she wants to do, the child develops a sense of initiative. Alternatively, if the child is discouraged to do, he/she feels lack of **self-confidence.**

4. **School Age:** When the child joins school from ages 6 to 12 years, he/she learns knowledge and skills. If the child makes progress compatible with his/her abilities, it develops in child a **sense of industry.** The opposite results in a **sense of inferiority.**

5. **Adolescence:** The children during their teenage period try to gain a sense of identity for them in the society. They do not want to become confused about themselves who they are. The autonomy, initiative and industry developed in earlier stages help the teenagers gain **identity** for them.

6. **Young Adulthood:** The young during their twenties try to develop deep and permanent relationship with others to have a feeling of **intimacy.** Failing in it results in a sense of **isolation.**

7. **Adulthood:** The adults during fourtees and fiftees of their ages face the situation of **generativity** or self-absorption. Adults who are productive in work, raise children with serious concern and guide to next generation are called generative. Self-absorbed adults do not look beyond themselves. They are absorbed in their career development and maintenance.

8. **Old (Sunset) Age:** The adult of **integrity** gains a sense of wisdom. He/she appreciates continuity of past, present and future and becomes fully satisfied. Fear of death is dispelled. The reverse situation results in a sense of **despair**, fear from death, desire for living second time and depressed.

Argyris Immaturity to Maturity Stages

Professor Chris Argyris[16] of Harvard identified distinct stages in one's personality development. He postulated that all healthy people seek such situations that can offer them autonomy, equality and the opportunity to show their ability and competency. According to him, the healthy people follow the following seven dimensions to move from immaturity to maturity.

1. From passivity to activity.
2. From dependence to independence.
3. From selective behaviour to diverse behaviour.
4. From shallow interest to deep interest.
5. From short-time perspective to long-time perspective.
6. From subordinate position to superordinate position.
7. From lack of self-awareness to self awareness and control.

Accordingly, the healthy people evince the behaviour of maturity while unhealthy demonstrate behaviour like childish. Argyris observes that most organisations tend to treat their employees like children *i.e.*, making them dependent on organisations.

Sheldon's Personality Development

Sheldon tried to explain personality development based on an individual's body build. He labelled different body builds reflecting certain personality characteristics. His three body builds with their personality characteristics are presented in Table 5.4.

Table 5.4: Body Builds vis-a-vis Personality Characteristics

Body Builds	Personality Characteristics
1. Endomorph (Fleshy)	Friendly, people oriented, seeks others when in trouble, slow to react, loves to eat.
2. Mesomorph (Athletic)	Seeks physical adventure, enjoys exercise, aggressive, risk taker, competition oriented.
3. Ectomorph (Thin)	Likes privacy, socially inhibited, quick to react and hypersensitive to pain.

5.6 HOW PERSONALITY INFLUENCES ORGANISATIONAL BEHAVIOUR?

By now, you have learnt various personality attributes and traits that help predict one's behaviour. In this section, you will learn how some of the attributes influence an individual's behaviour in organisations. Some of more important personality attributes that determine how one will behave are locus of control, machiavellianism, self-esteem, self-monitoring, risk-taking propensity and Type A personality. These are discussed one by one.

Locus of Control: Locus of control refers to one's belief that what happens is either within one's control or beyond one's control. The former is called internals and the latter is called externals. Those who have internal locus of control believe that they are masters of their own fate. On the contrary, those who have external locus of control see themselves as pawns of fate and believe that what happens to them in their lives is due to luck or factors beyond their control.

A large amount of research comparing internals with externals have proved that externals are less satisfied with their jobs and have higher absenteeism rates than internals. But, the dissatisfied internals are more likely to quit a dissatisfying job.

Machiavellianism: The personality characteristic of Machiavellianism (Mach) is named after Niccolo Machiavelli who wrote in the sixteenth century about how to gain and manipulate power. Thus, Machiavellianism refers to an individual's propensity to manipultate people for solving his/her interest. An individual high in Machiavellianism tends to be cool, logical and assessing the system around him, pragmatic, maintains emotional distance, tries to control people, events and situations by manipulating the system to his advantage. In sum, "if it works, use it" is consistent with a high Machiavellianism. They manipulate more, win more, are persuaded less and persuade others more than do individuals having low Machiavellianism. However, these high outcomes are moderated by situational factors.

However, the Machiavellianism can be considered as good in jobs that need bargaining skills (for example, labour negotiations) or in jobs offering substantial rewards for winning (such as commissioned sale). But, in jobs where ends cannot justify the means *i.e.* in jobs ethical consideration is involved, the Machiavellianism can not perform better.

Self-Esteem: An individual's liking or disliking oneself is callled self-esteem. This trait is bound to vary from individual to individual. Self-esteem is related to aspects individuals regard themselves as capable to achieve success. The research on self-esteem has revealed that individuals with high self-esteem tend to take on more challanging assignments and of unconventional nature. People with low self-esteem, on the contrary, are characterised by their susceptibility to external influences and approval seekers from others. They depend on the receipt of positive evaluations from others. As regards job satisfaction, individuals with high-self-esteem are found more satisfied with their jobs than those with low self-esteem.

Self-Monitoring: Self-monitoring is a personality trait that has recently received increasing attention. Simply speaking, self-monitoring is an individual's ability to adjust his/her behaviour to external factors/situations. Individuals with high self-monitoring trait show greater adaptability to adjust themselves with external situations. They can behave differently in different situations. Hence, there is very less behavioural consistency between who they are and what they do. It can be hypothesised that individuals high in self-monitoring are likely to be more successful managers who at times are required to play multiple, and even contradicting roles to perform their managerial activities. In other words, individuals with high self-monitors are capable of showing different faces for different audiences as per the requirements of the situations.

Risk-Taking: Individuals differ in taking risks. The propensity to assume or avoid risks affects a manager's behaviour in making decisions. Research has shown that managers with high risk-taking make more rapid decisions and use less information in making choices than do the low risk-taking managers. In practice, the propensity to assume risks varies depending upon the nature of the job. For example, a high risk-taking propensity may be good for a stock trader in a brokerage firm which demands rapid decision-making. But, the same personality trait may not be considered as good in auditing activities which require concentration and low risk-taking propensity.

Type A Personality: You have already learnt under title 5.3 Types of Personality who are type A Personalities. In brief, type A people are impatient and aggressive to achieve more and more in less and less time. These characteristics result in some specific behavioural outcomes. Working fast, emphasizing quantity over quality, working for long hours, making quick decisions etc., are some of the behavioural examples of Type A people.

In organisations, great salespersons are usually Type A's. The reason is, sales occurs in a competitive market which requires rigorous and aggressive efforts to sell one's product. But, senior executives are usually Type B's. The answer lies in the fact that promotions in corporate organisations usually go to those who are wise, tactful and creative rather than to those who are merely hasty and hostile in doing things.

5.7 A LOOK AT THE PERSONALITY TRAITS OF THE INDIAN MANAGERS

You have so far learnt that an individual's personality traits influence his/her organisational behaviour and, in turn, performance. Managers are not exception to it. Managers' personality traits and performance are intimately correlated. Therefore, it seems pertinent while studying personality in organisational behaviour to look at the personality traits that the Indian managers possess. Though it is difficult to list the generalised traits because various studies inform the various traits, an attempt has been made in the following paragraphs to give an overview of the personality traits by surveying some important studies undertaken in India.

Dwivedi's Traits[17]

R.S. Dwivedi studied personality traits of 52 managers working in public (22 managers) and private (30 managers) sectors. He reached to the findings that managers gave relatively high importance to the traits like co-operative, intelligent, energetic and sociable. Low importance was assigned to aggressive, confronting and independent. Other personality factors like flexible, persevering and self-monitored got moderate importance. The correlation coefficient between personality traits between public sector and private sector managers accounted for as high as 90.

Ghosh and Munerikar's Traits[18]

In a study carried out by Ghosh and Munerikar, the personality traits exhibited by managers included emotional, casual, tough, sensitive and tense. These personality traits were found inconsistent with their behaviour shown in situations faced by them.

Menon's Traits[19]

S.A. Menon studied personality traits of 26 managers working in corporate sector. His study established a positive relationship between the personality traits of the managers and their favourable attitudes towards the organisations. Personality traits like aggressive, communicative, relaxed, imaginative, high need achievement motive, work-oriented, open minded, less money-oriented and more sensitive helped the managers develop attitudes favourably towards their organisations.

Saiyadain and Monappa's Traits

Saiyadain and Monappa of the Indian Institute of Management (IIM), Ahmedabad also conducted a study on personality traits of 172 middle-level managers from both public and private sector organisations. The 172 managers represented major functional areas of the organisations. While studying the personality traits on two characteristics, namely, (*i*) authoritarian (these refer to the traits like rigidity, lack of tolerance, dominance over weak, adherence to traditional values), and (*ii*) Machiavellianism (which includes traits like cool and manipulative, indifferent to individual needs), an equal distribution between those on the high side and those on the low side of the scale was found. Yet another interesting finding of the study was that above two-thirds of the managers scored fairly higher than average on two personality traits like competence and need for achievement.

5.7 HOW TO MEASURE PERSONALITY

The need for measuring personality of people is imbued with multiplicity of justifications. The understanding of personality greatly influences several decisions like hiring personnel, establishing relationship, designing motivational packages, etc. To understand the personality of an individual, a number of measures and methods have to be used. This, in turn, underlines the need for developing the relevant methods to assess personality. Yes, the use of assessment method for undderstanding personality may vary from time to time and situation to situation depending on the very purpose of personality assessment. Among the various methods of assessing personality, three methods are being widely used. These are :

1. Personality Inventories
2. Projective Tests
3. Assessment Center

Let us discuss each of these in seriatim.

Personality Inventories

In fact, this is the most widely used method of personality assessment. As the nomenclature itself denotes, this method consists of a number of statements relating to a specific dimension of personality of the individual. These statements are combinedly called ' Personality Inventories' and become basis for prediction, or say, understanding of personaltiy. The individual is asked to indicate his/her degree of agreement or disagreement with regard to each statement. Even sometimes simply yes or no pattern of response is also sought. Since these responses, by and large, are expected to suffer from certain limitations such as faking and favourable responses. This underlines the need for making corrective measures to avoid and control these limitations so as to develop more and more reliable personal inventory. One way to do so is by asking both positive and negative statements for the same aspects of personality and also reversing the values of degree of agreement or disagreement.

Among the various personality inventories developed so far, the most popular one is the 'Locus of Control'developed by J.B. Rotter[21] during the sixties. According to Rotter, Locus of control as a method of personality assessment measures an individual's internal and external orientation along with his/her attitude toward control. Based on this, all individuals are broadly classified into two extreme categories. *One,* people who believe that they have complete control over their fate and luck called '*internal locus of control*'. *Second,* on the other extreme are the people who believe that what happens to them is absolutely at the mercy of forces that are beyond their control called *'external locus of control'*. Locus of control has its own bearing on their behaviour and performance. To quote, according to a study of Work Locus of Control administered over 1165 people conducted by P. Spector[22], internals tended to report more job satisfaction and less job stress. We have presented at the end of this chapter the Locus of Control Scale developed by Spector. You fill out the questionnaire and assess your own locus of control.

Closely related to these findings are the findings of the study conducted by S.K. Nair[23] who surveyed 260 supervisory cadre employees in technical and administrative work working in government and private organizations. The focus of the study was to examine relationship between locus of control and variables in a job-characteristic model. The findings of the study revealed quite positive relationship between internal locus of control and various job-characteristic such as skill variety, task identity, task autonomy, and performance feedback. Internal locus of control was also found positively related with critical psychological state, job satisfaction, and work motivation. The implications of these findings for managers are very clear. An understanding of the locus of control of employees can help managers design motivational packages and administer motivational practices more suited to the needs of the employees.

Projective Tests

Unlike inventory method of personality assessment, projective tests are basically designed to know the more subtle aspects of personality. Accordingly, these tests are based on the basic underlying assumptions that one's personality can be assessed by measuring some of his/her dormant feelings, aspirations, ambitions, and hopes. Over the period, a number of projective tests have been developed to assess personality. Inkblot Test, Thematic Appreciation Test (TAT), Sentence Completion Test, World Association Test, and Picture Frustration Tests are some of the projective tests to name. Among these too, inkblot test, also known as Rorschach Test developed by the Swiss psychiatrist named Herman Rorschach is the most widely used projective test to assess personality. In this test, Rorschach used ten ambiguous and unstructured pictures called inkblots consisting of one half being the same as another half. These pictures/inkblots are displayed to the individuals who are asked to indicate what they see in the inkblots/pictures. The interpretations they give for these inkblots reflect their feelings which become basis for assessing their personality[24].

Morgan and Murrary[25] have developed a projective test called Thematic Appreciation Test (TAT) also used to assess personality of an individual. It consists of twenty pictures representing different social situations. Unlike Rorschach Test, these pictures reflect a relatively defined picture of a situation. The individuals are asked to write a story of what might be happening in that social situation. It is noteworthy that the description of the situation is not warranted.

Assessment Centre

The concept of assessment centre was initially applied to military situations in the German army in 1930s. The basic purpose of this method was to assess candidates in a social situation. This concept travelled from army to the business world during 1960s. Unlike assessment centre as a method of performance appraisal conducted at a particular place, here it is a technique used to measure personality. The various simulated exercises used to evaluate personality include situational tests, management problems, in-basket exercises, business plan presentations, situation decision making exercises, and so on. The individuals are asked to participate in these exercises. The multiple trained assessors who could be from within the organization or from outside, observe the participants' behaviour and rate them based on predetermined dimensions, considered crucial in their work. The crucial diemsnions of a work are determined by conducting a job analysis. Each assessor prepares an evaluation report on each of the individual participating in assessment exercises. Finally, all the reports are integrated to get the profile of the particular employee.

The assessment centre method of personality evaluation benefits both the organization and employees on a symbiosis basis. Organisations get enough information about the employees to identify his/her strengths and weaknesses. This information helps the organization in planning for selection, training, promotion, and career path of the employees. On the other side, employees form positive impression about their job, promotional opportunities, and life-long attachment with the organization. There is ample research evidence available from both the Indian and outside contexts to suggest that assessment centre method of personality evaluation benefits employees, to a large extent. In this context, the findings of a recent study conducted by Purbani and Marjonohadi[26] are worth citing. The study reports that, after going through assessment centre, more than two-fifths of managers (42 per cent) were promoted and nearly one-third of them were rotated. Apart from these benefits, one of the benefit the assessment centre method of personality evaluation provides is that due to the composite and pooled judgement of several assessors, the personal biases, mistaken impression, and false inferences are minimized. In India, many companies such as Hindustan Lever, Eicher, Crompton Greaves, Modi Xerox, etc. have adopted this method to assess their employees. However, this method is not free from limitations. *One*, many of the stimulated techniques may not perfectly reflect the actual situation and, in turn, the participant may not behave in a true manner. *Second*, despite the fact that the employee will be assessed by several assessors, yet the halo effect with regard to personal skills may influence to the judgment.

LOCUS OF CONTROL – QUESTIONNAIRE*

Following are the 16 questions relating to Locus of Control. You mark these questions as frankly as possible using the following 6-point scale.

1. Disagree very much
2. Disagree moderately
3. Disagree slightly
4. Agree slightly
5. Agree moderately
6. Agree very much

* Adapted from P. Spector : Development of Work Locus of Control Scale, **Journal of Occupational Psychology**, Volume 61, 1988, pp. 335-340.

1.	----------	A job is what you make of it.
2.	----------	On most jobs, people can pretty much accomplish whatever they set out to accomplish.
3.	----------	If know what you want out of a job, you can find a job that gives it to you.
4.	----------	If employees are unhappy with a decision made by their boss, they should do something about it.
5.	----------	Getting the job you want is mostly a matter of luck.
6.	----------	Making money is primarily a matter of good fortune.
7.	----------	Most people are capable of doing their jobs well if they make effort.
8.	----------	In order to get a really good job you need to have family members or friends in high places.
9.	----------	Promotions are usually a matter of good fotune.
10.	----------	When it comes a landing a really good job, who you know is more important than what you know.
11.	----------	Promotions are given to employees who perform well on jobs.
12.	----------	To make a lot of money you have to know the right people.
13.	----------	It takes a lot of money you have to know the right people.
14.	----------	People who perform their jobs well generally get rewarded.
15.	----------	Most employees have more influence on their supervisors than they think they do.
16.	----------	the main difference between people who make a lot of money and people who make a little money is luck.

Follow the following instructions while scoring and instructions;

In order to find your Locus of control, subtract your score of responses to question 1, 2, 3, 4, 7, 11, 14, and 15 from seven. That is, if you gave a response of 4 to question 1, give yourself a 3, i.e. 7 minus 4. Similarly give scores to all 16 questions and add up all these to find your total score. Remember, your total score should be somewhere between 16 and 96. The implication of the total score is that the lower your score, the more internal you are, i.e. you believe what happens to you is a result of your own actions and efforts. On the contrary, the higher your score, the more external you are, i.e. you believe what happens to you is the result of a chance or luck. In Spector's survey of 1165 people working in a variety of occupations, the average total score was 38. This indicates that epople tended to believe themselves as more internals than externals.

SUMMARY

This summary is organized by the 'learning objectives' given on page no. 48 "

- *Personality is the totality of an individual's interaction with its sub-systems like environment and situation.*
- *Individual's external appearance and traits, their inner awareness of self and the person-situation interaction determine their personalities. Accordingly, personalities differ from individual to individual. While some personalities are classified as introverts and extroverts, others are categorised as Type A and Type B.*
- *Trait theory, psychoanalytical theory, social learning theory and self theory are the popular theories for studying personalities.*
- *Different psychologists have identified different stages through which personality develops from its infancy to maturity.*
- *An individual's personality is influenced and influences his/her behaviour in organisations.*

REVIEW QUESTIONS

1. What is personality? What are its major determinants?
2. What are the various theories of personality? According to you, which theory of personality is more comprehensive? Give reasons.
3. What are the various factors which affect personality development of an individual?
4. What are the factors that shape an individual's personality? Which of them, in your opinion, are more important in shaping personality?
5. Explain why personality is developmental in nature. What are the primary factors that influence the evolution of personality?
6. Describe locus of control, Machiavellianism and type A or B as types of personality.
7. How does personality relate to organisational behaviour?
8. How does the study of personality help in understanding organisational behaviour?
9. What behavioural predictions might you make if you knew that an employee had (*i*) an external locus of control? (*ii*) a low Mach score? (*iii*) low self-esteem? (*iv*) a Type A personality?
10. Write notes on:
    (*a*) Trait Theory
    (*b*) Machiavellianism
    (*c*) Introversion and Extroversion
    (*d*) Locus of Control
    (*e*) Type A and Type B Personalities
    (*f*) Fraud's Four Stages of Personality Development

REFERENCES

1. E.R. Hilgard, R.C. Atkinson and R.L. Atkinson: **Introduction to Psychology**, Oxford & IBH, New Delhi, 1975, p. 364.
2. Floyd L. Ruch: **Personality and Life**, Scott Foreman, 1963, p. 353.
3. Gordon W. Allport: **Personality**, Henry Holt, New York, 1937, pp. 43-47.
4. David C. McClelland: **Personality**, Willliam Sloam, New York, 1951.

5. W.G. Scott and T.R. Mitchell: **Organisation Theory**, Richard D. Irwin, Homewood Ill, p 1972, p. 91.
6. R.L. Hotz: Genetics, Not Parenting, Key to Temperament, Studies Say, **Los Angeles Times,** February 20, 1994, A1.
7. B.M. Staw and J.Ross: Stability in the Midst of Change: A Dispositional Approach to Job Attitudes, **Journal of Applied Psychology**, August 1985, pp. 469-480.
8. Fred Luthans: **Organisational Behaviour**, McGraw Hill, New York, 1995, pp. 119-121.
9. T. Newcomb: Intrafamily Relationship in Attitudes, **Sociometry**, 1, 1937, pp. 180-205.
10. Stephen P. Robbins: **Organisational Behaviour**, Printice Hall of India Private Limited, New Delhi, 1996, p. 92.
11. R.B. Cattell: Personality Pinned Down, **Psychology Today**, July 1973, pp. 40-46.
12. Gordon W. Allport: **Op. cit**., 1937, pp. 43-47.
13. R.B. Cattell: **Op. cit.**, 1973, pp. 40-46.
14. O.P. John: The Big Five Taxonomy: Dimensions of Personality in the Natural Language and in Questionnaires, In: L.A. Pervin (ed.), **Handbook of Personality Theory and Research**, Guilford Press, New York, 1990, pp. 66-100.
15. Carl C. Rogers: Counselling and Psychotherapy: New Concepts in Practice, Houghton, Boston, 1942.
16. Chris Argyris: **Personality and Organisations**, Harper, New York, 1957, pp. 51-53.
17. R.S. Dwivedi: The Relative Importance of Personality Traits among Indian Managers, **Indian Management,** April 1970, pp. 30-35.
18. P.K. Ghosh and Munerikar: In Search of Personality Characteristics of Managers, **Indian Journal of Applied Psychology**, January 1974, pp. 1-6.
19. S.A.Menon: Personality, Executive Training and Organisation, **Indian Journal of Industrial Relations**, July 1974, pp. 33-54.
20. M.S. Saiyadain and Arun Monappa: **Profile of Indian Managers,** Vidya Vahini, New Delhi, 1977.
21. J.B. Rotter: Generalised Expectancies for Internal versus External Control of Reinforcement, **Psychology Monographs**, Vol. 80, 1966, p. 609.
22. P. Spector: Development of Work Locus of Control Scale, **Journal of Occupational Psychology**, Vol. 61, 1988, pp. 335-340.
23. S.K. Nair: Relationship between Locus of Control and Job Characteristics Model Dimensions, **Indian Journal of Industrial Relations**, Vol. 32, No. 4, 1997, pp. 439-452.
24. R.K. Misra, M.K. Kharakwal, M.A. Kilroy and K. Thapa : **Rorschach Test : Theory and Practice**, Sage Publications, New Delhi, 1996.
25. C.D. Morgan and H.A. Murrary : A Method of Investigating Fantasies. The Thematic Appreception Test, **Archives of Neurological Psychology**, Vol. 34, 1935, pp. 289-306.
26. L. Purwani and V.K. Marjonohadi : **Learning from Assessment Centre : Concept and Its Practice in Glaxosmithkline India**, paper submitted to International Management Institute, New Delhi, 2002.

Case-5.1: Oberoi did it his way

It is not often acknowledged that Rai Bahadur Mohan Singh Oberoi, 100, chairman of an empire of 29 hotels spanning most of the world's landmass is also the man who pioneered India as a brand, way back when it was only a bazaar of begging bowls and exotica. At 90, he looked back in something close to awe and said, "I often wonder how I did it."

Certainly he did not give much of the credit to luck. True, he stood at the right time at the right place to confront his destiny, but this was just physical happenstance. What he did with the situation was amazing for a man from the boondocks of Bhaun, with little education, and really not to the manner born.

Indeed, if anything the Rai Bahadur made his fortune out of calamity. If his father hadn't died of cholera when he was only an infant, his mother would not have returned to the ancestral home which gave Oberoi the connections and contacts that helped him raise money later to buy his first hotel, the Clarke's at Simla. If he hadn't flunked the interview for his first job as clerk with the Government of India, he would never have made his way to the Simla Mall, gazed in wonderment at the glitter of the Cecil and made up his mind that he would work there. If a fatal bug in the water supply, hadn't laid low Calcutta's mighty Grand Hotel it would never have been up for grabs. Again Oberoi just chanced to hear about it at the Delhi railway station when he was leaving to return to base in Simla. He simply changed his ticket and his direction and went to mint millions out of war-time Calcutta—another catastrophe. Life served him lemons regularly, but with even greater regularity did the Rai Bahadur make lemonade.

The story of the Rai Bahadur is all the more impressive because there was nothing in his background to suggest that he would be able to create the world-class ambience and sophistication for which the group is now celebrated, that he would be able to foresee India's current positioning in the global market, while doffing a deferential hat to history when it was demanded.

For instance, when other hotels were cramming their lobbies with brassbound chests and colonial nostalgia, Oberoi created the first international business hotel, the Oberoi Inter-continental in Delhi. However, in the Mena House, Egypt, and the Windsor, Australia, he went to extraordinary lengths and expense to produce authenticity to the last detail, including countrywide searches for memories and memorabilia. In order to replicate the flooring in the Windsor, he tracked down the original supplier of the tiles in distant Stock-on-Trent, England.

Celebrating his 100th birthday with his mind almost as clear as it was 50 years ago, perhaps the one philosophy responsible might be his dictum, **"I never worry. It clutters the brain. The problem may not happen, and even if it does, worrying will only come in the way of a clear-headed solution."**

QUESTIONS

1. "Nature and nurture play a key role in personality development." Explain with reference to above case study.
2. In your opinion, what are the significant determinants in the making of Shri Oberoi's personality?
3. Which theory of personality does apply to Shri Oberoi's personality?

6

PERCEPTION

"When selecting an image, never try to be something you are not. People will see through the facade. Make every effort to put your best foot forward - but never at the cost of your identify or integrity." **– *William Gardner***

Learning Objectives

After studying this chapter, you should be able to:

- **Define** perception and distinguish it from sensation.
- **Discuss** the perceptual process and state the factors affecting it.
- **Suggest** ways how to improve the perceptual ability.
- **State** the application of perception in specific areas to understand organisational behaviour..
- **Define** impression management and also discuss the strategies used in impression management.
- **Give** Guidelines how to improve impression management.

6.1 INTRODUCTION

We all come across various objects or things in our everyday life. We are also constantly bombarded with various stimuli. Then, what we do in practice is while we receive some objects, we reject others. Further, we look at the same thing, yet perceive it differently. Looking at a painting, for example, some may perceive it as beautiful, the others as ugly. Then, the question arises is why the same object is perceived/understood differently by different people. The answer to it is perception which is a cognitive factor of human behaviour. Strictly speaking, perception lies at the base of every human behaviour. There can be no behaviour without perception. This chapter deals with various aspects of perception such as meaning of perception, process of perception, factors influencing perception and application of perception in organisational behaviour. Impression management which has direct implications for human behaviour, at the end of the chapter is also discussed.

6.2 WHAT IS PERCEPTION?

In simple sense, perception means perceiving *i.e.,* giving meaning to the environment around us. It is perceiving of objects what we are faced with. We can understand the meaning of perception in a better sense if we go through some important definitions of it given by some behavioural scientists.

According to Udai Pareek and others[1] "Perception can be defined as the process of receiving, selecting, organising, interpreting, checking and reacting to sensory stimuli or data".

Stephen P. Robbins[2] defines perception as "a process by which individuals organise and interpret their sensory impressions in order to give meaning to their environment".

Fred Luthans[3] opines that "Perception is an important mediating cognitive process through which persons make interpretations of the stimulus or situation they are faced with".

Now, perception can safely be defined as a process which involves seeing, receiving, selecting, organising, interpreting and giving meaning to the environment. The functioning of the whole process is influenced by the individual doing the perceiving, the objects or events being perceived, and the environment in which perception occurs.

6.3 PERCEPTION DIFFERS FROM SENSATION

People usually mean sensation and perception the same. But, there is a clear-cut distinction between the two. In simple words, sensation may be described as the response of a physical sensory organ to some stimuli. Our physical senses i.e., vision, hearing, touch, smell and taste are continuously bombarded by numerous stimuli that are both inside and outside of our body. Our physical sensory organs often react to these stimuli. The reaction of our eye to colour, ear to sound, nose to odor, and so on are the examples of our every day sensations. What these examples indicate is that sensation activates the functioning of the physical sensory organs[4]. Thus, sensation precedes perception. In this way, sensation serves as a raw input to be processed so as to make sense out of them to perceive the environment or stimuli around us.

Perception is much more than sensation. As noted before, perception depends upon the sensory raw data, yet it involves a cognitive process that includes filtering, modifying or even changing these sensation raw data to make sense out of them. In other words, the perceptual process adds to or/and subtracts from the sensory world. A simple illustration may be looking at an object. We see by means of our eyes. Remember, it is not our eyes but what we see and tend to see in its totality, with a figure and form against a background[5]. Thus, we find that eyes activate us to see an object, i.e., sensation and what is being seen, *i.e.*, perception. In this seeing process, though both sensation and perception are involved, yet perception process overcomes sensation process to make what is being seen.

Study the following examples. These will help you understand the difference between sensation and perception more clearly:

1. You buy a two-wheeler that you think is the best, but not the one that the engineer says is the best.
2. A subordinate's answer to a question is based on what he heard his boss says, but not on what the boss actually said.
3. The same Professor may be viewed by one student as a very good Professor and by another student of the same semester as a poor Professor.

4. The same item may be viewed by the manufacturing engineer to be of high quality and by a customer to be of low quality.

6.4 PERCEPTUAL PROCESS

We have already defined perception as a process of receiving, selecting, organising, interpreting, checking and reacting to stimuli. This is like an input-throughput-output process in which the stimuli can be considered as 'inputs', transformation of 'inputs' through selection, organisation and interpretation as 'throughputs' and the ultimate behaviour/action as 'outputs'. This whole perceptual process can be presented as follows:

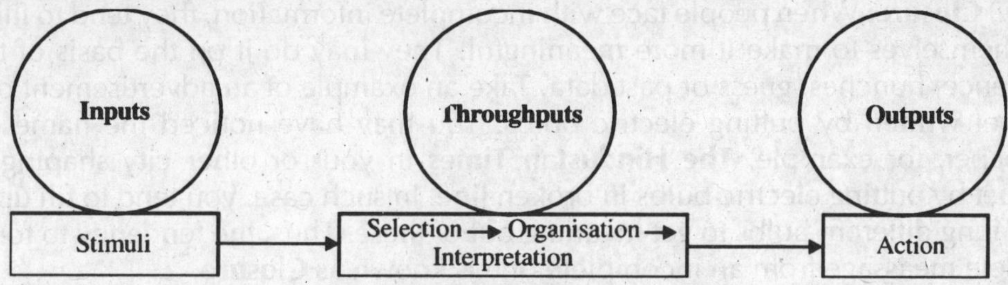

Fig. 6.1: Perceptual Process

Let us discuss each of these in turn :

1. **Receiving Stimuli:** The perception process starts with the reception of stimuli. The stimuli are received from the various sources. Through the five organs, we see things/objects, hear sounds, smell, taste and touch things. In this way, the reception of stimuli is a physiological aspect of perception process. Stimuli may be external to us (such as sound waves) and inside us (such as energy generation by muscles).

2. **Selection of Stimuli:** People, in their everyday life, are bombarded by myriads of stimuli. They cannot assimilate all what they observe or receive from the environment at a time. Hence, they select some stimuli for further processing to attach meanings to them while the rest are screened out. Selection of stimuli is not made at random, but depending on the two types of factors, namely, external factors and internal factors. While external factors relate to stimuli such as intensity of stimuli, its size, movement, repitition, etc., internal ones relate to the perceiver such as his/her age, learning, interest, etc. Normally, people selectively perceive objects or things which interest to them most in a particular situation and avoid those for which they are indifferent[6]. This is also called '**selective perception**'.

The 'selective perception' involves the following two psychological principles:

(*i*) **Figure Ground Principle:** As we just noted, we select stimuli for further processing that we consider important for us or which we cannot study. The meaningful bits and pieces of stimuli are called the "figure" and the meaningless ones are levelled as "ground". More attention is given to figure and less to ground.

(*ii*) **Relevancy:** Relevancy is yet another principle involved in selective perception. In practice, people selectively perceive things that they consider relevant to meet their needs and desires.

3. **Organisation of Stimuli:** Having selected stimuli or data, these need to be organised in some form so as to assign some meanings to them. Thus, organising the bits of information into a meaningful whole is called "organisation". There are three ways by which the selected data *i.e.,* inputs are organised. These are:

(*i*) **Grouping:** Grouping is based on the similarity or proximity of various stimuli perceived. The tendency to group stimuli *i.e.,* people or things appearing similar in certain ways has been a common means of organising the perception. For example, all the workers having similarity in certain aspects may be perceived have similar opinion about their boss. Similarly, all the workers coming from the same place may be perceived as similar on the basis of proximity.

(*ii*) **Closure:** When people face with incomplete information, they tend to fill the gaps themselves to make it more meaningful. They may do it on the basis of their experience, hunches, guess or past data. Take an example of an advertisement of an alphabet written by putting electric bulbs. You may have noticed the name of a newspaper, for example, **The Hindustan Times** in your or other city shaping the alphabet by putting electric bulbs in broken line. In such case, you tend to fill up the gap among different bulbs to get meaning out of these. Thus, the tendency to form a complete meassage from an incomplete one is known as **Closure**.

(*iii*) **Simplification:** When people find themselves overloaded with information, they try to simplify it to make it more meaningful and understandable. In this process, what they do is to subtract less salient information and concentrate on important ones only.

4. **Interpretation:** The data collected and organised remain meaningless for the perceiver till these are assigned meanings. Assigning meanings to data is called 'interpretation'. Thus, interpretation of data forms one of the most important element in the entire perceptual process. Strictly speaking, data collected and organised do not make any sense without interpretation. Several factors influence interpretation in organisations. The most important ones are halo effect, attribution, stereotyping, personality, situation, person perceived, etc. These are discussed one by one.

A brief description of these follows in seriatim :

(*i*) **Halo Effect:** Drawing a general impression about an individual based on a single characteristics or trait is called **halo effect**. But, it has an important implication for understanding or evaluating an employee in the organisation. An employee, based on halo effect, may be rated as bad in one trait, but good in other traits. Let us illustrate it with an example.

> The students of the MBA Ist semester are asked to appraise their one teacher teaching them OB. In doing so, the students may isolate a single trait/characteristics **enthusiasm**, for example, and do their appraisal/evaluation to be tainted by how they appraise the teacher on this one trait. If the teacher is quiet, assured, knowledgeable, and highly competent, but lacks zeal in his teaching style, he will be rated as poor or lower on this trait (enthusiasm) and a number of other traits and characteristics. This example well indicates how **hallo effect** can distort one's perception about another. In organisations, halo effect usually occurs in selection interviews and at the time of performance appraisal. Research studies[7] suggest that halo effect tends to be most extreme when (*a*) the traits to be perceived are ambiguous in behavioural terms, (*b*) when the traits imbibe moral overtones, and (*c*) when the perceiver judging the traits has had limited experience or knowledge.

(*ii*) **Attribution:** Explaining human behaviour in terms of cause and effect is called 'attribution'. However, attributing casual explanation to a particular human behaviour sometimes tends to distort perception. For example, if a prosperous worker does overtime on any day, it is perceived that he has done it in the interest of organisation. But, if a poor worker also does the same, the action or behaviour is perceived as being for money. A unique tendency is also observed among individuals is that they attribute their own behaviour to situational requirements but explain the behaviour of others by their personal disposition[8].

(*iii*) **Stereotyping:** When individuals are judged on the basis of the characteristics of the group to which they belong, this is called 'stereotyping'. The word stereotype was first, in 1922, applied by Walter Lipmann to perception. Since then, it has become a frequently used term to describe perception. In particular, it is employed in analyzing prejudice. Most stereotypes have favourable and unfavourable traits. That 'older workers cannot learn new skills', 'over-weight people lack discipline', 'Japanese are nationalistic', 'Indians are fatalistic', and 'workers are anti-management', are some common examples of stereotypes. The basic problem with stereotyping suffers is that it is so widespread that it does not give indepth truth. The fact otherwise remains that it may not contain even a shred of truth or may be irrelevant. Thus, stereotyping makes the perception inaccurate based on a false premise about a group.

(*iv*) **Personality:** Personality of the perceiver also affects what is to be perceived. In this context, researchers have reported that secure individuals tend to perceive others as warm not cold and indifferent and persons accepting themselves and having faith in their individuality perceive things favourable. These also imply that persons being insecure and nonaccepting themselves are less likely to perceive others around them.

(*v*) **Situation:** The situation or context in which we observe or see things also influences our perception about them. Just think. A management Professor may not notice his 20-years-old girl student in an evening gown and heavy makeup at a marriage party in a five-star hotel. Now, if the same girl student so attired attends his class on next day would certainly catch the Professor's attention alongwith that of the rest of the class. This indicates how situation affects our perception. Closely related to situation is time, light, heat or other situational factors that affect perceiver's perception about the things or events to be percieved.

(*vi*) **Perceiver:** So far we have learnt how factors residing in objects and situations affect one's perception about things and events. Factors residing in the perceiver himself/herself do also operate to shape and sometimes distort his/her perception. The perceiver's attitudes, motives, interests, past experience, and expectations are among the more relevant personal factors/characteristics that affect perception. Let us give an example how personal factors influence what he or she perceives.

> If you have bought a new Hero Honda, then you suddenly notice a large number of Hero Hondas just like yours plying on the road. Remember, it is unlikely that the number of such Hero Hondas suddenly increased. Rather, your own purchase (of Hero Honda) has influenced you so. You are now likely to notice them around you.

5. **Action:** Action is the last phase in the perceptual process. Action is the resultant behaviour of individual emerging from the perceptual process. The action may be positive or negative depending upon favourable perception held by the perceiver. As an example, a student may respond favourably to the motivational intentions of the Professor provided his understanding about his Professor is positive or favourable. The action also may be covert or overt. The covert action relates to change in attitudes, opinion, feelings, impressions, etc. The overt action may be in the form of one's behaviour easily noticeable and visible.

6.5. FACTORS AFFECTING PERCEPTION

Factors that influence perception relate to the perceiver, perceived and situation. All these factors are of two kinds — (*i*) Internal (Endogeneous) Factors, and (*ii*) External (Exogeneous) Factors. These are now discussed in detail.

Internal Factors

These factors reside in person concern. These include one's needs, desires, personality and experience.

(*i*) **Needs and Desires:** An individual's perception about stimuli is influenced by, **inter alia**, his needs and desires at that time. Perception varies depending upon variations in his/her needs and desires from time to time.

(*ii*) **Personality:** Closely related to needs and desires is the personality of the perceiver, which affects what is attended or perceived in the given situation. As mentioned earlier, research studies suggest that secure individuals tend to understand or perceive others as warm and self-accepting individuals perceive themselves as liked, wanted and accepted by others'.

(*iii*) **Experience:** Experience and knowledge serve as basis for perception. While one's successful experience enhances his/her perceptive ability, failure erodes his/her self-confidence. Successful experience also helps perceiver understand stimuli with more accuracy.

External Factors

The external factors relate to what is to be perceived and situation. These are size, intensity, frequency, status, etc.

(*i*) **Size:** The principle of size says that the larger the object, the more is the probability that it is perceived. Size attracts the attention of the individual. A full-page spread advertisement attracts more attention than a few lines in a classified section. The reason is not difficult to seek. The size establishes dominance and enhances perceptual selection.

(*ii*) **Intensity:** Intensity is closely related to size. The intensity principle of attention states that the more intense the stimuli, the more likely it is to be perceived. As an example, a loud noise or strong odour will be noticed more than a soft sound and weak odour. Following the intensity principle, the superiors may yell at their subordinates to gain attention. Advertisers also use intensity to attract and gain the consumer's attention.

(*iii*) **Frequency/Repetition:** The repitition principle states that a repeated external stimulus is more attention-getting than a single one. It is for this reason that advertisers go for repetitions advertising to gain the customers' attention to their product.

(*iv*) **Contrast:** As per contrast principle, the external stimuli which stands out against the background will receive more attention. For example, plant safety signs with black lettering on a yellow background or white lettering on a red background are more attention-attracting.

(*v*) **Status:** Status held by an individual also influences his/her perception about things or events. Researches suggest that people with high status often exert more influence on the perception of an individual as compared to those holding low status.

(*vi*) **Movement:** The movement principle says that people pay more attention to a moving object than the stationary ones. People will be attracted more by a running train than one standing on the plateform.

6.6 HOW TO IMPROVE PERCEPTION?

By now, you have learnt that perception precedes behaviour. How one (say, boss) will behave with others (say, subordinates) depends on how the former perceives the latter. More accurate the perception, the better will be behaviour and vice versa. Inaccurate perception distorts behaviour. And, in this lies the need for and importance of improving perception. Perception can be improved by making various attempts. Following are the important ones that can help one improve his/her perception.

1. **Perceiving Oneself Accurately**: In order to perceive others accurately, one first needs to perceive oneself accurately. Therefore, one needs to improve more awareness about himself/herself. Frequent and better interaction with peers; free, frank and open communication with others and mutual trust are some commonly adopted practices for perceiving oneself more accurately.

2. **Improving One's Self-Concept:** When people successfully accomplish what they want, it develops a sense of self-regard and self-esteem. It is called 'self-concept'. Research studies suggest that people having self-concept tend to perceive others more accurately. Abraham Maslow[9] also contends that self-actualising people have more accurate perceptions about themselves and others than those who are not self-actualising. It also indicates that correct perception about oneself helps perceive others also more accurately.

3. **Be Empathetic:** Empathy means to be able to see a situation as it is perceived by other people. In a way, it is like putting your feet in another's shoes. Looking at a problem from others' point of view enables the person to perceive the other side of the problem.

The role of empathy in improving perception can be appreciated by a story of '**A Puppy**'.

A PUPPY

A boy went to the pet store to buy a puppy. Four puppies were sitting together, priced at Rs. 1,000 each. Then there was one sitting alone in a corner. The boy asked if that was from the same litter, if it was for sale, and why it was sitting alone. The store owner replied that it was from the same litter and that it was a deformed one, and not for sale.

The boy asked what the deformity was. The store owner replied that the puppy was born without a hip socket and had a leg missing. The boy asked, "What will you do with this one?" The reply was it would be put to sleep. The boy asked if he could play with that puppy. The store owner said, "Sure." The boy picked the puppy up and the puppy licked him on the ear. Instantly the boy decided that was the puppy he wanted to buy. The store owner said "That is not for sale!" The boy insisted.

The store owner agreed. The boy pulled Rs. 200 from his pocket and ran to get Rs. 800 from his mother. As he reached the door the store owner shouted after him, "I don't understand why you would pay full money for this one when you could buy a good one for the same price." The boy didn't say a word. He just lifted his left trouser leg and he was wearing a brace. The pet store owner said, "I understand. Go ahead, take this one".

This is empathy.

4. **Having Positive Attitudes:** Positive attitude makes one's perception positive or more accurate. Hence, the managers need to try to overcome their personal bias, get rid of any negative feelings, if any, they have of others. These enhance an individual's perceptual skill.

5. **Avoiding Perceptual Distortions:** As discussed earlier, some factors such as halllo effect, stereotyping, attribution, first impression, etc. distort one's perception about things or problems. Therefore, sincere and contineous efforts should be made to guard oneself against such biases. This, in turn, improves one's perceptual ability.

6. **Communicating Openly:** Experience suggests that sometimes perception gets distorted due to communication gap or/and inadequate communication. In such case, effective communication needs to be developed to ensure that true and right message reaches at the right place and at the right time. This will enable to know the problem in a better perspective which, in turn, will improve person's perception about the problem.

In short, it can be summed up that perception skills can be enhanced/improved by:

- Knowing and perceiving oneself accurately.
- Seeing a situation/problem as it is experienced by others, i.e. empathy.
- Having positive attitude towards the problems and situations we are confronted with.
- Improving one's self-esteem or self-concept.
- Avoiding the common biases in perception.
- Making two-way/effective communication to dispel mis-communication or lack of communication.
- Making a conscious effort to avoid attribution.

6.7 PERCEPTION AND ITS APPLICATION IN OB

The word 'organisation', among other things, implies where host of individuals work together for achieving the organisational and individual goals. In this process, they are always judging each other on a continuous basis. One tries to evaluate how much effort his/her co-worker is putting into his/her job. Even when a new worker joins a department, he/she is immediately sized up by the other departmental workers. The perceptual process, as discussed earlier, suggests how one judges/assesses others largely depends upon how he/she perceives/understands them. In this way, perception tends to influence decision-making. Thus, perceptions, in many cases, have important effect on organisations. Let us briefly look at a few of the more obvious applications of perception in organisations.

Employment Interview: Interviewers make perceptual judgements that are often inaccurate. Different interviewers try to see different things in the same candidate and, thus, arrive at different perceptions about the same candidate. Who one thinks is a good candidate and who another thinks is a bad one may differ markedly. Importantly, interviewers form early impression about the candidate that weights in the final selection of the candidate. So to say, information elicited early in the interview carries greater weight than does information elicited later[10]. That is why a good candidate is characterised more by the absence of unfavourable characteristics than by the presence of favourable characteristics. In this way, it is clear that where interview is an important input into selection decision, the perceptual factors influence the decision who is to be selected. This, in turn, influences the quality of labour force selected in an organisation.

Performance Appraisal: Assessment of an employee's performance very much depends on the perception of the evaluator about the employee. In practice, an employee's future is closely tied to his or her performance appraisal. Promotions, pay raises and continuation of job are the most obvious and common outcomes of the employee's performance. Performance appraisal is both objective and subjective. It may be objective when performance can easily be quantified. For example, a salesman's performance can be assessed based on how many Rupees of sales he/she generated in his/her territory during a given period of time. However, many employees' jobs are evaluated in subjective terms. An impressive amount of evidence demonstrates that subjective measures are, by definition, judgemental. Judgements, as we discussed earlier, make one's perception more susceptible to distortions. Thus, subjective approach may influence the appraisal outcome.

Performance Expectation: New employees during their selection process acquire a set of expectations both about the organisation and about the job he is expecting to achieve. In case, there is a big difference between what expected and what actually acquired, it results in increased employee absenteeism and turnover.

Employee Effort: In many organisations, the level of an employee's performance is given high importance. Hence, an employee's future in an organisation depends on his/her effort made for achieving the organisational goals. However, assessment of an individual's performance is a subjective judgement and thus, susceptible to perceptual distortions and bias also.

Employee Loyalty: While assessing employees, the managers also make another important decision whether the employees are loyal to organisation or not. Like effort, assessment of loyalty is also a subjective judgement susceptible to perceptual distortions and bias. As an example, an employee looking for greener pastures outside the organisation may be labelled as disloyal to the organisation. As a resultant behaviour, the organisation may cut off his future advancement opportunities.

6.8. IMPRESSION MANAGEMENT

Simply stating, impression management is a process by which people try to control/manage the perception others hold of them. It is noticed that people try to present themselves in such a way so as to please or impress others in a way desirable to them. Based on this, impression management bears implications for organisation in areas such as performance appraisal, promotion, etc.

6.8.1 PROCESS OF IMPRESSION MANAGEMENT

As with other cognitive processes like perception, impression management also follows a process. Impression being cognitive is being studied in relation to aggression, attitude change, attributions, etc. There are two well identified components included in the process of impression management:[11]

1. Impression Motivation, and
2. Impression Construction.

Let us understand what these mean.

Impression Motivation: It is a situation especially in an employment when subordinates become motivated to present themselves how their boss perceives them. How much a subordinate is motivated to present or manage oneself in a way desired by the boss will depend on various factors like relevancy the impression has to the subordinate's goals, the value of these goals and the degree of discrepancy between the image the subordinate would like the boss to hold and the image or impression he/she believes the boss already holds.

Impression Construction: It is concerned with the specific type of impression people want to form and, then, how they go about doing it. While trying to construct or form a specific type of impression, they usually depend on five factors[12], namely, the self-concept, identity images, role constraints, target's values and current social image. These five factors influence the type of impression one tries to construct.

6.8.2 IMPRESSION MANAGEMENT STRATEGIES

Following are the two basic strategies[13] of impression management that people/ employees usually employ:

1. Demotion-Preventing Strategy
2. Promotion-Enhancing Strategy

A brief description of these follows.

Demotion-Preventive Strategy: This strategy is concerned with how people try to minimize responsibility for some (expected) negative event or try to remain out of trouble. To say it in another way, the demotion-preventive strategy is characterized by the following:

(*i*) **Excuses:** People/employees have a tendency to give excuses or justifications like not feeling well, having another priority assignment, etc. for not performing an action.

(*ii*) **Apologies:** In the absence of any logical way out (excuse), people/employees resort to apologize to the boss for negative action/event. Apologies serve two purposes. **One**, the individual/employee feels sorry. **Second**, it also gives an impression that the same (negative) action will not be repeated in future. This bears significance for organisational behaviour.

(*iii*) **Disassociation:** There is also a tendency noticed among the people that people try to disassociate themselves in future if anything/action has gone wrong. For example, an employee is a member of a committee that made a bad or wrong decision. He now tries to disassociate himself/herself by telling his/her boss that he/she fought for the right thing but was overruled by others.

Promotion-Enhancing Strategy: This strategy, on the contrary, involves the following :

(*i*) **Entitlements:** Under this approach, people demand for their rights or entitlements resulting from their actions/performance.

(*ii*) **Enhancement:** In such case, employees point out for more credit than what they really received.

(*iii*) **Association:** Under this approach, employees try to be associated with the right people at the right times. This gives a positive impression to the employees that they are properly associated with the matters/projects that will help get promotion in future.

6.8.3 HOW TO IMPROVE IMPRESSION MANAGEMENT ?

Impression being a cognitive process is susceptible to distortions. Following are some guidelines that will help especially organisational members, improve their impression management:

1. In the process of improving impression, one should always try to be on the lookout for high-positive impression. Recruiters, for example, should always be careful to separate self-promotion and legitimate claims for one's competence. Similarly, persons holding positions of power should be aware of subordinates' efforts to ingratiate them *i.e.*, **'buttering up the boss' or 'apple-polishing.'**

2. Attempts should be made to minimize personal, situational and organisational factors that tend to distort impression of others. Organisations having limited promotional avenues are examples of generating relatively high levels of ingratiation.

3. One needs to be influenced by ulterior motives, not by overly influences. This enables an individual to make an unbiased or fair assessment of others. This is found particularly relevant while the boss appraises his/her subordinates' performance in organisations.

In total, the best tactic how to improve one's impression management may be what is offered by William Gardner[14]. He views: **"When selecting an image, never try to be something you are not. People will see through the facade. In sum, make every possible effort to put your best foot forward-- but never at the cost of your identity or integrity".**

SUMMARY

This summary is organized as per the 'learning objectives' given on page no. 69:

- *Perception is a cognitive process of seeing, receiving, selecting, organising, interpreting and giving meaning to the environment around us. Sensation differs from perception in the sense that it activates through physical sensory organs to respond to some stimuli. In other words, sensation serves as a raw input to be processed for perceiving the stimuli around us.*
- *Perceptual process follows as inputs → throughputs, and → outputs.*
- *Two types of factors--internal and external-influence an individual's perception. The internal factors include individual's needs and desires, personality, experience, etc. Factors relating to size, intensity, frequency, contrast, status and movement constitute external factors that influence one's perception.*
- *Perception being a cognitive process is susceptible to distortions. Nonetheless, attempts made to perceive oneself accurately, improve self-concept, be empathetic, have positive attitudes avoid the common perceptual distortions and communicate openly help improve one's perceptual ability.*
- *The specific areas of application of perception in organisational behaviour include employee selection interview, performance appraisal, employee effort, employee loyalty, etc.*
- Impression management is a process by which people try to manage or control the perceptions others form of them. When people/employees try to minimize their responsibility for some negative event, it is called 'demotion-preventive strategy' characterized by excuses, apologies and disassociation. If they try to maximize responsibility for some positive outcome, it is known as 'promotion-enhancing strategy' characterised by entitlements, enhancement and association.
- To have high-positive impression, minimize distorting factors and be influenced by ulterior motives are some of the guidelines that help one improve one's impression management. To conclude, **"although there is nothing wrong with looking as good as one can, one must always be true to oneself".**[15]

REVIEW QUESTIONS

1. Define perception. Discuss the process involved in perception.
2. How does sensation differ from perception? Emplify.
3. How do external factors affect perception?
4. What does stereotyping mean? Give an example of how stereotyping can create perceptual distortion.

5. What is meant by halo effect? How does it affect perception?
6. "That you and I agree on what we see suggests we have similar backgrounds and experiences." Do you agree or disagree? Discuss.
7. In what way do you find perception relevant to understand organisational behaviour?
8. What does impression management mean? What is meant by impression motivation and impression construction?
9. What are major strategies employees can use in impression management?
10. Distinguish between impression and perception.

REFERENCES

1. Udai Pareek et. al: **Behavioural Process in Organisations,** Oxford and IBH Publishing Co., New Delhi, 1981, p. 27.
2. Stephen P. Robbins: **Organisational Behaviour,** Printice Hall of India, New Delhi, 1996, p. 132.
3. Fred Luthans: **Organisational Behaviour,** McGraw-Hill, Inc., New York, 1995, p. 108.
4. Fred Luthans: **Ibid,** 1995, p.87.
5. Peter J.R. Dempey: **Psychology and the Manager**, Pan Books, London, 1973, p.4.
6. D.C. Dearborn and H.A. Simon: Selective Perception: A Note on the Departmental Identification of Executives, **Sociometry,** June 1958, pp. 140-144. However, some of the conclusions in this classic study have recently been challanged in J.P. Walsh: Selectivity and Selective Perception: An Investigation of Managers' Belief Structure and Information Processing, **Academy of Management Journal,** December 1988, pp. 873-896.
7. J.S. Bruner and R. Tagiuri: The Perception of People; In : E.Lindzey (Ed.) **Handbook of Social Psychology,** Addison-Wesely, Cambridge, Mass, 1954, p. 641.
8. Spencer A. Rathus: **Psychology,** Holt, Rinehart and Winston, Fort Worth Text, 1990, pp. 613-614.
9. Abraham Maslow: A Theory of Human Motivation, **Psychological Review,** March/April, 1943, 50, pp. 370-396.
10. E.C. Webster: **Decision Making in the Employment Interview,** McGill University, Industrial Relations Centre, Montreal, 1964.
11. Mark R. Leary and Robin M. Lowalski: Impression Management: A Literature Review and Two-Component Model, **Psychological Bulletin**, Vol. 107, No. 1, 1990, pp. 34-47.
12. **Ibid,** pp. 40-42.
13. Robert A Giacalone: Image Control: The Strategies of Impression Management, **Personnel**, May 1989, pp. 52-55.
14. William M. Gardner: Lessons in Organisational Dramaturgy: The Art of Impression Management, **Organisational Dynamics**, Summer 1992, pp. 43-44.
15. Fred Luthans: **Op. cit.** 1995, p. 108.

An Exercise on Self-Perception and Development of the Self-Concept*

Goals:

1. To enable the students to consider their own self-concepts and to compare this with how they feel are perceived by others.

---

* Fred Luthans : **Organisational Behaviour**, Tata McGraw-Hill Publishing Company Limited, New Delhi, 2007, p. 323.

3. To stimulate student thinking about how management of human resources may involve perception and personality.

Implementation:

1. The students take out a sheet of paper and fold it in half from top to bottom.
2. The students write "How I See Myself" and "How I Think Others See Me".
3. The students write down five one-word descriptions (adjectives) under each designation that, in their opinion, best describe how they perceive themselves and how others perceive them.
4. The students then share their two lists with their classmates (in dyads, triads, or the whole class) and discuss briefly. Each person may communicate what he or she is most proud of.
5. The instructor may participate in the exercise by sharing his or her list of adjectives.

Case 6. 1 : Same Accident but Different Perceptions

The police report read that bus number 011-1234 while on its route from Ambattur to Madras on April 16, 1986, had an accident some 30 miles from Poonamallee–an apparent collision against a banyan tree. When the policeman on beat arrived at the scene around 1.30 p.m., he was unable to locate the driver. The passengers–some 35 of them were in a state of panic. All of them had got down from the bus and many were sitting under the shade of a nearby tree some distance from where the bus stood with its damaged front part. Children were crying and the women passengers were screaming as they saw the policeman walk towards them. The men were talking loudly, all at the same time. Nobody was able to state clearly what had happened or at what time exactly the accident had taken place. Estimates of when the accident occurred varied from 35 minutes to 2 hours earlier.

Three days later, the General Manager of Pandyan Transport was sitting at his desk looking at three different reports in front of him. One was the policeman's report which detailed the extent of damage to the bus, and the fact that the driver had abandoned the bus without telling the passengers where he was going or what they should be doing. The Regional Transport Officer (RTO) who was summoned to the scene two hours later also filed a report of his assessment of the damage. He stated that Thangavelu, the driver, whose record indicated that he had been a fairly safe driver for almost two decades, had been involved in a couple of minor accidents in the past six months. The first was when he hit a cyclist who fortunately sustained only some minor bruises and had his cycle intact, and the second when he drove into a ditch on a rainy night. Fortunately, again, there were no serious injuries to anyone and no damage to the bus. The RTO said that he had a suspicion that Thangavelu was perhaps driving under the influence of alcohol. Actually, according to the RTO, Thangavelu was found by one of the policemen inside a hut near the place of the accident drinking at 5.30 p.m. on April 16, and from there he was taken to the police station. The RTO felt that Thangavelu's behaviour was totally irresponsible inasmuch as he left the spot of the accident (something that the rules absolutely prohibited) and on top of that he was drinking just after the accident!

The third report in front of the manager was the one filed by Thangavelu himself. Thangavelu stated that in an effort to avoid a stray cow on the road, he swerved the bus and accidentally hit the tree on the side of the road on April 16. As soon as the accident happened, he wanted to report the incident to the police and to his head office. He also wanted to seek assistance so that the passengers could be put in another bus and his bus towed away. But he did not want to alarm the passengers and hence got down from the bus, signalled to the passengers that he will be back, and walked in search of a nearby telepone to contact the police and his head office.

Unfortunately, even after walking four or five miles, there was no telephone in sight, but he knew there definitely was one in the Tehsildar's home a few miles away. Hence he walked further but on reaching the place, he found the house locked. Knowing that the passengers would be in a state of franzy, he started to walk back to the bus, but on arriving at the spot he found neither the bus, nor the passengers. By this time, he was weary, and guessed that the police must have arrived at the spot, transported the passengers by another bus, and towed away the damaged bus. Since he was dead tired after all the walking and since his hours of duty were already over, he thought he would soothe his nerves with some toddy. That was the time when the policeman came into the hut and dragged him away. Thangavelu said that he did not walk away from the scene of the accident but he had acted in the best interests of his passengers. He did not want them to panic and thought he would find a telephone within a mile or so. He tried to be dutiful in the only way he knew how, and had no other option but to do what he did!

QUESTIONS

1. What kinds of perceptual processes were operating in the three different reports?
2. What additional information would you, as the manager of Pandyan Transport, seek to clarify your own perception of the incident?
3. Given the information provided in the case, how would you resolve the issue of whether or not to fire the driver?

Case 6. 2: When Otherwise Perception Caused Conflict*

Sunder Chemicals was established in the year 1945 with about 40 workers and was manufacturing a couple of pharmaceutical products. After three years of initial crisis, the company found itself in a very prosperous situation. In 1965, the company employed about 25,000 employees working in 15 different departments.

Mr. Parikh was incharge of the Tablet department having about 30 workers. In the day shift, Parikh was assisted by Mr. Patel for the general supervision of the department.

Mr. Joshi was one of the workers in the Tablet department about whom Patel did not have good opinion as Joshi was in the habit of remaining absent without leave. Patel often found him taking leave under false pretexts. Patel did not have any other complaint about Joshi.

One day Joshi approached Patel with a request to grant him leave for a week, as he wanted to go for a pilgrimage with his family. Patel this time flatly refused to grant

* MBA, Manipur University, 1999.

leave to him saying that he was not prepared to believe him considering his past record. Joshi felt very sorry about this and seemed to be disturbed.

During the lunch break, he was not in a mood to talk with his co-workers with whom he otherwise talked very cheerfully. On observing this, Mr. Solanki, a very old worker who was with the company from its inception, asked Joshi if there was something wrong with him. Joshi narrated the matter and broke into tears saying that his old parents would be unable to go on a pilgrimage.

Solanki was very popular among the group and always helped his co-workers by representing their case to management. He was, in general, very hostile towards the officers and they, in turn, did not have, good opinion about him. Solanki assured Joshi that he would certainly get his leave granted.

Solanki went to see Patel on the same day and found him giving instructions to some workers. Throwing the leave application on Patel's table, Solanki very arrogantly asked him why he was not sanctioning leave to Joshi. Patel felt very bad about the manner in which Solanki asked this and that too in front of his subordinates. But, controlling his emotions, he simply told him to ask Joshi to discuss the same with him. Solanki said that Joshi had authorised him to discuss this matter. He further accused Patel by saying that he unnecessarily harassed workers and that he will have to give up this habit, or he should be prepared to face the consequences. Patel, feeling very much insulted, asked him (Solanki) to get out of the department. On hearing this Solanki reacted very furiously and pushing Patel physically, and told him, "I will now straighten you". After saying this, he himself left the department. Immediately, Patel saw Parikh and briefed him about the incident. Parikh regarded this as a very serious matter, and informed the Personnel Officer, Mr. Amin, to take appropriate action in the matter. Considering this as a gross misconduct, Mr. Amin served Solanki with a chargesheet. The company had a consistent policy for disciplinary actions and in such cases the punishment would be that of discharge.

Solanki was a very active member of the representative union which had very good relations with the management. Management always supported this union against another union which was very aggressive and protested against all actions of the management. When workers of the department knew that Solanki was chargesheeted, they all approached the Secretary (of the recognised union) and strongly requested him to see that Solanki did not lose his job. They all agreed that Solanki was, to some extent, at fault. The Secretary, after hearing the full story, remarked that Solanki should have rather taken the constitutional course to deal with the matter. The workers said that in any case Solanki should not lose the job, as he fought for his co-worker and not for himself. Considering the insistence of the workers, the Secretary decided to see Amin. In the meantime, a written petition was also handed over to Amin by the workers.

The Secretary met Amin and conveyed to him the feeling of the workers. He pointed out that this was the first time when workers expressed their desire so forcefully. The Secretary further requested Amin to reconsider the case for the following reasons:

(*i*) All the workers were insistent and felt involved in the matter, and if they were dissatisfied, the popularity of the union may decline, thus, paving way for the other obstinate union.

(*ii*) The Secretary assured that he would see to it that Solanki does not misbehave like this in future.

Amin had been until now very consistent with the policy and he thought that this may become a very significant deviation from the rules. On the other hand, he thought that it would be rather difficult for him to observe consistency in this case, as otherwise he will have to displease the workers and perhaps the other union might take up the opportunity to establish a footing in the company. In the meanwhile, Parikh telephoned Amin and said that his workers had approached him and requested him to consider the case sympathetically. He insisted that he considered this as a very serious matter and that no mercy may be shown in Solanki's case.

QUESTIONS

1. What is the problem in the case?
2. Indicate the individual, managerial and organisational causes that have led to the problem.
3. What other realistic alternatives did Patel, Parikh and Amin have which could have avoided the problem? How can you explain Patel's behaviour?
4. Discuss the alternatives now available to Parikh and Amin. Discuss the consequences of these alternatives for the organisation and the feasibility of enforcing these alternatives.

7

ATTITUDES, VALUES AND JOB SATISFACTION

"Determine to like your work. Then, it will become a pleasure, not drudgery. Perhaps you do not need to change your job. Change yourself and your work will seem different." – ***Dr. Norman Vincent Peale***

"Keep your face to the sunshine and you cannot see the shadow."– ***Helen Keller***

Learning Objectives

After studying this chapter, you should be able to:

- **Define** attitudes, values and job satisfaction and also describe their types.
- **Explain** how attitudes and values are formed and measured.
- **Explain** what determines job satisfaction and how it is meassured?
- **State** the effects of values and job satisfaction on behaviour.
- **Identify** the reasons for employees' job dissatisfaction.

In previous two chapters 5 and 6, you have learnt how psychological factors such as personality and perception affect human behaviour at work. In this chapter, you will study the effects of other psychological variables such as attitudes, values and job satisfaction on employees' behaviour.

7.1 ATTITUDES

7.1.1 CONCEPT OF ATTITUDES

Attitudes are evaluative statements. They respond one's feeling either favourably or unfavourably to persons, objects or/and events. In other words, attitudes reflect how one feels about something. For example, Professor Philip Kotler says "I like teaching," he is expressing his attitude about his work.

Let us consider some important definitions on attitudes given by the behavioural thinkers to understand the meaning of attitude in a better manner: Krech and Crutchfield[1] define attitude as "an enduring organisation of motivational, emotional, perceptual, and cognitive processes with respect to some aspect of the individual's world."

According to Munn[2], "attitudes are learned predispositions towards aspects of our environment. They be positively or negatively directed towards certain people, serivce or institutions."

Now, attitudes can precisely be defined as a persistent tendency to feel and behave in a particular way towards some objects, persons or events.

Salient Features: The salient features of attitudes flowing from above definitions are summarized as follows:

1. Attitudes are related to the feelings and beliefs of people.
2. Attitudes respond to persons, objects or events.
3. Attitudes affect behaviour either positively or negatively.
4. Attitudes undergo changes.

Attitudes affect perception and, in turn, behaviour. This underlines the need for managers to understand different types of attitudes and their formation, how attitudes are measured and what causes change in attitudes. The subsequent sections unfold the same.

7.1.2 FORMATION OF ATTITUDES

Attitudes are not inherited. These are acquired or learned by the people from the environment in which they interact. The formation of attitudes is broadly classified into two sources:

1. Direct Experience, and
2. Social Learning

Direct Experience: One's direct experience with an object or person serves as a powerful source for his/her attitude formation. In other words, attitudes are formed on the basis of one's past experience in concerned object or person. Take your own case, for instance. How do you know that you like organisational behaviour or dislike financial management? The answer to it is that you have formed these attitudes from your experience in studying the two subjects. Research has shown that attitudes derived from the direct experience are more powerful, stronger, durable and are difficult to change than are attitudes that are formed through indirect experience[3]. This is because of their availability in our cognitive processes.

Social Learning: The process of deriving attitudes from family, peer groups, religious organisations and culture is called **social learning**. In social learning, an individual acquires attitudes from his/her environment in an indirect manner. Social learning starts from early age when children derive certain attitudes from their parents. This is often evident from when young children express their political preferences similar to those held by their parents.

Attitudes are derived from **peer groups** also. For example, if Ravi Saxena has been attending his duty late for some days but co-workers have always been on time, Ravi Saxena is likely to attend his duty on time.

Individuals acquire much of their attitudes by merely **observing their models** whom they admire and respect. The observer overhears their models expressing their opinion or watches them displaying a behaviour that reflects their attitude. Then, the same attitude is imbibed and displayed by the observer. So to say, individuals shape their attitudes to align with their models.

Learning attitudes from observation involves the following four processes:

1. **Attention:** Attention must be focussed on model.
2. **Retention:** What was observed from the model must be retained.
3. **Reproduction:** Behaviour must be practised again and again.
4. **Motivation:** The learner must be motivated to learn from the model.

An **individual's association** with others also shapes one's attitude about him/her. For example, the teacher's attitude, be it favourable or unfavourable, about X student will often be formed by associating him with Y student about whom the teacher had already formed an opinion or attitude.

Added to these is culture that also plays a definitive role in forming attitudes. Consider, for example, the contrast in thinking about earning income in India and America. People in India earn mainly for future requirements of life while their counterparts in America earn money to enjoy the present. The American attitude is: **'live to-day not tomorrow'**?

7.1.3 TYPES OF ATTITUDES

Though an individual can have numerous attitudes, but organisational behaviour focuses on job related attitudes only. As such, job-related attitudes are of three types-job satisfaction, job involvement and organisational commitment. A brief description of these follows.

Job Satisfaction: The term job satisfaction refers to an individual's pleasurable or positive emotional state toward his or her job. Job satisfaction is related with the five specific dimensions of the job: pay, the work itself, promotion opportunities, supervision, and co-workers. When people speak of employee attitude, more often than not, they mean job satisfaction. In fact, the two terms attitude and job satisfaction are frequently used interchangeably. Without question, job satisfaction has received bulk of attention in organisational behaviour. Therefore, this is discussed in considerable detail later in this chapter.

Job Involvement: Job involvement is the degree to which employees immerse themselves in their jobs, invest time and energy in them, and consider work as a central part of their overall lives. Employees with a high level of job involvement strongly identify with their jobs and take utmost care about the kind of job they do. Such employees seldom will be tardy and absent. They will attempt to be high performer.

Organisational Commitment: Organisational commitment is an attitude about employee's loyalty to their organisation. It is a process through which employees identify with the organisation and want to maintain membership in the organisation. In fact, like a strong magnetic force attracting one metallic object to another, organisational commitment is a measure of the employees' willingness to remain with a firm in the future also. It is usually stronger among longer-term employees, and those who have relished personal success in the organisation.

So, while **job involvement** means identifying with one's job, **organisational commitment** means identifying with one's employing organisation.

7.1.4 MEASUREMENT OF ATTITUDE

Our thoughts and feelings tend to compromise our attitudes towards anything from the other person, to the environment to the world. There is intention which is also shaped by our beliefs and which also influences the formation of our attitude. One could, then, say that between intention and action is attitude. An awareness of our attitude tells much about our self at any given moment. Attitude thinkers have identified five types of attitudes which are worthy of appreciation[4]:

1. Attitude of Kindness
2. Attitude of Mercy
3. Attitude of Compassion
4. Attitude of Forgiveness
5. Attitude of Humility and Self-respect

Each is worthy of discussion.

When you extend true love to everyone with selfless motivation that is an *Attitude of Kindness*

Three concepts meet and merge into one action - love, selflessness and kindness. These are rarely seen but are often aspired to. Then question is why? Most probably this is because the love has become more of a fuzzy idea, than a real and authentic gesture. That is why it seems 'love' is now one of the most misused words in our language. For example, if I say: 'I love my country', it is not true love, but just my identification. If I say: 'I love you (my wife)' sounds good, feels OK, but can easily be translated as I want you. It all means that only the speaker knows his or her own real motive. Therefore, true love is neither identification, stimulation, dependency nor desire. The extending of true love is simply the extending of the self as a conscious and benevolent connection is made with the other. It's not even motivated by the thought, "I want to give". That's nearly love, but even that is tinged by desire, and true love has no desire. Or does it? As soon as the self 'wants' then the energy of the self, which is love itself, ceases to radiate naturally. It ceases to flow outwards without distortion, and it tries to bring some part of the universe into itself. Ultimately love neither gives nor takes nor wants. It simply is and it simply does. Without the distorting 'intention' of giving, taking or wanting, the energy of the self simply radiates as it must, creating the appropriate action as it must and whoever it touches feels the gentle touch of kindness, they feel touched, and that's why we sometimes even say...'I was so touched'. Understanding the true nature of love seems to be one of the deepest challenges at this particular time. The fact remains that true love cannot be expressed in words. So to say, ultimately all words are inadequate to express true love.

When you send good wishes and pure feelings to those who are in deep sorrow that is an *Attitude of Mercy.*

Generally, we tend to 'sympathize' and create sorrow for ourselves under the illusion that by doing so we are giving support to those who are in sorrow. It means we have either forgotten or not yet learned the real meaning of empathy, which is to understand someone from their point of view by sensing perspective and their feelings/emotions without allowing ourselves to create the same emotions. Empathy is also rooted in the energy of love. It is love's natural response when faced with the suffering of another. Love is where empathy gets its strength not to be affected by the others' sorrows. The others' emotion is a symptom of their momentary weakness, and being in the company of someone who does not cry, but remains strong, can give them the strength to pull themselves up and out of their emotional trough. In a world where we learn that the loving thing to do is to 'cry with' the other, and thereby adding to their tears, it's not easy to not to join in and add to the sorrowfulness.

When you see the virtues rather than the weaknesses in others that is an *Attitude of Compassion.*

It also happens in this world that people not only look at the weaknesses of others but also more at the strengths i.e. positive side of others. Thus, they turn it into virtue. Yes, as much it is good to form virtue, it is not so easy and simple. It first requires that we be able to do the same for ourselves. We may do things that we may label bad or stupid but we are not an innately bad or stupid person. Self-criticism is both toxic and disabling. To know our own innate goodness and strengths becomes the only way we can see it genuinely in others. And as we do we give them the gift of a higher vision of themselves than that which they have for themselves in that moment. This is both a subtle and a spiritual empowerment. It empowers the other in a way they may not even notice at the time.

When you bless and uplift someone even as they defame you that is an *Attitude of Forgiveness.*

It is hard not to react and feel personally insulted when someone criticizes or defames us. By nature, we are conditioned to 'be offended'. But it's just another of ego's games. It is really the conditioning that is offended not the self. Whenever we take anything personally it just means we don't yet know ourselves as we truly are. We are still identifying with a false image we have given to our self. When we know ourselves as conscious beings with no self-image, when we are aware of our self only as consciousness, words cannot touch and, therefore, hurt us. The one who would insult us is then seen to be suffering within themselves. Their words, and the energy behind the words, are recognized as a symptom of their own discomfort. A need is discerned, so love as compassion arises. And that is forgiving. Love senses the need of the other and makes it available. This is because love is ultimately for giving.

When you tolerate a situation and take responsibility as well as give cooperation, even when not appreciated that is an *Attitude of Humility and Self-respect.*

Perhaps such attitude profiles a 'hero'. Who is a 'hero?' A hero is someone who saves the day. He has the courage to step up and put himself in danger, to take what seems to be a risk that few others would dare to take. The attitude of humility is only possible where there is the courage to let go of the illusion upon which the ego is based. It is always a false image that the self attaches to, perhaps even for a lifetime, hence the courage that is required is to let go or to 'see through' the illusion to the truth. "I am not that (image)". This is why humility cannot be pursued but arises only when there is the courage to let go of the illusion that the fear is real. All fear arises from the ego, and the ego is not real, so the fear is also unreal. Fear always loses its power when reality is restored. Only then, when the self stops being busy in ego's game of self-protection, can the self be fully available for all, which is cooperation in the most complete sense.

We have maintained that attitudes affect behaviour. Changes in attitudes make behaviour unpredictable. But, the managers need to know the dimension of attitude so as to anticipate employees' behaviour at work. One way to know the attitudinal dimension is attitude measurement.

Measurement in its broadest sense is the assignment of numerals, to objects or events according to rules. There are many methods of attitude measurement. All methods are classified into four types[5]:

1. Self-Report
2. Indirect Tests
3. Direct Observation technique
4. Psychological Reaction Techniques

However, attitude measurement of employees in organisations is most commonly carried out with **Self-Report Method.** Self-report usually elicits responses from employees through questionnaires dealing with their feelings about their work and related matters. Self-report is carried out through the use of attitude surveys.

Attitude surveys contain a set of statements or questions to be answered by the employees. A definite scale is assigned to each answer. Scaling-terms assigned are tailored to obtain the information what managers actually want. Table 7.1 illustrates what an attitude scaling might look like.

Statement in the questionnaire is: '**My job makes the best use of my abilities**'.

Table 7.1: Attitude Scaling for the Statements

Strongly Agree	5
Agree	4
Undecided	3
Disagree	2
Strongly Disagree	1

There are three types of attitude scaling commonly used in attitude measurement of employees in the organisations. These are:

1. Equal Appearing Interval Scales (L.L. Thurstone Scale[6])
2. Summated Rating Scales (Rensis Likert Scale[7])
3. Semantic Differential (C.E. Osgood et al Scale[8])

These are briefly discussed in the following paragraphs.

Equal Appearing Interval Scales: Perhaps the most widely used procedure of attitude measurement is L.L. Thurstone's technique of equal appearing interval scales. It is simple in application as it requires only one judgement for each item/statement. The statements range from pile 1 to pile 11 corresponding to the most favourable and the most unfavourable respectively. The other statements fall between these two extremes. The scales so prepared are then presented to the respondents for their responses on the statements. The responses given by the respondents are then summed up.

Summated Rating Scales: This scale is experimented by Likert for measuring attitudes. The scale has five points viz, always, often, sometimes, seldom and never. The statement is presented to the respondent who checks one of the five points assigned to each statements. These points indicate the degree of agreement or disagreement with the statements given to the respondents. Then, the scores or points given to the statements by the respondents are summed and averaged to yield an individual's attitude.

The Likert scale is considered better as compared to Thurstone's one because of its simplicity in making numerous statements which require only one statement for every aspect.

Semantic Differentials: Semantic differential refers to the successive allocation made of a concept to a score in a given multidimensional space by selection from a set of given scaled semantic alternatives. It comprises of many pairs of opposite alternatives having a scale value in between the extremes. The respondent marks the score along the scale for his/her attitude about the given object. Finally, the respondent's scores assigned to each statement are summed. The sum reflects the individual's attitude to the object, person or event, whatsoever it may be.

Apart from these, the other scales developed for attitude measurement include the Guttman technique, the error-choice method, and the sentence completion method. However, these have been least in use and hence have not been discussed here for want of space.

7.1.5 ATTITUDE CHANGE

As mentioned earlier, attitude formation involves three major components, namely, (i) congnitive (i.e, knowledge and awareness), (ii) affective (i.e. feelings), and (iii) conative (i.e. action or behaviour). As regards change in attitude, it covers all above three components. Several theories have been propounded to explain how attitude changes. Some of the prominent among them are discussed here.

Cognitive Dissonance Theory

Cognitive dissonance theory propounded by Festinger[9] is the best known and most researched framework pertaining to attitude change. According to this theory, attitude change is caused by inconsistency, or say, dissonance in beliefs. The reason is not difficult to seek. One cannot remain for long in inconsistent belief system. One needs to remove inconsistency in beliefs by resuming to one belief as good or right. To show how attempts to avoid cognitive dissonance may be involved in changing our own attitudes, let us consider an imaginary example.

Suppose, you say one thing but do another (e.g., claim you like administration (Job A) but take teaching (Job B). One attitude you hold is inconsistent with another (e.g., you cherish your health but also enjoy drinking alcohol). Then, an unpleasant state known as 'cognitive dissonance' arises. What happens is you feel uneasy about the inconsistencies between your words and deeds, or between your various attitudes, and you are tempted or motivated to change your attitude so as to resolve the dissonance. What we are saying, in its most general form, is that for the most cases, people's attitude toward selected alternatives tend to become more positive, and toward rejected alternatives become more negative. This is because people derogate the characteristics of an alternative they do not accept and tout the advantages of the one they take as an attempt to avoid cognitive dissonance.

Reinforcement Theory

This theory is propounded by Hovland et.al.[10] and is based on the effects of persuasive communication. According to this theory, change in attitude takes place due to the reward or incentive offered in the communication. More the communication persuasive, more likely is change in attitude.

Balance Theory

Developed by Heider[11], the balance theory explains that when one's beliefs are unbalanced, these create stress or tension. Then, one feels pressure to relieve stress by balancing, i.e., changing one's attitude. Two factors, namely, sentiment (e.g., liking, admiring) and unity (e.g., similarity, proximity) affect balance in one's beliefs. Balance occurs when sentiments or unity between beliefs about people or events or things are equally positive or negative. Imbalance happens when they are dissimilar in nature.

Comprehensive Theory

It was McGuire[12] who has been credited with the development of most comprehensive theory of attitude change. In his theory, Mc Guire has elaborated attitude change in five aspects, namely, attention, comprehension, yielding, retention, and action. According to him, change in attitude follows through these five stages. He has also showed that attitude change also follows a definite type of communication process comprising of five processes, namely, source, message, channel, receiver, and destination. While explaining how attitude changes, McGuire has suggested a matrix showing five stages (or modes) of attitude change on one axis and the five communication processes on the other axis (see Exhibit 7.1).

Exhibit 7.1: Mc Guire's Matrix of Attitudinal Change

Aspects of Attitude Change	Communication Process				
	Source	Message	Channel	Receiver	Destination
Attention					
Comprehension					
Yielding					
Retention					
Action					

Now, we shall briefly discuss each of communication processes in relation to attitude change.

Source

The source of communication has great influence on the first three phases of attitude change, i.e. attention, comprehension, and yielding. A source bears three characteristics in relation to attitude change, namely, credibility, attractiveness, and power. All three perform different functions in changing attitude. While credibility helps the receiver in internalising the message and attractiveness helps in identifying the receiver with the source, power of source helps in complying with the message.

Message

Like source, message also has four types of characteristics: suggestion, conformity, persuasion, and indoctrination. Suggestion is a repetitive presentation of message to target population / person with an objective to create an understanding about message in the minds of receivers. T.V. advertisements are such examples. As regards conformity, it refers to feedback given on the discrepancy between a person's behaviour and the norms or desired behaviour in this regard. For example, a T.V. advertisement shows a woman having long flowing hair by using Sun Silk Shampoo and, thus, emphasizes a discrepancy between the viewers' behaviour and espoused or desired behaviour, i.e., use of Sun Silk Shampoo. Persuasion is some what more active in the sense it also gives reasons for the acceptance of the particular behaviour. Appeals can be either rational or emotional, yet rational appeals are found more effective in influencing the receiver of the message. Similarly, compared to messages producing fear in the minds of receiver, messages offering pleasant feeling are found more likely to influence the receiver / people. The advantage of this tendency is taken by several organisations like banks when offering new products or services. For example, the Director of the National Institute of Financial Management (A Government of India Institute), Faridabad invited to its also faculty members to , Jaipur for two days to inform and impress upon them the new changes to be introduced in the institute from the academic year 2008-09. The rationale behind taking faculty members 200 kms. away from Faridabad to Jaipur is people are likely to be more positively susceptible and induced towards changes in pleasant atmosphere.

Channel

There are four variables related to a channel of communication. These are: direct experience, inter-personal communication, group discussion, and mass media. As regards the direct contact, the receiver's initial attitude - be favourable or unfavourable - toward the thing influences the change in attitude of the receiver. It is observed that direct experience for long often produces a favourable attitude. This is mainly because long contact produces and increases familiarly with the thing and, in turn, influences attitude. There is evidence to believe that increasing familiarly changes attitude from utter dislike to extreme liking. Long contact between husband and wife may be one such case. Regarding inter-personal communication, evidence suggests that spoken communication produces more influence than written communication on receiver. The reason is not difficult to seek. In case of spoken communication, the source of communication, i.e., the sender also becomes an added factor in persuasion. As far as mass media is concerned, research results on impact of mass media on attitude change have so far been inconclusive. Nonetheless, the findings are that mass media affects attention, comprehension, and yielding which are basic elements involved in attitude change.

Receiver

Receivers as individuals differ in personality characteristics and, in turn, in suggestibility and persuability[13]. While some individuals are easily influenced by suggesting them about what is expected of them, others cannot be. Similarly, some people are more susceptible to persuasion process, others are not. Active participation of individuals in the development of change programme is also found more effective in changing their attitudes toward positive direction.

Destination

Here, destination means the variables used to change attitude. There can be three major variables involved in the process of attitude change: (i) the duration of change, (ii) the delayed action effect, and (iii) developing resistance to counter the contrary effect. Regarding the duration of change, research findings report that attitude change through intensive persuasion lasts for a short - duration like 3-4 months and requires repetitive persuasion to make the change last for longer period. Some times there are some messages that produce impact on receiver only some time after the message sent. As far as immunization effect is concerned, it is produced through various ways. However, anchoring is found the most effective way to offset the influence of counter message on the receiver. Anchoring is done by linking a message with the core value of the individuals with whom the receiver wants to belong. This technique is generally used in T.V. advertisement by linking the advertisement message with models, hero's, celebrities, etc.

Attitudes affect behaviour. Hence, it is in the interest of the organisation to try for the favourable change in the attitudes. The following are some important ways that can be used for changing attitudes:

1. **Filling in the Information Gap:** Unfavourable attitudes are mainly formed owing to information gap or inadequate supply of information. Then, providing information to fill in the gaps can change attitudes. For example, workers may be anti-management because of the ignorance about the good intentions of management. If they are made known about the same, they may change their attitudes to pro-management.

2. **Use of Fear:** Researches report that attitudes can also be changed by giving fear. However, both low and high degree of fear arousal do not cause attitude change. The reason is while the former is often ignored, the latter makes the people stubborn in their held attitudes. In fact, only moderate level of fear arousal makes the people aware of the situations and induces to change their attitudes.

3. **Resolving Discrepancies:** Resolving discrepancies between attitude and behaviour, if any, is yet another way to change attitudes. For example, people try to have good attitude about the job they have held and negative ones about the jobs they did not choose to work.

4. **Impact of Peers:** Persuasion by peers with high credibility can also cause change in attitude. The same is not true with peers having low level of credibility.

5. **The Coopting Approach:** Coopting is also yet another way to change attitudes. In coopting approach, the people who are dissatisfied with a certain situation are taken to make them involved in improving things.

However, it would be naive to assume that attitude only affects behaviour. Sometimes, behaviour also, on reciprocal manner, influences attitudes, as this illustration demonstrates.

Nalini Pandey, a supervisor in Cachar Paper Mills, was resisting the implementation of personnel computers at work. After six months passed, Rupak Dayal, the General manager decided to purchase computers without wasting time to change supervisor's attitude. The computers were immediately installed and training on how to use computers was offered. Just after three weeks, Nalini emerged the most enthusiastic supporter for the computers and confided to her colleague: "We waited so long unnecessarily to get computers". Clearly, the General Manager's behaviour changed the supervisor's attitude.

Attitude affects performance. Hence, the need for positive attitude toward whatsoever work one does. Here is an interesting story of attitudes of three brick layers.

Three Brick Layerers

Three people were laying bricks. A passerby asked them what they were doing. The first one replied, "Don't you see I am making a living." when the same question was asked to the second one, he said, "Don't you see I am laying bricks to construct a wall". In answer of the same question, the third one replied, "I am building a beautiful cathedral/ monument." See, these three people doing the same thing had very different attitudes about their work. Their attitudes will certainly affect their performance. Third attitude is the example of pride of performance, i.e. positive attitude.

7.2 VALUES

7.2.1 CONCEPT OF VALUE

Values are one of the sources of individual differences which are discussed earlier in Chapter 4. Values are general beliefs tinged with moral flavour containing an individual's judgemental ideas about what is good, right or desirable. In other words, the answers to the questions-what is right or wrong and good or bad-are value laden. A few definitions of value will help us understand the meaning of value in a better manner.

Rokeach[14] defined value as "a specific mood of conduct or end-state of existence is personally or socially preferable to an opposite or converse mode of conduct or end-state of existence".

According to White and Bednar[15], "Value is a concept of the desirable, an internalised criterion or standard of evaluation a person possesses. Such concepts and standards are relatively few and determine or guide an individual's evaluations of many objects encountered in everyday life."

Thus, values are the basic convictions that give us a sense of right and wrong, good and bad. In this way, values form the basis for ethical behaviour. Like attitudes, an individual may have numerous values. A hierarchy based on a ranking of an individual's values in terms of their intensity forms his/her **value system**. All of us have a **value system.**

Values are learned. These change as individuals grow and mature. As changes in values change individual behaviour, managers have shown increasing interest in the study of values. This interest goes alongwith the emphasis on culture and ethics in organisations which we will discuss in Chapter 21. Here, our emphasis is confined to values as sources of individual differences at work.

Values and Attitudes

Both attitudes and values are tinged with moral. There are some similarities and dissimilarities between the two. The **similarities** are:

1. Both are learned or acquired from the same sources-experience with people, object, and event.
2. Both affect cognitive process and behaviour of people.
3. Both are endurable and difficult to change.
4. Both influence each other and, more often than not, are used interchangeably.

The sharp **differences** between attitudes and values are summarized in Table 7.2.

Table 7.2: Differences between Attitudes and Values

Attitudes	Values
1. Attitudes exhibit predisposition to respond.	Values represent judgemental ideas like what is right.
2. They refer to several beliefs relating to a specific object or situation.	They represent single belief focused on objects or situations.
3. These are one's personal experiences.	These are derived from social and cul tural mores.

7.2.2 TYPES OF VALUES

Milton Rokeach[16], a pioneer in studying human values, conducted a research survey on human values. On the basis of his research findings, he identified two basic types of values: **terminal value** and **instrumental value**.

Terminal Values: Terminal values represent the desirable end-states of existence; the goals an individual would like to achieve during his/her life time. Rokeach identified 18 terminal values (see Table 7.3).

Instrumental Values: Instrumental values reflect the way to achieving goals. In other words, these represent preferable modes of behaviour or means of achieving one's terminal values. Rokeach identified another set of 18 instrumental values, (see Table 7.3).

Both terminal and instrumental values work in concert to provide individuals with goals to strive for and acceptable ways to achieve the goals. A complete list of Rokeach's terminal and instrumental values is presented in Table 7.3.

Table 7.3: Terminal and Instrumental Values

Terminal Values		Instrumental Values	
1.	World Peace	1.	Honesty
2.	Happiness	2.	Forgiving Nature
3.	Equality	3.	Helpfulness
4.	Achievement	4.	Self-Control
5.	Inner Peace	5.	Independence
6.	Beauty in Nature	6.	Obedience
7.	Family Security	7.	Ambition
8.	Self-Respect	8.	Open-mindedness
9.	Salvation	9.	Cleanliness
10.	Friendship	10.	Affection and Love
11.	Mature Love	11.	Politeness
12.	Pleasure	12.	Rationality
13.	Freedom	13.	Responsibility
14.	Wisdom	14.	Courage
15.	Prosperity	15.	Competence
16.	National Security	16.	Cheerfulness
17.	Social Respect	17.	Intelligence
18.	Exciting Life	18.	Imagination

Source: **Adapted from Milton Rokeach:** The Nature of Human Values**, The Free Press, New York**, **1973.**

Allport and associates[17], in their **Study of Values,** identified six types of values as follows:

1. **Theoretical:** Accords high importance on the discovery of truth through a critical and rational approach.
2. **Economic:** Emphasises on the usefulness and practicability.
3. **Aesthetic:** Places the top most importance on form and harmony.
4. **Social:** Accords the highest value to the love and affection of mankind.
5. **Political:** Assigns importance to the acquisition of power and influence.
6. **Religious:** Have concern with the unity of experience and understanding of the cosmos as a whole.

Allport and associates developed a questionnaire containing a description of different situations. The respondents were asked to preference-rank a fixed set of answers. Based on respondents' answers, the two researchers ranked all the respondents in terms of the emphasis they accorded to each of the six types of values. One of their major findings, based on above ranking, was that people in different occupations give different importance to the six value types. For example, religious respondents gave the most value to religious values and rated the economic values least important. On the contrary, the purchasing executives placed the highest importance on economic values.

Values and Ethics: Sometimes some people consider values and ethics synonymous and use them interchangeably. However, the two mean the two different meanings. The major line of distinction between the two is that values are beliefs that affect an individual's judgemental ideas about what is good or bad. **The ethic is the way the values are acted out**. Ethical behaviour is acting in ways consistent with one's personal values and the commonly held values of the organisation and society.

7.2.3 FORMATION OF VALUES

Where do afterall our values come from? How are our values formed? The answers to these follow.

Research[18] has proved beyond doubt that a significant portion (40 per cent) of one's values is genetically determined. The rest of values, like attitudes, is learned and acquired through experiences with parents, school-mates, friends, peers, models and organisations.

Formation of values starts from family and is influenced by the parents. Recall your childhood when many of your mothers told you "Wash your hands and feet and brush your teeth." This they told because being lazy has been considered bad. Parents own behaviour to their everyday events also demonstrates what is good and bad, important and unimportant for the children. Thus, children imbibe many values from the parents.

Class-mates and peers also help shape one's values. As we grow and develop, our values also change. Here again, recollect your values during your school days. Your values about somethings, more often than not, had been the same as held by your parents. But, by now when you have grown up and exposed to several situations, might have changed.

Culture also influences the formation of values. As culture varies across the regions, so do values also.

Now, some reflection on how values affect behaviour before we leave this section on 'values'.

7.2.4 VALUES AND BEHAVIOUR

We have maintained throughout the section that values affect behaviour because they affect employee's views of what constitutes right and wrong. Therefore, the diversity of the work force makes it imperative that the managers understand difference in values. On the whole, an understanding of values is useful to a manager in the following ways:

1. **Values serve as foundations for attitudes**. In practice, individuals enter organisations with a pre-conceived notion of what "ought" and what "ought not" to be. These notions are value laden.

2. **Individuals hold their own interpretations of right and wrong.** Such situations cloud objectivity and rationality.

3. **Values affect both attitude and behaviour.** Let it be illustrated.

> Suppose, Ravi Shanker enters Cachar Paper Mills with the view that payment of salary on piece-rate system is right and on time-rate basis is wrong. He is likely to be disappointed if the Mill allocates salary on time-rate basis. His disappointment is likely to breed his job-dissatisfaction. This will, in turn, adversely affect his performance. His attitude and, in turn, behaviour would be different if his values are aligned with the organisation's reward/pay policy.

4. **Re-examining the established values poses challanges for the modern management.** That is why '**the value-based management**' has been receiving increasing attention in the recent years.

7.2.5 How to Develop Values?

That value, whether organisational or individual, are important for better conduct and performance is well established and accepted conclusion arrived at different studies. Then, a question arises is where do values come from? Are values inherited or these can be developed? If values can be developed, then, how? Research[19] has established that values can be developed, of course, not by sermons or preaches or lectures on values, but by role modeling and an examination of the gap between the values desired and values practiced. There is, more often than not, a gap between the espoused or desired values and the practiced ones, also called 'value incongruence'. Hence, there is a need to reduce or fill in the gap, i.e., value incongruence. In practice, the less the gap between the values desired and the values practiced, the more is the value congruence or vice versa in the organisation. Behavioural practitioners and researchers have conducted experiments or interventions to reduce the gap, i.e., incongruence in values. One most commonly suggested and used intervention for developing values in organisations is 'Value Clarification' originally suggested by Kirschenbaum[20]. A discussion on 'Value Clarification' follows subsequently.

Value Clarification

Interest on value clarification as an intervention used for developing values has increased and intensified over the period[21],[22]. One of such research on value clarification in the recent past is conducted by Uma Jain[23]. The following description on value clarification as an intervention for development of values has been extracted from Uma Jain's study.

According to Uma Jain, value clarification is done through a typical workshop which involves the following sequential steps:

- Participants are first of all asked to list their five most important values without giving them any input about values.
- Participants select the five most important values from an instrument, or call it, list that contains 27 values.
- With an objective to facilitate the participants to add to and / or appropriate their five values, a 'value auction'[24] is organized.
- Participants participate in the value auction to bid for and buy certain values they want. For this, they are made available a specific budget which they

can use the ways they like. They are also allowed to opt for two joint biddings while participating in the value auction.

- Once the above stage of participating in value auction is over, the participants are asked once again to list their final five most important values.
- Besides, the above individual value clarification exercises, the participants are also asked to form groups and then groups are asked to make decisions based on value criteria.
- Thereafter, each group presents its criteria used for their decisions and the other groups identify the values upheld by these decisions.
- In addition to individual and group value clarification, some other exercises like Psychic Power, Who to Retain and Discovery[25] are also used to appropriate values to the maximum extent possible?

However, experiences of value clarification workshops have revealed the negative feelings in terms of frustration, disappointment, and helplessness felt by the participants. This is because the participants cannot practice the values that they cherish and want because of one type or other constraints in organisations. In her study on value clarification intervention (workshop), Uma Jain has identified the following constraints found in work organisations:

- Unawareness on the part of participants about one's own values and practice.
- Decisions on values are based on others rather than own values.
- Use of differing criteria of values for oneself and others.
- Tendency to avoid pain rather willingly seek pleasure and meaning.
- Desiring others change their values but supporting maintaining *status quo* in own case.
- Terminal (ends) values not supported by instrumental (means) values.
- Incongruence of materialistic goals with spiritual goals or values.

Uma Jain also found some important changes in participants introduced through value clarification workshops. The following are the major ones:

- More clarity of one's own values.
- More awareness of the priority of one's values, or say, own 'value system'.
- Courage and willingness to pay the price.
- Setting materialistic goals in congruence with own values.
- Increased awareness of broader horizons of the things.
- Understanding, accepting, and respecting others' values.
- Identifying the gap between values exposed and values practiced and making efforts to remove the gap.

7.3 JOB SATISFACTION

In organisational behaviour, job satisfaction is the most important and frequently studied attitude. We have already discussed job satisfaction briefly earlier in this chapter. Here, we shall dissect the concept more carefully. What is after all the meaning of job satisfaction? What determines job satisfaction? How is job satisfaction measured? What are its effects on employee productivity, absenteeism, and turnover rates? This section answers to all these questions.

7.3.1 CONCEPT OF JOB SATISFACTION

Job satisfaction is a positive attitude toward one's job. A few important definitions on job satisfaction are produced here.

According to Feldman and Arnold[26], "Job satisfaction will be defined as the amount of overall positive affect (or feelings) that individuals have towards their jobs."

Locke[27] defined job satisfaction as "a pleasurable or positive emotional state resulting from the appraisal of one's job or job experience."

In the opinion of Davis and Newstrom[28], "Job satisfaction is a set of favourable or unfavourable feelings with which employees view their work."

Thus, job satisfaction means good or positive attitude or feeling toward one's job. It is important to mention that an individual may hold different attitudes toward various aspects of the job. For example, a university Professor may like his job responsibilities but be dissatisfied with the opportunities for promotion. Characteristics of individuals also influence job satisfaction. Individuals with high positive affectivity are more likely to be satisfied with their jobs. Reverse is true for individuals with high negative affectivity.

There are three important dimensions to job satisfaction. These are:

First, job satisfaction being an emotional response to a job, cannot be seen. As such, it can only be inferred.

Second, job satisfaction is often determined by how satisfactorily outcomes meet or exceed one's expectations.

Third, job satisfaction represents an employee's attitudes towards five specific dimensions of the job: pay, the work itself, promotion opportunities, supervision, and co-workers[29].

7.3.2 DETERMINANTS OF JOB SATISFACTION

What causes job satisfaction has been a very fertile topic for organisational researchers during the past across the globe including India. As such, there has been prodigious volume of research conducted on job satisfaction. Researchers have identified several factors that make employees satisfied or dissatisfied with their jobs. However, these factors fall into two broad categories- those relating to the organisation and those relating to the personal characteristics of the employees themselves as shown in the following Table 7.4 :

Table 7.4 : Determinants of Job Satisfaction

Organisational Determinants	Individual Determinants
• Pay • Work itself • Quality of Supervision • Working conditions	• Age • Gender • Status and Seniority • Marital Status

We will describe these determinants one by one.

Organisational Determinants

Pay: There are reasons and evidences available to believe that pay, also known as reward system, is highly related to job satisfaction[8]. The research reveals that employees are found satisfied with their jobs when they feel that they are remunerated in a fair manner. It was also found that flexible benefit plan gives more satisfaction to employees than a common benefit plan offered to all employees. One researcher[9] reasoned that salary per se does not give satisfaction to employees, rather salary received in recognition of one's good work does. Traditionally, a positive correlation between pay and satisfaction is taken for granted. However, some studies do not confirm such relationship between pay and job satisfaction[10].

Work Itself: The employees those who like and love their jobs experience job satisfaction. In other words, feeling of work is worship gives job satisfaction. As regards relationship between job (work) and job satisfaction, the views of Harvey McKay on it seem worth citing: "Find a job (work) what you love and you'll never have to work a day in your life". When people do work what they love and enjoy, then the journey rather than the destination becomes their greatest reward," Besides, flexibility, freedom, and recognition for good work performance contribute to employee job satyisfaction[11]. Jobs with ambiguity in tasks, confusing instructions, and unclear job analysis cause job dissatisfaction[12].

Quality of Supervision: Quality of supervision is yet another organisational determinant of job satisfaction. Research evidence reports that employees experience higher level satisfaction when their supervisors are competent, treat their employees with respect and dignity, and show their sincere concern for employees' welfare[13]. It has also been found that employees are found more satisfied with their jobs the more they have opportunities to communicate with their supervisors[14]. Poor quality of supervision and / or supervisory apathy toward employees has been found causing dissatisfaction to the employees. So much so dissatisfied employees leave the (poor) supervisor not the organisation[15].

Working Conditions: Though scholars have been inconclusive in listing what constitutes working especially quality of working conditions, the broad consensus is that the context in which work is performed constitutes working conditions. Research has indicated that quality of working conditions and job satisfaction has been positively related. On the contrary, poor working conditions such as overcrowded conditions, and dark, noisy environments with extreme temperatures and poor air quality cause job dissatisfaction. Just like quality of supervision, quality of co-workers also affects employee job satisfaction.

Individual Determinants

In addition to above mentioned organisational determinants of job satisfaction, there are also some personal factors that affect employee attitude toward his/her job (see Figure 7.1).

Age: Research indicates that younger employees are more satisfied with their jobs than their elder counterparts. This could be explained by the fact that younger employees have not yet gained especially much experience about the job and organisation and, hence, they like the job and feel job satisfaction. On the other hand, evidence generally indicates that an employee's loyalty with the job and organisation tends to decrease with advancement in his/ her age[16].

Gender: Evidence generally indicates that women are more satisfied with their jobs than their male counterparts[17]. The general tendency of men employees, to some extent, by the fact that persons at the higher level of organisational hierarchy usually enjoy better working conditions and higher level rewards than those placed at lower levels of hierarchy. Moreover, employees satisfied with their jobs stay with organisation for longer period than those less satisfied and/or dissatisfied employees. This also implies that dissatisfied or less satisfied will hardly reach to the highest echelons in the organisations.

Marital Status: The findings on relationship between marital status and job satisfaction are not in congruence. Some studies report no relationship between the two. But, some studies report that married women are less satisfied with their jobs mainly because of their role conflicts as an employee and a housewife. That married people with less number of children experience more job satisfaction is also reported in some other studies[18].

The various determinants or sources of job satisfaction can diagramatically be presented as follows :

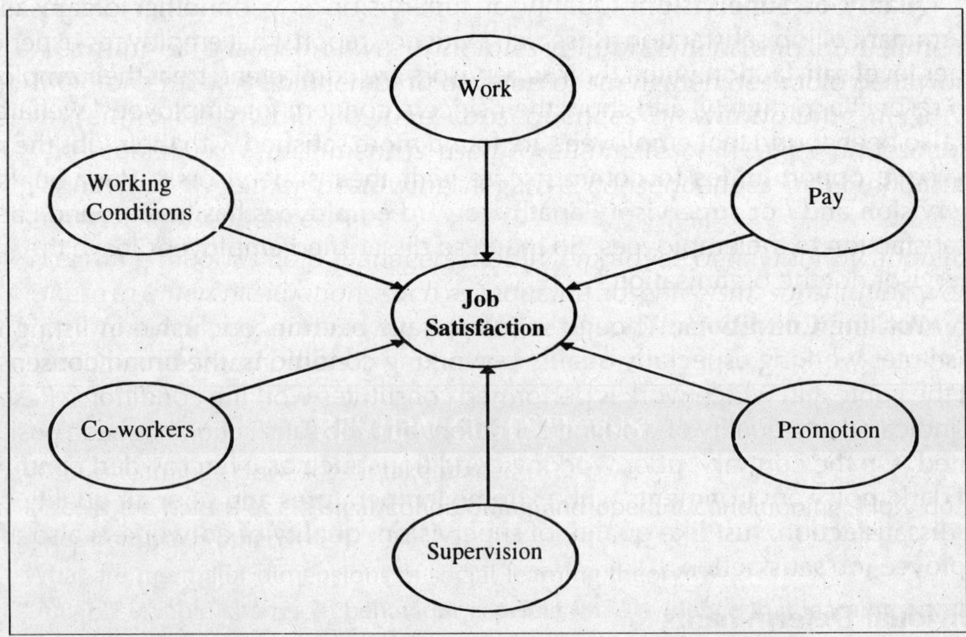

Fig. 7.1: Determinants or Sources of Job Satisfaction.

7.3.3 MEASURING JOB SATISFACTION

Like attitudes, there are a number of ways of measuring job satisfaction. The most common ways of measuring job satisfaction are: (1) Single Global Rating, and (2) Summation Score.

Single Global Rating: As implied from the terms, under single global rating, the employees are asked to respond to one question. An example of single question may be : "Considering all dimensions of the job, how satisfied are you with your job?" Employees need to respond by reporting "a figure" based on rating scale. Rating scales are from 1 to 5 as follows:

1. Highly Dissatisfied
2. Dissatisfied
3. No comment
4. Satisfied
5. Highly Satisfied

Thus, the rating, based on above scale, to a question given by the employee is a reflection of magnitude or measurement of employee's job attitude toward his/her job.

Summation Score: The summation score considers employees' attitudes towards the various aspects of the job. The important aspects of the job that would be included for rating score are the nature of the work itself, supervision, pay, promotion opportunities, and relationship with co-workers. The scores given to each of these aspects are then added up to create an overall job satisfaction score of an individual employee.

One may ask an obvious question: Which one of the two approaches discussed above is better or superior? It can be said, at least intuitively, that the second, i.e. summation score is likely to give a more accurate evaluation of job satisfaction because it covers all important aspects of the job. But, given the broad and inherent concept of job, the single-question global rating becomes a more inclusive measure of job satisfaction. This may be one of those rare instances in which simplicity (single rating) wins out over complexity (several ratings).

The following are some more ways of measuring job satisfaction:

Interviews: This is yet another method of measuring job satisfaction. Under this method, employees are interviewed personally. The responses given by them reveal their satisfaction or dissatisfaction towards their jobs.

Action Tendencies: Under this method, information is gathered about how the employees were inclined to avoid or join certain things relating to their jobs. This reflects their job satisfaction or disatisfaction.

Critical Incidents: This method is based on Herzberg's two-factor theory of motivation. In this approach, employees are asked to identify the specific incidents on their jobs in which they were particularly satisfied or dissatisfied. These incidents are further analysed to ascertain the aspects which were closely related to positive and negative attitudes of the employees towards incidents so identified.

7.3.4 EFFECTS OF JOB SATISFACTION

Finally, we address to the questions: What are the effects of job satisfaction on employees' productivity, absenteeism, and turnover rates? The following sections examine the same.

On Productivity: Are satisfied workers more productive than their less satisfied counterparts? Though research evidence does not establish any consistent positive relationship between satisfaction and performance, the general consensus is that, in the long run if not in short-run, job satisfaction leads to increased productivity. Research evidence indicates that the satisfied workers will not necessarily be the highest producers. In fact, the rewards employees receive results in greater performance[30]. There is also evidence to suggest that job performance leads to job satisfaction and not the other way round.

On Absenteeism: There is inverse relationship, though based on pretty research evidence, between satisfaction and absenteeism. When satisfaction is high, absenteeism tends to be low and vice versa. As in productivity, absenteeism is subject to modification by certain factors like the degree to which people feel that their jobs are important. Employees who believe that their work is important than do those who do not feel this way. It is also worth mentioning that a high degree of job satisfaction will not necessarily result in low absenteeism, while a low level of job satisfaction is likely to bring about high absenteeism.

On Turnover: Like between satisfaction and absenteeism, an inverse relationship, though at a moderate level, has been established between satisfaction and turnover. However, there are other moderating factors as well influencing the employees' turnover rates. Commitment to the organisation is one such factor. There may be some employees who cannot see themselves working anywhere else, so they remain in the organisation regardless of how much dissatisfied they feel in the organisation. Similarly, if the condition of the economy is such that people find it tough to find job, even the dissatisfied ones will stay where they are. Just the opposite tends to apply to the general economic conditions in which jobs are easily available. If green pastures are available, employees do not mind going in search of them, even when they are satisfied with their existing jobs.

Now, on an overall basis, it is accurate to say that job satisfaction affects turnover rates. Although absolute low turnover is not necessarily beneficial to the organisation, a low turnover rate is usually desirable because of training costs and the drawbacks of inexperience.

On Other Dimensions: Added to those noted above are the following other effects of job satisfaction:

1. Employees with high job satisfaction tend to have better mental and physical health.
2. They learn new job-related tasks more easily and quickly.
3. They commit less mistakes including on-the-job accidents.
4. They have and file less grievances about the job and the management.
5. Last but not the least, the satisfied employees tend to evince prosocial attitude towards their co-workers and customers.

7.4 THEORIES OF JOB SATISFACTION

Job satisfaction improves job performance. Hence, it is welcome. Then, some questions arise: what makes some people satisfied with their job or what makes some people more satisfied with their job than others? What gives people good feeling toward their jobs? Answers to these questions are provided by theories of job satisfaction. Though there are several different approaches to comprehend and understand what makes people satisfied with their jobs, two are the most influential approaches of job satisfaction. These are the *'Two-Factor Theory'* of Frederick Herzberg and the *'Value Theory'* of E. A. Locke. These are discussed in turn.

Frederick Herzberg's Two Factor Theory of Job Satisfaction

Nearly fifty years ago, Frederick Herzberg [31] tried among 200 accountants and engineers from Pittsburg to test what makes people especially satisfied and /or dissatisfied with their jobs. He analysed the information and found surprising results. The satisfaction and dissatisfaction stemmed from two different sources as shown in Table 7.5.

Table 7.5 : Herzberg's Two-Factor Theory

Job Satisfaction i.e., Motivators	Job Dissatisfaction i.e., Hygiene Factors
• Achievement • Opportunities for personal growth • Recognition • Responsibility • Promotion Opportunities	• Poor supervision • Pay • Company policies • Working conditions • Job security

Although one may expect that the presence of certain factors leads to job satisfaction, and absence of these leads to job dissatisfaction. But, this was not the case. It was found that job satisfaction was associated with conditions surrounding the job e.g., working conditions, pay, security, quality of supervision, etc. rather than the work itself. Hence, these factors prevent negative reactions, Herzberg referred to them maintenance or hygiene factors. By contrast, job satisfaction was associated with factors associated with the work itself or to outcomes directly derived from it such as achievement, promotion, appreciation, recognition and chances for personal growth. Because such factors were associated with the high levels of job satisfaction, Herzberg called them 'motivators'. This is precisely the Herzberg's distinction between hygiene factors and motivators; this is referred to as the *'Two-Factor Theory of Job Satisfaction.'*

While explaining his theory, Herzberg suggested that, as is believed by some people, the opposite of 'satisfaction' is 'no satisfaction' and the opposite of 'dissatisfaction' is 'no dissatisfaction.' Explaining alternatively, Herzberg opined that motivators when present at high levels contribute to job satisfaction but when these are absent also do not lead to job dissatisfaction, these just cause less satisfaction. Similarly, the presence of hygiene factors leads to dissatisfaction; however, the absence of them does not lead to satisfaction.

As regards the validity of Herzberg's job satisfaction theory, studies have yielded mixed results. While some studies[32] have supported the findings of Herzberg, others[33] have found that both hygiene and motivational factors exert strong effects on both satisfaction and dissatisfaction. Given such equivocal evidence, Herzberg's theory is heavily criticized for its validity. Notwithstanding, Herzberg's theory is useful for describing and understanding the conditions that people found satisfying and dissatisfying on the job. The theory has especially stimulated considerable research on job enlargement and job enrichment.

E. A. Locke's Value Theory

A second significant theory of job satisfaction called the *'Value Theory'* is proposed by E. A. Locke[34]. Locke's concept of job satisfaction states that it occurs when the job outcomes an employee receives matches with those that are desired by him / her. Accordingly, the more employees receive outcomes they value, the more satisfied they will be; the less they receive outcomes they value, the less satisfied they will be. The basic element in Locke's theory of satisfaction is the discrepancy between the present aspects of the job and one those that an employee desires. Thus, the greater is the discrepancy between the two, the less the job satisfaction and vice versa. In reality, employees experience discrepancy between the aspects of job one has and those one wants. Locke's theory is useful in the sense that it focuses attention on those aspects of the jobs that need to be changed for employees to feel satisfaction.

Beside, there are quite a few other theories of job satisfaction. The important among them are briefly discussed below:

Adam's Equity Theory

One yet more theory of job satisfaction called *'The Equity Theory'* is proposed by J. S. Adam[35]. The basic premise of this theory is that employees compare the ratio of their outcome over input with the ratio of others' outcome over input. On comparison, if they find that their ratio is greater than or lesser than that of the others', they feel dissatisfied because the inequity has occurred. If their ratio is equal to those of others, they feel satisfied. Like earlier theories, this theory is also not free from criticism. The major criticism labeled against this theory is its impreciseness because there are other alternate ways as well to deal with feelings of inequity. Still, the theory is useful in acknowledging that employees need to feel that they are fairly dealt with in order to feel satisfied.

Landy's Opponent Process Theory

This theory is proposed by F. J. Landy[36]. The basic element of this theory is that the constant input does not result in constant output. In other words, initiating some change in the job may increase worker's satisfaction but not necessarily the equal increase over period. Landy applied this concept to his goal-setting theory. He asserted that in the initial phase of their career, employees may resist goal-setting. But along with goal-setting and goal attainment, their resistance to goal-setting starts declining Conversely, pleasure or call it job satisfaction tends to increase. The most interesting implication of this theory is that measures aimed at increasing employees' job satisfaction may not necessarily prove useful in the initial stage[37]

7.5 JOB DISSATISFACTION

Employees may have positive (satisfaction) or negative (dissatisfaction) attitude towards their jobs. By now, you have learnt various aspects of positive job-attitude *i.e.*, job satisfaction. Now, some mention about job dissatisfaction as well before we leave the issue of job-attitude.

Though job dissatisfaction can be expressed in a number of ways. On an overall basis, job dissatisfaction reflects the employees' negative or unfavourable feelings towards their jobs. Like job satisfaction, job dissatisfaction also produces certain responses to be exhibited by the employees. The following section examines the most important of them.

Quit: The culmination of the employees' job dissatisfaction to a certain level pressurises them to quit the job or organisation and search for a new one.

Voice: Dissatisfied employees start raising their voices to improve the conditions that cause dissatisfaction to them.

Loyalty: They wait for the conditions to improve.

Neglect: In case the conditions seem not likely to improve, they allow conditions to worsen in the form of increasing shirking of responsibilities, absenteeism, lateness, mistakes, errors, etc.

Figure 7.2 exhibits how employees respond to their job dissatisfaction.

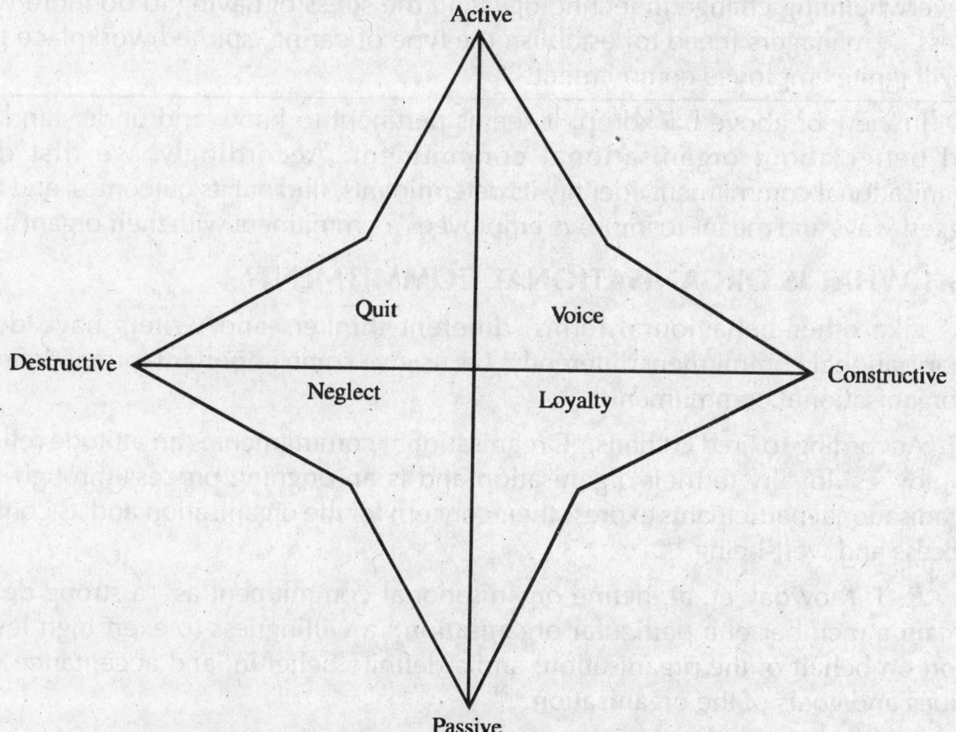

Figure 7.2: Responses to Job Dissatisfaction

While the two attitudes, *viz.*, voice and loyalty reflect employees' **constructive** and **active** attitudes towards their jobs, the other two quit and neglect represent the **destructive** and **passive** ones.

7.6 ORGANISATIONAL COMMITMENT

There is no denying the fact that job satisfaction has received the most attention of all the work-related attitudes. But, this does not necessarily mean that the employee who is satisfied with his/her job also feels positively toward his/her organisation. There is evidence to believe that even an employee satisfied with job hopes to get out the organisation as soon as possible. Just contrary may also hold true? An employee like a software engineer may like the organisation as wonderful place to work, but may be dissatisfied with his/her current job. Then, what does this suggests that in order to fully understand employees' work-related attitudes; we must go beyond the attitude toward job, i.e. job satisfaction but also consider employees' feelings toward their organisations. The employee attitude toward organisation is known as *'organisational commitment.'* Researchers have found a strong relationship between job satisfaction and organisational commitment in organisational performance and success. Of late, in the given business environment of downsizing, telecommuting, mergers and acquisitions, and globalisation, organisational commitment has emerged as a very important topic of curiosity and concern in the 21st century posed as follows:

> "Today's workplace is enveloped by the fear of downsizing, loss of job security, overwhelming change in technology, and the stress of having to do more with less ... managers [need to] establish the type of caring, spirited workplace that will ignite employee commitment.[38]"

In view of above backdrop, it seems pertinent to know and understand more and better about organisational commitment. Accordingly, we first define organisational commitment, identify its determinants, find out its outcomes, and finally suggest ways and means to improve employees' commitment with their organisations.

7.6.1 WHAT IS ORGANISATIONAL COMMITMENT?

Like other behavioural terms, different thinkers and writers have defined organisational commitment differently. Let us give some important formal definitions of organisational commitment.

According to Fred Luthans, "Organisational commitment is an attitude reflecting employees' loyalty to their organisation and is an ongoing process through which organisational participants express their concern for the organisation and its continued success and well-being.[39]"

R. T. Mowday et. al. define organisational commitment as: "a strong desire to remain a member of a particular organisation,; a willingness to exert high levels of effort on behalf of the organisation; and a definite belief in, and acceptance of, the values and goals of the organisation.[40]"

In the opinion of Robbins, Judge and Sanghi, "organisational commitment means the degree to which an employee identifies with a particular organisation and its goals and wishes to maintain membership in the organisation.[41]"

After having gone through above definitions, organisational commitment can be defined as the degree or extent to which employees identify themselves with and are involved with their employer organisations and are unwilling to leave them.

In simple words, organisational commitment is employees' loyalty toward the organisations they are working in.

7.6.2 DIMENSIONS OF ORGANISATIONAL COMMITMENT

With a view to make the understanding of organisational commitment easier and simpler, theorists have broken the concept down to its basic dimensions. The dimensions of organisational commitment include the two components, namely, foci of commitment and the bases of commitment. These are discussed in turn.

Foci of Commitment

The foci of commitment implies that employees can be committed to various entities in varying degrees towards their superiors, colleagues, subordinates, management, customers, or trade unions, i.e. any particular individual or group. Of course, the level of employee commitment may vary from entity to entity and from time to time in case of the same entity. In an attempt to categorize some of the foci, researchers drew a line of distinction between those whose commitment is concentrated at lower organisational levels, such as co-workers and supervisors, and those whose commitment is primarily concentrated on higher levels, such as top management and organisation as a whole[42]. They combined high and low levels of each of these and, thus, identified the four distinct commitment profiles as depicted in the following Figure 7.3:

ATTACHMENT TO SUPERVIOSR AND WORK GROUP	
Low	High
Uncommitted	Locally Committed

ATTACHMENT TO TOP MANAGEMENT AND ORGANISATION	
Low	High
Globally Committed	Committed

Figure 7.3: Four Distinct Commitment Profiles

A brief interpretation of the above four combinations follows:

Employees having low commitment to their supervisor and co-workers as well as low in commitment to top management and the organisation are labeled as uncommitted. On the contrary, employees high in commitment to both sets of foci are labeled as committed. There are two combinations in between. *One,* employees highly committed to their top management and organisation, but low commitment to their co-workers and their supervisor are labeled as globally committed. *Two,* those employees who have high commitment to their co-workers and supervisor but low to top management and organisation are termed as locally committed.

Bases of Commitment

To fully understand the concept of organisational commitment, we also need to know the motives employees have to be committed to their organisations. These are also called the bases of commitment. In an attempt to investigate into it, Meyer, Allen, and Gellatly[43] have identified three bases of organisational commitment. These are:

1. Affective Commitment: This refers to the employee's emotional attachment to, identification with, and involvement in the organisation. For example, a gardener may be affectively committed to the organisation because of its involvement with the plants from the day one of the organisation.

Continuance Commitment: This refers to the employee's motive to continue with the organisation because leaving may be costlier and he/she may not afford it. For example, an employee may not leave the organisation because of the loss of the seniority for promotion.

Normative Commitment: This kind of commitment refers to employee's moral obligation to remain with the organisation. For example, an employee (Professor) who is spearheading research activities in the National Institute of Financial Management, Faridabad may morally think to stay with the Institute because he feels his leaving would leave the institute in a lurch if he left.

To understand better the three bases of organisational commitments, these are now juxtaposed in the following Table 7.6:

Table 7.6: Bases of Organisational Commitments

Affective Commitment	Continuance Commitmen	Normative Commitment
1. I feel I strongly belong to my organisation.	1. At this point, I stay on my job because I have to more than because I want to.	1. I am reluctant to leave an organisation once I have been working there.
2. I feel I am emotionally connected to the organisation in which I work.	2. Leaving my job would entail a lot of personal sacrifice.	2. My employer would be very disappointed if I left.
3. I feel like I'm part of the family at my organisation.	3. I do not have any other choice but to stay on my present job.	3. I feel a strong obligation to stay on my job.
4. I'd be very pleased to spend the rest of my life working for this organisation.	4. Too much of my life would be disrupted if I left my present job.	4. I remain on my job because people would think poorly of me for leaving.

Source: *J. P. Meyer & N. J. Allen:* A Three-Component Conceptualization of Organisational Commitment, ***Human Resource Management Review,*** *1991, Vol. 1, pp. 61-89.*

7.6.3 FACTORS INFLUENCING ORGANISATIONAL COMMITMENT

As a matter of fact, research studies have listed many factors that may influence employees' commitment to their organisations. Here, we will now review some of the most important ones. These are as follows:

1. Job Characteristics: Employees tend to have greater commitment toward their organisations when they perform jobs with higher levels of responsibility. Similarly, organisational commitment tends to be high among the employees whose jobs are highly enriched. Since these job characteristics are present in abundance in self - employed jobs, it is, therefore, not surprising to find that the levels of organisational commitment are quite higher among self-employed people than those who are employed by organisations.

2. Job Rewards: Organisational commitment is also influenced by the type of rewards employees receive from the organisation. Research studies have shown that employees' commitment to their organisation is enhanced by the use of profit-sharing plan like 'Employee Stock Option Plan (ESOP).' The reason is that such job-related rewards give employees a feeling of ownership in the organisation and this enhances their commitment to organisation.

3. Availability of Alternative Job Opportunities: Expectedly, the greater possibilities for finding alternative jobs, less tends to be employees' commitment to the organisation and vice versa. This is particularly true of continuance commitment.

4. Personal Characteristics of Employee: There is evidence to believe that the personal characteristics of the employee also influence organisational commitment. It is found that the employees who have longer tenure with the organisation have greater organisational commitment than those with shorter stay with the organisation. The reason is not difficult to seek. It is an established fact that longer one serves an organisation, the more one is likely to have invested in it. As per the side-bets approach, one generally does not want to lose his/her investment in an organisation by leaving it. As regards gender differences in organisational commitment, it is generally noticed that women are less strongly committed to their job or organisation than men because of the type of jobs are traditionally performed by the women, on the one hand, and their family responsibilities, on the other. Yes, the scenario has been gradually changing when women are also assuming responsible and higher-level jobs along with their men counterparts.

7.6.4 MEASURING ORGANISATIONAL COMMITMENT

As our hitherto discussion has suggested, organisational commitment is desirable for improving organisational performance. Though it is difficult to exactly measure the level of organisational commitment of employees, but it is sure and certain that levels of organisational commitment is likely to vary from employee to employee and from time to time in case of the same employee. It is also certain that the higher the organisational commitment, better the organisational performance and vice versa. Then, the problem is how to measure and know employee's commitment to organisation. Behavioural scientists have evolved some methods to measure the organisational commitment of employees by knowing their feelings towards their organisation. For example, one way is to measure the employee's commitment to organisation is by allotting a specific rank to employee's feeling to organisation on the given point-scale. Then, find out the totals of different point-scales and average these all in order to arrive at overall level of organisational commitment.

As suggested by R. T. Mowday et. al.[44], following are fifteen statements that represent possible feelings that employees might have about their organisation where they work. Employees can express their feelings about each of the statement in terms of agreement and disagreement by checking a rank along the seven-point scale.

Sl. No.	Statements
1.	I am willing to put in a great deal of effort beyond what is normally expected in order to help this organisation be successful.
2.	I talk about this organisation to my friends as a great organisation to work for.
3.	I feel very little loyalty to this organisation.
4.	I would accept almost any type of job assignment in order to keep working for this organisation.
5.	I find that my values and the organisation's values are very similar.
6.	I am proud to tell others that I am a part of this organisation.
7.	I could just as well be working for a different organisation as long as the type of work was similar.
8.	This organisation really inspires the very best in me in the way of job performance.
9.	It would take very little change in my present circumstances to cause me to leave this organisation.
10.	I am extremely glad that I chose this organisation to work for over others I was considering at the time I joined.
11.	There's not too much to be gained by sticking with this organisation indefinitely.
12.	Often, I find it difficult to agree with this organisation's policies on important matters relating to its employees.
13.	I really care about the fate of this organisation.
14.	For me this is the best of all possible organisations for which to work.
15.	Deciding to work for this organisation was a definite mistake on my part.

The responses to each statement are measured on a 7-point scale with scale point anchors labeled: 1. Strongly Disagree, 2. Moderately Disagree, 3. Slightly Disagree, 4. Neither Disagree nor Agree, 5. Slightly Agree, 6. Moderately Agree, 7. Strongly Agree.

7.6.5 EFFECTS OF ORGANISATIONAL COMMITMENT

Like job satisfaction, organisational commitment greatly influences several key aspects of employee behaviour and, in turn, organisational performance. There is research evidence to believe that employees who feel deeply committed to their organisations behave differently, of course, positively than those who do not. Following are the major effects of organisational commitment on an organisation:

1. Evidences indicate that high levels of organisational commitment reduce absenteeism and turnover. The reason is not difficult to seek. More committed employees are less likely to look for green pastures. Evidences are also available to

believe that the levels of employees' commitment to organisation also deepen with the degree of warm and supportive organisational climate.

2. Organisational commitment also breeds 'organisational citizenship behaviour (OCB)". Employees deeply committed to their organisation perform roles beyond their formal job description. Such roles called 'extra-roles' improve organisational effectiveness.

3. Organisational commitment has also positive effects on individual employee concern. Generally, it is expected that those who are deeply committed to their organisation give less time to their non-work life. But, research findings report that those who were strongly attached and committed to their organisations tended to enjoy highly successful career and non-work life as well. The reason attributed to this is the job satisfaction such employees experience and relish helps them balance their career and home life[45].

On the whole, organisational commitment has positive effects on organisational performance. A committed workforce appears beneficial to both individual and organisation. Considering all above effects, steps designed to generate high levels of organisational commitment among employees seem worthwhile to which we turn our attention in the following paragraphs.

7.6.6 SUGGESTIONS TO ENHANCE ORGANISATIONAL COMMITMENT

Today's organisations are confronted with the dilemma of having workforce with self-motivation and high team spirit, on the one hand, and ever expanding business offering vast opportunities for employee attrition, on the other. Nonetheless, organisations need to have work force with high organisational commitment. Following are some guidelines as given by some organisational thinker to solve the current dilemma and enhance employees' organisational commitment[46]:

1. *Commit to People-First Values* : Put it in black and white, hire the right kind of managers, and also walk the talk.
2. *Clarify and Communicate Organisational Mission* : Clarify the organisational mission, ideology, and philosophy, shine it as charismatic, follow value-based hiring practices, and impart value-based training to the employees.
3. *Guarantee Organisational Justice* : Devise and follow a comprehensive grievance procedure, and provide for extensive two-way communications.
4. *Create a Sense of Community* : Lay foundation and build value-based homogeneity, share and subscribe values, foster barn raising, cross-utilization, and team-work spirit.
5. *Support Employee Development*: Enrich and empower, promote from within, provide developmental activities, provide employee security without guarantees, and actualize the employee potential.

SUMMARY

This summary is organized as per the 'learning objectives' given of page no. 86:

- Attitudes reflect employees' feelings towards their jobs. These are formed *through direct experience and social learning. Attitudes derived from direct experience are stronger because these are easily accessed and active in our cognitive process.*
- *Job satisfaction and job involvement are the two important types of job attitudes. The attitude is measured through the self-report or attitude survey.*
- *Attitudes endure and, hence, are difficult to change. Nonetheless, some of the ways of bringing about attitude changes are providing new information, use of fear, resolving discrepancies between behaviour and attitude, pursuation from friends or peers, and coopting.*
- *Values are the general beliefs that give us a sense of right or wrong and good or bad. A hierarchy of values in terms of their intensity is called 'value system'. Values are of two types—terminal and instrumental. The terminal values represent the goals to be achieved, while the instrumental values reflect the means to achieving it.*
- *While some values are genetically determined, most of the values are learned and acquired through experiences with family members, schoolmates, peers, colleagues and organisations. Values directly affect a person's attitude and, in turn, behaviour.*
- *Job satisfaction is a pleasurable or positive feeling toward the job. The work, pay, promotion, supervision, working conditions, and co-workers determine job satisfaction.* Single Global Rating and Summation Score are the two commonly used methods of measuring job satisfaction.
- *Job satisfaction improves the employees' productivity and reduces their absenteeism and turnover rates.*
- *Employees' negative or unfavourable attitudes towards their jobs are called job dissatisfaction. It is expressed through employees' behaviour directed towards leaving the job, raising voice and neglecting and shirking from responsibilities.*

REVIEW QUESTIONS

1. In your own words, what is an attitude? Discuss how attitudes are formed.
2. What are the various sources of attitude formation? Which source is stronger, in your own case?
3. Explain the various types of attitudes.
4. Assume that job satisfaction, job involvement, and organisational commitment are independent of one another-any one may be present without the others. Describe a situation in which an employee might be committed but not satisfied or involved. Tell what you would do with such an employee.
5. What are the various methods of attitude measurement? How does attitude measurement help the management?
6. Do you think it is possible to change attitudes? If yes, how can attitudes be changed?

7. Define values. Distinguish between terminal values and instrumental values. Are these values generally stable, or do they change over time?
8. What is the relationship between values and behaviour?
9. What is meant by the term 'job satisfaction'? What are some of the major determinants or factors that influence job satisfaction?
10. How is job satisfaction measured?
11. "A happy employee is a productive employee." Discuss this statement.
12. Assume that in a survey of the twenty employees in your division, 90 percent of them were basically satisfied with their jobs. What are the implications for you as a manager?
13. Prepare a series of questions, and interview your three teachers (one at each level) to determine their areas of satisfaction and dissatisfaction. Discuss the results.
14. How does job satisfaction affect the employees' productivity, absenteeism, and turnover rates?
15. What do you mean by job dissatisfaction? Contrast quit, voice, loyalty, and neglect as employee responses to job dissatisfaction.
16. Write note on:
Job Analysis and Job Description (IGNOU, MBA, June, 1999)

REFERENCES

1. D. Krech and R.S. Crutchfield: **Theory and Problem of Social Psychology**, McGraw-Hill, New York, 1948.
2. N.L. Munn, et al: **Introduction to Psychology**, Oxford IBH Publishing Co., New Delhi, 3rd Edition, p. 606.
3. R.H. Fazio and M.P. Zanna: On the Predictive Validity of Attitudes: The Roles of Direct Experience and Confidence, **Journal of Personality**, Vol. No. 46, 1978, pp. 228-243.
4. B. K. Mike George: Five Attitudes, Purity (A monthly magazine of Brahamakumari Ishawari Prajapati Vishwavidyalaya), June 2008, p.5.
5. G.F. Summers (Ed.): **Attitude Measurement**, Rand, Chicago, 1970.
6. L.L. Thurstone: **The Measurement of Values,** University of Chicago Press, Chicago, 1959.
7. Rensis Likert: A Technique for Measurement Attitudes, **Archives of Psychology**, No. 140, 1952.
8. C.E. Osgood, G.J. Suci and P.H. Tannenbaum: **The Measurement of Meaning**, The University of Illinois, Champaign, 1957.
9. I. Festinger: **A Theory of Cognitive Dissonance**, Stanford University Press, Stanford, C.A., 1957.
10. C.I. Hovland, I.L. Janis, and H.H. Kalley: **Communication and Persuasion**, Yale University Press, New Haven, 1953.
11. F. Heider: **The Psychology of Interpersonal Relations**, Wiley, New York, 1958.
12. W. J. McGuire: The Nature of Attitude and Attitude Change, In : G.Lindzey and E. Aronson (Ed.): **The Handbook of Social Psychology**, Volume Three, Addison - Wesley, New York, 1969, pp. 136-314.
13. I. L. Janis: Personality Correlates of Susceptibility to Persuasion, **Journal of Abnormal and Social Psychology**, Vol., 51, 1954, pp. 663-667.
14. P. Gupta and Pradip Khandelwal: Quality of Work Life in Relation to Role Efficacy, **Psychological Studies**, Volume 33, No. 1, 1988, pp. 34-38.

15. Gainful Play, **Human Capital**, Volume 11, No. 12, may 2008, p. 18.
16. A. N. Nazir: Perceived Importance of Job Factors and Overall Job Satisfaction of Bank Employees, **Indian Journal of Industrial Relations**, Volume 33, No. 4, 1998, pp. 477-496.
17. V. Malni: Job Commitment of Women Executives, **Management and Labour Studies**, Volume 26, No. 4, 2001, pp. 247-257.
18. V. Malni: *Ibid*, 2001, pp. 247-257.
19. Uma Jain: Value Erosion in Organisations and Society: Diagnosis and Change Through Value Clarification Intervention, In: Udai Pareek, Aahad M. Osma - Gani, S. Ramanarayan, and T.V. Rao (Eds.) : **Human Resource Development in Asia : Trends and Challages**, Oxford & IBH, New Delhi, 2002, pp. 297-308.
20. Howard Kirschenbaum: **Advanced Value Clarification**, Pfeffer & Co., San Diego, 1977.
21. Uma Jain: *op.cit.*, 2002, pp. 297-308.
22. S. Ramachandran: A Study of Congruence between Individual Values and Perceived Organisational Values and Its Impact on Commitment to the Organisation, **Xiever Labour Research Institute** (XLRI), Jamshedpur (Unpublished Doctorial Thesis), 2003.
23. Uma Jain: *op.cit.*, 2002, pp. 297-308.
24. Kirschenbaum: *op.cit.*, 2002.
25. Kirschenbaum: *ibid.*, 2002.
26. D.C. Feldman and H.J. Arnold: **Managing Industrial and Group Behaviour in Organisations,** McGraw-Hill, New York, 1983, p. 192.
27. E.A. Locke: The Nature and Cause of Job Satisfaction, In M.Dunnette (Ed.), **Handbook of Industrial and Organisational Psychology,** Rand McNally, Chicago, 1976, p. 1300.
28. Keith Davis and J. W. Newstrom: **Organisational Behaviour: Human Behaviour at Work**, Tata McGraw-Hill Publishing Company Limited, New Delhi, Ninth Edition, 1996, p. 195.
29. P.C. Smith, L.M. Kendall, and C.L. Hulin: **The Measurement of Satisfaction in Work and Retirement**, Rand McNally, Chicago, 1969.
30. P.M. Podsakoff and L.J. Williams: The Relationship between Job Performance and Job Satisfaction, In: E.A. Locke (Ed.), **Generalising from Laboratory to Field Settings,** Lexington Books, Lexington, Mass, 1986.
31. Frederick Herzberg: **Work and the Nature of Man**, World, Cleveland, 1966.
32. R. Saturia: Personal Needs and Two Factor Theory of Work Motivation, **Indian Journal of Industrial Relations**, Volume 6, 1980, pp. 219-232.
33. R. G. Sarveswara and G. Rao: A Study of Factors Contributing to Satisfaction and Importance of Industrial Personnel: A Test of the Two Factor Theory, **Indian Journal of Industrial Relations**, Volume 6, No. 2, 1973, pp. 233-262.
34. E. A. Licke: Job Satisfaction, In: M. Gruenberg and Y. Wall (Eds.): **Social Psychology and Organisational Behaviour**, Wiley London, 1984.
35. J. S. Adam: Towards an Understanding of Inequity, **Journal of Abnormal and Social Psychology**, Vol. 67, 1963, pp. 422-436.
36. F. J. Landy: An Opponent Process Theory of Job Satisfaction, **The Journal of Applied Psychology,** Volume 63, 1978, pp. 533-547.
37. N. Chimel; **Work and Organisational Psychology: A European Perspective**, Blackwell, Oxford, 2000,
38. ADL Associates: **Commitment: If You Build It ... Results Will Come**, ADL Associates, Lewisville, TX, 1998, p. 6.
39. Fred Luthans: **Organisational Behaviour**, Tata McGraw-Hill Publishing Company Ltd., New Delhi, 2002, pp. 235-236.

40. R. T. Mowday, L. W. Porter and R. M. Steers: **Employee- Organisation Linkages**, Academic Press, New York, 1982.

41. Stephen P. Robbins, Timothy A. Judge and Seema Sanghi: **Organisational Behaviour**, Pearson Printice Hall, Delhi, 2008, p. 91.

42. T. E. Becker and R. S. Billings: Profiles of Commitment: An Empirical Test, **Journal of Organisational Behaviour**, 14, 1993, pp. 177-190.

43. J. P. Meyer, N. J. Allen, and C. A. Smith: Commitment to Organizations and Occupations: Extension and Test of a Three-Component Conceptualization, **Journal of Applied Psychology**, 78 (4), 1993, pp. 538-551.

44. R. T. Mowday, R. M. Steers, and L. W. Porter: The Measure of Organisational Commitment, **Journal of Vocational Behaviour**, 14, 1979, p. 288.

45. B. S. Romzek: Personal Consequences of Employee Commitment, **Academy of Management Journal**, 1989, 39, pp. 641-661.

46. Gary Dessler: How to Earn Your Employees' Commitment, **Academy of Management Executive**, 13 (2), 1999, p. 65.

An exercise for you on Job Satisfaction

Ask yourself: How satisfied am I with this aspect of my job ?

VS means I am very satisfied with this aspect of my job.

S means I am satisfied with this aspect of my job.

N means I can't decide whether I am satisfied or not with this aspect of my job.

DS means I am dissatisfied with this aspect of my job.

VDS means I am very dissatisfied with this aspect of my job.

On my present this is how I feel about:	VDS	DS	N	S	VS
1. Being able to keep busy all the time					
2. The chance to work alone on the job.					
3. The chance to do difrerent things from time to time.					
4. The chance to be "somebody" in the community.					
5. The way my boss handles his employees.					
6. The competence of my supervisor in making decisions.					
7. Being able to do things that do not go against my conscience.					
8. The way my job provides for steady employment.					
9. The chance to do things for other people.					
10. The chance to tell people what to do.					
11. The chance to do something that makes use of my abilities.					
12. The way company policies are put into practice.					
13. My pay and the amount of work I do.					
14. The chances for advancement on this job.					
15. The freedom to use my own judgement.					
16. The chance to try my own methods of doing the job.					
17. The working conditions.					
18. The way my co-workers get along with each other.					
19. The praise I get for doing a good job.					
20. The feeling of accomplishment I get from the job.					

Case 7.1: Job Description vis-a-vis Job Satisfaction*

The Bharat Transport Service (BTS) has been experiencing severe difficulties with its bus drivers. Consumer complaints have tripled during the past six months. These complaints have focused on drivers failing to make scheduled stops, buses being filthy, and drivers not enforcing the rules of conduct posted on the inside of the bus.

Fearing loss of revenue and citizen support, Arvind, the BTS Managing Director, has called together members of both supervisory ranks and the drivers. He wants to settle the ongoing problem and make amends so that full, courteous service can be restored immediately. During the meeting, Arbind pinpointed the problem. The supervisors, as a group, had placed new demands on the drivers, demands that did not sit well with them. To retaliate, the drivers began their own show of strength. They invoked the better of their job descriptions. Among these were statements such as the following: "The driver has the right to refuse to board any passenger he believes may cause disorder in the bus", "Drivers will report to the authorities any inividual who disrupts the operation of the bus".

In better days, the drivers had handled almost everything themselves. But not now. As one driver stated, "It is not my Job"!

QUESTIONS

1. How could an accurate, updated, and well-defined job analysis have helped to prevent such a problem?
2. Realising that every aspect of the job cannot be identified because exceptions do exist, how can a job description be written so that these exceptions cannot be referred to as "not my job"?

Case 7.2 Paralysis Through Analysis**

One of the zonal office of a large organisation had a staff strength of more than a lakh of employees. A senior civil servant Mr. X with an excellent experience in various regulations, considered to be a veteran in the knowledge of rules and their interpretations, was posted to that zone office as a Deputy Chief of Personnel. Known for his acumen and integrity, he was workholic. In fact, in his entire service of 25 years, he had hardly gone on any vacation.

Mr. X had applied for two months leave and had gone on a vacation outing. He had cut short his sightseeing trip owing to some other urgent work at his headquarters and had returned back but did not join his duty since he felt the need to continue on leave for some more time due to various reasons.

Mr. Y was the Chief of Personnel in that office. He had come to the Personnel Division from some other discipline on option to work in the department which enabled him to get his due promotion. Though good at interpretation of rules theoretically, he was not very good at solving problems when any labour crisis arose.

---

* Berhampur University, MBA, 1996.

** N. Ramaswami : Paralysis through Analysis, **Indian Management,** October 1992, pp. 74-75.

One day a serious problem cropped up in one of the wings of that zone and this needed immediate attention. The chief had to interpret and analyse the problem immediately but he could not do it himself since the assistance available to him immediately was not of sufficient help. As he was not sure of himself and the matter was very important he wanted to consult someone of ingenuity. He immediately remembered that Mr. X was available in town and was quite relieved when, on phoning up, found Mr. X would be readily available and willing for consultations. However, Mr. X dictated a note himself and this was signed by Mr. Y and sent to the General Manager who was happy over the issue having been sorted out amicably and approved the note.

Mr. X, however, continued on leave till it was over and resumed duty on the due date.

After a couple of days of Mr. X's joining, Mr. Y sent for him in his chamber.

Mr. Y, started slowly talking of morals. Mr. X, being an expert in organisational behaviour, felt something fishy in the whole episode and asked the boss to be straightforward and tell him what was going on.

Mr. Y stated that Mr. X was being called for counselling. Mr. X was still perplexed and was feeling uneasy and wondered as to what had actually happened. Mr. Y explained that "it is not enough if one is honest but also should appear to be honest". Mr. X could not follow the whole episode at all. On this, Mr. Y showed a copy of the anonymous complaint written by some one to the vigilance department who in turn have asked the Chief to counsel his deputy. The complaint contained *inter alia* 2 points (1) the officer misused official vehicle for private purpose to visit office while on leave and (2) the officer had some specific ill motive to attend office when on leave since, in India, people are always happy to be away from office even while on duty. The vigilance had resorted to this action of writing to Chief and asking him to counsel Mr. X since they found, on investigation that, in fact Mr. X had attended office on that particular day, in official vehicle, about which there was an entry in the log book. They had also stated that on that day the office had received, during his presence in office, some of his dues, by calling the cashier. They had indicated that no serious action was being contemplated against the officer, since his integrity was always found to be above board.

The deputy, Mr. X, pointed out to his Chief that he had come to office on the beck and call of Mr. Y only, he spent his precious vacation period to sort out a problem of organisation, since he had the organisational goal in mind-not just to pleasure or oblige the boss but to ensure the good of the organisation. Mr. X also pointed out that in as much as there is ample proof to show that he was called and had done office official work, that period should be treated as duty duly cancelling his leave, so that his prestige before others are not lowered. He pointed out that Mr. Y should have explained the entire position to the vigilance and stated that there is nothing in the whole episode to feel sensitive about and after all counselling is nothing but a talk and not a punishment. Mr. Y also pointed out that the benefit as asked for by Mr. X cannot be given since another person was given the benefit of promotion in his place and allowing Mr. X the benefit of assumption to duty for a day would result in denial of all the benefits to a number of persons, as per rules and this will have a chain reaction. Mr. Y pointed out that he had agreed with the vigilance for counselling keeping only the organisational goal in view. However, Mr. Y said that he felt sorry for the whole affair and wanted it to be left at that. Mr. X pointed out that since the whole affair has gone on record, he was very unhappy, particularly because the whole episode has happened on account of his trying to keep the organisational goal in view, wanted to keep the boss pleased and also his colleagues by continuing on leave (particularly because the officer in his place was retiring shortly). Mr. X became a dejected person and his subordinates and colleagues with whom he had an excellent rapport were all demoralised. The output of the organisation also slowed down.

QUESTIONS

1. Is this an organisational systems failure? Analyse the personality of Mr. X and the attitude of Mr. Y.
2. How would you, if you were the boss, react to the views of the Vigilance Branch and what action would you take on the opinion expressed by the Vigilance Branch.
3. What do you feel about the action of the vigilance branch of the organisation with regard to their opinion?

Case 7.3: Car Incident*

Our company has eight levels of officers. Levels 1 and 2 are the supervisory level officers. Levels 3 and 4 are managerial levels called managers and assistant managers. Levels 5 and 6 are executives and senior executives. Levels 7 and 8 are deputy general managers and general managers. All the directors and general managers looking after centralised functions (personnel, finance, marketing, technical services etc.) are housed in the central building (head office). The department of technical services is a service department looking after all technical matters. The nature of our job requires that we frequently visit the various factory sites. Each of the factories has a general manager as the overall in-charge. These are located at different places within about 70 to 80 miles radius from the central office.

I am an executive of technical services (level 5). I was recently transferred from one of the factories to the head office. There are only a few cars in the head office. Whenever officers want to visit factory sites they have to ask for a car a day in advance. Officers in levels 4 and 5 below are expected to travel by bus or train. Level 5 officers can take a car when available provided at least two of them are travelling to the factory. Any officer of level 6 and above can take a car whenever he wants to go to the factory sites.

Soon after I had joined, I discovered that there were occasions when level 5 officers also made use of the car facility when they went to the factories alone. The cars are allotted by the administrative officer (AO) on the recommendation of the concerned General Manager (GM). Once I had to carry a lot of reports to distribute in one of the factories. These reports concerned some new scheme we were trying to introduce. I requested my GM to ask for a car to take me and the material to the

* Adapted from T.V. Rao: Indian Institute of Management, Ahmedabad, 1980

factory and bring me back that evening. An hour later the PA to GM rang me up to say the following :

"Sir, the AO informed the GM that no car could be spared tomorrow to take you to the factory. The GM has asked me to tell you that a car can be sent to pick you up from your house, and drop you and the material in the railway station. Arrangements could also be made by talking to the GM of the factory through a trunk call to have you picked up from the railway station there to take you to the factory". (It may be noted that the distance between the headquarters and my house is about 5 km and from my house to the railway station in the city is another 5 km. There is no railway station in the place where the factory is located. The nearest railway station is about 10 km from the factory. The first class railway fare between the two stations is Rs. 35. The distance by road between my house and the factory where I am to go is about 80 km).

I was upset with this response. I told the GM's PA, "Don't worry if a car cannot be spared. I will make my own arrangements. I don't need a car to drop me at the station because the car has to make so many trips here and also at the other station. The car has to make empty trips to come to my house and then from the station back, etc. I will make my own arrangements to go to the factory by bus and please tell the GM not to bother." (There is a bus service between the city where I live and the place where the factory is located. The bus stop is about 1/2 km from the factory).

I was upset because I generally don't ask for a car. I always travel by bus. This time I asked because I needed it. They can send a car to drop me at the station and pick me up from there but can't spare it. I thought there was a status question. Why this discrimination.?

A little while later the PA to GM again rang me up to say, "Sir, the GM says that if you are planning to go by bus he will arrange to send a car to pick you up from your house and drop you at the bus stand." To this, I said, "Don't worry, I don't want the company to incur any extra expenditure and I will manage on my own. Please tell the GM not to worry." I put the phone down and decided to go by bus.

There was another occasion when I had to go to the same factory. Again I had to carry some material with me. The day before I was scheduled to travel I asked for a car to be allotted. I was told that no car was available. I suggested that a private taxi be hired as the material I was carrying was rather heavy. Requisitions for company cars can go directly to AO but for private taxies they have to go through the GM concerned. I put up a note to the GM requesting him to approve of my hiring a private taxi, but he did not agree to it. He said there would be all kinds of complications for hiring a taxi, it would be misquoted, etc. He advised me to go by bus or train. Hence I had to go by bus. Generally when I go to the factory I make it a point to see the factory GM first. But that day he was busy in the factory and I could meet him only at 1.00 p.m during lunch. He asked me, "how did you come?", I answered, "by bus, sir".

He said, "Do you have a rule in your department that you and your boss should not travel together? I was surprised. I didn't know what to say. I asked him, "Is he here"? He said, "yes, he came in the morning." Since I didn't want to create a bad impression about my boss, I spoke a lie: "Sir, I was busy yesterday. So I couldn't meet him. I couldn't communicate to him my plans of coming here." He said, "So, you have a communication problem also?" Then he said, "You are a big officer, I am not going to let you travel by bus. After you are through this evening, you can take a car from my factory. It will drop you and come back."

I was embarrassed. Since I worked earlier in this factory I know many people who travel from here to the city where I now live. So whenever I go to the factory I generally travel back with them. Most of these are vendors. So I told the factory GM, "Sir, I have already made arrangements to go with some vendors."He said, "I know you have great friends in vendors, but take a car from here." I resisted although he was insisting.

After some time, around 2.30 p.m., I saw my boss (GM) walking out of the factory. I wished him and he wished me in return. Apparently he was going back to the headquarters. I left in vendor's car that evening.

The next morning I met the GM at the Head Office. He said, "Mr...yesterday it struck me just before I started at about 9.00 a.m. from here that you were also going to that factory. But by the time I realised it was too late. I thought you may have already left. So I didn't make any attempt to pick you up."

QUESTION

1. Go through the case and Analyse it.

8

LEARNING

"You cannot teach a man anything. You can only help him discover it within himself."
– Galileo

"Being ignorant is not as much a shame as being unwilling to learn."
– Benjamin Franklin

Learning Objectives

After studying this chapter, you should be able to:

- **Define** learning, reinforcement, and punishment.
- **Summarize** how learning theories provide insights into changing behaviour.
- **Distinguish** between classical and operant conditioning.
- **Appreciate** the role of reinforcement in learning.
- **Classify** the role of punishment in learning.
- **Establish** relationship between learning and behaviour.

A study on organisational behaviour will remain incomplete without studying learning. It is for this obvious reason that almost all complex behaviour is learned. If a manager wants to explain and predict human behaviour, he/she needs to understand how learning occurs or how people learn. Therefore, the purpose of this chapter is to discuss the nature, theory, and principles of learning. Towards the end, attempt has also been made to outline the managerial implications of learning.

8.1 MEANING AND DEFINITION

What is learning? In simple words, learning is a change in behaviour as a result of experience. Different psychologists and behavioural scientists have defined learning differently. Given below are a few important definitions of learning.

According to Stephen P. Robbins[1], "Learning is any relatively permanent change in behaviour that occurs as a result of experience."

Munn et. al[2] have defined learning as "The process of having one's behaviour modified, more or less permanently, by what he does and the consequences of his action, or by what he observes".

In the opinion of Steers and Porter[3], "Learning can be defined as relatively permanent change in behaviour potentiality that results from reinforced practice or experience."

Now, on an overall basis, learning can be defined as a change in behaviour acquired through experience.

The above definitions of learning reveal several **components** that deserve clarification.

First, Learning involves **change**, be it good or bad.

Second, the change in behaviour must be **relatively permanent**. For that matter, a temporary change in behaviour as a result of fatigue or temporary adaptations are not considered learning.

Third, only change in behaviour **acquired through experience** is considered learning. Therefore, a change in individual's thought process or attitudes, if accompanied by no change in behaviour, would not be learning. For example, the ability to work that is based on maturation, disease, or physical damages would not be considered learning.

Fourth, some form of **experience is necessary for learning**. Experience may be acquired directly through practice or observation or indirectly, as through reading.

Finally, learning is not confined to our schooling only. As a matter of fact, **learning is a life-long process**.

8.2 DETERMINANTS OF LEARNING

Now, let us understand what determines change in behaviour i.e., learning. The important factors that determine learning are motive, stimuli, response, reinforcement, and retention. A brief description of these follows:

Motive

Motives also called drives prompt people to action. They are the primary energisers of behaviour. They are the ways of behaviour and mainsprings of action. They are largely subjective and represent the mental feelings of human beings. They are cognitive variables. They arise continuously and determine the general direction of an individual's behaviour. Without motive, learning cannot occur. Motive and motivation are discussed in detail in the following Chapter 9.

Stimuli

Stimuli are objects that exist in the environment in which a person lives. Stimuli increase the probability of eliciting a specific response from a person. Viewed from this angle, stimuli may be of two types: generalisation and discrimination.

Generalisation: The principle of generalisation has important implications for human learning. Generalisation takes place when the similar new stimuli repeat in the environment. When two stimuli are exactly alike, they will have probability to elicit a specific response. It makes possible for a manager to predict human behaviour when stimuli are exactly alike.

However, the negative implication of generalisation is that the manager may make false inferences and conclusions based on the principle of generalisation. For example, halo effect in perception, as discussed earlier in last Chapter 6 occurs mainly because of generalisation.

Discrimination: What is not generalisation is discrimination. In case of discrimination, responses vary to different stimuli. For example, an MBA student may learn to respond to video teaching but not to the oral lecturing by his Professor.

Discrimination has wide applications in organisational behaviour in view of individual differences in various aspects. For example, a supervisor may respond to a high producing worker in a positive manner, but in a different manner to one producing very less.

Responses

The stimulus results in responses–be these in the physical form or in terms of attitudes or perception or in other phenomena. However, the responses need to be operationally defined and preferably physically observable.

Reinforcement

Reinforcement is a fundamental conditioning of learning. Reinforcement can be defined as anything that both increases the strength of response and tends to induce repetitions of the behaviour that preceded the reinforcement[4]. No measurable modification of behaviour can take place without reinforcement. Reinforcement is discussed in detail later in this chapter.

Retention

Retention means remembrance of learned behaviour over time. Converse is forgetting. Learning which is forgotten over time is called 'extinction'. When the response strength returns after extinction without any intervening reinforcement, it is called 'spontaneous recovery'. Both extinction and spontaneous recovery are discussed later.

8.3 LEARNING THEORIES

The most basic purpose of learning theory like any other is to better explain how learning occurs. Attempts have been made by the psychologists and behavioural scientists to develop theories of learning. To date, the most widely recognized theories of learning are four: classical conditioning, operant conditioning, cognitive and social learning theories.

Classical Conditioning

Classical conditioning is modifying behaviour so that a conditioned stimulus is paired with an unconditioned stimulus and elicits an unconditioned behaviour. Ivan Pavlov[5], a Russian psychologist developed classical conditioning theory based on his experiments to teach dog to salivate in response to the ringing of a bell. When Pavlov presented meat (unconditioned stimulus) to the dog, he noticed a great deal of salivation (unconditioned response). But, when merely bell was rung, no salivation was noticed in the dog. Then, what next Pavlov did was to link the meat and the ringing of the bell. He did this several times. Afterwards, he merely rang the bell without presenting the meat. Now, the dog began to salivate as soon as the bell rang. After a while, the dog would salivate merely at the sound of the bell, even if no meat was presented. In effect, the dog had learned to respond *i.e.,* to salivate to the bell.

The above cited example is logical, yet classical conditioning has real **limitations** in its applicability to human behaviour in organisations–for at least three reasons. **First**, human beings are more complex than dogs but less amenable to simple cause-and-effect conditioning. **Second**, the behavioural environment in organisations is also complex. **Third**, the human decision making process being complex in nature makes it possible to override simple conditioning. Skinner feels that the complex human behaviour is better learned through operant learning.

Operant Learning

What Pavlov did for classical conditioning, the Harvard Psychologist B.F. Skinner[6] did for operant conditioning. Skinner's operant conditioning is based on the notion that behaviour is a function of its consequences, which may be either positive or negative. He argued that creating pleasant consequences to follow specific forms of behaviour would increase the frequency of that behaviour. The consequences of behaviour are used to influence, or shape, behaviour through three strategies: reinforcement, punishment, and extinction. Thus, operant conditioning is the process of modifying behaviour through the use of positive or negative consequences following specific behaviours.

Difference between Classical Conditioning and Operant Conditioning

After going through classical and operant conditioning theories, a few lines of distinction between the two can easily be drawn as follows:

Classical Conditioning	Operant Conditioning
1. A change in stimulus elicits a particular response.	Stimulus serves as a cue for a person to emit the response.
2. The strength and frequency of classically conditioned behaviours are determined mainly by the frequency of eliciting stimulus.	The strength and frequency of operantly conditioned behaviours are determined mainly by the consequences.
3. The stimulus serving as reward is present everytime.	The reward is presented only if the organism gives the correct response.
4. Responses are fixed to stimulus.	Responses are variable both in types and degrees.

Table 8.1 better classifies the difference between classical conditioning and operant conditioning theories of learning.

Table 8.1: Difference between Classical and Operant Conditioning

	Classical Conditioning	
	(S) →	(R)
	Stimulus	**Response**
The individual:	is stuck by a pin	flinches
		is shocked by an electric

	current	jumps/screams
Operant Conditioning		
	(R)	(S)
	Response	**Stimulus**
	works	is paid
The individual:	enters a library works hard	finds a book receives praise and promotion

Adapted from: Fred Luthans: **Organisational Behaviour**, McGraw-Hill, Inc., New Delhi, Seventh Edition, 1995, p. 200.

Cognitive Theory

There are some psychologists who believe that neither of the two learning theories discussed so far can explain all the human learning that takes place. They view that most problem solving situations are hard to explain in the two manners. It is cognitive theory that explains such situations.

Let us first understand what cognition means. Cognition refers to an individual's thoughts, knowledge, interpretations, understandings or views about oneself, and his/her environment. Based on it, cognitive theory argues that the person tries to form his/her cognitive structure in memory, which preserves and organises all information relating to the events that may occur in learning situation. Let this be examplified by an example experimented by Kohler.

> Kohler presented two sticks to a monkey in the cage. Both sticks were too short to reach a banana lying outside cage. This produced an experience, or say, cognition, insight monkey. What monkey did without any prior exposure, joined both sticks together and pulled the banana inside the cage. Clearly, learning took place inside the mind of monkey. Thus, the learning process involved in this case is putting or organising bits of information in a new manner perceived inside the mind. This type of learning is very important in organisational behaviour for changing attitudes by the individuals. That is why, many researchers are currently interested in knowing the relationship between cognition and organisational behaviour.

Social Learning Theory

Individuals also learn by observing their models whom they admire. Much of what we have learned so far came from watching our models like parents, teachers, peers, superiors, motion pictures and television. Thus, learning through both observation and direct experience has been called **social-learning theory**[7].

In social learning, a person starts displaying his/her behaviour like that of someone else, *i.e.* model. For example, a person who has been promoted to a new job/position may imitate some of the behaviour of his/her predecessor. Like other learnings, social learning too can have negative consequences. For example, the subordinates of an organisation/department can learn to come late or display temper tantrums if their senior behaves in this manner.

Usually, the influence that a model will have on an individual is determined by the following four processes:

1. **Attention Process**: People can learn from their models provided they recognize and pay attention to the critical features. In practice, the models that are attractive, repeatedly available, or important to us tend to influence us the most.

2. **Retention Process:** A model's influence depends on how well the individual can remember or retain in memory the behaviour/action displayed by him/her when the model is no longer readily available.

3. **Motor Reproduction Process:** Now, the individual needs to convert the model's action into his/her action. This process evinces how well an individual can perform the modeled action.

4. **Reinforcement Process:** Individuals become motivated to display the modeled action if incentives and rewards are provided to them.

8.4 LEARNING PRINCIPLES

The most important principles of learning are two-reinforcement and punishment. A detailed description of these follows in turn.

8.4.1 REINFORCEMENT

Reinforcement may be defined as anything that both increases the strength of response and tends to induce repetitions of the behaviour that preceded the reinforcement. In other words, reinforcement is the attempt to develop or strengthen desirable behaviour by either bestowing positive consequences or withholding negative consequences. **Positive reinforcement** results from the application of a positive consequence following a desirable behaviour. Bonuses paid at the end of successful business years are an example of positive reinforcement. **Negative reinforcement** results from withholding a threatened negative consequence when a desirable behaviour occurs. For example, if the boss imposes a penalty on an employee for coming late is an example of negative reinforcement.

Besides, a behaviour can be modified and strengthened by keeping the negative consequence at bay. Take this example. An employee may be trying to avoid the work place simply because he/she does not feel ease and comfort with the colleagues he/she works in the office. In such case, merely a change in his/her work place like change in seating place may help him/her regain the enthusiasm. Similarly, taking away a positive consequence can serve as a source of negative reinforcement. A reduction in pay, *i.e.,* a source of reward, would serve as a negative reinforcer. Finally, an interesting effect is noticed when 'good' behaviour tends to continue to avoid negative consequence, or say, punishment. That is why employees come on time to avoid being reprimanded *i.e.* punishment.

Schedules of Reinforcement: Any analysis of reinforcement shows that it is not provided in a consistent manner. Following are some main types of reinforcement schedules:

(i) Continuous Reinforcement: In continuous reinforcement schedule, a desired behaviour is reinforced each and every time. For example, let us take the example of someone who always arrives at work late. Every time he is not tardy. His manager might compliment him on his desirable behaviour.

(ii) Intermittent Reinforcement: In case of intermittent reinforcement schedule, a desired behaviour is reinforced often enough to make the behaviour worth repeating but not every time it is demonstrated. In other words, in an intermittent schedule, each response is not reinforced. In extreme cases of intermittant scheduling, there is a little relationship between the occurance of a response and a reinforcement. Gambling is an example often cited as an intermittant scheduling. There is no relationship between the occurance of **Response** and **Reinforcement**. This kind of schedule leads to responses that hardly extinguish.

Intermittant or interval or ratio schedules can be of fixed or variable type.

Fixed-Ratio (FR): In a fixed-ratio schedule, rewards are initiated after a fixed or constant number of responses. A typical example of fixed ratio schedule is garment export industry. Each time a certain or fixed number of complete dresses are handed over, then only the payment (reward) is made.

Variable-Ratio(VR): When the reward varies relative to the behaviour of the person, it is called reinforcement on a variable-ratio schedule. Examples of such reinforcement schedule are salesmen who are rewarded with commission.

Fixed-Interval: In fixed-interval, rewards are spaced at uniform time intervals. The critical variable is time, and it is held fixed or constant. When your Professor receives his fixed salary after every month, he is rewarded on a fixed-interval schedule.

Variable-Interval: When rewards are distributed in time so that reinforcements are unpredictable, the schedule is of the variable-interval type. A series of randomly timed unannounced visits to a company office by the corporate audit staff is an example of a variable-interval schedule.

Now, all reinforcement schedules with their responses are juxtaposed in Table 8.2:

Table 8.2: Schedules of reinforcement and their effects

Schedule	Description	Effects Responding
Continuous	Reinforce follows	1. Steady high rate of performance as long as reinforcement continues to follow every response. 2. High frequency of reinforcement may lead to early situation. 3. Behaviour weakness rapidly (undergoes extinction) when reinforces are withheld. 4. Appropriate for newly emitted, unstable, or low-frequency responses.
Intermittent	Reinforcer does not follow every response before reinforcement occurs.	1. Capable of producing high frequencies of responding 2. Low frequency of reinforcement precludes early station. 3. Appropriate for stable or high frequency responses.

Fixed ratio (FR)	A fixed number of responses must be emitted	1. A fixed ratio of 1:1 (reinforcement occurs after every response) is the same as a continuous schedule. 2. Tends to provide a high rate of response which is vigorous and steady.
Variable ratio (VR)	A varying or random number of responses must be emitted before reinforcement occurs.	Capable of producing a high rate of response which is vigorous, steady, and resistant to extinction.
Fixed interval (FI)	The first response after a specific period of time has elapsed is reinforced.	Produces, an uneven response pattern varying from a very slow, unenergetic response immediately following reinforce to a very fast, vigorous response immediately preceding reinforcement.
Variable interval (VI)	The first response after varying or random periods of time have elapsed is reinforced.	1. Tends to produce a high rate of response which is vigorous, steady and resistant to extinction.

Source: Fred Luthans and Rober Kreitner: **Organisational Behaviour Modification,** Scott Foresman and Company, Glenview, p.51.

The following are some more aspects related to learning:

Learning Curve: Learning curve is a diagrammatic presentation of the amount learned in relation to time. A learning curve will show on the Y-axis the amount of learnt and on the X-axis the passage of time. Kolasa[8] has suggested the four types of learning curves (see Fig. 8.1).

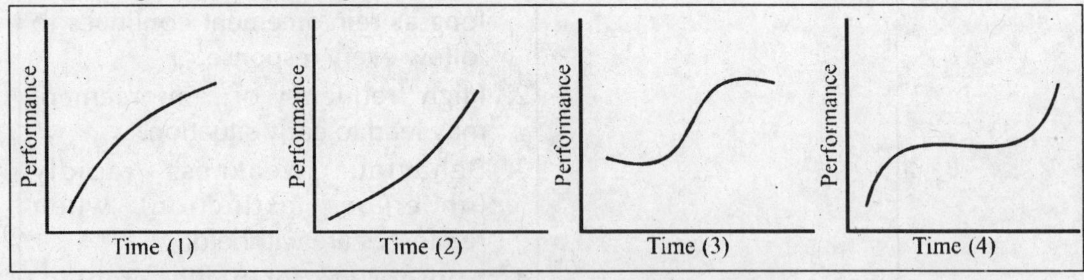

Fig. 8.1: Types of Learning Curves

Curve 1 is a negatively accelerated learning curve while curve 2 is a positively accelerated one. Curve 3 is the combination of both 1 and 2 with an S shape. Curve 4 is also a combination of both 1 and 2 but in the opposite direction. These curves focus on individual differences.

Let us also know what these imply. Curve 1 indicates that initially there is a spurt in learning. Usually, the graph levels off at some stage indicating that maximum performance has been achieved. This is because at the beginning of the learning process, the learner is highly motivated to exhibit a significant surge of effort. Curve 2 is just opposite of curve 1 indicating a rarer learning. It continues till the learning is completely unfamiliar to the learner. But, after some time learning starts taking better strides. Curve 3 represents the first both situations. Curve 4 shows a levelling off in performance after an initial spurt. This is called '**plateau.**' Such type of curve is usually found in trainning programmes in industry.

Extinction Principle: Extinction principle is related to reinforcement. According to Pavlov in his operant conditioning theory of learning, if the response is not reinforced by the consequence, the response will become extinct. In other words, extinction may be defined as a loss of memory. If response is not reinforced repeatedly, it eventually tends to disappear. Extinction principle can be practiced in organisations by not responding to the sarcasm (behaviour) of a colleague. It might also be preferable in other cases of undesirable behaviour.

However, extinction may not always be the best strategy. Punishment might be preferable in cases of seriously undesirable behaviour, such as employee embezzlement or other unethical behaviour.

Spontaneous Recovery: The return of response strength after extinction, without intervening reinforcement, is called '**spontaneous recovery**'. It may happen due to the fact that the conditioned response may not totally disappear during extinction, though it may get suppressed or inhibited. The spontaneous recovery may have its origin from demonstration effect, ego satisfaction, or one's desire for equality with the peers.

Generalisation: Generalisation is considered yet another determinant variable for learning. Generally, a conditioned stimulus results in a conditioned behaviour. Based on this, a new stimulus identical to the earlier conditioned stimulus is likely to result in behaviour identical to the conditioned behaviour. The same is called '**generalisation**'. The more the new stimulus is identical to the conditioned stimulus, the more probable it is that the new stimulus will produce the alike conditioned stimulus.

Discrimination: Discrimination is opposite to generalisation. The line of distinction drawn between the two is that generalisation is a reaction to similar stimuli, while discrimination is a reaction to differences. Let it be clarified with an example.

> There are two teachers equally competent, working in a University Department of Business Administration. Among them, one is sincere, polite and hardworking, and the other is rude and arrogant. Though, initially the response of the Head of the Department may be equal or similar to both, the Head over the period responds positively to the former and negatively to the latter. Thus, the Head of the Department discriminates between the two. The rude and arrogant teacher is not reinforced. Such discrimination enables the rude one to mend his behaviour and the polite one to improve further.

8.4.2. PUNISHMENT

Punishment is yet another way of changing human behaviour. It is inverse of the reward. As punishment is related to penalising or causing harm to a person, it is less talked of than reward. The purpose of punishment is to eliminate or weaken undesirable behaviour. It is done in two ways. One way to punish a person is through the application of a negative consequence following an undesirable behaviour. For example, a professional athlete who is excessively offensive to the refree on the football ground (undesirable behaviour) may be ejected from a game (negative consequence). The second way to be used to punish the person is through the withholding of a positive consequence following an undesirable behaviour. For example, a sales representative who makes few visits to companies and, in turn, makes sales well below quota (undesirable behaviour) is given less commission (positive consequence).

Punishment causes discomfort to the person being punished. Hence, it may have ill-effects. It may result in negative psychological, emotional performance, or behavioural consequences. For example, the person punished may become angry, hostile, depressed, or despondent. Experience suggests that work slow downs, subotage, and subversive behaviour are usually the ill-effects of punishment.

Hence, efforts need to be made to minimize the ill-effects of punishment. Research has shown that a hard punishment applied makes the person very anxious, decreasing his potential to be a good worker. In order to avoid these ill-effects, punishment needs to be followed by rewards to appropriate behaviour. For example, a worker who has been given a wage cut or forced to take casual leave (punishment) for coming late could be given a small wage hike (reward) for coming on time for a certain period like one month.

Solomon has suggested that punishment can become effective in changing behaviour if it is (*i*) applied before the undesirable behaviour has become very well learnt; (*ii*) fairly intense: (*iii*) followed immediately after the undesirable behaviour; (*iv*) specific to a particular act; (*v*) consistent across persons; (*vi*) applied everytime the act occurs; and (*vii*) accompanied by reward for the desired behaviour.

Douglas McGregor suggests the "**Hot Stove Rule**" to make the administration of punishment more effective in affecting human behaviour. The Hot Stove Rule suggests that administering punishment is much like touching a hot stove.

- The burn is *immediate*. When one touches hot stove, the burn is instantaneous, leaving no question of cause and effect.
- The person had an ample *warning*. Seeing the red colour of stove, the person knows what would happen if it is touched.
- The burn is *consistent*. Every time one touches hot stove, he/she gets the same response, i.e. one gets burned.
- The burn is *impersonal*. Regardless of who one is, if he/she touches a hot stove, the stove will burn anyone.

Thus, the comparison between touching a hot stove and administering punishment is apparent. Therefore, administration of punishment should also be immediate, with warning, consistent and impersonal. These guidelines are consistent with positive approach of punishment.

8.5 LEARNING AND BEHAVIOUR

We have maintained throughout the chapter that almost all human behaviour is learned. Learning is, therefore, considered vital for understanding human behaviour at work in organisations. Let us try to understand in a more orderly manner how learning helps managers change human behaviour in different organisational situations, such as reducing absenteeism, substituting well-pay for sick-pay, improving employees' discipline and developing training programme for the employees. These are discussed one by one.

Reducing Absenteeism Through Learning: Learning can help managers evolve programmes to reduce absenteeism. An example of such a programme may be rewarding employees for their satisfactory attendance. The management of a private software enterprise introduced lottery system to reward its employees with attractive prizes. Only employees with perfect attendance were eligible to contest for prizes. This lottery programme has a rousing success as it resulted in lower absence rates (about 30 per cent) among the employees.

Substituting Well-Pay for Sick-Pay: Paid sick leave is one of the fringe benefits provided to salaried employees by most of the organisations including Univeristies. However, research studies indicate that paid sick leave programmes reinforce the undesirable behaviour, i.e., absence from work. The reality is that employees use sick leaves all up, regardless of whether they are sick. As a consequence, organisations that provide paid sick leave experience quite more the absenteeism than organisations that do not provide paid sick leave[9].

As a matter of fact, organisations should reward attendance not absence. This calls for substituting **well-pay for sick-pay**. Hence, organisations should reward an employee in the form of bonus for remaining no absent from work for a definite period of time. There are researches[10] that report that well-pay produced reduced absenteeism, increased productivity, and improved employee satisfaction.

Improving Employee Discipline: Managers, at times, have to deal with employees' undesirable behaviour, such as drinking at work place, insubordination, stealing company property, arriving continuously late, etc. Usually managers respond to these with punishment like oral reprimands, written warnings, and even suspension. As mentioned earlier, punishment, however, provides only a short-term solution and has ill-effects on employee punished.

Evidences[11] suggest that discipline produces results in short-run.. In this lies the importance of fostering discipline in organisations. Learning helps the managers how to more effectively implement disciplinary actions so as to promote employee discipline. The managerial behaviours such as to respond immediately, provide time, state the problem specifically, allow the employee to explain his/her position, keep discussion impersonal, be consistent, take progressive action and obtain consensus agreement on change, if any, help the managers to more effectively implement disciplinary actions.

Developing Training Programmes: Learning also helps managers develop effective training programmes. Particularly, social-learning theory serves as a guide for this purpose. It suggests the organiser-managers that the training programme should offer a model to grab the trainee's attention, provide required motivational properties, provide adequate opportunities to practice the new behaviours, and also offer due rewards to the employees for accomplishment of tasks. In case of off-the-job training, the model should also allow the trainee some opportunity to transfer what he/she has learned to the job[12].

Summary

This summary is organized as per the 'learning objectives' given on page no. 125:

- *Learning is a relatively permanent change acquired through experience. Different processes are involved in learning.*
- *Classical conditioning involves the pairing of a neutral stimulus, resulting in the formation of a conditioned behaviour. The operant conditioning states that behaviour is a function of its positive and negative consequences. The social learning theory stresses upon the ability of an individual to learn by observing his/her models, such as parents, teachers, colleagues, peers, and others.*
- *The basic difference between classical and operant conditioning learning theories is that while a change in stimulus elicits a particular response in case of former, stimulus serves as a cue for a person to emit response in case of latter.*
- *Learning is based on two principles-reinforcement and punishment. Reinforcement is an attempt to develop or strengthen desirable behaviour by either bestowing positive consequences or withholding negative consequences. Punishment is used to eliminate or weaken undesirable behaviour by either bestowing negative consequences or withholding positive consequences.*
- *Learning theories help managers modify employee behaviour by applying these to different situations such as reducing absenteeism, substituting well-pay for sick-pay, improving employee discipline, developing training programmes, and others.*

REVIEW QUESTIONS

1. What is learning? How does it take place?
2. Discuss the nature of classical conditioning and operant conditioning. How do they differ from each other?
3. What are the major dimensions of social learning theory?
4. "Any observable change in behaviour is **prima facie** evidence that learning has taken place". Discuss.
5. How can reinforcement be used to generate change in behaviour?
6. What factors should be considered when using punishment for behaviour modification?
7. Which learning theory—the behavioural theory or Bandura's social learning theory-do you find more appropriate for people?

8. The branch manager of the State Bank of India, Tezpur has received numerous complaints that especially officers leave their chairs, apparently for some works, but do not return to their chairs for as long as 30 minutes. This causes great inconvenience to the customers/clients. In fact, the business has experienced a decline during the last 3 months. The branch manager wants to change the present situation.
If you were the manager of this branch of bank, what plan of action will you develop to alter this situation?

REFERENCES

1. Stephen P. Robbins: **Organisational Behaviour**, Printice Hall of India Private Limited, New Delhi, 1998, Eighth Edition, p.68.
2. N.L. Munn et al: **Introduction to Psychology**, Oxford and IBH Publishing Co., New Delhi, 1972, p. 201.
3. Richard M. Steers and Lyman W. Porter: **Motivation and Work Behaviour,** Mc Grawel, New York, 1975, p.478.
4. Fred Luthans: **Organisational Behaviour**, Mc Graw-Hill, Inc., New Delhi, Seventh Edition, 1995, p. 203.
5. I.P. Pavlov: **The Work of the Digestive Glands,** (trans. W.H. Thompson), Charless Griffin, London, 1902.
6. B.F. Skinner: **Science and Human Behaviour**, Free Press, New York, 1953.
7. A. Bandura: **Social Learning Theory**, Printice Hall, Englewood Cliffs, N.J., 1977.
8. Blair J. Kolasa: **Introduction to Behavioural Sciences for Business**, Wiley Eastern Limited, New Delhi, 1968, p. 180.
9. D.Willings: The Absentee Worker, **Personnel and Training Management,** December, 1968, pp. 10-12.
10. B.H. Harvey, J.F. Rogers, and J.A. Schultz: Sick Pay vs Well Pay: An Analysis of the Impact of Rewarding Employees for Being on the Job, **Public Personnel Management Journal**, Summer 1983, pp. 218-224.
11. R.H. Lussier: A Discipline Model for Increasing Performance, **Supervisory Management**, August 1990, pp. 6-7.
12. Stephen P. Robbins: ***op.cit.***, Eighth Edition, 1998, p.76.

Case 8.1 : Mr. Vice Chancellor Needs Learning Through Doings*

Often changes surface the organisations with the new Heads of the Organisations. So is ture in case of an infant Central University in the North-Eastern Region of India. As the Vice Chancellors in the University system are migratory birds for a certain period of 3 to 5 years to stay in the University, the previous Vice Chancellor left and the New Vice Chancellor joined the University with his own mission and vision for the Univerisity. He, from his first day in the University, started thinking and working to achieve his mission and vision. In order to monitor the things/ happening in the University in right direction, he formed an informal advisory committee consisting of some 20 Professors of the University. He also evolved a *modus operandi* for this advisory committee.

Fortnightly, he started holding meetings with the group of advisory committee in order to keep them informed and teach them the specifics of any new change in the Government and the University Grants Commission policies and procedures

---

* The case is real to the knowledge of the author. For ethical reasons, the actual names of the University and its Vice Chancellors are disguised.

that might affect their work. He also used to discuss priorities and assignments for them. This meeting was also a time and place when the members can share some of the problems and concerns of their respective departments. The meeting is shceduled to begin at 3 P.M. sharp every second and fourth Saturday of the month. Initially, when it was non-teaching duration, the members came on time. Lately, when classes in the Semester System gained momentum, the members have been filtering in every five minutes or until almost 4 P.M. This made the Vice Chancellor delay the start of the meeting until all the members arrive. During the last few weeks when classes are running in full swing, the meetings have not started until 4 P.M. In fact, at 3 PM, nobody has shown up. The Vice Chancellor could not understand what has happened. The facts unknown to him were that missing a single class in the semester system costs a lot, most of the Professors-Members were two-in-one *i.e.,* the Deans of the Schools and the Heads of the Departments, and non-availability of transport after 5 PM from the University Campus to the city with a distance of 20 kms. Though the Vice Chancellor was seeing the crowed of the students, teachers and non-teaching employees standing by the road-side waiting for highly irregular public transport, everyday while passing through the bus stop in his black glass official vehicle, but was oblivious to think over how they will come back to the city which is 20 kms away from the Campus.

The Vice Chancellor was only concerned how to conduct the Advisory Committee meetings on time. For a moment, he thought to start meeting at 3 P.M., so that meeting is over by 5 P.M. before the members leave for their homes. At the next moment, he felt that his hands are tied because, after all, the advisory committee is informal and, thereby, the members are volunteers by nature, and, therefore, he cannot push them or make them get to the meetings on time. On the other hand, the Professors-members, who are in no way less qualified than the Vice Chancellor, didn't care for this advisory committee meetings which are not under the purview of their official duties or jobs.

QUESTIONS

1. If you were a management consultant to the Vice Chancellor, what advice would you give to the Vice Chancellor?
2. In terms of reinforcement theory, explain what is happening here and what the Vice Chancellor needs to do to get the meetings started on time.

Case 8.2: The Dabbawalas of Mumbai**

The *dabbawalas* of Mumbai carry hot lunches from the homes of employees (customers) to their places of employment. The aluminium containers or 'tiffins' serve the dual purpose of keeping the food warn and preventing it from splashing out during the tiffin carrier's rushed and jostling journey. A typical tiffin carrier carries about 40 of these *dabbas* on a long, unwieldy tray on his head as he moves speedily through busy streets and cramped trains. The tray and tiffins have a combined weight of more than 60 kg. For distances over 4 km, the carriers often use bicycles; when carrying more than 40 tiffins, the carriers use handcarts.

** Based on Ashok Kumar, Stephen T. Margulis and Jaideep Motwani : An Efficient Real-World Food Delivery System; The Dabhawalas of Mumbai, *IIMB Management Review*, December 2001, pp. 7-13.

Each *dabbawala* is employed by one of the city's 800 contractors (*mukaddams*). The contractors and tiffin carriers both belong to the Mumbai Tiffinbox Carriers Association. It was registered as a trust in 1967, but was an informal guild for some 50 years before this.

There are two primary reasons why the tiffin carrier operations started and succeeded in Mumbai. First, the Indian value system places great emphasis on home-cooked meals, served hot. The problem for roughly eight out of ten white-collar workers in Mumbai is that they do not have time to go home for lunch. The tiffin carrier brings the security of an inexpensive, clean, tasty, and often still warm, home-cooked meal. Restaurant meals cost five to fifteen times more than home-cooked food and there is also the chance of falling ill, as many public eateries lack hygienci Kitchens. Second, Mumbai is the only city in India where the train traffic flows in the north-south direction and the pedestrian traffic flows in the east-west direction. Thus, tiffins are physically carried for relatively short distances from homes to train stations by one set of tiffin carried by ttrain for longer distances between stations, and finally carried by other tiffin carriers from the train stations to the designated workplaces. Therefore, Mumbai alone can sustain a tiffin carrier network of this size and complexity because of its quick, efficient and far-reaching suburban train service.

Most of Mumbai's tiffin carriers and contractors come from the Pune region, roughly 150 miles away from Mumbai. A tiffin carrier does not have to pay the contractor to be hired. There is absolutely no paperwork involved. Trust and loyalty are the main underpinnings of recruitment. Typically, no formal training is provided to the tiffin carrier upon being hired. However, for the first two days, the tiffin carrier follows his contractor of another dabbawala who shows the new recruit his route, the homes/apartments he would visit to pick up tiffins in the morning and to which he would return tiffin in the afternoon, and to which he would return tiffins in the afternoon, and explains the coding/identification system. a tiffin carrier will visit up to 40 homes each day and he must learn the location of all of them during his two-day orientation. All the training is done orally.

A *dabbawala* is usually paid a fixed/straight salary of Rs. 1,000 a month by his contractor. There are no other benefits provided to the tiffin carrier, except that he gets a week's vacation in March apart from public holidays. By contrast, contractors make between Rs. 6,000 and Rs. 8,000 a week. There is no policy regarding sick leave or absenteeism. A worker is expected to be at work. If a worker gets sick, other tiffin carriers in his group or his contractor may cover for him. The bond among tiffin carriers is as strong as the old school tie. They won't entertain any talk of dishonesty in the ranks. Trust is the essence of the business and a tiffin carrier typically sticks to his contractor.

The contractors basically run the business through two committees: the Mandal Committee and the Trust Committee. The members of the Mandal Committee are 11 elected contractors, each elected for five years. This committee collectively governs the Trust but its primary repsonsibilities seem to be dealing with brokering conflicts among contractors and addressing potential contractors. The Trust Committee, also comprises 11 elected contractors, each elected for a five-year period, is responsible for the operation of the courtesy inn (*dharmashalas*) back home in Pune. In addition, two contractors serve as staff to the Trust. The job of these two contractors includes: (1) resolving disputes and problems arising in day-to-day operations that cannot be resolved by contractors and their group, (2) entrolling new customers into the business, and (3) arranging and calling meeting of the Trust. The contractors, in turn, are responsible to The Mumbai Tiffinbox Carriers Association. The Mandal or 'Circle' (*i.e.,* the Association) organizes monthly business meetings. All contractors are required to attend the Mandal's monthly meetings. The tiffin carriers can also attend the monthly meetings if they so desire. The internal problems/disputes between the contractors are sorted out at these business meetings by the Mandal Committee. Additionally, the tiffin carriers and contractors meet socially once a month. These meetings are organized by the Trust.

Structure

Some of the salient points of the Trust in terms of structural dimensions are:

Standards: In the Trust, the work appears to involve output standardization because workers are given explicit work goals (e.g., tiffins to retrieve each morning). If goals do not change and each person completes his task, this is an important coordination mechanism.

Moreover, it appears that workers share beleifs about what is acceptable behaviour and what is not. This implies that output standardization is supplemented by norm standardization. The latter is encouraged by the tiffin carriers' functional unit grouping. In a functional unit grouping, everyone within a specific work group has similar tasks to perform.

Hierarchy: There is a relatively flat hierarchy of authority. There are only three levels within the organization: some 5,000workers, called carriers; some 800 supervisors or managers, called contractors; and the 11-member Mandal Committee. A flat organization such as this often implies a wide span of control. By contrast, here each manager manages a group of some four to ten employees. By Western standards, the span of control is narrow. However, we believe that this reflects an aspect of Indian culture—specifically, the tendency to have many supervisors in an Indian organization.

Specialization: There is a relatively high degtree of specialization. There are a limited number of different jobs and each involves a relatively narrow range of tasks. The jobs correspond to the three phases of the work: (*i*) the pick-up of filled tiffins from and the return delivery of empty tiffins to homes; (*ii*) train transportation of tiffins between residential and commercial districts; and (*iii*) the delivery of tiffins to and pick-up of tiffins from receivers (workers). A consequence of high specialization is increased task interdependence, hence the need for coordination mechanisms, such as standardization, to accomplish and results.

Complexity: The Trust is low in all types of structural complexity. Vertical complexity is low because the organization is flat; horizontal complexity is low because there are a slimited number of different jobs in the organization; geographical complexity is low because the organization is at one site only.

Staff: Professionalism is also low. There is very little formal education or employee training required for the work of contractors or carriers. As for personnel ratios, the administrative ratio is quite low, perhaps zero. There are only two line members (contractors) who have, as their additional responsibility, the completion of the staff functions of the organization.

Contextual Dimensions

There are four contextual dimensions—organizational size, organizational technology, external environment, and goals, and strategies. Some of the salient features of the Trust in these areas are:

Organizational Size. The Trust has some 5,800 members, making it a large-scale operation.

Organizational Technology. The technical complexity is low, as the Trust's organizational technology is labour intensive (uniform inputs, pre-coded inputs and few exception). Technical uncertainty is also low (variability in tiffins is low). The principal form of technical system interdependence is sequential interdepenuence across the three phases of work (see above) and with pooled interdependence within phases. This specific form of organizational technology is associated with low structural complexity and output standadization as effective coordination mechanism, both of which we have observed.

External Environment. The external environment is regarded as relatively stable by the Trust even though there are competitors in their task environment that are cutting into their business. Customers are the primary focus and they are satisfied with the service they are receiving. Nevertheless, consistent with our description of changing values towards meals, the customer base is shrinking because street vendors and restaurants offer active competition.

Goals and Strategies. Although strategies and goals are a central concern of organizations, the only stated goals we gathered from interviews with contractors and tiffin carriers was to continually provide this service in the best possible manner. The lack of strategic interest is even reflected in their passive approach towards threats to the very survival of their business.

A TYPICAL JOURNEY

To understand how the exchange and delivery of food take place (in other words, the activities involved in the supply chain), one of the co-authors accompained the tiffin carriers on their daily routes. Before describing the process in detail, we will present an overview. The process has three phases: The pick-up of the tiffin and its delivery to a train station, the train transportation of the tiffin to its final destination, and the delivery of the tiffin to the customer. This process occurs twice daily: From home to office and the tiffin's return from office to the home.

We will now describe a typical journey by following the tiffin of Raj Ramaswamy, a fictional accountant, on its daily trip from his home to office and back,

Step 1 Raj's tiffin carrier, who we call tiffin carrier 1, knocks at approximately 10 a.m. on the Ramaswamy's door. He is not wearing a watch. He quickly gets the tiffin from Mrs Ramaswamy and sprints down the stairs. His daily route covers 38 apartments (38 tiffins) spread over a two-mile radius. Each tiffin has a different symbol as each is bound for different destinations.

Step 2 At approximately 10:30 a.m., Raj's tiffin is transferred to tiffin carrier 2, who has been collecting all the tiffins with yellow characters. As tiffin carrier 2 pedals off to a nearby train station with his collected tiffins, tiffin carrier 1 continues to go from apartment to apartment to get lunch boxes which will soon be collected by other carriers.

Step 3 At the railway station, hundreds of tiffins have been desposited by different collectors. From them, tiffin carrier 3 quickly removes all of those with a red dot, Raj's included. He loads his consignment on a 'tray', a wooden crate 2.5 metres long. A typical tray loaded with 40 tiffins has a total weight of more than 60 kg. The carrier puts the tray on his head and runs to the platform just as the train rolls in. Raj's tiffin is now one of thousands riding this train into the city. Different characters on the tiffins tell the carriers at which stations en route they must pass on specific tiffins to other waiting carriers. The yellow alphanumeric character and the red dot on Raj's tiffin tell the carrier its destination is Churchgate Station, the hub of commercial Mumbai.

Step 4 At Churchgate Station, Raj's tiffin enters the last phase of its jorney. Tiffin carrier 4, waiting on the platform, picks it out together with other lunch boxes marked with similar characters. The second and third characters of the symbol indicate its exact destination: the Express Towers building at Nariman Point. by 12:30 p.m.,. the carrier has carried his tray up four flights of stairs and left Raj's lunch box, along with the others, outside the customers' offices.

At 2 p.m. the morning's delivery service tracks down the above steps in reverse, using exactly the same symbols that moved the tiffin forward previously. Tiffin carrier 1, now at the receiving end of the line, brings Raj's tiffin back to his wife at 4 p.m., guided to her house by the last character of the symbol. Of course, the exact location of the house is part of the memory database of tiffin carrier 1.

The Logistic Perspective

The logistics systems that have an exact one-to-one correspondence with the tiffin carrier system of Mumbai are the mail and parcel delivery systems in the United States of America and other countries. These systems have unique customer–supplier pairings for each delivery. Postal or parcel delivery systems are typically modelled as hub and then flown to their destination from the hub. These are multi-billion dollar systems that employ the latest technology for receiving and tracking deliverables. Major efficiencies are supposedly obtained through the hub-and-spoke structure of the logistical system. Despite large capital investments, highly sophisticated technologies, mature postal systems (zip codes and all), and other well-established identifications, these systems yield low delivery reliability and are unable to individualize operations. In contrast, the tiffin carrier system of India invests pennies, uses a very crude identification system, uses virtually no technology, and relies mainly on untrained, grossly under-educated (if not illiterate) personnel to obtain great delivery reliability and customer satisfaction.

The tiffin carrier system is a conjoined structure that falls squarely under arborescent systems. It involves the transfer of some 200,000 lunch boxes collected every day from an equal number of sources, and delivered to some 80,000 destinations the same day within a time window of three hours. The error rate of this system is remarkably low (less than 1 per cent) and it accomplishes its goals at the rate pf pennies per customer per day. In the US, large logistical systems that involve material transfer of the order of the lunch carrier system, are generally reduced to a hub-and-spoke structure (e.g., Federal Express, American Airlines) to gain efficiencies of time. they are also supported by state-of-the-art technologies, including computerized decision-making that exploits artificial intelligence and a very sophisctiacted telecommunication system. Their operating costs are typically in millions of dollars. By contrast and as noted, the tiffin carrier system uses virtually no technology (other than the trains and bicycles), is limited to face-to-face communication, employs virtually no computers, and is about as informal as a system of this size can be. What is particularly notable is the coding system to identify lunch boxes: it consists of just three to four symbols. Moreover, on-the-job training of operators is often accomplished within two days, which includes learning the delivery process and the specific locations of some 40 dwelling units of customers. Yet, it registers an outstanding performance on both counts—cost and reliability of delivery. That is, it operates literally at pennies a day per customer. It operates at a remarkably low error rate of less than 1 per cent, where errors include not only non-delivery within the time window, but also loss and breakage of lunch boxes. The tiffin carriers' error rate compares favourably with the error rates of lost suitcase at various airlines.

CONCLUSIONS

Our case study of a prosaic business supports two important principles: first, culture affects organizational form and functioning, human resource management, and the development of logistical systems. That is, it can result in systems that are not fully 'Western' in form and functioning. This leads to the second principle: A labour-intensive, technologically unsophisticated logistical system can be as efficient and as effective as a technologically sophisticated (Western) logistical system of the same design. The tiffin carriers are the unsophisticated counterpart of such sophiscated courier services as Federal Express and United Parcel Service, all of which are conjoined logistical system *i.e.*, where material is transferred from multiple sources to multiple sources to multiple destinations. We found that an organizational and logistical system that fits its cultural and geographic 'niche' can survive and, more importantly, prosper. and, in special cases where employee dedication results from family values, as is the case with the tiffin carrier system studied here, the performance could well be stunning!

QUESTIONS

1. What team and inter-team processes are reflected in the operation of the *dabbawala* system?
2. How has the *dabbawala* system responded to the changing context of the life of office-goers in Mumbai ?
3. What cultural factors have contributed to the spectacular success of the system?
4. What values and which aspects of positive perspective are reflected in the successful working of the *dabbawala* system ?

9

ORGANISATIONAL CITIZENSHIP BEHAVIOUR (OCB)

"Do unto others as though you were the others." – ***Anonymous***

"Render more service than that for which you are paid and you will soon be paid for more than you render. The law of 'Increasing Returns' takes care of this."

– ***Anonymous***

Learning Objectives

After studying this chapter, you should be able to:

- **Define** OCB.
- **Delineate** the theoretical perspective of OCB.
- **List** the determinants of OCB.
- **Identify** the predictors of OCB.
- **Suggest** the ways and means to cultivate and develop OCB in the Indian organisations.

9.1 INTRODUCTION

A question haunts most of the organisations is what ticks organisational success. Although there can be a number of alternative answers to this question, but the ultimate answer lies with the people, i.e., employees working therein. Employees' behaviour and performance are intimately related. Employees' behaviour is an outcome of employees' job involvement and organisational commitment. Then, the key questions arise are: Where do the employees' involvement and commitment come from? What makes employees to involve and commit themselves to organisation? In an attempt to answer these questions, researchers have defined all work behaviours exhibited by employees into two roles[1]. One is *'in role behaviour'*, i.e. role in accordance with organisational goals, objectives, and job description. Two is *'extra role behaviour,'* i.e. the employee behaviour which is beyond the formal job description, i.e. *'call of the duty.'* The extra role behaviour is also termed as 'Organisational Citizenship Behaviour (OCB).' There has been empirical research evidence to believe that employees' behaviour which is beyond traditional territory of job description, (i.e. OCB) does contribute to the organisational effectiveness[2]. That is why OCB as a competitive advantage has been gaining increasing significance in improving organisational effectiveness and success. The concept of OCB is widely studied in the West, but it is relatively of recent origin in India. Therefore, the concept of OCB needs to be explored and studied in depth and detail in the

Indian context. It is against this backdrop; the present chapter makes an attempt to explain the concept of OCB, investigate into its determinants and predictors, highlights its consequences, and submits suggestions to cultivate and develop OCB culture in the Indian organisations.

9.2 OCB DEFINED

As with many other behavoural terms, different people have described and defined OCB in different terms and senses. For example, various terms used to describe OCB include organisational citizenship behaviour[3], pro-social organisational behaviour[4], extra-role behaviour[5], organisational spontaneity[6], extra-role and organisational functional behaviour[7], and even counter-role behaviour[8]. Let us consider some of the important formal definitions of OCB that will help us better understand the meaning of OCB.

D. W. Organ[9] defines OCB as "individual behaviour that is discretionary not directly or explicitly recognized by the formal reward system, and that in the aggregate promotes the effective functioning of the organisation".

According to Turnipseed[10], "OCB includes pro-social behaviour, including helping others, innovating, volunteering, and the lack of undesirable behaviour."

Let OCB described and defined in any term, it means employee behaviour that goes beyond that which is formally prescribed by the organisation, but that behaviour does contribute to the overall organisational effectiveness. Thus, OCB is discretionary behaviour for which employees are neither explicitly rewarded for exhibiting nor are punished for not exhibiting nor employees are imparted training to perform OCB, nor such behaviour is a part of employees' job description. OCB goes far beyond the formal call of duty prescribed in job description. Extending help to a co-worker in finishing his pending work, not taking unnecessary leaves like casual leaves just because leaves otherwise may lapse, switching off lights, fans, and air conditioners while not in use not only that of one's own cabin or room but that of others also are some of the examples of OCB.

The major dimensions of OCB are: (i) extra-role or being going beyond "the call of the duty", (ii) discretionary or voluntary in nature, and (iii) not necessarily recognized by the formal reward system of the organisation. The full array of OCB includes behaviours such as constructive statements about the organisation, expressing interest in others' work suggestions for improvements, care of organisational property, house-keeping behaviours, punctuality, and other variables. At the same time, it also includes refraining from negative behaviours such as finding fault with others, expressing displeasure, starting arguments, and complaining about non-significant things.

9.3 THEORETICAL PERSPECTIVE OF OCB

During the past decade, OCB on the part of employees has received considerable attention in the human resource management and organisational behaviour literature. Yet metaphorically, the argument can be made that this construct is "old wine in a new bottle" in that it is indistinguishable from such accepted scientific constructs as altruism, collectivism, and organisational commitment which, unlike OCB, have been subjected to rigorous systematic research. There is also evidence to suggest and believe that the scholars who studied OCB cannot agree on its definition. For example, Organ (1988) defined OCB as spontaneous, modest, mundane employee behaviour that is not formally recognized in organisation's reward system, but nevertheless advances the effective functioning of the organisation. Graham[11] defined OCB as a behaviour that is supportive of collective rather than individual interests. She differentiated OCB from pro-social behaviour by describing the former as behaviour to help the organisation and the latter to help the individual; that is, altruism. Williams and Anderson[12] distinguished between OCB that benefits the organisation and OCB that benefits a specific individual.

In an organisational context, employee plays two roles to perform his / her job. These are nomenclatured as "in-role" and "extra-role." For better understanding of his performance, the performance is distinguished between "in-role" performance, and "extra-role" performance. While the in-role performance represents the results connected with the work output, including sales volume and commission earned, the extra-role performance is fundamentally related to the aspects of individual behaviour. Research has clearly demonstrated that both roles influence employee performance and, in turn, organisational success[13]. Therefore, managers while evaluating their employees for taking decisions regarding compensation, promotion, rewards, incentives, etc. keep both types of performance in mind.

The empirical evidence suggests that the "in-role" performance is an antecedent to job satisfaction, while the "extra-role" performance is seen as a consequence[14]. This is because of the fact that employees who are satisfied with their job have a feeling of gratitude towards their organisations and a desire to reciprocate, which manifests itself in their behaviour. In a sense, the "in-role" behaviour should be considered as an antecedent to organisational commitment, the "extra-role" behaviour is perceived as its consequence. Thus, the employees who are more committed to the firm want to give more of them with the intention of contributing to the overall well-being of the organisation[15]. Such relationship between commitment and performance has been widely analysed among the sales staff. This is, perhaps so because various aspects of services require non-mandated employee behaviour that can be critical to customer perception of service. Yes, while some type of behaviour can be explicitly defined, others are more abstract and are dependent on employee's attitude and motivation. Though, OCB is a type of discretional behaviour and is not directly rewarded or recognized in the formal structure of rewards, yet it is especially important for organisational effectiveness and success. Here, an important question arises is how does OCB help promote organisational performance and success? The simple answer to this question is that OCB promotes teamwork, eases communication between employees and management, improves the work environment, and reduces attrition and improves employee retention. As a result, employees who imbibe and develop this type of behaviour, usually help other employees to deliver quality service, that is, they are good candidates for encouraging and carrying out quality initiative in the organisation.

A review of literature on OCB identifies two main approaches employed in explaining the theoretical perspective of OCB. One approach considers OCB to be "extra-role" behaviour - individual contributions in the work place that go beyond the specified role requirements and are not directly or explicitly recognized by the formal reward system[16]. Another approach suggests that OCB must be considered separately from work performance, thus, obviating the problem of distinguishing between "in-role" and "extra-role" performances[17]. As per this approach, OCB must be conceived as a wider concept that includes all relevant positive behaviour of individuals within an organisation. The supporters of this approach also argue that it can be difficult for a firm to distinguish between "in-role" performance and "extra-role" performance, owing to certain factors. *First,* the perceptions of managers and employees about employees' performance and responsibilities do not necessarily correspond. *Second,* employees' perception of their performance and responsibilities is, more often than not, influenced by their satisfaction in the work place[18].

Now that a theoretical perspective is delineated, a discussion on the determinants of OCB seems logical in order.

9.4 DETERMINANTS OF OCB

OCB being extra-role behaviour, i.e. discretionary role does not happen with all always and automatically. Instead, it is determined by certain factors. Hence, it has become a very fertile topic for behavioural researchers to find out what determines OCB. Several behavioural scientists have tried to identify the determinants of OCB. For example, in their initial study, Natemeyer et. al.[19] identified four major determinants of OCB, namely, altruism, civic virtue, conscientiousness, and sportsmanship. Research conducted on OCB over the period has produced prodigious volume of research and have identified the number of factors that determine OCB. Based on these research findings, the following eight factors have been reported as the major determinants of OCB:

1. **Courtesy:** Courtesy includes informing others to prevent the occurrence of work-related problems. In other words, courtesy refers to the act of touching-base with others before taking actions and / or proactive information to avoid the unpleasant happenings at the work place[20].
2. **Altruism:** Altruism is defined as behaviour that is intended to benefit another person without any expectation of personal gain and in a self-sacrificial way promotes the welfare of other without concern for one's own self-interest. Very closer to altruism is collectivism, i.e., the subordination of personal goals to group goals and behaviours of solidarity and concern for others[21].
3. **Sportsmanship:** It describes tolerance of nuisance on the job (when employees endure impositions or inconveniences without complaint). Alternatively speaking, it denotes an employee's image or goodwill displayed

in tolerating the circumstances that are less than required or ideal without making much hue and cry or without making *'a mountain out of a molehill.'*

4. **Conscientiousness** : It refers to surpassing enforceable work standards and carrying out role behaviour well beyond the minimum required level[22]. In other words, it indicates employee's self-realization enabling him/her to work beyond the job requirement. Working beyond the official working hours and / or on holidays for the good of the company may be one such example of conscientiousness.
5. **Loyalty** : It implies employee's faithfulness and belongingness towards the organisation.
6. **Civic Virtue** : It manifests itself in the concern of the employee in participating in the life of organisation like attending organisational functions and meetings, and keeping up with organisational results that are not specially required[23].
7. **Extra-role Behaviour** : It refers to the individual's behaviour that extends beyond the standard behaviour normally expected by the employer for the good of the organisation.
8. **Commitment** : Organisational commitment refers to the extent and degree to which an employee aligns him / her with the organisation. This implies an employee's acceptance of the organisational goals and values and willingness to exert higher level efforts for achieving the goals and also remain a member of the organisation. Morrison[24] found positive relationship between affective commitment and several dimensions of OCB.

In an attempt to delineate dimensions of OCB, some researchers have suggested loyalty, obedience, advocacy participation, functional participation, and social participation as yet other dimensions of OCB[25]. Loyalty is an employee's identification with and allegiance to an organisation as a whole. Organisational obedience reflects acceptance and adherence to the rules and regulations governing organisational structure and job descriptions. Advocacy participation refers to employees' behaviour aimed at describing innovations, challenging and igniting others, and making suggestions for other's behavioural modifications. Functional participation personally focuses on behaviours that include participation through performing additional work activities, self-development, and volunteering for special assignments. Social participation refers to such participation that is non-controversial and involves interaction with other individual's inter-personal behaviours.

All in all, the review of literature indicates that researchers have primarily established motivational bases, employees' attitudes towards their job, and personality disposition determine OCB. Having known the determinants of OCB, what next is important to know is how to gauze the OCB. In other words, what reveals the various determinants of OCB? Research studies have identified several behavioural manifestations of the determinants of OCB. Following are 29 variables (statements) belonging to the eight factors of OCB.

Table 9.1: Factor-wise Classification of OCB Statements

Factors	Variables
Courtesy	1. Helping colleague, when he/she is in trouble.
	2. Always ready to help.
	3. Going to help others.
	4. Helping others even when busy.
	5. Co-operative towards new entrants.
Altruism	6. Keep organisation clean.
	7. Proper utilization of organisation resources.
	8. Attending non-compulsory meetings after work.
	9. Adhere to organisational rules and regulations.
	10. Understanding others problems.
	11. Release employees stress.
Sportsmanship	12. Consistent results towards organisation.
	13. Responsible attitude.
	14. Friendly and lively attitude towards employees.
	15. Updated with employees performance.
	16. Utilize spare time by increasing knowledge.
	17. Follow organisation's working procedure.
Consciousness	18. Appreciate constructive ideas of subordinate.
	19. Helping colleagues.
	20. Acting proactively.
Loyalty	21. Loyal towards my organisation.
	22. Sense of belongingness.
	23. Working above expectations.
Civic Virtue	24. Team work.
	25. Encourage peers to follow organisational policies.
	26. Remain committed towards organisation.
Extra-role Behaviour	27. Keeping personal and professional differences.
	28. Active participation in extra-curricular activities.
Commitment	29. Committed towards the organisation.

Based on above 29 statements, you can also ascertain your OCB by applying Rensis Likert's 5-point ranking method.

Attempts have also been made to see whether OCB varies across the organisations. One study revealed that employees tend to differ on various factors of OCB irrespective of the type of organisation. OCB in service industry is found significantly higher in comparison to the manufacturing sector employees[26]. Such finding can be credited to the nature of the industry as employees in service sector are supposed to be better in soft skills.

9.5 PREDICTORS OF OCB

OCB being a discretionary behaviour is not demonstrated by every individual and not all times. OCB though discretionary is yet rewarded. While rewarding OCB, it needs to be perceived rightly at least for two reasons. *One,* some times some employees try to demonstrate their extra-role behaviour as ingratiating. *Second,* it is also possible that the supervisors could perceive a single set of extra role behaviour in a different manner. This has underlined the need for identifying and understanding the predictors of OCB to better understand it. Researchers have reported certain predictors of and / or antecedents to OCB mainly based on job attitudes and / or personality dispositions.

Personality Variables: Personality variables vary from person to person. Research studies have found some personality variables correlated with OCB. To cite, conscientiousness[27], psychological contract[28], and collectivism[29] affect OCB.

Job Satisfaction: Job satisfaction implies one's pleasurable or positive feeling toward job. Research evidence reports that job satisfaction affects OCB and it is more strongly related to OCB than to job performance because of discretionary nature of behaviour[30]. The reason is that a satisfied employee is not always a productive employee, but his / her pleasurable feelings about job improve the effectiveness of the organisational environment. Job satisfaction being an attitude is comprised of both cognitive (knowledge-based beliefs) and affective (feelings) aspects. Of the two, cognitive aspect of job satisfaction is found more powerful predictor of OCB than the affective aspect[31].

Duration of Employee Relation with Organisation: Longer stay with the organisation makes employee earn investment, on the one hand, and becomes more involved in, committed to, and attached with organisation, on the other. This breeds employees' feelings to exhibit OCB for the effectiveness and success of organisation.

Psychological Contracts: Psychological contracts based on social exchange theory prepare employees to perform extra role behaviours. In other words, there is interplay between psychological contracts and OCB. There are two types of psychological contracts, viz., transactional and rational. Transactional contracts are primarily short-term economic exchanges. Rational contracts are rather like marriages; they are long-term attachments that encompass a broad array of subjective mutual obligations. Employees with a rational psychological contract are more willing to contribute their time and effort without expecting the organisation to pay back this debt in the short-term[32].

Leadership Ability: Leadership ability is to influence followers / others to willingly exert efforts for the achievement of organisational goals[33]. Transformational leadership theory is the best suited example to understand leadership as predictor of OCB[34]. Under this leadership, followers feel trust and develop respect towards the leader. This, in turn, increases followers' positive attitudes (e.g., job satisfaction, perceived fairness, and organisational commitment). Positive attitudes motivate people to do more and better than they are expected to do.

Organisational Culture: Organisational culture, i.e. the beliefs and values shared by the majority of organisational members, does also serves as antecedent to OCB[35]. Organ and Lingel[36] also found that OCB in the form of personality disposition like conscientiousness and agreeableness promotes OCB.

9.6 HOW TO CULTIVATE AND DEVELOP OCB ?

There is almost an agreement that OCB positively affects employee behaviour and, in turn, organisational performance. Growing evidence suggests that OCB enhances the pleasantness of workplace settings and, in turn, can contribute to increased performance and efficiency. Hence, organisations need employees who can display citizenship behaviour. Then, this prompts an important question: what steps organisations can take to cultivate citizenship behaviour among their employees? Behavioural scientists have tried to seek answer to this question. Their research reports that OCB is cultivated when organisations treat employees' fairly[37]. For example, one researcher[38] demonstrated that citizenship behaviours were strongly related to employees' perceptions of interactional justice, i.e., the extent to which employees are shown a high degree of courtesy, dignity, and inter-personal sensibility. Evidences confirm that the greater the extent to which employees felt that their supervisors had applied the formal procedures for distributing rewards in a fair and courteous manner, the greater the incidence of citizenship behaviour. The reason for this is not difficult to seek. The relationship between the employees and organisations help an organisation that does not appear to go out of its way to treat them with dignity and respect. Evidences are also galore to mention that the organisations that treat their employees in an interpersonally fair manner tend to reap the benefits of having employees who are good citizens. This is also duly supported by a growing body of research evidence indicating that interactional justice is strongly related to many kinds of behaviour in organisations[39]. Employee citizenship behaviour benefits both the employee and organisation. If organisations try, OCB can be easily cultivated. Yes, OCB once cultivated also needs to be managed, sustained, and further strengthened to reap its benefits for long time.

SUMMARY

This summary is organized by the 'learning objectives' given on page no. 144 :

- *OCB is employee's behaviour that goes beyond that which is formally prescribed by the organisation, but that behaviour does contribute to the overall organisational effectiveness. OCB is also called 'extra-role behaviour.'*
- *The major dimensions of OCB are: i) extra-role or being going beyond "the call of the duty,"' (ii) discretionary or voluntary in nature, and (iii) not necessarily recognized by the formal reward system of the organisation. The empirical evidence suggests that the "in-role" performance is an antecedent to job satisfaction, while the "extra-role" performance is seen as a consequence.*
- *The major determinants of OCB are courtesy, altruism, sportsmanship, conscientiousness, loyalty, civic virtue, extra-role behaviour, and commitment.*
- *The predictors or antecedents of OCB include personality variables, job satisfaction, psychological contracts, leadership ability, organisational culture, etc.*
- *The best way to cultivate OCB is to create pleasantness in the organisation by way of distributing rewards in a fair and courteous manner, showing the employees a high degree of dignity and inter-personal sensibility. So to say, OCB can be cultivated and developed by showing 'holier than thou" attitude by employers towards their employees.*

REVIEW QUESTIONS

1. What is meant by OCB? What determines OCB?
2. Delineate the theoretical perspective of OCB. How is OCB beneficial for the organisation?
3. "OCB though discretionary does contribute to the effectiveness of the organisation." Comment.
4. What predicts OCB? Do the predictors of OCB universally apply to all employees and organisations? Either in the case of yes or no, give justifications.
5. Can OCB be cultivated? If yes, elaborate how?
6. Take either your own case or any person known to you, elaborate your or his/her OCB with its dimensions. Is any change in OCB over the period? If yes, highlight the reasons and dimensions of change.
7. "OCB is old wine in new bottle." Comment on this statement.
8. Recall you own OCB during the recent times. List the various revelations of your OCB and find out which ones are more prominent and give reasons for their prominence.

REFERENCES

1. E. W. Morrison: Role Definitions and Organisational Citizenship Behaviour: The Importance of the Employee Perspective, **Academy of Management Journal,** 37 (6), 1994, pp. 1543-1567.
2. P. M. Podsakoff, and S. B. Mackenzie: Organisational Citizenship Behaviours and Sales Unit Effectiveness, **Journal of Marketing Research,** 31 (3), 1994, pp. 351-363.
3. D. W. Organ: **Organisational Citizenship Behaviour: The Good Soldier Syndrome,** Lexington Books, Lexington, M.A., 1988.
4. A. P. Brief and S. J. Motowidlo: Pro-social Organisational Behaviours, **Academy of Management Review,** 10, 1986, pp. 710-725.
5. Dyne Van, L. L. Cummings and J. M. Parks: Extra-role behaviours: In pursuit of Constructs and Definitional Clarity (a Bridge over Muddied Waters), **Research in Organisational Behaviour,** 17, 1995, pp. 215-285.
6. J. M. George and A. P. Brief: Feeling Good-doing Good: A Conceptual analysis of the Mood at Organisational Spontaneity Relationship, **Journal of Applied Psychology,** 112, 1992, pp. 310-329.
7. J. W. Graham: An Essay on OCB, **Employees' Responsibilities and Rights Journal,** 4, 1991, pp. 249-270.
8. L. L. Cumming and B. M. Staw: **Research in Organisational Behaviour,** JAI Press, Greenwich, C.T.,1990, pp. 43-72.
9. D. W. Organ: Motivational Basis of Organisational Citizenship Behaviour. In L. L. Cummings and B. M. Staw (Eds.): **Research in Organisational Behaviour,** JAI Press, Greenwich, CT, 1990, pp. 43-72.
10. David Turnipseed: Organisation Citizenship Behaviour: In Pursuit of Constructs and Definitional Clarity (a Bridge over Muddied Waters), **Research in Organisational Behaviour,** 17 (2), 1995, pp. 42- 47.
11. J. W. Graham: **Organisational Citizenship Informed by Political Theory,** Paper presented at the Annual Meeting of the Academy of Management, Chicago, Ill, 1986.
12. L. J. Williams and S. E. Anderson: Job satisfaction and Organisational Commitment as Predictors of Organisational Citizenship and In-Role Behaviours, **Journal of Management,** 17, 1991, pp. 601-617.

13. S. B. Mackenzie, P. M. Podsakoff, and R. Fetter: OCB and Objective Productivity as Determinants of Managerial Evaluation of Salesperson Performance, **Organisational Behaviour and Human Decision Processes,** 50, 1991, pp. 123-150.

14. D. W. Organ: 0p. cit., 3.

15. C. Hui, S. S. K. Lam, and J. Schaubroek: Can Good Citizens Lead the Way and Providing Quality Service? A Field Quasi Experiment, **Academy of Management Journal,** 44 (5), 2001, pp. 988-995.

16. D. W. Organ: op. cit., 14.

17. J. W. Graham: op. cit., 7.

18. E. W. Morrison: OCB as a Critical Link between HRM Practices and Services Quality, Human **Resource Management,** 35, 1995, pp. 495-512.

19. R. G. Netemeyer, J. S. Boles, D. O. McKee, and R. McMurrian: An Investigation into the Antecedents of Organisational Citizenship Behaviour in a Personal selling Context, **Journal of Marketing,** 61, 1997, pp. 85-98.

20. D. W. Organ: op. cit., 16.

21. R. G. Netemeyer, J. S. Boles, D. O. McKee, and R. McMurrian: **op. cit.,** 19.

22. ***Ibid.***

23. ***Ibid.***

24. E. W. Morrison: ***op. cit.,*** 1.

25. Dyne Van, L. L. Cummings and J. M. Parks: **op. cit.,** 5.

26. Garima Mathur and Silky Vigg: Organisational Citizenship Behaviour (A Study of Manufacturing and Service Organisations), **NICE Journal of Business,** 2 (2), July-December, 2007, pp. 57-68.

27. D. W. Organ, and K. Ryan: A Meta-analysis of Attitudinal and Dispositional Predictors of Organisational Citizenship Behaviour, **Personnel Psychology,** 48, 1995, pp. 775-802.

28. I. T. Robinson, and E. W. Morrison: Psychological Contract and Organisational Citizenship Behaviour: The Effect of Unfulfilled Obligations on Civic Virtue Behaviour, **Journal of Organisational Behaviour,** 16, 1995, pp. 289-298.

29. R. H. Moorman and G. L. Blakely: Individualism-Collectivism as an Individual Difference Predictor of Organisational Citizenship Behaviour, **Journal of Organisational Behaviour,** 16 (2), 1995, pp. 127-142.

30. D. W. Organ: ***op. cit.*** 20.

31. D. W. Organ and M. Konovsky: Cognitive versus Affective Determinants of Organisational Citizenship Behaviour, **Journal of Applied Psychology,** 74(1), 1989, pp. 157-164.

32. D. M. Rousseau: Psychological and Implied Contracts in Organisations, Employee **Responsibilities and Rights Journal,** Vol. 2, 1989, pp. 121-139.

33. R. J. House: Path-Goal Theory of Leadership: Lessons, Legacy, and Reformulated Theory, **Leadership Quarterly,** 7 (3), 1999, pp. 323-352.

34. James Burns: **Leadership,** Harper & Row, New York, 1978.

35. D. P. Kar and H. R. Tiwari: Assessing Organisational Culture as Antecedent of Organisational Citizenship Behaviour, **Management and Change,** 3 (1), 1999, pp. 115-127.

36. D. W. Organ and A. Lingl: **Personality, Satisfaction** and **Organisational Citizenship Behaviour,** Paper presented at the meeting of the Academy of Management, Las Vegas 1995.

37. J. Greemberg: Justice and Organisational Citizenship: A Commentary on the State of the Science, **Employee Responsibilities and Rights Journal,** 6, 1993, pp. 245-260.

38. R. H. Moorman: The Influence of Cognitive and Affective Based Job Satisfaction Measures on the Relationship between Satisfaction and organisational Citizenship Behaviour, **Human Relations,** 46, 1993, pp. 759-772.

39. J. Greemberg: *op. cit.* 37.

Vignette 1: Holier Than Thou*

Having visited to different locations in and around Almora throughout the day, the exhausted and deadly tired couple reached to a hotel late in the evening to stay in the night. When they enquired for room, the person present there said that all rooms are booked. Sorry, no room is available. It was very dark night and was raining very heavily outside. Other hotels were at some distances and it was also difficult to get transport at that time due to both (dark) night and rain. The signs of anxiety were clearly visible on the tired faces of the couple. The hotel person, whose education was only up to 11th standard, realized their problem that where they will go in such rainy night. It was also not sure whether they will get accommodation in other hotels. He thought to help them in any way.

An idea prevailed that let they take rest that night in his room allotted to him in the hotel. He told the couple to sit on the sofa and wait for some time. He called one of the room servants and ordered him to clean his room and make it in order. The room servant came after some time and reported that the room is ready. The person told the couple that I have arranged one room for your night stay. Though the room is not as good as other rooms are in the hotel, but I am sure that you would feel quite comfortable in that room. He told the couple: "Please you go in the room. I am sending two cups of hot coffee; it will give you comfortable sleep." The person passed that night on the sofa itself placed at the reception counter. Having passed their night comfortably, the couple thanked the hotel person and left for their next destination to Delhi.

After a few years, the couple constructed a magnificent multi-storied hotel in New Delhi. Advertisement was given for different hotel staff except the Hotel Manager. When asked why there was no advertisement for the post of hotel manager, the couple replied that they had already got a really very good manager for their hotel. He was the same person with an educational qualification up to 11th standard who offered his own room in his hotel to the couple in that rainy night in Almora. What an excellent example of OCB, or say, *"Holier than thou."*

Vignette 2: Service is Investment**

One summer evening I (David J. Schwartz) traveling by a car through Cincinnati. It was time for a gas-up. I stopped at an ordinary looking but surprisingly busy service station. Four minutes later I knew why this particular service station was so popular. After filling my car with gasoline, checking under the hood, and

---

***Source:** Asha Ram Ji: Aastha **Television Channel**, Saturday,10 December, 2005.

****Source:** David J. Schwartz : **The Magic of Thinking Big**, Simon & Schuster UK Ltd., London, 1979. pp. 214-215.)

cleaning the outside of my windshield, the attendant walked around to my side of the car and said, "Pardon me, Sir, it's been a dusty day. Let me clean the inside of your windshield." Quickly and efficiently he did a thorough job of cleaning the inside of my windshield, something not one service-station attendant in a hundred ever does.

This little special service did more than improve my night visibility (and it improved it a lot); it made me remember this station. It so happened that I made eight trips through Cincinnati during the next three months. Each time, of course, I stopped at this station. And each time I got more service than I expected to get. Interesting too was the fact that each time I stopped (once it was 4.00 A.M.) there were other automobiles filling up also. In all, I probably purchased about 100 gallons of gasoline from this station.

The first time I stopped the attendant could have thought to him, "This guy is from out of the state. Odds are 20 to one that he'll never be back. Why do more than give him the routine treatment? He's only a one-time customer."

But the attendants in that station didn't think that way. They put service first and that's why they were busy pumping gasoline while other stations looked almost deserted. If the gasoline was any better than a dozen other brands I didn't notice it. And the price was competitive.

The difference was service, i.e. OCB. And it was obvious that service was paying off in profits to the gasoline station.

10

EMOTIONS AND MOODS

"Nothing gives one person so much advantage over another as to remain always cool and unruffled under all circumstances." **– *Jefferson***

"Anybody can become angry-that is easy; but to be angry with the right person, and to the right degree, and at the right time, and for the right purpose, and in the right way - that is not within everybody's power and is not easy." **– *Aristotle***

Learning Objectives

After studying this chapter, you should be able to:

- **Define** emotions and moods and **distinguish** between the two.
- **Identify** the sources of emotions and moods come from.
- **Delineate** and **discuss** the different aspects of emotions.
- **Discuss** the major theories of emotions.
- **Establish,** with the help of 'Affective Events Theory (AET), the relationship between workplace events, emotions, and employee behaviour.
- **Justify** the need for and significance of emotional intelligence at work.
- **Reflect** on the implications of emotions and moods on employee behaviour at work.

Like attitude, perception, and personality, emotions and moods are yet another individual characteristics that also affect human / employee behaviour. Seeing the others behaviour or mode of conduct, we often comment like he / she is (highly) emotional or he / she is not in good mood. We also hear from some of our colleagues saying: "Today my mood is not good." Let emotions and moods be whatever they are, the fact remains that emotions and moods always remain with people and affect their behaviour. It is against this backdrop, the present chapter is devoted to discuss the various aspects of emotions and moods with their implications for organisational behaviour.

10.1 MEANING OF EMOTIONS AND MOODS

Emotions and moods vary from person to person and from time to time in case of same person and, accordingly affect the behaviour. Before we can proceed with our analysis, it seems pertinent first to clarify the terms emotions and moods and distinguish between the two.

The three terms affect, emotion, and mood are used interchangeably throughout much of the literature, without distinguishing between them. The confusion, to some extent, may be a result of the overlap among the concepts of three terms. Though we do not want to obsess over their definitions, let us define and clarify the differentiation between these three terms.

Of late, the term emotion has become a major variable in psychology and has been receiving increasing attention in the field of organisational behaviour. Similar to other psychological constructs, the exact definition and meaning of emotion are not totally agreed upon. Different authors have defined emotions differently. According to N. H. Frijda, "Emotions are intense feelings that are directed at someone or something[1]." In practice, we show our emotions when we are happy about something, angry at some person, and afraid of something. For example, we feel happy or glad when we see our friend after a long time, become angry when our directives are not followed by our subordinates, and we become afraid of technological changes to replace us in our organisation. Thus, emotions can best be described as how a person feels about something.

10.2 TYPES OF EMOTIONS

What are the types of emotions? Or how many emotions are there? Like the meaning of emotion, there is also not total agreement on the types of emotions. Some try to list as many number of emotions as they can. The list includes anger, contempt, enthusiasm, envy, fear, frustration, disappointment, disgust, happiness, hate, hope, jealousy, joy, love, pride, surprise, and sadness. There are other researchers who try to limit emotions into a few primary or basic ones such as anger, disgust, fear, happiness, sadness, and surprise. They argue that all the others are composed of some of these six basic emotions. Some researchers have tried to place these six basic emotions along a continuum ranging from happiness, surprise, fear, sadness, anger to disgust.

Table 10.1 summarizes the primary emotions and their descriptors mentioned in the psychological literature.

Table 10.1: Types of Emotions

Positive Primary Emotions	**Other Descriptors**
Love/affection	Acceptance, adoration, longing, devotion, infatuation.
Happiness/joy	Cheerfulness, contentment, bliss, delight, amusement, enjoyment, enthrallment, thrill, euphoria, zest.
Surprise	Amazement, wonder, astonishment, shock.
Negative Primary Emotions:	**Other Descriptors**
Fear	Anxiety, alarm, apprehension, concern, qualm, dread, fright, terror.
Sadness	Grief, disappointment, sorrow, gloom, despair, suffering, dejection.
Anger	Outrage, exasperation, wrath, indignation, hostility, irritability.
Disgust	Contempt, disdain, abhorrence, revulsion, distaste.
Shame	Guilt, remorse, regret, embarrassment, humiliation.

Source: Daniel Goleman: **Emotional Intelligence,** Bantam Books, New York, 1995, pp. 289-290.

Each of these emotions is common in the organisations and, hence, seems worthwhile to mention:

- (Late) Dhirubhai Ambani grew to ***love*** his team of engineers as they make Patalganga Project operational within the shortest possible time duly appreciated by Du Pont engineers.
- S. S. Khanka feels ***happy*** when the Vice Chancellor appreciated his research contribution the his Convocation Speech of the University.
- Ashutosh Das ***surprised*** to hear that the Director of his institute has resigned from the post.
- Arun Suri ***fears*** that nuclear deal with the US will be dangerous for India.
- Mrinmoy feels ***sad*** for Chandan because he contributed maximum to the development of the University but gets no recognition from the Vice Chancellor.
- Alok was ***angry*** over the Director because he was not considered for promotion to the post of Professor for the second time.
- Karan is ***disgusted*** with favouritism shown to his colleague Shekhar by the Director when the customized Management Development Programmes (MDPs) were allocated.
- Suresh Kumar Garg has a sense of ***shame*** for claiming expense reimbursement for a trip he did not take.

Plutchik[2], in his psycho-evolutionary theory of basic emotions has developed the following 10 postulates:

1. The concept of emotion being applicable to all evolutionary levels applies to animals as well as to humans.
2. Emotions have been evolutionary in various forms of expression in different species. Nonetheless, there are some common elements identifiable in different species.
3. Emotions served an adaptive role in helping organisms deal with key survival issues posed by the environment.
4. There common or prototype emotions are essentially small in their numbers.
5. All other emotions are mixed or derivative states; that is, they occur as combinations, mixtures or compounds of the primary emotions.
6. Primary emotions are hypothetical constructs in the sense that their properties and characteristics can only be inferred based on evidence.
7. All emotions vary in their degree of similarity to one another.
8. Each emotion can exist in depending on the varying degrees of intensity of arousal, emotions vary from each other.

Moods, on the other hand, tend to be less tense and also less fleeting than emotions. These are not directed at an object. Moods last for longer time than emotions. For example, one may wake up one morning feeling a bit down and stay that way for most of the day. One may also be sent into a mood by an unexpected event like, from the happiness of seeing a school day old friend to the anger of knowing cheated by a colleague. At times, one also just falls into a mood.

Difference between Affect, Emotion and Mood

There have been three inter-related terms namely, affect, emotion, and mood commonly used in the psychology literature. The meanings of emotion and mood have just been described. As regards affect, it is generic term that covers a broad range of feelings that people experience.

The specific differences between affect, emotion, and mood are summarized as follows:

"Emotions are reactions to an object, not a trait. They are object specific. You show your emotions when you are happy about something, angry at someone, afraid of something. Moods, on the other hand, are not directed at an object. Emotions can turn into moods when you lose focus on the contextual object. So when a work colleague criticizes you for the way you spoke to a client, you might become angry at him, i.e. emotion. But later in the day, you might find yourself just generally dispirited. This affective state describes a mood."[13]

That affect, emotion, and mood are closely connected and, in turn, influence each other is shown in the following exhibit 10.1:

Exhibit 10.1 : Close Connection between Affect, Emotion, and Mood

Affect

Defined as a broad range of feelings that people experience.

Affect can be experienced in the form of emotions and moods.

Emotions	**Moods**
Caused by specific event	Cause is often general and unclear.
Very brief in duration (seconds or minutes).	Last longer than emotions (hours or days).
Specific and numerous in nature.	More general (two main dimensions-positive affect and negative affect).
Usually accompanied by distinct facial expressions.	Generally not indicated by distinct expressions.
Action-oriented in nature	Cognitive in nature.

Source: Robbins, Judge, and Sanghi: **Organisational Behaviour,** Pearson Education, Delhi, 2007, p. 293.

10.3 SOURCES OF EMOTIONS AND MOODS

We all human beings experience and display emotions and moods. A human void of emotion and mood would be unable to function. Think for a moment, have we ever tried to know where our emotions and moods come from? Like types of emotions, researchers have identified not one source but more where emotions and moods come from. The main sources of emotions and moods are discussed subsequently:

1. Gender
2. Age
3. Personality
4. Time
5. Stress
6. Relaxation / Sleep
7. Exercise
8. Social Activities

Now, we will turn to discuss these main sources of emotions and moods one by one.

Gender : Like in many other matters, researchers have also tried to study and identify emotions and moods between men and women. There has been a general belief or assumption that women are more emotional than men. The research evidence confirms that women experience both positive and negative emotions more intensely and, in turn, also show greater emotional expression than men[4]. In contrasting genders, women react more emotionally and are better able to read emotions in others due to their stronger sixth sense, as believed in the Indian culture. Besides, women are better at reading and understanding non-verbal and paralinguistic cues than their counterpart men[5]. Several explanations are given to explain these gender differences in emotional reactions. Perhaps, the strongest explanation given is the social framework of the two genders. For example, men are taught to be strong and tough and, in turn, show emotions consistent with their image. In contrast, women are taught to be caring and loving. They, thus, socialize in a nurturing type of social framework. Gert Hofsteed nomenclatures the two cultural or social frameworks as masculinity and femininity[6]. As mentioned earlier, one more explanation to such gender difference is that women may have a better innate ability, also called sixth sense of women, to read and understand others and display their emotional reaction than do their counterparts, i.e., men.

Age: That age affects emotions is generally accepted, but the exact effect of age on emotions is so far not agreed upon. The general belief is that younger people experience more extreme and generally positive emotion as compared to older people do. The reason attributed to it is youthful exuberance characterized by high need for achievement.

But, research suggests contrary to it. One study reports that elder people experience less negative feeling / emotion than the younger do. Also the duration of positive emotion / mood of elder people lasted longer and the negative one faded relatively more quickly. Research has given two possible explanations. *One*, people gain experience with advancement in age that helps them better rationalize the things and experience emotions. *Second,* the intensity of negative feelings or emotions tends decrease as one becomes older and older in life[7].

Personality: What is personality? In simple words, personality is the unique and relatively stable pattern of behaviour, thoughts, and emotions shown by an individual. Research confirms that personality predisposes people to experience certain emotions and moods. Based on personality, people are classified into different types such as introverts and extroverts, and type A and type B.

You might have seen people with type A personality who experience emotions and moods very quickly like India's former cricket captain Saurav Ganguly. There are also people who are calm and cool no matter the situation like Rahul Dravin, the another cricket captain of India.. Rahul Dravin scores higher on emotional stability. Perhaps you are such one. People with emotional stability experience more positive and less negative emotions. Thomas Alwa is one such example. Extrovert and introvert personalities do also predispose people to experience emotions and moods differently in nature and degree. Let us illustrate with an imaginary example. Suppose two colleagues Ashutosh Das and Brijesh Kumar were scolded and rebuked by the chairman in a faculty meeting for not taking classes regularly and sincerely. While Ashutosh who is an extrovert, took it very positively to prove himself as a serious teacher in future, Brijesh an introvert by nature, felt it as an insult in front of colleagues and became very sad for about two days. In brief, extroverts are likely to be affected more by positive events and, in turn, positive emotions and moods. Conversely, negative events are more likely to affect the negative emotions and moods of introverts.

Time: Here, time means the day of the week and / or time of the day people experience emotions / moods. We generally work 5 days in a week from Monday to Friday. Generally, when people are to join work on Monday, they are usually low spirited perhaps because of the work load to be completed during the week ahead. But, mood starts becoming increasing with progress in work made day by day. It becomes highest positive towards the weekend with the feeling of weekend relaxation. That people tend to be in their worst mood, i.e. with the highest negative affect and lowest positive affect during the early week period and their best mood, i.e. with the highest positive affect and lowest negative affect towards the end of the week is shown by exhibit 10.2.

Exhibit 10.2 : Our Moods Are Affected by the Day of the week

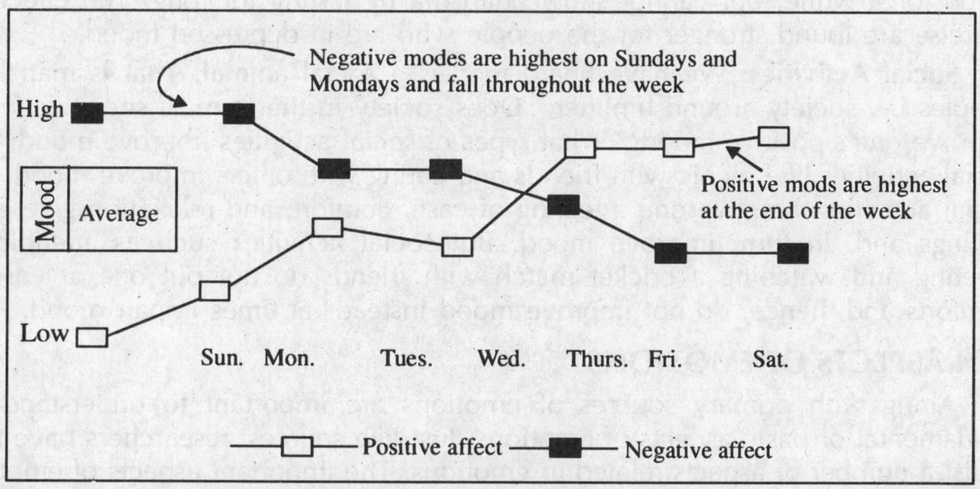

Source: D. Watson: **Mood and Temperament,** Gullford Publications, New York, 2000.

As regards time of the day, people are generally at lower positive mood in the morning which starts increasing with the joining of work till mid-day. The positive mood of the people starts decreasing towards evening as they get exhausted both mentally and physically and, in turn, feel low spirited.

Tension/Stress: Tension or stress also affects our emotions and moods. Remember, a particular stress does not remain with us life long. Stress emerges and dissipates too. To illustrate, we feel higher level of fear and tension before an interview for a job, but our fear dissipates once the interview is over. So is in case of students like you. You experience higher levels of fear or tension before an examination, but your fear/ tension dissipate once the examination is over. In a work place situation, boss's reprimand, an impending deadline, even a disturbing e-mail, and so on negatively affect our emotions and moods. Many times, such negative emotions and moods accompany us to our family also and get exhibited via our behaviour.

Rest/Relaxation: That the rest precedes the best performance is in conformity with *"a healthy mind rests in a healthy body"*. For good mind and physical health, rest or relaxations is necessary. Sleep is the best form of rest or relaxation. More the sleep and rest, better one's emotions and moods because person can coolly think over and make his/her decision. On the contrary, less sleep or no sleep causes greater feeling of fatigue, anger, and hostility. One of the reason why less or poor sleep or rest puts people in a bad mood is attributed to poor decision making and difficulty in controlling one's emotions. Besides the poor sleep previous night causes one tired, exhausted, fatigued, and irritative the next day which, in turn, impairs one's job satisfaction also. Job satisfaction also affects emotions and moods.

Exercise: Exercise is also called *"sweat therapy"* and enhances people's spirit, i.e., positive mood. Research evidence supports it. Recognizing that the exercise enhances positive moods, resulting in happier, healthier, and more productive employees, organisations have been providing fitness centers for their employees. No doubt, the effects of exercise on moods are consistent; nonetheless they are not stronger and do not last for longer period. It means exercise may improve one's mood for a while, but cannot show charisma by lasting for long. The effects of exercise are found stronger for the people who are in depressed mood.

Social Activities: We have heard man is a social animal. That is man likes peoples i.e. society around him/her. Does society in the form of social activities improve one's positive mood? What types of social activities improve mood? The social activities like picnic with friends and eating with others improve mood. The social activities that give one a feeling of ease, comfort, and relaxation give good feelings and, in turn, improve mood. But social activities such as attending a meeting and watching a cricket match with friends do not put one at ease or comforts and, hence, do not improve mood instead at times impair mood.

10.4 ASPECTS OF EMOTIONS

Along with primary sources of emotions are important to understand the fundamental or basic aspects of emotions. Just like sources, researchers have tried to list a number of aspects related to emotions. The important aspects of emotions are shown in the following exhibit 10.3:

Exhibit 10.3 : Aspects of Emotions

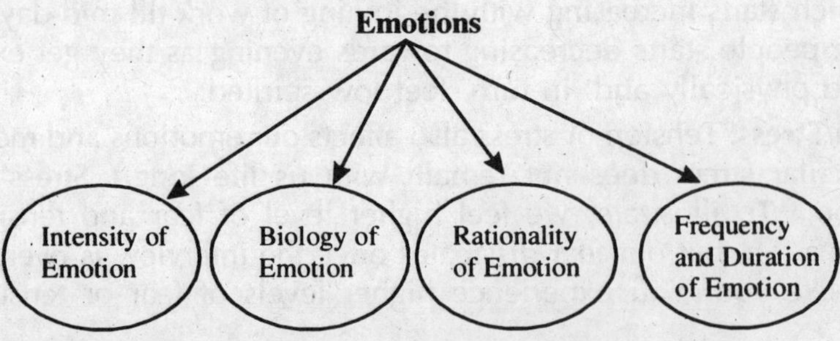

Let us discuss these in seriatim.

Intensity of Emotion: We all experience emotions but not in the same intensity in response to the same or identical stimuli. Look at the people around you be in the family or in the college or in the work organisation, you will find different people show their emotions in varying intensities. You may find people who seem to be on an emotional roller coaster. When they are happy, they are highly ecstatic. But, when they are sad, they are deeply depressed and too much low spirited. You may also find people who remain almost calm and cool, rarely get angry and seldom show anger. So to say, there are some people who hardly show their feelings. In nutshell, the intensity aspect of emotion is related to one's personality and it has just discussed a little ago. Intensity of emotion is also affected by the nature of job one holds. In practice, there may be some jobs where job holder needs to alter his / her emotional intensity as and when need arises. Lawyers and public administrators may be such examples.

Biology of Emotion: Emotions are cognitive in nature. A specific biology works how cognition takes place. Emotions originate in the brain's limbic system of the person[8]. The size of the limbic system of brain is about the size of a walnut. The relatively inactive limbic system makes a person to be happy, i. e. person experiences more positive than negative emotions. The nature of job a person holds also affects the intensity of emotion. For example, a receptionist, a traffic controller, and a moderator in a panel discussion need to be cool, calm, and controlled even in stressful situations. Contrary to it, the active limbic system of the person causes negative emotion when sadness dominance over happiness. To put simply, limbic system works like a lens. That is one finds things positive when limbic system is inactive and negative when limbic system is active.

Frequency and Duration of Emotion: Experience shows that responding to one's emotional demands depends not only on what emotions in what intensity need to be displayed, but also on how frequently and for how long one needs to display emotions. Let us exemplify this with an example. Suppose, Prof. Amarjyoti Choudhary, the Vice Chancellor of Gauhati University, is by nature a very quit and reserved person. He likes and enjoys his teaching job as an academician. But, he does not like to give speeches and attend social functions to make him known and visible in the society. But as a Vice Chancellor, he still has to attend programmes and give speeches. He expresses his experience: *"If I had to give large number of speeches and that too to large audiences every day, I would like to quit this job. I think this is good for me because I can fake the interest for a short time only, not for ever."*

Rationality of Emotion: Finally, rationality is yet another important aspect of emotions. That is, should a person experience and demonstrate emotion or not? There is, of course, no agreement on this. A group of thinkers including the famous astronomer Carl Sugan disapprove emotion in human conduct. Carl Sugan once viewed: *"Where we have strong emotions, we are liable to fool ourselves."* They view that emotion and rationality are in conflict with one another and demonstration of emotion is very likely to make one act irrationally[9]. Emotional display is likely to make us more often than not weak, down, discouraged, brittle, or irrational.

At the same time, there is also research evidence to believe that human devoid of emotion would be unable to function and remain alive as well. Emotions are found critical for rational thinking. Research studies on human brain found that losing the ability to emote led to the loss of the ability to reason. From this discovery, researchers learned that our emotions provide us with valuable information that improves our thinking process[10]. Emotions provide us information and knowledge about how we see and understand the things around us. Emotions, thus, help us rationalize things as good or bad. To sum up, emotions enable us to use both feeling and thinking which are considered the hallmarks of good decision making.

Some authors have identified three major aspects of emotions[11]. These are discussed in turn.

1. *Emotion is a feeling that is personal and subjective as well.* Of course, human beings can report an extraordinary range of states, which they can feel or experience. Some reports are accompanied by obvious signs of enjoyment or distress, but often these reports have no overt indicators to mention. In many cases, the emotions we note in ourselves seem to be blends of different states.

2. *Emotion is a state of psychological arousal, i.e., an expression or display of distinctive somatic and autonomic responses.* This emphasis suggests that emotional states can be defined by particular constellations of bodily responses. Specifically, these responses involve autonomously innervated visceral organs, like the heart or stomach. This second aspect of emotion allows us to examine emotions in both animals and human beings.

3. *Emotions are actions commonly deemed such as defending or attacking in response to a threat.* This aspect of emotion is especially relevant to Darwin's point of view of the functional roles of emotion. He said that emotions had an important survival role because they generated actions to dangerous situations.

10.5 THEORIES OF EMOTION

Emotions being an end, the psychologists and physiologists have tried to understand and explain what causes emotions. In other words, they have tried to identify the causes of emotions by developing cause-effect relationship between the two. The important theories of emotions are discussed as follows:

James-Lange Theory: This theory was proposed way back in 1884 by William James and Danish Physiologist Carl Lange and has been considered the oldest theory of emotion[12]. This theory is founded on the experiences we have in our lives that creates physiological reactions / events such as muscular tension, heart rate increases, perspiration, dryness of the mouth, etc. In essence, this theory proposes that emotions happen as a result of our reactions, rather than being the cause of them. While explaining his theory, William James mentions:

> "My theory ... is that the bodily changes follow directly the perception of the exciting fact, and that our feeling of the same changes as they occur is the emotion. Common sense says we lose our fortune, are sorry and weep; we meet a bear, are frightened and run; we are insulted by a rival, and angry and strike. The hypothesis here to be defended says that this order of sequence is incorrect ...

and that the more rational statement is that we feel sorry because we cry, angry because we strike, afraid because we tremble ... Without the bodily states following on the perception, the latter would be purely cognitive in form, pale, colorless, destitute of emotional warmth. We might then see the bear, and judge it best to run, receive the insult and deem it right to strike, but we should not actually feel afraid or angry[13]."

Despite being an old theory, it has also certain implications for managing emotions. That this theory also serves as a basis of behaviour modification approach can be exemplified with an imaginary example. Suppose, if a person wants to become democratic in his decision taking function, he/ she should consult and listen to others' views. If the person continues his consulting behaviour for some time, his/ her behaviour, thus, gets modified and starts enjoying the modified behaviour. Daniel Goleman explains such modification in behaviour by giving an example of 'managing' anger by one's changing behaviour[14].

Cannon-Bard Theory: This theory is also one of the oldest theories of emotions. According to this theory, emotions precede responses. In other words, action is the effect for which emotion is the cause. People feel emotions first as stimulus and then respond to action upon stimulus. Yes, actions may be of varied types like breathing, muscular tension, and perspiration. For example, when we see a snake, we become afraid (i. e. emotion) and start perspiration (action or response). In nutshell, this theory postulates that an action (response) is the effect for which emotion is the cause (stimulus).

Two-Factor Theory: Schachter and Singer have proposed this theory of emotions[15]. In a way, this theory resembles with the Cannon-Bard Theory of Emotion in the sense that it is also developed on the premise that people experience feelings (emotions) first and then try to know and understand its meaning. For example, when we suffer from fever, we try to find the cause of fever from its symptoms like shivering cold. Thus, this theory is based on the experience of physical arousal.

How to Express Emotions

As mentioned earlier, all living beings experience emotions or feelings. Emotions affect our action/ behaviour. In other words, emotions get expressions via behaviour. Hence, the need for understanding how to express emotions. It is easy to express emotions. Every one does it. But to express emotion in a right manner, at right time, and in right proportion is not so simple. It requires some thinking. There can not be a universally accepted and applicable way to all experiencing and expressing emotions. The reason is not difficult to seek. The manner used to express emotion may vary from person to person and from situation to situation. In fact, self-help approach may help on better respond to one's emotions. Following are some guidelines that may help one express his / her emotions in a better manner:

Accept and Recognize the Emotions: Remember that emotions do not emerge in vacuum. Instead, emotions succeed some happenings. For example, a student experiences sadness, or say, sad emotion on his failure in the examinations. A teacher feels happiness on the publication of his research article in an international journal of high academic repute.

Find Out the Alternative Ways to Express the Emotion: An emotion can be expressed in various manners and the person has to decide his / her manner to express the emotion. For example, in our above example, a student may have several options to express his sadness on failure in the examinations. He may keep regretting his failure for weeks together. He may give up the idea to reappear in the examinations. He may blame the examiner for awarding him less mark. He may ponder over the reasons for his failure and devise action-plan for hard study in future.

Besides, following are some relevant questions to be considered and answered while deciding the appropriate manner to express one's emotions[16]:

- Does the intensity of my feelings appropriate as per the situation?
- Do I also have other feelings that I need to pay due attention to?
- What are the options available to me to express my feelings?
- What are the merits and demerits of each option for me?
- What are the advantages and disadvantages of each option for others?
- What end result do I expect?
- What do I ultimately want to do?
- What will be the consequences if I do not do any thing?

10.6 AFFECTIVE EVENTS THEORY (AET)

By now, it is clear that emotions and moods are an integral part of our day-to-day life, more especially in our work lives. Then an obvious question arises is whether emotions and moods also affect our job behaviour and, in turn, performance. Attempts have been made by the researchers to examine the relationship between emotions and job performance. The two organisational psychologists Howard M. Weiss of Purdue University and Russell Cropanzano of University of Arizona developed a model to identify how emotions and moods influence job satisfaction and job performance. The model is popularly known as *'Affective Events Theory* (*AET*).[17]' The model proposes that organisational events are proximal causes of affective reactions.

What is event? The concept of event is not well defined in the literature. Weiss and Cropanzano[18] used definitions from the World Book Dictionary, i.e. "*a happening especially an important happening*" and from the Random House Dictionary, i.e. "*something that occurs in a certain place during a particular period of time.*" From the point of view of emotion, simply event is not important but affect-eliciting event is important. In other words, it is the appraisal, evaluation, and interpretation of events, rather than the events themselves that determine the emotion that is experienced[19].

The relationship between workplace events, emotions, and behaviour is summarized in the following exhibit 10.4:

Exhibit 10.4 Affective Events Theory

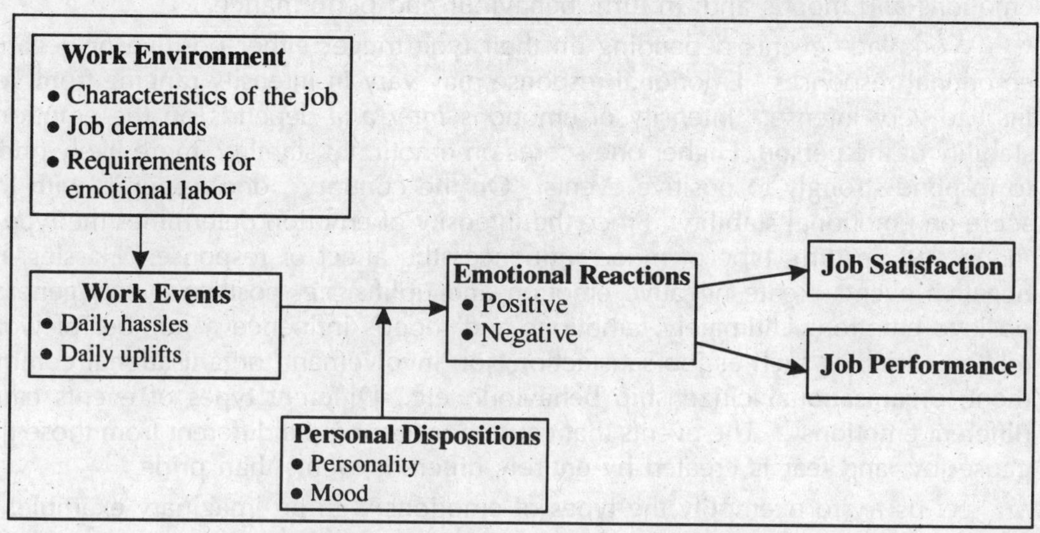

Source: N. M. Ashkanasy and C. S. Daus: Emotion in the Workplace: The New Challenge for Managers, ***Academy of Management Executive,*** February 2002, p. 77.

The AET is developed on the assumption that our emotions are response to an event in the work environment. In an organisational context, work environment refers to every thing surrounding the workplace. Examples of such things may be job varieties and their characteristics, autonomy, job demands, and emotional labour. The work environment creates work events that can be either hassles or uplift or even both. Hassle means happening that creates confusion. The common examples of hassle at the workplace are contradictory or confronting directives given by different superiors, avoiding to performing the assigned job, declining to perform some crucial task at the last moment, etc.

Many things happen at the workplace and, in turn, affect peoples' emotions and behaviour. A research study shows that people who sought out others, including co-workers, when good things happened to them were consistently happier than those who did not share their good news[20]. Added to this is if two people both have positive things happen to them, the happier person would be the one who shared the good news. Here, it is also important to mention that the response of person with whom good things or news are shared is also important to generate happiness. So to say, only genuine enthusiasm of others to one's good thing does generate happiness, the indifference or feigned response does not.

There is yet another type of workplace event that at times people experience one type of emotion but simultaneously display other type of emotion. The former is termed as *'felt emotion'* and the latter as *'displayed emotion.'* There can be many such workplace events. For example, the ritual look of delight on the face of the first runner-up as the *'Indian Idol'* is announced by the anchor is a display emotion of the loser to mask his/her felt sadness with a display emotion of happiness for the winner of the *'Indian Idol.'* This means employees need to display organisationally desired emotions during interpersonal transactions at the workplace. This is also called *'emotional labour.'* Obviously, emotional labour is likely to affect employees' emotions and moods and, in turn, behaviour and performance.

Workplace events depending on their type trigger either positive or negative emotional responses. Emotional response may vary in intensity ranging from very light to very intense. Intensity of emotions *inter alia* depends on the emotional stability of the person. Higher one scores on emotional stability, more likely one is to respond strongly to positive events. On the contrary, one responds with low score on emotional stability. Since the intensity of emotion determines the type of mood and, in turn, type of mood influences the affect or response. Hassles, i.e. negative events create negative emotion and uplifts, i.e. positive events generate positive emotion. Ultimately, emotions and moods influence a number of work-related variables such as job satisfaction, job involvement, organisational commitment, organisational citizenship behaviour, etc.. Different types of events cause different emotions[21]. The events that cause anger are quite different from those that cause joy, and fear is created by entirely different events than pride.

Let us try to exemplify the types of emotions with an imaginary example.

You have been working as a Professor in HRM in the National Institute of Financial Management, Faridabad (Haryana) for the last one year. Because of the forte of the Institute on financial management, you have just learned that the Institute is considering outsourcing of faculties in HRM and economics areas. Expectedly, the outsourcing event is likely to experience a fear, i.e. negative emotion that you might lose your job and income. Not only that, it also leads to a series of events called *'emotional episode'.* You approached the Director and the Director assures you that your job is safe. One faculty who is also a member in the Institute's Board of Management, tells you that the matter of outsourcing faculties is in the agenda of the Institute's next Board of Management (BOM) meeting. Someone also told you that the proposal of outsourcing faculties in the allied subjects has already been implemented in some other similar type of national institutes. Yet another colleague of yours told that Government is to rehabilitate the layoff faculties in some other national-level institutes. Just think how are you affected by above events? Some day you experience good or upbeat or positive emotion or other day you feel depressed or low or negative emotion. You, thus, experience emotional swings which affect your work attitude, behaviour, and performance.

In sum and substance, the AET offers the message that emotions and moods affect work attitude, behaviour, and, in turn, performance.

10.7 EMOTIONAL INTELLIGENCE

Before we discuss emotional intelligence, let us first define the two terms emotional and intelligence separately. In brief, emotion means a strong mental and instinctive feeling such as love or fear. Intelligence means the quickness of a person's thinking, reasoning, and understanding faculty. Psychologists have been uncovering other types of intelligences for some time now, and grouping them mainly into three clusters: *abstract intelligence* (the ability to understand and manipulate with verbal and mathematic symbols), *concrete intelligence* (the ability to understand and manipulate with objects), and, *social intelligence* (the ability to understand and relate to people).[22] Edward L. Thorndike defines social intelligence as *"the ability to understand and manage men and women, boys and girls - to act wisely in human relations.[23]"*

Howard Gardner has identified three distinct types of intelligence[24]:

1. **Linguistic Intelligence:** Persons who manifest this type of intelligence are good at writing, reading, telling stories or solving crossword puzzles.
2. **Logical-Mathematical Intelligence:** People high on logical intelligence are interested in patterns, categories and relationships. They are attracted to arithmetical problems, strategy games and experiments.
3. **Bodily-Kinesthetic Intelligence:** This type of intelligence processes knowledge through bodily sensations and such persons are often athletes, dancers or good at crafts such as sewing and woodwork.

Now that we have defined the two terms emotional and intelligence separately, we can now profitably explain the meaning of *'emotional intelligence (EQ).'* The concept of emotional quotient (EQ) was first coined by Reuven Bar-On in 1988 in his doctoral dissertation[25]. However, the term emotional intelligence was first used by the two American psychologists, Peter Salovey of Yale University and John Mayer of the University of New Hampshire[26]. They summed up emotional intelligence as human qualities such as empathy, self-awareness, and emotional control. Salovey and Mayor defined emotional intelligence as *"the ability to monitor the feelings of the self and others, discriminate among them and use this information to guide one's thinking and action."* For a while, the term they coined and used - emotional intelligence - languished in academic obscurity. Being a cognitive construct, different thinkers have defined EQ differently.

According to Bar-On and Parker: *"Emotional intelligence is an array of emotional, personal and social abilities which influence one's overall ability to cope effectively with environmental demands and pressures.[27]"*

It was the psychologist/journalist Daniel Goleman of The New York Times, who adopted the term 'emotional intelligence' and introduced it in his bestseller *'Emotional Intelligence - Why It Can Matter More Than IQ*[28]. He gave the term a new meaning of emotional intelligence. He defined emotional intelligence as: *"The capacity for recognizing our own feelings and those of others, for motivating ourselves, and for managing emotions well in ourselves and in our relationships."*

An Indian author Dilip Singh defined emotional intelligence in the Indian context in these words: *"Emotional intelligence is the ability of an individual to appropriately and successfully respond to a variety of emotional stimuli elicited from the inner self and the immediate environment.*[29]

The meaning of emotional intelligence can best be summed up by quoting the views of Aristotle: *"Anyone can become angry-that is easy. But to be angry with the right person, to the right degree at the right time, for the right purpose and in the right way is not that easy."*

There are four essential ingredients as corner stones for emotional intelligence[30]. These are:

1. Emotional Literacy
2. Emotional Fitness
3. Emotional Domain
4. Emotional Alchemy

Now, a brief description of these follows:

Emotional Literacy: Just as general literacy enables people to be aware of what is happening around them, emotional literacy helps people become more aware of their as well as other people's emotions. By managing emotions in others, problem-solving becomes easier and better. Emotional literacy also helps build self-confidence through emotional honesty, energy, emotional feedback, intuition, responsibility, and connection.

Emotional Fitness: What significant role physical fitness plays in doing physical/mental activities with confidence and resilience, so does emotional intelligence in the case of feelings. Emotional fitness strengthens one's resilience and believability for listening and managing conflict.

Emotional Domain: Emotional domain means realm of control by emotions. It explores the ways to align one's life and work with his / her unique potential and purpose.

Emotional Alchemy: Through emotional alchemy, one extends one's creative instincts and capability to flow with problems and pressures. It also enables one to compete for the future by building one's capacity to sense more readily and assess the hidden solutions and untapped potential and possibilities.

Emotional Competence

Effectiveness of emotional intelligence depends on emotional competence. What is emotional competence? An emotional competence can be defined as one's underlying capability that results in better and/or superior performance at work. Daniel Goleman, based on his research, has identified five broad dimensions of emotional competence, also called by some people as 'dimensions of emotional intelligence'[31]. These are:

Self-awareness: The ability to recognize one's emotions as well its effect on those around us.

Self-regulation: The ability to control one's impulsive judgement and reaction.

Self-motivation: The ability to pursue goals persistently as a higher calling and not for money or status alone.

Empathy: The ability to empathize with emotional state of others and respond accordingly. This is popularly expressed as "put your shoes in others shoe."

Social Skills: The ability to network and build rapport with others.

The above five dimensional framework of emotional competency is subsumed into twenty-five competencies as shown in the following Table 10.2:

Table 10.2 : Emotional Competency Framework

Major Dimensions	Sub-dimensions
Self-awareness	1. Emotional self-awareness 2. Accurate self-assessment 3. Self-confidence
Self-regulation	1. Self-control 2. Trustworthiness 3. Conscientiousness 4. Adaptability 5. Innovativeness
Self-motivation	1. Achievement drive 2. Commitment 3. Initiative 4. Optimism
Empathy	1. Service orientation 2. Developing others 3. Leveraging Diversity 4. Social awareness 5. Political awareness
Social skills	1. Influence 2. Communication 3. Leadership 4. Change catalyst 5. Conflict management 6. Building bonds 7. Collaboration and cooperation 8. Team capacity

Subsequently, some researchers[32], based on his factor analysis study on emotional competence, zeroed the above listed twenty five competencies to four major categories as shown in Table 10.3 . The classification labels one axis as awareness and management and the other axis as self and others.

Table 10.3: A Framework of Major Emotional Competencies

	Self (Personal Competence)	**Others (Social Competence)**
Awareness	*Self-awareness* (understanding feelings and accurate self-assessment)	*Social awareness* (reading people and groups accurately)
Management	*Self-management* (managing internal states, impulses and resources)	*Relationship management* (inducing desirable response in others)

Benefits of Emotional Intelligence

Should emotions be displayed at workplace or not has been a topic of debate among the scholars. According to conventional school of thought, the workplace is not the right place for emotions. The reason attributed to this belief is that emotions disrupt the organisational order carefully crafted over the years and causes indiscipline at the workplace. This is generally prompted by the mistaken notion that work is serious business and any display of emotions ought to be regarded with extreme suspicion. Hence emotions had to be reigned in, buttoned up, and locked away. However, the fast paced developments taken place in the business world since mid-eighties has intensified interest in emotional intelligence. Prodigious volume of research work carried out on the subject over the period has turned the tide. There is research evidence to believe that emotional intelligence proves competitive advantage for organisations. It is increasingly recognized that intelligence quotient (IQ) may account for only about 20 per cent of a person's success in life. The remaining 80 per cent depends largely on a person's emotional intelligence (EQ). It is also opined that one may get a good job with high IQ, but one must also have a high EQ to up the ladder. That emotional intelligence (EQ) helps one grow and develop in one's career and life can be exemplified with some examples.

Mother Teresa who was an ordinary nun could do so much service to poor and needy with no resources of her own. Mahatma Gandhi presents another example of high IQ as well high EQ to make India independent from the colonial regime. M. S. Oberoi and Dhirubhai Ambani rose from humble beginnings to build vast business empires all over the world. The college drop out Bill Gates succeeded to build a vast empire like Micro Soft for which he is envied by the entire world. There are many people who could not complete their education and dropped out, but went on to be extremely successful in business and life. Nelson Mandela also opines that a good head (IQ) and a good heart (EQ) are always a formidable combination for achieving success in career and life. Following is an anecdote of this type:

There is a tale about two MBA students - Peter and Mathew.

Emotional intelligence benefits people and, in turn, the organisations why they work in multiple ways. There is research evidence to believe that emotional intelligence helps managers or leaders create competitive advantage, i.e. a mantra for success in today's business[33]. Following is an abridged list of competitive advantages that emotional intelligence may offer to an organisation:

Table 10.4 : Competitive Advantages through Emotional Intelligence

1.	Increased Performance
2.	Effective leaders
3.	More teamwork
4.	Initiative and infectious enthusiasm result in quality customer service
5.	Improved and enhanced innovation
6.	Effective use of time and resources
7.	Restored trust
8.	Courage and resilience in times of adverse environment

Emotional intelligence is found more useful and effective in management which involves decision-making. This is so because Emotional Quotient) EQ enables managers to have skills motivating oneself, managing relationships, and being able to get along well with subordinates and teammates. Research studies have also established that emotional intelligence plays a prominent role in group effectiveness of an individual. It is often opined that one may get a good job with high IQ, but one must also have a high EQ to go up the ladder. EQ helps a manager manage him / her and others in a meaningful manner so that the goals - both individual and organisational - are achieved.

The major EQ ingredients with their contributions to the organisation are summarized in the following Table 10.5:

Table 10.5: EQ Ingredients and Their Contributions

EQ Ingredients	Their Contributions
• Motivating oneself as well as others around one.	• Multiplies achievements.
• Adopting empathy towards others.	• Works like magic.
• Controlling negative thinking.	• Checks from spoiling.
• Building confidence and developing trust.	• Returns from investments (you get when you give).
• Managing conflicts.	• Resolves what causes conflict.
• Building stress immunity.	• Adjusts one to cope with stressors.
• Controlling anger.	• Cools thoughts and feelings.
• Building and maintaining a cohesive team.	• Win cooperation, i.e. a must to perform group activities.

10.8 OB APPLICATIONS OF EMOTIONS AND MOODS

Before we leave this chapter, one last mention about application of emotions and moods to OB seems relevant. Emotions and moods being psychological constructs affect almost all aspects of human behaviour, i.e. OB. However, we shall examine here how an understanding of emotions and moods can affect OB with respect to employee selection, motivation, leadership, decision making, employee conflict, and job attitudes. Now, we shall reflect on these in seriatim.

Employee Selection

It will not be less than correct to mention that employee selection in like marriage between employee and employer, i.e. organisation and hence, needs good compatibility or harmonious match between the two for organisational success. Experience suggests that considering employees' emotions in selection process especially for the jobs that involve more social interaction helps hire right employees for the organisation. There is evidence to believe that employees with higher levels of positive emotions perform better than those with lower levels of emotions. A study of sales personnel showed that the sales persons scoring higher on emotional intelligence measures performed two-third more than those selected using traditional selection procedure[34]. This is the reason why increasing number of employers are, of late, not only using emotional intelligence measure to select employees but also impart training on emotional intelligence to their employees. For example, all new financial advisors in the American Express receive four days of emotional competence training.[35]

Motivation

Emotions and moods through AET also help motivate employees to exert more efforts for the attainment of organisational goals. As is generally believed, research also supports that good or positive emotions and moods motivate people to perform their jobs. In a research study, two groups of people were asked to solve some word puzzles. One group was shown a funny video clip with an objective to generate good or positive emotions and moods before starting to solve the puzzles. The other group, i.e. controlled group was not shown any video clip and it just started solving the puzzles. The results were quite different and encouraging. The first group with positive mood solved more puzzles and worked harder at them than the second, i.e. controlled group[36]. Thus, the study suggests that instilling and strengthening positive emotions and moods helps have more motivated workforce.

Leadership

Leadership is one's ability to influence followers to willingly exert higher level of efforts to achieve the organisational goals. Emotions and moods help leaders influence employees to act as per their vision. For this, leaders at times opt for the evocation, framing, and mobilization of their emotions to arouse affective feelings in their employees to accept and act for the leaders' vision. It is also seen that when leaders are in high spirit and enthusiastic for organisational cause, they may use emotional contagion to convey them a sense of self-efficiency, competence, internal locus of control, positively, etc. Research also reports that when leaders are in good mood, their followers are more positive and, in turn, more cooperative and productive as well[37].

Decision Making

Decision making involves selecting the best based on rationality amongst the alternatives available. Researchers have also tried to examine the role of emotions and moods in decision making activity. OB researchers are in agreement that positive emotions and moods help make good decision. However, they are in continuous debate on the effect of negative emotions and moods in decision making activity. Some researchers suggest that people in depressed or sad or negative mood make better decisions. For them the saying "sadder but wiser" holds true. But there are some other researchers who forward evidence to argue that people in depressed or negative mood make poorer decisions than people in happy and positive mood. The justification they give is that the depressed or sad people are poorer and slower in rationalizing the things involved in decision making activity. In contrast, happy people are better able to analyze and rationalize the issues involved in decision making activity and, in turn, making good / better decision.

Employee Conflict

Emotions and moods have been at the root of interpersonal compatibility and conflict between the employees. In other words, incompatibility in feelings or emotions causes conflict between the employees. The successes of a manager in conflict resolution, therefore, largely depends on identifying incompatible and / or deviant emotions and moods between employees and, then, try to resort to emotional compatibility. As mentioned earlier also, managers can use emotional mapping, evocation, and mobilization to establish emotional compatibility between the employees and thus, resolve inter-personal conflicts.

Job Attitudes

Job attitude means liking or disliking of job holder towards his / her job. A question asked is: Does job attitude affect employee's emotions and moods? Answer is generally in affirmative. If we ourselves introspect into our case we find that when we have a good day in the institution or organisation where we study or work, we tend to be in a good mood at home also that evening. Just contrary also holds true, i.e. when we had a bad day at work also tend to be in bad mood at home that evening. Depending on the intensity of the bad mood resulting from a bad day at work, it may also be carried over to the next day to work place. That is why we at times hear an advice: *"never take your work home with you."* But, this is easier sad than done because emotions and moods accompany a person just like his / her shadow does. Just as shadow cannot be seen all the times, similarly emotions and moods may not be felt all the times. Nonetheless, these are always with the person. No person may be devoid of emotions and moods.

SUMMARY

This summary is organised by the 'learning objectives' given on page no. 156 :

- *Emotions are intense feelings directed at someone or something. Moods are relatively less intense feelings that last longer than emotions. Affect is a generic term that covers a broad range of feelings that people experience in their lives.*
- *Emotions and moods come from various sources such as gender, age, personality, day and time, stress, exercise, social activities, etc.*
- *The aspects of emotions like intensity, biology, frequency, and rationality affect human behaviour.*
- *The major theories of emotions that explain cause-effect relationship between emotion and response include James-Lange Theory,Cannon-Bard Thoeory, and Two-Factor Theory.*
- *A model that explains the relationship between emotions and human (organisational) behaviour is called 'Affective Events Theory (AET)'.*
- *An individual's capacity for recognizing one's own feelings and those of others for managing emotions to deal well with others is called 'emotional intelligence'.*
- *The need for and significance of emotional intelligence lies in the fact that it improves human behaviour and, in turn, performance. Research reports that IQ accounts for only about 20 per cent of a person's success in life. The balance can be attributed to EQ, i.e., 'Emotional Intelligence.'*

REVIEW QUESTIONS

1. Define the terms emotion, mood and affect. Distinguish them with examples.
2. "Human beings devoid of emotions cannot function." Explain.
3. Where do emotions come from? Explain with your own case.
4. Explain with examples how 'Affective Events Theory' affects human emotions and behaviour.
5. Define emotional intelligence. Describe the dimensions of emotional intelligence with examples.
6. What is meant by emotional competence? Consider your own case and explain your emotional competencies.
7. "Performance depends 20% on intelligence and 80% on emotional intelligence." Elaborate.
8. Highlight, with examples, OB application of emotions and moods.

REFERENCES

1. N. J. Frijda: Moods, Emotion Episodes and Emotion, In: M. Lewis and J. M. Haviland (Eds.): **Handbook of Emotions,** Guilford Press, New York, 1993, pp. 381-403.
2. R. Plutchick: **Emotion: A Psycho Evolutionary Synthesis,** Harper & Row, New York, 1980.
3. Robbins, Judge and Sanghi: **Organizational Behaviour,** Pearson Education, Delhi, 2008, p. 292.
4. A. M. Kring and A. H. Gordon: Sex Differences in Emotion: Expression, Experience, and Physiology, **Journal of Personality and Social Psychology,** March 1998, pp. 686-703.
5. J. A. Hall: **Nonverbal Sex Differences: Communication Accuracy and Expressive Style,** Johns Hopkins Press, Batlimore, 1984.
6. Greet Hofstede: **Culture's Consequences: International Differences in Work Related Values,** Sage Publications, Beverly Hills, Calif, 1980.
7. L. L. Carstensen, M. Pasupathi, M. Ulrich, and J. R. Nesselroade: Emotional Experience in Everyday Life Across the Adult Life Span, **Journal of Personality and Social Psychology,** Vol. 79, No. 4, 2000, pp. 644-655.
8. J. Nolte: **The Human Brain,** Mosby, St. Louis, 2002.
9. www.womesmedia.com.
10. A. R. Damasio: **Descartes' Error: Emotion, Reason, and Human Brain,** Quill, New York, 1994.
11. http://library.thinkquest.org.
12. W. B. Cannon: The James-Lange Theory of Emotions, **American Journal of Psychology,** Vol. 39, 1927, pp. 115-124.
13. *Ibid.*
14. Daniel Goleman: **Emotional Intelligence,** Bantam Books, New York, 1995.
15. S. Schachter: **The Psychology of Affiliation,** Stanford University Press, Stanford, C. A., 1959.
16. Experiencing and Expressing Emotions, Self-Help Brochure of Counseling Center at the University of Illinois, *http://* www.couns.uiuc.edu

17. H. M. Weiss and R. Cropanzano: Affective Events Theory: A Theoretical Discussion of the Structure, Causes and Consequences of Affective Experiences at Work, **Research in Organisational Behaviour,** 1996, Vol. 18, pp. 1-74.
18. I. J. Roseman, M. S. Spindel and P. E. Jose: Appraisal of Emotion-Eliciting Events: Testing a Theory of Discrete Emotions, **Journal of Personality and Social Psychology,** Volume 59, No. 5, 1990, pp. 899-915.
19. cited by Robbins, Judge, and Sanghi: **Organisational Behaviour** 12th Edition, Pearson Education, Delhi, 2007, p. 302.
20. C. E. Izard: **The Psychology of Emotions,** Plenum Press, New York, 1991.
21. Edward L. Thorndike: **The Meaning of Intelligence,** Macmillan, New York, 1927.
22. *Ibid,* p. 228.
23. Howard Gardner: **Frames of Mind: The Theory of Multiple Intelligences** (10th Anniversary Edition), Basic Books, New York, 1993.
24. Reuven Bar-on: Emotional and Social Intelligence: Insights from the Emotional Quotient Inventory, In: Reuven Bar-on and J. D. A. Parker (Eds.) **Handbook of Emotional Intelligence,** Jossey-Bass, San Francisco, 2000.
25. P. Salovey and J. D. Mayer: Emotional Intelligence, **Imagination, Cognition and Personality,** Vol. 9, No. 3, 1990, pp. 185-211.
26. R. Bae-On and J. D. A. Parker (Eds.) **The Handbook of Emotional Intelligence,** Jossey-Bass, San Francisco, 2000.
27. Daniel Goleman: **Emotional Intelligence,** Bantam, New York, 1995.
28. S. S. Khanka: Use Emotional Intelligence to Climb, **Yojana,** February 2004, p. 39.
29. Daniel Goleman: What Makes a Leader?, **Harvard Business Review,** 1998, Nov.-Dec. 1998, pp. 93-102.
30. R. Boyatzis, D. Goleman, and K. Rhee: Clustering Competence in Emotional Intelligence: Insight from the Emotional Competence Inventory (ECI), In: R. Bar-On and J. D. A. Parker (Eds.): **Handbook of Emotional Intelligence,** Jossey-Bass, San Francisco, 2000.
31. R. S. Dwivedi: Identifying Emotional Intelligence Related Competencies among Highly Successful Managers for Corporate Success, **Paradigm,** Volume 6, No. 1, Jan-June, 2002, pp. 10-28.
32. R. Boyatzis: The Financial Impact of Competencies in Leadership and Management of Consulting Firms, **Development of Organisational Behaviour Working Paper,** Case Western Reserve University, Cleveland, 1999.
33. www.6seconds.org.2003
34. J. M. George: Emotions and leadership: The Role of Emotional Intelligence, **Human Relations,** August 2000, pp. 1027-1055.
35. D.M. Mathur: Emotional Intelligence in Effective Management, Indian Management, November 2000, pp.19-21.
36. *Ibid.*
37. Daniel Goleman: ***op. cit.,*** 1998.

Exercise 10.1 : Emotional Intelligence Test (Developed by N. K. Chadha)

The Test

1. **You have been ignored for a promotion by the management for which you were eligible. Moreover, one of your juniors has been promoted. You are upset and feel frustrated. What do you do?**
   a. Talk it over with your boss and ask for reconsideration of the management's decision.
   b. Start abusing the colleague who superseded you.
   c. Move to court and obtain a stay order to get justice.
   d. Identify your shortcomings and try to improve your performance.
2. **A freshly recruited professional graduate joins your organisation as a management trainee. After a few weeks, she complains to you that her superiors and subordinates were not taking her seriously. What will you suggest to her?**
   a. Ask her to handle the situation herself and not bother you with trivial matters.
   b. Tell her that such behaviour should be ignored.
   c. Ask her to be bold, face the challenge and overcome the problem.
   d. Empathies with her and help her figure out ways to get others to work with her.
3. **At the workplace, due to some misunderstanding, your colleagues stop talking to you. You are convinced that it was no fault of yours. How will you react?**
   a. Wait till they come and start talking again.
   b. Take the initiative, go forward and start talking to them.
   c. Let things take their own time to improve.
   d. Ask someone to mediate.
4. **You get into an argument with your colleague in the course of which you end up personally attacking him/her. However, you never intended to tarnish the image of your colleague. How will you tackle this ugly situation?**
   a. Sit calmly and consider what triggered off the argument and was it possible to control your anger at that point of time.
   b. Avoid future arguments and leave the scene.
   c. Apologies to your colleague.
   d. Continue with the argument till you reach some definite conclusion.
5. **Imagine you are an insurance salesperson approaching prospective clients to purchase insurance policies. A dozen people in a row slam the door on your face. What will you do?**
   a. Blame yourself and stop work for the day.
   b. Reassess your capabilities as an insurance salesperson.
   c. Come out with fresh strategies to overcome similar situations in future.
   d. Contact the clients again some other day.
6. **While speaking to an audience, you:**
   a. Find it difficult to convey your ideas.
   b. Find that only a part of the audience follows your speech.
   c. Are comfortable in conveying your ideas to the audience.
   d. Don't know if the audience is following you or not.

7. **You are on an aircraft and suddenly the pilot announces that it has been hijacked by the terrorists. Everyone is in a state of shock. What will be your reaction?**
   a. Blame yourself for choosing an inauspicious day for traveling.
   b. Be in emotional control and attend to the instructions of the pilot/air hostess.
   c. Continue to read your magazine and pay little attention to the incident.
   d. Cry out and vow not to travel by air in future.
8. **Imagine that you are a police officer posted in a sensitive area. You get information of violent ethnic clashes between two religious communities in which people have been killed from both sides and property damaged. What action will you take?**
   a. Decide not to visit the spot personally as there may be a danger to your life.
   b. Relax - this is not the first time riots have occurred.
   c. Try to handle the situation by taking all desired remedial measures.
   d. Reach the spot and assuage the feelings of the victims.
9. **Your grown up son starts arguing with you every now and then. He tells you that you cannot impose your outdated attitudes and irrelevant values on him. How will you tackle him?**
   a. Accept his statement in helplessness and take a low-profile position in the family.
   b. Send him to a psychologist to learn adjust with his environment.
   c. Manage your feelings and explain your point of view as patiently as possible.
   d. Talk to him and understand his feelings, beliefs and attitudes.
10. **In an argument, if you lose, you:**
   a. Feel totally beaten.
   b. Wait for the next opportunity to beat your opponents.
   c. Winning and losing are part of the game.
   d. Analyse the reasons for the loss.
11. **You are a professor in a college; while taking a class, a student comments that you have not prepared the topic properly and you are just passing the time. How will you react?**
   a. Report to the principal of the college about the behavior of the student.
   b. Ask the student to leave the classroom.
   c. Ask him/her to meet you after the class in your chamber to explain what he/she wants.
   d. Listen to the needs of the class and promise to prepare the topic properly in future.
12. **As the CEO of a company, while taking a meeting with the union, one of the union leaders levels serious allegations of corruption and favoritism against you. How will you react?**
   a. Continue with the discussion and listen to their demands with a cool head.
   b. Suspend the union leader from the job.
   c. Cancel further negotiation and ask the union leader to apologies first.
   d. Leave the room after assigning the responsibility to your subordinate to continue with the meeting.
13. **You had an argument with your spouse on some trivial family matter and are not on speaking terms for sometime. The situation is causing mental disturbance to both of you. What will you do?**
   a. Stick to your stand; after all you were never at fault.
   b. Ask your spouse to mend ways if he/she wants peace at home.

c. Try to break the ice by analyzing the reasons for the conflict and ease the situation.
d. Wait for your spouse to make the first move to restore normalcy.

14. You hail from a rural area and take admission in a city college. You find your classmates taunting you as you are not smart and are unable to speak good English. How do you react?

a. Ignore them.
b. Shout back and tell them to mind their own business.
c. Leave studies half way and go back to your village.
d. Accept their challenge and prove that you can match them.

15. When someone directly criticizes your behaviour:

a. Tend to close up and stop listening.
b. Carefully listen to their opinion.
c. Tend to get upset about it.
d. Think of ways to change your behaviour.

Your Name: ________________ Sex: ________________

Age: ________________ Profession: ________________

Response Sheet

Question No.	Response	Question No.	Response
1.	a. b. c. d.	2.	a. b. c. d.
3.	a. b. c. d. b.	4.	a. b. c. d.
5.	a. b. c. d.	6.	a. b. c. d.
7.	a. b. c. d.	8.	a. b. c. d.
9.	a. b. c. d.	10.	a. b. c. d.

11.	a. b. c. d. b.	12.	a. b. c. d.
13.	a. b. c. d.	14.	a. b. c. d.
15.	a. b. c. d.		

Scoring key

Calculate your score using the following table.

Question	Response	Score	Explanation
1.	a. b. c. d.	20 0 5 15	*Emotional Competency:* When frustrated people respond in ways which are emotionally not intelligent. Response A is most suitable.
2.	a. b. c. d.	0 5 5 15	*Emotional Sensitivity:* Empathising and helping people in distress reflects high EQ. Response D is best.
3.	a. b. c. d.	0 20 5 10	*Emotional Competency:* Learning to avoid ego problems and have healthy interpersonal relations reflects high EQ. Response B is best.
4.	a. b. c. d.	20 10 5 0	*Emotional Competency:* Emotional self-control during angry situation helps to cool down temper. Response A is best.
5.	a. b. c. d.	0 20 15 10	*Emotional Competency:* The situation measures levels of optimism. Response B is best.

6.	a. b. c. d.	5 10 20 0	*Emotional Competency:* Communicating yourself to others effectively is an important emotional competency. Response C is best.
7.	a. b. c. d.	0 20 15 0	*Emotional Maturity:* Adapting to a given situation reflects high EQ. Response B seems most appropriate.
8.	a. b. c. d.	5 0 20 15	*Emotional Sensitivity:* Interpretation of human expressions and responding to them with sensitivity and human touch reflects emotional intelligence. Response C appears most suitable.
9.	a. b. c. d.	0 5 20 15	*Emotional Maturity:* Appreciating others' point of view requires high EQ. Response C seems most appropriate.
10.	a. b. c. d.	0 5 5 20	*Emotional Competency:* Learning to avoid negativity of emotions is a sign of emotional intelligence. Response D appears most appropriate.
11.	a. b. c. d.	5 5 5 20	*Emotional Sensitivity:* Maintaining rapport, harmony and comfort while dealing with groups reflects high emotional intelligence. Response D is most appropriate.
12.	a. b. c. d.	20 0 5 5	*Emotional Maturity:* Delaying the gratification of reacting to the situation instantaneously, you may come out a winner. Response A is most suitable.
13.	a. b. c. d.	0 5 20 5	*Emotional Competency:* Tackling ego problems in interpersonal life is a sign of emotional competency. Response C is most appropriate.
14.	a. b. c. d.	5 10 0 20	*Emotional Competency:* Handling an inferiority complex reflects high EQ. Response D is most appropriate.

15.	a. b. c. d.	5 20 0 10	Emotional Sensitivity: To understand how others evaluate and relate to you reflects high EQ. Response B seems most appropriate.

Your total score =

Interpretation of scores

Your Score	**Percentile**	**Interpretation**
285 and above	P-90	Extremely high EQ
250-274	P-75	High EQ
200-249	P-50	Moderate EQ
150-199	P-40	Low EQ
149 and below	P-15	Try some other day

11

TRANSACTIONAL ANALYSIS (TA)

"I do not understand my own actions." – ***Saint Paul***

"There are five fingers to the palm. We point out, where we come across a bad man, with the pointing finger. When you point at others, only one finger points out at them and three fingers point back to you. So, when you point out one fault in others, you must be able to examine three times whether there is a fault in you."–

Satya Sai Baba

Learning Objectives

After studying this chapter, you should be able to:

- **Define** the meaning of transactional analysis.
- **List** and **explain** the different ego states of human beings.
- **List** and **explain** the different life positions of people go through.
- **Show** the effects of ego states and life positions on human behaviour.
- **Explain** the term 'script analysis' in the context of transactional analysis.
- **Discuss** stroking in relation to inter-personal relationships.

11.1 INTRODUCTION

Every day we all have some interaction or relation with some persons for some purposes, be at home, in the school, at the work place, in the market, on the road, and so on. Our own experiences in this regard suggest that we experience joy in some relationships, upset in some others, and unaffected at all in some others. Why does this happen like this? An understanding of our different relationships giving different experiences will help us develop and improve our relationship with others. This becomes particularly important in our formal relationships at work places where we have to interact with others for meeting our specific purposes. For example, a person on the work in an organisation has to interact or deal with three types of persons: superiors, colleagues, and subordinates. Besides these, the same person has also to interact or deal with different types of other persons like consumers, customers, suppliers, public, and government officials. There is no gainsaying of the fact that one's success in meeting his/her purposes from others depends on how effectively he/she deals or interacts with others. Effective relationship or interactions with others depends on knowing oneself and others as well, i.e., improved inter-personal skills. Transactional analysis (TA) helps in developing and improving inter-personal relationships. The present chapter is, therefore, devoted to give a detailed account of 'transactional analysis' such as its meaning, ego states and life positions people go and experience, and their impact on human behaviour.

11.2 MEANING OF TRANSACTIONAL ANALYSIS (TA)

Before we define the term 'transactional analysis (TA)', let us first define its antecedent, that is, 'inter-personal style.' People at work places use some individual style while dealing with others to meet their purposes. Inter-personal style can be defined as a unique, self-consistent and enduring pattern of behaviour in interacting or transacting with other persons. Behavioural experiences suggest that the enduring nature of behaviour of a person has its roots in the personality orientation of the person, as reflected in his/her attitudes, values, beliefs, and culture. Transactional analysis provides one useful conceptual framework to understand an individual's inter-personal style.

TA is founded on interaction between people. The interaction whether assertive or non-assertive, involves two persons in which one person responds to another. Such transaction is called social transaction. Thus, transactional analysis (TA) can be defined as a study of social transactions between people that helps them improve inter-personal communication and relationship. The main objective of TA is to provide a framework to the people to transact or relate with one another so that they can improve inter-personal communication and develop inter-personal relations.

Having defined TA, it seems pertinent to give a brief account of the roots of TA. TA is one of the most accessible and applicable theories of modern psychology. History from all standpoints - be it philosophy, medical sciences, and religion - confirms that each individual has a multiple nature. It was Sigmund Freud who, in the early twentieth century, through his clinical tests established that the human psyche is multi-faceted and that each one of us has warring factions in our subconscious. Since then, other scholars continued to put forward their experiments and convictions that each one of us has parts of our personality which surface and affect our behaviour according to different circumstances.

A great fillip came to this conviction in 1951 with Dr. Wilder Penfield's series of scientific experiments[1]. Penfield established, using conscious human subjects, by touching a part of the brain (the temporal cortex) with a weak electrical probe, that the brain could be caused to 'play back' certain past experiences, and the feelings associated with them. In his experiments, the patients 'replayed' these events and their feelings despite not normally being able to recall them using their conventional memories. He carried on his experiments over several years which resulted in wide acceptance of the following conclusions:

- The human brain acts like a tape recorder. While one may forget his / her experiences, but the brain still has them recorded.
- Along with series of events, the brain records the associated feelings, and both feelings and events stay locked together.
- It is possible for a person to exist in two states simultaneously. This is based on the patients replaying hidden events and feelings could talk about them objectively at the same time.
- Hidden experiences when replayed are vivid, and affect how one feels at the time of replaying the event. There is a certain connection between mind and

body, i.e. the link between the biological and the psychological, e.g. a psychological fear of spiders and a biological feeling of nausea.

TA has wide applications in clinical, therapeutic, organisational and personal development, encompassing communications, management, personality, relationships and behaviour. Eric Berne, during 1950s, developed his theories of TA and reached to the conclusion that verbal communication, particularly face to face, is at the centre of human social relationships and psychoanalysis[2]. His starting point in his theory of TA was that when two people encounter each other, one of them will speak to other. This Berne called the 'Transactional Stimulus.' The reaction from other person he called the 'Transactional Response.' The person sending the 'stimulus' is called the 'agent.' The other person who responds is called the 'respondent.' In a sense, TA is a method of examining the encounter, or say, transaction: "I do something to you, and you do something back." Two TA concepts have been very popular in understanding interpersonal transactions: the ego states and the life positions. We shall discuss the both concepts in detail in turn.

11.3 EGO STATES

Let us first understand the meaning of ego states. In simple words, ego states are psychological positions such as parent, adult, and child that form the basis for social transactions. According to Eric Berne, each person is made up of three alter ego states and is involved in transaction with others with these ego states. The three ego states are:

1. Parent Ego
2. Adult Ego
3. Child Ego

The above three terms have different definitions and meanings than in common parlance. Their meanings in the context of TA are discussed as follows :

Parent Ego

The parent ego is characterized by ingrained voice of authority, absorbed conditioning, learning and attitudes from when we were young[3]. Recall, we get conditioned during our childhood and adulthood from our real parents and other elders like uncles, aunts, teachers, relatives, neighbours, etc. Alternatively speaking, parent ego is formed by external events and influences upon us as we grow through early childhood to adulthood. Yes, it can be changed also, but this is easier said than done. Just like our parents, parent ego is characterised by protective, nurturing, commanding, and directing. People with parent ego dogmatically prescribe norms and standards while transacting with others. For example, one may refer to: "Go through the leave rules and follow it squarely."

Adult Ego

The adult ego is characterized by our ability to think, analyse, and determine action for ourselves, based on received inputs like information, knowledge, and data. This ego state tries to improve and upgrade our decisions by seeking facts, processing data, estimating probabilities, and holding factual discussions. The formation of our adult ego starts at when we are ten months old. Experiences suggest that adult ego serves as a means to control our both child and parent egos. This also means that if we wish to change our parent and child, we must start it through our adulthood itself. Yes, this is also easier said than done.

Child Ego

Child ego is characterized by our feelings to external events during our childhood. In other words, our child ego is formed by seeing, hearing, feeling and emotional body of data within us. Our feelings like anger and despair dominate reasons and decide our behaviour / reaction to external events. Like an actual child, the child ego state desires approval from others and prefers immediate rewards. It may be featured by spontaneous, dependent, creative, or rebellious nature. Like parent and adult egos, child ego can also be changed. However, it is not always easier.

The above mentioned three 'egos' can be summarized as follows:

- Parent ego refers to our *'Taught'* concept of life.
- Adult ego refers to our *'Thought'* concept of life.
- Child ego refers to our *'Felt'* concept of life.

Having gone through the three ego states, some major conclusions about them stand out:

- *First,* conversations often are a mixture of reactions from Parent, Adult, and Child.
- *Second,* each ego state has both positive and negative features, i.e. it can add to or subtract from another person's feelings of satisfaction.
- *Third,* ego state can be detected by carefully observing the words and tone used postures, gestures, and facial expressions shown.
- *Fourth,* ego states are more apparent in two-person transactions than in group transactions.

11.4 TYPES OF TRANSACTIONS

All transactions taking place between individuals can be classified into two types:

1. Complementary Transactions
2. Non-complimentary Transactions

Complimentary Transactions: When the receiver of the message responds the message in the same ego state he / she receives it, such transaction is called "complementary transaction" or "parallel transaction." In other words, transactions are complimentary when the ego states of the sender and receiver in the opening transaction are simply reversed in the response. For example, the supervisor sends message with parent ego state to the employee who receives it with child ego state and also responds the message in child ego state itself. Here the communication was effective inasmuch as it accomplished what it was supposed to. Following is one such example of complimentary transaction:

Example: The supervisor speaks to the employee, "Ajanti, I want you to stop what you are doing for a few minutes and go to the finance section to bring a cheque they have for me." The employee, i.e. Ajanti responds, "Though I am busy, but I will because you are my boss."

Non-complimentary Transaction: When the receiver of the message responds the message with different ego state than the ego state he / she receives message, such transaction is called 'non-complimentary transaction." In other words, in case of non-complimentary transaction, the ego states in receiving and responding the message are non-parallel but cross each other. That is why non-complimentary transaction is also called "crossed transaction." For example, the employee receives message from his / her supervisor in child ego state but responds to the supervisor from adult ego state. So to say, in case of non-complimentary transaction, both stimulus and response are not parallel in ego states. Here is one such example:

Example: The supervisor says to the employee in an adult-to-adult ego state, "Let we both sit together to discuss and find out why you are not performing as efficiently as before." The employee responds in a child-to-parent ego state, "I do not know why you always pick on me only for every poor performance in my section."

The two types of transactions are shown in the following figure 11.1:

Figure 11.1: Types of Transactions

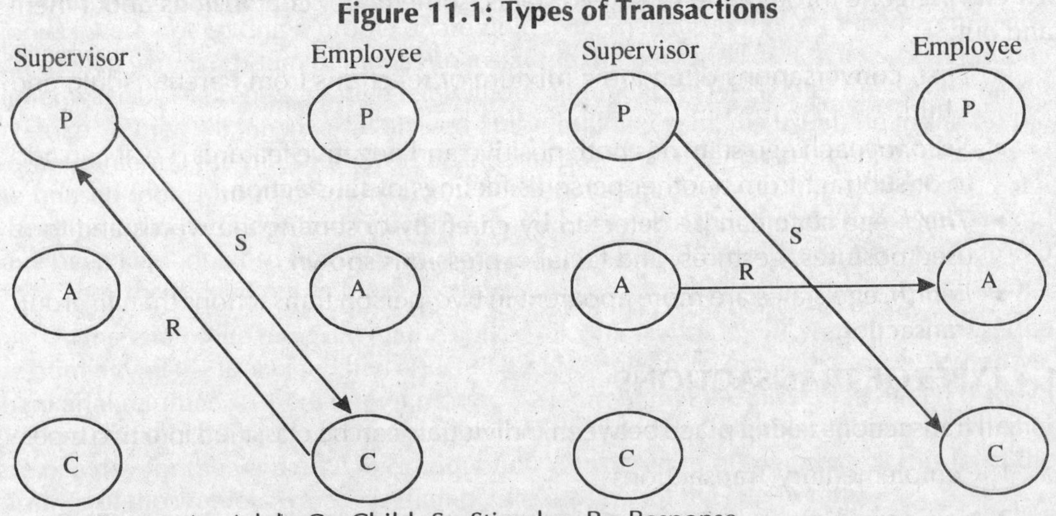

P= Parent, A= Adult, C= Child, S= Stimulus, R= Response

Complimentary Transaction	Non-Complimentary Transaction
Example:	***Example:***
Supervisor: You are late again to-day.	**Supervisor:** Is the presentation ready?
Employee: I'm sorry, Sir.	**imployee:** Do you think I have no other important works to do?

Theoretically, all the three ego states are important for the composition of a person. In numerical sense, the three ego states should account for about 33 per cent each. The same is true of sub-ego states under each ego state. For example, the three sub-ego states of child (i.e., reactive, creative, and adaptive) should be about 33 per cent each with respect of their composition of the full child. Similarly, the two sub-ego states of parent (i.e., regulating and nurturing) should be 50 per cent each of the full parent. However, these proportions are likely to vary in reality. The different sub-ego states under ego states are discussed in more structured manner subsequently under 'life positions.'

11.5 LIFE POSITIONS

Life Positions

Based on Penfield's conclusions that the human brain performs three functions: (i) recording, (ii) recalling, and (iii) reliving[4], Thomas Harris developed human life positions on the assumption that our earliest experiences , though ineffable, are recorded and do replay in the present[5]. Eric Berne terms life positions as existential positions. That life positions start forming since conceptions is illustrated by Harris with an example of a child.

When a child a conceived he/she is hopefully at peace and waiting to emerge into the world outside of the womb. If nothing untoward happens, he/she will emerge contented and relaxed. In such case, the child is likely to perceive the world from the perspective of "I am OK" and "You are OK".

In case the birth is difficult or even life threatening, the child may, even at the somatic level, experience and perceive the life as scary. In such case, the child's perception goes into "I am not OK" and "You are not Ok."

Assuming that the pregnancy went well and the birth was easy enough. The child's life experiences will start reinforcing his'/her initial somatic level life position. For example, the child is treated punitively, talked down to, and not welcomed; the child then begins to believe. "I am not OK" and "You are OK."

Supposing that he/ she is picked on and bullied as a child, the child feels himself / herself stronger. In such case, the child begins to perceive. I" am OK" and "You are not OK".

Based on the beliefs held by a person with respect to oneself and others, Harris has classified life positions into four types :

1. I'M NOT OK - YOU'RE OK
2. I' AM NOT OK - YO'RE NOT OK
3. I'M OK - YOU'RE NOT OK
4. I'M OK - YOU'RE OK

The above mentioned life positions can be used to understand one's style of working or transacting with others. Style can be simply defined as a consistent and stable way of interacting with others. The above four life positions give four transactional styles people may use while transacting with others:

1. Avoidant/Averse (A) Style
2. Bossing (B) Style
3. Competent/Confident (C) Style
4. Diffident (D) Style

These are depicted in the following Figure 11.2 :

Figure 11.2: Four Transactional Styles of Four Life Positions

	I'm not OK	I'm OK
	A	**B**
You're not OK	Avoidant/ Averse	Bossing
	D	**C**
You're OK	Diffident	Competent/Confident

There are a number of ways of diagramming the life positions. Franklin Ernst drew the life positions in quadrants, which he called the OK Corral[6]. Figure 11.3 presents the diagrammatical presentation of his OK Corral.

Figure 11.3: Franklin Ernst's OK Corral

You are Okay with me

I am Not Okay with me			I am OKay with me
	I am not OK **You are OK** one down position Get away from Helpless	**I am OK** **You are OK** healthy position Get on with Happy	
	I am not OK **You are not OK** hopeless position Get nowhere with Hopeless	**I am OK** **You are not OK** One-up position Get rid of Angry	

You are Not Okay with me

11.6 ELABORATION OF TRANSACTIONAL STYLES

Both ego states and life positions are inseparable in inter-personal transactions. One way to elaborate transactional analysis is to combine all the six ego states with the four life positions which give 24 transactional styles (see Figure 11.4).

Figure 11.4: Ego States vis-à-vis Life Positions

		A I'm not OK You're Not OK	**B** I'm OK You're Not OK	**C** I'm OK You're OK	**D** I'm not OK You're OK
Parent	Regulating Nurturing	Traditional Overindulgent	Prescriptive Patronizing	Normative Supportive	Indifferent Ingratiating
Adult		Cynical	Task-Obsession	Problem-Solving	Overwhelming
Child	Adaptive Reactive Creative	Sulking Withdrawn Humorous	Complaining Aggressive Bohemian	Resilient Confronting Innovative	Dependent Intropunitive Satirical

Different transactional styles are now discussed one by one.

I'm Not OK You're not OK - A (Avoidant/ Averse Style)

This is the life position characterized by no respect for oneself or others. In other words, the person feels himself/herself worthless or useless. The result is person tries to avoid transacting with others. Depending upon the various ego states, the person is likely to exhibit the following types of transactional styles:

1. Regulating Parent and Traditional Style: Under the regulating parental role, the person ensures that the norms of behaviour are duly followed. He/she, just like regulating parent, disapproves the deviation from the established norms of behaviour. Since the person does not have faith on himself/herself or others, he/she, therefore, just tries to follow the laid down norms and regulations of behaviour. For example, a trainer may exhibit this type of style by doing what he/she has learnt as a participant in some training programme.

2. Nurturing Parent and Over Indulgent Style: Since the person does not have faith on himself/herself and others, hence he/she provides excessive support and protection to others without exactly knowing how much to provide. In other words, a person like a nurturing parent shows more then necessary indulgence while dealing with others.

3. Adult and Cynical Style: The adult ego state by nature is concerned with the job. As the person follows the avoidant style, he/she becomes tempted to make cynical remarks on others. Such style can be shown by a manager who knows that nothing serious and meaningful can be achieved, he/she produces cynical attitude toward others.

4. Adaptive Child and Sulking Style: The adaptive child by nature accepts the norms of elders and, in turn, enjoys others' approval. But, if such child has no-okayness feeling about oneself and others, he/she does not disclose his feelings with others but simply sulks the same. For example, an employee dissatisfied with his/her job may not disclose his/her dissatisfaction to the superior / manager. One possible reason for such adaptive nature may be to ensure the security of the job. Since such style will have adverse effects on employee performance, hence such adaptive style is also termed as 'dysfunctional adaptation.'

5. Reactive Child and Withdrawn Style: In such style, the person reacts but by withdrawing himself/herself from the matter. The examples of such style may include a manager withdrawing himself/herself by showing his/her disinterest and a trainer may withdraw himself / herself by discontinuing his / her relationship with the client.

6. Creative Child and Humorous Style: Humorous style can be used just to avoid the situation not genuinely to enliven the situation. A manager, for example, may opt for using humors to show his/her creative nature to make a serious situation to a ludicrous one.

I'm OK You're Not OK - B (Bossing Style)

7. Regulating Parent and Prescriptive Style: In this style, the person prescribes norms and regulations for people to follow and also ensures that the same are duly followed. So to say, when people do not follow the prescribed norms, he / she become unhappy about the same. For example, a trainer lays down the detailed rules and regulations for the participants to be properly followed. Non-adherence of the same makes the trainer unhappy towards the participants.

8. Nurturing Parent and Patronizing Style: In this style, a person nurtures people by extending support and makes them realize that he/she is taking care of them. Alternatively speaking, both nurturance and support are provided to others by almost imposing oneself on them. That a manager provides support to his/her employees, and also makes them clear that he is doing a favour to them, else they are not in the position to take care of them.

9. Adult and Task-Obsessive Style: In task-obsessive style, the person - be manager or consultant or trainer - has concern for task completion only. Accordingly, he/she involves himself/herself in taking responsibility for completing the tasks and involves others in the secondary types of roles.

10. Adaptive Child and Complaining Style: Such style is characterized by the person's attitude to adapt him / her to situations to ensure his/her security, but also complains the reasons responsible for the situation. In simple words, the person adapts the situation but still complains that he/she does not have what he/she actually deserves. For example, a manager finds faults with the organisational policies for his / her low performance.

11. Reactive Child and Aggressive Style: A person using this style is likely to exhibit his aggressiveness in various forms like infighting with others, placing unrealistic demands, repeating the same issue again and again with an intension not to allow these to be amicably settled. Such behaviour is often going back to the issues, and never allowing these to be settled. The result of all such behaviour is that he gets alienated; people do not take such a person seriously any more.

12. Creative Child and Bohemian Style: A bohemian person is characterized by creativity. He / she does not stay with one idea but is obsessed with finding out new ideas all the time. When he / she gets new ideas, informs it to the peers, subordinates, and others relating to him with joy and overwhelms. It is due to this creative attitude, he /she is always in search of inputs for new ideas while transacting with others.

I'm OK You're OK - C (Confident Style)

Persons in this life position are characterized by competence, confidence, and creativity. They have faith on themselves as well as on others. Such persons may exhibit the following six types of transactional styles while dealing with others:

13. Regulating Parent and Normative Style: People in this life position set behavioural norms but with involvement of others like subordinates, clients, participants, etc. They also ensure that the set norms are followed by others. The advantage of this style is that the involvement of others in setting norms makes their adherence easier.

14. Nurturing Parent and Supportive Style: The person in this style provides the necessary support needed by others with whom he transacts. The distinguishing feature of this style as compared with previous nurturing style is that support is provided only when solicited by others.

15. Adult and Problem Solving Style: The distinguishing feature of this style is that the person in this life position is very much concern to solve the problem with others. This style is different from over task-obsession in the sense that the person wants to accomplish the task with proper means and solutions, not by all means. Yes, it is possible that at times concern for task may affect problem solving.

16. Adaptive Child and Resilient Style: The people in this life position are ready to adapt but to the extent it suits to them. In other words, people react and oppose the situation if it does not suit to them. Hence, this style is also called as functional adaptation. This is, in a sense, like *'Management by Exceptions'* where manager takes decisions as per the situations prevalent to suit to him.

17. Reactive Child and Confronting Style: Aggressiveness is the main characteristic of this style. What is important in this style is one's aggressiveness is not always dysfunctional but some times it is functional as well. It becomes functional when the person does not give up and perseveres till the problem is not solved or task is not completed. Here, a distinction also needs to be made between pseudo-confrontation and real confrontation. While the former is just expression of aggression to others, the latter is aggression expressed with an objective to solve the problem.

18. Creative Child and Innovative Style: A person in this life position is characterized by his desire to solve the problem or perform the task always in newer ways. Thus, the person who practices this style is not satisfied with one style of working but always is in search of newer and better ways of doing the work. Yes, he may also be serious to stabilize the existing one method till new one is not innovated.

I'm Not OK, You're OK - D (Diffident Style)

In this life position, the person does not have confidence and faith on him but on others. As such, he/she is unable to assert but surrenders before others. So to say, the person in this style depreciates oneself. The person may show six types of styles in this life position:

19. Regulating Parent and Indifferent Style: In this style, the person leaves the adherence of norms to the discretion of others. As such, he/she has least concern whether the people have properly understood the norms or not. Not only had that, due to his lack of confidence in him, he at times overlooks if the laid down norms followed or not. He does not have enough trust in his ability to help people develop proper norms and follow such norms. A manager who ignores the question of propriety of behaviour of his subordinates may be the example of such transactional style.

20. Nurturing Parent and Ingratiating Style: This style is characterized by one's deliberate effort to please or placate other for serving one's purpose. For example, a manager in an organisation may invite his subordinates to social parties at his/her home and also visit occasionally to their places with the thinking that this style of transaction will help him / her in getting work done by subordinates.

21. Adult and Overwhelmed Style: A person in this position is always concerned with the task he/she has to complete. As such, he/she always feels overburdened with work and is at times confused what to do. He/she becomes workaholic.

22. Adaptive Child and Dependent Style: Such person for his/her own security remains over dependent on others. The manifestations of such style may be working the others want one to work and seeking others' approval for one's working. For example, a dependent manager may go blindly by what his subordinates tell him to do for approval. Similarly, a dependent consultant is guided primarily by his / her clients' wishes and instructions.

23. Reactive Child and Intropunitive Style: A person with this style shows pity on self. He blames himself for his/her ineffectiveness and shows aggression and anger on self only.

24. Creative Child and Satirical Style: This style is characterized by pungent form. In other words, the person with this style is creative about ideas and solutions but, at the same time, keeps himself/herself away from any conflict and confrontation by resorting to satire.

11.7 SCRIPT ANALYSIS

Just the script of a play before us reveals what will happen in each act and how the play will finally end, life script also is a plan that indicates how the person will live and die. According to Eric Berne, people decide early in childhood how they will live their life and finally die. It was Steiner who for the first time studied life script in a structured and systematic manner[7]. Later, he did extensive work on script analysis and became well known for this work. His script analysis is based on the belief that people since their childhood plan about their life stages and try to live accordingly. Sometimes people may not realize that they have set a plan for their lives but can find this out they ask themselves what and how was their childhood, who were their favourite characters and whom they identified with. Then, consider the beginning, middle, and end of the story. According to Steiner, just that happens with all of us.

Different people have listed different elements involved in script analysis. For example, Eric Berne has suggested seven elements in the script apparatus[8]. Here, we are discussing the four generally accepted elements involved in a script apparatus. These are:

Pay-off or Curse: In this case, the parents plan script for their children. That is to say, the parents through verbal or non-verbal messages tell the children either to live or die as per their plan. The script pay-off takes place, according to Eric Berne, only when the script is accepted by the children.

Injunctions or Stoppers: As per the literary meaning of injunction, it refers to negative command from the superior to the subordinates. A father's command to his son *"Get Lost"* is one example of injunction. In practice, injunctions are accepted by the people when these are accompanied by punishment for not abiding by the command. In place of the term injunction, Eric Berne preferred to use the term "stoppers" to imply the quality by which an injunction may stop a person in his behaviour as and when it is replayed in future.

Counter Script: This is the next element in progression in the script apparatus. As seen above, pay-off and injunction are given during the childhood (up to six years).

Counterscript messages are given in the later ages. Recall your post-childhood script stage, you might have got messages like "work hard'" "be honest", etc are the examples of counterscript messages. Different script elements affect person differently. For example, while pay-offs shape one's destiny; counterscripts determine one's personality style. Berne opines that counterscript messages influence one more internally than externally.

Programme or Pattern: Programme denotes the blue print the parents teach their children to follow to live their lives. For this, parents usually suggest some models to their children to emulate and live alike. Such scripts are also known as process script classified into six types as follows:

Never	The person with this life script is characterized by the view: *"I never got what I deserved."*
Always	The person with this script has a motto to follow a role once and for all the times. For example, parents tell their children: *"Always respect the elders."*
Until	This is the script which denotes that the thing will not happen unless something does not happen. *"You cannot appear in the public service examination until you are not graduate"* is one such example.
After	This script type is just the converse of until. Accordingly, it states that the thing will happen only after happening something. For example, *"in order to get good things today, I will pay for it next week."*
Almost	The person with this script repeats the same behaviour again and again irrespective of success or failure. For example, *"a basket ball player tries to put the ball in the net again and again irrespective of his success."*
Open-ended	As the term itself denotes, the person in this script finds himself / herself in the open air like *'pie in the sky.'* This is a script in which person reaches to a life stage with all his parental messages and then does not know what to do next.

11.8 STROKING

What is stroking? The literary meaning of stroke is a blow or mode of striking or attracting sudden attention. In general, while transacting with others, we expect attention or recognition of our behaviour by others. Any act or behaviour of ours as a recognition by others is called *'stroking.'* In transactional analysis, the compliments and general ways of giving recognition are called "strokes". For example, when a teacher enters the class expects students to say "Good Morning, Sir,' or 'standing up'. John W. Newstrom and Keith Davis has defined stroke "as performing any act of recognition for another person."[9] Stroking, or say, recognition can be physical, verbal, and non-verbal. While telling to one's subordinate, "Shyam Sunder, you had a mesmerising style of teaching your subject," is an example of verbal stroke, "patting on the back of the student for his excellent presentation style," is an example of physical stroke.

Strokes can be positive, negative, or mixed. The stroke that makes one cheerful and feels good is called positive stroke. Words of affection, appreciation, recognition, cuddling, pat on back, firm handshake, and pleasant smile are the examples of positive stroke. For example, the boss pats on the back of his subordinate Ashwini Goel and says: "I like you for your honesty and sincerity." Positive strokes contribute to the recipient's sense of being OK. On the other hand, negative strokes make one feel sad. Criticism, hatred, and scold are the examples of negative strokes. For example, the boss says" Om Prakash, I don't like your insincerity." Negative strokes make the recipient feel less OK about her or him/self. Mixed stroke makes one feel both good and bad. The comments of the Director of a Management Institute: "Rakesh, your teaching style is good, considering the small amount of experience you have in teaching," is the example of mixed stroke. In this instance, the Director is communicating to his faculty under Parent-to-Child life position where both good teaching style as positive stoke and less teaching experience as negative stroke are involved.

Strokes can also be of conditional and unconditional types. The difference between conditional and unconditional strokes is that while former is stoking for doing, the latter is a stroke for being. For instance:

"I like you when you smile". – Conditional stroke.

"I like you." – Unconditional stroke

As negative strokes, these might be:

"I don't like you when you are sarcastic". – Negative conditional stroke.

"I don't like you." – Negative unconditional stroke.

Employees hunger and need for strokes, mainly positive ones. That the occasional reluctance shown by the superiors to use positive strokes at times dampens employees' feeling is demonstrated in the following imaginary conversation between the Director and an Associate Professor of a Management Institute: Tulsi Gupta, an Associate Professor and Coordinator of the PGDM Course, had just made a presentation to the Expert Team of the Association of the Indian Universities (AIU), for the equivalence of PGDM with MBA. Later, he excitedly asked his Director how he had done. "You made a nice presentation," said the Director (Tulsi's eyes lit up in pleasure). The Director further added: "Yours was not a great presentation, but just a nice presentation." Although Tulsi did not show his disappointment, we can guess that his spirits were considerably dampened by the Director's qualified remarks. One week later, Tulsi requested the Director to relieve him from the co-ordinatorship of the PGDM(FM). He was subsequently relieved and the most buttery faculty A. P. Sharma was appointed the Coordinator of the PGDM course.

SUMMARY

This summary is organized as per the 'learning objectives' given on page no. 184 :

- *Transactional Analysis (TA) is the study of social transactions between people so as to develop improved communication and human relationships.*
- *There are three ego states people experience in their lives: Parent Ego, Adult Ego, and Child Ego. The parent ego is characterised by protective, nurturing, commanding, and directing. People with parent ego dogmatically prescribe norms and standards while transacting with others. The adult ego is characterized by our ability to think, analyse, and determine action for ourselves, based on received inputs like information, knowledge, and data. The child ego is featured by spontaneous, dependent, creative, or rebellious nature.*
- *Life Position is one's basic beliefs about self and others, which are used to justify decisions and behaviour in social transactions. People go through four life positions, namely, (i) I am OK, you are OK, (ii) I am not OK, you are Ok, (iii) I am not OK, you are not OK, and (iv) I am OK, you are not Ok.*
- *Script analysis is a plan that indicates how the person will live and die. The nature of script governs one's behaviour towards others.*
- *Performing any act of recognition for another person is called stroking. Stroking can be positive, negative or mixed which elicits behaviour from others accordingly.*

REVIEW QUESTIONS

1. What is interpersonal style? Explain the importance of it.
2. Explain transactional analysis and its relationship to understand Interpersonal style?
3. Explain different types of Interpersonal styles.
4. What is script analysis? Discuss with examples the various types of scripts.
5. What is meant by stroking? Take the examples of your own strokes and explain how the stroking affects inter-personal styles.

REFERENCES

1. W. Penfield: Memory Mechanism, **A.M.A. Archives of Neurology and Psychiatry,** 67, 1952, pp. 178-198.
2. Eric Berne: **Transactional Analysis in Psychotherapy,** Grove Press, New York, 1961.
3. John W. Newstrom and Keith Davis: **Organisational Behaviour** (**Human Behaviour at Work**), Tata McGraw-Hill Publishing Company Limited, New Delhi, 2007, p. 324.
4. W. Penfield: *op.cit.,* 1952, pp. 178-198.
5. Thomas A. Harris: **I'M OK-YOU'RE OK,** Arrow Books, Great Britain, 1995, p. 38.
6. Franklin Ernst: Lecture on "**Listening**" delivered at the Institute for Transactional Analysis, Sacramento, California, 18th October, 1967.
7. C. Steiner: **Scripts People Live,** Grove Press, New York, 1974.
8. Eric Berne: **Games People Play,** Grove Press, New York, 1964, p. 29.
9. John W. Newstrom and Keith Davis: op. cit., 1997, p. 325.

Exercise 11.1: An Exercise for You*

Assume that you are a manager. Read each statement below and write your response (how often you will behave this way) in the space to the left, according to the key.

Key

Write 1 if you rarely or never behave this way.
Write 2 if you occasionally behave this way.
Write 3 if you sometimes behave this way.
Write 4 if you often behave this way.
Write 5 if you almost always behave this way.

______ 1 I would assure my people of my availability to them.

______ 2 I would delay doing things that I do not like.

______ 3 I would help my people to see the ethical dimensions of some of our actions.

______ 4 I would communicate strong feelings and resentment to my colleagues and seniors without caring whether this will affect my relationship with them.

______ 5 I would collect all the information needed to solve various problems.

______ 6 I would overwhelm my colleagues with new ideas.

______ 7 I would respect and follow organisational traditions that seem to give the organisation its identity.

______ 8 I would provide my people with the solutions to their problems.

______ 9 I would zealously argue my point of view in organisational meetings.

______ 10 I would admonish my people for not acting according to my instructions.

______ 11 I would try out new things.

______ 12 I would collect information and data even when these are not immediately needed or used.

______ 13 I would help my people to become aware of some of their own strengths.

______ 14 I would not express my negative feelings during unpleasant meetings but would continue to be bothered by them.

______ 15 I would raise questions with my people about what should or should not be done.

______ 16 I would champion my people's cause even at the cost of organisational effectiveness.

______ 17 I would think out several alternative solutions to problems before adopting one for action.

______ 18 I would try out new ideas or methods without waiting to consolidate the previous ones.

---

*Adapted from Udai Pareek: **Understanding Organisational Behaviour**, Oxford University Press, New Delhi, 2004, pp. 200-201.

______ 19 I would accept others' suggestions that appeal to me.

______ 20 I would instruct my people in detail about work problems and their solutions.

______ 21 I would express my feelings and reactions frankly in meetings with seniors and colleagues.

______ 22 I would clearly prescribe standards of behaviour to be followed in my work unit.

______ 23 I would try out new ways and see each problem as a challenge.

______ 24 I would work primarily on organisational tasks, overlooking the feelings of people.

Scoring

Total your responses for the following items and write down the totals in the given space.

	Pn	Pr	A	Cc	Cr	Ca
(a)	1+13 ____	3+15 __	5+17 ___	11+23 _____	9+21 ___	7+19 ___
(b)	8+20 ___	10+22 ___	12+24 _____	6+18 _____	4+16 ___	2+14 ___
Difference in totals (a minus b)	____	____	_____	____	____	___

Find the difference for each pair (a minus b), keeping the algebraic sign. The totals in each case will range between 8 and -8. The positive scores show an OK position and the negative scores show a not-OK position. Reflect on your scores.

12

MOTIVATION : CONCEPTS

"People are like icebergs. What you see above the surface (i.e. performance) is only a small part. A large part of the attributes needed to perform excellently in a future job, which I call potential, is not immediately visible."

– ***K.Ramchandran, Vice-President, Philips India Ltd.***

"What makes life dreary is the want of a motive." – ***George Eliot***

Learning Objectives

After studying this chapter, you should be able to:

- **Explain** the concept of motivation.
- **Outline** the nature and process of motivation.
- **Describe** the need for and significance of motivation in modern organisations.
- **Discuss** the major theories of motivation.

We have so far discussed the cognitive variables, such as personality, perception, attitudes, values and learning that affect human behaviour at work. There is yet another cognitive variable, namely, motivation that also affects human behaviour. Motivation cannot be seen, but all that can be seen is behaviour. Some people work harder or exert more effort than others. In other words, individuals with lesser ability can; and do, outperform their more gitted counterparts. In fact, this is because of motivation. Therefore, while studying human behaviour, motivation cannot and should not, be underrated. This chapter is, therefore, devoted to discuss various explanations of why some people exert more effort on their jobs than others. The applied aspects of motivator are discussed in the next chapter 13 on **Motivation: Application**.

12.1 MEANING OF MOTIVATION

Motivation originally comes from the Latin root word *movere,* which means "to move". It is derived from the word 'motive'. Motive may be defined as an inner state of our mind that activates and directs our behaviour. It makes us move to act. It is always internal to us and is externalized via, behaviour. Motivation is one's willingness to exert efforts towards the accomplishment of his/her goal. Let us consider a few important definitions on motivation that will help us understand the meaning of motivation in more clear sense.

According to Fred Luthans[1]. "Motivation is a process that starts with a physiological or psychological deficiency or need that activates behaviour or a drive that is aimed at a goal or incentive."

In the opinion of Stephen P. Robbins[2], "Motivation is the willingness to exert high levels of effort toward organizational goals, conditioned by the effort ability to satisfy some individual need".

Gray and Strake[3] defined motivation as "the result of processes, internal or external to the individual, that arouse enthusiasm and persistence to pursue a certain course of action."

Thus, motivation can be defined very simply as the willingness to exert toward the accomplishment of goal or need.

12.2 NATURE OF MOTIVATION

Having gone through the meaning of motivation, the nature of motivation emerges out as follow:

1. Motivation is internal to man: Motivation cannot be seen because it is internal to man. It is externalized via behaviour. It activates the man to move toward goal.

2. A single motive can cause different behaviours: A person with a single desire to earn prestige in the society may move towards to join politics, attain additional education and training, join identical groups and change his outward appearance.

3. Different motives may result in single behaviour: The same or single behaviour may be caused by many motives. If a person buys a car, for example, his this buying behaviour may be caused by different motives, such as to look attractive, be respectable, gain acceptance from similar group of persons, differentiate the status and so on.

4. Motives come and go: Like tides, motives can emerge and disappear. Motives emerged at a point of time may not remain with the same intensity at other point of time. For instance, a boy overly concerned about his hair and dress styles during his adolescence age may turn his concern towards other things like health and education once he grows up and attains youth.

5. Motives interact with the environment: The environment in which we are at a point of time may either trigger or suppress our motives. You probably have experienced environment or situation when the intensity of your hunger picked up just you smelled the odour of palatable food. You may desire an excellent performance bagging the first position in your examination but at the same time may also be quite sensitive to being shunned and disliked by your class-mates if you really perform too well and get too much of praise and appreciation. Thus, what this indicates is that human behaviour is the result of several forces differing in both direction and intent.

12.3 MOTIVATION CYCLE OR PROCESS

As stated earlier, motivation is a process or cycle, aimed at accomplishing some goal. The basic elements included in the process are **motives, goals** and **behaviour**. These are discussed as follow:

Motives: Almost all human behaviour is motivated. It requires no motivation to grow hair, but getting a hair cut does. Motives prompt people to action. Hence, these are at the very heart of motivational process. Motives provide as activating thrust toward reaching a goal. The examples of the needs for food and water are translated into the hunger and thrust drives or motives. Similarly, the need for friends becomes a motive for affiliation.

Goals: Motives are directed towards goals. Motives generally create a state of physiological or psychological imbalance. Attaining goal restores balance. For example, a goal exists when the body of the man is deprived of food and water or one's personality is deprived of friends or companions.

Behaviour: Behaviour is a series of activities to be undertaken. Behaviour is directed to achieve a goal. For example, the man goes to saloon to cut his hair.

Diagrammed simply, the process or cycle of motivation is presented in Figure 12.1.

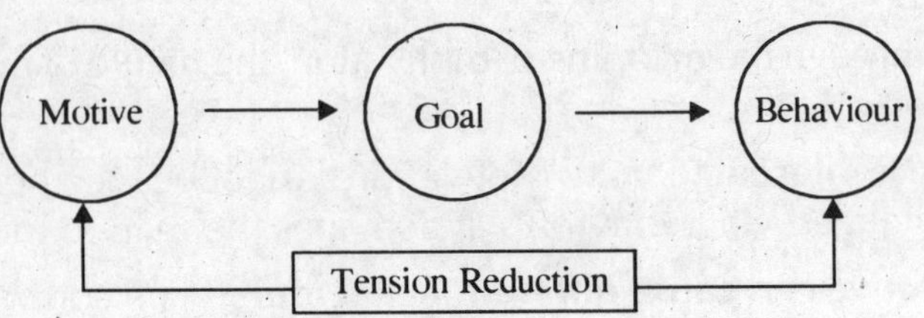

Fig. 12.1: Motivation Process

12.4 NEED FOR MOTIVATION

Among the behavioural concepts, motivation has received the most attention in the study of organisational behaviour. The following factors justify the need for and significance of motivation in organisations:

1. Organisations are run by people. Hence, managers cannot afford to avoid a concern with human behaviour at work. This is because the motivated employees are more productive and quality-conscious than apathetic ones.

2. Motivation as a pervasive concept affects and is also affected by a host of factors in the organisational milieu. It enables managers to understand why people behave as they behave.

3. Organisational effectiveness becomes, to some extent, the question of management's ability to motivate its employees. Hence, an appreciation of motivation helps the managers how to motivate their employees.

4. Machines become necessary in case of complex technology. However, these remain inefficient vehicles of effective and efficient operations without man to operate them. Therefore, orgnaisations need to have employees with required capability and willingness to use the advanced and complex technology to achieve the organisational goals.

5. With the realisation that organisations will run in more complex milieu in future, an increasing attention has been given to develop employees as future resources (a 'talent bank'). This facilitates the managers to draw upon them as and when organisations grow and develop.

Finally, the need for and significance of motivation for an organisation can be put as: **"If we compare management with driving, while the organisation is the vehicle than motivation is the power or fuel that makes the vehicle moving".**

Difference between Motivation and Incentive

Sometimes, some people consider motivation and incentive mean the same. However, these mean two different meanings.

- Motivation is individual-oriented and is 'will to do.' For example, the policy of promotion on the basis of one's outstanding performance motivates employees to perform well.

- Incentive is something introduced in work environment to encourage employees to perform better. Proportional increase in salary in proportion to increase in production is an example of incentive.
- Seen in above context, incentive is a 'means,' whereas motivation is an 'end.'
- Alternatively speaking, incentive creates motivation.

12.5 THEORIES OF MOTIVATION

From the very beginning, when the human organizations were established, various thinkers have tried to find out the answer to what motivates people to work. Different approaches applied by them have resulted in a number of theories concerning motivation. These all theories are broadly classified into two categories:

12.5.1 Content Theories

These theories are people-centered that explain 'what'. The main theories that fall under this category are:

(i) Abraham Maslow's Need Hierarchical Theory
(ii) Herzberg's Two Factor Theory
(iii) Douglas McGregor's Theory X and Theory Y
(iv) Alderfer's ERG Theory
(v) David C. McClelland's Three-Need Theory

12.5.2 Process Theories

These theories are work-centered that explain 'how.' Following are the main theories under this category:

(i) Vroom's Expectancy Theory
(ii) Porter and Lawler's Expectancy Theory
(iii) Adam's Equity Theory

These are discussed in that order.

12.5.1 Content Theories

Maslow's Need Hierarchy Theory

It is probably safe to say that the most well-known theory of motivation is Maslow's need hierarchy theory[4]. Maslow's theory is based on the human needs. Drawing chiefly on his clinical experience, he classified all human needs into a hierarchical manner from the lower to the higher order. In essence, he believed that once a given level of need is satisfied, it no longer serves to motivate man. Then, the next higher level of need has to be activated in order to motivate the man.

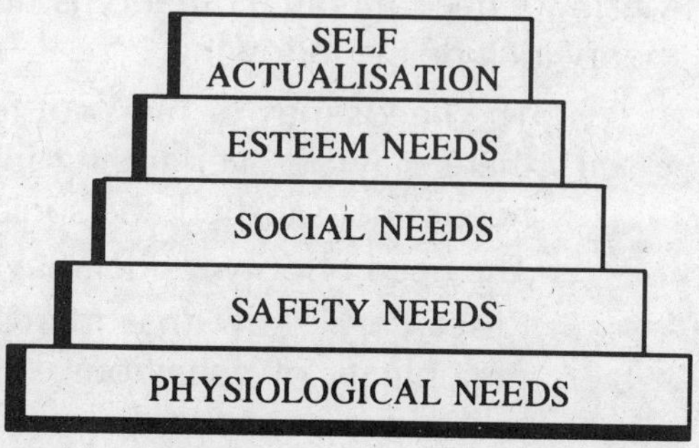

Fig. 12.2: Maslow's Need Hierarchy

Maslow identified five levels in his need hierarchy as shown in figure 12.2.

These are now discussed one by one.

1. Physiological Needs: These needs are basic to human life and, hence, include food, clothing, shelter, air, water and other necessities of life. These needs relate to the survival and maintenance of human life. They exert tremendous influence on human behaviour. These needs are to be met first at least partly before higher level needs emerge. Once physiological needs are satisfied, they no longer motivate the man.

2. Safety Needs: After satisfying the physiological needs, the next needs felt are called safety and security needs. These needs find expression in such desires as economic security and protection from physical dangers. Meeting these needs requires more money and, hence, the individual is prompted to work more. Like physiological needs, these become inactive once they are satisfied.

3. Social Needs: Man is a social being. He is, therefore, interested in social interaction, companionship, belongingness, etc. It is this socializing and belongingness why individuals prefer to work in groups and especially older people go to work.

4. Esteem Needs: These needs refer to self-esteem and self-respect. They include such needs which indicate self-confidence, achievement, competence, knowledge and independence. The fulfillment of esteem needs leads to self-confidence, strength and capability of being useful in the organization. However, inability to fulfil these needs results in feelings like inferiority, weakness and helplessness.

5. Self-Actualisation Needs: This level represents the culmination of all the lower, intermediate, and higher needs of human beings. In other words, the final step under the need hierarchy model is the need for self-actualisation. This refers to fulfillment. The term self-actualisation was coined by Kurt Goldstein and means to become actualized in what one is potentially good at. In effect, self-actualisation is the person's motivation to transform perception of self into reality.

According to Maslow, the human needs follow a definite sequence of domination. The second need does not arise until the first is reasonably satisfied; and the third need does not emerge until the first two needs have been reasonably satisfied and so on. The other side of the need hierarchy is that human needs are unlimited. However, Maslow's need hierarchy theory is not without its detractors. The criticisms of the theory include the following:

1. The needs may or may not follow a definite hierarchical order. So to say, there may be overlapping in need hierarchy. For example, even if safety need is not satisfied, the social need may emerge.
2. The need priority model may not apply at all times in all places.
3. Researches show that man's behaviour at any time is mostly guided by multiplicity of behaviour. Hence, Maslow's preposition that one need is satisfied at one time is also of doubtful validity.
4. In case of some people, the level of motivation may be permanently lower. For example, a person suffering from chronic unemployment may remain satisfied for the rest of his life if only he/she can get enough food.

Notwithstanding, Maslow's need hierarchy theory has received wide recognition, particularly among practicing managers. This can be attributed to the theory's intuitive logic and easy to understand. One researcher came to the conclusion that theories that are intuitively strong die hard[5].

Herzberg's Two Factor Theory

The psychologist Frederick Herzberg extended the work of Maslow and proposed a new motivation theory popularly know as **Herzberg's Two-Factor (Motivation Hygiene) Theory**[6]. Herzberg conducted a widely reported motivational study on 200 accountants and engineers employed by firms in and around western Pennsylvania. He asked these people to describe two important incidents at their jobs: (1) When did you feel particularly good about your job, and (2) when did you feel exceptionally bad about your job. He used the critical incident method of obtaining data.

The responses when analysed were found quite interesting and fairly consistent. The replied the respondents offered were consistent. The replies respondents gave when they felt good about their jobs were significantly different from the replies given when they felt bad. Reported good feelings were generally associated with job satisfaction whereas bad feelings with job dissatisfaction. Herzberg labeled the job satisfiers **motivators,** and he called job dissatisfiers hygiene or **maintenance factors**. Taken together, the motivators and hygiene factors have become known as Herzberg's **two-factor theory of motivation.**

Herzberg's motivational and hygiene factors have been shown in the Table 9.1.

According to Herzberg, the opposite of satisfaction is not dissatisfaction. The underlying reason, he says, is that removal of dissatisfying characteristics from a job does not necessarily make the job satisfying. He believes in the existence of a dual continuum. The opposite of 'satisfaction' is 'no satisfaction' and the opposite of 'dissatisfaction' is 'no dissatisfaction'?

According to Herzberg, today's motivators are tomorrow's hygiene because the latter stop influencing the behaviour of persons when they get them. Accordingly, one's hygiene may be the motivator of another.

However, Herzberg's model is labeled with the following criticism:

1. People generally tend to take credit themselves when things go well. They blame failure on the external environment.
2. The theory basically explains job satisfaction not motivation.
3. Even job satisfaction is not measured on an overall basis. It is not unlikely that a person may dislike part of his/her job, still thinks the job acceptable.
4. This theory neglects situational variable to motivate an individual.

Regardless of criticisms, Herzberg's 'two-factor motivation theory' has been widely read and a few managers seem unfamiliar with his recommendations. The main use of his recommendations lies in planning and controlling of employees work.

Distinction between Maslow's and Herzberg's Theories

Both Maslow and Herzberg theories focus on motivational factors. However,

Hygiene: Job Dissatisfaction	Motivators: Job Satisfaction
	Achievement
	Recognition
	Work itself
	Responsibility
	Advancement
	Growth
Company Policy and Administration	
Supervision	
Interpersonal Relations	
Working Conditions	
Salary*	
Status	
Security	

* Because of its ubiquitous nature, salary commonly shows up as a motivator as well as hygine.

both differ from each other in their approaches. As discussed earlier, Maslow's motivation theory is based on the hierarchy of needs. According to this theory, only unsatisfied needs motivate individuals. Once a need is satisfied, it ceases to be a motivating factor. But, Herzberg's motivation theory is based on motivational and hygiene or maintenance factors. According to Herzberg, hygiene or maintenance factors prevent job dissatisfaction but do not provide motivation to workers. In his view, Maslow's lower order needs like physiological, safety and social needs act as hygiene or maintenance factors.

McGregor's Theory X and Theory Y

Douglas McGregor formulated two distinct views of human being based on participation of workers. The first basically negative, labeled **Theory X**, and the other basically positive, labeled **Theory Y**[13]. Theory **X** is based on the following assumptions:

1. People are by nature indolent. That is, they like to work as little as possible.
2. People lack ambition, dislike responsibility, and prefer to be directed by others.
3. People are inherently self-centered and indifferent to organizational needs and goals.
4. People are generally gullible and not very sharp and bright.

On the contrary, **Theory Y** assumes that:

1. People are not by nature passive or resistant to organizational goals.
2. They want to assume responsibility.
3. They want their organization to succeed.
4. People are capable of directing their own behaviour.
5. They have need for achievement.

What McGregor tried to dramatise through his theory X and theory Y is to outline the extremes to draw the fencing within which the organisaitonal man is usually seen to behave. The fact remains that no organizational man would actually belong either to theory X or theory Y. In reality, he/she shares the traits of both. What actually happens is that man swings from one set of properties to the other with changes in his mood and motives in changing environment.

Urwick's Theory Z

Much after the propositions of theories X and Y by McGregor, the three theorists- Urwick, Rangnekar, and Ouchi-propounded the third theory labeled as Z theory[14]. The two propositions in Urwick's theory are that:

(*i*) Each individual should know the organizational goals precisely and the amount of contribution through his efforts towards these goals.

(*ii*) Each individual should also know that the realization of organizational goals is going to satisfy his/her needs positively.

In Urwick's view, the above two make people ready to behave positively to accomplish both organizational and individual goals.

However, Ouchi's Theory Z has attracted the lot of attention of management practitioners as well as researchers. It must be noted that Z does not stand for anything, but is merely the last alphabet in the English Language.

Theory Z is based on the following four postulates:

1. Strong Bond between Organisation and Employees.
2. Employee Participation and Involvement.
3. No Normal Organisation Structure.
4. Human Resource Development.

Ouchi's Theory Z represents the adoption of Japanese management practices (group decision making, social cohesion, job security, holistic concern for employees, etc.) by the American companies. In India, Maruti-Suzuki, Hero-Honda, etc. apply the postulates of Theory Z.

Alderfer's ERG Theory

Clayton reexamined Maslow's Need Hierarch Theory with the help of empirical research. Thus, he developed another need-based theory called 'Existence, Relatedness and Growth (ERG) Theory.' Alderfer classified all human needs into three broad needs as follows:

1. *Existence Needs*: These are basic material needs for one's existence or survival.

2. *Relatedness Needs*: These refer to desire to establish, maintain, and develop inter-personal relations.

3. *Growth Needs*: These refer to one's intrinsic desire for one's development to the extent one can.

A comparison of Alderfer's Theory with Maslow's Theory reveals the following similarities and dissimilarities between the two:

Similarities: (i) Alderfer's 'existence' needs are similar to Maslow's physiological needs.

(ii) What is Alderfer's 'relatedness' needs is the same Maslow's 'social' needs.

Dissimilarities: (i) According to Maslow, a person stays at one level of need till it is not satisfied. But as per Alderfer's ERG theory, if (higher level) need is not satisfied, the person's desire to increase a lower need takes place. In other words, frustration due to non-satisfaction of some need may lead to a regression to a lower need. For example, one's inability to satisfy social need might increase the desire for more money to satisfy his/her security need.

(ii) Maslow considers that there exists a rigid hierarchy of needs where one can progress to higher need only after the lower level need is fully satisfied. But, Alderfer's ERG theory considers needs as flexible ones. For example, a person can be working on growth needs even though existence or relatedness needs are not satisfied.

David C. McClelland's Three Need Theory

Another well-known need-based theory of motivation, as opposed to hierarchy of needs or satisfaction-dissatisfaction, is the theory developed by McClelland and his associated[7]. McClelland developed his theory based on Henry Murry's[8] developed long list of motives and manifest needs used in his early studies of personality. McClelland's need theory is closely associated with learning theory, because he believed that needs are learned or acquired by the kinds of events people experienced in their environment and culture. He found that people who acquire a particular need behave differently from those who do not have. His theory focuses on Murray's three needs: achievement, power and affiliation. In the literature these three needs are abbreviated **"n Ach", n Pow"** and **"n Aff"** respectively[9]. They are defined as follow:

Need for Achievement: This is the drive to excel, to achieve in relation to a set of standard, and to strive to succeed. In other words, need for achievement is a behaviour directed toward competition with a standard of excellence[10]. McClelland found that people with a high need for achievement perform better than those with a moderate or low need for achievement, and noted regional/national differences in achievement motivation. Through his research, McClelland identified the following three characteristics of high-need achievers:

1. High-need achievers have a strong desire to assume personal responsibility for performing a task of finding a solution to a problem.
2. High-need achievers tend to set moderately difficult goals and take calculated risks.
3. High-need achievers have a strong desire for performance feedback.

Need for Power: The need for power is concerned with making an impact on others, the desire to influence others, the urge to change people, and the desire to make a difference in life[11]. People with a high need for power are people who like to be in control of people and events. This results in ultimate satisfaction to man.

People who have a high need for power are characterized by:

1. A desire to influence and direct somebody else.
2. A desire to exercise control over others.
3. A concern for maintaining leader-follower relations.

Need for Affiliation: The need for affiliation is defined as a desire to establish and maintain friendly and warm relations with other people[12]. The need for affiliation, in many ways, is similar to Maslow's social needs. The people with high need for affiliation have these characteristics:

1. They have a strong desire for acceptance and approval from others.
2. They tend to conform to the wishes of those people whose friendship and companionship they value.
3. They value the feelings of others.

Figure 9.2 is a summary chart of the three need theories of motivation just discussed. The chart shows the parallel relationship between the needs in each of the theories. Maslow refers to higher-lower order needs, whereas Herzberg refers to motivation and hygiene factors.

	Maslow		Herzberg	McClelland
Higher order needs	Self-actualisation	Motivational Factors	The work itself : • Responsibility • Advancement • Growth	Need for achievement
	Esteem		Achievement	
	Socialisation		Recognition	Need for power
Lower order needs	Safety and security	Hygiene Factors	Quality of inter-personal relationships	Need for affiliation
	Physiological		Job security	
			Working condition	
			Salary	

Argyris's Theory

Argyris has developed his motivation theory based on proposition how management practices affect the individual behaviour and growth[15]. In his view, the seven changes taking place in an individual's personality make him/her a mature one. In other words, personality of an ndividual develops from immaturity to maturity as follow:

Immaturity	Maturity
Passivity	Activity
Dependence	Independence
Capable of behaving in a few ways	Capable of behaving in many ways
Shallow interest	Deep interest
Short-term perspective	Long-term perspective
Subordinate position	Superordinate position
Lack of self-awareness	Self-awareness and control

Argyris views that immaturity exists in individuals mainly because of organisaitonal setting and management practices such as task specialization, chain of command, unity of direction, and span of management. In order to make individuals grow mature, he proposes gradual shift from the existing pyramidal organization structure to humanistic system; from existing management system to the more flexible and participative management. He states that such situation will satisfy not only their physiological and safety needs, but also will motivate them to make ready to make more use of their potential in accomplishing organizational goals.

12.5.2 Process Theories

Vroom's Expectancy Theory

One of the most widely accepted explanations of motivation is offered by Victor Vroom in his Expectancy Theory[16]. It is a cognitive process theory of motivation. The theory is founded on the basic notions that people will be motivated to exert a high level of effort when they believe there are relationships between the effort they put forth, the performance they achieve, and the outcomes/rewards they receive.

The relationships between notions of effort, performance, and rewards are depicted in Figure 12.3

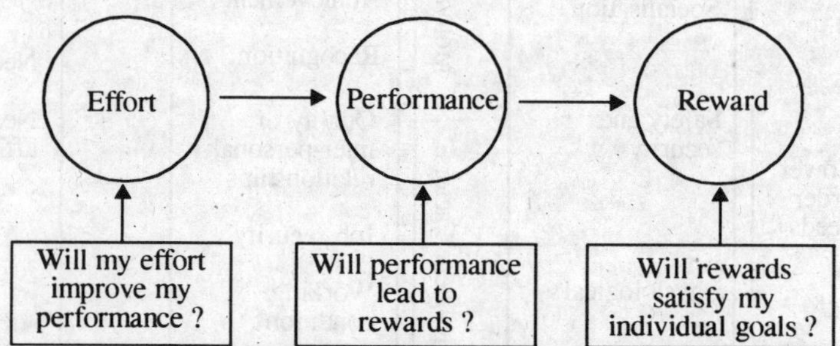

Fig. 12.3: Varoom's Expectancy Model of Motivation

Thus, the key constructs in the Varoom's expectancy theory of motivation are:

1. Valence: Valence, according to Vroom, means the value or strength one places on a particular outcome or reward.

2. Expectancy: It relates efforts to performance.

3. Instrumentality: By instrumentality, Vroom means, the belief that performance is related to rewards.

Thus, Vroom's, motivation can also be expressed in the form of an equation as follows:

Motivation = Valence × Expectancy × Instrumentality

Being the model multiplicative in nature, all the three variables must have high positive values to imply motivated performance choices. If any one of the variables approaches to zero level, the possibility of the so motivated performance also touches zero level.

However, Vroom's expectancy theory has its critics. The important ones are:

1. Critics like Porter and Lawler lebeled it as a theory of cognitive hedonism

which proposes that individual cognitively chooses the course of action that leads to the greatest degree of pleasure or the smallest degree of pain.

2. The assumption that people are rational and calculating makes the theory idealistic.
3. The expectancy theory does not describe individual and situational differences.

But the valence, or value people place on various rewards varies. For example, one employee prefers salary to benefits, whereas another person prefers to just the reverse. The valence for the same reward varies from situation to situation.

In spite of all these critics, the greatest point in the expectancy theory is that it explains why a significant segment of workforce exerts low levels of efforts in carrying out job responsibilities[17].

Porter and Lawler's Expectancy Theory

In fact, Porter and Lawler's theory[18] is an improvement over Vroom's expectancy theory. They posit that motivation does not equal satisfaction or performance. The model suggested by them encounters some of the simplistic traditional assumptions made about the positive relationship between satisfaction and performance. They proposed a multi-variate model to explain the complex relationship that exists between satisfaction and performance. What is the main point in Porter and Lawler's model is that effort or motivation does not lead directly to performance.

It is, in fact, mediated by abilities and traits and by role perceptions. Ultimately, performance ends to satisfaction. This is depicted in the following Fig 12.4

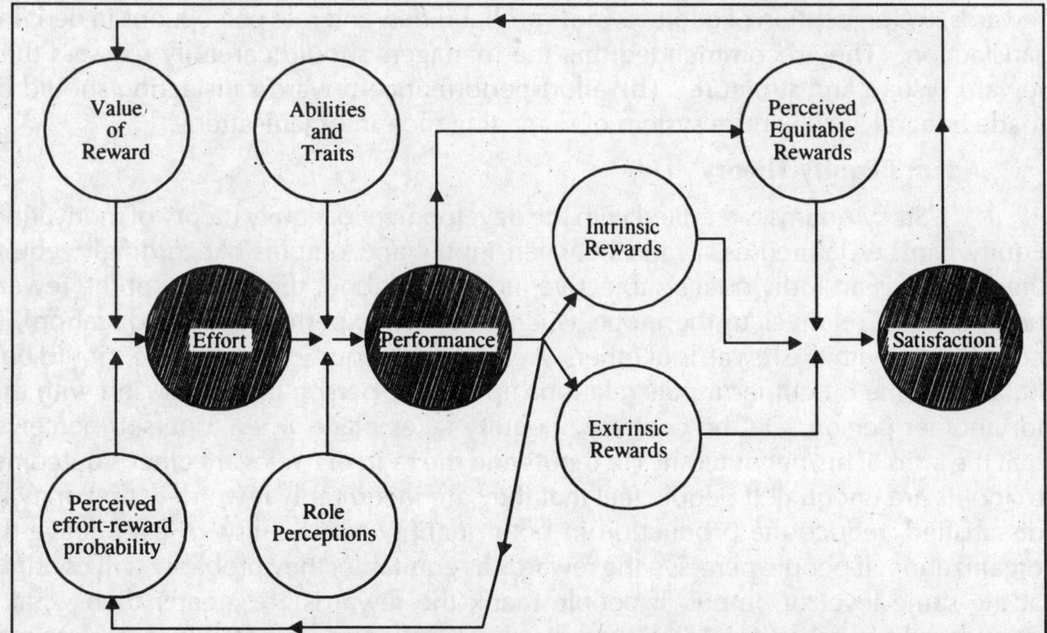

Fig. 12.4: The Porter and Lawler Motivation Model

Adapted from: L.W. Porter and E.E. Lawler: ***Managerial Attitude and Performance***, Richard D. Irwin, Homewood III, 1968, p.195.

Let us briefly discuss the main elements of the model:

Effort: Effort refers to the amount of energy an employee exerts on a given task. How much effort an employee will put in a task is determined by two factors – *(i)* value of reward and *(ii)* perception of effort – reward probability.

Performance: One's effort leads to his/her performance. Both may be equal or may not be. However, the amount of performance is determined by the amount of labour and the ability and role perception of the employee. Thus, if an employee possesses less ability and/or makes wrong role perception, his/her performance may be low in spite of his putting in great efforts.

Satisfaction: Performance leads to satisfaction. The level of satisfaction depends upon the amount of rewards one achieves. If the amount of actual rewards meet or exceed perceived equitable rewards, the employee will feel satisfied. On the contrary, if actual rewards fall short of perceived ones, he/she will be dissatisfied.

Rewards may be of two kinds – intrinsic and extrinsic rewards. Examples of intrinsic rewards are such as a sense of accomplishment and self-actualisation. As regards extrinsic rewards, these may include working conditions and status. A fair degree of research[19] supports that the intrinsic rewards are much more likely to produce attitudes about satisfaction that are related to performance.

There is no denying of the fact that the motivation model proposed by Porter and Lawler is quite complex than other models of motivation. In fact, motivation itself is not a simple cause-effect relationship rather it is a complex phenomenon. Porter and Lawler have attempted to measure variables such as the values of possible rewards, the perception of effort-rewards probabilities, and role perceptions in deriving satisfaction. They recommended that the managers should carefully reassess their reward system and structure. The effort-performance-reward-satisfaction should be made integral to the entire system of managing men in organisations.

Adam's Equity Theory

J. Stacy Adams is credited with the development of equity theory of motivation. Equity can be defined as a ratio between inputs and outputs. Accordingly, equity theory means an individual's subjective judgments about the fairness of the reward he or she got relatives to the inputs (such as effort, experience, and education), in comparison with the rewards of others. According to equity theory, there should be a balance of the outcomes/inputs relationship for one person in comparison with that for another person. On the contrary, inequity takes place when a person perceives that the ratio of his/her outcomes to inputs and the ratio of a relevant other's outcomes to inputs are unequal. If people feel that they are inequitably rewarded, they may be dissatisfied, reduce the production in both quantity and quality, or even leave the organization. If people perceive the rewards as equitable, they probably will continue at the same level of output. If people thank the rewards are greater then what is considered equitable, they may work harder. It may also be possible that some may discount the rewards. These three situations are illustrated in the following figure 12.5.

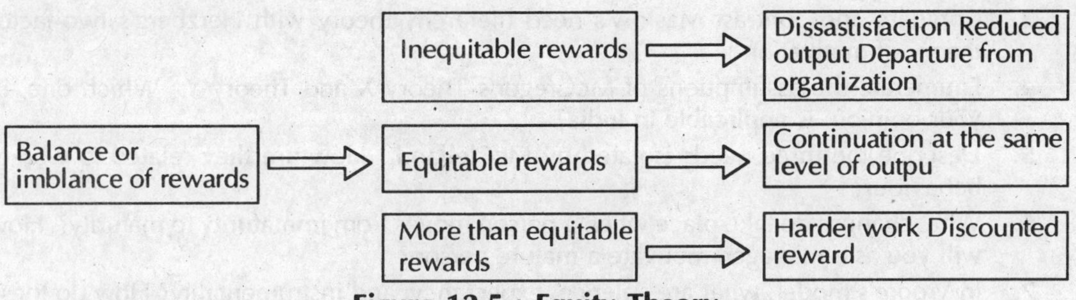

Figure 12.5 : Equity Theory

However, the equity theory suffers from some problems also. People may overestimate their own contributions and the rewards other receive. Employees can tolerate certain inequalities for some time, but prolonged feelings of inequity may result in strong reactions to a minor incident. For example, an employee reprimanded for being a few minutes late may get angry and may decide to quit the job, not so much because of the reprimand but because of long-standing feelings that the rewards for his/her contributions are inequitable in comparison witfeelings that the rewards for and may decide to quit the job, not so much becauLikewise, a person may be very satisfied with a weekly salary of Rs.1000 until he or she knows that another person doing the similar job receives Rs. 20 more.

SUMMARY

This summary is organized by the 'learning objectives' given on page no. 200 :

- Motivation can be defined as one's willingness to exert his/her maximum efforts for the accomplishment of certain goals or objectives.
- Motivation starts with motive. Motive is activating, invisible force. One motive may result in different behaviours. Motive may change over times. Motives are goal-directed and prompt people to action.
- Motivation involves a process that includes motive, goal, and behaviour. The significance of motivation lies in the fact that if serves as fuel or power to make an organization move toward the accomplishment of its goals.
- The models and/or theories of motivation explain what actually makes the people exert more toward the accomplishment of their goals. All motivation theories or models are broadly classified into three types. **Human need-based theories** suggest that people are prompted to work to satisfy their needs. That the nature of personality content activates one to put in efforts for the accomplishment of goals is the substance of **nature-based theories.** Contrary to these, **the expectancy-based theory** says that human effort is the basis for motivation and that people want their effort to lead to performance and rewards. Finally, theories of motivation are found culturally bound and differences occur between nations.

REVIEW QUESTIONS

1. Define motivation. Appreciate its importance to a modern enterprise.
2. What are the five categories of motivational needs described by Maslow? Give an example of how each can be satisfied.

3. Compare and contrast Maslow's need hierarchy theory with Herzberg's two-factor theory of motivation.
4. Enumerate the assumptions of McGregor's Theory X and Theory Y. Which one, in your opinion, is applicable in India?
5. Describe the three needs isolated by McClelland. How are they related to worker behaviour?
6. What changes do take place when a person moves from immaturity to maturity? How will you as a manager, motivate a mature person?
7. In Vroom's model, what are valence, expectancy, and instrumentality? How do these variables relate to one another and to work motivation?
8. Critically examine Porter-Lawler model of motivation. How do performance and satisfaction relate to each other?
9. "Motivation is a product of values one seeks and one's estimation of the probability that a certain action will lead to those values." Discuss the idea contained in this statement.
10. Do you believe you can do a better job of studying than you are currently doing? Do you think you would get better grades if you did a better job (study)? Do you care about the grades (rewards) in your University? Discuss.
11. What do you mean by motivation? Discuss the Maslow's theory of motivation.

QUESTIONNAIRE*

Goals:

1. To experience firsthand the concepts of one of the work-motivation theories-in this case, the popular Maslow hierarchy of needs.
2. To get personal feedback on your opinions of the use of motivational techniques in human resource management.

Implementation:

The following questions for the Motivation Questionnaire on the next page have seven possible responses:

1. Please mark one of the seven responses by circling the number that corresponds to the response that fits your opinion. For example, if you "strongly agree," circle the number "+3."
2. Complete every item. You have about 10 minutes to do so.

	Strongly Agree	Agree	Slighly Agree	Don't Know	Slightly Disagree	Disagree	Strongly Disagree
1. Special wage increases should be given to	+3	+2	+1	0	-1	-2	-3
employees who do their jobs very well.	+3	+2	+1	0	-1	-2	-3
2. Better job descriptions would be helpful so that employees will know exactly what is expected of them.	+3	+2	+1	0	-1	-2	-3
3. Employees need to be reminded that their jobs are dependent on the company's ability to compete effectively.	+3	+2	+1	0	-1	-2	-3

4. Supervisors should give a good deal of attention to the physical working conditions of their employees.	+3	+2	+1	0	-1	-2	-3
5. Supervisors ought to work hard to develop a friendly working atmosphere among their people.	+3	+2	+1	0	-1	-2	-3
6. Individual recognition for above-standard performance means a lot to employees.	+3	+2	+1	0	-1	-2	-3
7. Indifferent supervision can often bruise feelings.	+3	+2	+1	0	-1	-2	-3
8. Employees want to fee that their real skills and capacities are put to use on their jobs.	+3	+2	+1	0	-1	-2	-3
9. The company retirement benefits and stock programs are important factors in keeping employees on their jobs	+3	+2	+1	0	-1	-2	-3
10. Almost every job can be made more stimulating and challenging.	+3	+2	+1	0	-1	-2	-3
11. Many employees want to give their best in everything they do.	+3	+2	+1	0	-1	-2	-3
12. Management could show more interest in the employees by sponsoring social events after hours	+3	+2	+1	0	-1	-2	-3
13. Pride in one's work is actually an important reward.	+3	+2	+1	0	-1	-2	-3
14. Employees want to be able to think of themselves as "the best" at their own jobs	+3	+2	+1	0	-1	-2	-3
15. The quality of the relationships in the informal work group is quite important.	+3	+2	+1	0	-1	-2	-3
16. Individual incentive bonuses would improve the performance of employees.	+3	+2	+1	0	-1	-2	-3
17. Visibility with upper management is important to employees.	+3	+2	+1	0	-1	-2	-3
18. Employees generally like to schedule their own work and to make job-related decisions with a minimum of supervision.	+3	+2	+1	0	-1	-2	-3
19. Job security is important to employees.	+3	+2	+1	0	-1	-2	-3
20. Having good equipment to work with is important to employees.	+3	+2	+1	0	-1	-2	-3

Scoring:

1. Transfer the numbers you circled in the questionnaire to the appropriate places in the following chart.

Statement No.	Score	Statement No.	Score
10	________	2	________
11	________	3	________
13	________	9	________
18	________	19	________
Total	________	Total	________

(Self-actualization needs)
6 ________ ________ 1
8 ________ ________ 4
14 ________ ________ 16
17 ________ ________ 20
Total ________ ________ Total
(Esteem Needs) (Basic Needs)
5 ________ ________
7 ________ ________
12 ________ ________
15 ________ ________
Total ________ ________
(Belongingness needs)

2. Record your total scores in the following chart by marking an X in each row below the number of your total score for that are of needs motivation.

3.

	-12	-10	-8	-6	-4	-2	0	+2	+4	+6	+8	+10	+12
Self-actualization													
Esteem													
Belongingness													
Safety													
Basic													

Low Use High Use

By examining the chart, you can see the relative strength you attach to each of the needs in Maslow's hierarchy. There are no right answers here, but most work-motivation theorists imply that most people are concerned mainly with the upper-level needs (that is, belongingness, esteem and self-actualization.

REFERENCES

1. Fred Luthans: *op. cit.*, p. 141.
2. Stephen P. Robbins: *op, cit.*, p. 168.
3. J.L. Gray and F.A. Starke: **Organisational Behaviour-Concepts and Applications**, Merrill Publishing, Co., Columbus, 1988, p. 104.
4. Abraham Maslow: A Theory of Human Motivation, **Psychological Review,** March/April 1943, 50, pp. 370-396.
5. M.A. Wahba and L.G. Bridwell: Maslow Reconsidered: A Review of Research on the Need Hierarchy Theory, **Organisational Behaviour and Human Performance**, April 1976, pp. 212-240.
6. F. Herzberg, . Mausner, and B. Snyderman: **The Motivation to Work**, John Wiley, New York, 1959.

*The "Motivation Questionnaire" is reprinted from "Motivation: A Feedback Exercise," in John E. Jones and J. William Pfeiffer (Eds.), ***The Annual Handbook for Group Facilitators,*** University Associates, San Diego, Calif., 1973, pp. 43-45, and is used with permission.

7. David C. McClelland: **The Achieving Society**, Free Press, New York, 1961: Also J.W. Atkinson and J.O. Raynor: **Motivation and Achievement,** Winston, Washington, D.C., 1974.
8. H.A. Murray: **Explorations in Personality: A Clinical and Experimental Study of Fifty Men of College Age**, Oxford University Press, New York, 1938.
9. David C. McClellan: Towards a Theory of Motive Acquisition, **American Psychologist**, Vol. 20, 1965, pp. 321-333.
10. David C. McClelland: Achievement Motivation can be Learned, **Harvard Business Review**, 43, Nov. Dec. 1965, pp. 6-24.
11. David C. McClelland and D. Burnham: Power is the Great Motivator, **Harvard Business Review**, 54, 1976, pp. 100-111.
12. S. Schachter: **The Psychology of Affiliation**, Stanford University Press, Stanford, 1959.
13. Douglas McGregor: **The Human Side of Enterprise**, McGraw-Hill, New York, 1960.
14. F.L. Urwick: Theory Z, **Indian Administrative and Management Review**, Jan.-March 1974; Sharu S. Rangnekar: The Last Alphabet of Management Theory Z, **Industrial Times**, June 1972; and William Ouchi: **Theory Z,** Addison-Wesley, 1981.
15. Chris Argyris: **Personality and Organisation**, Harper & Row, New York, 1957.
16. Victor H. Vroom: **Work and Motivation,** Wiley, New York, 1964.
17. Stephen P Robbins: *op. cit.,* 1998, p. 189.
18. L.W. Porter and E.E. Lawler: **Managerial Attitude and Performance,** Richard D. Irwin, Home Wood, III, 1968.
19. Gary Blau: Operationalizing Direction and Level of Effort and Testing their Relationships to Individual Job Performance, **Organisational Behaviour and Human Decision Processes,** June 1993, pp. 152-170.
20. Referred in **Motivation, Job Design and Appraisal,** MS-2, Block 3, Indira Gandhi National Open University, New Delhi, 1991 (reprint), p.37.

Case 12.1: A Qualified but Hesitant Teacher

Vikram earned his Post-Graduate Degree from a University in the North-East India. He hails from a poor farming family with rural background. Vikram studied with great hardship. For him, it was 'earn while you learn'. He used to walk on foot ten kms. Village road while he was pursuing his Graduation Degree. He proved "where there is a will, there is a way." With his self-help, the God also helped him. Vikram, just after the declaration of his Post-Graduation result, got a regular teaching post in the same college. For Vikram, one battle was over but new and more challenging battle just started.

Though Vikram was hard working, but not ready to accept challenges of new environment. Some of his faults were to enter the class often five to ten minutes late, to get irritative when the students ask questions while he teaches, not update his knowledge in the subject he teaches, and bringing petty and routine matters to the Head of his Department or to peers for decisions. Somuchso, when ever he does anything even preparing his class lecture, brings it to the Head of the Department. Complaints about Vikram from the students started pouring even written complaints to the Head of the Department that the students are not getting any thing meaningful from ..... In fact, it became a real problem for the Head how to tackle the same.

The Head, over the six months period, found Vikram as plain and innocent by heart. He therefore, decided to motivate Vikram by saying that "each new teacher, even myself, faces such problem. These are overcome over the period through sincere efforts. I am sure that you are doing the same and keep it up. Be more objective and specific in your efforts. I see potential in you to emerge as a very effective teacher in days to come." Vikram imbibed all this and assured the Head to honour his advices. He, then left for his class with new challenge and determination to excel in his task. Just within a week, Vikram improved his teaching and the students reported their satisfaction to the Head of the Department over Vikram's teaching.

QUESTIONS

1. If you were the Head of the Department, how would you improve Vikram?
2. In your opinion, which motivation theory can help motivate Vikram?

Case 12.2: Gopal Cotton Mills Limited*[1]

In 1952 Mr. Ramachandra Shah, the managing director of Gopal Cotton mills, went to Japan on a trade mission. On his way back to India, he visited several Southeast Asian countries to make a survey of Indian testiles. In the course of talking with many merchants and customers, he learned that they preferred Japanese products to Indian ones because of the former's faultless weave. Customers were not interested in buying Indian cloth which, being manufactured on monautomatic looms, contained frequent flaws. Mr. Shah decided, therefore, to introduce automatic looms in his mills.

On his return to Ranchipur, Mr. Shah drew up a plant of build a new loomshed for automatic looms to replace those in the existing loomsheds. He consulted the weaving superintendent about the plan. Later he called in Mr. Shankarlal, the supervisor in the shed which was to be replaced, and explained the new system to him. He also told Mr. Shankarlal that he would be considered for promotion as soon as operations started in the new automatic shed.

The loomshed to be replaced was the smallest of the three in the company's compound. It had 100 looms running on two shifts. All the weavers working in this shed belonged to the same community: they were Gujarati Patels. In line with tradition, each jobber (mechanic or first line supervisor) selected his own workers. So a jobber brought workers from the rural areas of his own community. All the weavers in Mr. Shankarlal's department lived in the same locality and almost all of them had been working in the shed for at least 10 years, some for as long as 25 years. Although he lived in a different part of the city, he joined the workers on festive occasions, when they held sing-songs or performed dramas. Weavers from the other sheds did not join in; they came from different communities.

The old loomshed was hot, humid, poorly illuminated and very noisy. The machinery was old and a large number of breakdowns and accidents took place. But the workers were proud of the loomshed. They boasted that even with such old looms their production was higher than that of the other sheds with powerlooms. Each worker minded two looms and was paid according to his output. He had no helper to assist. When he had to leave his looms running while he went to bring bobbins, carry cloth, go to the washroom, drink water, or talk with people, his neighbours would look after them. In fact, the workers took turns to go out for a break, and a group could always he found outside, away from the noise, talking, smoking and drinking water. Although the management was not in favour of this practice, all attempts to stop it had failed.

Mr. Shankarlal made it a practice to make two rounds in the loomshed every day

* Adapted from Lynton Rolf P. and Harriet, R. Asian Cases, Aloka Ltd., Hyderabad, India, 1960, pp. 137-139.

and to talk with any worker in difficulty. Several times each day he stood outside the door of the shed and chatted with workers who were coming in or going out. Many weavers consulted him about their personal problems. When the managing director or the superintendent was on his rounds, Mr. Shankarlal passed the word to the workers so that they could go back to their looms in time. When any of his workers were called to the folding department to explain bad work, Mr. Shankarlal went along to plead for them and to minimize the fines imposed on them by the folding clerks.

The erection of the new loomshed was completed in September, 1953. It had up to date lighting and humidification equipment, and comfortable washrooms and toilets inside the building. The machinery consisted of looms driven by separate motors and was spaced more generously than in the old shed. The plan specified one weaver to eight looms. Each weaver would have the assistance of a helper to take care of all the auxiliary work so that he would not have to leave the looms at all. The weavers were to be paid according to output. The helpers would be paid a fixed wage somewhat lower than the weaver's pay. All workers from the old shed were needed in the new shed, so the question of retrenchment did not arise. They would be either weavers or helpers. Those having the longest service with the company would be weavers. These points were covered by an agreement which Mr. Shah made with the labour union to which 60 per cent of the workers in the shed belonged.

Mr. Shankarlal went around and talked about the new plan to the workers individually and in small groups. He told them about the better working conditions and assured them that their earnings would soon be higher than before. He also told them that helpers would be given weaver's positions just as soon as the older weavers retied. But after over a whole week devoted to convincing the workers of the advantages of working in the new shed, only 16 workers agreed. This number was too small to start the new section. For two more weeks Mr. Shankarlal kept up his efforts to persuade the workers but got no response.

At the end of this period, Mr. Shankarlal was called to the director's office and asked to explain the situation. Mr. Shah told him that the workers would be given an ultimatum: if they were not willing to abide by the agreement made by the company and the union leaders, new workers would be recruited.

Back in the shed, Mr. Shankarlal went round again and told the workers of the director's decision. As far as he could judge, the workers were adamant in their refusal and unafraid at the threat of losing their jobs. They hardly stayed to listen to what he had to say. They raised no questions and were altogether silent in his presence. This silence became characteristic of the relationship between the workers and Mr. Shankarlal. They no longer came to him with their problems: and if they saw him outside the shed they would either stay away from him or go inside.

About a week after Mr. Shah had spoken to him, Mr. Shankarlal called a meeting of the workers and gave a talk about the importance of the new shed. He told them that foreign competition forced the company to have automatic looms, whether they liked it or not; that they should give the new idea a try. He finished his talk by asking them for any questions that they might have about any aspect of the change. Nobody spoke and the meeting broke up. The next day Mr. Shankarlal put up a notice signed by Mr. Shah . It stated the terms of the agreement with the union had set a limit of seven days for the workers to agree to work on the new looms.

During that week the workers were persuaded by the union leaders to work in the new shed and they finally agreed. At the same time, the company proceeded with all arrangements to start the new section.

On the eighth day after the notice was put up, work started in the new section. The changes went according to plan. Mr. Shankarlal was promoted to Assistant Weaving Master and put in charge of the new section. He was very satisfied to notice that production climbed steadily. Within two months the shed had reached the target of 88 per cent efficiency. Mr. Shankarlal then turned his attention to learning more about the automatic looms. He cut down his rounds in the loomshed and spent as much time as he could with the expert technician from the firm that had supplied the looms.

But an increasing amount of his time was taken up with listening to complaints from the workers. The complaints were mostly about bad working conditions: that the walking distance between looms was too great, that the yarn breakage rate was too high for automatic looms, that the light was too glaring, that the toilet and drinking water place should not be in the same room, and so on. Production fell to 84 per cent efficiency. Mr. Shankarlal made it a practice to check the production of individual workers and to call to his office those whose production was the lowest. He asked them to explain the decline in production. In reply the workers stated more grievances.

One day, three representatives of the workers came to his office. They told him that the Mills were getting enormous profit from the automatic loom weaving, but that the workers were not getting a proper share of it. Mr. Shankarlal replied that the company had spent a very large sum of money in installing the new shed and that it could not pay higher wages. The representative left without argument. A week later the workers went on strike. When Mr. Shankarlal arrived at the mill at 7 a.m., as usual, he found all the workers entering the old shed. Mr. Shankarlal saw that the management had removed the unused looms from the old shed. The workers sat down on the empty floor, each where his loom had been and refused to move. They said that the old loomshed should have been kept intact so that, if they wanted to, they could have gone back to their old jobs. They threatened not to leave the floor until all the old looms had been replaced.

At the end of the third day of the strike, Mr. Shankarlal fell ill. He complained that the humidity of the loomshed had affected his lungs and took a month's leave. When Mr. Shankarlal returned to work after a month, he learned that the strike had ended through the persuasion of the union leaders and with the assurance from the company of a higher rate of a pay for the workers. But production was down to 80 per cent; at this level the earnings of the workers were less than before, in spite of the rise in rate.

One week later, Mr. Shah replaced Mr. Shankarlal as Assistant Weaving Master. The new man was a technical graduate with four years' experience of automatic loom weaving. Mr. Shankarlal was offered a new job: Assistant Weaving Master in charge of Labour Control for all three sheds. He readily accepted it and so assumed charge of hiring and firing workers, taking disciplinary action, carrying out drives for higher production, and keeping the superintendent and the director generally informed on all labour problems.

QUESTIONS

1. If you were Mr. Ramchandra Shah, what would you do?
2. Which theory of motivation do you use to motivate the weavers and why?

13

MOTIVATION : APPLICATION

"Motivation will almost always beat mere talent." **– *Norman R. Augustine***

"The significance of man is not in what he attains, but rather in what he longs to attain." **- *Kahlil Gibran***

Learning Objectives

After studying this chapter, you should be able to:

- **Explain** the rationale for motivational selectivity.
- **Classify** different types of incentives offered to employees to motivate them.
- **Describe** how job design alongwith its various approaches is used for motivating employees at work.
- **Describe** the types of motivational patterns used to motivate employees in the Indian organisations.

Having learned various theories or models of motivation in the previous chapter, now you as a manager need to see how to use them. In this chapter, you will learn how to apply motivational theories/models into practice.

13.1 MOTIVATIONAL SELECTIVITY

As discussed earlier, motives are cognitive variables. They prompt people to action. They arise on continuous basis and influence what people notice, how they see and think, and what they learn from their environment. Such influence of motivation on cognitive process is called **motivational selectivity.** For example, a person who has an intense desire for having something would be searching for that particular thing, thus, forgetting or neglecting other things. In such situations, the stimuli that are relevant to the active motive tend to stand out focally, whereas the irrelevant ones tend to fade into the background. The reason being, people cannot assimilate all what they observe or receive from the environment at a time. Hence, they selectively perceive objects/things which interest to them most in a particular situation and avoid those for which they are indifferent[1]. Such selectivity involves the two psychological principles of (*i*) figure ground, and (*ii*) relevancy, discussed earlier in Chapter 6. It means that people actively resist certain aspects or objects while accepting the desirable ones. This is called **perceptual defense.** Perceptual errors are yet another type of motivational selectivity. If an employee wants to see his/her leader as an ideal or noble and a student wants to see his/her Professor as a noble, it will be his/her tendency to neglect or resist evidences and instances on the contrary.

Evidences suggest that when a particular motive-effort becomes fruitful, people consider it as an incentive to direct their motive/effort in the same direction. In a nutshell, the motivational selectivity aspects like attention and perception, thinking and learning, remembering and forgetting,fantasy and dreams, and levels of awareness assume great importance in motivating people at work. Hence, success of motivation to a large extent, depends upon selection of appropriate motivational tools befitting the given situation and motivational selectivity.

13.2 MOTIVATIONAL TOOLS

Motivational tools are instruments that prompt people to action. Hence, while using motivational tools, these should be adequate and capable enough to motivate employees to make their maximum efforts to accomplish the set goals. Various motivational tools used to motivate employees in business organisations are broadly classified into monetary and non-monetary tools or incentives. These are discussed in more details subsequently. Here, we will focus on why motivational tools need to be appropriate to activate people to action.

Man is a wanting animal. He works to satisfy his needs in a prepontency order. Therefore, motivational tools need to be effective enough to satisfy human needs. As human needs vary between people and between different points of times in case of the same person, motivational tools are, therefore, bound to vary accordingly. For example, while increase in salary may satisfy one's physiological needs, recognition may satisfy the esteem needs.

When needs are not satisfied, people become frustrated. Yes, there may be both environmental and personal factors resulting in one's frustration. Apathy, indifference, aggresion, antagonism, open conflict, physical violence, etc. are the common responses to frustration observed in organisations. These are detrimental to organisational efficiency.

It is true that reaction to frustration may vary from person to person, yet the behavioural pattern of individuals is likely to be identical in identical situations. As such, it makes easier for the motivator/manager to apply the appropriate motivational tools, if the behavioural pattern of the individuals is known to him. Job frustration is discussed, in detail, later in chapter 23.

Thus, it can be concluded that motivational tools are expected to be need satisfying, and hence, need to be person-oriented. Better the motivational tools, greater would be its effect on the individual behaviour. This would, in turn, lead to organisational effectiveness. And in this lies the need for and significance of motivational tools to be used to motivate employees in business organisations.

13.3 INCENTIVES

The term incentive means an inducement which rouses or stimulates one to action in a desired direction. An incentive has a motivational power. A large number of incentives the modern organisations use to motivate their employees may be broadly grouped into (*i*) financial incentives, and (*ii*) non-financial incentives. These are discussed one by one.

Financial Incentives

Money is an important motivator. Common uses of money as incentive are in the form of wages and salaries, bonus, retirement benefits, medical reimbursement, etc. Management needs to increase these financial incentives making wages and salaries competitive between various organisations so as to attract and hold force[2].

Money plays a significant role in satisfying physiological and security/social needs. As money is recognized as a basis of status, respect and power, it also helps satisfy the social needs of the people. It is important to mention that once the physiological and security needs are satisfied, money ceases to be motivator. Money then becomes, what Herzberg termed, hygiene and maintenance factor.

The presence of hygiene factor, of course, prevents job dissatisfaction but do not provide 'on the job satisfaction' to the employees in the organisation. In such case, money cannot be considered as motivator. Then, in order to motivate employees, according to Herzberg, it is necessary to provide other incentives for the satisfaction of **ego, status,** and **self-actualisation** needs. However, these needs are experienced generally by employees working at higher levels in the organisations. People in higher positions getting higher monetary rewards are not motivated by increased monetary rewards. Yes, they may be motivated by money only when increase is large enough to raise their standard of living and status in the society to which they belong to.

What follows from above discussion is that money is not the only motivator and also it is not always a motivator. In order to satisfy different kinds of human needs, management needs to provide non-financial incentives such as job enlargement, participative management, recognition, praise, etc. These also motivate employees at their works.

Non-Financial Incentives

As mentioned earlier, man is a wanting animal. Once money satisfies his/her physiological and security needs, it ceases to be a motivating force. Then, higher order needs for status and recognition and ego in the society, emerge. The following non-financial incentives help management satisfy its employees' these needs:

1. **Appreciation of Work Done:** Appreciation or praise for work done, be it at home, at school/University or at work place, serves as an effective non-financial incentive. Appreciation satisfies one's ego needs. However, managers need to use this incentive with great degree of caution because praising an incompetent employee may create a resentment among competent employees.

2. **Competition:** If there exists a healthy competition among the employees both at individual and group levels, it will prompt them to exert more to achieve their personal or group goals. Thus, competition serves as a non-financial incentive for employees to put in more efforts at their works.

3. **Group Incentives:** Some times, group incentives act as more effective than individual incentives to motivate the employees. Particularly, when the prestige or even existence of a group is at stake, the group members work with a team spirit. This results in high morale and, in turn, increase in its productivity.

4. **Knowledge of the Results:** Knowledge of the results of work done leads to employee satisfaction. An employee derives satisfaction when his/her boss appreciates the work he/she has done just as an MBA student gets satisfaction when his/

her Professor appreciates the seminar he/she presented in the class.

5. **Workers' Participation in Management:** Inviting workers to participate in organisational management gives worker's a psychological satisfaction that their voices are also heard. This imbibes a sense of importance among the workers.

6. **Opportunity for Growth:** Man is not only a wanting animal but an ambitious creature also. People always need to grow in their career. So, if the employees are provided proper opportunities for growth and career advancement and chance to develop their personality, they feel much satisfied and become more committed to the organisational goals.

7. **Suggestion System:** Suggestion system is yet another non-financial incentive to be used to motivate employees. Following this, some organisations make use of cash awards for giving useful suggestions. They sometimes publish the worker's name with his/her photograph in the company's magazine with a motive to motivate other workers to search for useful suggestions for the company. Thus, suggestion system acts as an incentive for the workers to be in search of something useful for the company.

8. **Job Enrichment:** Job enrichment simply means adding the contents to a job leading to increased responsibility, scope and challange in its performance. Particularly, the executives working at the higher levels often prefer to job enrichment because it makes job more challenging. They derive higher satisfaction by performing more and more challanging jobs. Thus, job enrichment as an incentive motivates the executives to exert for accomplishment of their goals. Job enrichment is a by-product of job design which is discussed subsequently.

13.4 JOB DESIGN

The job a worker does is a significant aspect of his/her life for more than one reasons. It provides worker not only a living, but also helps in achieving his/her other goals such as economic, social, political and cultural. Somuchso, work is philosophised and treated as "**worship**". People who work for living spend a significant period of their lives at work. Hence, job needs to provide them satisfaction to sustain their interest in jobs. This is done through job design. While other incentives, as discussed in the preceding section, provide extrinsic motivation, job design provides intrinsic motivation to the workers.

A job can be defined as a grouping of tasks within a prescribed unit or units of work. Job design is a deliberate attempt made to structure the tasks and social relationships of a job to create optimal levels of variety, responsibility, autonomy and interaction. In fact, the basic objective of job design is to maintain a fit between a job and its performer so that the job is performed well and the job performer derives satisfaction from doing job.

The important approaches or strategies a job design involves are job enlargement, job enrichment, job simplification, job rotation, quality of work life and goal-setting. Fig. 13.1 summarizes the various approaches to job design.

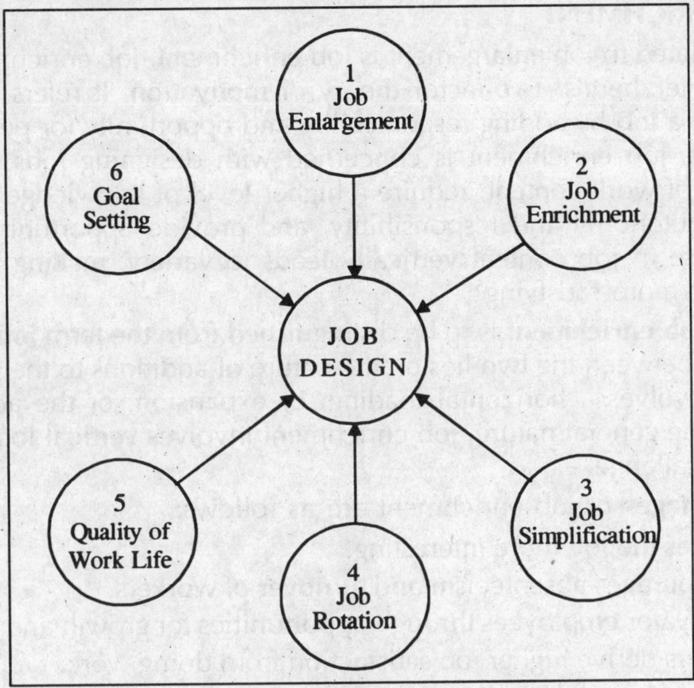

Fig. 13.1: Approaches to Job Design

Each of these approaches are now discuss one by one.

13.4.1 JOB ENLARGEMENT

Job enlargement consists of making a job larger in scope by combining additional task activities into each job through expansion. This is called **horizontal loading**. It, thus, focuses on enlarging jobs by increasing tasks and responsibilities. An example of job enlargement in a University may be assigning a Professor the task of looking after the NSS activities besides his/her teaching in his/her Department. Similarly, a clerk in an office who is doing the typing work only may also be assigned the task of drafting letters, sorting of incoming mails and filing of letters.

Following are the **advantages** of job enlargement :

1. Job enlargement avoids monotony which is the result of high degree of specialisation and division of labour.
2. It improves workers satisfaction, decreased production costs, and increased quality[3].
3. It also improves the worker's efficiency at work.

In spite of above advantages, certain **disadvantages** of job enlargement cannot be lost sight of. These are:

1. Workers may require additional training for performing enlarged tasks. Thus, the training costs tend to rise.
2. Moreover, productivity may fall during the introduction of new system based on job redesigning.
3. Lastly, workers often argue for increased pay because of the increased work load as a result of job enlargement.

13.4.2 JOB ENRICHMENT

Closely related to job enlargement is job enrichment. Job enrichment is a direct outgrowth of Herzberg's[4] two-factor theory of motivation. It refers to the vertical enlargement of a job by adding responsibility and opportunity for personal growth. In other words, job enrichment is concerned with designing jobs that include a greater variety of work content, require a higher level of knowledge and skill, give worker more autonomy and responsibility, and provide opportunity for personal growth. Increase in job content vertically leads to variety, making repetitive jobs less boring but more satisfying[5].

The term **job enrichment** is to be distinguished from the term **job enlargement**. The difference between the two lies on the nature of additions to the job. While job enlargement involves a horizontal loading, or expansion, or the adding of more tasks of the same general nature, job enrichment involves vertical loading, addition giving more challange.

The **advantages** of job enrichment are as follows:

1. It makes the job more interesting.
2. It discourages absenteeism and turnover of workers.
3. It motivates employees through opportunities for growth and advancement.
4. Workers derive higher job satisfaction from doing work.
5. The enterprise also gains through improvement of output both in quantity and quality.

However, job enrichment is not an unmixed blessing. It suffers from the following **limitations** or **disadvantages** also:

1. Technologically, it may not be easy to enrich all jobs.
2. Enrichment of jobs has proved to be a costly preposition in certain cases as the expenditure exceeds gains.
3. Adding challanges to highly skilled jobs may not necessarily bring satisfaction for highly professional ones.
4. All those who prefer to job enrichment may not have the requisite capability to meet the new challanges.

Go through the following short case of job enrichment applied in Dynamo Corporation Limited, Rampur. It will help you understand how job enrichment motivates workers to improve their job performance.

Job Enrichment in Dynamo Corporation Limited, Rampur

An interesting study in job enrichment was undertaken at the Rampur unit of Dynamo Corporation Limited. The corporation was set up for 10 years and produced items for the "core" sector (heavy engineering equipment). The study was conducted on managers, supervisors, and workers of a unit producing auxiliary equipment. An initial survey revealed that none of the workers was emotionally committed to the product, there was forced idle time because of task interdependence and uneven distribution of work load. Having worked for a long time at the same job, workers did not find it sufficiently challenging.

These findings were placed before the total unit, which agreed on setting up a rotating task force with representatives from each category and the introduction of a new work system. The new work system consisted of having a group of employees taking charge of a complete task and gradually taking on each other's job after training. Thus a welder did the job of a fitter, and a fitter did that of a welder or a gas cutter. Each worker became multiskilled. Three things were noted: (1) Monotony was partially eliminated; (2) the traditional hierarchical concept of trade was minimized, and (3) a positive attitude towards co-workers and the work was developed.

Monthly data for targets set and percentages of fulfilment of targets were plotted. From April 1975 to November 1975, rising trends were noticed both in the fulfilment of targets and the overall efficiency against clocked time. There was an increase of 6.9 per cent and 45.3 per cent in relation to the targets and the overall efficiency respectively. Thus, changes in job content, greater variety, and freedom contributed to the performance of the employees.

13.4.3 JOB SIMPLIFICATION

In case of job simplification, a job is broken down, to the extent possible, into smaller parts as is done in assembly line operations. Doing so fragmented task repetitively leads to increase in worker's productivity. However, the other side of doing the repititive task is that job may produce boredom and monotony to the workers. This may, in turn, lead to a tendency of absenteeism among them. Nonetheless, such type of job may be suitable for workers having low levels of skills and knowledge.

13.4.4 JOB ROTATION

Some people have suggested job rotation also as a motivational strategy. In job rotation, a worker moves from one job to another, at the same level, that has similar skill requirements. Job rotation reduces boredom and monotony through changing employee's activities. This has almost the similar effects as the job enlargement has. However, job rotation has certain drawbacks also. The important ones are: (*i*) Work suffers from obvious disruption caused by change in job; (*ii*) Job rotation becomes less useful as specialisation proceeds, and (*iii*) It may demotivate intelligent and ambitious employees who seek specific responsibilities in their chosen speciality.

13.4.5 QUALITY OF WORK LIFE (QWL)

There have been divergent views as to what really is quality of work life (QWL). According to Sangeeta Jain[7], QWL consists of a whole parcel of terms and notions all of 'which really belong under the Quality of Working Life Umbrella'. Walton[8] viewed it as consisting of all those work conditions that give satisfaction to workers while doing their jobs/tasks. In simple words, QWL refers to the favourableness or unfavourableness of a total job environment for people. The elements included in a QWL programme like open communication, equitable reward system, employees' job security and satisfaction, participative management, development of employee skill, etc. make job environment favourable.

Though one can catalogue a long list of factors that contribute to quality of work life, the following four are the broad and common ones:

1. Job Involvement
2. Job Satisfaction
3. Sense of Competence
4. Job Performance and Productivity

Now, in what follows is their brief description one by one.

1. **Job Involvement:** Job involvement indicates the extent a worker identifies himself/herself with the work. Workers involved in their jobs spent more time on their jobs. Challanging jobs make workers to get involved with their jobs. Besides, people with high need for achievement and high work ethic are also found to be involved with their jobs.

2. **Job Satisfaction :** Job satisfaction refers to one's good or positive feeling toward his/her job. Job satisfaction improves work performance and reduces employee absenteeism and turnover.

3. **Sense of Competence:** Job involvement ultimately results in sense of competence. Sense of competence denotes the feelings of confidence that one has in one's own ability, skill or competence. High sense of competence and job involvement combinedly produce high levels of job satisfaction and productivity.

4. **Job Performance and Productivity:** The aforesaid three factors - job involvement, job satisfaction, and sense of comptence---boil down to improved job performance and productivity of employees.

How to improve QWL? Suggestion and measures given by behavioural scientists do not tally but vary. The simplest solution to improve QWL may be improving the existing job environment. Some researchers[9] consider two directions to improve QWL. One direction concerns the alleviation or removal of negative aspects of work and working conditions and the other direction concerns the modification of aspects of work and working conditions. Measures to improve QWL in India, as suggested by one researcher[10], include participative community development projects, job sharing and creating part-time jobs, choice of appropriate technology, involving unions, education and training and lagislative measures. Besides, the conditions that contribute to motivation (equitable salaries, financial incentives, effective employee selection, etc.) also contribute to improving the quality of work life (QWL)[11].

Q§WL is discussed, in detail, in the penultimate Chapter 24.

Job Analysis

Closely related to job enlargement, enrichment, simplification, and rotation is job analysis. Job analysis is a statement mentioning who will do what. Absence of job analysis may adversely affect the performance of a task just as exemplified as follows:

> This is a story about four people named Everybody, Somebody, Anybody and Nobody. There was an important job to be done and Everybody was sure that Somebody would do it. Anybody could have done it, but Nobody did it. Somebody got angry about that because it was Everybody's job. Everybody thought Anybody could do it, but Nobody realized that Everybody wouldn't do it. It ended up that Everybody blamed Somebody when Nobody did what Anybody could have done!

13.5 GOAL SETTING

What is a goal? Goal is a target and objective for future performance. It helps focus employees' attention on items of greater importance to the organisation and stimulates employees towards goal attainment. Goal setting refers to setting of attainable goals for an organisation as well as for an employee.

It was Locke[12] who did the seminal work on a theory of goal setting way back in 1968. His theory has generated a considerable research on goal setting. Goal setting works as a motivational tool because it creates a discrepancy between current and expected performance. Goal setting results in a feeling of tension which is diminished through goal attainment. Individuals attaining goals successfully tend to set even higher goals in the future. Self-efficacy contributes a lot to success of goal setting. Self-efficacy is an internal belief regarding one's job-related capabilities and competencies. It differs from self-esteem, which is a broader feeling of like or dislike for oneself.

The presence of the folllowing four elements in goal setting makes it more effective in improving job performance:

1. Goal Acceptance
2. Specific Goals
3. Challenging Goals
4. Performance Monitoring/Feedback.

These are shown in Fig. 13.2.

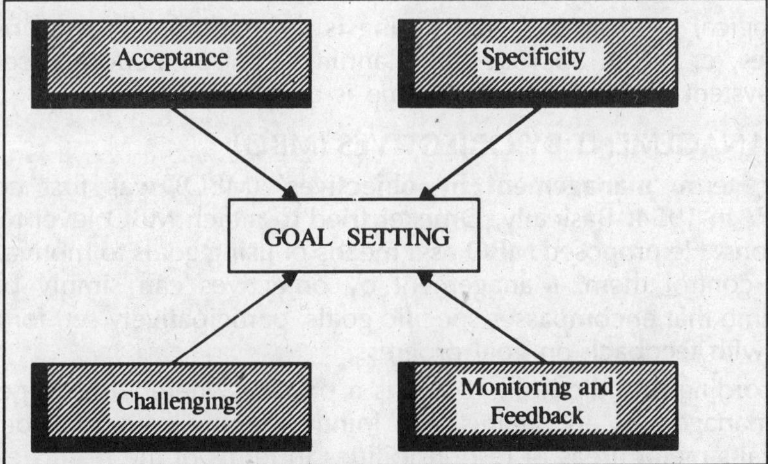

Fig. 13.2: Elements Making Goal Setting Effective

A brief description of these follows :

Goal Acceptance: Effective goals need to be not only understood but also accepted. Accepted goals arrived at through participation seem preferable to assigned goals. There is ample evidence to suggest that people who set their goals through participation, and who own their own goals, perform better than those who are told what their goals are going to be.

Specific Goals: Goals need to be as specific, clear, and measurable as possible. Specific goals are always better than vague or general goals such as "do your best," "do better", or "work harder". Giving a salesperson a specific quota or a worker an exact number of units to produce should be preferable to setting a goal such as "try as hard as you can," or "try to do better than last year".

Challenging Goal: Research shows that most employees work harder when they have difficult goals to attain rather than easy ones. Take the case of MBA students itself, for example. They work harder in papers e.g. Financial Management,

Statistics for Managers, etc. which they treat/consider hard or difficult and their surprise they perform better in these papers than in easy or simple ones, e.g. Principles of Management, Marketing Management, etc. However, challenging goals must be attainable/reachable and no so difficult that they would be frustrating.

Monitoring and Feedback: Besides setting well-defined and challenging goals, the two closely related elements, viz monitoring and feedback, are also important to complete the process of goal-setting. Performance monitoring is observing one's behaviour, inspecting output, etc. This heightens their awareness of the role they play in contributing to organisational effectiveness.

Monitoring needs to be followed by performance feedback to enable employee to have an idea how successful he/she is. Man, by nature, is hungry for information about how well he/she is performing. Just as a football team needs to know the score of the game, the woodchoper needs to see the chips fly and and pile of firewood grow, and the student of MBA like you needs to know how he performed in his assignment-seminar, the same is true of a worker working in an organisation. In sum, performance feedback tends to increase better job performance, and self-generated feedback is an especially powerful motivational tool.

A logical extension of goal setting is the traditionally used **management-by-objectives**, or MBO, approach to planning, control, performance appraisal, and overall system performance. The same is discussed next.

13.6 MANAGEMENT BY OBJECTIVES (MBO)

The, term **'management by objectives'** (MBO) was first coined by Peter Drucker[12] in 1954. Basically, Drucker tried to attach MBO level to result-oriented evaluations. He proposed MBO as a means of using goals to motivate people rather than to control them. Management by objectives can simply be defined as a programme that encompasses specific goals, participatively set, for an explicit time period, with feedback on goal progress.

According to Odiorne[13], "MBO is a process whereby the superior and subordinate managers of an organisation jointly identify common goals, define each individual's major areas of responsibilities in terms of the results expected of him, and use these measures as guides for operating the unit and assessing the contribution of each of its members."

MBO provides specific objectives for each succeeding level (*i.e.*, divisional, departmental, individual in the organisation). In other words, MBO is a process by which objectives cascade down through the organisation as depicted in Fig. 13.3.

An MBO programme or process consists of four common ingredients. These are: specificity, participative decision making, an explicit time period, and performance feedback. A brief description of these follows.

1. **Specificity:** The objectives in MBO should be clear and precise that can be measured and evaluated. To state a desire to cut costs, for example, may not be enough. Instead, to cut costs by 5 per cent will be more clear, exact and measurable objective.

2. **Participative Decisions/Objectives:** In MBO goals are not imposed on people. The superior and subordinate jointly set objectives to be attained.

3. **Explicit Time:** Each objective is to be completed within a specific time period, be it three months, six months or a year.

4. **Performance Feedback:** The final ingredient in an MBO programme is feedback on performance. It includes continuous and systematic measurement and review of performance. Based on these, corrective actions are taken to achieve the planned objectives.

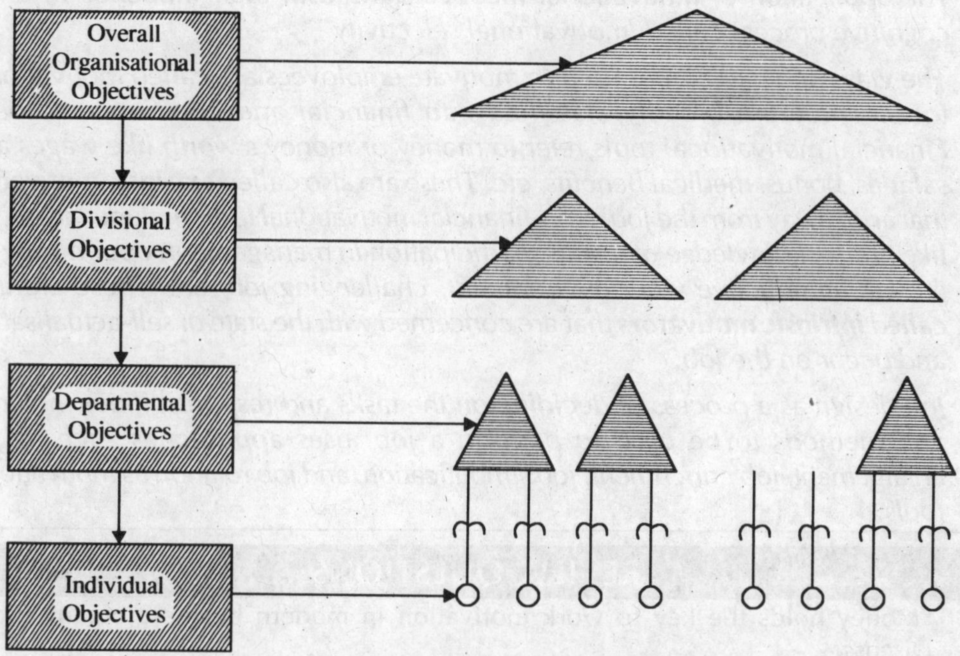

Fig. 13.3. Management by Objectives

Advantages of MBO

Following are the advantages of MBO:

1. The need to clarify objectives is stressed and suggestions for improvement are obtained from all levels of management.
2. All managers have a clear idea of the important areas of their work and of the standards required.
3. The performance of staff can be assumed and their needs for improvement highlighted.
4. Greater participation may improve morale and communication.
5. It makes individuals more aware of organisational goals.

Disadvantages of MBO

MBO suffers from the following disadvantages also:

1. It takes a few years to be effective.
2. Some companies always tend to raise goals. If these are too high, employees become frustrated.
3. Appraisals are sometimes made on personality traits rather than on performance.
4. Some employees do not want to be held responsible and goals forced upon them may lead to ill-feeling.

SUMMARY

This summary is organized by the 'learning objectives' given on page no. 221 :

- *The application of motivational theories starts with their influence in one's cognitive process called 'motivational selectivity'.*
- *The ways and techniques used to motivate employees are called motivational tools. These are broadly classified into financial and non-financial tools. Financial motivational tools refer to money or money's worth like wages and salaries, bonus, medical benefits, etc. These are also called* ***extrinsic motivators*** *that arise away from the job. Non-financial motivational tools include incentives like praise, knowledge of results, participation in management, opportunity for growth, conductive work environment, challenging job, etc. These are also called* ***intrinsic motivators*** *that are concerned with the state of self-actualisation and occur on the job.*
- *Job design as a process of deciding on the tasks and responsibilities included and methods to be used to perform a job, uses approaches such as job enlargement, job enrichment, job simplification, and job rotation as motivational tools.*

REVIEW QUESTIONS

1. "Money holds the key to work motivation in modern business organisations". Discuss.
2. What is job design? What are the various approaches to job design? Discuss.
3. What is job enrichment? With what theory of motivation can you link job enrichment?
4. Differentiate job enrichment from job enlargement. Which is in your opinion, more powerful as a motivator?
5. What do you mean by quality of work life? Discuss the impact of job design on quality of work life.
6. "There is no universally consistent motivational device applicable to everyone. What motivates people is situation." Discuss the statement.
7. Study an organisation, unit, or an individual (for example, your own Professor) and suggest ways and means to motivate him to perform more effectively.
8. Write short notes on:
   (*a*) Job Enrichment
   (*b*) Job Enlargement
   (*c*) Job Rotation
   (*d*) Quality of Work Life (QWL)
   (*e*) Management by Objectives (MBO)
   (*f*) Goal Setting
9. What do you mean by MBO? Discuss the elements involved in an MBO programme.
10. "MBO is an extension of goal setting approach to job design". Do you agree? Comment.

REFERENCES

1. D.C. Dearborn and H.A. Simon: ***op. cit.,*** 1958, pp. 140-144.
2. S.W. Gellerman: **Management by Motivation,** American Management Association, New York, 1968, p. 173.
3. David J. Cherrington: **Organisational Behaviour,** Allyn and Bacon, Boston, 1994, p. 225.
4. Fredrick Herzberg: **Work and Nature of Man,** World Publishing Co., Cleveland, Ohio, 1966.
5. Nitish De : Training Strategy for Change in Attitude: Micro-Level Experiences, **Economic Times**, 26 February, 1976.
6. Mirza S. Saiyadain: **Job Enrichment: Prospects and Problems**, Indian Institute of Management, Ahmedabad, 1976.
7. Sangeeta Jain: **Quality of Work Life**, Deep & Deep Publications, New Delhi, 1991, p. 17.
8. Richard E. Walton: Quality of Working Life: What is it? **Sloan Management Review**, Vol. 15, No. 1, Fall, 1973, pp. 11-21.
9. John W. Newstrom and Keith Davis: **Organisational Behaviour** (Human Behaviour at Work), Tata McGraw-Hill Publishing Company Limited, New Delhi, Third Reprint, 1996, pp. 345-346.
10. Loins E. Davis and Albert B Cherns: **The Quality of Working Life II;** The Free Press, New York, 1975, p. 349.
11. J.P. Singh: Improving Quality of Working Life in the Indian Context **Productivity,** 22(4) 1982, pp. 13-20.
12. Edwin A. Locke: Toward a Theory of Task Motivation and Incentives, **Organisational Behaviour and Human Performance,** May 1968, pp. 157-189.
13. Peter F. Drucker: **The Practice of Management,** Harper & Row, New York, 1954.
14. G.S. Odiorne: **Management by Objectives,** Pitman, New York, 1965, p. 8.

AN EXERCISE FOR YOU

You have already learnt Abrahim Maslow's need-hierarchy theory of motivation which includes five needs from lower to higher order. Based on these needs, L.W. Porter in his study of **"Job Attitudes in Management : Perceived Deficiency in Need Fulilment as a Function of Job Levels"**, developed a 13-item questionnaire to measure the need deficiency and the importance of these needs to an individual. These 13-items are presented below.

You read each of these statements and rate each of them three times following the 7-point rating scale. For your convenience, you can circle your ratings.

The Three – Times are nomenclatured as:

1. How much of the characteristic is there now?
2. How much ideally should it be?
3. How much important is the characteristic to you?

Statements	How much is there now? Min Max	How much should there be? Min Max	How important is this to me? Min Max
1. The feeling of security in my position.	1 2 3 4 5 6 7	1 2 3 4 5 6 7	1 2 3 4 5 6 7
2. The opportunity in my position to give help to other people.	1 2 3 4 5 6 7	1 2 3 4 5 6 7	1 2 3 4 5 6 7
3. The opportunity to develop close friendship in my position.	1 2 3 4 5 6 7	1 2 3 4 5 6 7	1 2 3 4 5 6 7
4. The feeling of self-esteem a person gets from being in my position	1 2 3 4 5 6 7	1 2 3 4 5 6 7	1 2 3 4 5 6 7
5. The prestige of my position inside the company.	1 2 3 4 5 6 7	1 2 3 4 5 6 7	1 2 3 4 5 6 7
6. The prestige of my position outside the company.	1 2 3 4 5 6 7	1 2 3 4 5 6 7	1 2 3 4 5 6 7
7. The authority connected with my position.	1 2 3 4 5 6 7	1 2 3 4 5 6 7	1 2 3 4 5 6 7
8. The opportunity for independent thought and action in my position.	1 2 3 4 5 6 7	1 2 3 4 5 6 7	1 2 3 4 5 6 7
9. The opportunity in my position for participation in the setting of goals.	1 2 3 4 5 6 7	1 2 3 4 5 6 7	1 2 3 4 5 6 7
10. The opportunity in my position for participation in the determination of methods and procedures.	1 2 3 4 5 6 7	1 2 3 4 5 6 7	1 2 3 4 5 6 7
11. The opportunity of personal growth and development in my position.	1 2 3 4 5 6 7	1 2 3 4 5 6 7	1 2 3 4 5 6 7
12. My feeling of self-fulfilment a person gets in my position.	1 2 3 4 5 6 7	1 2 3 4 5 6 7	1 2 3 4 5 6 7
13. My feeling of worthwhile accomplishment in my position.	1 2 3 4 5 6 7	1 2 3 4 5 6 7	1 2 3 4 5 6 7

The 13-items fall under the five need-hierarchies as follows:

1. Security Needs	Item	1
2. Social Needs	Items	1 and 2
3. Esteem Needs	Items	4,5 and 6
4. Autonomy Needs	Items	7, 8, 9 and 10
5. Self-Actualisation Needs	Items	11, 12 and 13

Calculation of Deficiency Score

	Total Score of how much should be there	------------
Less	Total Score of how much is there	------------
	Defiency	------------

Now, add up the deficiency score on all the items that belong to a particular need hierarchy/category. Divide this total by the number of items. The quotient will be the average score for those items. Thus, you will have now comparative averages of different needs. You can see in which need category your need deficiency is high.

The ***Importance Score*** will tell you how much important is that deficiency to you.

Case 13.1 : Job Redesign in the Bharat Heavy Electricals Limited (BHEL), Haridwar*

During the mid 70s, a pilot project on job redesign was started at the BHEL plant located at Haridwar. Following intensive interaction with the management, the trade unions and the supervisory staff, Block V where 25 workmen were engaged in fabrication of the upper part of the condenser unit, was selected for the pilot experiment. Some of the criteria for selection of this work unit were its compact character, reasonable layout and the favourable attitude of the manager and the shop floor trade union leaders. Moreover, the productivity in the shop was low (appx. 30% in May 1975). The break up of the 25 workers in terms of their assigned jobs was 9 fitters, 3 fettlers, 3 welders, 2 gas cutters, 1 crane operator, 2 riggers, 2 helpers, and 3 workmen involved in material supplies.

The workers participated in a series of meetings with both internal and external consultants and agreed that there was a need to redesign the work. Diagnosis of the existing work system with their help revealed the following bottlenecks that came in the way of improving efficiency:

1. Each worker was concerned exclusively with his own trade. None of them identified himself with the product.
2. There was invariable forced idle time because when a particular worker was engaged at a given location, another who was required to work in close proximity had to wait until the first worker had finished his job.
3. There was uneven demand of the services of the materials supplies group, the crane operator and the riggers.

To initiate action on job redesign, the workers decided to set up a task force consisting of representatives of each category of workers together with the supervisor. Membership of the task force was to be on rotational basis except in the case of two workers with leadership skills and the supervisor. The task force consisted of eight members. An Industrial Engineer was associated with the task force as a Consultant. The Manager in charge of the shop could also participate in the task force deliberations if he wished. The task before this group was to evolve an alternative system of work which would improve the workers' motivation as well as productivity.

The task force in association with the rest of the workers came up with the following decisions:

1. Formation of Direct Production Group consisting of 1 welder, 3 fitters and 1 fettler with responsibility for the complex task.
2. Doing one another's job by undergoing on-the-job training.
3. Crane operators and riggers to learn each other's skills.
4. Gas cutters, helpers, and material supplies group to be integrated into the new work system at a later stage.

---

* Source: N.R. De: **India: New Forms of Work Organisation, Volume 2,** International Labour Organisation, Geneva, 1979.

The above reorganization led to several benefits; a welder now started working as a fitter and training in other trades was given to fitters, fettlers, gas cutters and others.

In September 1975, the workers, based on the confidence generated in them through the new work system, attempted further redesign of their job and decided that the workforce should be distributed in two shifts: Shift one consisting of five fitters, five welders, one gas cutter and one fettler and shift two comprising four fitters, four welders, one gas cutter and one fettler.

In addition, there would be crane operators in both the shifts. Each shift group became integrated and self-contained. It was decided that one shift would fabricate the right side of the upper part of the condenser unit, the other shift would do the same with the left side.

The above reorganization led to the following advantages:

1. Productivity rose from 30% in May 1975 to over 75% in February 1976.
2. One-man-one-job concept was replaced by multiple skill acquisition.
3. Individual system of working gave way to team work.
4. Groups were self-managed, the traditional supervisory functions of work allocations, coordination, monitoring and control being performed by the groups.
5. Identification with the total product and concern for quality became a reality.
6. Personal idle time (wasted in gossiping, loitering, and in unauthorized absence from workplace) was dropped considerably.
7. Workers' supervisor and the manager showed a high degree of work commitment.

QUESTIONS

1. What made workers and management to go for a job redesign?

2. What were, in your opinion, contributing factors to make the BHEL experiment of job redesign a successful one?

3. If you were asked to suggest an alternative job redesign strategy, which one will you suggest and why?

14

MORALE

"Morale is the capacity of a group of people to pull together persistently and consistently in pursuit of a common purpose."
– Alexander H.Leighton

Learning Objectives

After studying this chapter, you should be able to:

- **Define** the term 'morale' and **distinguish** it from motivation.
- **Enumerate** and **discuss** the factors that affect morale.
- **Identify** the symptoms of low and high morale.
- **Suggest** the ways and means how to improve employee morale.
- **Establish** relationship between morale and productivity.

Closer to motivation is 'morale'. Though some people consider the two terms, i.e., motivation and morale as synonymous, these mean two different things. Both are intangible and influence people behaviour and performance. Hence, both become inescapable in the study of organisational behaviour. You have just read employee motivation in the previous chapter 12 and 13. We shall discuss, in this chapter some main aspects of employee morale such as its meaning, causes, symptoms, and impact on productivity. Let us begin with the meaning of the term 'morale'.

14.1 MEANING OF MORALE

Morale is an intangible term. Like other intangible terms, it means different things to different people. It generally relates to stressful or controversial context. When discussing the morale of a group, morale is known as *esprit de corps* and is defined from different standpoints. For example, it means enthusiasm to accomplish the assigned task in military, self-confidence of a team in sports, eagerness to learn by students in education, and desire to achieve the goal. In general sense, morale means the capacity of the people to maintain belief in oneself or others, or a goal or an institution. It is an overall attitude of an individual or group towards all aspects of work, whatsoever it is. Following are some important formal definitions of morale:

According to Alexander H. Leighton, "Morale is the capacity of a group of people to pull together persistently and consistently in pursuit of a common purpose."[1]

In the opinion of Dale Yoder: "Morale is a feeling, somewhat related to *esprit de corps*, enthusiasm or zeal. For group of workers, morale refers to the over - all tone, climate or atmosphere of work, perhaps vaguely sensed by the members."[2]

Edwin Flippo has described morale, "as a metal condition or attitude of individuals and groups which determines their willingness to co-operate. Good morale is evidenced by employee enthusiasm, voluntary confirmation with regulations and orders and willingness to co-operate with others in accomplishment of an organisation's objectives Poor morale is evidenced by surliness, insubordination, a feeling of discouragement and dislike of the job, company and associates."[3]

According to **Michael J. Jusius,** morale consists of: What it is? What does it do? Where does it reside? What does it affect? He answers to these questions as follows:

What is it? : It is an attitude of mind, an *esprit de corps*, a state of well being, and an emotional force.

What does it do? : It affects output, the quality of a product, costs, co-operation, enthusiasm, discipline, initiative, and other ingredients of success.

Where does it reside? : It resides in the minds and emotions of individuals and in the reactions of their group or groups.

What does it affect? : It affects the employees and executives in their interactions. Ultimately, it affects consumers and the community.

Whom does it affect? : It affects an employee's or group's will to work and co-operate in the best interests of the individuals or groups and the organisations for which they work.

Now morale can simply be defined as an overall state of group's emotional health, arousal and enthusiasm. Morale is a composite attitude of various individuals employed by an organisation. It is generated by the group and may be considered as a by product of the group. It must be noted that it is not an average of individual attitudes. Morale is unrelated to morality, i.e. the ability to distinguish right and wrong.

Now that we have understood the meaning of the term morale, we can profitably distinguish morale and motivation.

14.2 DIFFERENCE BETWEEN MOTIVATION AND MORALE

Motivation and morale are conceptually different. They could be distinguished along the following lines:

1. Motivation is an individual's state of disposition, and to do or not to do things, to behave or not to behave in a particular way, in response to given stimuli, whether internal or external, while morale is more a group situation.
2. Motivation is only one of the factors which explains 'why' of individual behaviour and performance. Morale represents the totality of impact of several interacting factors and forces in the atmosphere of a group.
3. A well-motivated individual tends to experience a high degree of morale also. As regards this, a group characterized by a high state of morale may or may not have a high degree of motivation to perform.
4. It is possible to build up motivation in an individual or group by a combination of rewards and penalties, but morale can be built up by positive and favourable means only.
5. Organisations, in general, devote more direct attention towards motivational aspects or people's behaviour than to aspects of morale.

6. The field of motivation is more extensively explored and intensively studied and researched by theorists, and several theories on motivation have been evolved but morale has remained a less directly studied and researched area.

14.3 FACTORS AFFECTING EMPLOYEE MORALE

Despite the intangible nature of morale, material factors affect the morale. But, history is also filled with stories that organisations with poor or inferior material set up have shown very high level of employee morale. For example, the Army of Northern Virginia displayed morale to the very end even with very poor supply of material in the American Civil War. Nonetheless, there are some important factors that affect employee morale within the workplace. These are discussed subsequently.

Job Security: An average Indian worker/employee wants a life - time secured job or employment. The reasons for this are not difficult to seek. A secured job offers employee a secured income which, in turn, ensures a secured living. This keeps employee morale high and, in turn, improves performance both in quantity and quality. On the contrary, insecurity of job lowers employee morale which adversely affects his/her behaviour and performance. In a sense, both job security and job insecurity are contagious to employee behaviour and performance.

Job Satisfaction: While doing a job, an employee not only gets remuneration, but also experiences some feeling toward job. Employee's good or positive feeling toward job is called job satisfaction. Job satisfaction relates to job related aspects such as pay, promotion, working conditions, co-workers, and supervision. More favourable these job related aspects are, more satisfaction an employee derives from his / her job and vice versa. Research evidence shows that job satisfaction fosters employee morale which, in turn, improves employee performance. That is why "a satisfied employee is considered a productive employee."

Organizational Culture: Organizational culture refers to beliefs, values, traditions, etc. shared by the majority of members. Experience shows that better the compatibility between organisational culture and employee culture, gives the latter a high level of enthusiasm, i.e., morale to work for the organisation. Just contrary is also true.

Management Styles: The managerial style used by the managers also influences employee morale. For example, the custodian or paternistic style of management gives the employees feeling of caring by managers which raises their enthusiasm to work more and more for the organisation. On the contrary, authoritative style of management creates a feeling of neglected and uncared among the employees. Such a negative feeling causes demoralization among the employees which, in turn, leads to employee attrition. How much the managerial style matters in employee demoralization and attrition lies in the research evidence that most of the employees do not leave organisations but they leave managers and/or leaders.

Self Concept of the Employee: Self-concept means one's self-respect, self-confidence, self-value, etc. There is evidence to believe that the employees who have self-confidence show high level of morale. Those who lack in self-confidence suffer from either low or lack of morale.

Perception of Work and Reward: Employees join organisation with a perception about their work and career opportunities. If the employees after joining the organisation find their work interesting and honorable with possibilities for career progression, their morale is high. If work is perceived boring and monotonous and possibilities for reward as remote and bleak, they suffer from low level of morale.

Here is an example of how employee perception of his/her work affects morale toward the job.

> "Three people were laying bricks. A passerby asked them what they were doing. The first one replied, "Don't you see I am making a living." When the same question was asked to the second one, he said, "Don't you see I am laying bricks to construct a wall." In answer of the same question, the third one replied, "I am building a beautiful cathedral/ monument." See, three people doing the same thing had very different attitudes about their work. Their attitudes will certainly affect their performance. Third attitude is the example of pride of performance, i.e. "positive morale."

14.4 SYMPTOMS OF LOW MORALE

Employee morale affects organisational performance. While high morale causes more increase in performance, low morale causes less increase or even decrease in performance. As such, it is imperative for the organisation to have employees with high morale and / or improve low morale to high morale. The question is how? Just as coming events cast their shadows before, low morale is also characterized by certain symptoms. Low morale initially unnoticeable gradually becomes perceptible with certain relatively permanent features also called 'symptoms.' It is prudent on the part of the organisation to recognize the symptoms of low morale at an early stage and accordingly take proactive measures to avoid the evil effects of low morale on organisational performance. As per researchers, following are the commonly observed symptoms of low morale:

1. Tardiness
2. Lack of positive feeling toward work
3. Lack of pride in work
4. High rate of absenteeism
5. High rate of turnover
6. Bad or disturbed mood
7. Poor inter-personal relations
8. Poor or lack of group cohesiveness
9. Increasing employee indiscipline
10. Bad industrial relations
11. Strikes and sabotages
12. Increasing accidents
13. Increasing wastages and spoilages
14. Decline in the quality of goods
15. Decrease in the quantity of goods

14.5 SYMPTOMS OF HIGH MORALE

Just like low morale, high morale is also characterized by certain symptoms. Since high morale is the opposite of the low morale, the symptoms of high morale are accordingly just the opposite of the low morale. Following are the main symptoms of high morale:

1. Feeling of belongingness
2. Group cohesiveness
3. Team spirit
4. Commitment to organisational goals
5. Feeling of organisational citizenship
6. Longer stay with organisation
7. Less need for employee supervision
8. Better inter-personal and industrial relations
9. More peaceful and harmonious atmosphere in the organisation
10. Increased adaptability among the group members
11. Less or no strikes and sabotages
12. Less or no wastages and spoilages
13. High level of pride in work
14. Increase in quantity and quality of work performance.

14.6 HOW TO BOOST MORALE?

The preceding description clearly suggests that for organisational development, there is need for boosting employee morale. Then, the million dollar question is how to boost employee morale? Experiences suggest that employee morale can be boosted through various concerted efforts. Following are the examples of such efforts:

Motivate employees with your example: Correction starts from oneself, i.e. individual. Show good conduct and character in the manner you want your employees imitate and behave. Always try to demonstrate the best of you like your positive attitude, discipline, code of conduct, etc. Remember that your example can make or mar employees' day and, in turn, performance. Therefore, enter the work place with smile, greet people, walk tall and confidently, and exchange pleasantries to your employees. In other words, always practice "walk the talk" or "example is better than preach." Research and analyze what motivates workers at work. Ensure the same and it will certainly boost the employee morale.

Establish clear and good communication with employees: Good communication removes barriers and brings the parties together. Here, the views of Martin Luther King about the need for and significance of communication seems worth citing: *"People do not get along because they fear each other. People fear each other because they do not know each other. People do not know each other because they have not communicated with each other."* Clear and effective communication removes ambiguity, confusions, doubts, and misunderstanding about work matters. Therefore, it calls for telling employees your objectives for the company and then promptly sharing news that affect the organisation. This will enable employees know clearly what the organisational expectations are.

Enrich employees' jobs: Always try to enrich employees' jobs to make the jobs interesting to them. In other words, reduce the job discontentment by adding more challenging job contents. Experiences suggest that some employees like difficult and serious kind of jobs and performing such jobs helps improve their morale. The reason is not difficult to seek. Enriching a job opens opportunities for jobholders for greater recognition, responsibility, and growth. Performing difficult and serious but interesting jobs gives job satisfaction, provides learning and, in turn, boosts morale.

Challenge employees to perform better: Some times, employee morale remains lying dormant. In other words, employee can perform big and better but his / her performing desire remains idle and dormant. Such employee's morale can be boosted by shaking him / her to perform better. One way to do so is to challenge such employee to put his / her best efforts to perform the job as the only and only option left for him / her. History is replete with such examples where challenging employees has performed miracles. Here, the example of the Hindi movie *"Chak de India"* is worth citing.

"The coach of the Indian hockey team, i.e., Shah Rukh Khan challenged his cricket team players in the dressing room to play their best game on the day of their clash in the final match with the world champion Australian hockey team. Shah Rukh Khan challenged his team members by saying: Today I am not telling you how to play. "Today I am telling you that you have only 75 minutes and only 75 minutes to be lived, loved, and remembered. Decide yourself what and how to perform". The effect of this challenging the players was amazing. It boosted players' morale like anything and each and every player played like fire fighter. As a result, the Indian hockey team had firstly tie up with 2-2 goals with the Australian team and finally, with its upbeat morale, the team won the world cup with 5-4 goals in penalty stroke."

Let us substantiate the above point with yet another anecdote.

"Despite the intangible nature of morale, improvements in material factors (such as remuneration, food and shelter) can also improve the morale. However, history is filled with stories of the self-will and determination of a poorly supplied army maintaining morale of the very end, such as the Army of Northern Virginia in the American Civil War.[5]"

Involve employees as equal members of your team: Try to make employees feel valued and connected to organisational cause. Evidences suggest that feeling valued is ranked right up as an important actor that consistently boosts the morale of employees. The reason is not difficult to seek. When organisation cares for employees, in turn, they do also care for organisation. This reciprocity between organisation and employees can be exemplified with an imaginary example.

The employees of XYZ organisation have this ritual in their office where a volunteer (employee) is sent in everyday to gauze the boss's mood (much like that hoary Panchatantra tale of the lion and the rabbit). If the boss has walked in with a spring in his step and a ditty on his lips, then all is well with the world. But woe betides if he has stomped into the office, barking orders all the while. The message is loud and clear - stay away if you know what's good for you.

Consult your employees before implementing policies that will affect them. Instead of handling down rules like a dictator, allow employees to give feedback and input into creating their own environment.

Empower your employees: Always try to recognize the talent and potential of your employees useful for organisational purposes. Then, challenge them with new opportunities to use and develop their skill and talent. Give employees a chance to set their job roles. This all will encourage employees to take responsibility for their work and put bigger efforts to the work.

Acknowledge and appreciate employees' performance: Recognize even small successes with kind and encouraging words for a job well done. This breeds the feeling of recognition for employees. Organizations can recognize and reinforce the commendable performance further by giving inexpensive rewards like *"thank you for the good work"* or, *"job well done"* cards, or *"appreciation certificates"* or larger expensive gifts. Showing appreciation lets employees know on a constant basis how much pride you take in them and in their efforts. It is a grave mistake on the part of organisation to only interact with workers when there is a problem.

Show care about your employees: Employees live two lives: personal life and work life. Hence, organisations also need to show care and concern for both lives of employees. Recognize employees' personal life and permit them to be and live like human. Show concern and interest in their personal lives and get to know what's important to them. Employees will appreciate the care and interest shown and assistance given to them to deal with their personal issues. So to say, you have to be your employees' monitor, advisor, trainer, and a shoulder to cry on. By doing so, organisations can help them perform their jobs well and, in turn, achieve their goals.

Create healthy work environment: A very important factor in improving employee morale is creating the work environment. Psychological research shows that work ambience and environment greatly and directly affect the motivation and morale and feeling of well being of the employees in a work place. Wherever possible, providing comfortable and aesthetically pleasing furniture is one way that researchers suggest to boost employee morale at workplace. Added to these, proper lighting, flowers, and artwork can also help improve employee morale. Admittedly, providing a pleasant atmosphere at workplace is not always possible. Factories and repair works are such workplaces. In such types of workplaces, provisions like a pleasant break room or relaxation area helps improve employee morale. Besides, providing workers safe and comfortable conditions also improve employee morale by giving workers a reasonable sense of security.

Do some personal things: A little personal effort managers can do to improve employees' morale may include the following things:

I. Be friendly and interested in your employees. Show a warm smile and a sincere query about how an employee is doing. Try to know your employees by names and personalize the work environment. Such things inspire employees to help you more and more.

II. Respond to problems, concerns, and questions of employees. Remember that leaving things unaddressed tells employees you do not care for them. Non - addressing problems and / or inconsistency in problem - solving hinders employees' motivation and morale which is contagious.

III. Be fair about employee discipline. One way to maintain fairness in employee discipline is follow Douglas McGregor's *"Hot - Stove Rule"* in dealing with employee discipline.

Now that we have understood morale in its various aspects, it seems in the fitness of the context to see relationship between morale and productivity.

14.7 MORALE AND PRODUCTIVITY

As regards the relationship between morale and productivity, there have been ample evidences to believe that these are positively related. So to say, positive or high employee morale benefits organisational performance. Evidences reveal that compared to employees with high or positive morale, disengaged employees (employees with low morale) are less efficient, miss more workdays, and cost organisations thousands of dollars in lost productivity. A recent HR study points out that a company of 100 employees could stand to lose nearly $75,000 per year due to low morale leading to absenteeism, turnover, and tardiness. Though positive or high morale generally boosts employee productivity, yet there are some studies which disagree with this positive relationship between morale and productivity. According to these studies, just as a satisfied employee is not always a productive employee, high morale may also not lead always to high productivity. Instead it may cause, in some cases, decrease in productivity. It is also important to mention that the relationship between morale and productivity may not be proportional. For example, an increase of 20% in morale may not lead 20% increase in productivity. This is because of the type of relationship between the two. Researchers have classified the relationship between morale and productivity into four combinations. These are: (i) High morale and high productivity, (ii) high morale and low productivity, (iii) Low morale and high productivity, and (iv) Low morale and low productivity. These four combinations of relationship between morale and productivity are depicted in the following figure 14.1:

Figure14.1 : Four Combinations of Morale and Productivity

Productivity	Low (Morale)	High (Morale)
High	2 Low Morale and High Productivity	1 High Morale and High Productivity
Low	4 Low Morale and Low Productivity	3 High Morale and Low Productivity

Morale

Now, a brief description about each of these combinations follows:

1. High Morale and High Productivity: This situation indicates that the employee is satisfied with the work and organisational environment which raises employee's morale high. Both, in turn, improve employee's productivity.

2. Low Morale and High Productivity: This refers to the situation in which employees' morale is low but organisational environment in terms of strict rules, regulations, procedures, prescriptions of punishment for poor performance, and use of better equipment and technology makes employees perform more and better. In a sense, organisation by using strict control and showing fear forces employees to perform more and better. So to say, organisation follows Douglas McGregor's motivation theory of 'Theory X.'

3. High Morale and Low Productivity: This situation is just opposite of above mentioned combination 2. In this type of relationship-combination, employees are satisfied with their work and environment which boosts employees' morale high. Nonetheless, incompetent leadership, ambiguity in individual and organisational goals, inadequacy of facilities required to perform a job may lead to low productivity.

4. Low Morale and Low Productivity: This is the situation marked by negative characteristics, i.e. low morale and low productivity. In this situation, employee's morale is low and in the absence of strict control and fear given to employees, they perform less and, in turn, leads to low productivity.

Thus, it becomes clear from above four relationship-combinations that the relationship between morale and productivity is complex and unpredictable. It is also well worth noting that the relationship between the two may differ from organisation to organisation and from time to time in the same organisation. However, among the above four combinations, the number 1 combination is the most desirable one for improving organisational productivity. The other three combinations need to be improved to make these favourable for improving organisational performance and productivity.

SUMMARY

This summary is organized by the 'learning objectives' given on page no. 237 :

- Morale also known as *esprit de corps* means overall state of group enthusiasm toward its work or task. Morale and motivation are conceptually different in the sense that morale is more a group enthusiasm whereas motivation is an individual's state of enthusiasm.
- The factors that affect employees' morale include job security, job satisfaction, organisational culture, management style, self concept of the employee, etc.
- Tardiness, absenteeism, turnover, accidents, wastages, and spoilages are the major symptoms of low morale. On the other hand, greater loyalty, commitment, citizenship behaviour, longer stay with organisations, etc. are the symptoms of high morale.
- Improvements in material factors such as remuneration, food, shelter, healthy work environment, etc. and intangible factors such as concern for employees, acknowledgement and recognition for performance, employee empowerment, etc. can improve employee morale.
- Morale and productivity are generally positively related. However, the relationship between the two has not always been proportional and positive.

QUESTIONS

1. What is meant by morale? How is morale different from motivation?
2. Discuss the key factors that affect morale in a business organisation.
3. List and discuss the key symptoms of low and high morale.
4. Discuss the ways and means that can be used to improve employee morale in an organisation.

5. Show the relationship between employee morale and productivity.
6. "An employee with high morale is not always a productive employee." Comment.

REFERENCES

1. Alexander H. Leighton: **Human Relations in a Changing World: Observations on the Use of the Social Sciences,** 1949.
2. Dale Yoder:
3. Edwin B Flippo: **Personnel Management,** McGraw-Hill, New York, 1984.
4. Michael J. Jucius: **Personnel Management,** Richard D. Irwin, Homewood III, 1980.
5. http: www.confidencecenter.com
6. Miller and Form quoted by Shashi K. Gupta abd Rosy Joshi: **Human Resource Management,** Kalyani Publishers, New Delhi, 2004, p. 21.3.
7. Douglas McGregor: **The Human Side of Enterprise,** McGraw Hill, New York, 1967.

AN EXERCISE FOR YOU

Now, here is an exercise for you. Different things boost different peoples' morale. Here is a list of such things. Go through the following nine statements and find how much each of these is important for you to boost your morale.

Statements	Moderately important or less	Quite important	Extremely important
How important is ... ?			
a. The amount of pay you get.			
b. The opportunity to develop your skills and abilities.			
c. The amount of job security you have.			
How important is ... ?			
a. Your chances for getting a promotion.			
b. The chances you have to accomplish something worthwhile.			
c. The amount of freedom you have on your job.			
How important is ... ?			
a. The respect you receive from the people you work with.			
b. The praise you get from your supervisor.			
c. The friendliness of the people you work with.			

CASE 14.1: ESSAR'S WAY TO BOOST EMPLOYEE MORALE*

Essar Steel Ltd. has implemented a performance reward scheme with a view to boost employee morale towards higher performance on the job. This has helped the organisation in identifying good performers in all departments and boosting others' morale to become performers and, thus, help achieve the set business targets.

---

* Biswajeet Pattanayak: **Human Resource Management,** Printice-Hall of India Private Limited, New Delhi, 2003, pp. 188-190.

The scheme is intended to identify the following in each of the following groups:

Best employee of the month — Best employee of the quarter

Best employee of the year — Best employee of the ESSAR Steel

For the purpose of this scheme, the following groups comprising of departments as indicated below are nominating executives from respective groups. They are as follows:

Group	No. of Executives to be Nominated
HBI & CPP - I	3
SMP	5
HSM	3
DSC	2
Material handling logistic & shipping	2
Utilities, projects, CGS & technology cell	2
PPC, QA / QC, ERIM and fire & safety	1
Corporate strategic planning, human resources, administration & training	2
Finance, accounts, commercial & directors office	2
Sales & marketing	2
Pelletization plant	1
Total	**25**

The numbers of nominations indicated above are based on the assumption that for every 80-90 people one person can be considered as good performer for that month.

Each group will be required to nominate the abovementioned number of executives under this scheme as per the details mentioned below:

1. Best Employee of the Month

The head of the department with the involvement of the respective unit HR officers draws the nominations from each group. The nominations for a particular month should reach the head of human resources on or before fifth of the subsequent month along with a brief write up on each such nomination.

The entire list of nominations are to be compiled by the HR department and all those employees, nominated would be felicitated with an appreciation letter on the tenth of the subsequent month in the presence of the departmental heads and the chief of operations.

Each of the nominees would be entitled to movie tickets (self & family) and dinner at any hotel in the city, the total cost of which should not exceed Rs. 750/- (Rupees Seven Hundred and Fifty).

2. Best Employee of the Quarter

The list of all employees nominated as *'best employee of the month'* would be compiled by the HR department for the last quarter and the same would be forwarded to the head of departments with respect to their respective groups. This list is to be forwarded to the departmental heads by tenth of the subsequent month after the three-month period.

The nominations for the best performer of the quarter should reach the head of human resources on or before fifteenth of the subsequent month along with a brief write-up on each such nomination. There will be only one nomination from each group for this reward.

The entire list of nominations is to be compiled by the HR department and all those employees nominated would be felicitated with an appreciation letter in the presence of the departmental heads and the chief of operations. The employees nominated and their family members would be entitled for two-day vacation at any nearby holiday resort the choice lies with the employee. The cost of such a trip not to exceed Rs. 3,000/- (Rupees three thousand) per family.

3. Best Employee of the Year

The list of all employees nominated as *'Best employee of the month'* would be complied by the HR department for the last twelve months and the same would be forwarded to the heads of departments with respect to their respective groups.

The nominations of the best performer for the year should reach the head of human resources within fifteen days of receipt of the list along with a brief write-up on each such nomination. There will only one nomination from each group for this reward.

The entire list of nominations is to be compiled by the HR department and all those employees nominated would be felicitated with an appreciation letter in the presence of the department heads and the chief of operations. The employees nominated and their family members would be entitled for seven day vacation at any hill station in India (the choice lies with the employee). The cost of such a trip not to exceed Rs. 25,000/- (Rupees twenty five thousand) per family.

4. Best Employee of Essar Steel

The entire list of nominations for best employee of the year is to be compiled by the HR department and forwarded to a committee formed. The composition of the committee would be as follows:

Director/chief of operations (Chairman)

Head of human resource

Head of two manufacturing units

Head of either marketing or finance & accounts departments (can be co-opted on alternative years)

The committee to interview all the 11 nominated executives and evaluate them on set parameters to be worked out in detail later.

The top scorer out of this process to be awarded with a rolling shield at ESSAR SANGAM of the subsequent year. The winner along with his/her spouse would also be entitled for a one-week holiday tour abroad.

The employee selected under this scheme would be entitled only for the reward as announced under the **'best employee of Essar Steel scheme.'**

For the purpose of this scheme, the period of one year would be between January to December.

PART THREE

GROUP DYNAMICS

- Foundation of Group Behaviour
- Team Building
- Organisational Conflicts and Negotiations
- Job Frustration
- Job Stress
- Communication
- Leadership
- Power and Politics

15

FOUNDATION OF GROUP BEHAVIOUR

"The path to greatness is alongwith others." ***- Baltasar Gracian***

"If you do not believe in co-operation, look what happens to a wagon that loses a wheel." ***- Anonymous***

Learning Objectives

After studying this chapter, you should be able to:

- **Define** group and list its characteristics.
- **Explain** the theories of group formation.
- **Explain** why people join groups.
- **Describe** the different types of groups typically found in organisations.
- **List** the stages of group development.
- **Describe** group norms, goals, role, and conflicts.
- **Delineate** the process involved in group decision making.
- **Suggest** how to make group decision making more effective.

You have already read the individual persepective of human behaviour from chapter 4 to 14 in this book. This and next 7 chapters will deal with the group dynamics/perspective of human behaviour.

Groups have been a central part of our everyday lives. At any given time, we are members in many different (small) groups, such as our family, student clubs, work groups, sport clubs, professional associations, and political parties. At any one time, the average individual belongs to five or six different groups[1]. The behaviour of individuals both affects and is affected by the group. Thus, groups have a great role to play in what goes on in organisations. What is it that makes employees form or join groups? How do these groups form? How do these groups behave and make decisions? How can the role of groups be made more effective? These are the basic questions to the topic of group dynamics and team work, the two major foci of this chapter.

We begin with defining a group.

15.1 DEFINITION AND CHARACTERISTICS OF GROUP

A group is a collection of two or more individuals, interacting and interdependent, who have come together to achieve particular common objectives. A group is, thus, an aggregation of people who interact with each other, are aware of one another, have a common objective, and perceive themselves to be a group[2]. Now, a group may be defined as a collection of people who have a common purpose or objective, interact with each other to accomplish the group objectives, are aware of one another and perceive themselves to be part of group.

Mere collection of people cannot constitute a group. For example, a crowd in front of a shop in the market watching India vs Pakistan one-day cricket match on T.V. will not be called as **group** because people do not interact with one another, do not know one another, and also do not share a common purpose.

Now, based on above definitions of group, the following **characteristics** of group can be listed:

1. **Two or More Persons:** A single individual can't form a group. For group formation, at least two persons are must. There is no specific limit on the maximum number of persons to form a group.

2. **Collective Identity:** Each group member knows one another. Each member of the group perceives that he/she is a part of group.

3. **Interaction:** There is an interaction among the members of the group. Each member shares his ideas with others through different communication methods such as face-to-face, in writing, over the telephone, and accross a computer network.

4. **Common Purpose:** The members of the group work to achieve some common objective or purpose. In fact, it is the common purpose that binds the group members together.

15.2 WHY DO PEOPLE FORM AND JOIN GROUPS ?

People form and become members of groups for a variety of different reasons. Any one or more of the following explain why people join groups :

1. **Safety and Security Needs:** Groups provide protection to their members from outside pressures. That is why workers join trade unions to feel safe and secure. This holds true at all walks of life. Even in the nursery class, when the teacher asks the small kids who broke the toy, he seldom gets an answer. What happens is all the kids keep mum or quiet. Although young, they protected their member by not disclosing any kid's name or pointing out at any one in group.

2. **Relatedness or Belongingness Needs:** People being social beings, belonging to or relating to groups satisfies a number of their social needs. In every organisation, there are many persons who are very isolated or who prefer to be absent from work most of the times. Studies show, such phenomena occur more where people are unable to belong to groups.

3. **Esteem Needs:** When one is a member of a group and does some good piece of work, gets a praise from others. This, in turn, brings a sense of recognition to the group member, on the one hand, and also a sense of fulfilment of one's need for growth towards higher achievement of work and better career prospects, on the other.

4. **Power:** One of the appealing aspects of groups is that they represent power and also offer power to their members. Workers enjoy much greater power by joining groups than they do as individuals. This is because of at least two reasons: (*i*) **There is strength in numbers,** and (*ii*) **United we stand, divided we fall.**

5. **Identity:** As a member of a group, an individual gets identity `Who am I ?[3] In practices we understand ourselves through the behaviour of others towards us. For example, when others praise us, we feel we are great, if others laugh at us, we see ourselves as funny ones.

15.3 THEORIES OF GROUP FORMATION

Though a number of theories have been propounded by various experts to explain the dynamics of group formation, the most important ones are discussed hereunder:

1. **Homans's Theory:** Homans's theory[4] of group formation is based on three elements, namely, **activities, interaction,** and **sentiments.** According to Homans, these three elements are directly related to each other. The required activities are the assigned tasks to people to work. The required interaction takes place when any person's activity takes place or is influenced by the activity of any other person. As regards sentiments, these are the feelings or attitudes of a person towards others, *i.e.,* his likes or dislikes, approval or disapproval.

The following imaginary example will help you understand Homans's theory in a better manner.

Suppose, you the students of Business Administration are in queue to deposit your examination fees in the UCO Bank. All of you have a common purpose, that is, to deposit fees when your turn comes. You see, a student from Mass Communication Department comes and breaks the queue to go ahead. The student whose turn was dislocated by the queue breaker tells the queue breaker not to do so and pushes him out. This influences all other students standing in the queue to follow the student whose turn was dislocated, in telling him not to break the queue. In this example, you can see activities and interactions taking place among the students. When the students actually disapprove the queue breaker in doing so, it reflects their sentiments towards each other. In sum and substance, all these activities took place because of the sentiments or feelings of the students/people. Such group formation you might have often seen in case of railway reservation queue.

2. **Exchange Theory of Reward and Cost Outcome:** Thaibaunt and Kelly[5] put forward their theory of group formation, stating the outcome of interaction as the basis of group formation. According to them, the outcome of interaction should result in attraction and affiliation, also called rewards, among the persons of a group. In case, the interaction incurs anxiety or frustration or embarrassment or fatigue to the members of a group, it is, then, called cost for the members rather than a reward. In exchange theory, affiliation, interaction and common attitude play an important role.

3. **Balance Theory:** This theory was propounded by Newcomb[6]. According to this theory, groups are formed on the basis of attractions of people towards each other having similar attitudes and values. Rao and Barman form relationship because of their common attitudes and values. They try to maintain a symmetrical relationship between the attraction and common attitudes and values. As and when, their relationship becomes unbalanced, both try to restore balance. However, if balance cannot be restored, then their relationship gets dissolved. Thus, you will

appreciate that both attraction and interaction play a significant role in balance theory.

Let us now turn our attention to various types of groups found in organisations.

15.4 TYPES OF GROUPS

There are mainly two ways of classifying groups into types: formal and informal groups. Different kinds of formal and informal groups are listed in the following Table 15.1.

Table 15.1: Types of Groups

Formal Groups	Informal Groups
Command Group Task Group Project Group Committees	Friendship Group Interest Group Reference Group

A brief description of each of them follows.

Formal Groups

Groups established by the organisation to achieve organisational goals are called **formal groups**. In formal groups, the behaviours that a member should exhibit are stipulated by organisation and directed towards organisational goals. It is possible to further sub-classify formal groups into the following ones:

Command Group: A command group is composed of a supervisor (manager) and the subordinates who report directly to that supervisor. A command group is determined by the organisational chart. In the Department of Business Administration of a University, for example, the Head of the Department and the other faculty members in the department would comprise a command group.

Task Group: A task group comprises of persons working together to complete a common task. However, a task group can cross command relationships. In a University, for instance, if a student is accused of a campus crime, it may involve interaction among the head of the department, the dean of the shcool, the dean of the student's welfare, the proctor, and the registrar of the university. Here, it should be noted that all command groups are task groups, but task groups can cut across the organisational boundary, the reverse need not be true.

Project Group: Likewise, project groups are formed to complete a specific project. The life of the project group normally coincides with the length of the project. Assigning a research project to a university Professor by the University Grants Commission is an example of project group.

Committees: Committees are usually created outside the usual command group structure to solve recurring problems. The life of a committee may be relatively long or short. An example of committees is a University's Examination Discipline Committee created to solve desciplinary problems relating to examination.

Informal Groups

Groups which are not formal are informal. In other words, these are groups that are neither formally created nor controlled by the organisation. These groups are natural formations in the work environment that appear in response to the need for social contact. Four employees belonging to four different departments taking their lunch together represent an example of an informal group. The various kinds of informal groups are:

Friendship Groups: Friendship groups are associations of people who like each other and who like to be together. Such groups are formed because members have one or more common characteristics, such as age or ethnic heritage, political beliefs, religious values, and other bonds of attraction.

Interest Groups: Interest groups are composed of individuals who may not be members of the same organisation (command or task groups), but they are united by their interest in a common issue. Example of interest groups may include a group of university Professors who organise a seminar on Law and Order Problems in the North-Eastern Region of India.

Reference Group: A reference group is a special type of informal group that people use to evaluate themselves. A reference group may not be an actual one that meets together, it can be an imaginary group. The reference group for a new university Lecturer, for example, may be other scholars in the same discipline working in other universities.

15.5 STAGES OF GROUP DEVELOPMENT

Different researchers have reported different stages of group development. For example, Bernard M. Bass and Edward C. Ryterband[7] report that groups typically develop through a four stage process : (1) mutual acceptance, (2) communication and decision making, (3) motivation and productivity, and (4) control and organisation. However, the most widely accepted four stages of group development are ones as reported by B.W. Tuchman and M.A. Jensen[7]. These are : forming, storming, norming and performing. These are summarised in Figure 11.1.

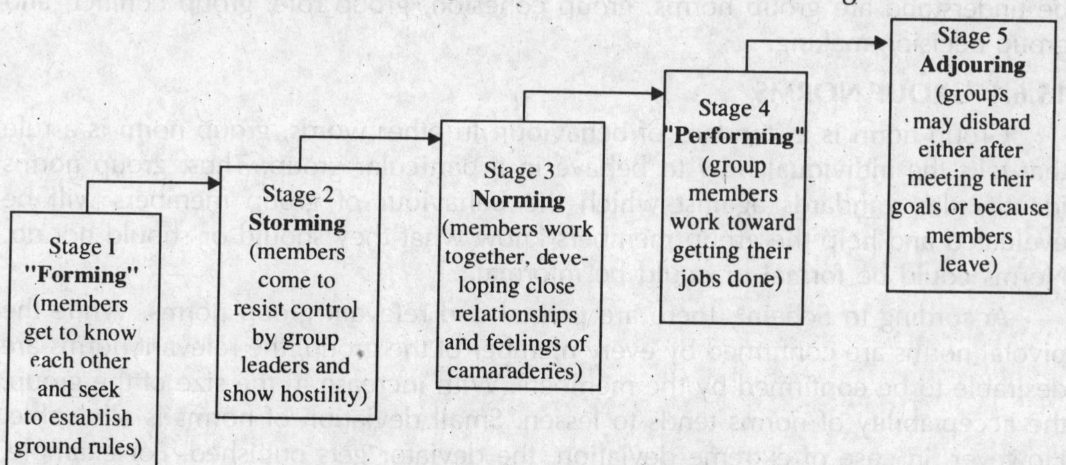

Fig. 15.1: Stages of Group Development

Forming Stage: The first stage for almost every group is an orientation stage. This stage is marked by a great deal of caution, confusion, courtesy and uncertainty about the group's purpose, structure, and leadership. The formal leader exerts a great influence in structuring the group and shaping member expectations. This stage is complete when members of the group have begun to think of themselves as part of a group.

Storming Stage: This stage is characterised by conflict, confrontation, concern, and criticism. Struggles for individual power and influences are common. In case, the conflict becomes extremely intense and dysfunctional, the group may dissolve or continue as an ineffective group that never advances to higher levels of group maturity.

Norming Stage: This is the stage in which close relationship among the members develops. The group evinces cohesiveness. The group now assumes to certain identity and camaraderie.

Performing Stage: This is the highest level of group maturity. This stage is marked by teamwork, role clarity, and task accomplishment. Conflict is identified and resolved through group discussion. The members of the group are aware of group's processes and the extent of their own involvement in the group.

Adjourning Stage: Groups are adjourned for two reasons. **First,** the group has completed its task. **Second,** the members decide to disband and close the group with sentimental feelings.

15.6 GROUP BEHAVIOUR

Groups are composed of individuals. Hence, the group behaviour means behaviour of its members. In practice, each member of the group affects the behaviour of other members and, in turn, is also affected by them. The nature and patterns of reinforcement the members receive through their interaction with one another is also determined by the group itself. This is because the behaviour of individual members in a group becomes different than their behaviour outside the group situation. Therefore, while studying group behaviour, the factors that should be understood are group norms, group cohesion, group role, group conflict, and group decision-making.

15.6.1 GROUP NORMS

Group norm is a standard of behaviour. In other words, group norm is a rule that tells the individual how to behave in a particular group. Thus, group norms identify the standards against which the behaviour of group members will be evaluated and help the group members know what they should or should not do. Norms could be formal or could be informal.

According to Schein[8], there are pivotal and relevant group norms. While the pivotal norms are confirmed by every member of the group, the relevant norms are desirable to be confirmed by the members. With increase in the size of the group, the acceptability of norms tends to lessen. Small deviation of norms is allowable. However, in case of extreme deviation, the deviator gets punished. For example, when the union is on strike, its members attending to work are punished by being boycotted by the group.

Thus, the group norms have following characteristics:

1. As personality reveals an individual, so group norms do for groups.

2. Norms serve as the basis for behaviour of group members.
3. They predict and control the behaviour of members in groups.
4. Norms are applied to all members of the group, though not uniformly.

15.6.2 GROUP COHESION

Group cohesion means the degree to which the group members are attracted to each other and remain within the group[9]. It is usually reflected by its resiliency to disruption by outside forces. Group cohesion develops out of the activities, interactions and sentiments of the members. Cohesiveness binds all the group members to work as one man to attain the set goals.

How to Increase Group Cohesiveness

There are various factors that improve group cohesiveness. The most popular factors are given in the following Table 15.2.

Table 15.2. Factors Increasing Group Cohesion

1.	Inducing agreement on group goals.
2.	Increasing membership homegeniety.
3.	Increasing interactions among group members.
4.	Down-sizing of the group.
5.	Encouraging competition with other rival groups.
6.	Allocating rewards to the groups not to the members
7.	Keeping the members isolated from other groups.

Relationship between Group Cohesiveness and Productivity

It will be interesting to look into how group cohesiveness affects the productivity of group members. Evidences such as Hawthorne studies, indicate that highly cohesive groups are more effective than those with less cohesiveness. It is also reported that a high degree of cohesiveness is both a cause and effect of high productivity. However, the relationship between the two is moderated by the degree to which the group attitudes are aligned with the organisational goals[10]. This can be understood with an example of a hockey team. Here, the successful performance of the players depends upon both cohesiveness among them and their attitudinal alignment with their organisational goal.

Given the favourable group attitude or norms, the productivity of a cohesive group tends to be higher than a less cohesive group. But, if group cohesiveness is high and group norms are not favourable, the group productivity will be lower. If group cohesiveness is less, on the one hand, and group norms are not favourable, on the other, there seems to be no significant effect of group cohesiveness upon productivity.

Lastly, a high group cohesiveness also offers job satisfaction to its members. Job satisfaction helps reduce absenteeism, tardiness and turnover among the group members. As regards its effect upon productivity, it depends upon reconciliation between the group goals and the organisational goals.

The cohesive groups have important implications for managers mainly for two reasons. **First,** a cohesive group being united commands control over its members. It enables the group to command a powerful bargaining power. **Second**, if the cohesive groups are not managed and motivated effectively, its productivity is sure to be low. Therefore, it is imperative for the management to work in close cooperation with the cohesive groups to attain higher productivity.

15.6.3 GROUP ROLE

What is a role? The social scientists use the term role in much the same way as a director of a play would refer to the character who plays a part. Thus, the part one plays in the overall group structure is what we mean by a role. In other words, a role means a set of expected behaviour pattern attached to a position or post in a social context. In an organisation, an employee's role is briefly indicated by a position title and elaborately specified by a job description. As regards group roles, these are designated and assigned in formal groups. These roles are prescribed by the organisation with a view to make division among workers and assign them responsibility. But, group roles are usually not explicitly prescribed in informal groups. That is why in informal groups, one group member may perform several roles or several members may also perform the same role. Roles is, thus, many hats we wear.

Types of Group Roles: In practice, the group members may be expected to perform a variety of different roles. A complete listing of these group roles would be very lengthy. However, the three most relevant group roles are discussed as follows:

(*i*) **Work Roles:** These roles relate to task-oriented activities involved in accomplishing the group tasks or group goals. Developing a strategy for accomplishing the task, assigning jobs, evaluating work progress and clarifying the group goals are the examples of work roles related to task-oriented activities.

(*ii*) **Maintenance Role:** These roles relate to social-emotional activities of group members that help maintain their involvement and commitment to group. Examples of these roles may be encouraging other fellow members to participate, praising and rewarding other members for their excellent contribution, and similar other activities designed to maintain a friendly group atmosphere.

(*iii*) **Blocking Roles:** These are the activities that disrupt or destroy the group. These activities may include such things as dominating the discussion, attacking other group members, disagreeing unreasonably with other group members, and distracting the group by unnecessary humor.

Role Identity: There are certain attitudes and actual behaviours consistent with a role. These create the role identity. Role identity is better when the roles are clearly defined. On the contrary, if the roles are ill-defined, the role identities become clouded.

People shift roles rapidly when there is change in situation and demand for change is also recognized. For example, when the union leaders were promoted to foremen positions, their attitudes changed from pro-workers to pro-management within a month of their promotion.

Role Ambiguity: Role ambiguity refers to the discrepancy between the defined role and perceived role. This is a confusion resulting from the delegation of job responsibilities. Many times, some jobs do not have job description in writing and when employees are asked to do something, they are confused. Role ambiquity is harmful for employees. The evil consequences of job ambiguity are frustration, job dissatisfaction, and stress or tensions. However, extreme role ambiguity creates an unhealthy condition leading to absenteeism and turnover.

Role Conflict: People in their lives perform several roles. While on the job, one performs the role of the servant, when the same person is off the job, he performs roles like a husband, a father, a brother, and so on. Many of these roles are compatible, whereas some roles create conflict[2]. Thus, when a person is confronted by divergent role expectations, this is called **'role conflict'.** Role conflict emerges when the compliance with one role requirement makes difficult the compliance with another one. In some extreme cases, two or more roles may turn to be mutually contradictory or conflicting.

Role Expectations: In simple words, role expectations are what other people believe you should behave in a given situation. How you behave is determined ***inter alia*** by the role defined in the context you are behaving or acting. For example, the role of a Professor is believed as having sincerity and dignity, whereas a football coach is viewed as aggressive, dynamic, and inspiring to his players.

15.6.4 INTER-GROUP BEHAVIOUR

Organisations are composed of individuals and groups. Organisation being a system, both individuals and groups cannot remain independent but dependent on each other. For example, one group may depend on others for raw materials, information and other assistance. The nature of interdependence among different groups can be classified into the following four categories:

(*i*) **Pooled Interdependence:** When the groups belonging to the same parent organisation depend on each other, it is called 'pooled interdependence'. Such groups have limited interaction among them. Manufacturing divisions producing independent products are examples of pooled interdependence.

(*ii*) **Sequential Interdependence:** Group activities occuring in a sequential manner create sequential interdependence. For example, A group's activities or operations precede and act as prerequisite for B group's operations. Assembly line departments represent such sequential interdependence.

(*iii*) **Reciprocal Interdependence:** When a group relies on the other to perform its own job effectively, it is called 'reciprocal interdependence'. Relationship between union and management is an example of reciprocal interdependence.

(*iv*) **Team Interdependence:** The reciprocal interdependence gets multiplied with interaction among multiple groups. The examples of multiple groups may be various departments such as sales, advertising, and market research in marketing division.

The nature and degree of interdependence among groups will influence the degree and quality of inter-group behaviour. Accordingly, groups tend to have the following two types of interactions:

(*i*) **Inter-Group Openness and Co-operation:** Groups being parts of an organisational system, each group co-operates with others to achieve organisational objectives. However, a co-operative relationship does not mean absence of competition among the groups. This is because the groups may not compete with each other but still groups may not be co-operative. The groups may be just indifferent. Factors like superordinate goals, lateral communication, suitable structural arrangement help establish co-operation among various groups.

(*ii*) **Intergroup Closure and Competition:** Intergroup relationship becomes as competitive in the following situations:

(*a*) One group sees other groups as the enemy.

(*b*) With decrease in interaction and communication, hostility of one group towards others tends to increase.

(*c*) While interacting with each other, the groups try to defend own viewpoints and finding faults with the other.

As such relationship among groups benefits none—neither groups nor organisations. The managers need to take timely actions to overcome these problems.

15.6.5 INTER-GROUP CONFLICTS

Conflict arises out of inconsistency. Inconsistency in different matters among groups in an organisation creates inter-group conflicts. One union vs. another union, one functional group like production vs. another functional group like marketing are the examples of group conflicts or inter-group conflicts. The inter-group conflicts usually arise when (*i*) there is a felt need among groups for a joint decision-making; (*ii*) there is differentiation in goals of the groups; and (*iii*) there is differentiation in perceptions of reality by the groups:

A brief description about each of these three follows.

1. **Need for Joint Decision-Making:** The need for a joint decision-making is felt by the groups in the following situations :

(*i*) The limited resources at the disposal of the organisation need to be shared by the groups.

(*ii*) The timely completion of interdependent jobs needs to have scheduling for them.

(*iii*) The different departmental heads require joint decision-making for establishing co-ordination at the higher levels of the organisation.

2. **Differences in Groups Goals:** Goals vary among groups for the following reasons:

(*i*) If an individual is the member of different groups, he/she faces role conflict because there are differences in sub-goals of various groups.

(*ii*) The members of different groups also differ in terms of their family background, culture, education, training, etc.

(*iii*) Pattern and frequency of interaction among the group members also leads to differences in goals.

3. **Differences in Group Perceptions:** The following factors create differences in perception of people:

(*i*) Perceptions differ depending upon differing views about goals.

(*ii*) Perceptions of the members about group goals may differ because of differences in their family background, education, training, culture and value system.

(*iii*) Different sources of information to different members may also affect their perception about organisational and group goals. Inadequacy of information may also affect perception of the members.

Now, let us know how groups make decisions to solve the various problems and accomplish the set goals.

15.7 GROUP DECISION-MAKING

What is decision-making? Decision-making is the process whereby a final but best choice is made among the alternatives available. When a group makes decision, it can be either through the consensus mode or through majority vote. When all members of the group agree to the decision arrived at, it is called 'consensus'. If majority of the group members agree to the decision arrived at, it is called majority vote. Whether the decision arrived at will be consensus or majority mode depends mainly on the size of the group.

Let us also understand the process a group follows in decision-making.

Group Decision-Making Process

Group decision making process involves the following four steps as depicted in Fig. 15.2:

1. **Diagnosing the Problem:** Decisions are made to solve problems. Hence, the first step involved in decision making process is to identify the problem to be solved.

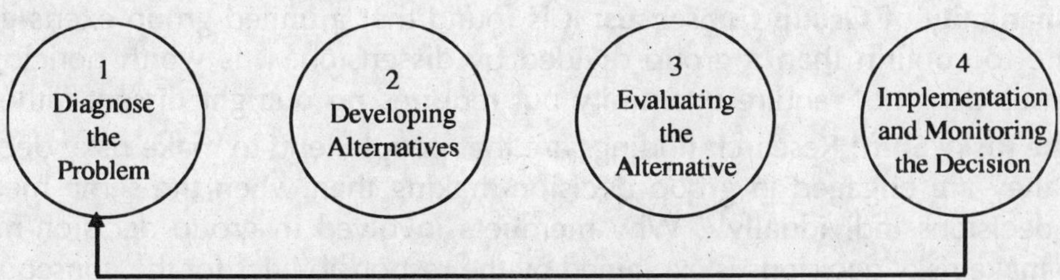

Fig. 15.2: Decision-Making Process

2. **Developing Alternatives:** Decisions are made out of alternatives. Therefore, alternatives are developed through different sources like experience, practices in other organisations, and ideas and suggestions from different parties related to the diagnosed problem.

3. **Evaluating the Alternatives:** Having alternatives being developed, these are evaluated one by one to know their plus and minus points. Then, finally the most

appropriate alternative is selected.

4. **Implementing and Monitoring the decision:** The last step involved in the decision-making process is implementing the selected alternative and then monitoring it. Monitoring may include activities like seeing whether the activities are taking place according to plan or not, whether the workers/subordinates are performing according to expectations or not. If not, appropriate measures need to be taken to correct the situation.

Though decision-making is supposed to pass through a definite process as delineated above, group decisions in practice are made differently. The same is discussed hereunder.

15.7.1 HOW DO GROUPS MAKE DECISION ?

Group Size: Research indicates that as the number of members in problem-solving groups increases beyond a certain point, the quality of decisions made by the group tends to decrease. This is because the group pressure tends to increase to influence the decision. Though the size of an ideal group has not been determined, groups consisting of five to seven members have been found to be effective for decision-making. This is because the members of a group of this size get adequate opportunities to express their opinions, listen to each other, seek clarifications on points that are not clear, and reach to a unanimous decision. This does not happen in case of large groups. Nonetheless, larger groups may be necessary where variety of skills, knowledge, experience, and expertise from different functional areas is required for making decisions on critical issues like developing a new product.

Group Composition: The qualifications of group members also influence the group decision. Group members with higher status, either due to their background or expertise, are likely to exert subtle pressures, manipulate, coerce, or otherwise alter or sway the thinking of the other group members in a particular direction[11]. Minority group members tend to be highly influenced by such group pressures.

Unanimity of Group Consensus: It is found that a united group exerts greater pressure to confirm than a group divided by dissension. It is worth noticing that consensus does not require unanimity but requires no outright dissent either.

The Risky Shift: Research findings are that people tend to make risky decisions when they are engaged in group decision-making than when the same members make decisions individually[12]. Why members involved in group decision-making like to make risky decisions is explained by the responsibilities for the consequences of the decisions will be shared by all the group members rather than one individual member shouldering the entire burden. Such phenomenon for groups to make risky decisions is known as the **risky shift.** Individuals tend to make conservative decisions because the consequences of the decisions will be borne by the individual alone.

Advantages of Group Decision-Making

The group decision-making offers the following advantages:

1. Compared to an individual, the groups usually have a greater knowledge, expertise, and skill base to make better decisions.
2. Larger number of members provide more perspectives of the problem. As such, the narrow vision of a single perspective is avoided in making decisions.
3. With larger number of group members, the participation also increases that helps reach at a quality decision.
4. Following increased group participation, comprehension of final decision arrived at is usually high.

Disadvantages of Group Decision-Making

All is not good with group decision-making. It suffers from the following disadvantages also:

1. Group decision-making is a time consuming process.
2. Influence groups usually manipulate the group decision in a direction of their liking and interest.
3. Sometimes decisions made by the group members are simply a compromise between the various views and options offered by the group members.

In view of above disadvantages, there is a need to improve group decisions. What follows next is the same.

15.7.2 HOW TO IMPROVE GROUP DECISIONS MAKING ?

Efforts have been made by the social scientists to develop strategies to make group decision making more and more effective. Four such techniques developed are **brain-storming, nominal group technique, delphi technique,** and **consensus mapping.** A brief description of these follows :

1. Brainstorming: Brainstorming technique was originally adopted by Alex Osborn[13] in 1938 in an American company for encouraging creative thinking in groups of six to eight people. According to Osborn, brainstorming means using the brain to storm the problem. In brainstorming, the participants should be connected with the problem directly or closely. It is based on the following four basic guidelines:

1. Generate as many ideas as possible.
2. Be creative, freewheeling, and imaginative.
3. Build upon piggyback, extend, or combine earlier ideas.
4. Withhold criticism of others' ideas.

There are two principles that underlie brainstorming. **One** is deferred judgement, by which all ideas are encouraged without criticism and evaluation. The **second** principle is that quantity breeds quality. As more ideas come forth, it facilitates to develop the higher-quality ones. The success of brainstorming depends on each member's capacity and willingness to listen to others' thoughts, to use these thoughts as a stimulus to spark new ideas of their own, and then feel free to express them[14]. Brainstorming sessions last from ten minutes to one hour and do not require

Although brainstorming technique is found useful for all types of decisions, it is particularly useful for simple and well-defined problems. It stimulates members to generate new ideas for solving a particular problem.

2. **Nominal Group Technique (NGT):** As mentioned earlier, the two disadvantages of group decision making are it is time-consuming and the decisions are influenced by the dominant members. The nominal group technique (NGT) minimizes these problems. In the NGT, a nominal group exists in name only. The members have minimal interaction prior to making a decision[15]. The NGT follows the following process:

1. Members are brought together and presented a problem.
2. Each member develops solution or ideas independently and writes them on cards.
3. Each member presents his/her ideas to the group in a round-robbin procedure.
4. When the presentation of ideas by each member is over, brief time is allotted to clarifications of ideas or solutions.
5. Group members individually rank their preferences for the best alternatives by secret ballot.
6. Based on above, the group decision is announced.

The advantages of the NGT include the integration of both group creativity and individual creativity and the equal participation by all members in group decision making. The disadvantage of the NGT is reported that the members do not have the opportunity to benefit from cross-fertilization of ideas.

3. **Delphi Technique:** The name Delphi indicates a shrine at which the ancient Greeks used to pray for information about the future. In Delphi technique of decision-making, members are scattered over large distances and do not have face-to-face interaction for decision-making. Members are selected because they are experts or have relevant information to share. A typical approach involved in decision-making works as follows:

Firstly, a small group of members designs a questionnaire which is administered in a larger group. The results so obtained are then tabulated and used in developing a revised questionnaire. The questionnaire is then completed by the larger group. The results of the first round are fed back to the respondent group to use these in their subsequent responses. The process is repeated several times until the response converses satisfactorily or a consensus is reached[16].

The effectiveness of the Delphi decision-making technique depends on adequate time, participants' expertise, communication skill, and motivation of the members to immerse themselves in the task. The major advantages the delphi technique offers include:

1. Elimination of interpersonal problems among panelists.
2. Efficient use of experts' time.
3. Adequate time for reflection and analysis by respondents.
4. Diversity and quantity of ideas generated.

The major disadivantage of the Delphi technique, if any, is its complexity and high cost involved in administering the series of questionnaires.

4. **Consensus Mapping:** Consensus mapping is yet another technique of group decision-making. In this technique, an attempt is made to arrive at a decision by pooling the ideas together generated by several task sub-groups. It begins with developing ideas by a task sub-group. The facilitators encourage participants to further develop clusters of ideas. The ideas so generated by the task sub-groups are developed and narrowed in smaller number of ideas. Then, all ideas are consolidated into a representative structure called **'strawman map'** for the all ideas generated by the sub-groups. Strawman map is further narrowed down to arrive at a mutually acceptable solution.

Consensus mapping technique is found best suited for problems that are multi-dimensional, have interconnected relationships, and involve many sequential steps in problem solving.

15.8 QUALITY CIRCLE (QC)

The concept of quality circle (QC) originally emerged in Japan is of a recent origin in the Indian organisations. Quality circle is a work group of employees who meet regularly to discuss their quality problems, investigate causes, recommend solutions, and take corrective measures[17]. QC is a small group of employees who work voluntarily on company time, to address work related problems such as quality control, cost reduction, production planning and techniques, and even product design.

Quality circle is used to achieve the following objectives :

1. Improvement in quality of product manufactured by the organisation.
2. Improvement in methods of production and productivity.
3. Development of employees participating in QC.
4. Promoting morale of employees.
5. Respect humanity and create a happy workplace worthwhile to work.

How to Introduce Quality Circles in Organisations ?

Like any organisational change, QC being a new concept is most likely be opposed by the employees. Therefore, QC should be introduced with great concern and precaution as discussed below:

1. **Publicising the Idea of QC:** Implementation of QC is just like an organisational change programme. Hence, like an organisational change programme, the workers need to be convinced about the need for and significance of QC from the point of view of the organisation and the workers. Participation in QC being voluntary, its publicity among the workers is necessary. To begin with, management can also arrange for initial training to some workers who want to form quality circles.

2. **Constitution of Quality Circles:** Workers doing similar type of work are drawn voluntarily to constitute quality circles. The membership of a QC should be limited to ten to twelve members.

3. **Initial Problem Solving:** The members of the QC should discuss the problem at threadbare and prepare a list of alternative solutions. Each alternative solution

should be evaluated and final solution should be arrived at on the basis of consensus.

4. **Presentation and Approval of Suggestions:** The final solution arrived at should be presented to the management either in oral or in written form. The management may evaluate the solution by forming a committee for this purpose. The committee may also meet the members of the quality circle for clarifications. Presentation of solutions to the management helps improve the communication between management and workers and reflects management's interest to the members of QC.

5. **Implementation:** Once the suggestion/solution is approved by the management, the same is being put into practice in a particular workplace. Quality circles may be organised gradually for other workplaces or departments also. Thus, following this process, the entire organisation can have quality circles.

Problems in Implementation of Quality Circles and Their Solutions

Though QC concept has many positive points, it has failed miserably in many organisations due to certain problems and pitfalls. Following are some major problems of QC implementation and their suggested remedies:

1. **Negative Attitude:** Both employees and managers having negative attitude toward QC often resist its implementation. Managers feel that QC dilutes their authority and importance in the organisation. This negative attitude can be dispelled by imparting appropriate training to employees as well as managers about the real concept and contributions of QC.

2. **Lack of Ability:** The Indian workers are characterised by their low level of education and lack of leadership abilities. This problem can be overcome by initiating workers' education programme.

3. **Lack of Management Commitment:** Lack of management commitment toward QC is demonstrated by not permitting the members to hold QC meetings during the working hours. Therefore, the top management should permit workers to hold QC meetings periodically during the working hours and should also extend all required and timely assistance for the smooth functioning of QC.

4. **Non-Implementation of Suggestions:** The members of the QC feel disheartened in case their suggestions are not accepted and implemented without convincing reasons. Instead, the suggestions rendered by QC should be given due consideration and weightage and should be implemented. This will enthuse the members of the QC to improve quality of their goods and services. QC benefits both organisation and workers.

15.9 WORK TEAMS

Now that you have a clear understanding of groups and how they function, we can compare them to another type of collection of individuals known as '**teams**' This section is, therefore, devoted to define what is meant by teams and how they are different from groups. We will then present some guidelines for creating teams in organisations.

Meaning of Team

A team can be defined as an association of individuals who, by generating positive synergy, is committed to achieve some common goal. According to Katzenbach and Smith[18], "A team is a group whose members have complementary skills and are committed to a common purpose or set of performance goals for which they hold themselves mutually responsible."

A team is characterised by the following features :

- It creates positive synergy
- It creates and fosters comraderies among the members through regular and repeated interactions.
- It encourages members to sublimate their individual goals for those of the team.
- It also encourages members' involvement in the team work.

How Teams Differ from Groups ?

At this point, it is probably not entirely clear to you exactly how a team is different from an ordinary group. This confusion probably stems in part from the fact that people often refer to their groups as teams, although they are really not teams. As a matter of fact, there are several important distinctions between them. The major bases of distinction between team and a group are presented as follows:

Bases	Team	Group
Performance	On both individual member's work and collective work.	On the work of individual workers.
Accountability	On both individual and mutual accountability.	On group as a whole.
Connection to management	Usually self-managed or autonomous.	Responsive to demands placed on it by management.
Skills	Complementary.	Random and varied.
Synergy	Positive synergy.	Often neutral synergy, sometimes even negative synergy, called 'social loafing'.

Jon R.Katzenbach and Douglas K. Smith [19] distinguish between a group and a team based on performance results. They note :

"A working group's performance is a function of what its members do as individuals. A team's performance includes both individual results and what we call "collective work–products." A collective work-product is what two or more members must on together....(it) reflects the joint, real contribution of team members."

Like a group as seen earlier in this chapter, a team's development also passes through five stages, viz., forming stage, storming stage, norming stage, performing stage, and adjourning stage.[20]

Types of Teams

Based on purpose, power and period, Mohrman [21] has classified teams into three broad types:

1. Problem-Solving Team
2. Self-Managed Team
3. Cross Functional Team

These are discussed in seriatim.

Problem-Solving Team : Problem-solving team, also known as corrective action team, is constituted to solve some specific problem an organisation or its some department is facing. The members in such teams are drawn from the sections or departments that are related to the problem to be solved. Quality circles are the example of such teams.

Self-Managed Team : This is natural work group that is given substantial autonomy and, in return, is asked to control its behaviour and produce significant results. Hence, it is also called 'autonomous' or 'empowered team'. Self-managing team is characterised by empowerment, self plan, self goal, self inspection, and self responsible for the results. Over the last few years, emphasis on building self-managed teams has remained high because of the advantages these teams offer. For example, Howlett–Packard has discovered that when its teams are empowered and allowed to organise the work themselves, productivity can skyrocket.[22]

Cross Functional Team : Cross-functional teams are made up of members drawn from a host of different departments or functional specialities, particularly from those functional areas which have high interdependance. The basic objective in forming such team is to solve problem that cannot be done by a particular or functional department. Such team is usually disbanded when the problem is solved.

Besides, 'time' is one more dimension or criterion taken to classify teams. Accordingly, some teams are only 'temporary' and are formed for a specific project with a finite life. For example, a team formed to develop a product would be considered temporary. As soon as its job is done, it disbands. Other kinds of teams are 'permanent', and last as long as the organisation is operating. For example, teams focussing on providing effective customer service tend to be permanent parts of many organisations.

Team Building

Why team building ? The need for team building, according to Baltasar Grasaifi, a Spanish priest and writer, lies in the fact that : "The path to greatness is along with others." The successful stories of work teams benefitting both the organisation and team members abound in the business world. For example, a comprehensive meta-analysis covering seventy studies concluded that self-managed teams had a positive impact on productivity and specific attitudes like motivation, absenteeism, turnover, etc. relating to the members of a team. That is why work teams have assumed increasing attention in the recent years.

However, experiences also indicate that as the work team is very important for the organisation, it is not so easy and simple to build an effective team. In fact, building an effective team involves serious concern and consideration. According to Hackman[23], building an effective team involves a process that proceeds four distinct stages. These are :

Stage 1 : Do Prework

This stage is in a way forming stage of team building. This stage is marked by decisions like what is the need for building a team, what authority the team should have, and alike. In addition, an inventory of the skills needed to do the job should also be made.

Stage 2 : Create Performance Conditions

In this stage, the concerned officials have to ensure that proper conditions are created for a team to perform its job, whatsoever is decided at stage one. It involves making both material resources (e.g., tools, equipment, and money) and human resources (e.g., appropriate blend of skilled personnel) available to the teams. In addition, support from management is also ensured to let the team do its own work. Team is bound to fail without support from the management /organisation.

Stage 3 : Form and Build the Team

This stage involves three things to be done to help a team make good start. *First,* establish clear demarcational boundaries to clarify who is and is not a member of a team. This is required because ambiguity causes confusion and frustration. *Second,* arrive at an agreement about the overall mission and purpose is inevitable. *Third,* clarify the behaviour expected of each member.

Stage 4 : Provide Ongoing Assistance

Once a team has started functioning, it needs to be provided with needed and timely assistance to keep it ongoing. For this, managers may intervene to eliminate team problems, if any. For example, they may need either to counsel the disruptive team members or replace them by new ones. Similarly, material resources also may need to be replenished or upgraded. Yes, it may be unwise for managers to intervene in the successful affairs of a team, on the one hand, and to neglect opportunities to help a team do even better, on the other.

Examples are also gallore to mention that all teams all the times do not contribute to organisational performance and, therefore, are considered ineffective. A recent in-depth interview survey of 4,500 teams at 500 organisations uncovered a host of individual and organisational factors behind team ineffectiveness. Following were the individual problems :

1. Either team members are not willing to give up past practices or set aside power and position vested in them.
2. Not all team members possess ability, knowledge, skill, etc. to contribute to the team work. Team result slows because some members show the 'social loafing'attitude.
3. At times, what suits to the team does not suit to the individual member. Then, this causes conflict for the individual.
4. The social facilitation too at times impairs individual performance. This is because sometimes an individual is found to perform better alone than in the presence of others.

As regards the organisational level problems, the survey uncovered the compensation and reward solely based on individual performance as a major problem impairing team performance.[25]

How to Make Teams More Effective ?

Teams can be made more effective by overcoming what has made them ineffective, *i.e.* problems. Viewed from this angle, most suggested guidelines revolve around training and evaluation systems. Following are the training guidelines suggested by Paul E. Brauchle and David W. Wright for developing effective teams:

Training Guidelines for Developing Team Effectiveness

Steps of Training	Summary
1. Establish credibility	The trainers must first establish their knowledge and believability.
2. Allow ventilation	The trainees must have their anxieties and unresolved issues cleared before starting.
3. Provide an orientation.	The trainers should give specific verbal directions and provide clear expectations and models of behavior.
4. Invest in the process	Early on, have the team identify its problems and concerns.
5. Set group goals.	The trainees create, through consensus, their own mission statement and then set goals and specific activities and behaviors to accomplish these goals.
6. Facilitate the group process.	The trainees are taught about how groups function and are given techniques, such as nominal grouping and paired comparison.
7. Establish intra-group procedures.	This involves setting up a meeting format that might include reporting minutes, making announcements, discussing problems and issues, proposing solutions, taking action and making new assignments.
8. Establish inter-group . processes	Although the team is self-managed, leaders must be selected in order to interact with others, such as supervisors, managers, and other teams.
9. Change the role of the trainers.	As the team becomes more experienced and empowered, the trainers take on a more passive role.
10.	End the trainers' involvement. At this point, the team is on its own and is self-managing.

Having the teams trained, their functioning must also be evaluated and monitored on a continuous basis to inact them effective. One expert suggests the ways teams be evaluated as follows :

"At any point, team members can slide back to a lower level of effectiveness if they do not continually work together as a team, listen and communicate effectively, recognize each others contributions, provide honest feeback and demonstrate other characteristics of an effective team."

As regards monitoring of teams, this involves specifying the following five areas and then closely monitoring them :

1. Team Mission
2. Goal Achievement

3. Empowerment
4. Open and Honest Communication
5. Positive Roles and Norms.

If evaluation and monitoring of teams is done carefully, teams can be more effective and contribute to the performance of the organisation.

SUMMARY

This summary is organized by the 'learning objectives' given on page no. 251 :

- *A group is a collection of people who interact with each other, know one another and work together to achieve a common objective.*
- *People form groups to satisfy their various needs like safety and security, esteem, belonginginess, getting power and identify.*
- *The important theories of group formation are Homans's Theory, Exchange Theory of Reward and Cost Outcome, and Newcomb's Balance Theory.*
- *Groups established by the organisations to achieve organisational goals are called formal groups. Groups that are neither formally created nor controlled by the organisation are called informal groups.*
- *Formation of a group involves four stages, namely, forming stage, storming stage, norming stage, and performing stage.*
- *Group behaviour is influenced by group norms, group cohesion, group role, group conflict, and group decision-making.*
- *Four steps involved in group decision-making are : diagnosing the problem, developing alternatives, evaluating alternatives and implementing and monitoring the decision.*
- *Brainstorming, nominal group technique, delphi technique, and consensus mapping are the main techniques developed to improve group decision-making.*
- *When workers doing similar type of work meet voluntarily to discuss their quality problems, it is called quality circle (QC).*

REVIEW QUESTIONS

1. Define the term"group". Why are groups formed?
2. Distinguish between formal and informal groups.
3. Define group dynamics. Why informal group comes into existence? What factors influence group cohesiveness?
4. What are group norms? Why do they develop?
5. "Both formal and informal groups are necessary for the group activity just as two blades are essential to make a pair of scissor workable". Comment on this statement.
6. Define group cohesiveness. Explain the relationship between group cohesiveness and productivity.
7. How are group decisions made? How can group decisions be made more effective?
8. What is meant by quality circle? How can this concept be introduced in an organisation?
9. Write a note on how groups are formed.
10. Distinguish between team and group. How is an effective team developed ?
11. Write short notes on:
    (*a*) Informal Group

(*b*) Group Cohesion
(*c*) Quality Circle
(*d*) Group Conflict
(e) Self-Managed Team

REFERENCES

1. P.M. Mills: **The Social Psychology of Small Groups,** Printice-Hall, Eaglewood Cliffs, N.J., 1967.
2. E.H. Schein: **Organisational Psychology**, Printice-Hall of India Private Limited, New Delhi, 1973.
3. H. Joseph Reitz: **Behaviour in Organisations,** Richard D. Irwin, Illinois, 1977, p. 299.
4. G.C. Homans: **The Human Group,** Harwart, Brace and World, New York, 1950, pp. 43-44.
5. John W. Thaibaut and Harold H. Kelly: **The Social Work,** 1959.
6. Theodre M. Newcomb: **The Acquaintance Process**, Halt, New York, 1961.
7. Bernard M. Bass and Edward C. Ryerband : **Organisational Psychology**, Allyn and Bacon, Boston, 1979 (2nd ed.), pp. 252-254. Also see, B.W. Tuckman and M.A. Jensen: Stages of Small-Group Development Revisited, **Group and Organisational Studies**, December 1977, pp. 419-427.
8. E.H. Schein: ***op. cit.***, 1973.
9. John W. Newstrom and Keith Davis **Organisational Behaviour: Human Behaviour at Work,** Tata McGraw-Hill Publishing Company Limited, New Delhi, 1998, p. 362.
10. Stanley E. Seashore: **Group Cohesiveness in the Industrial Work Group**, University of Machigan Survey Research Centre, Ann Arbor, 1954.
11. Uma Sekaran: **Organisational Behaviour: Text and Cases,** Tata McGraw-Hill Publishing Company Limited, New Delhi, Seventh reprint, 1998, p.124.
12. J.A.F. Stoner: **A Comparison of Individual and Group Decisions Involving Risk**, Masters Thesis, MIT Sloan School of Industrial Management, Cambridge, Mass, 1961.
13. Alex F. Osborn: **Applied Imagination**, Charles Scribner's Sons, New York, 1953.
14. John W. Newstrom and Keith Davis: ***op. cit.***, 1997, p. 354.
15. William M. Fox: Anonymity and Other Keys to Successful Problem-Solving Meetings, **National Productivity Review,** Spring 1989, pp. 145-155.
16. Robert E. Erffmeyer et at.: The Delphi Technique: An Empirical Evaluation of the Optimal Number of Rounds, **Group and Organisation Studies,** March-June 1986, pp. 120-128.
17. Joel E. Ross and William C. Ross: **Japanese Quality Circles and Productivity**, p.2.
18. Jon R.Katzenback and Douglas K. Smith : The Discipline of Teams, **Harvard Business Review**, March-April 1993, p. 112.
19. *Ibid*, p. 113.
20. Bruce W. Tuckman and Marry Ann C. Jensen : *op. cit.*, 1977, pp. 419-427.
21. S.A. Mohrman : Integrating Roles and Structure in the Lateral Organisation, In : J.R. Galbraith & E.E. Lawler III (Eds.) : **Organising for the Future**, Jossey-Bass, San Francisco, 1993, pp. 109-41.
22. Stratford Sherman : Secrets of HPs 'Muddled' Team, **Fortune**, March 18, 1996, pp. 116-120.
23. J.R. Hackman : The Design of Work Teams, In : J.W. Lorsch (Ed.) : **Handbook of Organisational Behaviour**, Printice Hall, Englewood Cliffs, NJ., 1987, pp. 315-342.
24. Work Teams Have Their Work Cut Out for Them, **HR Focus**, January 1993, p. 24.
25. *Ibid*, 1993. Also see John Beck and Neil Yeager : Moving Beyand Team Myths, **Training and Development**, March 1996, pp. 51-55.

CASE 15.1* Union Behaviour in Modern Textiles Limited

Modern Textiles Limited is one of the leading textile mills in the south, having a work force of more than 1500 employees, engaged in the manufacture of cotton yarn of different counts. The company has a well-established distribution network in different parts of the country. It had modernised most of its plants, with a view to improve the productivity and maintain quality. To maintain good human relations in the plants and the organisation as a whole, it extended all possible facilities to the employees. Compared to other mills, the employees of Modern Textiles Limited were placed in reasonably high wage brackets.

The company has a general manager, followed by a line of executives in-charge of different functional areas. The Industrial Relations Department was headed by the Industrial Relations Manager with supporting staff. The company earned profits every year and distributed reasonable amounts as bonus to the employees. The employees were represented by six trade unions—A, B, C, D, E and F (unions are alphabetically presented based on membership)—out of which the top three unions were recognised by the management for purpose of negotiations. All the unions maintained good relations with the management individually and collectively. In a particular year when the bonus issue was placed before the management, it had series of discussions with all recognised unions and finally announced a bonus, which was, in turn, agreed upon by all recognised unions. The very next day when the management prepared the representatives, while unions A and C signed the same, the leader of union B refused to do so and walked out, stating that the amount decleared as bonus was not sufficient. The next day, union B issued a strike notice to the management asking for higher bonus. The management tried its level best to avoid an unpleasant situation, but in vain. As a result, one morning, members of union B went on strike. They were joined by members of union D. During the strike, the management could probe the reason for the deviant behaviour of union B leader: it was reported that leader of union A, soon after the first meeting had stated in the presence of a group of workers "because of me the management has agreed to declare this much amount of bonus to the employees. Some representative unions, particularly union B, had miserably failed in its talks with the management for want of initiative and involvement". This observation somehow reached the leader of union B on the very day it was made, as a result of which he felt insulted. Soon after identifying this as the reason for B's strike call, the management in the presence of the Industrial Relations Manager brought about a compromise between the union leaders, A and B. Immediately after this meeting, the strikers (members of union B and D) had resumed work and the settlement was signed for the same amount of bonus, as was originally agreed upon.

QUESTIONS

1. Was the leader of union A justified in making remarks that caused offence to the leader of union B ?
2. Could the strike have been avoided had A not made his remarks before a group of workers?
3. If you were manager, what should your long term strategy be for ensuring against the recurrence of inter-union differences on issues affecting the welfare of workers?

* IGNOU, MBA, June 1999

16

TEAM BUILDING

"One and one make eleven." ***– Anonymous***

"Bringing people together is beginning, keeping people together is progress, and working with people is success." ***– Henry Ford***

Learning Objectives

After studying this chapter, you should be able to:

- **Define** the term team and **differentiate** it from group.
- **Classify** teams into various types.
- **Delineate** the process involved in team building.
- **Discuss** the roles played by teams.
- **Identify** the causes that make a team failure.
- **Suggest** the measures to make teams more effective.
- **Explain** the meaning of social loafing and **suggest** the measures to minimize social loafing.

16.1 MEANING OF TEAM

We have just read group and its behaviour in the preceding chapter 15. Very closer to the word 'group' is the word 'team'. By now, the words team and team building have become buzzwords in the corporate lexicon. Among various OD interventions, as we shall see later in Chapter 28, team building is the most important and widely applied intervention for organization development. French and Bell have appreciated the importance of team building as an OD intervention in these words: *"probably the most important single group of interventions in the OD are the team building activities, the goals of which are the improvement and increased effectiveness of various teams within the organization."* Team building by now has emerged as a phenomenon in organizational effectiveness and development. Hence, it seems pertinent to know about team building right from its formation to functioning in organizations. Let us begin with understanding the meaning of the terms 'team' and 'team building.'

What is a team? Merely a collection of individuals in one place may be only a crowd. A group of individuals working in a face-to-face relationship for a common goal, having collective accountability for the outcome of its efforts is called team.

According to Katzenbach and Smith, "A team is a group whose members have complementary skills and are committed to a common purpose or set of performance goals for which they hold themselves mutually accountable[1]."

Thus, a team is characterized by the following salient features:

1. Team members are driven by a common purpose, have shared understanding of the performance measure, and are guided by a common approach to achieve the team purpose.

2. Members of the team possess the complementary capabilities / skills to perform and achieve the common goal or purpose. The complementary capabilities of team members can be visualized as pieces in a jigsaw puzzle - individually they convey no meaning; collected they still do not project a clear picture; meaning comes out clearly only when they are placed in their respective positions.

3. All members of the team are mutually accountable to the common purpose, goal, and approach.

4. Team members work individually but outcome is always collective.

5. Every member shares three levels of accountability - (i) for individual performance, (ii) for the performance of other members of team, and (iii) for mutual outcome/performance.

The two terms, namely, team building and team work are profusely used and discussed while discussing team performance. While the process of making teams effective is called 'team building,' the practice of working in teams is called 'team work.'

Teams are different from work groups

At this point, it is not entirely clear to you exactly how a team is different from an ordinary work group. This confusion probably stems in part from the fact that people often refer to their groups as teams, although they are really not teams. In fact, teams are distinct from groups on several counts. The important ones are as follows:

First, in teams, any single member is not sufficient to accomplish the team task, whatsoever it is. Each team member is dependant on other members to perform his/her function. But, in groups, work performance typically depends on the work of individual members.

Second, in case of group, members usually do not take responsibility for any results other than their own. By contrast, members of a team, focus on both individual and mutual accountability. So to say, team members work together to produce an outcome that represents their joint contribution, and each member of the team shares responsibility for that joint outcome.

Third, Members of a group are required to be responsive to demands regularly placed on them by management. By contrast, members of a team are usually to some degree self managing - that is, they are free to set their own goals, timing, and the approach that they wish to take, usually without management interference.

Finally, whereas members of a group may share a common interest goal, team members share a common commitment to purpose but usually with greater deal of commitment and involvement in its purpose.

The major bases of distinction between team and a group are presented as follows:

Bases	Team	Group
Performance	On both individual member's work and collective work.	On the work of individual workers.
Accountability	On both individual and mutual accountability.	On group as a whole.
Connection to Management	Usually self-managed or autonomous.	Responsive to demands placed on it by management.
Skills	Complementary	Random and varied.
Synergy	Positive synergy.	Often neutral synergy, sometimes even negative synergy, called 'social loafing.'

Katzenbach and Smith[2] distinguish between a group and a team based on performance results. They note:

"A working group's performance is a function of what its members do as individuals. A team's performance includes both individual results and what we call "collective-work products." A collective work-product is what two or more members must on together ......(it) reflects the joint, real contribution of team members."

They have tabulated the difference between a group and a team as follows:

Bases	Team	Group
Purpose	Specific	Same as organization
Work products	Collective	Individual
Process	Discuss, decide, do.	Discuss, decide, delegate
Leadership	Shared	A single leader
Meetings	Open, problem solving	Efficient
Accountability	Individual and mutual	Individual
Evaluation	Direct (collective work product)	Indirect (e.g. financial)

Thus, it becomes clear that all teams are groups, but all groups are not teams.

16.2 TYPES OF TEAMS

Depending on construction, purpose, power, duration, etc, there may be different types of teams in an organization. Nonetheless, the common type of teams generally found in organizations are cross-functional teams, lead teams, problem solving teams, and self-managing teams. A brief description about these follows in seriatim.

Lead Teams

This is the most common form of team found in the most parts of an organization. The members of a lead team consist of managers and direct subordinates. The basic objective of a lead team is to plan and executive business activities in its specified area of responsibility. A lead team, follows the approach of *'do as I do'* rather than the conventional *'do as I say'* approach and, thus, demonstrates the example of team work. Team work creates the team spirit among the members which, in turn, generates synergy in organizational performance.

Problem-Solving Teams

As the name itself denotes, a problem-solving team is formed to solve the specific problem faced by the organization. The team consists of the members from the department facing the problem. Yes, the members in such teams are drawn from the sections or departments that are related to the problem to be solved and have intimate knowledge of the problem. Quality circles are the example of such teams. The team applies the decision making methodology to solve the problem. It includes the identification of the problem, developing alternative solutions to problem, evaluating the alternative solutions, and finally selecting the most suitable solution.

Self-Managed Teams

In today's knowledge economy, increasing emphasis has been given o formation of self-managed teams, also known as 'empowered' or 'autonomous teams'. These teams are characterized by the following features:

- They are empowered to plan, control, and implement their work processes.
- Set own goals, develop work schedule.
- Prepare their own budget, order material, and maintain required inventory.
- Own responsibility for their performance.

Over the last few years, emphasis on building self-managed teams has assumed increasing emphasis because of the advantages these teams offer. For example, Hewlett-Packard has discovered that when its teams are empowered and allowed to organize the work themselves, productivity can skyrocket. However, formation of empowered teams or self-managed teams is advisable when the members are quite matured and competent to manage the team by themselves effectively. Otherwise, empowered teams may become liability for the organization.

Cross-Functional Teams

Cross-functional teams are made up of members drawn from a host of different departments or functional specialties, particularly from those functional areas which have high inter-dependence. The basic objective in forming such teams is to solve problem that can not be done by a particular functional department. Such team is usually disbanded when the problem is solved.

Virtual Teams

The work teams that work across space, time, and organizational boundaries with links strengthened by webs of communication technologies are called 'virtual teams.' While members from the same organization in the same location meet face-to-face in traditional teams, members of virtual teams coming from cutting across organizational boundaries interact through web-based technologies. A research team having members from different countries working on a common research project is the example of 'virtual team.'

Besides, 'time' is one more dimension or criterion taken to classify teams. Accordingly, some teams are only 'temporary''' and are formed for a specific project with a finite life. For example, a team formed to develop a product would be considered temporary. As soon as its job is done, it disbands. Other kinds of teams are 'permanent' and last as long as the organization is operating. For example, teams focusing on providing effective customer service tend to be permanent parts of many organizations.

While discussing team building, it seems pertinent to first know how a team is formed or what life cycle a team actually passes through. B.W. Tuckman[3] has delineated the process of team formation consisting of five stages, namely, forming, storming, norming, performing, and adjourning. Since these stages have already been discusses earlier in Chapter, the same has not been discussed here for the sake of repetition.

16.3 TEAM BUILDING PROCESS

Team building as an evolving concept involves certain stages to proceed from beginning to its building. These are shown in the following figure 16.1.

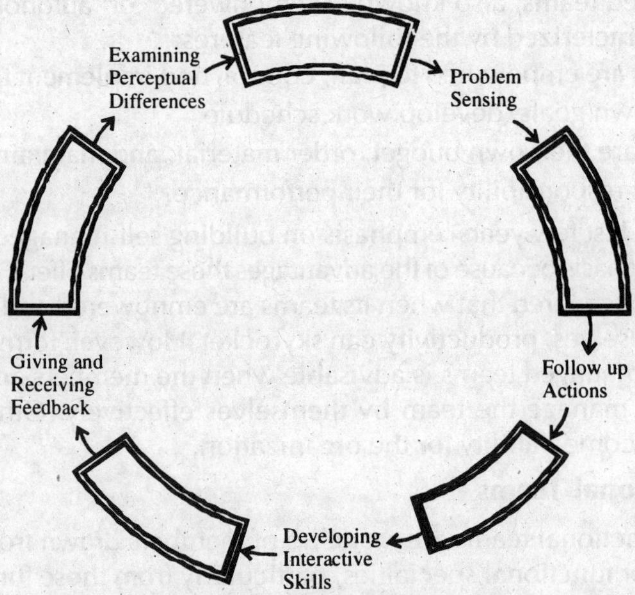

Figure 16.1: Team Building Process.

As seen from Figure 16.1, team building process proceeds in a lockstep manner. The various steps involved in team building process are discussed one by one.

Problem Sensing and Identification

Team building process begins with problem sensing and identification with a view how to solve the problem and improve team effectiveness. The members think over and come forward with points as to what the real problems are hindering team effectiveness. Expectedly, the problems may range from the organizational to group to personal problems. Nonetheless, emphasis is given on consensus problem while identifying the problem to be solved.

Examination of Differences

Individuals vary in several respects like backgrounds, personality dimensions, attitudinal aspects, values, cultures, etc. As such, individuals differ in perceptions about the problems team suffers from. Hence, efforts are made to reduce or remove individual differences in perceiving the problems or issues through specially designed communication and training sessions. This helps make the team cohesive to the extent possible. More the team cohesive, more it is effective.

Feedback

Realizing that members while forwarding their arguments about the problem may not be well versed with and fully conscious of what they are arguing, hence they need to be given feedback about the same so as to improve upon their perception about the problem. The feedback given to the members may include their feelings, approach, way, staying with the topic and going off on tangents, who were talking more and / or who were arguing less, who were avoiding or distorting the solution, etc. Thus, feedback provides the members opportunity to evaluate, introspect, understand, and know themselves. Johari Window can be one way to understand and know oneself better and perform more effectively in future.

Developing Argumentative Skills

This is the penultimate stage in team building process. The basic objective of this stage-cum-process is to increase the ability among the people as to how they should interact with others and engage in constructive behaviour. Following are the examples of constructive and negative behaviours.

Constructive Behaviour

A. *Building:* developing and expanding the ideas of others.
B. *Bringing in:* harmonizing, encouraging others to participate.
C. *Clarifying:* resting, ensuring, understanding, seeking relevant information.
D. *Innovating:* bringing in new relevant ideas, information, feelings, etc.

Negative Behaviour

A. *Overtalk*: interrupting, talking together with speaker.
B. *Attacking*: deriding, belittling, criticizing person.
C. *Negative*: cooling, cynicism, undermining morale.

At the time of discussion of feedback, people take themselves assignments to increase specific constructive behaviours and decrease specific negative behaviours. If this process is adopted several times, there is a strong possibility that members may learn constructive behaviours and leave negative behaviours. This is quite helpful in developing teamwork.

Follow-up Action

This is the final stage in team building. At this stage, the total team is convened to review what has been learned and to identify what the next step should be. Follow-up action also helps in overcoming the drawback involved at the initial stages of team building. It involves deciding who will take care of each area of the team's responsibilities and who will be responsible for team projects in a group that has not developed a satisfactory division of responsibility: clarifying and setting differences in perception concerning responsibility and authority in the team, with complex division of responsibility and authority among members.

These attempts bring co-operative and supportive feelings among people involved in the team functioning. When this exercise is undertaken at the initial stage, it contributes positively towards the feelings of the people. However, to encourage and sustain such feelings, management should take such actions at regular intervals so that members feel reinforced and sustain their positive behaviour. Such actions will go a long way in shaping the organizational climate quite conductive to members for their efficient working.

16.4 TEAM ROLES

Having discussed so much by now about work teams, now one obvious question arises is how does a team perform to achieve its objectives. Various researchers have identified various roles- both formal and informal ones. Parker[4] has enlisted the four roles played by team members. These are contributor, collaborator, communicator, and challenger. A brief description about each of these follows in turn.

Contributor: These are the members who have primary concern to complete the task for which the team is formed. For this, they as a team set high standards of performance to be achieved. They collect and provide necessary inputs like information and resources to the team to share these with other members of the team.

Collaborator: They collaborate with team in different ways. For example, these members focus their attention on the ultimate purpose of team in the given organizational context in which the team has to function. They remind the team as and when required to review and change and/or modify the team goals.

Communicator: They are the team members who have concern and who show their focus on the process of team functioning. This they do by encouraging other team members to participate in team decision-making,

How to Evaluate Team Building ?

As mentioned earlier, team building as an OD intervention has attracted maximum attention. Many research studies have also confirmed the positive contributions of team building on the organisation's outcomes though in different degrees". In general, team building contributes to the organisational performance in the following manner:

1. It improves the organization's problem-solving and decision-making ability.
2. It helps in developing effective interpersonal relationships by stimulating the group members for that.
3. It helps in developing communication within the group and inter-group and overcoming many psychological barriers that block communication flow.

Here is an example to illustrate how teamwork really works:

Teamwork That Really Works

Nature offers this outstanding example of teamwork, which is also one of Zig Ziglar's classic stories:

Have you ever noticed a flock of (Canadian) geese flying overhead? You'll observe three interesting things.

1. They always fly in a distinctive V formation.
2. One leg of the V is always longer than the other.

3. Geese move up from the back to the front to take over the lead position.

The lead goose is setting the course for the group. Because he is out front all alone, he creates a partial vacuum off both wing-tips, as does each goose down the line. In the process of fighting the strong head-wind, the leader grows tired faster than the other geese. To maintain speed, others move up to replace him. It was discovered in wind tunnel tests that due to the V formation, a flock of geese can fly seventy-two percent farther than an individual goose flying alone with the same amount of energy!

Have you ever wondered why one leg of the V is always longer than the other? It's because one leg has more geese in it!

Source: Walter Doyle Ataples: **How to Win in Life,** UBSPD UBS Publishers' Distributors Ltd., New Delhi, 1999, p. 76.

However, team building has been termed as one-sided effort and it suffers from the following limitations:

1. It focuses only on work groups and other major organisational variables such as technology, structure, etc., are not given adequate attention.
2. Team building becomes a complicated exercise when there is frequent change in team members. New member may find it difficult to adjust with the team because of his confusion over his roles in terms of task performance and building good relationships.

In spite of these problems, team building has a positive outlook. However, it is not that effectiveness is in isolation. Therefore, there have been calls for combining team building with organisation behaviour modification approaches. One such suggestion is to use a task hierarchy to reinforce the team as it progresses up a behaviour skill hierarchy (for example, listening, communicating, monitoring, and feedback skills)".

16.5 WHAT CAUSES TEAM FAILURE ?

We mentioned earlier in this chapter that teams results in synergy and, in turn, success. However, evidences are available to believe that teams always do not result in success, but teams sometimes fail also. Hence, the question is what causes team failure? Experiences indicate that some teams experience certain obstacles and / or pitfalls that cause teams to fail. Knowledge of and avoidance of these obstacles to team success is, hence, imperative. Based on past experiences, the following obstacles or reasons have been reported as the causes of team ineffectiveness:

1. Team members' unwillingness to cooperate with each other.
2. Failure of teams to receive support from management.
3. Managers' unwillingness to relinquish control.
4. Lack of co-operation among teams.

16.6 HOW TO MAKE TEAMS SUCCESSFUL ?

Corporate history is replete with successful teams. Based on experience-analyses of successful teams, it is possible to identify several things that teams can do to become successful. Katzenbach and Smith[4] have listed the following tips for the success of work teams:

Tip	Rationale
Make the team's task urgent.	Team members are prone to rally around challenges that compel them to meet high performance standards.
Skill-based selection of team members.	While forming team, members should have required skills to contribute to team task.
Frame clear-cut behavioural norms and rules.	It must me made clear to the members about what is and what is not expected of them.
Recognize intermediate performance goals.	Set sub-goals to motivate members to achieve them before the final goal.
Challenge and charge the team with new information and facts	New facts and feedback will provide team members right direction to move on.
Meet Regularly	Meet the team members to remind them of their obligations to be met.
Acknowledge and Appreciate vital contributions from team members	Acknowledging and appreciating members for their contribution further motivates them to perform better.

16.7 SOCIAL LOAFING

What is social loafing? It relates to the size of a team and its motivation. It is the tendency for individuals to expand less effort when working collectively than when working individually. In other words, social loafing is a situation in which people exert less effort (or usually perform at a lower level) when working in teams than when working alone[5]. It is contrary to synergy. It, thus, directly challenges the stereotype logic that the productivity of the group as a whole should at least equal the sum of the productivity of each member in the team. This is due to shirking or free-riding by some members in the team work. Here is solid research evidence to confirm the social loafing behaviour of work teams.

Way back during late 1920s, a German psychologist named Max Ringelmann compared the results of individual and group performance on a rope-pulling task[6]. He expected that the group's effort would be equal to the sum of the efforts of individuals within the group. That is three people pulling rope together should exert three times as much pull on the rope as one person, and eight people should exert eight times as much pull. But, the results did not confirm this stereotype expectation. The results were: (i) one person pulling on a rope alone exerted an average of 63 kilograms of force. In groups of three, the per person force dropped to 53 kilograms and in groups of eight, it largely fell to 31 kilograms per person. What do these results reveal is that team performance increases with group size, but the additions of new members to the team has diminishing return on productivity. This exercise also suggests that social loafing is most likely to occur when members work in large-size groups where team members work alone toward a common output pool i.e., they have low task interdependence and individual output is difficult to identify.

Some thinkers have tried to explain the phenomenon of 'social loafing' by, what is called, 'social impact theory'[7]. What is, then, social impact theory? This theory refers to the impact of any social force acting on a group is divided equally among its members. According to this theory, the impact of the force on any one member decreases with increase in the number of members in a team. Or say, the larger the size of the team, lesser is the share of each member's contribution in team performance. This happens because the more the people to contribute a team's performance, the less pressure each member feels to perform more and better in the group. The reason is not difficult to seek. This is because the responsibility for doing the job is diffused over larger number of members. As a result, each team member feels less responsible for behaving appropriately and, in turn, social loafing occurs.

From the point of view of human behaviour at work, an important question arises is what causes social loafing effect? Several reasons can be attributed to it.

(i) The members believe that they will receive their share of team rewards regardless of their low individual contribution8.

(ii) It may also happen due to a belief that other members in the team are not exerting their fair share. Seeing other members, thus, lazy or inept, one can also think to reestablish equity by reducing his/her effort to team work.

(iii Social loafing might also happen when the task to be performed by the team is not challenging enough or the members do not find the task interesting enough or when team members are not adequately rewarded

(iv) Yet another explanation to the social loafing behaviour is the dispersion of responsibility. That is the results of team cannot be attributed to any single member. This is because of vague relationship between a member's effort and the team's effort. Such a situation makes team members tempted to become "free riders" and coast on the team's efforts.

(v) When team members think that why poor performers should be benefited from their higher level performance.

The biggest disadvantage of social loafing is that it demotivates other team members, resulting in a *"sucker effect"* where good performing team members tend to put their less efforts, because they do not want others to take advantage / more benefit of them.[8] As such, the team does not achieve whatever it is capable of achieving.

However, social loafing effect has some implications for OB to motivate work teams. The effects of social loafing have a Western bias. That is, it is consistent with individualistic cultures, like the U. S. and Canada dominated by self-interest. Contrarily, it is inconsistent with collectivism cultures like People's Republic of China and Israel because they value their group membership and believe in working for achievement of group objectives[9].

How to Minimize Social Loafing ?

By understanding the causes of social loafing, we can identify ways to minimize this problem. The ways may be of two types[10] - (i) by making each member's performance more viable and (ii) by increasing each member's motivation to perform his / her task within the group. These include:

1. Form Smaller Team
2. Specialize Tasks
3. Measure Individual Performance
4. Increase Job Enrichment
5. Select Motivated Employees.

SUMMARY

This summary is organized as per the 'learning objectives' given on page no. 274.

- Team is a group whose members have complimentary skills and are committed to a common purpose or set of performance goals for which they hold themselves mutually accountable. Team differs from group in the sense that each team member is dependant on other members to perform his/her function whereas an individual can independently perform his/her function.
- Teams are classified into lead teams, problem-solving team, self-managed team, cross-functional team, and virtual team.
- The major steps involved in team building process include problem sensing and identification, examination of differences, feedback, developing argumentative skills, constructive behaviour, negative behaviour, and follow-up action.
- Teams play roles as contributor, collaborator, and communicator.
- Lack of cooperativeness among the team members, lack of support from management, and managers' lukewarm attitude toward teams are the major reasons that cause team failure.
- Measures like making the team's task urgent, selecting skilled people as team members, framing behavioural do's and don't do's, holding regular meetings of teams, and acknowledging and appreciating vital contributions made by teams can make teams more effective.
- The tendency for group members to exert less individual effort on an additive task as the size of the group increases. To form smaller teams, assign specialized tasks, measure individual performance, increase job enrichment, and select motivated employees as team members can help in minimizing the tendency for social loafing.

Here is an exercise for you.

Form 2 or 3 groups of your class. Analyse the evolution of the Lagaan (the Hindi film produced by film actor Amir Khan) cricket team. Then, share your findings in the total class.

REFERENCES

1. J. R. Katzenbach and D. K. Smith: The Discipline of Teams, **Harvard Business Review**, March-April, Vol. 71, No. 2, 1993, pp. 111-120.
2. Wendell L. French and Cecil H. Bell: **Organisation Development**, Printice-Hall, Englewood Cliffs, N.J. 1981, p.119.
3. B.W. Tuckman: Development Sequence to Small Groups, **Psychological Bulletin**, No.63, 1965.
4. J. R. Katzenbach and D. K. Smith: *Op. Cit.,* 1993, pp. 111-120.
5. J.M. George:- Extrinsic and Intrinsic Origins of Perceived Social Loafing in Organisations, **Academy of Management Journal**, Vol. 35, 1992, pp.191-202.

6. W. Moede: Die Richtlinien der Leistungs-Psychologie, Industrielle Psychotechnik, Volume 4, 1927, pp. 193-207. See also D. A. Kravitz and B. Martin: Ringelmann Rediscovered: The Original article, **Journal of Personality and Social Psychology**, May 1986, pp. 936- 941.
7. B. Latane and S. Nida: Social Impact Theory and Group Influence: A Social Engineering Perspective, In: P. B. Paulus (Ed.): **Psychology of Group Influence**, Lawrence Erlbaum Associates, Hillsdale, 1980, pp. 3-34.
8. J. Sweeney: An Experimental Investigation of the Free-Rider Problem, **Social Science Research**, Vol.2, 1973, pp. 277-292.
9. D. Johnson and F. Johnson: **Joining Together: Group Theory and Group Skills** (6th Ed.), Allyn & Bacon, Boston, 1997.
10. P.C. Earley: Social Loafing and Collectivism: A Comparison of the U.S. and the People's Republic of China, **Administrative Science Quarterly**, Vol.34, 1989, pp.565-581.

Vignette 16.1: The Story of a Hare and a Tortoise

A Hare and a Tortoise lived in the world famous Kaziranga National Park in Assam. They were very close friends and some times used to have a dig at each other. What happened that, one day the Hare in a joking mode ridiculed the Tortoise for his slow pace. The Tortoise felt bad and reacted very sharply challenging the Hare to a race from Kaziranga National Park to Tezpur. On 15th June 2008, the two met at the starting point and started the race. As expected, the Hare dashed off like a flash. After crossing the midway point Chakalabanda, the Hare thought a short sleep i.e., nap would do no harm to him. But short nap turned out relatively a long nap. Meantime, the Tortoise crossed the mid point Chakalabanda and reached the destination, i.e., Tezpur before Hare. The Hare awoke from his slum, and dashed off to Tezpur. He found the Tortoise taking a nap at the finish point Church field in Tezpur. *The lesson of the study is slow and steady wins the race.* But the story does not end here.

The Hare went home and pondered over his defeat in the race. He understood the complacency and over-confidence were the reasons for his defeat. He resolved not to commit such mistake again. He went to the Tortoise and invited him to another race. The Tortoise also agreed. They met at the appointed day and time and begun the race. This time the Hare dashed off to the finishing point without any nap and break and won the race comfortably. *The moral of the story is fast and steady also wins the race.* The story does not end here also.

This time the Tortoise made introspection about his defeat and realized that the Hare could not be defeated by speed. He pondered over his core-competence in relation to the Hare. The Tortoise invited the Hare to race from Tezpur to Nagaon. As usual, the Hare this time too dashed off in a flash and arrived at the bank of the Brahamputra. He did not know how to swim. After some time, the Tortoise also arrived at the Brahamputra bank and saw the Hare standing helplessly at the bank. The Tortoise looked at the Hare in sympathy and coolly entered into the water. He swam to the other side and reached Nagaon. *The lesion of the story is core competence wins the race.* But, the story does not end here also.

The two friends decided enough of racing against each other. The finally found a way by which they could together travel from Nagaon to Guwahati Airport in the minimum possible time. On the appointed day and time, the two met. The Tortoise sat on Hare's back and dashed off from Nagaon to Guwahati Airport. After arriving at the bank of Brahamputra, the Hare got on to the back of the Tortoise. The Tortoise swiftly crossed the river. On reaching the other bank, the Tortoise again climbed on to Hare's back. The Hare again dashed off in a flash to reach to Guwahati Airport. Thus, the both friends made it possible to reach Guwahati Airport in the fastest possible time.

The moral of the story is innovation and team work win the race...

Exercise 16.1: The Social Loafing Effect: A Classroom Demonstration

The greater the number of people contributing to your group's task output, the less your individual productivity is likely to be. This phenomenon, known as social loafing, can have serious adverse influences on group performance (see pp. 306-309). The following exercise is designed to demonstrate this effect.

Procedure

1. Select an additive task that may be conveniently performed in class. For example, you may form groups whose members combine their individual contributions to any of the following tasks: (a) copying entries from a telephone book into index cards, (b) counting the number of sheets in a large stack of paper, or (c) folding letters and inserting them into envelopes.
2. Performs the task for ten minutes, in groups of different sizes. Try to do your best. Select one person at random to perform the task alone. Combine the remaining students into groups of two, three, four, and so on until the largest possible group is formed (remaining students can simply be included in the largest group). Make random selections by drawing names written on folded slips of paper.
3. After ten minutes, count the number of units you have produced (be it entries copied, sheets counted, letters folded and inserted, or whatever output results from the task performed).
4. Each group computes the average number of units produced by its individual members.
5. At the board, the instructor will record this information in graph from, plotting the average number of units produced per individual (on the vertical axis) as a function of the size of the individuals' work group (on the horizontal axis).

Points of Consider

1. Did the general pattern of performance obtained reveal the social loafing effect? What basis is there for this conclusion?
2. If you did not find evidence for the social loafing effect, why do you think this happened? Might it have been because you expected it to occur and refrained from the natural tendency to lower your individual performance in groups? To test this possibility, repeat the exercise using participants who do not know about this phenomenon. Compare the results.
3. How did members of different-size groups feel about the contributions they were making to the task they performed? Specifically, did members of larger

groups feel more dispensable, or that they could easily get away with doing less?

4. What could have been done to counteracts any "free riding" that may have occurred in this demonstration?

TEAM-BUILDING EXPERIENTIAL EXERCISE

Game Objectives

1. Building a team orientation.
2. To sensitize the participants about the dynamics of the team.
3. To help them appreciate the roles that need to be played in the team.

Resources Required

Waste cardboard sheets, gunny bags, wooden planks, flat metal plates, newspapers, packing materials, thermacool sheets, etc.

Time Required

2 hours including briefing, game, and debriefing after the game.

Things to be Arranged Before the Game Begins

1. Arrange for a common room for briefing, and separate locations (syndicate rooms) where teams will sit and plan the team activity.
2. Ensure that members from different teams are not allowed to interact with each other during the game.
3. Arrange the lots of the materials for auction in a separate room; ensure that there are sufficient lots of materials for teams to plan their work.
4. Choose an outdoor location, and fix the destination for all the teams to reach there.

Briefing Before the Game

Divide the class into multiple teams of 10-12 members each.

Announce to the class:

The game will be played in multiple phases. All the teams have to reach a specified destination as fast as possible. The team that reached there first will be considered the winner. The conditions is this, that the team members will stick together as a team; not creating gaps while walking; the team will construct a bridge with the material bought by them in the auction, and walk only on that material-not touch the ground with any part of their body; the team members will not speak to each other while walking; and team members will only walk forward, and not backwards. In the course of walking, the team will also dismantle the bridge-no material or part of it should be left behind by the team.

Describe the phases of the game to all the team members (common briefing).

Phase I: Resource inspection phase

The teams will select two delegates each who will inspect the distance to be traveled, and the material available in the lots. During this phase, the inspectors will not be allowed to speak and discuss anything with each other. However, they can note down the details in a notepad. This phase will last for five minutes.

Phase 2: Bid preparation

The inspectors go back to their teams who collectively plan for the bidding of the material. The teams have Rs 100 each as initial working capital for purchasing the lots. They also select one bidder from among themselves. This phase will last for fifteen minutes.

Phase 3: Bidding

The oral bidding of the lots begins with the auctioneer announcing the base price. If any team is bidding for a lot of items, the initial bid amount should be at least as much as the base price. The other team member can bid for the same lot, provided his bid is at least Re 1 more than the price quoted. Once the bidding phase is over, no more resources can be procured from anywhere.

Phase 4: Plan the walk

In this phase, the bidders will go back to their respective teams with the materials bought. The team members will not be allowed to talk to each other during the final phase. However, they may develop a code/sign language for communication with each other. The teams have five minutes to plan the walk.

Phase 5: Walk the plan

In this phase, the teams actually walk the distance. Every member of the team has to cover the distance, the entire bridge is to be dismantled with no material being left behind, and the team has to have a positive balance (in rupees). The first team to achieve this will win the game. The winning team will get Rs. 50 as reward.

The teams get penalty points while walking (in Phase 5) for:

1. Talking-Rs 5 per work spoken
2. Touching the floor-Rs 10 each time

Role of the Observer

It is advisable to appoint one observer for each team when the teams are working separately, doing their planning, etc. If possible, the whole process can be video recorded for accuracy and assistance in debriefing.

Debrief them on

1. The way the teams defined thé agenda
2. The problem-solving approach adopted by the teams
3. The planning of resources
4. The stages of team development
5. The participation of various members in the planning
6. The various roles played by different members
7. How the group handled conflict/disagreements
8. The support provided, if any, in the team
9. The role of norms
10. How the team handled the success/failure, after the game was over?

17

ORGANISATIONAL CONFLICTS AND NEGOTIATIONS

"Progress flows only from struggle." – ***Louis Dembitz Brandeis***

"Have you fifty friend? - It is not enough. Have you one enemy? - It is too much."

– ***Italian Proverb***

Learning Objectives

After studying this chapter, you should be able to:

- **Define** conflict.
- **Distinguish** between competition and conflict.
- **Identify** the main sources of conflict.
- **List** the different types of conflicts and **diagnose** functional and dysfunctional conflicts.
- **Outline** the conflict process.
- **Describe** the techniques for managing conflict.

You have already learnt that organisations are composed of individuals and their groups. Human beings experience conflict in their every day life. Hence organisations are not free of it. Conflict has considerable influence on organisational as well as individual performance. Conflict management has, therefore, become a matter of great concern for the managers to make the organisation effectively run. Hence, this chapter is devoted to discuss the various aspects of conflict such as its meaning, sources, process and resolution. Let us begin with clarifying what is meant by conflict.

17.1 DEFINITION OF CONFLICT

Like other behavioural terms, the term conflict has also acquired divergent meanings. In simple sense, conflict is a tension or collision or disagreement. Here, we are producing some important definitions of conflict to make its meaning more clear.

Chung and Megginson[1] have defined conflict as the struggle between incompatible or opposing needs, wishes, ideas, interests, or people. Conflict arises when individuals or groups encounter goals that both parties cannot obtain satisfactorily.

Thomas[2] has defined conflict as a process that begins when one party has negatively affected or is about to negatively affect, something that the first party cares about.

According to Kolb and Bartinek[3], conflict can be a disagreement, the presence of tension, or some other difficulty within or between two or more parties. Conflict can be public or private, formal or informal, or be approached rationally or irrationally.

Now, conflict can simply be defined as disagreement, be it in violent or subtle form between two persons or parties.

Conflict Differs from Competition

Like conflict, competition occurs when two or more parties engage in activities that are in some sense incompatible. Since both parties cannot win, the success of one prevents the other from achieving success. Though conflict and competition seem the same, they differ in the degree of self-interest displayed by each side. The same distinguishes one from the other.

Competition does not involve direct action by one party to interfere with the activities of the other. But, in case of conflict, one party tries to prevent or to inhibit the success of the other. This difference can be exemplied by a sport example.

Track events are examples of competition rather than conflict because each runner attempts to run faster than the others but no one is allowed to trip or interfere with the others. In contrast, games of football, and hockey involve both conflict and competition because each team acts directly to interfere with the activities of the other. Yes, the degree of conflict is limited by the rules of the game, and penalties are assessed when players violate the rules.

Conflict designed to destroy other party is not uncommon in organisations. For example, price wars involve conflict between organisations, with one company trying to drive its competitors out of business. Conflict between union and management is also common in modern organisations.

17.2 SOURCES OF CONFLICT

Conflict can arise from a variety of sources. They can be classified into two broad categories: **structural factors,** which stem from the nature of the organisation and the way in which work is organised, and **personal factors,** which arise from differences among individuals. Following Fig. 17.1 summarizes the causes/sources of conflict within each category.

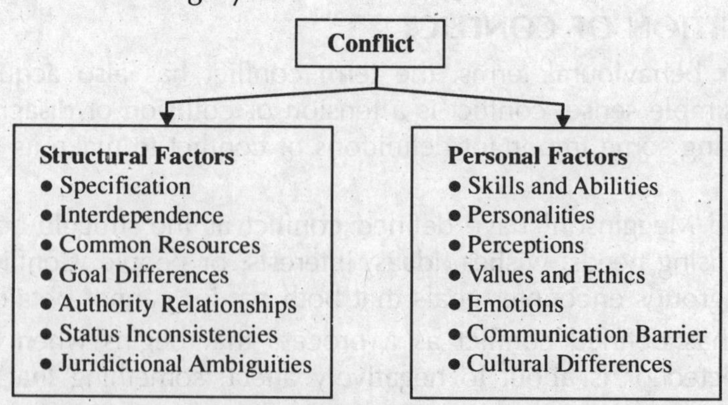

Fig. 17.1: Sources of Conflict in Organisations

The structural factors and the personal factors are also called as the external factors and the internal factors respectively. The most important of these are, now, discussed here under.

Specialisation

When jobs are highly specialised, employees become experts at certain tasks. For example, in case of a software company, while there is one specialist for data bases, another for statistical packages, and yet another for expert systems. As the highly specialised people have little awareness of the tasks that others perform, such a case leads to conflict among the specialists.

Interdependence

Interdependence occurs when two or more groups depend on each other to accomplish their tasks. Depending on other people to work done is good when the process works smoothly. However, when problem arises, it becomes easy to blame other party, and as such, conflict escalates. The potential of conflict increases as the degree of interdependence increases.

Three types of task interdependence have been identified :

(*i*) **Pooled Interdependence:** A condition of pooled interdependence occurs with additive tasks when the performance of different groups is simply combined or added together to achieve the overall performance.

(*ii*) **Sequential Interdependence:** It occurs when the task of one group cannot be completed unless the preceding group has completed its task. For example, in case of assembly line manufacturing, the products must first pass through department A before they can proceed to department B.

(*iii*) **Reciprocal Interdependence:** Such an interdependence also occurs with conjunctive tasks when each group depends upon the performance of each of the other group. While A group depends upon B and C, B and C groups depend upon each other and as well as A. Reciprocal interdependence can be seen in hospitals where various department like the X-ray unit, the blood laboratory, the nursing unit, the emergency centre, and the anesthesiology staff all depend on each other to provide skilled patient care.

Goal Differences

Sometimes different work groups having different goals have incompatible goals. For example, in a cable television company, the salesperson's goal was to sell as many new installations as possible. This created problem for the service department, because its goal was timely installations.

Juridictional Ambiguities

It refers to the presence of unclear lines of responsibility within an organisation. Recall, have you ever contacted your own University administration for some problem and had you been asked to go to different people and departments ? This happens because of the juridictional ambiguities among the departments.

The sources or causes of conflict just discussed are external or structural in nature. There are other conflicts also that come from differences among individuals, also called personal/internal sources or causes of conflict.

Skills and Abilities

Work force in an organisation/department is composed of people with varying levels of skills and abilities. Such diversity in skills and abilities leads to conflict, especially when jobs are interdependent. Workers may find it difficult to work with a new boss, fresh from University knowing a lot about managing people but unfamiliar with the technology they are working.

Personalities

We pointed out in Chapter 5 that personality also causes individual differences. It is differences in personality that neither the manager likes all of his co-managers and subordinates nor all of them like the manager. This creates conflict among them. Research studies[4] report that usually an abrasive personality is rejected by others. An abrasive person is one who ignores the interpersonal aspects of work and feelings of colleagues.

Perception

Like personality, differences in perceptions can also lead to conflict. One area in which perceptions can, for example, differ may be the perception of what motivates employees. Managers, for example, usually provide what they think employees want rather than what employees really want.

Values and Ethics

People also hold different beliefs and adhere to different value system. Older workers, for example, value company loyalty and probably would not take a sick day when they were not really sick/ill. But, the younger workers, valuing mobility, may take a sick day to get away from work.

Emotion

The moods of the people can also be a source of conflict in the work place. Problems at home often spill over into the work arena, and the related moods can be hard for others to deal with.

Communication Barriers

Communication barriers such as physical separation and language can create distortions in messages, and these, in turn, can lead to conflict. Value judgement also sometimes serves as barrier. Many other communication barriers that can create conflict are discussed in Chapter 15.

17.3 TYPES OF CONFLICTS

Conflict can take on any of several different forms in an organisation. It can occur within an employee, between individuals or groups, and across orgnaisations. Thus, the different types of conflicts are: intrapersonal, interpersonal, intergroup and interorganisational conflicts. It is important to note that the prefix **intra** means "within", whereas **inter** means "between". A brief description of each of these follows :

Intrapersonal Conflict: When conflict occurs within an individual, it is called **intrapersonal conflict**. It emerges as a result of conflicting role taken by the individual. One such type of conflict many employees experience is work/homeconflict, in which their role as worker clashes with their role as spouse or parent. For example, when a child gets sick at school, the parent often must leave work to care for the child.

Interpersonal Conflict: Conflict between two or more people is called **interpersonal conflict.** Individual differences create interpersonal conflicts. Wide differences are noticed between people in terms of personalities, perceptions, values and attitudes which we have already discussed in Chapters 5, 6 and 7.

Intergroup Conflict: When conflict occurs between groups or teams, it is known as **intergroup conflict**. Such conflict emerges when one group sets out to undermine the other, gain power, and improve its image. Conflicts also arise from such causes as different viewpoints, group loyalties, and competition for resources. Such group conflicts have negative consequences like aggression, hostile, and prejudice toward the other group. But, some group conflicts can be constructive also. Conflicts can have predictable effects within each group, such as increased group cohesiveness, increased focus on tasks, and increased loyalty to the group[5].

Interorganisational Conflict: Conflict that occurs between two or more organisations is called **interorganisational conflict**. Such conflict may include conflict between organisations pursuing similar objectives, conflict between government agency and organisation and conflict between head office and manufacturing unit. Competition among organisations also can spur inter-organisational conflict.

12.3.1 ANALYSING INTERPERSONAL CONFLICT

Research studies have established beyond doubt that interpersonal conflict has been the major reason for organisational conflict. Hence, there is the need for understanding the dynamics of interpersonal behaviour. Joseph Luft and Harry Ingham (popularly known as *Johari*) have developed a very popular descriptive framework for analysing and understanding the dynamics of inter-personal behaviour and, for that matter, inter-personal conflict. The name '*Johari*' is a combination of the first names of its originators, Joseph Luft and Harry Ingham. The framework developed by Johari is termed as '*Johari Window*'.

The Johari Window: This model is based on four types of interactive forms of interpersonal interaction/behaviour as shown in Figure 12.2. The term 'self' used in the model refers to 'me' and 'others' to 'you'. There are certain things that the person/self knows about himself or herself and there are also certain things he/she does not know.

	The person knows about the other	The person does not know about other
The person knows himself or herself	1 Open Self	2 Hidden Self
The person does not know about himself or herself	3 Blind Self	4 Undiscovered Self

Figure 17.2 : Johari Window of Interpersonal Behaviour

Similarly, there are certain things the person knows about other and certain things does not know. Based on such knowledge about oneself and other, there can be four types of interpersonal relationships, termed as 'cells', viz., open, hidden, blind and undiscovered. What each of these cells means need to be explained.

1. **Open Self :** In this form of interactive cell, the person knows both about oneself and other. Since there will be openess in interaction between the two, there would be less chances for interpersonal conflict.

2. **Hidden Self :** This is the situation in which person knows about oneself but does not know about the other one. As such person remains hidden from the other with the fear how the other might react. In other words, the person may hide his/her true feelings from other. As such, the situation becomes source for potential conflict.

3. **Blind Self :** This situation is opposite of hidden self. Person knows about other person but does not know about himself or herself. The result is that the person might unintentionally arguing and then irritating to the other. As in the hidden self, here too lies potential for interpersonal conflict.

4. **Undiscovered Self:** In this situation, the person neither knows himself or herself nor the other person. Such situation creates misunderstanding between the two and becomes the most explosive situation for interpersonal conflict.

17.4 ASPECTS OF CONFLICTS

We have already mentioned in the beginning of the Chapter that conflict is inevitable in organisations. Hence, this poses a question whether the conflict is good or bad for an organisation. In other words, the management needs to know what are the good or bad aspects, if any, of conflict in orgnaisation. Viewed from this angle, conflicts are characterised by having two aspects, namely, functional and dysfunctional conflicts. These are discussed one by one.

17.4.1 FUNCTIONAL CONFLICT

Conflicts that support the goals of the group and improve its performance are known as **functional conflicts**. Studies have suggested that some conflicts not help but may be a necessary condition for creativity/improvement. These are also called 'constructive conflicts'.

Following are some of the positive or functional aspects of conflicts that may occur in organisations:

- Conflicts bring cohesiveness in groups.
- Conflicts motivate group members to have concern for organisation.
- Conflict sbreed creativity among the members.
- Conflicts lead to innovation.
- Conflicts promote change.
- Conflicts lead to high quality decisions.

As mentioned earlier, there is a close relationship between conflict and organisational performance. Moderate or optimum level of conflict contributes to high organisational performance. On the contrary, both extremely low or extremely high level of conflicts adversely affect organisational performance. In this context, Boulding[6] also recognizes that some optimum level of conflict and associated personal stress and tension are necessary for progress and productivity, but he portrays conflict primarily as a potential and social cost.

17.4.2 Dysfunctional Conflict

The destructive forms of conflict that hinder group performance are called dysfunctional conflicts. Such conflicts hinder or destroy the achievement of organisational or group goals. The performance of an organisation tends to deteriorate when conflict becomes too great. In Universities, for example, intense conflict between employees and administration destroys the working relationships between them and seriously reduces the level of organisational efficiency and performance.

Fig. 17.3 reflects the relationship between conflict and organisational performance.

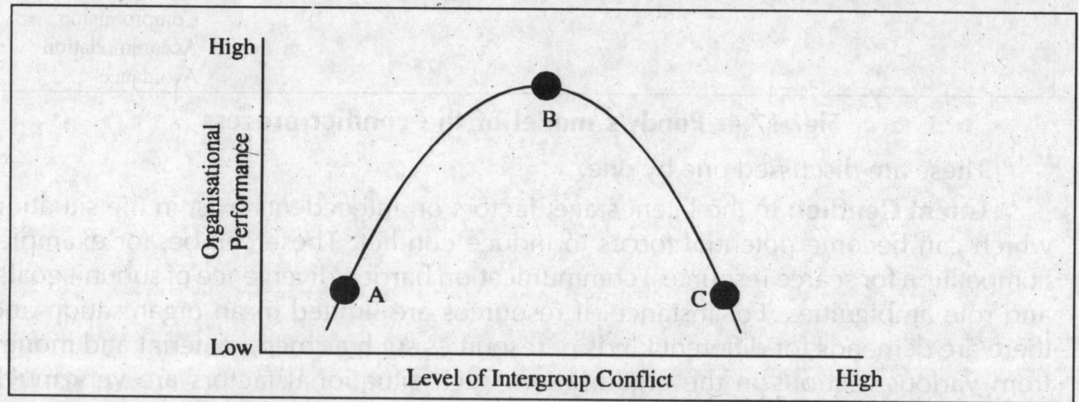

Fig. 17.3: Relationship between Conflict and Organisational Conflict

Organisational performance is low when level of conflict is either extremely low or extremely high. When level of conflict is low at point A, performance is low because of a lack of arousal and stimulation. When conflict is at a too high level at point C, it causes inadequate coordination and cooperation. In consequence, the performance tends to decline. When conflict is at an optimum or moderate level, at point B on the curve, organisational performance becomes the maximum. This is because of sufficient conflict stimulates new ideas and makes a creative search for solutions to the problems.

In fact, the line of demarcation between functional and dysfunctional conflict is neither clear nor precise. As a matter of fact, no one level of conflict can be considered as acceptable (functional) or unacceptable (dysfunctional) under all conditions and cases. The fact remains that the type and level of conflict that creates healthy and positive contribution toward one group's goals today may, in another group or in the same group at another time, be regarded as highly destructive or dysfunctional.

17.5 CONFLICT PROCESS

Having learnt sources and types of conflicts, it seems pertinent to know how conflict develops or escalates. Pondy[7] developed a process model of conflict which is very useful in understanding how conflict starts and different stages it goes through. Pondy's model of the conflict process, what he terms, *conflict episode*, is adapted and portrayed in Fig. 12.4 wherein he delineates the five stages involved in conflict episode. These are: latent conflict, perceived conflict, felt conflict, manifest conflict, and conflict aftermath.

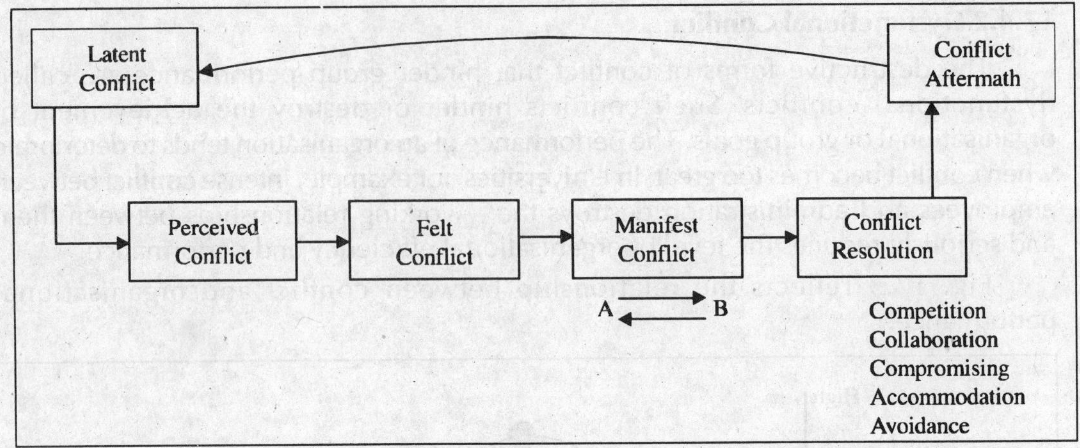

Fig. 17.4: Pondy's model of the conflict process

These are discussed one by one.

Latent Conflict: In the latent stage, factors or antecedents exist in the situation which can become potential forces to induce conflict. These can be, for example, competition for scarce resources, communication barrier, divergence of subunit goals, and role ambiguities. For instance, if resources are limited in an organisation and there are demands for different kinds of resources such as men, material and money from various sections in the organisation, such situational factors are very much conflict-inducing.

Perceived Conflict---Sometimes conflict may be perceived when latent conditions are not in existence in the system. Such a situation arises when one party perceives the other to be likely to thwart or frustrate his/her goals. Let it be clarified with an imaginery example.

> Suppose, the production manager hears the marketing manager saying that he requires more sales persons to achieve the set target for the year 2003-04. As the production manager also requires more mechanists to step up production, he perceives the likelihood of a conflict developing between him and the marketing manager. This is because, given the limited resources of organisation, if more sales personal are hired, less money will be available to hire more mechanics for the production division.

Felt Conflict: Emotional involvement in a conflict creating anxiety, tenseness, frustration, and hostility is known as felt conflict. It is that stage when the conflict is not only perceived but actually felt and cognized. In the above example, when the Chairman fixed a meeting of the heads of the department to discuss resource allocation, both the managers may literally feel the impact of the impending confrontation between them in the forthcoming meeting because of the likely powerful exchange of words and sentences between them.

Mainfest Conflict: This is the stage where conflicts become visible. In this stage, the two confronting parties engage themselves in behaving different forms such as open aggression, apathy, sabotage, withdrawl, and perfect obedience to rules. In other words, the behaviour of the conflicting parties includes the statements, actions, and reactions to each other.

Conflict Aftermath: Finally, the action-reaction-resolution interplay between the confronting parties results in certain consequences. Whether the consequences will be positive, or say, functional or negative, or say, dysfunctional depends upon how the conflict is resolved. If the conflict is genuinely resolved to the satisfaction of all the parties involved in conflict, it will result in positive consequences. On the other hand, if the conflict is merely suppressed but not resolved, it will still have residual tension left in the parties which will serve as basis for latent conflict for the next conflict episode. As our model (see Fig. 12.3) demonstrates, the conflict aftermath is a direct function of the results of the conflict resolution styles adopted and exercised to manage conflict in a given situation of an organisation. Hence, we now turn our attention to conflict management.

17.6 CONFLICT MANAGEMENT

Before we leave this chapter, one last question to address is how to manage or resolve conflict? Several styles or techniques have been suggested for managing conflict. Based on styles' assertiveness (the extent to which one wants one's goals met) and cooperativeness (the extent to which one wants to see the other party's concerns met), Thomas[8] has classified conflict management styles into five styles: avoiding, accommodating, competing, compromising, and collaborating. Following Fig. 17.5 graphs these five conflict management styles using these two dimensions.

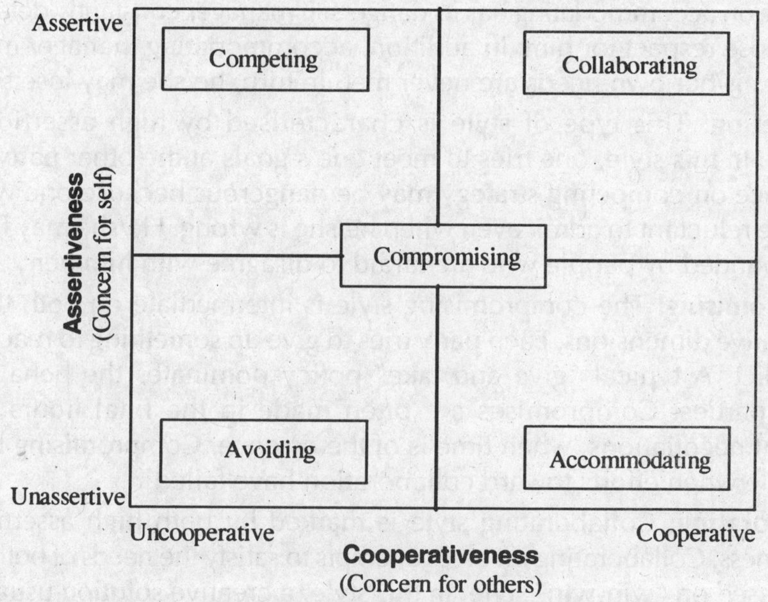

Fig. 17.5: Conflict Management Styles

Each of these styles is discussed now.

Avoiding: Avoiding is a style low on both assertiveness and cooperativeness. Avoiding is a deliberate decision to sidestep a conflictful issue, postpone addressing it till later or withdraw from a conflicting situation. In certain situations, it may be appropriate to avoid a conflict. For example, when parties are much angry and need time to cool down, it may be best to use avoidance. Avoiding conflict can be very functional when the issue involved in the conflict is trivial. However, research shows that overuse of this style results in negative evaluations from others in the workplace[9]. Here is an example of the avoiding style of conflict management in use.

> The head of a large MNC stayed regularity in a posh five star hotel in Delhi. On one such trip, he forgot to remove the "Do Not Disturb" sign from his door when he left for work in the morning. He came back late at night to find his room as he had left it: the sheets unchanged, the breakfast tray still there, and the room unswept. The sign on the door was intact.
>
> His reaction? He charged down to the reception, sign in hand, and proceeded to scream the hotel down. When the receptionist said that they were merely following his instructions, he got even more agitated, saying that he could have died in his room, and nobody would've disturbed him.
>
> The situation was rapidly spiralling out of control, when the hotel's General Manager stepped in. Within minutes, he had pacified the charged executive, apologising profusely instead of arguing with him. He then put him in a better room till his room was made up, and sent him dinner. Suitably mollified, the guest was soon tucking into his food all anger forgotten, and the staff heaved a sigh of relief.

Accommodating: A style in which one is concerned that other party's goals be met but relatively unconcerned with getting one's own way is called accommodating. In this style, one party is willing to self-sacrifice in the interest of the other party. Overreliance on accommodating has its dangers. If manager constantly defers to others, others may lose respect for him. In addition, accommodating manager may become frustrated as his/her own needs are never met. In turn, he/she may lose self-esteem.

Competing: This type of style is characterised by high assertion and low cooperation. In this style, one tries to meet one's goals at the other party's expense. Much reliance on competing strategy may be dangerous because one who does so may become reluctant to admit even when he/she is wrong. He/she may find himself/herself surrounded by people who are afraid to disagree with him/her.

Compromising: The compromising style is intermediate on both the assertive and cooperative dimensions. Each party tries to give up something to reach a solution to the conflict. A typical "give and take" policy dominates the behaviour of the conflicting parties. Compromises are often made in the final hours of union—management negotiations, when time is of the essence. Compromising becomes an effective style when efforts toward collaboration have failed[10].

Collaborating: Collaborating style is marked by both high assertiveness and cooperativeness. Collaborating involves attempts to satisfy the needs of both the parties. Thus, it is based on "win-win" style. In this style, a creative solution usually emerges because of the joint efforts of both the parties who are keen on both gaining from the situation without hurting the other.

Now, appropriate situations for using each conflict management style are listed in Table 17.1.

Table 17.1: Uses of Five Styles of Conflict Management

Conflict-Handling Style	Appropriate Situation
Competing	1. When quick, decisive action is vital (e.g., emergencies). 2. On important issues where unpopular actions need implementing (e.g., cost cutting, enforcing unpopular rules, discipline). 3. On issues vital to company welfare when you know you are right. 4. Against people who take advantage of noncompetitive behaviour.
Collaborating	1. To find an integrative solution when both sets of concerns are too important to be compromised. 2. When your objective is to learn. 3. To merge insights from people with different perspectives. 4. To gain commitment by incorporating concerns into a consensus. 5. To work through feelings that have interfered with a relationship.
Compromising	1. When goals are important, but not worth the effort or potential disruption of more assertive modes. 2. When opponents with equal power are committed to mutually exclusive goals. 3. To achieve temporary settlements to complex issues: 4. To arrive at expedient solutions under time pressure. 5. As a backup when collaboration or competition is unsuccessful.
Avoiding	1. When an issue is trivial, or more important issues are pressing. 2. When you perceive no chance of satisfying your concerns. 3. When potential disruption outweighs the benefits of resolution. 4. To let people cool down and regain perspective. 5. When gathering information supersedes immediate decision: 6. When other can resolve the conflict more effectively. 7. When issues seem tangential or symptomatic of other issues.
Accommodating	1. When you find you are wrong to allow a better position to be heard, to learn, and to show your reasonableness. 2. When issues are more important to others than to yourself to satisfy others and maintain cooperation. 3. To build social credits for later issues. 4. To minimize loss when you are outmatched and losing. 5. When harmony and stability are especially important. 6. To allow employees to develop by learning from mistakes.

SOURCE: K.W. Thomas, "Toward Multi-Dimensional Values in Teaching: The Example of Conflict Behaviours", **Academy of Management Review** 2(1977), 484-490.

17.7. CONFLICT MANAGEMENT IN INDIA : SOME RESEARCH EVIDENCES

As seen earlier, conflict is inevitable to take place in organisations. It affects human behaviour and, in turn, performance. Hence, there is always a need to resolve conflict as and when it surfaces among the members of an organisation. Before we close this chapter, it seems pertinent to examine how employee conflict is resolved in the Indian organisations. So far, good number of researches on conflict management are conducted in India. Depending on the nature of focus of these researches, these are broadly classified into two categories :

1. Researches focusing on strategies for conflict management.
2. Researches focusing on the factors effecting the choice of conflict resolution strategies

Some of the important researches undertaken under each of these categories are reviewed here.

Strategy Focused Studies. In order to know the preferred style of conflict management in the Indian organisations, Sayeed[11] in his study titled "Conflict Management Styles : Relationship with Leadership Styles and Moderating Effect of Esteem for Co-workers", studied two sets of managers, i.e. 101 and 157 managers working in wide variety of industrial organisations. The study revealed that the preferred styles of conflict management the managers were using were confronting, toning down, and adhering to rules and regulations in force in the organisations, in that order. Similarly, in another research study of 50 managers working in a computer manufacturing company also revealed toning down followed by accommodating, compromising, consulting and following rules and regulations in that order as their preferably used styles of conflict management[12].

Factor Focused Studies

Several studies are undertaken to find out what factors and how do these affect the choice of conflict management strategy. In his study of 225 managers, Bhawan[13] found that managers working in a power-oriented organisational climate prefer to use the avoiding style of conflict management. Types of leadership styles the managers exercise are also found exerting their influence on the choice of styles used for conflict resolution. For example, while managers using participative leadership styles prefer to collaborating strategy of conflict management, those exercising the autocratic style of leadership usually prefer to the authoritative, or say, competing strategy of conflict resolution.[14]

In addition to these, the research studies also report that the use of strategy of conflict resolution also varies across the levels of managers. While junior level managers prefer to humanistic approach, the middle level ones follow rules and regulations, and the senior level managers exercise confronting style of conflict management Added to these are some other strategies of conflict management that the Indian managers use. In their study of 60 first line managers, Singh and Sengupta[15] found that forming and promoting team work in the organisations lead to reduction in employee conflict and, in turn, increase in productivity. In the same way, setting the superordinate goals and the accepted by the employees was found as powerful factor in conflict avoidance by the employees. There are also research evidences[16] to cite that managers, especially at the top level, use flexibility as a paradigm shift in managing conflict in their organisations. The reason attributed to the adoption of such paradigm to manage conflict was a host of factors ranging from personal to organisational to environmental factors. It is also important to note that the paradigm may shift from variable to variable from time to time depending upon the type of environmental, organisational, and personal factors are in existence. This, in a way, suggests that the Indian managers at times adopt situationally relevant strategies of conflict management that is, to a large extent akin to the "Contingency Theory of Leadership" propounded by Fred E. Friedler.

17.8 NEGOTIATIONS

Just think back through last week's events. You may find there were divergent goals of yours and your co-worker or employer. You would have resolved your conflict with your co-worker through interaction or negotiation or bargaining. In organizations, negotiation permeates of almost all working in groups. For example, employees negotiate with management and vice versa. Management negotiates with the Government. Thus, negotiation has been one of methods of conflict resolution. Simply stated, negotiation is a bargaining between the conflicting parties to arrive at a decision to resolve their conflict or confrontation about something.

Different thinkers have defined negotiation differently. For example, Neale and Bazerman have defined negotiation as "a decision-making process among inter-dependent parties who do not share identical preferences. It is through negotiation that the parties decide what each will give and take in their relationship."[18] J.A. Wall defines negotiation as "a process in which two or more parties exchange goods or services and attempt to agree on the exchange rate for them."[19] According to McShane, Glinow and Sharma, "Negotiation occurs whenever two or more conflicting parties attempt to resolve their divergent goals by redefining the terms of their interdependence."[20] Now, negotiation can be simply defined as a process of bargaining in a settlement when parties differ on some issue. We will use the terms 'negotiation' and 'bargaining' interchangeably. In this last section of this chapter, we will present the negotiation strategies, outline the process involved in negotiation, list the situational influences on negotiation, and suggest some guidelines for effective negotiations. We shall also briefly reflect on third party negotiation.

17.8.1 NEGOTIATION STRATEGIES

While engaging in negotiations, conflicting parties follow either of the strategy or approach to resolve the conflict - distributive bargaining or integrative bargaining.[21] These two bargaining strategies are now discussed one by one.

Distributive Bargaining: Distributive Bargaining is done following win-lose approach. This type of bargaining is based on the belief that there is only a set amount of goods of services, called fixed pie, to be divvied up between the parties It means every more unit of pie in one party's pocket is a unit out of counterparty's pocket. Each party bargains aggressively and treats the other party as an opponent to be defeated. In practice, we knowingly or unknowingly engage in distributive bargaining. How? When we approach a house owner for taking his house on lease rent, we try to give less rent while house owner tries to get more rent. In this bargaining process, every rupee less as rent we pay becomes our gain and the same as cost for the house owner. In organizational context, probably the most widely cited example of distributive bargaining is union-management negotiations over wages. The union leaders bargain to get as much as possible out of management. What happens that every rupee more that union leaders bargain increases cost for management.

In distributive bargaining every party has an initial offer to opponent party, a target point as realistic goal for final settlement, and a resistance point beyond which party will not make further concessions. The gap between target point and resistance point is called 'bargaining' or 'negotiation zone.'[22] The following figure displays one such possible bargaining zone.

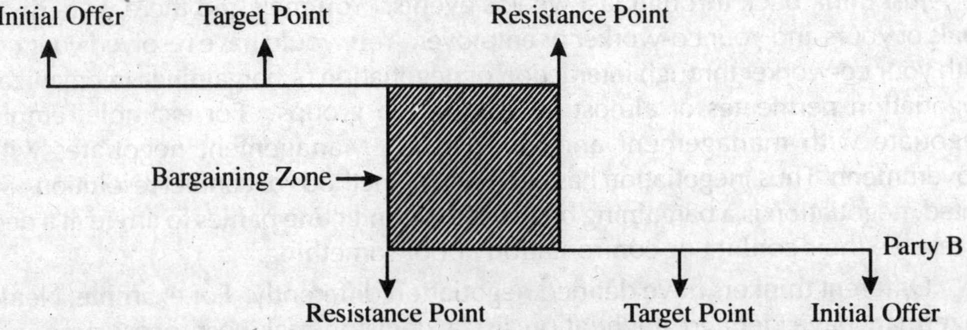

Figure 17.6 : Bargaining Zone Model of Negotiation Integrative Bargaining.

Integrative Bargaining: In contrast to distributive bargaining, integrative bargaining assumes that though resources might be limited, yet are expandable. How? The reason is not difficult to seek. It focuses on the merits of each party to have access to them. For this, a broad range of alternatives is created by the parties to reach at a "win-win" solution. Thus, integrative bargaining can be defined as a process that seeks one or more settlements that can create win-win solution. Let it be exemplified with an imaginary example.

Karan approaches the HDFC Ltd. for a house loan for Rs. 10 lacs. Since the HDFC Ltd. does not know the credit worthiness of Karan, it refuses to lend money to Karan. The HDFC Ltd. told Karan if he can provide a guarantor for his loan, it will lend loan to Karan. Karan provides his friend Dharam as his loan guarantor and the HDFC Ltd. lends loan to Karan. This house loan negotiation is an example of integrative bargaining, i.e. win-win settlement for both Karan and HDFC Ltd.

This suggests that integrative bargaining requires parties to be creative to reach a win-win settlement. Let us cite here the classic example where two sisters are arguing over who gets an orange. Unbeknownst to the other party, one sister wants the orange to drink the juice, whereas the other sister wants the orange peel to bake a cake. If one sister simply capitulates and gives the other sister the orange, then they never would have forced to explore their reasons for wanting the orange, and, thus, they would have hardly reached the win-win situation.

Generally, integrative bargaining is preferable to distributive bargaining on more counts than one. *One,* former cements long-term relationships between the opposing parties. *Two,* it brings and bonds the negotiating partners closer. *Third,* in case of former, all parties win whereas, in case of latter one gains and other loses. This suggests that we should have more integrative bargaining. However, that's actually not the case. Why? This is because the conditions necessary for such negotiation to succeed often do not exist. These include parties open with information and candid concerns, one's sensitivity toward other's need, and ability to trust one another.

Now that we have understood both distributive and integrative bargaining, we can distinguish between them. This is borne out by Table 17.2 :

Table 17.2: Distributive versus Integrative Bargaining

Bases of Difference	Distributive Bargaining	Integrative Bargaining
Goal	Get maximum of the pie.	Expand the pie to make both parties win.
Information sharing	Low	High
Motivation	Win-Lose	Win-Win
Interest	Opposed	Congruent
Duration of relationship	Short-term	Long-term

17.8.2 NEGOTIATION PROCESS

Negotiation for conflict resolution is as useful is not so simple. Negotiation to be effective needs to be made thoughtfully. As shown in figure 17.7, negotiation being a process involves five steps: preparation and goal setting, clarify the ground rules, communicate effectively, make concessions for bargaining, and implementation.

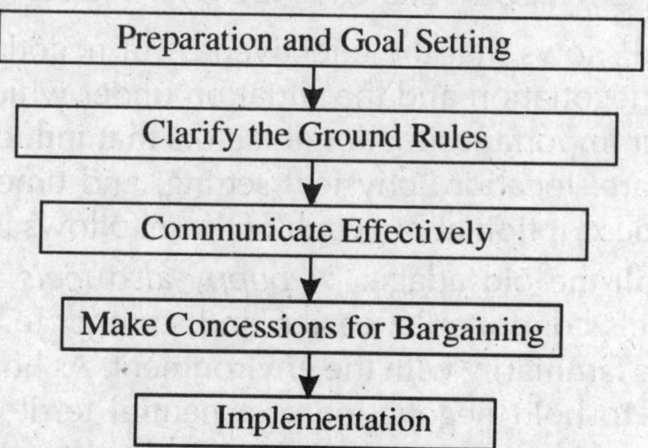

Figure 17.7 : Negotiation Process

A brief description of these follows in seriatim.

Preparation and Goal Setting: Well begun in half done. There is research evidence to believe that negotiations engaged with thoughtful preparation and clear-cut goals are more effective.[23] Preparation for negotiation includes deciding your initial offer, target point, resistance point, underlying assumptions, alternative strategies in case of one strategy fails, and goals to be achieved through negotiation. Equally important is sizing up the other party by researching what it wants from negotiation and its negotiating assumptions and strategies. A negotiating party should also determine its and the other party's 'Best Alternative to a Negotiated Agreement

(BATNA)'. A CEO appreciates the significance of preparation or home work for effective negotiation in these words: "You have to be prepared every which way about the people, the subject, and your fallback position. Before walking into the room for the actual negotiation, I ask my colleagues to throw some curve balls at me."[24]

Clarifying the Ground Rules: Having completed the preparation for negotiation, what follows next is to decide the rules of game (Negotiation). These include deciding the negotiators; the place negotiation will take place; time limit, if any; issues of negotiation; and any specific procedure to be followed in case of negotiation impasse. Parties start exchanging their initial offers at this stage of negotiation.

Communicate Effectively: The hallmark of effective communication is its effective relationship between the parties. The effective negotiators structure their message in such a way that it does not irritate other party and the party understands and accepts the message. Effective communication removes the walls of differences between the parties.

Make Concessions for Bargaining: While engaged in bargaining, making concessions are imbued with multiplicity of justifications. For example, concessions make the parties to move towards the bargaining zone and symbolize party's good intention to bargain. In fact, the essence of making concessions lies in the actual give - and - takes in trying to hash out a settlement acceptable to all parties.

Implementation: Once a settlement is arrived at, it needs to be implemented and monitored. If required, a procedure necessary for implementation and monitoring is worked out. Finally, the negotiation is closed or over by handshake between the negotiating parties.

17.8.3 SITUATIONAL INFLUENCES ON NEGOTIATION

The experience shows that the effectiveness of negotiations depends on both the preparation for negotiation and the situation under which the negotiations take place. There are four important situational factors that influence the effectiveness of negotiation. These are: location, physical setting, and time passage and audience characteristics[25]. A description about each of these follows in seriatim:

Location: Recall the old adage: *"A puppy also feels stronger in its street."* A negotiating party feels comfortable, easier, and stronger to negotiate on one's own turf because of one's familiarity with the environment. As home turf is a minor factor, some parties prefer to hold negotiation at a neutral territory. Of late, information technology in terms of electronic messages, telephones. mobiles, teleconferencing have, to a great extent, avoided territorial issues in negotiations. Nonetheless, face-to-face communication or negotiation has been found more touching and effective. Here, the views of Frank Lowy, cofounder of retail property giant Westfield Group seem worth citing: "Telephones are too cold for negotiating. From a voice I do not get all the cues I need. I go by touch and feel, and I need to see the other person."[26]

Physical Setting: Seating arrangement for negotiating parties also influences the negotiation settlement. One of the elements in sitting arrangement is the distance between the parties. Experience reveals that the negotiating partners sitting face-to-face are more likely to develop win-lose orientation towards the conflict resolution.

On the contrary, deliberately interspersing negotiation participants around the negotiation table tend to indicate orientation towards win-win situation.

Time Passage: Time duration and its deadline are yet other factors that influence negotiation settlement. How? The more time participants devote in negotiations, the stronger becomes their commitment in reaching a settlement. However, investing more time in negotiation also implies more tendencies to make unwanted concessions with an intention not to allow the negotiation to impasse.

As regards time deadlines, these may be useful to the extent that they motivate the parties to complete negotiations. However, time deadlines at times also prove costly for negotiations on different counts. For example, information is not properly processed due to time pressure. Negotiators tend to make excessive and unwanted concessions and soften their demands more rapidly as a deadline approaches.

Audience Characteristics: There is anecdotal evidence that negotiators' behaviour varies depending on the characteristics of the audience. Most negotiators have audiences, i.e. any one who has stake in the negotiation and its outcome. It is seen that negotiators tend to act differently when their audience observes the negotiation and/or has sufficient information about the process, compared to situations in which the audience is interested in the end results only. Also, when the audience has direct surveillance over the proceedings, negotiators tend to be more active, aggressive, and competitive. They show less or least orientation towards making concessions but more inclined to use creative tactics to bargain maximum of the pie for their audience. Such a "hard-line" type of behaviour exhibited by the negotiators assures the audience that the negotiators are working in their sheer interest. Behaving in such manner under the surveillance of audience also helps negotiators save their face.

17.8.4 GUIDELINES FOR EFFECTIVE NEGOTIATIONS

We have just seen in the preceding section that preparation, i.e. homework for negotiation and situational factors influence the effectiveness of negotiations. We have also seen that negotiation has been one of the important methods to resolve conflict. However, negotiation is as much useful in resolving conflict is not so simple. Along with above mentioned situational factors, the following guidelines should also be followed while engaged in negotiation:

- Do sufficient homework for participating in negotiations
- Participate with positive overture
- Participate with positive mood
- Have win-win approach
- Have empathy for opponent party
- Address the problem, not the person
- Have open discussion and communication
- Create a climate of mutual trust
- Have empathy for opponent party
- Use and insist the other party to use objective criteria in negotiation
- Consider and adapt cultural differences while negotiating
- Consider the gender differences while negotiating

The first eight guidelines mentioned above are self-explanatory. However, the last two guidelines need some elaboration.

Cultural Differences in Negotiations: Cultural differences abound across the countries- due to differences in values, perceptions, time orientations, emotional versus rational approach to problem solving, and other relevant factors. Research studies have reported that cultural differences affect the approach and style of negotiations.[27] For example, Americans rely on facts and figures and appealing to logics as the negotiating strategy. They counter opponents' arguments with objective facts. In contract, Arabians appeal to the emotional aspects of an issue as a negotiating strategy. Russians have difficulty in making concessions of any sort, and consider it as a sign of weakness when opponents make them. French take relatively long time to reach a settlement. On the contrary, Americans are impatient to reach a solution. Majority of negotiators from India, Japan, China, and France tend to adopt win-win approach while engaged in negotiations. On the contrary, Britishers, Germans, and Mexicans adopt give - and - take approach while sitting in negotiations. Thus, it becomes clear that one needs to take cultural differences into account when negotiating with opponents hailing from different cultural backgrounds. Equally important is to keep in touch with one's own cultural biases and nuances to protect these from exploitation by the savvy negotiators hailing from other cultures.

Based on his research study, L. Khosla[28] has highlighted how cultural differences affect negotiators' (American Managers) negotiating styles.

- Italians, Germans, and French don't soften up executives with praise before they criticize. Americans do, and to many Europeans this seems manipulative.
- Israelis, accustomed to fast-paced meetings, have no patience for American small talk.
- British executives often complain that their U.S. counterparts chatter too much.
- Indian executives are used to interrupting one another. When Americans listen without asking for clarification or posing questions, Indians can feel the Americans aren't paying attention.
- Americans often mix their business and personal lives. They think nothing, for instance, about asking a colleague a question like, "How was your weekend?" In many cultures such a question is seen as intrusive because business and private lives are totally compartmentalized.

Gender Differences in Negotiations: Some people ask question: Does gender affect the negotiation outcomes? Or, are men more effective in negotiating than women? There are no unanimous answers to both the questions. Some people hold the stereotype belief that men are better in negotiating issues because of the higher positions held by them in the organizations. Some people hold the belief that women are nicer then their men counterparts in negotiations because of the low positions held by them. Research evidence suggests that low-power managers, be men or women, try to placate their opponents and use softly persuasive tactics rather than direct confrontation. Added to this, research studies report that it is possible that a few hundred dollars more in salary or the corner office is less important to women than forming and maintaining an interpersonal cordial relationship[29].

17.8.5 THIRD-PARTY NEGOTIATION

We conclude our discussion of negotiation by dealing with third-party negotiation. So far, we have discussed bargaining through direct negotiations. Evidences also suggest that sometimes, the parties involved in direct negotiations do not reach to any settlement but a stalemate takes place called *'bargaining impasse.'* In such cases, the parties may look for an outside neutral person called 'third party' to help them resolve the conflict. Third-party conflict negotiation simply means any attempt by a relatively neutral person to help the parties resolve their differences. In practice, there are generally three types of third-party roles involved in dispute resolution activities: arbitration, inquisition, and mediation. Scholars have tried to classify these three roles of third-party by their level of control over the process and control over the decision as given in the following Figure. 17.8 :

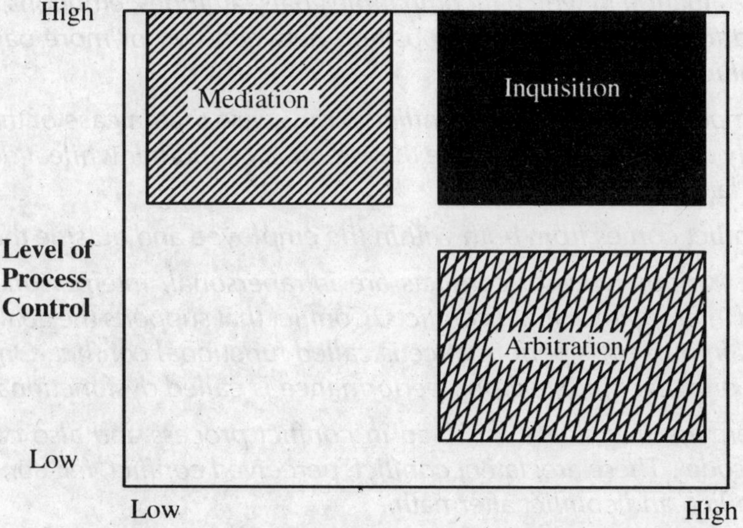

Figure 17.8 : Types of Third-Party Negotiations

Arbitration: Arbitration can be voluntary (requested) or compulsory (forced on the parties by law or contract). Arbitrator as a third party is bestowed with the authority to dictate a settlement between the conflicting parties. Arbitrators have high control over the final decision but low control over the process. Nonetheless, the degree of authority an arbitrator can exercise may vary depending upon the set of rules set by the negotiators. The strong point with arbitration is that it always results in a settlement because of the authority vested with the arbitrator. However, arbitration suffers from certain shortcomings also especially when the arbitrator is heavy-handed. The conflict resolution based on arbitrator's heavy-handed authority may cause other party overwhelmingly defeated and dissatisfied. As such, the conflict may again surface at any time in future.

Mediation: Mediation is done by a neutral third party who facilitates negotiation by using reasoning and persuasion. Mediators have high control over the intervention process and are widely used in labour-management negotiations. As per past experiences, the success rate of mediation in resolving conflicts is reasonably high. Mediation is found more effective under moderate levels of conflict. The mediators have little or no control over the conflict resolution decision because it is ultimately the parties only that decide how to resolve their differences.

Inquisition: Inquisitors control all discussion about the conflict. Like arbitrators, they do also enjoy high decision control by choosing the form of conflict resolution. But, at the same time, they also have high process control because it is they only who decide which information to examine and how to examine it. How the conflict resolution process will go about is also decided by the inquisitors only.

SUMMARY

This summary is organized by the 'learning objectives' given on page no. 289

- *Any situation in which incompatible goals, attitudes, emotions, or behaviour lead to disagreement or opposition between two or more parties is called conflict.*
- *Competition defers from conflict in the sense that in case of the former, one party does not try to frustrate the attempts of another while it does in case of the latter.*
- *Conflict comes from both within the employee and outside the employee.*
- *The various types of conflicts are intrapersonal, interpersonal, intergroup and interorganisational conflicts. Conflict that supports the goals of the group and improves its performance is called functional conflict. On the contrary, the one that hinders group performance is called dysfunctional conflict.*
- *There are five stages involved in conflict process and also called 'conflict episode'. These are: latent conflict, perceived conflict, felt conflict, manifest conflict, and conflict aftermath.*
- *Conflict needs to be managed when it becomes dysfunctional. The five styles adopted for conflict management are: avoiding, accommodating, competing, compromising, and collaborating.*

REVIEW QUESTIONS

1. Define conflict. How does it defer from competition?
2. Identify the structural (external) and personal (internal) factors that contribute to conflict.
3. Discuss the differences between functional and dysfunctional conflicts.
4. Discuss the major forms of conflict in organisations.
5. Explain the conflict process.
6. What are the styles of conflict management? Discuss.
7. Identify and discuss what causes you the most conflicting at the University Department of your study.

REFERENCES

1. Kae H. Chung and Leon C. Megginson: **Organisational Behaviour,** Harper and Row, New York, 1981, p. 252.
2. K.W. Thomas: Conflict and Negatiation Processes in Organisations, in M.D. Dunnette and L.M. Hough (Eds.) **Handbook of Industrial and Organisational Psychology,** Consulting Psychologists Press, Palo Alto, 1992, and pp. 651–717.
3. D.M. Kolb and J.M. Bartinek (Eds.) **Hidden Conflicts in Organisations**, Sage Publications, Newbury Park, CA, 1992.
4. J.C. Quick and J.D. Quick: **Organisational Stress and Preventive Management**, McGraw-Hill, New York, 1984.
5. M. Sherif: **Intergroup Conflict and Cooperation,** University Book Exchange Norman, Okla, 1977.
6. Kenneth E. Boulding: **Conflict and Defence**, Harper, New York, 1962, p. 305.
7. L.R. Pondy: Organisational Conflict: Concept and Models, **Administrative Science Quarterly,** 1967, Vol. 12, pp. 296-320.
8. K.W. Thomas: Conflict and Conflict Management, in M.D. Dunnette, ed., **Handbook of Industrial and Organisational Psychology**, Rand McNally, Chicago, 1976, p. 900.
9. R.A. Baron, S.P. Fortin, R.L. Frei, L.A. Hauver, and M.L. Shack: Reducing Organisational Conflict: The Role of Socially Induced Positive Affect, **International Journal of Conflict Management,** (1) 1990, pp. 133-152.
10. K.W. Thomas: Toward Multidimentional Values in Teaching: The Example of Conflict Behaviours, **Academy of Management Review**, (2), 1977, pp. 484-490.
11. O.B. Sayeed : Leadership Effectiveness and Managerial Response to Conflict Strategies, **Productivity**, 34 (1), 1993, pp. 99-108.
12. R.A. Sharma and R. Samantare : Conflict Management in Indian Firm, **Indian Journal of Industrial Relations**, 30 (4), 1995, pp. 439-453.
13. M. Bhawan : Perceived Organisational Climate and Interpersonal Conflict Handling Strategies, **Indian Journal of Industrial Relations**, 35 (1), 1999, pp. 43-54.
14. S. Samiullah, G. Kateswarajah and K.S. Reddy : Styles of Conflict Resolution among Employees of Different Organisations, **Indian Journal of Applied Psychology**, 34 (1), 1997, pp. 14-18.
15. S.Singh and Sengupta : the Brighter Aspects of Conflict, **Indian Journal of Industrial Relations**, 33 (2), 1998, pp. 327-348.
16. P. Mishra, V. Dhar and S. Dhar : Restrategising the Management of Conflict : An Empirical Study, **Indian Journal of Industrial Relations**, 35 (2), 1999, pp. 160-174.
17. Fred E. Fielder : **A Theory of Leadership Effectiveness**, McGraw Hill, New York, 1947.
18. Margaret A. Neale and Max H. Bazerman: Negotiating Rationally: The Power and Impact of the Negotiator's Frame, **Academy of Management Executive**, August 1992, p.42.
19. J.A. Wall Jr.: **Negotiation: Theory and Practice**, Foresman, Glenview Il, 1985.
20. Steven L. McShane, Marry Ann Von Glinow, and Radha R. Sharma: **Organisational Behaviour**, Tata McGraw-Hill Publishing Company Limited, New Delhi, 2008, p.408.
21. R.E. Walton and R.B. McKersie: **A Behavioural Theory of Labour Negotiations: An Analysis of a Social Interaction System**, McGraw-Hill, New York, 1965.
22. R. Stagner and H. Rosen: **Psychology of Union-Management** Relations, Wadsworth, Belmont CA, 1965.

23. S. Doctor off: Reengineering Negotiations, **Sloan Management Review**, Vol.39, March 1998, pp.63-71; D.C. Zetik and A.F. Stulhmacher: Goal Setting and Negotiation Performance: A Meta Analysis, **Group Processes & Intergroup Relations**, January 2002, pp.35-52.

24. B. McRae: **The Seven Strategies of Master Negotiators**, McGraw-Hill, Toronto, 2002, pp.7-11.

25. J.W. Salacuse and J.Z. Rubin: Your Place or Mine? Site Location and Negotiation, **Negotiation Journal**, Volume 6, January 1990, pp.5-10.

26. J. Margo: The Persuaders, **Boss Magazine**, 29 December 2000, p. 38.

27. L. Khosla: You Say Tomato, **Forbes**, May 21, 2001, p. 36.

28. A. F. Stuhlmacher and A. E. Walters: Gender Differences in Negotiation Outcome: A Meta-analysis, **Personnel Psychology**, Autumn 1999, pp. 653-677.

29. L. L, Putnam: Beyond Third Party Role: Disputes and Managerial Interventions Intervention, **Employee Responsibilities and Rights Journal**, Vol. 7, 1994, pp. 23-36.

Self-Assessment Exercise

This Self-Assessment exercise is designed to help you identify your preferred conflict management style.

Go through the following 25 statements given in the chart. Select your response using the five-point ranking scale for all 25 statements and write your closest agreement on the left side of each statement.

The Five-Point Rating Scale is :

1. Do not agree at all
2. Mildly agree
3. Moderately agree
4. Strongly agree
5. Extremely agree

------------- 1. I try to solve conflicts by finding solutions that benefit both me and other person.

------------- 2. I go along with suggestions from other members even if I don't agree with them.

------------- 3. I keep my opinions to myself rather than disgree with others.

------------- 4. I integrate good ideas of others to arrive at a joint decisions.

------------- 5. I try to keep away from issues where there is disagreement.

------------- 6. I try to use my influence to get my ideas accepted.

------------- 7. To reach an agreement, I give up some things in exchange for others.

------------- 8. I depend on my own expertise to make decision.

------------- 9. To resolve an impasse, I try to find a middle course.

------------- 10. In negotiations, I hold on to my position rather than give in.

------------- 11. I give and take so that a decision is arrived at.

------------- 12. To resolve the issue in the best possible way, I involve all concerns in the decision.

-------------- 13. I try to satisfy the opinions of others.

-------------- 14. I try to avoid open differences to be discussed openly with others.

-------------- 15. I try to work with others to meet mutual expectations.

-------------- 16. I prefer to negotiate to arrive at a compromise decision.

-------------- 17. I try to respect others' opinions to arrive at a decision.

-------------- 18. I try to stay away from disagreement with others.

-------------- 19. I try to help others to make decision in their favour.

-------------- 20. I try to propose some middle course to break the deadlock, as and when it is there.

-------------- 21. I try to hold on to my solution to the problem.

-------------- 22. I try to give concession to others to arrive at a decision.

-------------- 23. To reach an agreement, I try not to stick to my difference with others.

-------------- 24. To get the decision on my terms, I like to use my power.

-------------- 25. To make others not to feel hurt, I try to withheld my disagreement to myself.

ANSWER KEY

Accommodating	Avoiding	Collaborating	Competing	Compromising
2	3	1	6	7
13	5	4	8	9
17	14	12	10	11
19	18	15	21	16
22	25	20	24	23

Case 17.1: Who Pays and When ?

"Why haven't I received reimbursement for the two business trips I made last month? asked R. Chidambaram as he entered Uma Sekaran's Office Chamber. Sekaran was the budget officer for the manufacturing division of Cachar Paper Mills, a manufacturer of news paper. Chidambaram was a technical troubleshooter who worked in manufacturing but frequently dealt with customer complaints that were channelled through sales representatives and national sales director's office.

Sekaran responded, "you know it takes nearly four weeks for expense reimbursement, and for one of those trips, your travel request was processed after you returned. The vice-persident of manufacturing does not like to approve reimbursement after-the-fact. All travel is supposed to be preapproved and funds encumbered for travel".

"I know that", said Chidambaram, "but some of these sales representatives want immediate attention to customer problems. They want me to go to the customer's warehouse to inspect our shipment when the customer refuses acceptance. I cann't wait three days for approval. If I did, we would lose customers. You know that the sales representatives want answers right away so that they can get their full commissions".

"Furthermore", continued Chidambaram, "sometimes I have to charge lodging and meals on my own credit card, and the bill comes due before I get reimbursed."

"Request an advance," countered Sekaran.

"There isn't time to get an advance, besides, advances are for only 80 per cent of expected expenses. I still have to pay some expenses out of my own pocket," Chidambaram stated, frustrated.

"That's easy to handle. Overestimate your expenses by 20 per cent, and you can get an advance for 100 per cent of expenses," Sekaran suggested.

"I think these emergency trips should be charged to sales rather than manufacturing," Chidambaram offered.

"You know I requested that last year and I lost," Sekaran remarked.

"Well, you need to fight that battle again or change some of the reimbursement procedures. I am tired of bankrolling the company," complained Chidambaram as he left Sekaran's office.

QUESTIONS

1. Identify and describe the form of conflict. What are the causes of the conflict?
2. Is the conflict functional or dysfunctional? What approach can be taken to resolve the conflict? Explain.
3. Is Chidambaram, Sekaran, or both being difficult? If so, identify the type of difficult person each represents.

Case 17.2: When Conflict Boiled between the Superior and the Subordinate*

The National Globe Company of Delhi put in an advertisement in the 'Situation Vacant' column of the Statesman in April, 1997, for a typist in their Typing Section in the grade of Rs. 1600-2500 (exclusive of dearness allowance). The office of the company was flooded with applications from all over the country. After screening of applications, only twelve applicants were called for interview. Ten days after the interview, Ram Din, 25 years old and a graduate of the Lucknow University, received an appointment letter from the company.

Ram Din joined the comapny on June 1, 1997. He was asked to report to the Section Officer incharge of the typing section. Ram Din was on probation for a period of six months.

During the first month, it was observed that Ram Din did his work on time and intelligently. According to one filling clerk, he grasped his work so quickly and easily that it made some of his colleagues green with envy. Usually after having finished his own assignment, he helped other people in the section.

After about six months, when the probation was over, the Section Officer noticed that Ram Din started leaving his room too often. Having observed Ram Din for about a week in his new habit, the Section Officer, Miss Saxena called him in her room.

Miss Saxena	:	Ram Din, I see you leaving your seat too often these days.
Ram Din	:	When I finish my work, I go to the canteen to take my tea.
Miss Saxena	:	It is against office discipline to go to the canteen during the working hours. You can go to the canteen during the

* C.A., Intermediate (New), May 1998

lunch interval.

Ram Din : You should be satisfied as long as I do my work. If my visits to the canteen interfere with my work, then I will stop going out.

Miss Saxena kept Ram Din under close observation as a follow-up to her conversation with him. She found that Ram Din not only went out as frequently as he did before, he also took a few colleagues along. The Section Officer started giving Ram Din more work than was due to him. One morning there was an unpleasantness between Ram Din and Miss Saxena. Miss Saxena had asked to carry out an additional assignment.

Ram Din : Ever since I started going to the canteen for tea, you have been wanting my blood. If I default in my assignments, you have every right to pull me up. When I do my job regularly, why should I be persecuted for relaxing after every two hours. You are now giving me an assignment which is in addition to my normal work. Is it fair?

Miss Saxena : You are exceeding your limits, Ram Din. In this office, you have to accept what I say. You have to carry out my instructions. You will have to do this assignment or else be prepared to suffer the consequences...

Ram Din : You are now threatening. I know your motive. The motive is not to get work done. It is to teach me a lesson.

Miss Saxena : I warn you. Your behaviour is undesirable.

Ram Din : I know what you are driving at. I might as well tell you it is not easy to dismiss me. Even if you succeed in dismissing me, there is no dearth of jobs for a good typist.

Having said this, Ram Din walked out. Miss Saxena reported it to Ravi Mohan, Manager incharge of the section. The Manager called him and administered a strict warning.

Ravi Mohan : Miss Saxena has told me everything. You have to observe office discipline regardless of your efficiency. And also, avoid using strong language when talking to superiors.

Ram Din : Yes, Sir, May I state my side of the story?

Ravi Mohan : No, Miss Saxena has already told me everything... Try to mend your ways. That is all I want to tell you.

QUESTIONS

Read the above case carefully and answer the following questions after analysing it:

(*a*) What is the real problem in the case?

(*b*) Who is at fault and why?

(*c*) What remedial action would you suggest if you were a manager there, to resolve the problem?

18

JOB FRUSTRATION*

"Prosperity is a great teacher, adversity is a greater. Possession pampers the mind, deprivation trains and strengthens." – ***William Hazlitt***

Learning Objectives

After studying this chapter, you should be able to:

- **Define** frustration.
- **Identify** the sources it comes from.
- **Exemplify** the effects of frustration on the behaviour of the frustrated person.
- **Suggest** ways and means how frustration can be reduced or managed.

18.1 INTRODUCTION

Human activities are purposive and goal directed. Accomplishment of one goal gives genesis to another goal, usually of higher order[1]. Hence, man is called a 'wanting animal'. However, all human goals are not achieved. While achieving goals gives satisfaction, not achieving creates otherwise feeling producing a sense of deprivation in the person. The sense of deprivation may result in, what is called, **'frustration'.** Thus, frustration is a natural and unavoidable feature of human life. Frustration causes harm to both person and organisation where one works. In this lies the need for and importance of understanding frustration.

The present chapter, therefore, tries to address to certain questions while studying human behaviour at work. What is frustration ? Where does frustration come from ? What are the effects of frustration ? and How can frustration be managed ?

18.2 WHAT IS FRUSTRATION ?

Human behaviour being goal-directed, an individual undertakes a series of activities to achieve a goal. If a goal is not achieved, it produces a sense of deprivation in individual. This may result in frustration. Frustration is, thus, the resultant feeling caused by a sense of privation (lack of something), deprivation (blocking or interfering with) or conflict in relation to the goal-directed activities[2]. In other words, frustration is the blocking or slowing down a goal-directed activity. Frustration is a sort of disappointment that people face in their every day life.

* This chapter draws heavily from S.S. Khanka : Frustration Management, **Prabandh**, January-June 2002, pp. 81-85.

18.3 WHERE DOES FRUSTRATION COME FROM ?

There can be three sources where frustration comes from. These are :

1. Privation
2. Deprivation
3. Conflict

A brief mention of these follows :

Privation : When an individual experiences lack of something relevant to a desired goal, it may produce frustration for him/her. If a student, for example, preparing hard to seek admission in an Indian Institute of Management may not pursue his goal because of lack of required financial resources, may feel frustration caused by **'privation'.**

Deprivation: Blocking or interfering with one's goal-directed activities may also produce frustration. If an employee preparing hard for a career advancing examination falls ill and is forced to take rest, may feel frustrated due do deprivation factor.

Conflict: Frustration may also be caused by conflict between two goals : be these equally attractive goals, equally unattractive goals, or attractive-unattractive goals. Let these be clarified.

The conflict of a Reader working in the IGNOU, New Delhi between joining the post of Professor in a Central University in the North-Eastern Region of India where circumstances do not allow him to take his family and remaining in the IGNOU at New Delhi as a Reader is an example of conflict-caused frustration[3]. Such a conflict is called "**approach-approach conflict**". The conflict between two equally unattractive goals is called "**avoidance-avoidance conflict**." A bank employee's option to choose between a higher position in a far off remote place and giving up chances of promotion by staying at his home town is an example of "**avoidance-avoidance approach**". When an attractive goal also has some unattractive aspects, it produces "**approach-avoidance conflict**". Getting an attractive offer of employment in a highly distrubed region is an example of such conflict.

It is clear from the preceding description that frustration is caused by goal-related factors. Let us see what factors cause frustration. Here is an example of Anup who felt frustrated because he worked hard and his boss promised him to promote him. But, when the announcements were made, Anup did not get the higher position. In this case, several factors that caused frustration to Anup are listed in the following formula:

$F = fL\ V \times O + I + P$, where

F = Frustration

f_L = the function

f = Expectation to achieve the goal

V = Valence (attractiveness of the goal)

O = Opportunity to achieve the goal in the near future (very low)

I = Investment of effort and other inputs in achieving the goal

P = Publicity of the expected achievement of the goal to others.

In the above example, if Anup had no expectation to get promoted, he would have no or very little frustration even if he did not get promoted. Similarly, more the goal attractive, more will be frustration and vice versa. The low possibility to get promoted in near future caused more frustration to Anup. Higher efforts put into achieving a goal produce more frustration if the goal is not achieved. Knowing of more people that Anup is likely to get promotion caused more frustration to him compared with a situation in which no one or a very few knew that Anup was to be promoted.

18.4 HOW DOES FRUSTRATION AFFECT BEHAVIOUR ?

People experience frustration quite often in their every-day life. Hence, it will be interesting to know how frustration affects them *i.e.*, their behaviour. People manifest wide range of reaction to frustration. We are illustrating it with an example of Rupak. Rupak, a General Manager in Cachar Paper Mill, promoted from production manager, faced with frustration caused by fall in productivity in the mill. He may behave in various ways. He may be angry with his staff *i.e.*, **aggression**. Having experience in production job, he himself may rush to solve the production problem, *i.e.*, **regression**. He may explain the problem to his boss, *i.e.*, **flight**[4, 5]. He may also, with his staff, take decision to improve the situation, *i.e.*, **exploration**.

Even the above mentioned four modes of his behaviour can take several forms. A brief description of these follows :

Aggression

Aggression is the most common reaction to frustration. It may take the forms of **general aggression** like kicking, knocking, stambing foot, breaking etc.; **target-directed aggression** such as anger expressed towards the boss or subordinate; **self-directed aggression** by blaming oneself for frustated situation; and **displaced aggression** when anger is diverted to some other person(s) than the person(s) seen causing disappointment as a manager cannot express his/her anger to the superior or boss but may express anger to weaker ones such as wife and subordinates.

Regression

Regression is characterised by reverting to the previous mode of behaviour. It may take the form of **Retrogression** when one reverts to one's past behaviour. In our cited example, Mr. Rupak may behave like a production manager under frustrated situation; **Primitivation** reflecting primitive or less mature modes of behaviour under frustration; and **Stereotype** making the person show repetitive behaviour. Such a regression is best demonstrated in gambling when a gambler repeats the same approach and loses in a series of moves.

Flight

One reaction to frustration is escaping or flight from frustrating situation. It may take several forms like **Apathy** when one neglects the frustrating situation; **Withdrawal**, that is, not attend such situations; **Fantasy** say dreaming pleasant things and creating fantasies of doing something one cannot do in real life; and **Rationalisation** when one attributes certain reason for not getting what was expected (like **the fox seeing the grapes sour**).

Exploration

The exploration mode of reaction to frustration is problem solving. In this mode of reaction, the individual explores alternative strategies with others to solve the frustrating problem. It may take forms like Alternative Generation, Self Action, Action by Others and Joint Action.

18.5 HOW TO MANAGE FRUSTRATION ?

Frustration is inevitable in human life. There is, therefore, no way out but to manage it or cope with it. The following are some steps that may help managers effectively manage frustration of their employees. These are subsumed under two general categories, viz., diagnostic and constructive steps.

Diagnostic Steps

The phenomenon of frustration is highly individualistic in nature. hence, it first needs to be diagnosed before trying to combatting it. The following steps may help the managers diagnose the frustration:

To know the feeling of the frustrated employees: The first step involved in diagnosing the frustration is listening to the feelings of the frustrated employees. One way to ensure the employees that the manager has listened to their feelings is to restate the employees' feelings, points of view, etc. at the end of the session.

To share own feelings of disappointment: The next step is to express and share one's own feelings of disappointment, if any, for the employees' frustration. If an employee is not duly rewarded, for example, it may cause disappointment to the manager also. Similarly, if the manager has partly contributed to the frustration of the employee by arousing high expectations as happened in case of Anup, for example, the manager should also share his feelings of guilt for the same. These acts may help cement the rapport between the manager and employees, on the one hand, and help the employee own up his own feelings of disappointment or frustration, on the other. Yes, cementing relationships needs to be done with honesty, not as a gimmick. Thus, diagnosing the frustration by clearing the feelings will help the employee-manager team move forward to fight with the frustrating situation.

Constructive Steps

This state consists of combatting measures. One such step is to help the frustrated employees realize and assess damages frustration is causing to them. Frustration causes damages in terms of **physical effects** (such as sleeplessness, tension, loss of appetite), **social effects** (such as distortion in social relationships, reduced social contacts), and **effects on work** (like absenteeism, work errors, fall in work quality, neglect of work). The realisation of these effects of frustration pampers the frustrated employees to think of steps to be taken to combat frustration. Accordingly, the employees may generate alternatives in dealing with the problem of frustration. Engaging oneself in physical exercise, sports activities, mediation, self-management techniques, and managing the work-to-home transitions are some ways that help dissipate the dysfunctional consequences of frustration and, thereby, cope with frustration.

SUMMARY

This summary is organized by 'learning objectives' given on page no. 314 :

- *Frustration is the blocking or slowing down a goal- oriented activity.*
- *The sources of frustration where it comes are privation, deprivation, and conflict.*
- *Frustration affects behaviour in the form of aggression, regression, flight, and exploration. Culmination of effects of frustration leads to stress.*
- *Various ways to cope with frustration include physical exercise, sports activities, mediation, relaxation, and other self-management techniques.*

REVIEW QUESTIONS

1. What is frustration ? What are the symptoms of job frustration ?
2. Take a frustrated employee and identify the various sources of frustration he/she is experiencing from.
3. What are the sources of frustration for you as a student ?
4. "Frustration causes harm to employee experiencing it." Explain.
5. What will you suggest, as a manager, to reduce employee frustration ?

REFERENCES

1. Abraham Maslow views that human needs follow a hierarchical order from lower to higher. He classified all human needs into five neat all-inclusive categories : Physiological needs, safety needs, social needs, esteem needs, and self-actualisation. See Abraham Maslow : A Theory of Human Motivation, **Psychological Review**, March-April, 1943, Vol. 50, pp. 370–396.
2. Udai Pareek: **Organisational Behaviour Processes,** Rawat Publications, New Delhi, 1996, pp. 155–164.
3. N. Panchanatham and V. Shanmuga Ganeshan: The Effect of Psychological Stress on Academic Achievement, **Journal of Community Guidance and Research**, Vol. 9, No.2, 1992, pp. 139–149.
4. C.K. Poddar: Retention of Employees–H.R. Manager's Challenge, **The Hindu**, Jan. 10, 1996.
5. Salma Ahmad reports that 'Job Hopping' has slowly become a rule rather than an exception. Even in case of a premier institute in management (IIM, Ahmedabad), 23 out of 61 faculty members fled during 1991–95 due to disappointment with job. See Salma Ahmed : Talent Retention: A Challenge, **Personnel Today**, Vol. 18, No.2, July–September 1997, pp. 37–38.
6. S.S. Khanka : Coping with Stress : Self-Management Approach, **The Chartered Accountant**, October, 1999, pp. 19–22.

19

JOB STRESS*

"It's better to bend than to break." – ***Aesop.C***

"Stress is spice for life. Absence of it is death." – ***Hans Selye***

Learning Objectives

After studying this chapter, you should be able to:

- **Define** stress and scan its symptoms.
- **Explain** how to measure stress.
- **Trace** out the causes of stress called, 'stressors'.
- **Discuss** the various consequences of stress.
- **Show** the impact of stress on task performance.
- **Suggest** strategies for coping with stress or managing stress.

The origin of the concept of stress predates antiquity. Derived from the Latin word 'stringere,' stress was popularly used in the seventeenth century to mean hardship, strain, adversity, or affliction. It was used in the eighteenth and nineteenth centuries to denote force, pressure, strain, or strong efforts with reference to an object or person.[1]

In the modern times, stress has become a buzzword and legitimate concern for people of all walks of life. In fact, no one is immune to stress. Right from the time of birth till death, an individual is invariably exposed to various stressful situations. Hence stress is a subject which is hard to avoid. Stress has been a much and widely talked about phenomenon in corporate (western) world because it is a costly business expense that affects both employee health and corporate profits.[2] To quote, studies of stress among American workers reveal that 69 percent of workers reported that health problems related to stress made them less productive, 30 percent executives believe their work has adversely affected their health, and the number of stress-related workers' compensation claims tripled in one decade, jumping from 5 percent to 15 percent of all claims.[3]

Stress featured in the Indian corporate world since 80's when the Indian market turned competitive. But now, it has become a subject of great concern and action. As regards the consequences of stress, what is true of corporate America is true of corporate India also. As confirmed by research studies, stress bears debilitating effects on both the employee and the employer.

At the Escorts Heart Institute in Delhi, India, routine cardiac screening indicate that most executives are in the advanced stages of stress. "Corporate India is finally

* This chapter draws heavily from S.S. Khanka : Coping with Stress : Self-Management Approach, **The Chartered Accountant,** *Volume XL VIII, No. 4, October 1999, pp. 25-28.*

waking up to the fact that a lot of human potential is being drained away because of stress and burnout," says Shekhar Bajaj, CEO of the Indian consumer, electronics manufacturer Bajaj Electricals.[4] In this lies the need for and importance of preventing or managing stress.

Accordingly, in this chapter we discuss what stress is, what causes stress, and, how it affects negatively both the individual and the organization. We conclude the chapter by discussing various techniques to be used for managing or coping with stress.

19.1. WHAT IS STRESS ?

The concept of stress is borrowed from the natural sciences. It was first introduced in the life sciences by Hans Selye in 1936. What is stress? Different people have different views about stress as different people experience it from a variety of sources. For example, the businessman views stress as frustration or emotional tension; the air traffic controller sees it as a problem of alertness and concentration; and the biochemist thinks of it as a purely chemical event. Not only that, the term stress is used variously by scholars of different disciplines and professions. To quote, in physics, stress is a force which acts on a body to produce strain. In physiology, the various changes in the physiological function in response to evocative agents donate stress(rather than strain). In psychology, stress refers to a particular kind of state of the organization resulting from some interaction between him / her and the environment.

In general sense, stress is the pressures people feel in life due to their reaction to situation. Hans Selye[5] defines stress as "an adoptive response to the external situation that results in physical, psychological, and /or behavioural deviation for organizational participants ". However, individual differences account for a wide range of reactions to situations and, in turn, to stress. For example, a task viewed as challenging by one person may produce high level of anxiety, or say, stress in another. According to Beehr and Newman [6], stress is a condition arising from the interaction of people and their jobs and characterized by changed within people that force them to deviate from their normal functioning. This side of stress is called *distress.* There is also a positive side if stress, called *eustress.* Eustress refers to the healthy, positive, constructive outcome of stressful events and the stress response. Eustress is the stress experience that activates and motivates people to achieve their goals and succeed in their life's challenges. This means people need some stress to survive. That is why Hans Selye views stress as the spice of life and absence of stress is death.[7] However, the negative side of stress, i.e. distress has attracted much attention and concern as it adversely affects the employees mental and physical health and, in turn, their performance. Consequently our subsequent discussion will focus on distress side of stress.

GENERAL ADAPTATION SYNDROME (GAS)

Hans Selye, a pioneer in stress research, developed about 50 years ago a comprehensive model to explain that people have a fairly consistent physiological response to stressful situations. This response, called **General Adaptation Syndrome** (GSA) provides an automatic defense system to help people cope with external/ environmental demands. The defense system occurs in three stages: alarm reaction, resistance, and exhaustion. A diagrammatic view of these stages is shown in Figure 19.1. The line in this figure shows the individual's energy and ability to cope with the stressful situation, i. e. the normal level of resistance.

Alarm Reaction. In the alarm reaction stage, also called 'initial/shock phase', the perception of a threatening or challenging situation causes the brain to send a biochemical massage to various parts of the body that, in turn, make the defense mechanisms active. This stage is characterized by increased respiration rate, heart beat, blood pressure, muscle tension, adrenalin discharge, and gastro intestinal ulceration. At first, the individual's energy level/resistance capacity and coping effectiveness decrease in response to the initial shock. The extreme shock may result in incapacity of individual to cope with stress. In most situations, the alarm reaction alerts the person to the environmental condition and prepares the body for the resistance stage.

Resistance. The bodily signs characteristics of the alarm reaction disappear and the body has activated various biochemical, psychological, and behavioural mechanisms. As a result, the person's resistance increases above the normal level during this stage. However, if the stress persists, or the defensive mechanism proves ineffective, the person's organism deteriorates to the next stage of exhaustion.

Exhaustion. People have a limited resistance capacity. When the resistance adaptation capacity is exhausted, the signs of alarm reaction reappear. Resistance level begins to decline abruptly. Finally, the organism gets collapsed.

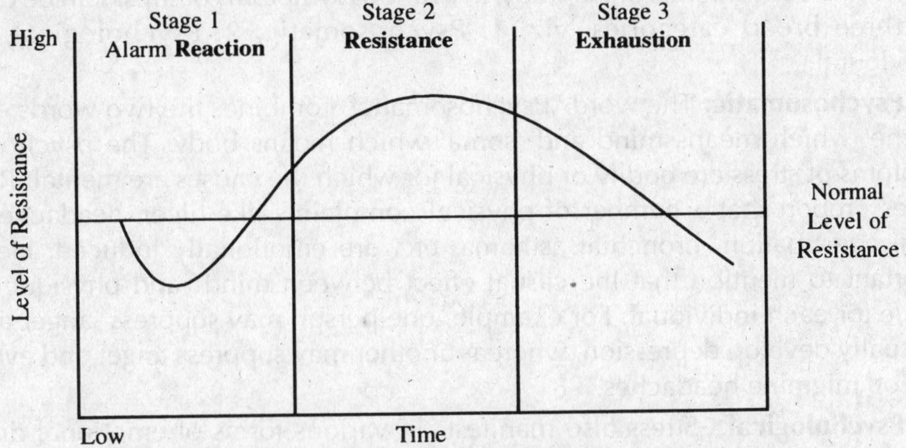

Fig. 19.1 Hans Selye's General Adaptation Syndrome.

We have just seen how the General Adaptation Syndrome describes the stress experience. But, this is only part of the picture. To effectively manage work- related stress, we must understand its symptoms, causes and consequences. What follows next is the same.

19.2. SYMPTOMS OF STRESS

As already mentioned, stress is a pressure people feel in life. When stress persists and becomes excessive, it culminates to strain and, in turn, adversely affects a person's physique, psychology and behaviour. The body prepares itself for "fight' or 'flight'.

The excessive stress develops various symptoms that harm the employee's job performance and health, and threaten their inability to cope with the environment. The various symptoms of stress are diagrammatically presented in Figure 19.2 :

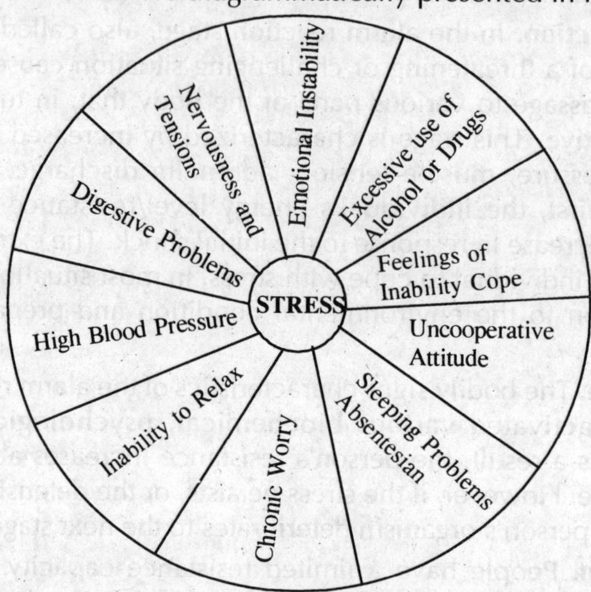

Fig. 19.2 Symptoms of Stress

For the convenience of the study, the various symptoms of stress can be classified into three broad categories, viz, 1. Psychosomatic, 2. Psychological, and 3. Behavioural.

Psychosomatic. The word "Psychosomatic" combines the two words, namely, 'psyche' which means mind and 'soma' which means body. The psychosomatic symptoms of stress are bodily or physical for which the causes are mental. Research studies[8] report that a number of physical complaints like ulcer, headaches, chest pains, constipation, bronchial asthama, etc. are emotionally induced. Here, it is important to mention that the casual effect between mind and physique will be unique for each individual. For example, one person may suppress anger and may eventually develop depression, whereas another may suppress anger and eventually develop migraine headaches.

Psychological. Stress also manifests in various forms of emotional disorders. Researches[9] have found that stress gets its reflection in the form of anxiety, depression, helplessness, hopelessness, and anger. The stressful people with the slightest provocation are easily induced to anger and anxiety and become unable to relax. In his study, Dua[10] reports that the employees suffering from occupational stress generally tend to have low psychological commitment to the organization.

Behavioural. Job stress also bears behavioural symptoms which are easily observable also. There is general agreement that a high degree of job stress drives people adopt certain easily visible behavioural symptoms such as sleeplessness, excessive drinking, smoking, absenteeism, obesity, and gluttony. Job stress can also lead to less visible behavioural symptoms in the form of bad decision-making, negative internal politics, reduced creativity, apathy, and so on. According to a recent survey[11], about 25 percent of Indian executives and 44 per cent of middle level executives report that job stress drives them to high level of alcohol consumption.

19.3. MEASUREMENT OF STRESS

Just as a doctor needs first to measure the intensity of the health problem of his / her patient to prescribe the right treatment for its cure, so does need the level of stress also to be measured before applying right kind of strategy for coping with stress. Hence, the researchers have felt the need for measuring stress and have developed some instruments for its measurement. Though various instruments have been developed in the West to measure stress, in India, there are so far mainly two techniques developed which have been extensively used to measure stress. These are:

1. Organisational Role Stress (ORS)
2. Occupational Stress Index

Organisational Role Stress (ORS)

Organisational Role Stress, popularly known as ORS, is developed by Udai Pareek [12] to measure stress in the Indian context. Pareek's ORS instrument is based on integration of an employee's job role with overall"organizational structure within he/ she works. In other words, in his instrument, Pareek assumes that the role assigned to an employee is linked with different parts and persons of an organization and it is through this role the employee interacts and integrates himself with the entire organizational structure. Here, it is important to mention that the type of organizational structure within which employee works influences the role he/ she plays at times producing strain and stress for the role performer/ employee. This is because different significant persons of organization, even including the employee, have different expectations from the job role assigned to an employee. In course of role performance, the expectations of different persons may clash and, in turn, produce stress for the employee. Pareek [13] explains this stressful experience with the help of two closely related concepts of 'role space' and 'role set'.

Role Space. In practice, each individual occupies and plays several different roles simultaneously. For example, a person can be and play the roles of an executive, a son, a father, a husband, a club member, and so on at the same time. All these roles assumed and played by the individual constitute 'role space'. But, self stands at the centre of the role space. Thus, role space can be defined as "the dynamic interrelationship between the self and the various roles an individual occupies."

Role Set. What role an individual plays is influenced by the expectations of other significant roles and those of the individuals himself/ herself . In this sense, role set can be defined as " the pattern of relationship between the role being occupied and other roles related to an individual."

Pareek developed his ORS scale based on 50 items measuring ten types of organisational role stresses. The ORS scale with 50 items is given at the end of this chapter. The ten different types of organisational role stresses are:

(*i*) **Inter-Role Distance (IRO).** It emerges when there is a conflict between organisational and non-organisational roles.

(*ii*) **Role Stagnation (RS)** . It is the feeling of being stuck to a specific role.

(*iii*) **Role Erosion (RE).** It is the feeling of the role occupant that some roles which should belong to his / her role are assigned to some one else.

(*iv*) **Role Expectation Conflict (REC).** Stress is caused by varying expectation of significant persons like superiors, subordinates, peers, family members and role performer's dilemma as to whom to please.

(*v*) **Role Overload.** The feeling of the role occupant that there are too many expectations from his /her role.

(*vi*) **Role Isolation (RI)** . This refers to the felt distance between the occupied role and other roles in the same role set.

(*vii*) **Personal Inadequacy (PI).** It arises when the role occupant feels that he lacks in required skill or training to effectively play his/ her role.

(*viii*) **Self- Role Distance (SRD)** . This refers to the role occupant's feelings that the role occupied by him/her is against his / her self concept.

(*ix*) **Role Ambiguity (RA)** . It is the confusion about the expectations of role one occupies.

(*x*) **Resource Inadequacy (RIn)** . It arises when role occupant feels that he / she is not given enough resources for performing his / her role.

Occupational Stress Index

Occupational Stress Index as an instrument to measure stress was constructed by Srivastava and Singh[14]. The index consists of 46 items relating to all relevant components of a job life causing stress in one way or other, Like Pareek's 'organisational role stresses', the 46 items of the index measure twelve different types of occupational stresses. These are:

1. Role Overload	7. Powerlessness
2. Role Ambiguity	8. Poor Peer Relations
3. Role Conflict	9. Instrinsic Improvement
4. Group and Political Pressures	10. Low Status
5. Responsibility for Persons	11. Strenuous Working Conditions
6. Under Participation	12. Unprofitability

19.4. CAUSES OR SOURCES OF STRESS

Management of stress is difficult unless the individual experiencing stress is not aware of the specific causes or sources of stress. As we will soon see, many things/ conditions can cause stress. Conditions that cause stress are called 'stressors' or 'Loads'.

Stressors can be defined as the causes of stress, including any environmental conditions that place a physical or emotional demand on the individual. Stress emanates from a misfit between environmental demands and personal adequacies to meet these demands. Different researchers have tried to classify the various causes of stress into different categories. For example, Motowidlo and others[15] have classified the causes of stress into two broad categories: organisational stressors and life stressors. Pestonjee[16] has identified three important sources where stress emanates from. These are: (a) job and organisational, (b) social sector, and (c) intra psychic sector. For purposes of our discussion, the various causes of stress are classified into four broad categories: Environmental , Organisational , Group and Individual Causes or Stressors. These are briefly discussed below:

Environmental Causes. Environmental factors do also have impact on employee stress. The environmental factors to which an employee responds mainly include things such as fast technological change, family demands and obligations, economic and financial conditions, race, caste, class, ethnic identity and relocation and transfers. 17

Of late, the phenomenal rate of social and technical change also has had its great impact on people's life style which is carried over into their jobs. To mention, while medical science has increased the life span of the people by eradicating or reducing the life claiming threats of many dreaded diseases, on the one hand, the modern living style caught up in the rush -rush, mobile, urbani sed and crowded has deteriorated the wellness and increased the potential for stress on the job, on the other. For most people in the recent years, their weak financial position has forced them to do extra job or the spouse has had to join work to meet ever increasing ends. This situation reduces time for recreation, relaxation and family activities. The overall effect is more stress on the employees. These are, according to some stress researchers[18], examples of stressors as unresolved environmental demands.

The physical environmental conditions, such as excessive noise, poor lighting, safety hazards, poorly designed office space, lack of privacy, and poor air quality also cause stress. For example, a study[19] found that clerical employees experience significantly higher stress levels in noisy open offices than in quiet areas.

Here is an example of stress caused by physical environment.

Ravi Sachdeva, an employee of BSNL was transferred from a small hill town Nainital to a very large city Delhi where his commuting time to work was nearly one hour. He disliked city noises, heavy traffic, and crowds, and he felt he was wasting his time while commuting. Besides these, his new job also had more responsibilities.

Within a few months he developed intestinal problems. When medical examination showed no medical cause of his difficulties, he was sent to a counselor. There was only slight improvement and finally his counselor in cooperation with his physician recommended that he be transfer red to a small city. His firm arranged his transfer to Kashipur and within a short time, his problems disappeared.

Organisational Causes /Stressors

Stressors occur not only outside the organisation, but within it also. Oranisational stressors may come in many forms, such as organisational policies, procedures, and structure. As we shall learn in Chapter 28, most forms of organisational change are stressful. For example, downsizing (reducing the number of employees) is extremely stressful to both employees who lose their jobs and also who remain in the organisation.

As a result of downsizing, the remaining workers have been forced to pick up the slack of the workers who have left. For example, a research study[20] found that the percentage of employees suffering from high blood pressure doubled after the company laid off 10 percent of its work force. The reason being the fear of lay off and over burden of work. The long-term sick leave taken by remaining employees doubled after the down sizing. Organisational policies, such as unfair performance evaluation, rotation of work, inequality in remuneration and incentives etc. also serve as Stressor. There is also research evidence[21] that the difference between perceived actual leadership style and expected leadership style leads to a conflict and dissonance between the managers and subordinates. This conflict and dissonance serves as a source of stress.

Whether the position held by one in the organisation has something to do with stress or not, the research findings are inclusive. For example, Ray[22] in his study of 53 scientists (23 junior and 30 senior) revealed that junior scientists experienced greater occupational stress then their senior counterparts. On the contrary, there is one research evidence [23] that the level of stress experienced does not vary much across the positions. For example, there is not much significant difference in the level of stress experienced by the executives and supervisor.

Group Causes/Stressors

People are usually member of various formal and informal groups. The department, division or section to which one belongs, for example, is formal group. As already seen in Chapter 11, group bears tremendous influence on individual member's behaviour. Therefore the group can also be a potential source of stressor. These group stressors' can be categorized into three broad categories.

(*i*) **Lack of Group Cohesiveness.** The famous Hawthorne studiese [24] have made it clear that cohesiveness, or say, togetherness provides satisfaction to the employees. Lack of cohesiveness creates conflict and tension which serves as potential stressor for the employees. According to Selye[25], learning to live with other people in a work setting is one of the most stressful aspects of life. There are three crucial relationships at work an employee has to maintain- with superiors, with subordinates, and with colleagues. At times, these relationships can produce stress for an employee.

(*ii*) **Lack of Social Support.** There is an old saying "*Misery loves company.*" With respect to stress, this statement implies that we as the members of groups look for support from other co-workers in terms of stress or difficulty. If we get this social support, we feel much better off. If such support is lacking for an individual employee, the same can cause stress for him /her [26].

When individuals believe that they have co- workers and friends to support them at times of sorrow or difficulty, their ability to resist the adverse effects of stress seems to increase. Several mechanisms come into play. **First**, having people/ friends to turn to in times of difficulty may help individuals perceive stressful events as less threatening and more under their control would otherwise be the case. **Second**, friends can often suggest useful strategies for dealing with sources of stress. **Third**, by providing a pleasant distraction, friends can help reduce the negative feelings that often result from stressful events. It is for these reasons, social support serves as an important buffer against the effects of stress.

(*iii*) **Interpersonal and Inter Group Conflict.** The incompatibility in terms of needs and values between co- workers /colleagues usually creates interpersonal conflicts. Likewise, variance in objectives and goals between groups leads to inter-group conflict. Conflict studies indicate that such dysfunctional conflicts can also lead to considerable stress for individuals.

Individual Causes / Stressors

Apart from the stressors discussed so far (environmental, organisational and group stressors), there are individual factors also that cause stress, These are:

(*i*) **Role Conflict.** People play various roles in organisations. When people face conflicting demands in discharging their roles, it is called 'role conflict' . When two roles conflict with each other, it is called 'Inter role conflict'. For example, sales staff in the Indian banking industry experience inter role conflict in trying to balance the needs of their bank 'and the needs of customers. Role conflict also occurs when an employee receives contradictory massages from different people about how to perform a job. It is called 'intrarole conflict'.

(*ii*) **Role Ambiguity.** Role ambiguity occurs when employees are uncertain about several aspects of their jobs (e.g. duties, performance expectations, level of authority, and other job conditions). This ambiguity tends to occur when people enter new situations, such as joining the organisation or taking a foreign assignment, because they are uncertain about task and social expectations. Ivancevich and Matteson[27] have identified role conflict, role ambiguity, and degree of responsibility for others as major sources of stress. In another study, Chand and Sethi[28] have found significant positive relationship between job-related strain and role overload and role conflict.

(*iii*) **Workload.** When the phrase" *work- related stress*" is mentioned, usually people envision scenes in which employees are asked to do more work than they can do in a given period of time. This is a case of work overload. In fact, in today's business environment, where downsizing is common, fewer employees are often required to do more work than ever before. This causes stress. A distinction needs to be made, however, between '*quantitative overload*', situations in which employees are asked to do more work than they can complete in a specific period of time, and' *qualitative overload*', the employees' beliefs that they lack the required skills or abilities to perform a given job. Both types of overload are unpleasant and can lead to high levels of stress. Work overload is such common problem in Japan that death from overwork has its own name *Karoshi* [29]. For Example, whereas the average American spends about 1,600 hours working per year, the comparable figure for Japanese is 2,159 hours.

As work overload can be stressful, so can be work inderload also. Work underload is a situation of receiving too little work ('*quantitative underload*') or having tasks that do not sufficiently use the employee talent ('*qualitative overload*') Both types of work underload serve as a possible stressors. This is because as the saying goes; " *The hardest job in the world is doing nothing - you cann't take a break.*"

(*iv*) **Life Events.** Life events, such as the death of a spouse, divorce, injury to one's family members, unwanted pregnancy etc., have dramatic effect on people. This was first studied by Holmes and Rahe[30], who asked large groups of people to assign arbitrary points (from 1 to 100) to various life events according to how much readjustment each had required. They proved that more the person experiences sudden life events like death and divorce of spouse ,the more is stress experienced and, in turn, the poorer will be his consequent health.

(v) **Personality Traits.** Personality affects behaviour. Different people possess different kinds of personality (discussed, in details, in chapter 5). Individual characteristics of personality moderate the extent to which people experience stress. That is why different people experience different levels of stress for the same stressors. Why people experience different levels of stress for the same stressors might be for three reasons: **One**, each of us depending on our self-efficacy perceives the same situation differently. Self - efficacy refers to one's belief that he or she has the ability and motivation to perform the task successfully. **Second**, different people have different thresholds of resistance to a stressor. **Third**, different people use different coping strategies for the same stressors. Even, some people tend to ignore the stressor, hoping that it will go away its own.

There is some evidence (although still inconclusive) that women cope with stress better than their male counterparts.[31] The reason attributed to it is women are more likely to seek emotional support from others in stressful situations, whereas men try either to change the stressor or use less effective coping strategy. However, we must remember that exceptions are always there.

People are classified into two types of personality dimensions – Type A and Type B. Type A people are hard -driving, competitive, impatient, loose temper, talk rapidly, and interrupt others during conversations. In contrast, those with type B dimensions work steadily, take a relaxed approach to life, and be even-tempered. Heart researchers[32] report that type A employees experience considerable stress than type B employees.

19.5 CONSEQUENCES OF STRESS

By now, you are probably convinced that stress stems from many sources, and that it exerts important effects on the people who experience it. What may not yet be apparent, though, is just how powerful and far reaching such effects can be. In fact, so widespread are the detrimental effects of stress that it has been estimated that its annual costs exceed 10 per cent of the US gross national product[33]. The general adaptation syndrome, introduced earlier in this chapter, describes how chronic stress diminishes the individual's resistance, resulting in adverse consequences for both the employee and the organisation. The various consequences of stress are classified into physiological, psychological, and behavioral consequences.

Physiological Consequences. Stress takes its toll on human body. People experience tension, headaches, high blood pressure, high level of cholesterol, ulcers, arthritis etc. due to stress. Studies have found that upto 90 per cent of patients complain of stress related symptoms and disorders[34].

According to medical researchers, the long-term effect of stress on the heart goes something like this: Wherever people are stressed, their blood pressure goes up and down. That frequent pressure change causes injury to the blood vessel walls, which eventually makes them constrict and function abnormally. Overtime, this sequence leads to heart disease. Unfortunately, we often cannot tell when we are physiologically stressed. For example, researchers have found that people think they are in a low -stress state when, in fact, their palms are sweating and their blood pressure has risen.[35]

Psychological Consequences. Apart from physical consequences, stress produces various psychological consequences also. Job dissatisfaction, moodiness, depression, anger, anxiety, nervousness, irritability and tension are the manifestations of the psychological consequences of stress[36]. Emotional fatique is another psychological consequence of stress and related to job burnout.

What is job burnout? Different people have described job burnout differently. Some contend that burnout is type of stress itself. Others describe it as the process of emotional exhaustion, depersonalization, and reduced personal accomplishment resulting from prolonged exposure to stress.[37] Following Table 19.1 compares and contrasts between stress and burnout.

Table 19.1: Stress vs Burnout

Stress	Burnout
The person feels fatigued	The individual encounters chronic exhaustion
The person is anxious	The individual is hypertensive
The person feels moody	The individual feels impatient, irritable, and unwilling to talk others.
The person feels guilty	The individual encounters mental depression
The person experiences increased blood pressure and heart beat.	The individual begins to voice psychosomatic complaints

Behavioural Consequences. When stress becomes distress, it adversely affects the employee's behaviour. The consequences of high level of stress are undereating or overeating; sleeplessness, obesity, increased drinking and smoking, and drug abuse. Over stressed also tend to have higher levels of absenteeism. There might be two reasons for it. One reason is that stress makes people sick. The other reason is that absenteeism is a coping mechanism, Absenteeism is a temporarily withdrawing from the stressful situation so that the stressful employee has an opportunity to re-energize. There is sufficient research evidence to confirm such consequences of stress. In a recent study, Babani[38] shows that 1 in 4 Indian executives suffer from obesity and 44 percent of middle -level executives report that job stress drives them to high level of alcohol consumption. Besides, high level of stress also impairs our ability to remember information, make effective decisions, and take appropriate action. You have probably experienced this level of stress, or call it distress, in an examination or emergency work situation.

19.6. STRESS AND TASK PERFORMANCE

Having studied the various consequences of stress, it also seems pertinent to see the impact of stress on employee's task performance and, in turn, organisational performance. A number of studies[39] have been undertaken to examine the impact of stress on empolyee's task performance. The research evidence shows that stress is both helpful and harmful to task performance. In other words, stress is both a friend and a foe[40]. Absence and too low level of stress does not stimulate the employee to work more or and perform better. Instead, increasing research evidences show that increase in stress level till its mild level serves as a stimulus to activate employee to respond to the challenges of task and, in turn, facilitates employee's task performance. Such mild level of stress can be called ***eustress***. People in certain jobs such as journalists and television announcers, who work under time pressures would seem to benefit from a mild level of stress, You also probably would have benefitted from mild stress caused by time pressure to write your examinations better and more speedily. Yes, the mild level of stress will vary from individual to individual depending on how long it continues, how much complex the task is, and how strong the individual's resilience power is.

But, if the stress level continues to increase beyond the employee's resilience capacity, it causes emotional, mental, and physical exhaustion, also called '*job burnout*' to the employee exposed to stress Such exhaustion distracts and interferes with the employee's task performance.

How both no or too low and too high stress levels interfere with one's performance can be exemplified with tennis players' experience of stress.

> In tennis, upsets occur often at Wimbledon when an unseeded tennis player who is " not supposed to win" rises to the occasion and later admits to having felt only mild stress. The vanguished opponent, who took the match too lightly, may have experienced either no or too low stress to stimulate his/ her early performance. When the match appears to be slipping away, the losing player begins experiencing too much stress to play his /her optimum game. Here, what does it imply is that the athletes like tennis players need to maintain the right balance between their stress and performance.

Newstrom and Devis [41] have compared the relationship between stress and performance with that of strings and music on a violin, Just as either too little or too much tension on the strings does not produce suitable music and the violin strings need to be readjusted to accommodate the changing conditions, such as increased humidity, either too low or too high stress level interferes with employee's performance and, therefore, stress level needs to be periodically adjusted and moderated. Generally, the relationship between stress and performance on many tasks is believed to be curvilinear. Figure 19.3 shows such curvilinear relationship between employee stress and his/ her task performance.

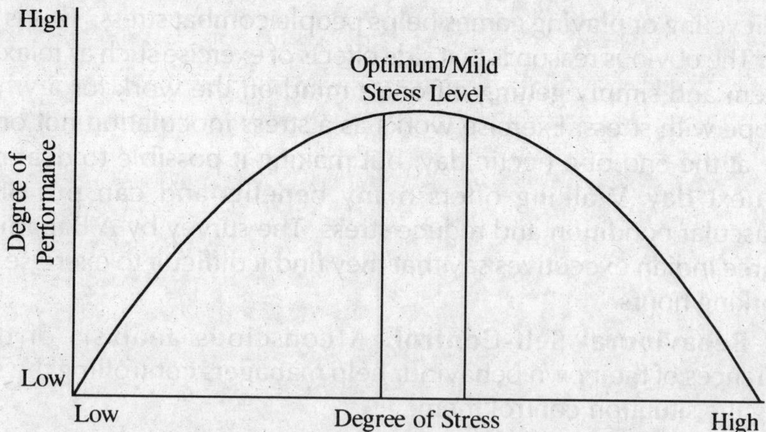

Fig. 19.3 Employee Stress and Task Performance

Having said all this, we must also note that there are exceptions to this curvilinear hypothesis of stress and task performance. While even relatively mild or moderate stress level can interfere with task performance, because the prolonged or repeated exposure to mild stress may have harmful effects on employee's health, too high level of stress can produce better performance by making the person rise to the occasion. Both types of examples abound in organisations.

Having mentioned all this, now the most reasonable conclusion we can give concerning stress and task performance it that the precise impact of stress on performance depends on different factors, such as the duration of stress continues, the complexity of the task peiformed, the resilience power of the person exposed to stress, and one's previous experience with the task. Therefore, in view of such complexities, generalization about the impact of stress on task performance should be made with considerable caution.

19.7 HOW TO MANAGE OR COPE WITH STRESS ?

It is better to bend than to break. Hence, the need for coping with stress. Though stress is helpful, but it is usually harmful as it impinges on employee's health and his/her task performance. Therefore, stress needs to be managed or coped with to minimize its debilitating effects. The word 'managing' or 'coping' bears two connotations in stress literature[42]. It has been used to denote the way of dealing with stress, or the effort to master conditions of harm, threat, or challenge when routine or automatic response is not readily available. Researchers have indicated various strategies to be used to manage or cope with stress. However, these strategies vary from person to person and in the same person from time to time. Nonetheless, the various strategies can be classified into two broad categories:

1. At Individual Level
2. At Organisational Level

At Individual Level

Individual strategies are based on 'self-help' or 'do yourself approaches. Some specific techniques that individuals can use to effectively manage their job stress are:

(*i*) **Physical Exercise.** Exercise in any form, be it walking, jogging, swimming, riding, bicycling or playing games helps people combat stress. This is excellent stress modifier. The obvious reason is that side effects of exercise such as relaxation, enhanced self-esteem and simply getting off one's mind off the work for a while help people better cope with stress. Exercise works as a stress inoculation not only relieving the pressure at the end of a hectic day, but making it possible to deal more effectively with it next day. Walking offers many benefits and can put one in excellent cardiovascular condition and reduce stress. The survey by A Babani shows that two out of three Indian executives say that they find it difficult to exercise regularly due to long working hours.

(*ii*) **Behavioural Self-Control.** A conscious analysis of the causes and consequences of their own behaviour help managers controlling the situation instead of letting the situation control them.

(*iii*) **Social Support.** "*Misery loves company.*" Studies have suggested that social support moderates the effects of stress on personal well-being. It is one of the important aspects of the quality of social milieu. We see in practice people give and receive different types of social support, such as money, material and emotional help. Adequate social support may reduce intensity and frequency of stressors.

(*iv*) **Yoga and Meditation.** Yoga and mediation which are of the Indian origin, also affect the psychological well-being of people. Researchers have reported that mediators were less anxious than non-meditators. Yoga is, according to Patanjali, a " suspension" of the functions of the mind. It is an integrated system which emphasises harmony of body and mind. Yoga can help managers lead a stress free life and be more effective.

Yoga teaches us to follow a set of behaviours called ,yam and niyam. There are five yam: non-violance (*ahimsa*) , truthfulness (*satyam*) , non-stealing (*asteya*) ,continence (*brahmcharya*), and non-convetousness (*aparigriha*). Similarly, there are five niyam also: purification (*saucha*), contentment (*santosh*), austerity (*tapas*), study (*swadhaya*) , and self-surrender to the lord (*iswara pravichara*). In total, both *yam* and *niyam* are guidelines for an enlightened lifestyle. Lack of adherence to these guidelines lessens the positive effects of yoga on the physical, psychological, and spiritual well being of managers.

Closely related to yoga is asan that also helps reduce the debilitating effects of stress and tension of life. According to Patanjali, comfortable bodily posture is asan. There are a variety of assans varying from simple to complex ones. Swami Shivananda in Yogasana has suggested a few asan useful for the managers to reduce stress. These asans are: *padnasana* (the lotus posture) , '*Siddhasana* (the perfect posture) , *Sirshasana* (the topsyturvy posture) and *sarvangshamasana.* A manager needs to learn asans from a trained yoga teacher before he begins the asans.

Meditation relates to a pscho-spiritual processes. Meditation is one step further to concentration. While concentration focuses on an object, meditation opens it. In meditation, both self and external world blend together harmoniously. Rajneesh has defined meditation as " a state of mind". In meditation, there is nobody inside, nothing outside. Research has proved that both concentration and meditation have positive effects on physiological ,psychological and spiritual processes which buffer stress. Like asans , managers must learn meditation from a learned mediator -teacher.

(*v*) **Changing Gears.** Changing gears involves shifting one's attention from main work to something else, such as a hobby. Yet, while changing gears, the changed work needs to capture the worker's attention. Changing gears helps in removing one's attention from pressure of work, on the one hand, and draining of pent-up tensions, on the other.

(*vi*) **Pampering Oneself.** We pamper others when they experience a crisis in life. We send flowers to a friend who is admitted in the hospital struggling with his life and death. We do these because they break routine and help cope with stress. One can pamper oneself in many ways. A manager may plan a series of short-vacations instead of one long vacation. The objective is to break routine.

(*vii*) **Warming Up Oneself.** A manager also needs to warm up before starting work just as the football player warms up before the buzzer sounds to start the game. The basic object in warming up is to set tone for the day. Warming up, thus, prepares one for the tensions he will have to encounter during the day.

(*viii*) **Rearranging One's Job Schedule.** Researchers have revealed that managers taking their job seriously, working harder and assuming increasing responsibilities become more susceptible to job stress, One of the ways of releasing job pressure is to rearrange one's schedule. An effective way to deal with job stress is to confront difficult tasks when one is fresh.

At Organisational Level

Like an individual, an organisation can also help manage stress through various proactive interventions. Some of these interventions are listed below:

(*i*) **Setting Clear Objectives.** Organisations should set clear objectives for its members. This helps minimize role ambiguity which usually filters down the organisation in the form of neuoris.

(*ii*) **Stress Audit.** Pestonjee[43] has suggested stress audit as one of the effective proactive intervention to combat stress. According to him, when an organization decides to have a scientific peep into mental and physical health status of its backbone group (executives) , the exercise is called a stress audit. It involves an attempt that organisations make to study, explore, and control various types of stresses which the individual executives experience by virtue of their organisatinal membership.

Stress audit as an OD intervention involves the following **four stages**:

Phase - I : Conducting an exploration of 'Stress Tolerance Limit' (STL) with the help of psychometric instruments in terms of anxiety, depression, anger, dominant motive/ need profile and alike.

Phase - II: Identify the dominant organisational role stress dimensions by measuring Role Efficacy Index (REI) for the executives,

Phase - III : Collecting both qualitative ad quantitative information on stress variable and their impact on individual health and task performance with the help of conducting **structure** interviews.

Phase - IV : Suggesting remedial ways and means for introducing desired changes and modifications made in organizational activities and practices. This might also include organizational restructuring of slight of minor nature.

(*iii*) **Counselling:** Counselling is yet another proactive strategy to be used by organisations to deal with stress. Counselling to employees in the matters like career planning to provide them clarity in their job roles, helping them in identifying their strengths and weaknesses help them better cope with stress[44]. Dissemination of information to employees on how to face stressors within the organisation and outside proves useful for employees in dealing with stress.

(*iv*) **Spread the Message:** Spreading the message about the importance of regular habits of work, leisure, proper diet, exercise, and mental peace among the organisational members helps them better cope with stress.

(*v*) **Fit between Person and Work:** Research evidence[45] shows that striking a fit between worker and his / her work environment serves as one of the best strategy to manage stress. This congruence can be attained by linking the worker to the job characteristics, for high internal motivation, high quality performance, high work satisfaction, and low absenteeism and turnover.

(*vi*) **Clarity in Roles:** There is enough evidence[46] to show that defining individual' roles through role efficacy helps them reduce their role- shared stresses. This is so as a result of an individual's movement from a reactive *i.e.* role taking behaviour to a proactive *i.e* role -making behaviour. Role efficacy is found negatively related with role stress and role efficacy helps in overcoming the experience of role stress.

SUMMARY

This summary is organized by 'learning objectives' given on page no. 319 :

- *Stress is non- specific response to demands from environment that result in physical, psychological and / or behavioural deviations for people. No one is immune to stress.*
- *Stress in work settings stems from different sources such as individuals, group, organisational, and environmental.*
- *Though the precise impact of stress is difficult to predict, it adversely affects the physiological, psychological, and behavioural aspects of people experiencing to it. Effects of stress vary from person to person depending on their resilience capacity, perception of stimuli, prior experience to it, and complexity of task to be performed.*
- *Stress can be managed at both the individual level and the organisational level. Individual approaches to manage stress include exercise, behavioural control, proper diet, meditation, relaxation, etc. Organisational*
- *Strategies to manage stress include clarity of employee roles, procedures, policies and rules, change in organisational structure, counseling, spread of message of evil effects of stress, and so on.*

REVIEW QUESTIONS

1. What is job stress? Is it always bad for the individual? Explain.
2. Where does stress come from? Describe three sources of your own stress.
3. Bring out the impact of stress on performance and satisfactiori of employees.
4. How can stress be coped with ?

4. Breathe easily and naturally through your nose, concentrating on each individual breath. Each time you exhale, repeat the word" one" (or any similar simple sound) silently to yourself. (this is your mantra) .
5. Continue this process for about ten to twenty minutes, (It's OK to open your eyes occasionally to check the clock, but do not use an alarm!) After you're finished, do not jump up; remain quietly seated for a few minutes longer and then slowly rise.

Hints: Don't obsess about reaching a deep level of concentration. You probably won't be able to do so at first. But with practice, you will be able to achieve relaxation very quickly. When distracting thoughts enter your mind, simply ignore them and return to repeating your mantra. Practice the technique once or twice daily, but never within two hours after eating a meal(the process of digestion interferes with the ability to relax). It might take several weeks (or even months) to get to the point where you can relax without mental interference, so be patient.

Remember the Following points

1. Were you skeptical about this process at first? How did trying this technique change the way you feel? Did you become a greater believer in the benefits of relaxation?
2. At first, how long did it take you to achieve deep relaxation? With practice, were you successful in reducing this time?
3. Did you find that the more you practiced this technique, the less you became distracted by outside thoughts entering your mind?
4. Did this technique to work for you? In other words, has it helped relieve stress in your life? If so, what particular sources of stress were most effectively alleviated?
5. How did your experiences with this technique compare to those of your classmates? Why do you think some were able to use the technique effectively while others were not?

Organisational Role Stress (ORS) Scale **

People have different feelings about their roles. Statements describing some such feelings are given below. Read each statement and indicate in the left hand side space how often do you have the feeling expressed in the statement in relation to your role in your organisation.

Use the following scheme to indicate your feeling. If you find that the category to be used in answering does not adequately indicate your own feelings, use the one which is closest to the way you feel. Do not leave any item unanswered.

0 = if you never or rarely feel this way
1 = if you occasionally (a few times) feel this way
2 = if you sometimes feel this way
3 = if you frequently feel this way'
4 = if you very frequently or always feel this way

1. My role tends to interfere with my family life.

Adapted from U. Pareek : **Making Organisational Roles Effective, Tata Mc-Graw Hill, New Delhi 1993.

5. "Job stress can have physiological, psychological, and behavioural effects". E
6. List and discuss the four major sources of stress in your life during the last two
7. Examine yourself whether you are primarily type A or type B person. Discu reasons for your. choice. Make a list of your five main type A and type B charac tics.
8. Two individuals exposed to the same situation may experience sharply contras levels of stress. Why ? Explain.

Here is an exercise for You to assess your own stress-related behaviour

None is immune to stress. So are you too. Following are some statements relate to stress behaviour of a students like you. Evaluate yourself with regard to each c criteria listed below by circling the number that indicates your assessment of the degree you experience in case of each statement. Total the scores from the items.

Examine the range of class scores and compute the average. Note that a higher score suggests the possibility of greater current stress in life.

	Low Degree				High Degree
1. Inadequate privacy	1	2	3	4	5
2. Living on a tight budget	1	2	3	4	5
3. Low quality of food	1	2	3	4	5
4. Concern about personal safety	1	2	3	4	5
5. Worry about career prospects	1	2	3	4	5
6. Parental pressure for grades	1	2	3	4	5
7. Transportation problems	1	2	3	4	5
8. Ethical conflicts (e.g. alcohol, drugs)	1	2	3	4	5
9. Self- consciousness about appearance	1	2	3	4	5
10. Lack of intellectual challenge	1	2	3	4	5
Total Score..........................					

1. What interpretation for your own and other's scores can you provide?
2. Which items seemed to produce the greatest stress among class members?
3. Which actions would you suggest for the reduction of students stress?

That relaxation helps control stress is exemplified below for your benefit *

One of the most effective things we can do to control our own stress levels is to relax. Relaxation helps reduce the physiological strain on the body, minimizing the long term damage that may be caused by exposure to stressors, Although you already know how to relax, we are talking about a deeper kind of relaxation than normal. Keep an open mind, and give it a try.

Here is the procedure to follow

As in other things, preparation is crucial. Find a quiet, comfortable place where you can be free from distractions for approximately twenty minutes. Then follow each of these steps.

1. Sit quietly in a comfortable position.
2. Close your eyes.
3. Starting at your feet, and working your way up toward your head, deeply relax each of your muscles. (This will take some concentration and practice).

---

* Adapted from J.C. Quick and J.D. Quick : **Organisational Stress and Preventive Management** Mc Graw-Hill, New York, 1984.

2. I am afraid I am not learning enough in my present role for taking up higher responsibility.
3. My workload is too heavy.
4. Other role occupants do not give enough attention and time to my role.
5. I do not have adequate knowledge to handle the responsibilities in my role.
6. I have to do things in my role that are against my better judgement.
7. I am not clear on the scope and responsibilities of my role (job).
8. I do not get the information needed to carry out responsibilities assigned to me.
9. I have various other interests (social, religious, etc) which remain neglected because I do not get time to attend to these.
10. I am too preoccupied with my present role responsibility to be able to prepare for taking higher responsibility.
11. I am not able to satisfy the conflicting demands of the various peer level people and my juniors.
12. Many functions of what would be a part of my role have been assigned to some other role.
13. The amount of work I have to do interferes with the quality I want to maintain.
14. There is not enough interaction between my role and other roles.
15. I wish I had more skills to handle the responsibilities of my role.
16. I am not able to use my training and expertise in my role.
17. I do not know what the people I work with expect of me.
20. I do not get enough resources to be effective in my role.
21. My role does not allow me to have enough time with my family.
22. I do not have time and opportunities to prepare myself for the future challenges of my role.
23. I am not able to satisfy the demands of clients and others, since these are conflicting with one another.
24. I would like to take more responsibility than I am handling at present.
25. I have been given too much responsibility.
26. I wish there was more consultation between my role and other roles.
27. I have not had pertinent training for my role.
28. The work I do in the organisation is not related to my interests.
29. Several aspects of my role are vague and unclear.
30. I do not have enough people to work with me in my role.
31. My organisational responsibilities interfere with my extra organisaional roles.
32. There is very little scope for personal growth in my role.
33. The expectations of my seniors conflict with those of my juniors.
34. I can do much more than what I have been assigned.
35. There is a need to reduce some parts of my role.
36. There is no evidence of involvement of several roles(including my role) in joint problem solving or collaboration in planning action.
37. I wish I had prepared myself well for my role.
38. If I had full freedom to define my role I would be doing some things different from what I do now.
39. My role has not been defined clearly and in detail.

40. I am rather worried that I lack the necessary facilities needed in my role.
41. My family and friends complain that I do not spend time with them due to heavy demands of my work role.
42. I feel stagnant in my role.
43. I am bothered with the contradictory expectations different people have from my role.
44. I wish I had been given more challenging task to do.
45. I feel overburdened in my role.
46. Even when I take initiative for discussions or help, there is not much response from the other roles.
47. I need more training and preparation to be effective in my work role.
48. I experience conflict between my values and what I have to do in my role.
49. I am not clear as to what are the priorities in my role.
50. I wish I had more financial resources for the work assigned to me.

Answer Sheet for ORS Scale

Transfer your answers to 50 questions in the table below,

1......	11......	21......	31......	41......	....	....	IRD	I
2......	12......	22......	32......	42......	....	....	RS	2
3.......	13......	23	33......	43......	....	....	REC	3
4......	14......	24......	34......	44......	....	....	RE	4
5......	15......	25..	35......	45......	....	....	RO	5
6......	16......	26..	36......	46..	....	....	RI	6
7......	17......	27......	37......	47......	....	....	PI	7
8......	18......	28......	38......	48......	....	....	SRD	8
9.......	19......	29......	39......	49......	....	....	RA	9
10......	20......	30......	40......	50......	....	....	Rin	10

The answer sheet can be used for scoring. The total scores on each of role stressors range from 0 -20. You can also add all the scores on 10 stressors to get an overall score. By and large, the higher the scores on any of the 10 stressors or on overall total, the greater the possibility of experiencing high stress.

REFERENCES

I. D.M.Pastonjee: **Stress and Coping** (**The Indian Experience**), Sage Publications, New Delhi, Second Edition 1999, pp.15-16.
2. Susan L. Lind and Fred L. Otte : Management Styles, Mediating Variables, and Stress among HRD Professionals, **Human Resource Development**, Winter 1994, p. 301.
3. Leslie Brooks Suzukama: Fed Up , Fired Up or (Gulp) Fired, Duluth News Tribune, February 26, 1996 ,pp. IB,4B; and also see Jennifer 1. Laabs: Job Stress, **Personnel Journal**, April 1992, p.43.
4. N. Chowdhury and S. Menon: Beating Burnout, **India Today**, June 9, 1997,p.86. 5. Hans Selye : The Stress of Life, Mc Graw Hill Book Company, New York, 1956.
6. Terry A Beehr and J.E. Newman: Job Stress, Employee Health and Organisational Effectiveness, **Personnel Psychology**, Winter, 1978,pp. 665-669.
7. Hans Selye : ***op.cit***, 1956.

8. B.B Brown: **Stress and the Art of Biofeedback**, Harper and Row, New York, 1977.
9. AP. Singh and B. Singh: Stress and Strain among Indian Middle Managers, **Indian Journal of Industrial Relations**,. 28(1), 1992,pp.71-84.
10. J. Dua : Job Stressors and their Effects on Physical Health, Emotional Health and Job Satisfaction in a University, **Journal of Educational Administration**, 32, 1994, pp.59-78.
11. A Babani : Men are Like This Only, **Outlook**, May 6, 2002 , p.112. Also Jagdish : Perceived Occupational Stress and Employees' Attitude towards Job and Management, **Indian Journal of Industrial Relations**, 23(1), 1987,pp.80-92.
12. Udai Pareek: **Organizational Role Stress Scale: Manual**, Navin Publications, Ahmedabad, 1983.
13. Udai Pareek: Managing Stress and Coping, In : D.M. Pestonjee, U.Pareek and R. Agarwal (Eds.) : **Studies in Stress and Its Management**, Oxford & IBH, New Delhi., 1999.
14. AK.Srivastava and AP. Singh: Construction and Standardisation of an Occupational Stress Index : A Pilot Study, **Indian Journal of Clinical Psychology**, Volume 8, 1991,pp.133-136.
15. Stephen J. Motowidlo, John S. Packard, and Michael R. Manning : Occupational Stress: Its Causes and Consequences for Job Performance, **Journal of Applied Psychology**, Vol. 71,1986, pp.618-629.
16. D.M. Pestonjee : **Stressors or Loads: A Diagrammatic Presentation of the Stress Phenomenon**, Unpublished Manuscript, Indian Institute of Management, Ahmedabad, 1983.
17. D.M.Pestonjee: Executive Stress: Should it be Avoided ? **Vikalpa**, 12(1),1987,pp.20-30.
18. Rabi S. Bhagat and Stephen M. Allie: Organisational Stress, Personal Life Stress and Symptoms of Life Strains: An Examination of the Moderning Role of Sense of Competence, **Journals of Vocational Behaviour**, Volume II, 1967, pp.213-218.
19. G. Evans and D. Johnson: Stress and Open Office Noise, **Journals of Applied Psychology**, 85,2000, pp.779-783.
20. M. Kivinaki, J. Vahtera, J. Pentti, and J. E. Ferrie: Factors Underlying the Effect of Organisational Downsizing on Health of Employees: Longitudinal Cohort Study, *BMJ*: **British Medical Journal**, April 8, 2000, pp 971-975.
21. Jagdish: Perceived Occupational Stress and Employees' Attitude towards Job and Management, **Indian Journal of Industrial Relations**, 23 (1), 1987. pp. 80-92.
22. A. Roy: Executive Stress and Social Support: An Exploratory Study, **Abhigyan**, 15 (4), 1997,pp.25-31.
23. B. Pattanayak: Effect of Shift Work and Heirarchical Position in Satisfaction Commitment Stress and HR Climate, **Management and Labour Studies,** 25(2), 2000, pp. 126-135.
24. Elton. Mayo: **The Human Problems of an Industrial Civilization**, Harvard University Press, Cambridge, Mass, 1933.
25. Hans Selye: ***op.cit.,*** 1956.
26. Nazimuddin Ahmed and S.S. Jha: Job Stress: Strain and Social Support, **Indian Journal of Training and Development**, May- June 1989, pp. 16-20.
27. J.M. Ivancevich and M.T. Matteson: **Stress and Work**, Scott Foresman, Glenview, Ill, 1980.
28. P. Chand and AS. Sethi: Organisational Factors in Development of Work Stress, **Indian Journal of Industrial Relations,** 32 (4),1997, pp. 453-462.
29. S. Efron: Jobs Take a Deadly Toll on Japanese, **Los Angeles Times**, April 12, 2000, p. A1.

30. T. H. Holmes and R.H.Rahe: Social Readjustment Rating Scale, **Journal of Psychomatic Research**, 1967, Vol. I I. pp. 213-218.
31. S.M. Aditya and AK. Sen: Executive under Stress: A Comparison of Men and Women, **Journal of the Indian Academy of Applied Psychology**, Vol. 19, 1993, pp 1-6.
32. M. Friedman and R.Rosenman: The Central Nervous System and Coronary Heart Disease, **Hospital Practice**, Vol. 6, 1971, pp. 87-97.
33. S.E. Sulljivan and Rabi S. Bhagat: Organisational Stress, Job Satisfaction, and Job Performance: Where Do We Go from Here? **Journal of Management**, 1992, Vol.18, pp. 353-374.
34. A Bhandarker and P. Singh: Managerial Stress: A Study in Cyclical Perspective, **Abhigyan**, Autum, 1998, pp. 7-42.
35. D.K. Sugg: Study Shows Link between Minor Stress, Early Signs of Coronary Artery Disease, **Battimore Sun**, December 16, 1997, p. A3..
36. R. D. Lele: Stress and Tension: A Medical Review, **B.M.A. Review**, Vol. 4 & 6, November- December 1993, pp 36-40..;.
37. C. Maslach: **Burnout: The Cost of Caring**, Printice- Hall Englewood Cliff, 1982.
38. A Babani: ***op. cit.***, May,6, 2002.
39. J. Dua: Assessment of Positive and Negative Effect as a Result of Thoughts and Real Life Experiences, **Behaviour Change**, Vol. 7, 1990. pp. 62-65; J. Dua: Job Stressors and their Effects on Physical Health, Emotional Health and Job Satisfaction in a University, **Journal of Educational Administration**, Vol. 32, 1994, pp.59-78; D.M. Pesronjee: Executive Stress: Should It Always the Avoided?, **Vikalpa**, Vol. 12, 1987, pp. 23-30.; And T.R. Rajeshwari: Employee Stress: A Study with Reference to Bank Employees, **Indian Journal of Industrial Relations**, Vol. 27, No.4 1992, pp. 419- 429.
40. S. Batliwala: **Stress: Your Friend or Foe ?**, Wagle Process Studies and Press Pvt, Ltd., Mumbai, 1990.
41. John W. Newstrom and Keith Davis: **Organisational Behaviour: Human Behnviour at Work**, Tata McGraw-Hill Publishing Company Ltd., New Delhi 1998, pp. 440.
42. R. S. Lazarus: The Psychology of Coping: Issues of Research and Assessment, In G.V. Coelho, D.A. Humburg and T.E. Adams (eds.) **Coping and Adaptation**, Basic Books, New Delhi, 1974.
43. D.M. Pestonjee: ***op.cit***, 1999.
44. N. Panchanathan: Effects of Stress Reduction on the Creative Personality of Executives through Counselling, **Sankalpa**, Vol. 6,No.I, Jan-June 1998, pp. 8-15.
45. N.M. Agarwal: **Application of Job Characteristics in Management of Organisational Stress**, Unpublished Manuscript, IIM, Ahmedabad, 1984.
46. U. Pareek: Managing Stress and Coping,. In: D.M. Pestonjee, U. Pareek and R Agarwal (eds), **Studies in Stress and Management**, Oxford & IBM, New Delhi, 1999; and O.B. Sayeed: Role Stress and Role Making Behaviour, **Managerial Psychology**, Vol. 6, 1985, pp 35-57.

Case 19.1: LASTLY STRESS AND STRAIN BROKEDOWN*

Alok Tiwari left his home in East Delhi at 5.20 A. M. and moved for the 30-mile drive to Gurgaon. He hoped he had left early enough to be in front of the rush hour traffic entering the city. He was not thinking about distance, but only for a job opportunity he had to pursue, as Mr. Tiwari had not been employed full-time for nearly two years. Though he was an electrician with over seven years of experience, he had failed the licensing test to become a master electrician three times. Although

* The case is real to the knowledge of the author. However, for ethical reasons, the names of the individuals are disguised.

he had had more time to study and prepare for test in recent months because of lack of work, many days he did not work were occupied with house-hold chores and caring for his two young children—a daughter and a son. Both were of school age.

Alok's wife, Sushma was teaching Science and Math at middle school standard in the Ahlcon Public School, Delhi for the last twelve years. Her work had been interrupted two times for the birth of their children. When Alok was employed full time and Sushma was teaching, their daily lives were very hectic. Both had to get up very early in the morning to get sufficient time to wake up the children, give them bath, feed them and get them dressed, and take them to school and day care. As Alok had to report for work by 7.00 A.M., Sushma used to handle the children and arrive at her school by 8.30 A.M. Alok's finishing time to his work day was also unpredictable than Sushma's. Many days Alok was required to work beyond 6.00 P.M. Naturally, only Sushma had to pick up the children from day care, prepare evening meal, help the children in their home works, and perform other household tasks without Alok's assistance. The fact remains that both Alok and Sushma were obviously extremely busy and nearly exhausted by early in the evening. Moreover, Sushma usually had school work (assignments, tests to evaluate, and students' other performance to evaluate) also to complete in the evening itself because she did not get time in the morning. Though she enjoyed teaching very much, but she was becoming increasingly frustrated. The reason being more of her teaching day was taken up with student discipline problems, meetings with parents, and other non-teaching tasks. She along with her other colleagues had concluded that 13- and 14- year olds were undoubtedly the toughest age group to teach effectively.

Despite the difficulties Alok and Sushma had while both worked full-time, neither of them anticipated the problems associated with Alok's under-employment. For the last year Alok has worked, on everage, two days a week. On Sundays, he would arrange for repair and other minor electrical works for neighbours and others. Uncertainty of his future work and irregularity of his work not only reduced family income but also created much disruption of their daily lives. Their already complicated situation culminated to the breaking point shortly after Alok arrived home from Gurgaon at 7.15 P.M. from his first full day of work in nearly four weeks.

As Alok pulled the gateway of his home, he was greeted by a police inspector: What happened late today in the school day, an seventh class student, namely, Bharat Dogra, who had not only been difficult, but at times abusive also, badly confronted Sushma and struck her with his belt. By this time, the school medical officer gave first aid and had bandage on Sushma's forehead. The police inspector had come to their home to gather additional information for the filing of the charges against the difficult boy-Bharat Dogra. When Alok entered the house, he found Sushma in a very emotional and distraught condition. Her face turned bright red. The moment Sushma saw Alok, she brokedown and started sobbing. She told Alok that she could not go to the school the next day and that she wanted to quit teaching. Later in the night, Alok concluded that she might be having a nervous breakdown backed by heavy work stress and strain.

QUESTIONS

1. Identify and analyse sources of stress for both Alok and Sushma.
2. Briefly outline a programme of preventive stress management for Sushma.

20

COMMUNICATION

"People do not get along because they fear each other. People fear each other because they do not know each other. People do not know each other because they have not communicated with each other." – ***Martin Luther King***

"Barriers break when people talk." – ***Airtel Advertisement***

Learning Objectives

After studying this chapter, you should be able to:

- **Explain** the meaning of communication
- **Describe** the nature of and need for communication.
- **Outline** the process involved in communication
- **Discuss** channels of communication.
- **Identify** major barriers inhibiting effective communication in organisations.
- **State** the problems of communication.
- **Suggest** how communication can be made effective.

In order to accomplish the organisational goals, the managers have to frequently communicate their employees the necessary information, decisions, ideas, suggestions, so on and so forth. As per same studies, more than 75% of manager's time is spent in communicating with others[1]. In fact, this underlines the significance of communication in organisations. The success of an organisation depends, to a great deal, on effective communication. It is, therefore, important to understand the dynamics of communication. This chapter, therefore, addresses the meaning, functions, process, barriers to and problems of communication. At the end, it also discusses how communication can be made effective.

20.1 WHAT IS MEANT BY COMMUNICATION ?

The word 'communication' is derived from the Latin word *'communis'* which means common. If a person affects a communication, he has established a common ground of understanding. Thus, communication involves imparting the common meaning in another person. Let us also consider some definitions of communication.

According to Hudson[2], "Communication in its simplest form is conveying of information from one person to another."

In the words of Allen[3], "Communication is the sum of all things one person does when he wants to create understanding in the mind of another. It is a bridge of meaning. It involves a systematic and continuous process of telling, listening and understanding."

Stephen P. Robbins[4] views that communication refers to transference and understanding of meaning.

Thus, communication means transference of messages or exchange of ideas, facts, opinion or feelings by two or more persons. It is the act of making one's ideas and opinions known to others. Thus, communication does not simply involve sending of a message by one person. It also involves the receiver listening to it, interpreting it, and responding to it or acting according to it.

20.2 NATURE OF AND NEED FOR COMMUNICATION

The very nature of communication flowing from above definitions may be outlined as follows:

1. Communication involves two parties, one who transmits and one who receives the message.
2. The two respective parties must have ability to convey and listen to what the sender has to communicate.
3. Communication includes sending the message and also receiving the response to the message.
4. The message may be conveyed verbally, in writing, by means of signs, gestures or symbols.
5. Communication is a contineous process. It pervades the entire organisation.

The need for communication is best explained by the fact that an idea, no matter how great, is useless until it is transmitted and understood by others. The need for communication is also felt for the following reasons:

1. Adequate and timely communication helps managers discharge their functions of planning, organising, staffing, directing, and controlling.
2. Effective communication ensures willing cooperation of others. This, in turn, contributes to higher efficiency in job performance.
3. A good communication system communicating quality information contributes positively to the quality of decisions.
4. Communication by flowing information throughout the organisation maintains coordination of activities across departments in the organisation.
5. Effective communication also helps in moulding attitudes and building up employee morale. It also helps in developing harmonious labour-management relations.

20.3 PROCESS OF COMMUNICATION

The process of communication includes the following seven elements: (1) communicator, (2) encoding, (3) message, (4) medium, (5) decoding, (6) receiver, and (7) feedback. These are shown in Fig. 20.1. Each of these components needs due elaboration.

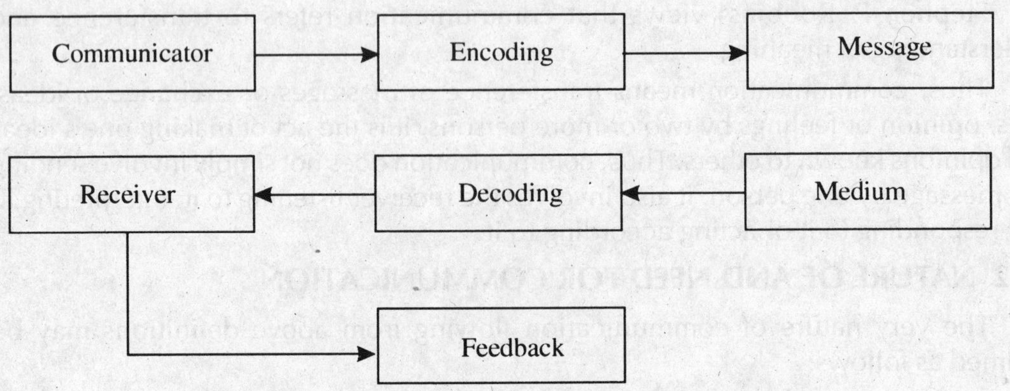

Fig. 20.1: Elements of Communication Process

1. **Communicator:** The communication process begins with the who has an intended message to communicate. The characteristics of the communicator influence the communication process. For example, while a sensitive communicator will look at the communication process from the receiver's perspective, an insensitive one will be primarily concerned with his/her own interest[5].

2. **Encoding:** It refers to converting a communication message into symbolic form. Encoding is necessary because information can only be transmitted from communicator to receiver through symbols or gestures.

3. **Message:** The message is the actual physical product from the source of encoding. When we speak, the speech is the message. When we write, the writing is the message. When we gesture, the movements of our arms, the expressions on our face are the message. Thus, message is what is communicated.

4. **Medium:** Medium is a channel through which a communication message travels. Medium is the link that connects the communicator (sender) and the receiver. Face-to-face verbal communication, use of telephone, use of memorandum, notice, circulars, statements, etc. are the various means available as media of communication. Besides, non-verbal media like signals, symbols, gestures, etc. may also be used. The choice of medium assumes significance as the use of proper medium also determines the effectiveness of communication. The medium/channel is discussed, in detail subsequenty, under 20.4 **Channels of Communication.**

5. **Decoding:** Translating the sender's message by the receiver is called **decoding.** Decoding is the process by which the receiver draws meaning from the symbols encoded by the communicator or sender. One's knowledge, attitude, and cultural background influence one's ability to encode or receive, just as they do the ability to send.

6. **Receiver:** The person who receives the message is called receiver. The communication process is incomplete without the existence of receiver of message. Communication to be effective needs to be receiver-oriented.

7. **Feedback:** The actual response of the receiver to the message communicated to him is known as "feedback". In other words, if a communicator or sender decodes the message that he encodes, if the message is put back into his system, we have feedback[6]. Feedback enables the communicator to check whether or not the message received has been properly understood by the receiver.

20.4 CHANNELS OF COMMUNICATION

The channel is the medium or path through which the message travels. The channels of communication can be divided on the following three bases:

(a) Based on Relationship

(b) Based on Direction of Flow, and

(c) Based on Method Used

Fig. 20.2 also depicts the channels of communication based on these bases.

Now, a brief description of these follows :

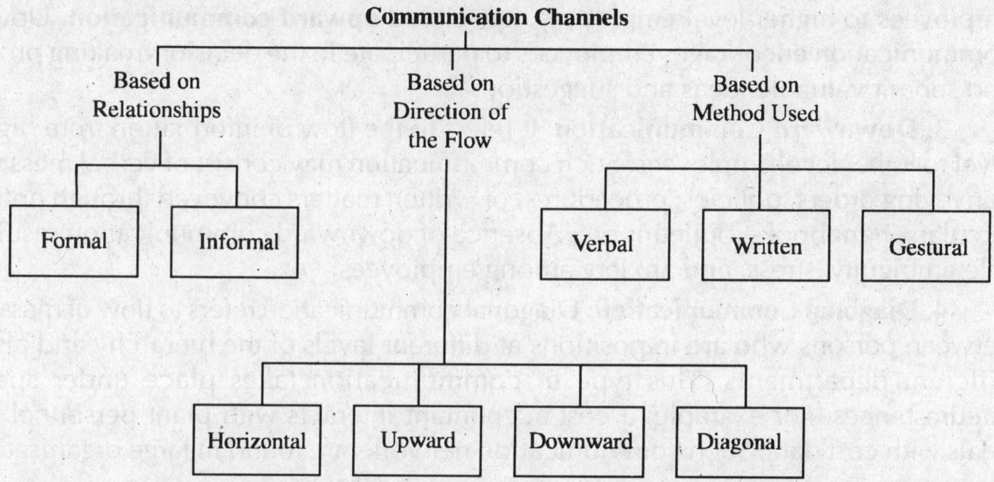

Fig 20.2: Types of Channels of Communication

(a) Based on Relationship

Based on relationship, communication may be of two broad types: (1) formal, and (2) informal.

1. **Formal Communication:** The channels of communications established formally by the management are called **'formal communication'**. In other words, the formal chennels of communication are used for the transmission of official messages within or outside organisation. It derives its support from scalar chain of organisation[7]. However, formal communication which intends to travel through more than one level suffers from delay and also chances of distortion.

2. **Informal Communication:** Communication which takes place on the basis of informal or social relations among people in an organisation is known as informal communication. Thus, informal communication can take place between persons cutting accross positions held by people working in different divisions and units. Hence, it is also known as *'grapevine'*.

One characteristic feature of informal communication is that it spreads very rapidly among people. Distortions may appear in the transmission of such messages through grapevine in the form of rumours and gossips. No one is held responsible for it, nor is it taken seriously[8].

(b) Based on Direction of Flow

Based on direction of flow, chennels of communication are of four types: (1) horizontal, (2) upward, (3) downward, and (4) diagonal.

1. **Horizontal Communication:** Also called lateral communication, horizontal communication takes place between peers. In other words, it refers to transmission of information among positions of the same level. This facilitates coordination among peers or people working on the same levels. Horizontal communication is more of informal nature[9].

2. **Upward Communication:** When communication flows from lower-level employees to higher-level employees, it is called **upward communication.** Upward communication encourages employees to participate in the decision-making process and submit valuable ideas and suggestions[10].

3. **Downward Communication:** It refers to the flow of information from higher-level to lower level employees. Such communication may consist of verbal messages, conveying orders, policies, procedures, or written matters conveyed through notices, circulars, handbooks, bulletins etc. Absence of downward communication results in role ambiguity, stress, and anxiety among employees.

4. **Diagonal Communication:** Diagonal communication refers to flow of messages between persons who are in positions at different levels of the hierarchy and also in different departments. This type of communication takes place under special circumstances. For example, a cost accountant interacts with plant personnel who deals with cost data. Such communication networks are found in large organisations.

(c) Based on Method Used

On the basis of methods used for the purpose, communication may be: (1) verbal, (2) written, and (3) gestural.

1. **Verbal Communication:** When the message is conveyed orally, it is called **verbal communication**. It produces in communication a personal touch. Verbal communication is the most economical both in terms of time and money[11]. However, its greatest drawback, if any, is its non-applicability especially when the communicator and receiver are at places far away from one another and the number of persons to be communicated is large.

2. **Written Communication:** Communication that takes place between people in written form is callled **written communication**. Formal communication is usually in written form such as orders, instructions, reports, bulletins, etc. Communication being in written form is permanent, tangible, and verifiable. It is useful when subject matter to be communicated is lengthy and it intends to be communicated to a large number of people. Limitations of written communication are that it is time-consuming, lacks personal touch and unfolds the secrecy about the written message.

3. **Gestural Communication:** When the message transmitted through some gestures, it is called **gestural communication**. People use different gestures such as moving hands and eyes to communicate their views, ideas, etc. If the superior pats his subordinate on his back, it is understood as appreciation for work. This is an example of gestural communication.

20.5 COMMUNICATION NETWORKS

What is communication network? Simply stating, a communication network is defined as a channel by which information flows. In other words, a communication network is the pattern of communication channels between group members or among positions in an organisational structure. The channels are one of two varieties : either formal or informal. These are just discussed in the preceding section. Communication networks influence the functioning of a group, and different types of networks have been studied to examine their effects on such things as the speed of problem solving, accuracy in transmitting information, and the satisfaction of the group members.

In organisations, communication flows among groups of individuals in different patterns. Fig. 20.3 illustrates the five most common communication networks. These are the circle, the wheel, the chain, the Y, and the all-channel networks.

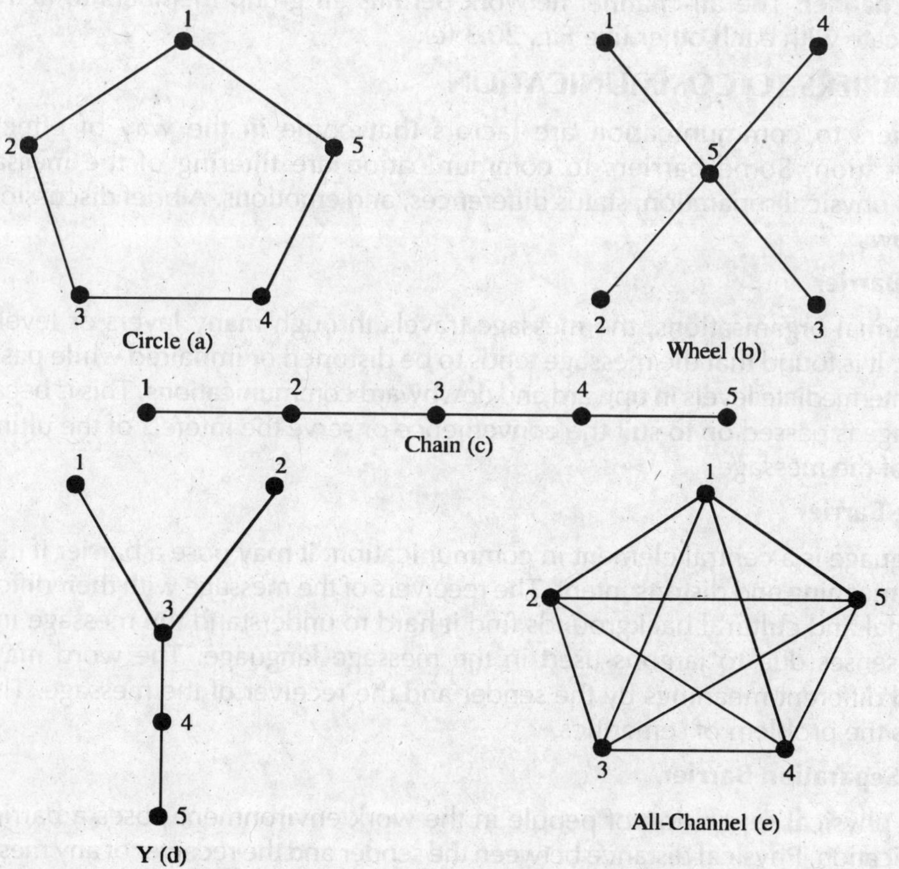

Fig. 20.3: Communication Networks.

Circle: It is the network where each member of the group can interact with the adjoining member, as illustrated by Figure 20.3 (*a*). The circle network is the highly decentralized because each position can communicate directly with two other positions in the network. No one can communicate directly with everyone.

Wheel: In case of wheel network, one person (a supervisor for example) can communicate with (say) four workers, but the workers do not communicate with each other. The wheel relies on the leader to act as the central conduit for all the group's communication [Fig. 20.3 (*b*)]. Since all communication passes through the center position, the wheel is the most centralized communication network.

Chain: The chain rigidly follows the formal chain of command. In this network, one person transmits information to another as per the chain in the organisational hierarchy. For example, the president informs the vice-president who then passes on the same information to the head of the department, who tells his/her manager, who passes on to the supervisor, who then informs the employee. Fig. 20.3 (*c*) represents such a chain.

Y Network: In this type of network, two people report to a superior or boss who occupies two positions above as shown in Fig. 20.3 (*d*).

All-Channel: The all-channel network permits all group members to actively communicate with each other like Fig. 20.3 (*e*).

15.6 BARRIERS TO COMMUNICATION

Barriers to communication are factors that come in the way of effective communication. Some barriers to communication are filtering of the message, language, physical separation, status differences, and emotions. A brief discussion of each follows.

Filtering Barrier

In formal organisations, the message travels through many layers or levels of hierarchy. It is found that the message tends to be distorted or impaired while passing through intermediate levels in upward and downward communications. This is because the message is passed on to suit the convenience or serve the interest of the ultimate receiver of the message.

Language Barrier

Language is a central element in communication. It may pose a barrier if its use obscures meaning and distorts intent. The receivers of the message with their different educational and cultural backgrounds find it hard to understand the message in the senders' senses due to jargons used in the message language. The word may be attributed different meanings by the sender and the receiver of the message. This is known as the problem of semantics.

Physical Separation Barrier

The physical separation of people in the work environment poses a barrier to communication. Physical distance between the sender and the receiver of any message serves an obstacle to effective communication. This is because the difficulty involved in evaluating whether the receiver has understood, accepted, and acted upon the message sent to him when his workplace is far away from that of the sender of the message.

Status Barrier

Status differences related to power and the organisational hierarchy pose another barrier to communication among people at work, especially within manager-employee pairs. It is due to the status difference that subordinates often suppress or withhold information which may not be liked by their superiors, or pass on distorted information to please their superiors[12]. On the other side, status consciousness of the superiors prevents them from fully communicating information to their subordinates.

Emotional Barrier

When people are eloquent with emotions, it influences their understanding of the message accordingly. Psychological barriers do also impair effectiveness of communication. When the subordinates hold favourable image of the superior, they become psychologically more inclined to accept and respond positively to the message sent by the superior. Obviously, it does not happen so when they have an unfavourable image of their superior. The image is built on the basis of experience and interaction between the superior and the subordinate. Any change when its effects are uncertain also creates psychological barriers to effective communication in an organisation.

20.7 HOW TO MAKE COMMUNICATION EFFECTIVE ?

In view of the barriers to effective communication, the following specific suggestions can be made to ensure the effectiveness of communication:

1. **Language:** Experience suggests that complex language, technical terms, and jargon make communication difficult to understand and frustrating to the listener. It is not true that complex ideas require complex words to explain them. Hence, while preparing the communication message, its language should be relatively simple and the ability of the receiver to interpret the message accurately should be kept in view. Efforts should be made to explain abstract ideas and avoid the vague expressions.

2. **Regulating the Flow of Communication:** Priority of messages to be communicated should be determined so that the managers may concentrate on more important messages of high priority. Similarly, the messages received should be edited and condensed, to the extent possible, to reduce the chances of overlooking or ignoring important messages.

3. **Feedback:** Communication is complete when it receives feedback. Feedback may include the receiver's response in terms of acceptance and understanding of the message, his/her action, and the result achieved. Thus, the two-way communication is considered to be more helpful in establishing mutual understanding than one-way communication.

4. **Repitition:** Repitition of message helps improve effectiveness of communication. It helps the listener interpret messages that are ambiguous, unclear, or too difficult to understand the first time they are heard. Repitition also helps avoid the problem of forgetting. A popular strategy to help the managers remember the main points is **"Tell them what you're going to tell them, then tell them what you've told them."**

5. **Restraint Over Emotions:** As strong feelings and emotions on the part of either the sender or receiver of the message distort the meaning of the message. One may, therefore, defer the communication for some time. He/she should respond to communication with a composed mind only.

6. **Mutual Trust and Faith:** Communication becomes effective having mutual trust and faith between the sender and receiver of the message. The honesty of the purpose is the best means breeding trust and faith between the two parties, *i.e.* sender and receiver.

7. **Listening Carefully:** Misunderstanding and confusion are often caused by the half-hearted attention to the communication[13]. Therefore, a receiver-listener needs to be patient mentally well composed, and avoid distractions while receiving the message. He/she should seek clarification, if necessary, on the message. At the same time, the sender of the message must also be prepared to listen to what the receiver has to say, and respond to his questions, if any.

8. **Pygmalion Effect:** In the ancient Greek mythology, a sculptor named Pygmalion carved the statue of a most beautiful woman. The result was so perfect that the sculptor fell in love with the statue and sat in front of it for a long time. He sat in front of it hoping that some day the statue will come to life – and it ultimately happened. Since then, this is called the '**Pygmalion Effect**'. Thus, the Pygmalion effect refers to power of one's expectation. In other words, people's expectations determine their behaviour. Let it be clarified with an example. If a Professor believes that a particular student is not very hard working and sincere, then all his/her communication, be it verbal or non-verbal, will communicate this message to the student. What will happen is in the long run, a perfectly hard-working student may become lazy and insincere.

Ten Tips to Becoming a Better Listener

The following are ten tips to help one become a better listener:

1. **Stop talking.** You cannot listen if your mouth is moving.
2. **Put the speaker at ease.** Break the ice to help the speaker relax. Smile!
3. **Show the speaker you want to listen.** Put away your work. Do not look at your watch. Maintain good eye contact.
4. **Remove distractions.** Close your door. Do not answer the telephone.
5. **Empathize with the speaker.** Put yourself in the speaker's shoes.
6. **Be patient.** Not everyone delivers messages at the same pace.
7. **Hold your temper.** Do not fly off the handle.
8. **Go easy on criticism**. Criticizing the speaker can stifle communication.
9. **Ask questions.** Paraphrase and clarify the speaker's message.
10. **Stop talking.** By this stage, you are probably very tempted to start talking, but do not. Be sure the speaker has finished.

Following are ten commandments of good communication developed by the **American Management Association:**

1. Clarify before attempting to communicate.
2. Examine the purpose of communication.
3. Understand the physical and human environment when communicating.
4. In planning communication, consult others to obtain their support, as well as the factors.

5. Consider the content and overtones of the message.
6. Whenever possible, communicate something that helps, or is valued by the receiver.
7. Communication, to be effective, requires following up.
8. Communicate messages that are of short-run and long-run importance.
9. Actions must be congruent with communication.
10. Be a good listener.

SUMMARY

This summary is organized by the 'learning objectives' given on page no. 342.

- *Communication means transmission of messages or exchange of ideas, facts, opinion or feelings by two or more persons. Communication does not only involve sending a message but also its acceptance by the receiver.*
- *Communication involves two parties, one sender and other receiver of the message. The message may be communicated verbally, in writing, through gestures, signs or symbols. Communication is a continuous process in organisations. It involves seven elements; (1) communicator; (2) encoding, (3) message, (4) medium, (5) decoding, (6) receiver, and (7) feedback.*
- *Communication channels may be of two broad types: Formal and Informal. Formal channels are based on organisational relationship. These correspond to the chain of command. Informal channels are based on personal relationship and are not established by the management. Both formal and informal channels may be of different types such as, horizontal, vertical, diagonal, verbal, written, and gestural.*
- *The channel by which the message flows is called communication network. The most common channel networks found in organisations are the circle, the wheel, the chain, the Y, and the all-channel networks.*
- *Filtering, language, physical separation, status differences, and emotions are potential communication barriers that can be overcome.*
- *Specific suggestions like language simplicity, regulating the flow of communication, repitition, restraint over emotions, mutual trust and faith, and listening carefully may help make communication more effective.*
- *Communication plays a vital role in leadership and power and politics. These are discussed in the next two chapters.*

REVIEW QUESTIONS

1. Define communication. Why is communication of vital importance to management?
2. Explain the elements of the communication process.
3. Discuss in detail the various channels of communication which are generally used in modern business enterprises.
4. What are the common barriers to effective communication ? How can they be overcome?
5. What is meant by communication network? Discuss the various types of communication networks.

6. What do you understand by upward and downward communication in an organisation? What are the rules of effective communication?
7. Write notes on:
   (*a*) Status Barrier to Communication
   (*b*) Communication Channels
   (*c*) Communication Network
   (*d*) Formal Communication
   (*e*) Verbal Communication
   (*f*) Language Barrier

REFERENCES

1. H. Mintzberg: **The Nature of Managerial Work,** Harper and Row, New York, 1973.
2. Cyril L. Hudson: **Business Organisation and Operation,** Staples Press, London, 1970, p. 158.
3. Louis A. Allen: **Management and Organisation**, McGraw-Hill, Tokyo, 1958, p. 154.
4. Stephen P. Robbins : ***op. cit.,*** 1998, p. 310.
5. Kae H. Chung and Leon C. Megginson: **Organisation Behaviour,** Harper and Row, New York, 1981, p. 193.
6. D.K. Berlo: **The Process of Communication,** Rinehart & Winston, Holt, New York, 1960, p. 103.
7. Keith Davis: **Human Behaviour at Work**, Tata McGraw-Hill, Bombay, 1977.
8. L.M. Prasad: Formal and Informal Communication in India, **ISTD Review,** May-June 1976, pp. 17-20.
9. Dalton E. Mc Farland: **Management**: **Foundations and Practices**, Macmillan, New York 1979, p. 568.
10. L.M. Prasad: An Assessment of Upward Communication in a Public Sector Organisation, **Lok Udyog**, July 1976, pp. 35-41.
11. Rekha Agarwal: Communication Behaviour and Technological Environment of a Manufacturing Organisation, **Indian Management**, February 1974, pp. 39-43.
12. L.M. Prasad: Why Subordinates are not Willing to Communicate up? **Integrated Management**, June 1977.
13. Ralph G. Nichols: Listening is Good Business, **Management of Personnel Quarterly**, Winter, 1962, pp. 2-9.

Case 20.1: Misunderstanding between Workers and Management

For Mr. Ranjan, the General Manager of a textile manufacturing company, personal successes have come as though they had been programmed by a computer. During a long career at the company, which he had joined as an humble assistant, promotions came one after another culminating in his elevation to the present post.

But no sooner had Mr. Ranjan taken over the new job then problems began to pile up for him. The most upsetting of these was a threatened strike by the workers of the company on the

question of bonus. The workers demanded five months bonus as against months bonus conceded by the company which, even as it was, was more than any identical unit in the industry had given for a year.

Though the proposed strike did not materialise as a result of intervention by the local administration, the workers were not convinced of the rightness of the company's stand. They had a feeling that the management deliberately understated profits so as to deny the workers their legitimate due. Many other stories had been circulating about an alleged wickedness on the part of management in that it spent lavishly on the maintenance of the managerial staff, but was very stingy when it came to providing benefits to workers. As one labour leader put it "Let the management not gloat over its victory. They do not know how terribly they are harming the interests of the company by alienating workers. Secretiveness in management is all right to some extent. But it should not be practised so as to render the workers, who are no less important members of the organisation, strangers in their own work place."

QUESTIONS

1. Do you think the present situation in the company is due to lack of proper communication between management and workers?
2. What steps would you suggest to bridge the communication gap? (*Utkal University, MBA, 1998*)

Case 20.2: Communication Problem with Communication Manager

Mr. Gautam Ghosh founded a small radio manufacturing plant in Western India in the late sixties. From this small beginning came one of the country's largest radio, television and allied products companies. By 1996, it had recorded annual sales of Rs. 800 million, with 25,000 employees and 8 manufacturing locations. Throughout its growth, the founder remained an active, imaginative and driving force behind his company. In earlier days, every manager and worker knew him, and he was able to call most of them by their first names; so even after the company grew fairly large, people felt they knew the founder and chief executive, and their strong feeling of personal loyalty had much to do with the fact that the company's workers never formed a union.

However, as the company prospered and grew, Mr. Ghosh thought that it was losing its "small company" spirit. He also felt that communications were suffering, that his objectives and philosophy were not being understood in the company, that much wasteful duplication was occurring through poor knowledge of what others in the company were doing, and that new product development and marketing were suffering as a result. Likewise, he was concerned that he had lost touch with the people. To solve the communication problem, he hired a Director of communications reporting directly to him. The issues were discussed in detail between the two. They then put into effect every communication device they found in other large companies, namely:

(*a*) bulletin boards in every office and plant throughout the country,

(*b*) a revitalised company newsletter carrying detailed company and personal news affecting all locations, (*c*) "Company Facts Book" for every employee, giving significant information about the company,

(*d*) regular profit-sharing letters,

(*e*) company-sponsored courses to teach communication methods,

(*f*) monthly one-day meetings at headquarters for the Top 100 executives,

(*g*) annual three-day meetings of 900 executives at all levels, at a resort town, and

(*h*) a large number of special committees to discuss company matters.

After much time, effort and expense spread over a year, Mr. Ghosh was disappointed to find that his problems of communication and of the "small company" feeling still existed and that the results of his programmes did not seem to be significant.

Read the above case carefully and answer the following questions after analysing it in the light of your knowledge about the subject-matter of communication.

QUESTIONS

(*a*) Why do you think Mr. Ghosh was disappointed? Should he have been?

(*b*) What do you see as the company's real communication problem?

(*c*) What would you suggest to improve communication in the company?

(*d*) Was Mr. Ghosh right in believing that communication would help him maintain the 'small company' spirit? [*C.A. Intermediate (New), May 1999*]

21

LEADERSHIP

"To lead the people, walk behind them." — ***Lao-Tzu***

"Leadership is about creating a vision, communicating that vision to one's followers, and exhorting them to move towards that vision." — ***N.R. Narayana Murthy***

Learning Objectives

After studying this chapter, you should be able to:

- **Define** leadership and distinguish between leadership and management.
- **Discuss** the functions performed by leaders.
- **Describe** the major styles of leadership.
- **Explain** major theories of leadership.
- **Examine** the leadership styles exercised in the Indian organisations.
- **List** and **describe** the major determinants of effective leadership.
- **Differentiate** between transactional and transformational leadership.
- **Identify** and **describe** "substitutes for," or "neutralisers of" leadership.

People working in organisations need to be led to work on a definite direction to accomplish the organisational goals successfully. This is because without leadership, an organisation would be only a confusion of people and machines, just as an orchestra without a conductor would be only musicians and instruments. Hence, like orchestra, organisations also require leadership to use their precious assets to the fullest. As such, leadership become the focus and conduit of most of other areas of organisational behaviour. This chapter is, therefore, intended to discuss the various aspects of leadership in organisations. To begin with, first let us clarify what we mean by the term **leadership**.

21.1 WHAT IS LEADERSHIP ?

Leadership is a term that conjures up different images in different people. While to some it means charisma, to others, it means power and authority. One expert[1], puts that there are almost so many definitions of leadership as there are persons who have attempted to define the term. Let us present a few important definitions of leadership.

According to George K. Terry[2] "Leadership is the activity of influencing people to strive willingly for group objectives.

Koontz[3] et. al. have defined leadership "as the art or process of influencing people so that they will strive willingly and enthusiastically towards the achievement of group goals."

In the opinion of Chester Barnard[4], "Leadership is the quality of behaviour of individuals whereby they guide people or their activities in organising efforts."

After going through the above definitions of leadership, it can safely be defined as a process of influencing group activities towards the achievement of certain goals. **Formal leadership** occurs when an organisation officially bestows upon a leader the power and authority to guide and direct others in the organisations. **Informal leadership** occurs when others in the organisation unofficially accord a person the power and influence to guide and direct their behaviour.

The person who guides or influences the behaviour of others is called 'leader' and people guided or influenced are called the 'followers'.

The main characteristics flowing from the preceding definitions of leadership are as follows :

1. Leadership is a continuous process of influencing others' behaviour.
2. Leadership is basically a personal quality that enables leader to influence the subordinates' behaviour at work.
3. The success of a leader depends on the acceptance of his leadership by the followers. Of course, the situational variables also affect the effectiveness of leadership.
4. There is a relationship between leader and followers which arises out of functioning for a common goal.

Following are yet some more hallmarks of effective or successful leadership:

- The best example of leadership is leadership by example.
- A leader is one who knows the way, goes the way, and shows the way.
- The function of leadership is to produce more leaders, not more followers.
- The leader takes people where they want to go – A great leader takes people where they don't necessarily want to go, but ought to go.
- A leader must have courage to act against experts, advice.
- Management is doing things right – leadership is doing the right things.
- He that cannot obey cannot command.

21.2 LEADERSHIP DIFFERS FROM MANAGEMENT

Some people treat leadership and management as 'synonymous'. However, leadership differs from management. While leadership, as you have already learnt, involves influencing people to strive towards the achievement of group goals, management involves planning, organising, staffing, directing and controlling group activities to accomplish organisational goals. In sum and substance, managers manage things, while leaders lead people[5]. Leadership is a part of management but not all of it. This implies that a strong leader can be a weak manager because he/she is weak in other managerial activities like planning and organising. The reverse is also possible. A manager can be a weak leader and still be an acceptable manager, especially if he happens to manage people who have strong inner achievement drives[6].

Differences between leadership and management on various bases are tabulated in the following Table 21.1.

Table 21.1: Differences between Leadership and Management

Leadership	Management
1. Leader leads people.	Manager manages things.
2. Leader can use his/her informal influence.	Managers hold formal positions.
3. Leaders create a vision and inspire others to achieve this vision.	Managers achieve results by directing the activities of others.
4. Leader possesses non-sanctioned influencing ability.	Manager enjoys formal designated authority.
5. Leader inspires enthusiasm.	Manager engenders fear.

Warren Bennis and Burt Nanus[7] have differentiated leadership from management by stating that **"managers are people who do things right, and leaders are people who do the right thing. Management's efficiency lies in climbing the ladder of success, leadership determines whether the ladder is leaning against the right wall."**

Zaleznik's distinction between leaders and managers is similar to the distinction made between transactional and transformational leaders discussed later in the chapter.

Table 21.2: Leaders and Managers

Personality Dimension	Manager	Leader
Attitudes toward goals	Has an impersonal, passive, functional attitude; believes goals arise out of necessity and reality.	Has a personal and active attitude; believes goals arise from desire and imagination.
Conceptions of work	Views work as an enabling process that combines people, ideas, and things: seeks moderate risk through coordination and balance.	Looks for fresh approaches to old problems; seeks highrisk positions, especially with high payoffs.
Relationships with others	Avoids solitary work activity, preferring to work with others; avoids close, intense relationships; avoids conflict.	Is comfortable in solitary work activity; encourages close, intense working relationships; is not conflict averse.
Sense of self	Is once born; makes a straightforward life adjustment; accepts life as it is.	Is twice born; engages in a struggle for a sense of order in life: questions life.

Having made distinction between leadership and management, let us know what leaders actually do in organisations.

21.3 FUNCTIONS OF LEADERSHIP

Leadership functions of a manager are closely related with managerial functions he performs. Nonetheless, the leadership functions are somewhat different. As a leader, the manager has to perform some other functions as well. Following are the important ones:

1. **Developing Team Work:** One of the primary functions of the leader is to develop and combine his followers as a team. Given the followers' competence, potential and needs, the leader needs to create a congenial and healthy working environment for his work-team.

2. **Representing the Team:** In organisations, the leader serves as a linking-pin between his/her team members and management. As and when required, the leader communicates the problems and grievances of his subordinates to the management, and also helps solve problems by participating in problem-solving process.

3. **Counselling the Work Men:** When team members face problems in doing their work, they seek guidance and advice from their leader. The problems may be technical or emotional in nature.

4. **Managing Time:** One of the functions of the leader is to ensure the timely completion of activities undertaken by his/her team members. He has to appreciate the trite saying **"a stich in time saves nine."**

5. **Using Proper Power:** Leader has to exercise his power and authority over his subordinates as per the demand of the situation. Exercise of power needs to stimulate positive response from the subordinates.

6. **Securing Group Effectiveness:** The manager leader needs to provide for a reward system to improve the efficiency of capable workmen, delegate authority, and invite participation of employees in decision making. Availability of necessary and adequate resources and communicating necessary information to the employees also help leader secure effectiveness of group-effort.

21.4 LEADERSHIP STYLES

The ways the leader influences his/her followers is called 'leadership styles'. There are three basic styles of leadership:

1. Autocratic or Authoritative Style
2. Democratic or Participative Style
3. Laissez-Faire or Free-Rein Style.

Let us discuss these in details.

Autocratic or Authoritative Style

In autocratic style, the leader centralises power and decision-making in himself/herself. The leader commands complete control over the subordinates who are compelled to obey the orders. The subordinates have no opportunity to make suggestions or take part in decision-making function. The autocratic leader has little concern for the well-being of employees. In turn, employees have a tendency to avoid responsibility and try to work as little as possible. They also suffer from frustration and low morale.

The autocratic leadership style is subject to several **limitations**. The main ones are:

1. It results in low morale and job dissatisfaction.
2. Employees efficiency tends to decline over period.
3. Potential manager-leader employees do not get opportunity to exhibit their capabilities.

However, the autocratic style of leadership is **suitable** in the following situations when:

1. The subordinates are incompetent and inexperienced.
2. The leader wants to be active and dominant in decision-making.
3. The leader is highly competent for making a right decision.

Democratic or Participative Style

In democratic style of leadership, the leader takes decision in consultation with the subordinates. In other words, the subordinates participate in decision-making function. Hence, the style is also known as participative style. Participation in decision-making enables subordinates to satisfy their social and ego needs. It also makes them more committed to their organisations. Frequent interaction between the manager-leader and subordinates also helps build up mutual faith and confidence.

Several **benefits** offered by the democratic style of leadership are:

1. It gives opportunity to the subordinates to develop their potential abilities and assume greater responsibilities.
2. It provides job satisfaction, on the one hand, and improves the morale of subordinates, on the other.
3. Subordinates' participation in decision-making helps make right decision because **'two heads are better than one'.**

Despite the above benefits, democratic style of leadership cannot be regarded as the best style under all situations. It also suffers from the following **limitations**:

1. Decision-making is a time-consuming process in democratic style.
2. There is possibility that a few dominant subordinates may influence decision in their favour.
3. The responsibility for implementing decision cannot be fixed on an individual subordinate but on the whole group.
4. Sometimes the decisions taken become the distorted one because **'many cooks spoil the broth'.**

However, the democratic style is found suitable in the following situations when:

1. Subordinates are competent and experienced.
2. The leader prefers participative-decision making.
3. The organisation has made its objectives transparent to the employees.
4. Reward and involvement are used as the primary means of motivation and control.

Laissez Faire Style

Laissez faire style is just the opposite of autocratic style. In laissez faire style, the manager-leader leaves decision-making to the subordinates. The leader completely gives up his/her leadership role. The subordinates enjoy full freedom to decide as and what they like. The biggest **limitation** of this style is that, due to full freedom to subordinates, it creates chaos and mismanagement in decision-making.

Nonetheless, laissez faire style is found **suitable** in the following situations when:

1. Leader is able to fully delegate the powers of decision-making to his/her subordinates.
2. Subordinates are also well competent and knowledgeable.
3. Organisational goals and objectives are well communicated to the employees.

Look at Fig. 21.1 which shows diagramatic representation of all these three styles of leadership:

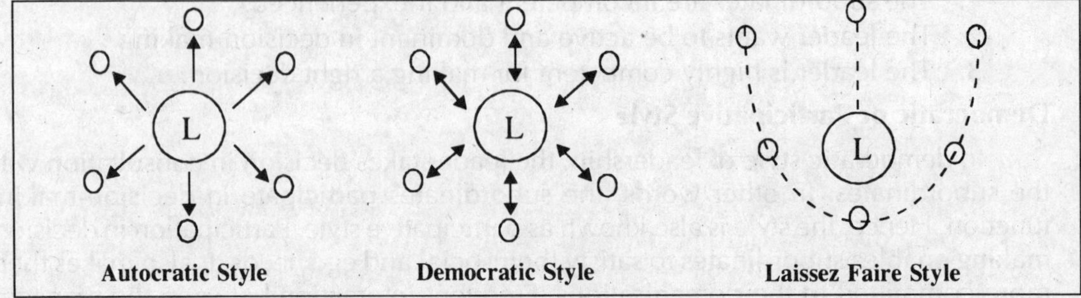

Fig. 21.1: Diagramatic Representation of Leadership Style

Studies on Leadership

Let us also go through some studies on leadership that will help us understand the leadership styles better.

Hawthorne Studies

Studies undertaken by Mayo and Roethlisberger in an electricity company at Illinois in USA, from 1924 to 1932, are popularly known as **Hawthorne Studies**[8]**.** In one phase of their study, the researchers tried to find out if changes in illumination, rest period, and lunch breaks can affect workers' productivity. To the utter surprise of the researchers, it was found that less light, shorter and also fewer rest periods and shorter lunch breaks led to increase in workers' productivity. When all these changes were eliminated and the normal working condition were resumed, it was again found that the workers' productivity and the feeling of being together went up. The reason for increase in the workers' productivity was attributed to the positive attitude of workers towards each other and high feeling of togetherness. This finding is known as Hawthorne effect. These findings enabled Mayo and Roethlisberger to conclude that a leader has not only to plan, organise, lead and control, but also consider the human element which needs recognition and well being. An effective leader needs to incorporate such human elements in his/her style of leading the subordinates.

Iowa Leadership Studies

In 1939, Lippitt and White under the guidance of Lewin, studied three different styles of leadership of ten-year old boys in three groups[9]. The **authoritarian** leader of the group was found not allowing any participation by group members. He was very directive. In another group, the **democratic** leader encouraged participation of the group members in decision-making process. The **laissez-faire** leader of the third group completely gave up leadership and allowed full freedom to the group members in making decisions. In fact, each member of the group was let alone.

The researchers in this study selected boys of the same intelligence level, all making soap carvings in the same room. It was found that the three group leaders assumed different styles as they shifted every six week from group to group. Nineteen out of twenty boys liked the democratic style of leadership. The only boy who liked authoritarian style of leadership happened to be the son of an army officer. Seven out of ten boys preferred the laissez-faire style of leadership to the autocratic one.

One comment made on Iowa studies is that a study on ten years old boys cannot be compared to leader behaviour of adults that too with complex jobs. Despite the above comment, Iowa studies are considered a pioneering effort in understanding leadership styles from the point of scientific methodology. Another significance of these studies lies in the fact that they also threw light on how different styles of leadership can produce different complex reactions from the same or similar groups.

Michigan Studies on Leadership Styles

In his study, Likert[10] of the University of Machigan identified two major styles of leadership orientations **employee orientation** and **production orientation.**

The employee orientation style dealt with the aspects of an individual's job. Such leader poses his/her trust as well as confidence on the subordinates. They feel free to discuss matters relating to their jobs with the leader. Leader also invites ideas and suggestions from the subordinates.

In production orientation, the leader emphasises on production and technical aspects of job. Subordinates are looked as tools to accomplish the organisational goals. In this style, work, working conditions and work methods are understood in depth and detail.

While relating these orientations to the employees' performance, Likert found that the employee-oriented style resulted in higher performance compared to production-oriented one. However, Likert did not find any direct relationship between the satisfaction and productivity of the employees.

Ohio State Studies on Leadership Styles

Stogdill[11], at the Bureau of Business Research in Ohio State University initiated a series of researches on leadership in 1945. The two independent leadership dimensions identified through the researches were **'consideration'** and **'initiating structure'.** The studies were conducted on Air Force Commanders and members of bomber crews, officers, civilian administrators in the Navy Department, executives, teachers, principals and leaders of various civilian groups. The above two concepts were identified by using two types of questionnaires. One was 'Leader Behaviour Description Questionnaire' (LBDO) and the other was Leader Opinion Questionnaire (LOQ).

Consideration reflected the behaviour of the leader indicating his/her relationship with the subordinates. In case of initiating structure, the leader deals with the relationship between himself/herself and the subordinates and tries to define and structure own roles and those of their subordinates towards goal accomplishment.

The observed behaviours of the leader under consideration and initiating structure are shown in Fig. 21.2.

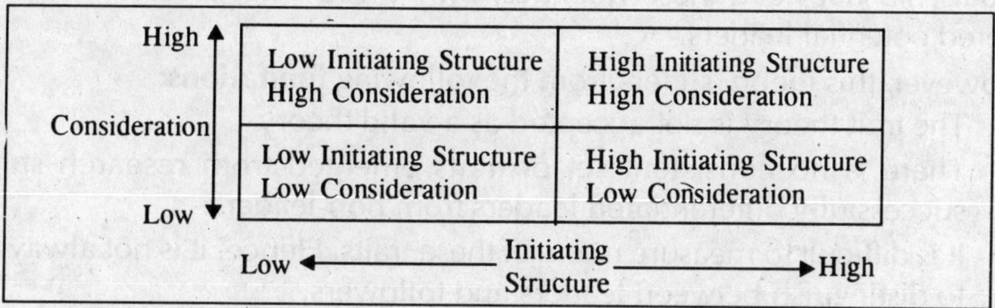

Fig. 21.2: The Ohio State Leadership Quadrants

However, the Ohio State studies suffer from the following two major **limitations**:

1. These studies did not consider other factors such as one's social status within the group, type of technology employed, the psychological rewards from working with a particular type of leader, one's expectation of a particular style that also affect leadership effectiveness.
2. The two types of questionnaires administered at the subordinates and at the leader levels have come in severe criticism because the two are not likely to agreę. This causes a serious measurement problem how is leadership style measured.

Scientific Manager's Style

F. W. Taylor[12] developed a scientific method to manage men at work. His scientific thought of management was based on two scientific experiments, namely, time study and motion study to determine standard time and standard work respectively. According to Taylor, scientific methods used to do jobs help improve workers' performance and, in turn, maximize profits. Scientific management style emphasises that management of a work organisation must be divorced from human affairs and emotions. In fact, people need to adjust to the management and not management to the people. Taylor believes that the leader is supposed to be the most competent individual in planning and organising the work of his/her subordinates. The way he/she does it is called his/her leadership style.

That our familiarity with some important theories of leadership will enrich our understanding of various styles of leadership, we, therefore, now turn our attention to some important theories of leadership.

21.5 LEADERSHIP THEORIES

There are a number of theories which provide explanations regarding various aspects of leadership phenomenon. Here, we are discussing some of the important theories only.

Trait Theory

This is the earliest theory as described by Kelly[13] attempting to classify what personal characteristics like physical, personality and mental, are associated with leadership success. Illustrated traits which researchers attributed to leaders were such aspects as height, weight, physique, good health, high level of energy, good appearance, intelligence, scholarship, good judgement and decision-making, insight, originality, dominance, persistence, self-confidence, ambition, and so on[14]. Since all individuals did not have these qualities, only those who possess them would be considered potential leaders.

However, this theory suffers from the following **limitations:**

1. The trait theory is not accepted as a valid theory.
2. There is no consistent set of traits emerged from research studies that successfully differentiated leaders from non-leaders.
3. It is difficult to measure many of these traits. Hence, it is not always possible to distinguish between leaders and followers.

These limitations made researchers to give up the study of traits to understand leadership and started to focus their efforts on observing the behaviours of leaders. Hence, the behavioural theories of leadership came into existence.

Behavioural Theories

According to the behavioural theories of leadership, leadership can be described in terms of **what leaders do rather than what they are.** In other words, leadership can be identified by reference to their behaviour in relation to the followers. Behavioural theories have been presented mostly on the basis of research studies.

Behavioural theories differ from the trait theories in at least two ways. **First**, actual leader behaviours, not the personal traits were the main focus. **Second**, while most trait theories endeavoured to distinguish between leaders and non-leaders, behavioural theories attempted to determine how different kinds of behaviours affect the performance and satisfaction of the followers.

The two important behavioural theories are Ohio State Unversity studies and the studies of Michigan University. These are already discussed in the preceding section 21.4 **Leadership Styles.**

Fiedler's Contingency Model

According to the contingency theories of leadership, the success of leadership depends upon the situation in which the leader operates. Fred E. Fiedler[16] developed a contingency model of leadership. According to him, a leader's effectiveness depends upon the following three situational factors:

1. **Leader-followers relations**, that is the degree of followers' trust, confidence and respect for the leader.
2. **Task structure**, that is the nature of task performed by the subordinates.
3. **The status power,** that is the degree of power associated with the position or status held by the leader in the organisation.

The most favourable situation for leaders to influence their group is one in which they are well liked by the members, the task performed is highly structured and the leader has enough power attached to his/her position in the organisation. On the other hand, the most unfavourable situation for leaders is one in which they are disliked, the task is highly unstructured and little power is attached to the leader's position.

Path-goal Leadership Theory

Robert House[16] has developed a path-goal theory of leadership initially presented by Martin Evans[17]. This theory is based on the expectancy theory of motivation. The theory states that leaders can exercise four different kinds of styles[18]: **directive leadership** (giving directions to the subordinates rather than seeking their cooperation), **supportive leadership** (being friendly and approachable to subordinates), **participative leadership** (asking for suggestions from subordinates before making decisions), and **achievement-oriented leadership** (setting challenging goals and assignments for subordinates). The path-goal theory postulates that leaders become effective due to their influence on followers' motivation, ability to perform, and their satisfaction. Leader motivates the employees by influencing their expectancies relating to the performance and attractiveness of goal. The subordinates feel satisfied when they believe that their job performance will lead to desirable outcomes. They will be able to achieve their goals with hard work.

Situational Leadership Theory

The situational leadership model is developed by Paul Hersey and Kenneth Blanchard[19] which suggests that the leadership effectiveness depends upon the situation in which leadership is exercised. In their model, the authors have employed two dimensions of leader behaviour as were used in Ohio State University studies as discussed earlier. The two dimensions were task (production-oriented) and relationship (people-oriented). The level of followers' development, or say, maturity is categorized into four levels based on their ability and willingness to accept responsibility for completing their task. Followers who are unable and unwilling are categorized as the least mature, and those who are both able and willing are termed as the most mature. The model suggests that the two different types of styles are used to influence the followers of four different levels of maturity as is depicted in Fig. 21.3.

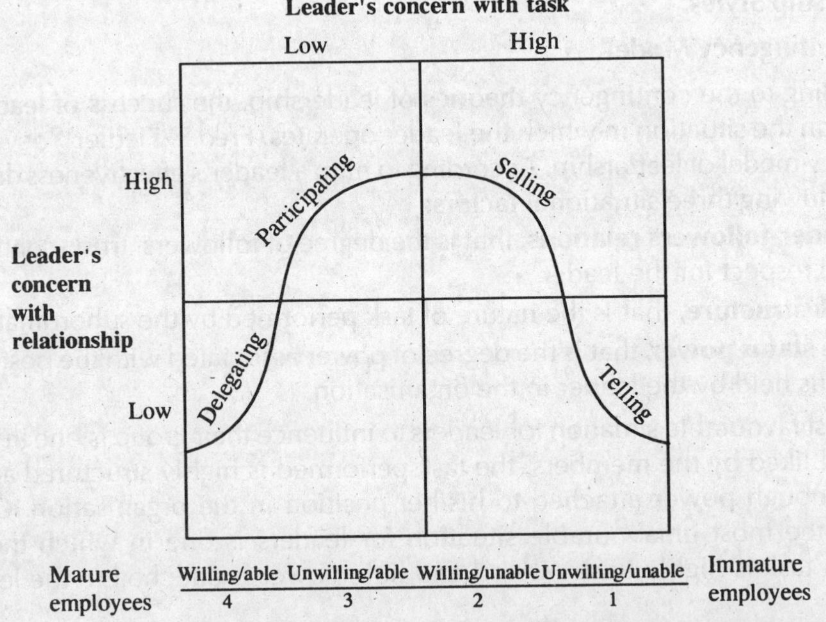

Fig. 21.3: The Hersey-Blanchard Model of the Situational Leadership Model

It is seen from the Fig. 16.3 that the leadership style varies across the levels of followers' maturity. A leader needs to use a telling style of leadership with immature followers who are both unable and unwilling to take responsibility for completing their work. Once the followers mature to the second level, the leader needs to exercise a selling style. Followers further matured *i.e.*, able but unwilling, need to be led by employing participating style by the leader. Finally, the most mature followers who are able as well as willing require to be led by a delegating style of leadership for the simple reason because the followers accept responsibility entrusted upon them.

What leadership style should be employed at which maturity level of followers is now tabulated as follows:

Table 21.3 Followers' Maturity Level vis-a-vis Leadership Style

Maturity Level	Recommended Leadership Style
1. Low ability, low willingness	Telling (directive, low support)
2. Low ability, high willingness	Selling/coaching (directive, supportive)
3. High ability, low willingness	Participating/supporting (supportive/low direction)
4. High ability, high willingness	Delegating (low direction, low support)

However, one key limitation of the situational leadership model is the absence of central hypotheses that could be tested[20]. It also does not have a widely accepted research base[21] which would make it a more valid and reliable theory of leadership. Nonetheless, the theory has intuitive appeal and is widely used for training and development in corporations. It has achieved considerable popularity and also awakened many managers to the idea of situational approaches to leadership styles.

The Managerial Grid

One of the most widely known styles of leadership is the managerial grid developed by Blake and Mouton[22]. The grid is based on two underlying dimensions labeled as **Concern for Production** and **Concern for People**. Based on these two dimensions, the authors have generated a 9 by 9 grid representing concern for production along the horizontal dimension and concern for people along the vertical dimension. The authors have identified the five distinct managerial styles as shown in Fig. 21.4.

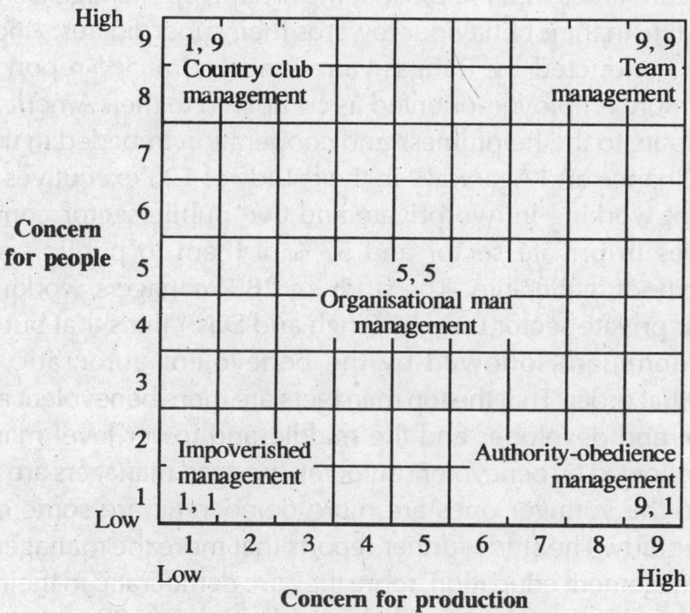

Fig. 21.4: The Managerial Grid

A brief description of these five leadership styles follows:

The **impoverished manager** (1.1) has low concern for both production and people. He exerts the minimum efforts to get essential work done, while maintaining organisational membership. This style of management is similar to the laissez-faire style as discussed earlier.

The **country-club manager** (1.9) has high concern for people but low concern for production. Good feelings towards followers are the hallmarks of such manager.

The **authority-obedience manager** (9.1) has more concern for production but low concern for people. Production maximization is the hallmark of such manager. This style is similar to the autocratic style of leadership.

The **team-manager** (9.9) has high concern for both production and people.

The **organisation man manager** (5.5) has moderate levels of concern for both production and people. Such manager goes along to get along, conforming to and maintaining *the status quo.*

The best style for all managers, in all organisations, and under all situations is the 9.9 **team manager style.**

21.6 LEADERSHIP STYLES IN THE INDIAN ORGANISATIONS

Having known different leadership styles, now it seems pertinent to examine the leadership styles exercised in the Indian organisations. We think that the review of research in leadership styles in India will help us know the leadership styles prevalent in the Indian organisations. Here follows the same.

Myers[23] in his study of leadership behaviour in both Indian and foreign owned organisations concludes that the most of the Indian top managers exercise relatively authoritarian style in their behaviour towards their subordinates. Another study of 56 top managers conducted by Rangaswamy and Helmick[24] report that the Indian managers are more employee-oriented as compared to their American counterparts. This, they attribute to the helpfulness and cooperation imbeded in the Indian culture and religion. Elhance and Agarwal[25] in their study of 123 executives at various levels of management working in two private and two public sector companies find that 67% executives in private sector and 57% of them in public sector units adopt democratic style of leadership. The study of 280 managers working in two public sector and four private sector units by Singh and Das[26] finds that bureaucratic style is the most predominant followed by the benevolent autocratic, developer and democratic in that order. That the top managers are more benevolent autocrat followed by democratic and developer and the middle and lower level managers are more bureaucratic followed by benevolent autocrat; the aged managers are more benevolent autocratic and the younger ones are more democratic are some of the interesting findings of the study. The study further reports that more the managers are exposed to the formal management education, more they are democratic in their leadership style. Similar results are reported by Jaggi[27] also in his study of 120 managers. He indicates that leadership style is influenced by various factors such as age of the managers, their levels and responsibilities, and the size and structure of the organisation. Accordingly, the younger managers in the bigger organisations are less authoritarian while the managers in production and technical areas are more authoritarian in their styles. Similarly, Gupta[28] in his study of leadership styles also concludes that various variables such as organisational culture, one's confidence in own plans, probability of success, and relative importance of task undertaken affect the style a leader will actually adopt.

On the whole, leadership in Indian organisations has generally been found to be, at best, of the benevolent authoritarian type. Given the changing demographics of the workforce, a question to be asked is whether such a leadership style will be functional in the future also. Those working in urban organisations in India are younger, better and more educated, and technically trained than their counterparts of the previous generation[29]. Obviously, a different leadership style is called for to better utilize the talent and skill of the work force with changed composition. This view is duly supported by the continued emigration of the Indian scientists and technocrats to the west where they find proper outlets for their creativity and innovation. A more egalitarian organisational relationship prevalent in the west facilitates one's creativity and innovation to blossom and flourish. If such is the case, situational style of leadership taking the abilities and aspirations of the employees into consideration, would be more appropriate for the Indian organisations of today and tomorrow.

21.7 WHAT MAKES LEADERSHIP EFFECTIVE ?

Although deciding what makes leadership effective seems as if it should be a simple decision, the theories and research reviewed earlier illustrate the complexity of the issue. By now, you know that leadership means taking along people in the fulfilment of certain desired goals or set objectives. Leadership does not mean imposing will on unwilling working under one in an office or a factory. In practice, people are always impressed by something extraordinary and great and are prepared to follow it if it really touches their hearts. Thus, leadership needs to win the hearts of others to attain some desired goals. The following points will be of great help in this regard:

1. **Mental and Physical Health:** A healthy mind rests in a healthy body. A leader needs to have sound health both mental and physical to be able to bear the pulls and pressures of his role as leader. He must also possess stamina and balanced temperament.

2. **Knowledge and Intelligence:** One most important requirement of a leader is to have required knowledge of human-behaviour, psychology and professional competence. In order to evince his convincing competency, the leader also must update himself continuously and keep renewing himself[30].

3. **Clear-cut and Worthy Goals:** Actions without clearut directions lead nowhere. That is why there is very little achievement inspite of a lot of movement in life. Hence, a leader needs to be very clear in mind about what to achieve, how to achieve and then reinforce it by a strong will-power and conviction.

4. **Conviction:** Swami Vivekananda said **"Great convictions are the mothers of great deeds".** It is always man and women with convictions who influence others.

There are millions with opinions but very few with convictions. Leader must have courage of conviction to impress upon his subordinates.

5. **Sense of Responsibility:** A leader also must have sense of responsibility for the task assigned to him. In other words, a leader must discharge his responsibility thrusted upon him willingly and cheerfully. This enjoins upon us to put our heart and soul into the work, with single minded dedication, and devotion. This ensures our success in performing the particular task[31].

6. **Motivation:** Effective motivation comes from within not from outside. Strictly speaking, real motivation cannot be imposed or injected from outside. In order to inculcate motivation from within the subordinates, a leader needs to have capacity to appreciate others and look at things from his subordinates' angle.

7. **Initiative and Drive:** As electric energy locked up in the power house is of no use unless it is flown through the cables and manifested itself through the medium of various gadgets so as to be beneficial, so is in case of leader also. Passive goodness of leader is never helpful unless it is action-oriented and result producing. Initiative and drive are, therefore, the essential prerequisites of effective leadership.

Besides, some writers have identified a number of other factors that influence leadership effectiveness. The important ones are:

1. The leader's own personality, past experience and expectations.
2. The expectations and behaviour of his superiors.
3. The subordinates' characteristics, expectations and behaviour.
4. The requirements of tasks to be performed by subordinates.
5. Expectations and behaviour of fellow managers (peers).
6. Organisational culture (climate) and politics.

21.8 TRANSACTIONAL AND TRANSFORMATIONAL LEADERSHIP

Another kind of leadership style is transactional and transformational leadership identified by Burns[32]. A brief description of these follows:

Transactional Leadership: Transactional leaders manage the transactions between the organisation and its members so that the organisational objective is achieved. They get things done by giving contingent rewards in terms of recognition, pay hike and advancement for those who perform better. They often use management-by-exception principle to get expected things done through their subordinates.

Transformational Leadership: These leaders focus on changing the attitude and assumptions of their employees towards building commitment for organisational mission and objectives. Leaders of this type generate awareness and acceptance of the purposes and mission of the group. They stir their subordinates to look beyond their own self-interest for the good of the whole group/organisations.

The distinguishing characteristics between the two types of leadership are presented in the following Table 21.4.

Table 21.4 Characteristics of Transactional and Transformational Leadership

Transactional Leadership	Transformational Leadership
• **Contingent Reward:** Contracts exchange of rewards for effort, promises rewards for good performance, recognizes accomplishments.	• **Charisma:** Provides vision and sense of mission, instills pride, gains respect and trust.
• **Management by Exception(active):** Watches and searches for deviations from rules and standards, takes corrective actions.	• **Inspiration:** Communicates high expectations, uses symbols of focus efforts, expresses important purposes in simple ways.
• **Management by Exception** (Passive): Intervenes only if standards are not met.	• **Intellectual Simulation:** Promotes intelligence, rationality, and careful problem solving.
• **Laissez-Faire:** Abdicates responsibilities, avoids making decisions.	• **Individualized Consideration:** Gives personal attention, treats each employee individually, coaches, advises.

21.9 SUBSTITUTES FOR LEADERSHIP

Evidences are available to state that while some situations constrain leaders, there are some other situations that make leadership unnecessary and redundant. Such variables are referred to as **substitute variables.** This is so because they substitute for leadership either by making the leader's behaviour unnecessary or by rendering leader's role ineffective. Examples of such variables that tend to substitute for, or neutralize leadership are long and rich experience of the subordinates, their sound professional competency, routine type of work, group cohesiveness, etc. In other words, the substitutes, or neutralizers may be found in subordinate, task, and organisation characteristics.

Some of the variables that tend to substitute for, or neutralize leadership are illustrated in Table 21.5.

Table 21.5 Substitutes and Neutralizers for Leadership

Substitute or Neutralizer	Leader Behaviour Influenced	
	Supportive Leadership	**Instrumental Leadership**
A. **Subordinate Characteristics:**		
1. Experience, ability, training		Substitute
2. "Professional" orientation	Substitue	Substitute
3. Indifference toward rewards offered by organization	Neutralizer	Neutralizer
B. **Task Characteristics:**		
1. Structured, routine, unambiguous task		Substitute
2. Feedback provided by task		Substitute
3. Intrinsically satisfying work	Substitute	

C. **Organisation Characteristics:**		
1. Cohesive work group	Substitute	Substitute
2. Low position power (leader lacks control over organizational rewards)	Neutralizer	Neutralizer
3. Formalization (explicit pains, goals, areas of responsibility)		Substitute
4. Inflexibility (rigid, unyielding rules and procedures)		Neutralizer
5. Leader located apart from subordinates with only limited communication possible	Neutralizer	Neutralizer

Source: Adapted from Stephen Kerr and J. Jermier, "Substitutes for Leadership: Their Meaning and Measurement," **Organisational Behaviour and Human Performance, vol.** 22(1978).

However, the existence of substitutes for leadership does not necessarily mean that leadership is unimportant or leaders do not really matter much. Instead, it presents the complexity of the world in which leaders have to function. Researches support that leadership is an extremely important function that bears enormous influence on the effective functioning of groups in organisations, business or non-business organisations. However, the complexity of the situation may sometimes prevent us from knowing in advance which particular leadership style will be the most effective.

SUMMARY

This summary is organized by the 'learning objectives' given on page no. 355:

- *Leadership is a process of influencing group activities towards the achievement of set goals. Leadership differs from management in the sense that the former leads people and latter manages things.*
- *Leaders perform functions such as developing team work, representing the team, counselling the team members, securing group cohesiveness, etc.*
- *Autocratic, democratic and laissez-faire are the popular styles of leadership.*
- *The prominent theories of leadership are trait theories, behavioural theories, contingency theory, path-goal theory, situational theory, the managerial grid, etc.*
- *Leadership in Indian organisations has generally been found to be, at best, of the benevolent authoritarian type.*
- *Factors such as mental and physical health, knowledge and intelligence, clear-cut goals, strong conviction, sense of responsibility and motivation help make leadership effective.*
- *Transactional leadership means managing transactions between the organisations and its members through contingent rewards. Transformational leadership involves changing the employees' attitudes towards building their commitment to organisational objectives and missions.*
- *The variables that make leader's behaviour unnecessary or redundant are referred to as substitutes for leadership.*

REVIEW QUESTIONS

1. What is "leadership" and who is a "leader"?
2. "A leader is developed and not born." Do you agree with this? Explain with reasons.
3. How will you distinguish leaders from managers?
4. What do you understand by leadership styles? Discuss the main styles of leadership.
5. Examine the different styles to the study of leader behaviour. Is there a best style?
6. Bring out the relationship and differences between Ohio State Leadership Studies and Blake and Mouton's Managerial Grid.
7. Discuss the concept of "maturity" in the light of the Situational Leadership Theory of Hersey and Blanchard and suggest the styles that are relevant for different levels of maturity.
8. Between Fiedler's theory and House's Path-Goal theory, which would you say more appealing to you? Why ?
9. Examine the leadership styles followed by the Indian managers. Can you suggest a right style?
10. Apply Fiedler's contingency theory of leadership by identifying two extremely different situations, one extremely unfavourable, and explain why a task-oriented (LPC) leader is most effective in each situation.
11. What is meant by 'substitutes for", and "neutralisers of", leadership? Give some subordinate, task and organisation examples of these substitutes and subordinates.
12. When might leaders be irrelevant?

REFERENCES

1. R.M. Stogdill: **Handbook of Leadership**: **A Survey of the Literature,** Free Press, New York, 1974, p. 259.
2. George R. Terry: **Principles of Management**, Richard D. Irwin, Inc., 1979, p. 342.
3. Harold Koontz et. al: **Essentials of Management**, McGraw-Hill Book Company, 1986, p. 397.
4. Chester I. Bernard: **The Function of the Executive**, Harvard University Press, Cambridge, Mass, 1938.
5. Warren Bennis: Why Leaders Can't Lead ? **Training and Development Journal**, Vol. 43, April 1989, pp. 35-39.
6. John W. Newstrom and Keith Davis: ***op. cit.***, 1997, p. 201.
7. Warren Bennis and Burt Nanus: **Leaders: The Strategies for Taking Charge**, Harper and Row, New York, 1985, p. 21.
8. Elton Mayo : **The Human Problems of an Industrialised Civilization,** Harvard University Press, Mass, 1939.
9. K. Lewin, R. Lippitt, and R. White: Patterns of Aggressive Behaviour in Experimentally Created Social Climates, **Journal of Social Psychology**, Vol 10. 1939, pp. 271-299.
10. R. Likert : **New Patterns of Management,** McGraw-Hill, New York, 1961, pp. 166-169.
11. R.M. Stogdill: **Handbook of Leadership**, Free Press, New York, 1974.
12. F.W. Taylor: **The Principles of Management,** Harper and Row, New York, 1947.
13. J. Kelly: **Organisational Behaviour,** Homewood, Irwin, 1974.
14. R.M. Stogdill : ***op. cit.***, 1974.
15. Fred Fiedler : **A Theory of Leadership Effectiveness**, Mc-Graw Hill, New York, 1967.

16. Robert J. House: A Path Goal Theory of Leader Effectiveness, **Administrative Science Quarterly**, 1971, pp. 321-338.
17. M.G. Evans: The Effect of Supervisory Behaviour on the Path-Goal Relationship, **Organisational Behaviour and Human Performance,** 1970, pp. 277-298.
18. Uma Sekaran: **Organisational Behaviour: Text and Cases**, Tata McGraw-Hill Publishing Company Limited, New Delhi (Seventh Reprint), 1998, p. 158.
19. Paul Hersey and Kenneth Blanchard: **Management of Organisational Behaviour: Utilizing Human Resources**, Printice Hall, Englewood Cliffs, NJ, 3rd ed. 1977, pp. 170-77.
20. B. M. Bass: **Bass and Stogdill's Handbook of Leadership: Theory, Research, and Managerial Applications**, Free Press, New York, 3d. ed., 1990.
21. Critical persepectives on the Hersey-Blanchard situational leadership model appear in Barry-Craig P. Johenson: Situational Leadership: A Review of the Research, **Human Resource Development Quarterly**, Spring 1990, pp. 73-85.
22. R.R. Blake and J.S. Mouton: **The Managerial Grid,** Gulf Publishing, Houston, 1964.
23. C.A. Myers: **Industrial Relations in India**, 1960, p. 180.
24. G. Rangaswamy and D. Helmick: A Comparative Study of Indian and American Executives' Leadership Styles, **Indian Administrative and Management Review,** July-September, 1976.
25. D.N. Elhance and R.D. Agarwal: **Delegation of Authority,** Progressive Press, Bombay, 1975.
26. P. Singh and G.S. Das: Management Style of Indian Managers : A Profile, **ASCI Journal of Management,** Sept. 1977.
27. B.L. Jaggi: Management Leadership Styles in Indian Work Organisations, **Indian Manager,** April-June 1978.
28. I. Gupta: Leadership Styles, **Business India,** April, 1980.
29. Uma Sekaran: ***op. cit.,*** 1998 p. 162.
30. Madhurendra K. Verma: Pragmatic Approaches to Leadership, **Personnel Today**, April-June 1998, pp. 14-15.
31. K.K. Chopra : Leadership in Management, In: Sunil Kumar (Ed.) **Managerial Effectiveness,** Excell Books, New Delhi, 1998, pp. 12-19.
32. James M. Burns: **Leadership,** Harper & Row, New York, 1978.

Case 21.1: The Overheard Complaint

Ms Dipshikha Paul has been supervising eight accounting clerks in the budget and planning department of a paper industry, namely, Cachar Paper Mills, Panchgram, Assam. Though none of the clerks had earned certificate in the Chartered Accountancy, but all were quite skilled in handling records and figures. They primarily prepared budgetary plans and analyses for various operating departments of the mill. The required data inputs were secured from the departments and mills records. Dipshikha has been assigning projects to the clerks on the basis of their interests and skill acquired. Some projects were more desirable than others because of prestige, challange, the contacts required, or other factors. Thus, there were sometimes occassional conflicts over which one clerk was to receive a desirable project. But one clerk who seemed especially eager and sensitive and regularly complained about this issue was Ms Rajyashree Dutta.

Meantime, Dipshikha received a desirable project and assigned it to Ms. Nayana Pal Choudhury depending on her proven skill and conpetency. This time Rajyashree

Dutta was particularly distressed because she felt she should have had this assignment/ desirable project. She was so distressed that she immediately retaliated by gathering up her present assignment and putting it away in her desk. Then, she took a magazine from her bag and started reading it. All other seven clerks being sitting in the same room, most of them observed Ms Dutta's actions. Very soon, she announced to Ms Rebecca Ao, who was sitting by Dutta's right hand side, in a voice loud enough to be heard by others, "Nobody around here ever gives me a desirable/good project."

Ms Dipshikha clearly overheard Dutta's comment and looked up from her cabin, noting what was happening. Dipshikha was electrified with anger. Somehow, she controlled herself and sat on her seat for about five minutes wondering what to do. Meanwhile, Ms Dutta continued reading her magzine.

QUESTIONS

1. In your opinion, what leadership issues are raised in this case incident?
2. Discuss what actions Dipshikha should take. Consider the pathgoal model of leadership before making your decision.

Case 21.2: When Leadership floundered in NASA*

When astronaut Neil Armstrong set foot on the moon, it was the culmination of everything the National Aeronautics and Space Administration (NASA) had worked toward for ten years. Plenty of money and strong management, along with high level political support, guided NASA to the moon. But since then NASA's leadership has floundered.

Part of the problem is lack of money. Another problem is that one third of NASA's top managers are of retirement age, and the agency's relatively low pay has hampered efforts to recruit younger replacements. And, since the explosion of the space shuttle Challenger, NASA has been plagued with launching delays and mishaps, as well as more serious problems, such as the flaws in the $1.5 billion Hubble Space Tele cope.

Those problems have led to reduced political and popular support. In addition, costs consistently exceed budgets. Many of NASA's planned projects, notably the Freedom Space Station, are considered too expensive by Congress.

Bruce Murray, a former director of NASA's Jet Propulsion Laboratory, is among those who believe that NASA engineers have been ordered to cut corners to save money and maintain projects that will keep the agency alive. But leadership that encourages cost cutting, he says, simply doesn't work. "We're headed for real disasters. The plan is sin now, pay later," Murray says. "Good managers drop things they might otherwise do when money is tight" says Alton D. Slay, a retired Air force general who led a shuttle safety inquiry after the Challenger disaster.

A panel of experts, established by NASA at the request of President George Bush, says that to get back on track, NASA must first control costs. Runaway costs, the panel said, cause poor management, which in turn causes low employee morale.

The panel also recommended that NASA's top management structure in Washington, D.C., be revamped and that outside contractors be hired to run NASA's regional research centres.

---

* MBA, Manipur University, 1999.

Originally intended to be "think-tanks", which would specialize in different aspects of research and development, the centers have become minifiefdoms, varing with each other for both funding and manpower. The lack of centralized planning for major projects adds to the lack of leadership.

Before the Apollo Manwalk, leadership at NASA's had come directly from the top-in this case, the White House during the administrations of Presidents John. F. Kennedy and Lyndon B. Johnson. But subsequent Presidents did not show the same strong support for the agency. They also did not set clear goals for NASA.

President Bush has tried to reverse the lack of White House leadership. He has called for a manned flight to Mars and further moon exploration. He has also estabilished the National Space Council, headed by Vice President Dan Quayle. The council has been a political supporter of NASA, but has clashed with the agency over future projects.

NASA has attempted to solve some of its own problems. The agency estabilished an Engineering Council, composed of two dozen senior executives who review new projects to keep costs in line. But the agency has been slow to consider new ways of doing things or to look at ideas suggested by those otuside of NASA.

One of those suggestions is that NASA should concentrate on those projects that could pay for themselves, such as shuttle luanches of commercial cargo.

To do that, NASA to centralize responsibility for the shuttle, which is now split between the agency and Lockheed Space Operations Co. Although it has a $1.6 billion contract with NASA, Lockheed is not responsible for making sure that parts manufactured by other companies will work. With a prime contractor overseeing the shuttle project, it would be easier to ensure performance. Says Phillip E. Culbertson, a former NASA general manager. "It's an intriguing idea to ensure greater accountability."

Lack of accountability coupled with lack of money, were behind the major problems discovered in the Hubble Space Telescope after it was launched. The telescope's mirrors, designed to be the most technology advanced ever, were flawed, affecting the clarity of the photographs the telescope was able to transmit.

NASA blamed the main contractor, which in turn blamed subcontractors. Ultimately, it became clear that no one had overall supervision of the project. The result was a demoralized NASA work force and a drop in political support and public confidence.

The debate over what to do about NASA is likely to continue. But without greater funding and strong leadership, it is unlikely that the agency can return to its glory days.

QUESTIONS

1. In what negative ways has NASA's management influenced employees ?
2. By encouraging employees to cut corners, how has NASA management shown a lack of leadership and undermined employee morale?
3. Who could be considered the ultimate leader at NASA?
4. What style of leadership has prevailed at NASA? What style do you think would work best?

22

POWER AND POLITICS

"Authority intoxicates." – ***Samuel Butler***

"Not everything that counts can be counted, and not everything that can be counted counts." – ***Albert Einstein***

Learning Objectives

After studying this chapter, you should be able to:

- **Define** power and **distinguish** between power and authority.
- **Describe** the bases or sources of power a manager uses to influence other people.
- **Identify** the symbols of power and powerlessness in organisations..
- **Explain** the meaning of organisational politics.
- **State** the various reasons for emergence and existence of organisational politics.
- **Discuss** the ways managers can manage politics in organisations.

You know that organisations are built by the aggregations of people who work for achieving the organisational goals. The behaviour of the people needs to be influenced in a required manner so that the set objectives are successfully achieved. The power and politics ***inter alia*** help manager influence the subordinates' behaviour to achieve the organisational goals. Hence, any discussion on organisational behaviour is likely to remain incomplete without a reference to power and politics. This chapter is, therefore, devoted to discuss various aspects of power and politics exercised and played in organisations.

22.1 MEANING OF POWER

As seen so far, the various terms and concepts used in the subject of organisational behaviour seldom have universally agreed upon definitions. Similarly, the concept of 'power'may have ever more diverse definitions than most. Almost all authors who write about power define it differently. For example, the famous pioneering sociologist Max Weber[1], quite way back in 1947 defined power as "the probability that one actor within a social relationship will be in a position tò carry out his own be in a position resistance". According to Homan[1], "power is an exchange ... between an agent and a target." "Power is an exchange relationship that occurs in transactions between an agent and a target. The agent is the person who uses the power, and target is the receipt of the attempt to use power.[1] White and Bednar[2] have also defined people or things, usually obtained through the control of important resources.

In simple words, power is one's ability to influence other people.

Sometimes, people consider power, influence and authority as synonymous. However, these mean different meanings. We have just defined power as the ability to influence someone else. Power being an ability, individuals can learn to use it effectively. **Influence** is the process of affecting the thoughts, behaviour, and feelings of another person. **Authority** is the right to influence another person[3]. In other words, authority is a legitimate right to influence others.

22.2 DISTINCTION BETWEEN POWER AND AUTHORITY

Having understood the meanings of power and authority, the two can be distinguished from each other as follows:

1. Authority is right to influence others but power is ability to influence people or things.
2. Authority is legitimate while power is not.
3. Authority confers legitimacy to power but power itself need not be legitimate.

22.3 BASES OR SOURCES OF POWER

Where does power come from? French and Raven have answered this question by identifying five sources from a manager derives power. They are reward, coercive, legitimate, referent, and expert power[4].

Reward Power: Reward power is based on the agent's/manager's ability to control rewards the target/employee wants. The common examples of reward power are managers control rewards of salary increases, bonuses, and promotions. This power is based on old saying that **'wealth is power'.** People comply this power because they get benefits out of its compliance.

Coercive Power: Coercive power is opposite of reward power. Coercive power is based on a manager's ability to cause an unpleasant experience for its people. To coerce someone into doing something means to force the person to do so, often with threats or punishment. In organisational situation, it may be in the form of action for or threat for dismissal, suspension, demotion, or other method of embarrassment for the people working in organisations.

Legitimate Power: Legitimate power is power that is based on position and mutual agreement. Both the agent and target agree that the agent has the right to influence his employees. In organisational setting, such legitimate power is in the form of authority which is delegated to the positions of organisational members. In our culture, age has still certain premium and the aged people have legitimate power and the members of the society believe in his right to influence the decisions in their lives.

Referent Power: Referent power is an elusive power that is based on interpersonal attraction. The agent has referent power over the target because the target identifies with or wants to be like the agent. Charismatic individuals are often thought to have referent power. Such power may take place without organisational context as most of the people take somebody as ideal and behave accordingly upto a certain stage. Advertisers use this type of power when they use celebrities, such as movie stars or sports figures, to do testimonial advertising. Research has found that arguments, especially emotional ones, are more influential which come from beautiful people.

Expert Power: Expert power exists when the agent has information or knowledge that the target needs. It is based on the proverb, **'knowledge is power'.** For expert power to work, three conditions need to be fulfilled. **First**, the target must trust that the information given by the agent is accurate and correct. **Second**, the information given should be relevant and useful to the target. **Third,** the target must consider the agent as an expert. It is important to mention that if an agent considers himself/herself as an expert but not the target, then the expert power will not be effective.

22.4 ACQUISITION OF POWER

We know that some people enjoy more power than others. Then, the question arises is what makes them enjoy more power. The answer is they do so because of the following doings:

1. **They do extraordinary things.** Doing things in a routine manner does not contribute much to personal power. It is non-routine or extraordinary works that involve risks increase one's power. In organisational context, negotiating a new contract, developing a new product, or formulating a new programme are the examples of extraordinary activities that contribute to power.

2. **They do the right things:** Doing right and relevant activities does also increase one's power. Simply performing the assigned roles may not necessarily increase an individual's power.

3. **They do visible activities:** Even extraordinary activities not known to others do not generate much power. Therefore, activities need to be visible or known to others. Instead of individuals **'blowing their own trumpets',** their activities announced and appreciated by the people of higher echelons bring more power to the people.

4. **They cultivate right people:** Individuals can also increase their personal power by developing their interpersonal relationships with their superiors, subordinates, and peers.

5. **They form coalitions:** Coalescing is yet another way to earn power. In practice, individuals or groups often combine their resources to pursue common goals and objectives. The philosophy behind joining together is gaining increased capability to influence others. In organisations, a labour union comprising many labourers with a view to promote the collective interest of workers is an outstanding example of coalescing.

6. **They co-opt:** In addition to coalescing, individuals can increase their personal power by co-opting people or groups whose support is needed into positions of limited influene. Coopting is different from coalescing. Co-opting specifically seeks to eliminate threats and opposition to an individual's base of power.

Closely related to power acquisition is symbols of power and powerlessness to which we turn our attention in the subsequent paragraphs.

22.5 SYMBOLS OF POWER AND POWERLESSNESS

As we mentioned earlier, people may have authority, but may have no power. Organisation charts, of course, show who has authority, but they do not reveal much about who has power. Hence, it becomes interesting to look at symbols of power and powerlessness. Kanter[5] has identified several symbols of power or characteristics of powerful people in organisations. These are:

1. **Ability to intercede for someone in throuble.** An individual who can pull someone out of a jam has power.
2. **Ability to get placement for favoured employees.** Arranging and getting a key promotion for an employee is a sign of power.
3. **Exceeding budget limits.** A manager who can go beyond and above budget limits without being reprimanded has power.
4. **Procuring above-average raises for employees.** A manager who can pull incentives above-average for his/her employees has power.
5. **Getting items done on own terms at meetings.**
6. **Access to early information.** Having access to information before anyone else is an indication or signal that a manager is holding key position plugged to key sources.
7. **Top managers seeking out opinion.** Top managers when facing a problem may seek advice from their lower-level managers. These lower-level managers, thus, have power.

A theme that runs through Kanter's list is doing things for others, *i.e.* for people in trouble, for employees, for bosses reflects power.

Unlike Kanter, Michael Korda[6] takes a different look at symbols of power in organisations. He identified three symbols of power: office furnishing, time power, and standing by. A brief description of these follows :

1. **Office Furnishing:** Office furniture is not only a facility but a message about power one has. Locked file cabinets are signs that the manager has important confidential information in his office. Size of the manager's table conveys the amount of power the manager has. Similarly, most executives' preference to have large, expensive, and attractive desks speaks of power they have.

2. **Time Power:** Korda says that the powerful executives value time much. For that matter, a full calendar of the day is a proof of manager's power. Personal planners are left open on the desk of the executive to display his/her busy schedule.

3. **Standing By:** Standing by is a game in which people are obliged to stay close to their phones so that the executive can have access to them. The idea is that the more you can impose your schedule on your people, the more power you have. Korda says that closely tied to this is the ability to make others perform simple tasks for you, such as getting your coffee or fetching the mail.

How to Measure Power ?

How much power one holds can be measured by using some tests. Here is one example.

Indicate how strongly you agree or disagree that each of the following statements accurately describes your supervisor. Answer by using the following numbers:

My supervisor can :

— 1. See that I get a raise

— 2. Give me jobs I dislike

— 3. Make sure I get the promotion I desire

— 4. Make my work life miserable

— 5. Explain my responsibilities

— 6. Give me good advice on getting the job done

— 7. Understand the tasks that I have to accomplish

— 8. Make me feel good

— 9. Give me the benefit of his/her technical know-how

—10. Give me to feel important.

Follow the following directions :

To score add your responses to numbers 1 and 3. This measures your belief about your supervisor's reward power.

The sum of 3 and 4 measures coercive power.

The sum of numbers 5 and 7 measures legitimate power.

The sum of numbers 6 and 9 measures expert power.

Finally, the sum of 8 and 10 measures referent power.

This is an illustrative questionnaire and exercise. This will give you a good idea of how social scientists measure individual in an organisational context.

Symbols of Powerlessness

Kanter has also identified certain symptoms of powerlessness *i.e.*, a lack of power in managers at different levels of the organisation. For example, the first-line supervisors often display three symptoms of powerlessness. These are : (*i*) overly close supervision, (*ii*) inflexible adherence to rules, and (*iii*) a tendency to do the jobs themselves rather than educating and training their subordinates to do these.

One symptom of powerlessness is to use mask of powerfulness or business. Here is one interesting story of how people put on a mask to show them what they are not.

Putting on a Mask

A middle level manager was promoted to the executive cadre. However, he could not reconcile himself to his new office and position. There was a knock at his door. To show how important and busy he was, he picked up the phone and then asked the visitor to come in. As the man waited for the executive, the executive kept talking on the phone, nodding and saying,"No problem, I can handle that." After a few minutes he hung up the phone and asked the visitor what he could do for him. The man replied, "Sir, I am from the BSNL office and am here to connect your phone."

As regards staff professionals such as accountants and lawyers, when they feel powerless, they often tend to resist change and try to protect their turf.

Top executives can also feel powerless at times. They display different symptoms of powerless such as focusing on budget cutting, punishing others, and using dictatorial, top-down communication.

In addition to managers, employees also at any level can feel powerless. When placed on jobs that are powerless, they may react passively as well as display overdependence on their boss[7]. There may be another sign of powerless. Employees may fall prey to frustration and disrupt the work-group[8].

Then, the problem is how to overcome powerlessness. In sum and substance, the key to overcome powerlessness is to share power *i.e.*, empowerment and delegate tasks to subordinates.

Power Tactics

Having reviewed where power comes from, it's logical to know how employees translate their power bases into actions. The ways in which people/employees translate power bases into desired actions are called 'power tactics'.

Recent research has shown that people use different types of power tactics to make others do what they want. Based on their comprehensive research, Yukl and his associates have found nine tactics that are used by people to translate their power bases into specific actions or behaviours. These are given in Table 22.1.

Tactic	Description
Rational persuasion	Using logical arguments and facts to persuade another that a desired result will occur
Inspirational appeal	Arousing enthusiasm by appealing to one's values and ideals
Consultation	Asking for participation in decision making of planning a change
Ingratiation	Getting someone to do what you want by putting her in a good mood or getting her to like you
Exchange	Promising some benefits in exchange for complying with a request
Personal appeal	Appealing to feeling of loyalty and friendship before making a request
Coalition	Persuading by seeking the assitance of others , or by noting the support of others
Legitimating	Pointing out one's authority to make a request, or verifying that it is consistent with prevailing organisational policies and practices
Pressure	Seeking compliance by using demands, threats, of intimidation

Source : G. Yukl, C.M. Fable and J.Y. Youn : Patterns of Influence Behaviour for Managers, **Group & Organisational Management,** Vol. 18, 1993, pp. 5-28.

In general, the most popularly used tactics to influence people at all levels are consultation, inspirational appeal, and rational pursuation.

22.6 ORGANISATIONAL POLITICS

Closely related to power is politics. The term politics in organisations conjures up a few negative images. However, politics is not necessarily negative. Politics relates to the ways people gain and use power. Thus, organisational politics means the use of power and influence in organisations. Let us also consider a few definitions on organisational politics.

According to Farrell and Peterson[9], Organisational politics refers to those activities that are not required as part of one's formal role in the organisation, but that influence, or attempt to influence, the distribution of advantages and disadvantages within the organisation."

Tushman[10] has defined politics as "the structure and process of the use of authority and power to affect definition of goals, directions and the other major parameters of the organisation. Decisions are not made in a rational and formal way but rather through compromise, accommodation and bargaining.

In practice, people with power use various tactics and strategies to use power to influence people. Some of these tactics and strategies are acceptable to the organisation, while others are not. Thus, actions not officially sanctioned or acceptable by an organisation that are taken to influence others in order to meet personal goals[11], refer to politics.

There is a controversy surfaced among managers whether there should be politics in organisations or not. While some managers view organisational politics as favourable, others see it as detrimental to organisation. In one study[12], 53 per cent managers considered politics had a positive impact on the achievement of organisational goals. On the contrary, 44% managers reported organisational politics distracting organisation members from focusing on goals. In a different study[13], about nine-tenth managers viewed that managers must be good politicians also. In contrast, nearly three-fifth managers were of the opinion that workplaces that were free of politics were more satisfying to work performance. Any way, these studies pointed out that the politics remains very much in existence in organisations regardless it is desirable or not. Hence, it will be interesting to know why there is politics in organisations.

22.7 REASONS FOR ORGANISATIONAL POLITICS

Organisational politics is a natural phenomenon in every organisation. There are many reasons that contribute to political behaviour in organisations. Some more prominent cnes are as follows:

1. **Unclear Goals:** Organisations or human groups work for achieving certain goals. The more unclear and complex the goals are, the more politics will be.

2. **Autocratic Decisions:** In case of autocratic style of leadership, the leader dictates the decisions or orders, and the subordinates have no right to point out, as discussed in the previous Chapter 16. Workers are made aware of what to do, but not why. This leads to lower employee morale, on the one hand, and doubts about what the manager-leader decides, on the other. Therefore, in order to safeguard their interests, workers involve in politics by forming coalitions and associations.

3. **Discretionary Authority:** Organisations provide positions with discretionary authority that is used based on individual judgement. In a University, for example, the Vice Chancellor may be given discretionery authority to appoint adhoc lecturers in the case of shortage of teaching faculty without advertising the posts. Appointments of adhoc lecturers under such discretionary authority becomes the basis for politics in the University or organisation.

4. **Power Politics:** Managers like power to exercise over people and things because it is satisfying to them. Like other resources, power is also limited in supply. Hence, there is a competition among managers/executives to acquire more and more power. In doing so, they involve themselves in manoeuvring the things in a manner that may enable them to acquire more power and resources than their competitors. Managers' such behaviour beocmes quite dysfunctional from organisational view point.

5. **Biased Performance Appraisal:** In organisations, there are cases when employees' performance evaluation cannot be based on any concrete achievement. One such case may be when performance cannot be measured quantitatively, for example, the job performance of a personnel or research manager. In such case, performance appraisal is made on the basis of the judgement of the superior. As such, the performance appraisal is likely to be subjective and biased. This may force the subordinates into dysfunctional political behaviour. Subordinates liking to be closer to the superior for providing him personal satisfaction rather than organisational performance may be such type of dysfunctional politics.

6. **Saturation in Promotion:** Some people resort to politics after they have reached saturation level of career. Having felt that they have reached the maximum level as per their talent and skills, they feel dissatisfaction and resort to the organisational politics. This is what **Peter principle** describes, that is, in a hierarchy, every employee tends to rise to the levels of incompetence and he/she will have no other option than to resort to politics that have usually undesirable consequences. Yes, exceptions are always there. Some people may like work performance more than positional achievement and, therefore, may not resort to politics.

22.8 MANAGING ORGANISATIONAL POLITICS

It has already been observed that politics is a natural phenomenon of every organisation where groups of human beings work together for achieving a goal. Therefore, in a discussion of managing organisational politics, it will be futile to try to restrict politics in organisations. What one can do is to make efforts to minimise the dysfunctional effects of politics. Given on next page are some guidelines that can help minimise the dysfunctional effects of politics in organisation.

1. **Jobs need to be clearly defined.** Our accumulated experience suggests that much of the political behaviour is caused in organisation in the absence of clarity in job definitions. Therefore, much of dysfunctional behaviour can be restricted if the jobs are clearly defined. This is because clarity in jobs helps in minimising favouritism, unfairness, nepotism and so on that give genesis to dysfunctional behaviour of people in organisations.

2. **Management should discourage the dysfunctional behaviour of people.** Dysfunctional form of political behaviour occurs only when top management

encourages it directly or indirectly. In organisational situations, subordinates look to their superiors for standards in many respects including behaviour. Then, when top management itself is engaged in dysfunctional behaviour, the people at lower levels also follow it. Things happening on top percolate down. Therefore, instead of indulging in dysfunctional behaviour, they should discourage it by making provisions to penalise such behaviour.

3. **Actions should be taken to nip the dysfunctional behaviour in the bud**. As and when the first sign of dysfunctional behaviour is evident, management should apply offensive tactics to curb and curtail it. The decision makers should not be allowed to pass the buck for making wrong decisions, but should be made responsible for wrong decisions taken by them.

4. **People should be rewarded objectively.** Much of dysfunctional form of political behaviour can be checked if the people are rewarded for their positive behaviour and penalised for the negative one. People engage themselves in dysfunctional behaviour when inefficiency goes unnoticed and unpenalised, and rewards are given to those who are near the boss and who project themselves busy without any contribution. Therefore, management needs to follow objective criteria for setting objectives for individuals and also rewarding of them.

Burton and Thakur[14] has suggested the three strategies to minimise the dysfunctional effects of politics. These are:

1. Open Communication
2. Reduction of Uncertainty
3. Awareness

Look at following Fig. 22.1. It will help you understand how the dysfunctional effects of political behaviour can be minimised.

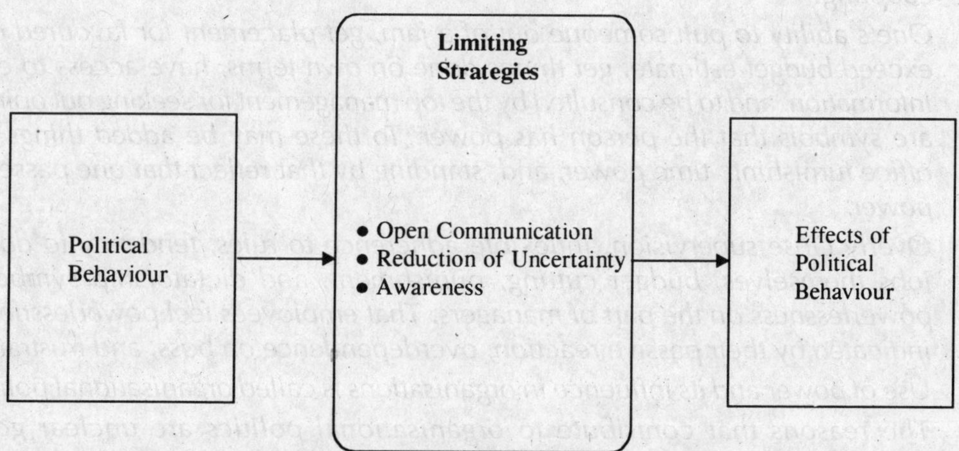

Fig. 22.1: Limiting the Effects of Political Behaviour.

Source: Burton and Thakur: **Management Today**, Tata McGraw-Hill Publishing Co., New Delhi, 1995, p. 371.

A brief description of these follows:

Open Communication: As stated earlier also, clarity helps in minimising dysfunctional effects of political behaviour. A clearly defined procedure for allocating scarce resources, for example, helps reduce tendency of people to involve in political manoeuvring. Also, open communication among people help stop control over information and, in turn, discourages political behaviour among them.

Reduction in Uncertainty: Uncertainty in terms of ambiguous goals, unrealistic and nonprogrammable decisions, technological, and organisational change breeds dysfunctional behaviour of politics. Therefore, reduction of uncertainty helps curb political behaviour in organisations.

Awareness: Making people aware of the causes and consequences of politics make them resist temptations of resorting to political behaviour.

The above mentioned strategies, being long-term course of action, require a suitable and conducive organisational climate. Since the organisational climate is largely set by the top management, it is the top management which can take a lead in limiting the dysfunctional effects of political behaviour in organisations.

SUMMARY

This summary is organized by the 'learning objectives' given on pager no. 375:

- *Power is the ability to influence other people. Influence is the process of affecting the thought, behaviour, and feelings of another person. Authority is a legitimate right to influence others. The basic difference between power and authority lies in the fact that power is capacity to influence and authority is right to influence others.*
- *The main sources or bases from people derive power are reward, coercive, legitimate, referent and expert power. People acquire power by doing right, extraordinary and visible things, cultivating right people, coalescing and coopting.*
- *One's ability to pull someone out of a jam, get placement for favoured one, exceed budget estimate, get things done on own terms, have access to early information, and to be consulted by the top management for seeking out opinion are symbols that the person has power. To these may be added things like office furnishing, time power, and standing by that reflect that one passesses power.*
- *Overly close supervision, inflexible adherence to rules, tendency to do the jobs themselves, budget cutting, punishment, and dictatorship symbolise powerlessness on the part of managers. That employees feel powerlessness is indicated by their passive reaction, overdependence on boss, and frustration.*
- *Use of power and its influence in organisations is called organisational politics.*
- *The reasons that contribute to organisational politics are unclear goals, autocratic decisions, discritionery authority, power politics, baised performance appraisal, and saturation in promotion.*
- *Strategies such as defining jobs clearly, discouraging dysfunctional behaviour of people, and rewarding people objectively help manage organisational politics. Added to these are open communication, reduction in uncertainty, and awareness that also contribute to curb political behaviour of people in organisations.*

REVIEW QUESTIONS

1. What is power? How does it differ from authority?
2. What are the sources of power? How is power acquired in organisations?
3. What are the symbols of power? What are the symptoms of powerlessness?
4. Who is the most powerful person you know personally? What is it that makes the person so powerful?
5. Do you see your Head of the Department as powerful, or powerless, or both? On what symbols or symptoms are you basing your perceptions?
6. What do you mean by organisational politics? Why do organisational politics emerge? Discuss the measures to avoid organisational politics.

REFERENCE

1. Max Weber : **The Theory of Social and Economic Organisation**, Free Press, New York, 1947, p. 152. Also see G.C. Homans: Social Behaviour as Exchange, **American Journal of Sociology**, No. 63, 1958, pp. 597-606.
2. Donald D. White and David A. Bednar: **Organisational Behaviour,** Allyn and Bacon, Boston, 1986, pp. 445-446.
3. R.D. Middlemist and M.A. Hitt: **Organisational Behaviour: Managerial Strategies for Performance,** West Publishing, St. Paul, Minn., 1988.
4. J. R. P. French and B. Raven: The Bases of Social Power, in D. Cartwright (Ed.): **Group Dynamics: Research and Theory**, Row, Peterson, Evanston, III, 1962.
5. R. Kanter: Power Failure in Management Circuits, **Harvard Business Review**, July-August 1979, pp. 31-54.
6. M. Korda: **How to Get It, How to Use** It, Random House, New York, 1975.
7. L. Mainiero: Coping with Powerlessness: The Relationship of Gender and Job Dependency to Empowerment Strategy Usage, **Administrative Science Quarterly**, Vol. 31, 1986, pp. 633-653.
8. B.E. Ashforth: The Experience of Powerlessness in Organisations, **Organisational Behaviour and Human Decision Processes,** Vol. 43, 1989, pp. 207-242.
9. D. Farrell and J.C. Peterson: Patterns of Political Behaviour in Organisations, **Academy of Management Review,** July 1982, p. 405.
10. M.I. Tushman: A Political Approach to Organisations: A Review of and Rationale, **Academy of Management Review**, 1977, p. 217.
11. B.T. Mayes and R. T. Allen: Toward a Definition of Organisational Politics, **Academy of Management Review,** No. 2, 1977, pp. 672-678.
12. D.L. Madison, R. W. Allen, L.W. Porter, and B.T. Mayes: Organisational Politics: An Exploration of Managers' Perceptions, **Human Relations**, No. 33, 1980, pp. 92-107.
13. J. Gandz and V. Murray: The Experience of Workplace Politics, **Academy of Management Journal**, No. 23, 1980, pp. 237-251.
14. Burton and Thakur: **Management Today**, Tata McGraw-Hill Publishing Co., New Delhi, 1995, p. 371.

Case 22.1: People Power at Jet Airways

Selection and placement are the two most critical decisions that all organisations make. Like other organisations, various inputs such as competence tests, personality assessments, letters of recommendations, interviews, and so on lead Jet Airways also to the final decision. Besides, Jet Airways follows a unique and unconventional selection process. One classical example of such process is the case of a highly qualified and experienced pilot who was interviewed for the position of cockpit in the late 1990s. He was duly certified to fly all of the aircraft in the Indian territory or inventory. He enjoyed quite good letters of recommendation as well. He also presented himself very well. He had an excellent and impressive interview with a panel of six pilots from Jet Airways, Air India, and Indian Airlines. The panel gave him Consensus rave reviews. The promising pilot assumed his competence and expertise alongwith his relationship with peer group constitute his power base.

Jet Airways has a unique organisational culture to it where all people regardless of job description and roles are considered important. For example, unlike other organisations having a personnel department, Jet Airways has a "people department". People in Jet Airways has their own influence over selection decisions.

For that matter, the Travel Agent who booked the pilot's flight from Calcutta to Mumbai had his input into the final decision in pilot's selection. Similarly, the coordinator who arranged the pilot's interviews also contributed his input into the final decision. The receptionist who received the pilot at Bombay for his scheduled interviews had her own say in the final decision of pilot's selection. What it does mean is power at Jet Airways is in the hands of the people working in it.

However, the pilot failed to obtain the job at Jet Airways despite his recognized competence as a pilot, his strong recommendations, and quite high grades awarded by the panel of six pilots. These factors were undoubtedly very much in his favour. But he was rude to the travel agent who booked his air ticket from Calcutta to Mumbai. He was not polite to the coordinator who arranged his schedule of interviews in Mumbai. Finally, he failed to be polite to the receptionist when he arrived for his interview in the Head Office of Jet Airways at Mumbai. What happened? Three strikes and he was out.

QUESTIONS

1. What made the pilot fail the job in Jet Airways ?
2. What lessons, as a prospective job seeker, will you draw for yourself from this case ?

PART FOUR

DYNAMICS OF ORGANISATION

- Introduction to Organisation
- Organisational Structure
- Organisational Theory
- Organisational Climate
- Organisational Culture
- Organisational Change and Development
- Organisational Effectiveness
- Quality of Work Life
- International Organisational Behaviour

23

INTRODUCTION TO ORGANISATION

"The best way to handle stiff competition and a fast changing world is to build your organization on enduring principles." – ***Herb Kelleber***

Learning Objectives

After studying this chapter, you should be able to:

- **Define** organisation and **state** its characteristics.
- **Classify** organisations into types.
- **Explain** organisational goals and **discuss** how the goals are determined.
- **Define** the terms goal succession, goal displacement, and goal distortion.

We have so far studied how individual and group dynamics influence human behaviour at work in organisations. Though strange but true that organisations do also influence human behaviour at work. Before we try to know how organisation exercises its influence on human behaviour, it seems pertinent first to know about basics of organisation. What is organisation? What are its characteristics?, What are various types of organisations?, and How are organisational goals determined? These are the foci we consider in this chapter.

23.1 MEANING OF ORGANISATION

The term 'organisation' is used every day in different context to mean different things. For instance, we hear people say "This organisation is full of red tape." "He needs to improve his organisational skills" These underline the need for understanding the meaning of the term 'organisation'? Let us consider a few definitions of organisation.

According to Pfiffner and Sherwood[1], "Organisation is the pattern of ways in which large numbers of people, too many to have intimate face to face contacts with all others, and engaged in a complexity of tasks, relate themselves to each other in the conscious, systematic establishment and accomplishment of mutually agreed purposes."

To Schein[2], "An organisation is the rational coordination of the activities of a number of people for the achievement of some common explicit purpose or goal, through division of labour and function, and through a hierarchy of authority and responsibility".

Robbins[3] defines an organisation as "a consciously coordinated social entity, with a relatively identifiable boundary, that functions on a relatively continuous basis to achieve a common goal or set of goals."

Now, we can define an organisation as a purposeful system with several subsystems where individuals and activities are organised to achieve certain predetermined goals through division of labour and coordination of activities. The important characteristics that flow from the definitions of organisation are now scanned and presented in the subsequent section 18.2.

23.2 CHARACTERISTICS

The main characteristics of an organisation are:

Co-ordination: The fact remains that the very idea of organising stems from the saying **"United we stand and divided we fall."** Or **"Unity is the strength."** Human beings require several things to survive such as food, shelter and safety. Some of these things usually are either unattainable by individuals working alone or, if attainable individually, are achieved more efficiently through group efforts. People can do more by coordinating their efforts than one could have done singly. Ever growing popularity of Co-operative Group Housing Societies in our country is the clearest example of co-ordinating group efforts to fulfil the individual needs of shelter.

Common Goal: Though organisational members have their own individual goals, but they also share a common goal to be achieved. The consensus organisational goal is supported the individuals outside the organisation who have expectation about what the organisation should be doing[4]. For example, universities like Assam Central University, are expected to educate people, hospitals are supposed to treat the sick, and manufacturing companies are expected to produce products.

Division of Labour: Organisation consists of many sub-systems, popularly known as 'division of labour'. Division of labour implies dividing work into narrow parts to perform the work efficiently. In a way, the idea of division of labour is closely linked to the idea of differentiation of operation or function. Every function is assigned to the employee who is the most fit to perform the particular function. People vary in their skill, competency, knowledge, etc. Here lies the one consideration of forming the organisation to have people with different skills and knowledge to perform varied types of functions to be performed to achieve the common goals, whatsoever it may be. Your own MBA programme is an appropriate example where different specialized papers are taught by the teachers having the relevant specialisation.

Integration: Different functions performed by different persons in an organisation need to be combined together so as to achieve the consensual goal of the organisation. This is called '**integration**'. If different departments work independently, without having regard to each other, it may lead to chaos and may make achievement of the common goal uncertain and difficult. Hence, the efforts made by different people working in different functional areas need to be integrated through hierarchy of authority like superior-subordinate relationship indicating who will report whom.

Conscious Rationality: There is a deliberate attempt on the part of orgnisation to specify norms and standards for every action and behaviour of its members. Members' behaviour is expected to be logical. The behaviour is governed by reward and penalty system of the organisation which acts as a binding force on its members. The desirable behaviour is rewarded and undesirable one is penalised.

However, rationality has its limitations. Experience suggests that no stable system can develop without boundaries to rationality[5]. Hence, organisations are intendedly rational.

Continuing System: An organisation may outlast its creator by century. Members may join and leave the organisation. But, organisation continues and enjoys eternal entity. There are organisations like General Motors, being in existence for centuries.

Structure: The coordination and integration of human activities require a structure wherein various individuals are fitted in. Organisation structure refers to how tasks are to be allocated, who reports to whom, and the formal coordinating mechanisms and interaction patterns that will be followed. Structure, thus, serves as a means for attaining the objectives and goals of an organisation[6]. You will know organisational structure, in detail, in the next Chapter 19.

What does Organisational Behaviour Study of Organisation ?

The study of organisational behaviour focuses **on three characteristic aspects of organisation.** These are: behaviour, structure, and processes. These are discussed, in brief, as follows :

Behaviour: Organisations are created by people to benefit people. Therefore, in order to understand organisational behaviour, we must be able to understand the behaviour of individuals. The study of perception, job satisfaction, motivation, and learning, discussed in Chapters 6 to 10, are all concerned with the behaviour of individuals. In nutshell, the study of behaviour includes how individuals respond to situations exposed to them.

Structure: The term **structure** refers to the fixed and formal relationships of the organisation such as how jobs are assigned to various departments, who reports to whom, and how the jobs and departments are arranged in an organisational chart. The structure of an organisation has a large influence on the behaviour of individuals working therein and the effectiveness of the organisation.

Processes: The term **processes** in the context of organisation refers to the interactions among the members of the organisation. Communication, leadership and power are examples of some of the major organisational processes. These topics have already been discussed in chapters 15 to 17.

23.3 TYPES OF ORGANISATIONS

Organisations are an inescapable part of modern human life. Our whole life is a continuous process of traversing from one organisation (e.g. family, school, college, university, office, company, etc.) to another. Thus, organisations bear pervasive influence on human lives[7]. Yes, organisations in the past were limited in number and small in size. But, at present, we have organisations large in both number and size. To-day, we have numberous TNCs and MNCs working in the country. Organisational impact on individual behaviour varies from one organisation to another depending upon the types of organisations, or say, typology of organisations. Hence, there is a need for understanding the types of organisations.

Organisations can be variously classified. One simple classification may be based on their **size**, such as small, medium, large, and giant: **evolution**, such as formal and informal; **ownership**, such as public, private, and mixed; **legal forms**, such as sole proprietor, partnership firm, joint stock company, corporation, and co-operative society; and **area of operation**, such as local, regional, national, and international. Etzioni[8] has used compliance as the basis for classifying the organisations into three types: (*i*) **Coercive organisations** based on application of physical means such as prisons, (*ii*) **Utilitarian organisations** based on application of material means of control such as business organisations, and (*iii*) **normative organisations** using symbolic means of prestige, esteem, and acceptance such as religious organisations.

Hughes[9] has classified organisations in the form of : (*i*) voluntary association, (*ii*) military organisation, (*iii*) philanthropic organisation, (*iv*) corporation, and (*v*) family business. Thompson and Tuden[10] have classified organisations on the basis of decision-making strategies.

Using beneficiary of organisations' output as basis for classifying organisations Blau and Scott[11] have classified organisations into the following four categories:

1. Mutual-Benefit Associations,
2. Business Organisations,
3. Service Organisations, and
4. Commonwealth Organisations.

Above four are the most widely accepted types of organisations. Therefore, a discussion on these seems pertinent.

1. **Mutual-Benefit Associations:** These are associations which come up voluntarily for mutual benefit. Political parties, trade unions, professional associations, etc. are the common examples of such mutual-benefit organisations. Though all members in such associations are equal, these still suffer from membership apathy and oligarchical control[12]. Such organisations are confronted with internal democracy. This makes the associations islands of vested interest.

2. **Business Organisations:** In case of business organisations, the owners or the proprietors are the prime beneficiaries. The owners' main concern is the maximum return on investment at minimum cost in order to further survival and growth. The main problem encountered in such organisations is the problem of maximising operating efficiency. The owners are obsessed with the problem of how to reduce costs and improve productivity. In long run, other social groups such as employees, customers, government, society, etc. also derive benefits from business organisations under the umbrella of **social responsibility of business.**

3. **Service Organisations:** In this case, the prime beneficiaries are the clients or those who come in the direct contact with the organisations with whom and on whom its members work. Examples of such organisations are schools, universities, hospitals, social welfare agencies, etc. Such organisations suffer from the problem of beneficiaries' control over them. As they do not know what means will best serve their interest and fall prey to exploitation at the hands of the professionals who run such organisation. Therefore, professionals in such organisations need to assure that their self-interest carries no sense if they seek to promote it at the expense of optimum service to the

clients[13]. Therefore, the professionals should not lose sight of the welfare of clients for enhancing his own status. They should also ensure at the same time that they do not become the captive of the clients.

4. **Commonwealth Organisation:** The basic characteristic of such organisations is that the public at large is their beneficiary. The prominant examples of commonwealth organisations are post office, army, police department, fire fighting departments, etc. Such organisations are plagued with problems of developing creativity, bravery and so on. Further, public at large is the prime beneficiary of these organisations but they do not have control over them. In fact, such organisations are governed on bureaucratic pattern/basis.

23.4 ORGANISATIONAL GOALS AND THEIR DETERMINATION

What is organisational goal? It has already been noted at the outset of the chapter, organisations members have a goal that is commonly shared by members and there is sufficient agreement among people about the organisations' goals to unite them in a common purpose. Thus, an organisational goal is something which an organisation seeks and something towards its resources and efforts are directed. The goal is variously referred to as 'purpose' 'mission', 'goal', 'target', or 'objective'. No organisation can exist without goal. Every organisation has a goal to achieve. However, some people argue that organisations do not have goals, rather individuals engaged in them have goals[14]. Nonetheless, organisations being deliberate and purposive creation, have certainly some goals. Yes, the organisational members may have goals different from the organisation's, and the organisation may have several goals. A business organisation, for example, has earning profit as its main objective, but it also has a series of other goals or purposes like satisfaction of workers' interest, satisfaction of customers' interest', etc.

Researchers[15] for the convenience of the study have classified organisational goals into two types: (*i*) **Official goals,** and (*ii*) **Operating goals. Official goals** are the general mission or purpose of the organisation. **Operative goals**, on the other hand, are more specifice and describe what the organisation is actually trying to accomplish, regardless of what the official goals are.

Setting organisational goals provides several benefits for the organisations. The important ones are listed as follows:

1. **Legitimacy:** The official goals of an organisation provide a symbol of legitimacy both to the employee and to external constituencies. Goals describe the purpose of the organisation, so people know what it stands for and accept its existence.

2. **Employee Motivation:** Research on goal setting has shown that the performance of employees can be significantly increased by realistic goals. Operative goals provide a sense of direction and motivation for employees.

3. **Decision Guidelines:** Goals provide a standard for evaluating performance. These can, therefore, serve as the criteria against which management decisions are made.

4. **Reduce Uncertainty:** The process of setting mutually accepted goals tends to reduce uncertainty for members of the organisation especially for top management.

Having understood organisational goals, let us now understand how these are determined.

Determination of Organisational Goals

As already stated, organisations are created for certain purposes or goals. Goals provide direction to perform required activities. However, specific goal-setting is not always possible in certain situations[16]. Examples of such situations may be (*i*) when the organisation is in its normative period of development, (*ii*) when the environment in which the organisation operates is unstable and uncertain, owing to social, economic, technological or legal changes; and (*iii*) when members cannot build enough trust or agreement to decide upon a common goal. But, specific goal-setting becomes appropriate in the conditions characterised by (*i*) when the managers want to narrow the focus and efforts of members; (*ii*) when the environment is relatively stable and certain; (*iii*) when the organisation is exposed to severe time or resource constraint, and (*iv*) when the organisational members require more defined conditions.

Days are gone when organisational goals were supposed to fulfil the owner's expectations of organisation. Now, having social responsibility attached to organisations, their goals need to fulfil the requirements of all those having stake in them, be these owners, workers, customers, suppliers, financing institutions, the government or so on. In other words, organisational goals should be set as per the requirements of its environment in which the organisation operates. Then, we can say that owners, managers and workers cannot achieve something on their own which customers, suppliers and the public at large do not permit them. Or say, no organisation can survive for long if it is oblivious of its relevant environment.

In practice, organisational goals are often set in a complicated power play involving the various components of the organisational environment. Therefore, while setting organisational goals, the organisations must adopt suitable strategies for coming to terms with the environment. Thompson and McEwen[17] have suggested alternative strategies for dealing with the organisation environment as either competitive or cooperative. These are competition, bargaining, co-operation, and coalition. These strategies allow outsiders to intervene and limit organisational decisions regarding goals. However, the entry of outsiders varies from strategy to strategy. These strategies are discussed below:

1. **Competition:** The term competition implies rivalry. Competition is seen widespread in different spheres of our society. For example, when various political parties compete for the same vote, business organisations compete for the same customers, and the management departments in the Universities compete for the same qualified students. Then, the obvious question is who will succeed ? The simple answer is that one who offers the maximum attraction to its clientele for which it is competing. Therefore, in order to deal with its environment, organisation needs to develop its competitive strength by adapting itself to the environmental situation.

2. **Bargaining:** Bargaining refers to a process of arriving at an agreement between two or more parties for the exchange of goods and services. The often witnessed examples of bargaining are agreements arrived at between the management and the trade union leaders, and the university authorities and students, seller and buyer, etc.

However, agreements arrived at once cannot be taken for granted for ever. In fact, the agreements need to be rearrived at in the face of changing environment. Thus, bargaining affects the goal-setting of an organisation. However, unlike competition, bargaining involves direct interaction with other organisations in the environment, rather than with a third party. It is how bargaining invades the actual decision process regarding goal-setting.

3. **Co-operation:** Cooperation is defined as the process of absorbing new elements into the policy-making structure of an organisation as a means of averting threats to its stability or existence[18]. It is a process of power sharing among different parties of an organisation. For this, organisations coopt members from other organisations or groups who represent and safeguard the group interests they represent. Thus, like bargaining, cooperation also makes inroads on the process of organisational goal-setting.

4. **Coalition:** The term coalition implies a combination of two or more individuals, groups, or organisations for a common goal. Coalition is often formed to mobilise joint resources so as to influence the outcome of a contest or struggle. In our country, coalition concept is very common in political parties where two or more political parties combine to jointly fight against the third. A 13 party coalition government led by the Bhartiya Janta Party (BJP) is the classical example of political coalition of our times. Coalition philosophy takes place in business organisations as well[19]. As you know, business organisations consist of a number of groups such as owners, managers, suppliers, employees, governmental agencies/agents, etc. They all combine to increase business strength of the organisation. Thus, their coalition, like bargaining, makes inroads on the process of organisational decisions regarding goals.

Closely related to organisational goals are the terms '**goal succession**', '**goal displacement**', and '**goal distortion**'. These are discussed in seriatim.

Goal Succession: Organisational goals are set in tone with the given environment. Hence, goals need to be changed with change in environment. Change in goals or adoption of new goals is called **'goal succession'.** This may happen when (*i*) the existing goals have been achieved and the organisation still wants to continue; (*ii*) the earlier goals have become irrelevant in the existing changed environment; and (*iii*) the existing goals can no longer be achieved. In fact, organisations which do not respond to their environment, are often faced with extinction.

With changing environment, goal succession has become a reality in the organisational world. There are several famous organisations known worldwide which had faced the situation of goals succession. For example, the Red Cross which was established primarily for helping those who suffered from the World War I later shifted its goal of preserving and improving public health. Similarly, in response to changes in the social environment, the YMCA has changed its goal from religion spirituality to recreation and physical exercise. These are new goals in addition to Old ones. Thus, goal succession is quite usual characteristic of most of the organisations. So much so, goal succession phenomenon happens in case of human beings also . Academician converting into politician Dr. Manmohan Singh, for example, represents a case of goal succession. Goal succession is also known as goal expansion and goal multiplication.

Goal Displacement: As stated earlier, goals are of two types: (*i*) official goals, and (*ii*) operating goals. Sometimes operating goals tend to shift when environmental factors impinge upon the organisation. Etzioni[20] has termed this situation as **goal displacement**. In case of goal displacement, the official goals remain unchanged but the organisation pursues goals different from the stated ones *i.e.,* official goals. While goal succession is deliberate, goal displacement happens unconsciously or unintentionally. However, if it is deliberate, it is not publicly announced.

Goal displacement may occur in the following four conditions:

(*i*) Substitution of legitimate (official) goals for some other goals;

(*ii*) Pursuation of goals for which the organisation was not created;

(*iii*) Pursuation of goals for which resources were not allotted to it; and

(*iv*) Seeking a goal which is not known to serve.

The major factors that lead to goal displacement are reversing means and ends, shifting priority, and over-measuring.

Goal Distortion: Goal distortion is the extreme form of goal displacement. In other words, goal distoriton is the misunderstanding or misapplication of organisational goals. Distortions in goal may occur for different reasons like over emphasis on certain aspects of goals, blockages in communication, mismatching of code books, sub-unit goal internalisation, and remote view of goals at lower level. Some of these have been discussed here :

1. **Over emphasis on Certain Aspects of Goals:** Overemphasis on certain aspects of goals leads to goal distorition as overmeasurement leads to goal displacement. A classical example of goal distortion is Entrepreneurship Development Programmes (EDPs) whose real goal is to develop the entrepreneurial skill among the prospective entrepreneurs. But, the organisations conducting the EDPs mainly concentrate on how to conduct the maximum EDPs neglecting the effectiveness of the EDPs.

2. **Blockages in Communication:** At times, either communication gets blocked in the transmission process or the entire information is not passed on to the concerned parties. These create misunderstandings between the concerned parties and, thus, tend to distort the organisational goals.

3. **Mismatching of Code Books:** Sometimes, code books of the sender and receiver of the communication do not match or tally. Such a mismatching affects the intended message and, in turn, tends to distort goals.

4. **Sub-unit Goal Internalisation:** Following the division of labour, organisational tasks are assigned to employees working in different divisions. Accomplishment of the assigned tasks becomes the goal of every division. At times, it so happens that the divisional goals assume uppermost importance for the divisional employees which may not coincide with the main goal of the organisation. Somuchso, conflict may crop up between the divisions while striving for achieving their divisional goals. Such a situation causes problem of goal distortion.

5. **Remote View of Goals at Lower Level:** Sometimes, employees working at lower levels of organisation do not have overall view of organisational goals. This

may happen because of certain reasons like internalisation of sub-goals and distance between goal setting units and goal operating units. Obviously, such distance blocks the understanding of the organisational goals on the part of lower level employees *i.e.*, goal operating employees. Such a situation, then, causes distortion in organisational goals for the employees working at lower levels.

SUMMARY

This summary is organized by the 'learning objective' given on page no. 389:

- *An organisation is a purposeful creation where individuals and activities are organised to achieve certain predetermined and commonly accepted goals through coordinated activities.*
- *In practice, there are four types of organisations found, i.e, mutual-benefit associations, business organisations, service organisations, and commonwealth organisations.*
- *Organisations are created to achieve certain goals or objectives. Organisational goal is something which an organisation seeks and something towards its resources and efforts are directed. Organisational goals are classified into two types: official goals and operative goals. While official goals are the general mission or purpose of organisation, operative goals are what the organisation is actually trying to accomplish.*
- *Both internal and external factors influence the setting of organisational goals. Competition, bargaining, cooperation, and coalition are the major factors taken into consideration while setting organisational goals.*
- *Adoption of new goals is called 'goal succession'. When an organisation pursues goals different from its official goals, it is called 'goal displacement'. When goals are misunderstood or misapplied, it is called 'goal distortion'.*

REVIEW QUESTIONS

1. Define organisation and bring out its important characteristics.

2. "Organisations are coalitions of individuals and groups." Comment. (*Delhi University, M.Com. 1977*)

3. Discuss some important typologies of organisations. Is a prison a commonwealth organisation or a service organisation?

4. How are organisations classified on the basis of prime beneficiary? Point out the problems which these organisations have to face.

5. What do you mean by organisational goal? How are organisational goals determined?

6. Explain the process of translation of general goals into operational goals in an organisation. Why do distortions occur in the hierarchy of organisational goals? (*Delhi University, M.Com. 1978*)

7. How does goal succession differ from goal displacement? When does goal displacement turn into goal distortion?

8. How does environment influence organisational goals? How does coalition make inroads on the process of organisational goal-setting?

REFERENCES

1. J.M. Pfiffner and F.P. Sherwood: **Administrative Organisation**, Printice-Hall of India, New Delhi, 1968.
2. E.H.Schein: **Organisational Psychology,** Printice-Hall of India, New Delhi, 1973.
3. Stephen P. Robbins: **Organisation Theory** (Structure, Design and Applications), Printice-Hall of India Private Limited, New Delhi, 1998, p. 4.
4. David J. Cherrington: **Organisational Behaviour,** Allyn and Bacon, Massachusetts, 1994, p. 14.
5. R. A Sharma: **Organisational Theory and Behaviour**, Tata McGraw-Hill Publishing Company Limited, New Delhi, 1998, p. 3.
6. Madhukar Shukla: **Understanding Organisations** (Organisational Theory and Practice in India) Printice-Hall of India Private Limited, New Delhi, 1996, p. 61.
7. Madhukar Shukla: ***Ibid,*** New Delhi, 1996, p. ix.
8. Amitai Etzioni: **Modern Organisations**, Printice-Hall of India Private Limited, New Delhi, 1972.
9. Evertt C. Hughes : Memorandum on Going Organisations, Quoted in Richard H. Hall: **Organisations: Structure and Process,** N. J. Printice Hall, Englewood Cliffs, 1972, p. 5.
10. J.D. Thompson and A. Tuden: Strategies, Structures, and Processes of Organisational Decision; in: J.D. Thompson, et. al. (Eds.), **Comparative Studies in Administration**, University of Pittsburgh Press, Pittsburgh, 1959.
11. P.M. Blau and W.R. Scott: **Formal Organisations: A Comparative Analysis,** Chandler Publishing Company, San Francisco, 1962.
12. Barber Bernard: Participation and Mass Apathy in Associations' in Alwin W. Gouldner (Ed.): **Studies in Leadership,** Harper, New York, 1950, pp. 486-487.
13. Talcott Parsons: **Essays in Sociological Theory,** Free Press, New York, 1954, pp. 34-39.
14. Richard M. Cyert and James G. March: **A Behavioural Theory of the Firm**, Printice-Hall, Englewood Cliff, N.J., 1965, p. 26.
15. Charles Perrow: **The Analysis of Goals in Complex Organisation**, American Sociological Review, Dec. 1961, p. 855.
16. Michael B. McCaskey : A Contingency Approach to Planning : Planning with Goals and Planning without Goals, **Academy of Management Journal,** June 1974, pp. 281-291.
17. James D. Thompson and William J. McEwen: Organisational Goals and Environment, in Amitai Etzioni, (ed.): **A Sociological Reader in Complex Organisations,** Rine-hart and Winston, New York, 1969, pp. 187-196.
18. P. Selznick: **IVA and the Grass Roots**, University of California Press, Berkeley, 1949.
19. James G. March: The Business Firm as a Political Coalition, **Journal of Politics,** No. 24, 1962, pp. 662-678.
20. Amitai Etzioni: ***op. cit.*** 1972, p. 10.

24

ORGANISATIONAL STRUCTURE

"Hierarchies remain; our belief in their efficacy does not."

– Marlene Solomon

Learning Objectives

After studying this chapter, you should be able to:

- **Define** organisation structure and **state** its need.
- **Discuss** important elements involved in an organisation structure such as division of labour, delegation of authority, span of control, centralization and decentralization.
- **Classify** various types of organisational structure.
- **List** the factors that favour different organisational structures.
- **Identify** and **describe** the types of organisational structure suitable at different stages of an organisation's life cycle.
- **State** the ways organisational structure might affect employee behaviour.

In the previous chapter, an organisation was defined as a purposeful creation by a group of individuals to achieve the mutually accepted goals of the organisation. Now, this chapter describes how the group activities are structured. The theme behind it is that structures vary across the organisations and these structures have a bearing on employees' auitudes and behaviour.

Let us first understand what an organisation structure means.

24.1 WHAT IS ORGANISATIONAL STRUCTURE ?

The term 'organisational structure' is highly abstract, and is not visible in the same way as a mechanical structure. An organisational structure is the established pattern of relationships among various components or parts of the organisation. Let us consider a few definitions of organisational structure.

Child[1] defined structure as "the formal allocation of work roles and administrative mechanisms to control and integrate work activities, including those which cross formal organisational boundaries."

Stoner[2] opined that "Organisational structure indicates the organisation's hierarchy and authority structure, and shows its reporting relationships. It provides the stability and continuity that allow the organisation to survive the comings and goings of individuals and co-ordinate its dealings with the environment."

According to Robbins[3], "An organisational structure defines how job tasks are formally divided, grouped, and coordinated".

Thus, organisation structure means the way in which the job holders' positions, their duties or roles, and the lines of authority in the system are configured so as to attain the organisational goals. In other words, organisation structure indicates the manner in which an organisation divides groups into specific tasks and establishes coordination among these tasks.

Now, what flows from the definitions of organisation structure is that the creation of an organisation structure requires to respond to two basic issues: (*i*) division of labour among its members, and (*ii*) coordination of what has been divided. For doing so, an organisational structure needs five key elements to be addressed : division of work/labour, departmentalisation, span of control, delegation of authority, centralization, and decentralization.

24.2 WHY ORGANISATIONAL STRUCTURE ?

As stated earlier, organisation structure means division of task among different people and coordination of the same. In the absence of any structure, no one will be knowing what to do and whom to respond. There will be a chaotic situation. As such, management will be rendered ineffective. The existence of an organisational structure, not only overcomes the limitations of individuals, but also serves many other purpose, on the other hand Some of these are discussed here:

1. **It facilitates management:** A well designed organisation structure facilitates the managers to discharge their duties effectively through clearcut authority and responsibility delegation, communication, control, and coordination. That is why successful managers always try to develop a good structure for their organisation. For this, even separate units for organisational analysis are created.

2. **It encourages growth and diversification:** The organisation structure provides a framework for enterprise growth. The structure, therefore, needs to be flexible enough to incorporate changes in enterprise : be these expansion or diversification. In other words, structure should be possible to be modified because the structure that is appropriate today may be not so in the changed conditions in future.

3. **It facilitates the optimum use of technological improvement:** In order to attain goals effectively, organisations need to make use of improved technologies on a continuous basis. An organisation can take advantage of improved technology by having a suitable organisation structure. An ideal organisation structure facilitates the management to blend the two : cost of technology and advantages it offers to the organisation.

4. **It encourages proper use of human resources.** Human beings are distinct from other factors of production because they have feelings and sentiments. They do not only want income but also satisfaction. Research studies report that a human being contributes the best when his/her satisfaction is the most. And, most of satisfaction, particularly psychological one, is derived from one's work, relationship, and work environment. A good organisation structure is one that provides satisfaction to the people working in the organisation.

5. **It stimulates creativity:** Organisation structure being based on division of work *i.e.,* specialisation fosters and stimulates creativity. Doing a specialized task facilitates one to think new ways of doing things. This serves as seedbed for creativity.

24.3 ELEMENTS OF ORGANISATIONAL STRUCTURE

As discussed earlier, organisational structure encompasses various elements that facilitate attainment of goals. Here, we propose to elaborate upon some of the important elements of organisational structure.

24.3.1 DIVISION OF LABOUR

The term '**division of labour**' refers to the process of dividing the total task of an organisation or unit into successively smaller jobs. Another term related to the division of labour is '**job specialisation**'. Job specialisation is based on the philosophy that everyone cannot do everything particularly those tasks that are considerably more specialized than others. The essence of division of labour or job specialisation is that, rather than an entire job being done by one individual, it is broken down into steps/parts, each step being completed by a separate individual. In essence, individuals perform better and specialize in doing part of an activity rather than an entire activity.

> Early in this century, Henry Ford by building automobiles on an assemby line exemplified how work can be performed more efficiently if employees are allowed to specialize. Ford assigned every worker a specific and repititive task. For example, one worker would just put on the right front wheel and another would install the right front door. Thus, by breaking jobs up into small standardized tasks, which could be performed over and over again, Ford became able to produce cars at the rate of one every ten seconds, while using employees who had relatively limited skills.

In fact, division of labour or job specialization has become the buzzword in group activities in the present times.

While analyzing the results of a division of labour, a distinction is often made between line and staff activities. **Line activities** are functional activities such as engineering, assembling, painting, and shipping, whereas **staff activities** are supportive ones that provide advice to the line personnel. Examples of staff activities might include the personnel, legal, and accounting departments of an organisation. Hence, some mention about '**departmentalization**' seem pertinent.

24.3.2 DEPARTMENTALIZATION

Once jobs are divided into specialized parts, these now need to be grouped together so that common tasks can be coordinated. The basis by which jobs are grouped together is called '**departmentalization**'. The central issue regarding departmentalization is the degree of similarity among the jobs within the department. The terms used to denote the departments may vary among different types of organisations. For example, in business organisations, such terms as department, division, and section are used. But, in case of a government organisation, these are referred to as branch, section, department, and bureau. In military, altogether different terms are used to denote departments, such as, regiment, battalion, group and company. However, our discussion here is relating to departments in business organisations.

Jobs can be grouped into various departments by applying different bases or criteria. The bases most commonly used for departmentalization of business enterprises include function, product, process, territory and clientele *i.e.* customers. A brief description of these follows:

Functional Departmentalization: One of the most popular ways to group activities is by functions performed by the organisation. The word function refers to the principal activities of an organisation. Therefore, departmentalization by function can be used in all types of organisations. As a matter of fact, only the functions change to reflect the organisation's objectives and activities. For example, while a manufacturing enterprise may have departments like, engineering, production, personnel, finance, and purchasing, a hospital might have departments such as research, patient care, and accounting.

It is important to mention that functional departmentalization may also be carried out at the lower levels of the organisation as long as there exists a sound base for further differentiation. Activities in the marketing department, for example, may be further classified into three groups, namely, marketing research, sales and advertising.

Look at figure 24.1. It will help you better understand the functional departmentlization of a manufacturing enterprise.

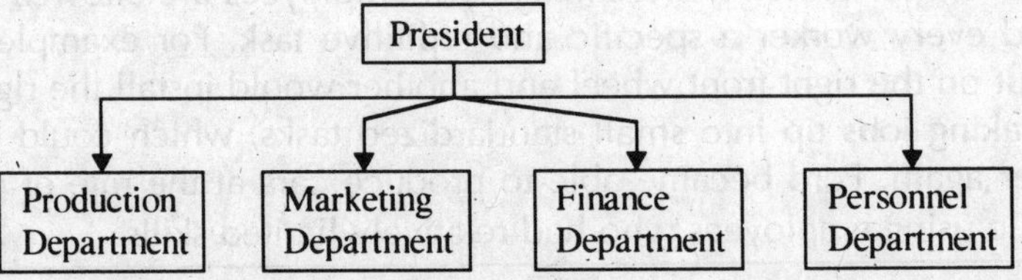

Fig. 24.1: Functional Departmentalization

Advantages

1. It is the most logical form of departmentalization.
2. It helps in obtaining effeciencies by putting specialists together.
3. It seeks to achieve economies of scale by placing people with common skills and orientations into common units.
4. It facilitates delegation of authority and, thus, reduces the burden of the chief executive in the enterprise.

Disadvantages

1. Too much emphasis on specialization hampers the broadening of outlook of various people.
2. At times, it may create conflicts between departments. For example, sales department may not honour the delivery date promised because of delay on the part of production department.
3. Coordination and control of the activities performed by the different departments becomes difficult.
4. It may so happen that managers may try to build their functional empires.

Product Departmentalization: Organisational tasks can also be departmentalized by the type of product organisation produces. In other words, in case of product departmentalization, departments are created on the basis of products produced by the organisation. Product departmentalization is especially useful when product expansion and diversification, and the engineering, manufacturing and marketing characteristics of the product are of primary concern[4]. For example, in a petroleum product company, the three major product areas (fuels, lubricants and waxes, and chemicals) are placed under the authority of a vice-president who is a specialist in, and responsible for, everything having to do with his or her product line. This will be more clear from the following figure 24.2:

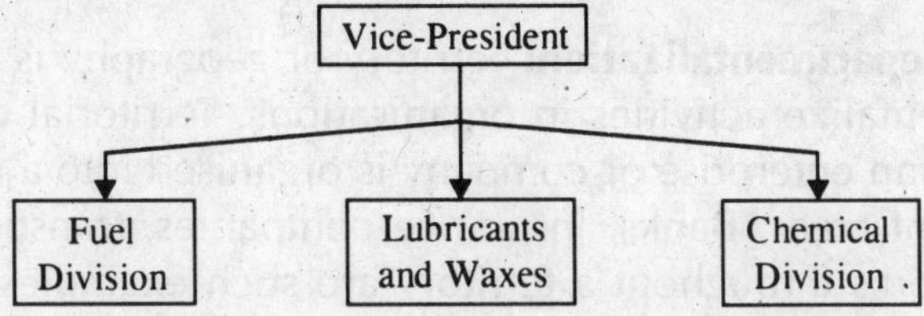

Fig. 24.2: Product Departmentalization

Advantages

1. Coordination problems created by functional departmentalization are reduced in product departmentalization.
2. It facilitates product expansion and diversification.
3. It takes due care of each product line.
4. It fixes increased accountability for product performance.
5. It makes evaluation and comparison of performance of various product divisions easier.

Disadvantages

1. Maintaining separate facilities and functional personnel causes duplication of physical facilities and many functions.
2. In case of insufficient demand for product, plant may remain under-utilized.
3. Advantages of centralization cannot be achieved.

Process Departmentalization: In this method, various manufacturing processes are taken as basis for dividing the activities into departments. A textile enterprise, for example, may departmentalize its activities on the basis of production of equipment involved, into spinning, weaving, calendering and dying. Similarly, an engineering industry may also use this type of departmentalization as shown below :

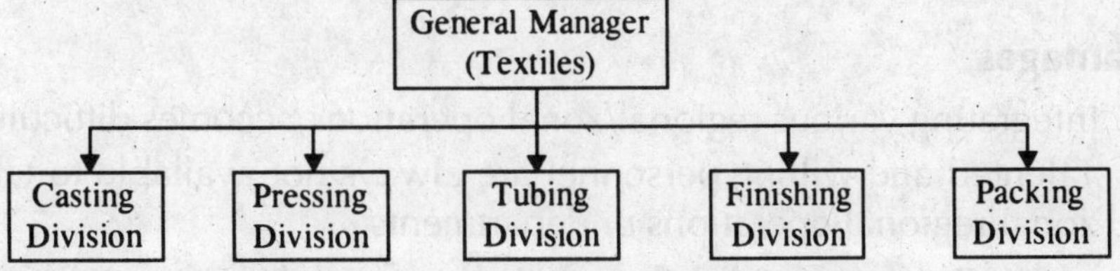

Fig. 24.3: Process Departmentalization

Advantages

1. It is especially helpful when equipments to be used require special operating skill.
2. It enables the organisation to reap the benefits/fruits of specialisation.
3. It is better suited to the manufacturing enterprises.
4. Finally, it also offers a basis for the homogeneous categorizing of activities.

Disadvantages

1. In case of process departmentalization, coordination of various functions and products becomes difficult.
2. At times, it creates conflicts between different managers cutting across their levels.

Territorial Departmentalization: Territory or geography is used as yet another basis to departmentalize activities in organisations. Territorial departmentalization takes place when an enterprise or company is organised into a number of divisions located in different areas. Banks, insurance companies, transport companies, and distribution networks throughout a territory are such examples. These enterprises/organisations divide their activities into zones, divisions and branches. Life Insurance Corporation (LIC) of India is a classical example that follows territorial departmentalization as shown by the organisation chart of the LIC given in Fig. 24.4.

Advantages

1. It helps in achieving the benefits of local operations.
2. It facilitates better coordination of activities in a zone or location through setting zonal/regional divisions.
3. It promotes expansion of business in different localities/regions.

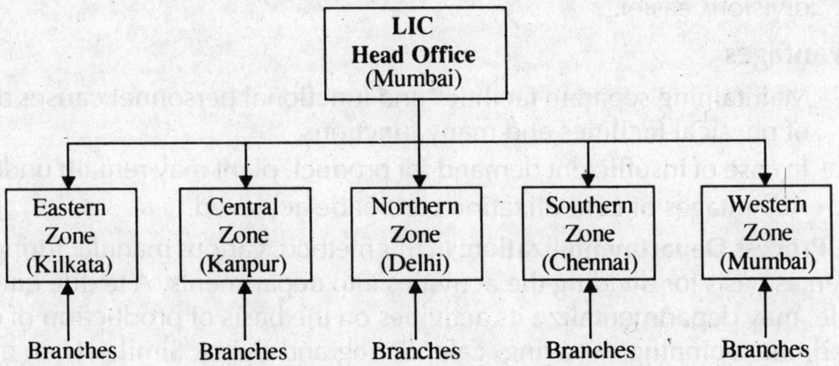

Fig. 24.4: Territorial Departmentalization

Disadvantages

1. Integrating various regional/zonal operations becomes difficult.
2. Talented and willing personnel are always not available to take charge of zonal/regional operations or departments.

Customer Departmentalization: A final type of departmentalization is to use the particular type of customer the organisation seeks to cater. The basic idea behind this departmentalization is to provide services to clearly identified groups of customers. Thus, a marketing organisation may group its activities according to the classes of customers served by it. Accordingly, an organisation may group its marketing activities into wholesale, retail and export as shown below.

General Manager
Marketing Manager
Wholesale
Retail
Export

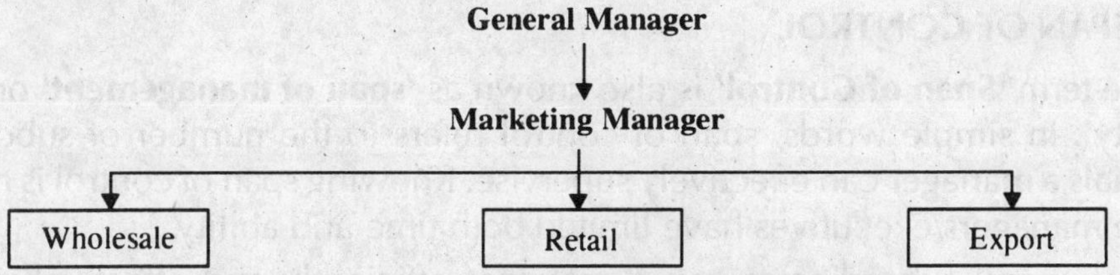

Fig. 24.5: Customer Departmentalization

Advantages

1. It meets customers' demands more satisfactority.
2. It helps attract customers.
3. It enables to gain advantages of specialization also.

Disadvantages

1. It may not consider all customers, their varied interests, habits and customs.
2. It may discriminate between rich and poor customers.
3. It creates coordination problem between sales personnel and production personnel.

Departmentalization of TATA SSL LIMITED in existence in June 1999 is presented in Fig. 24.6.

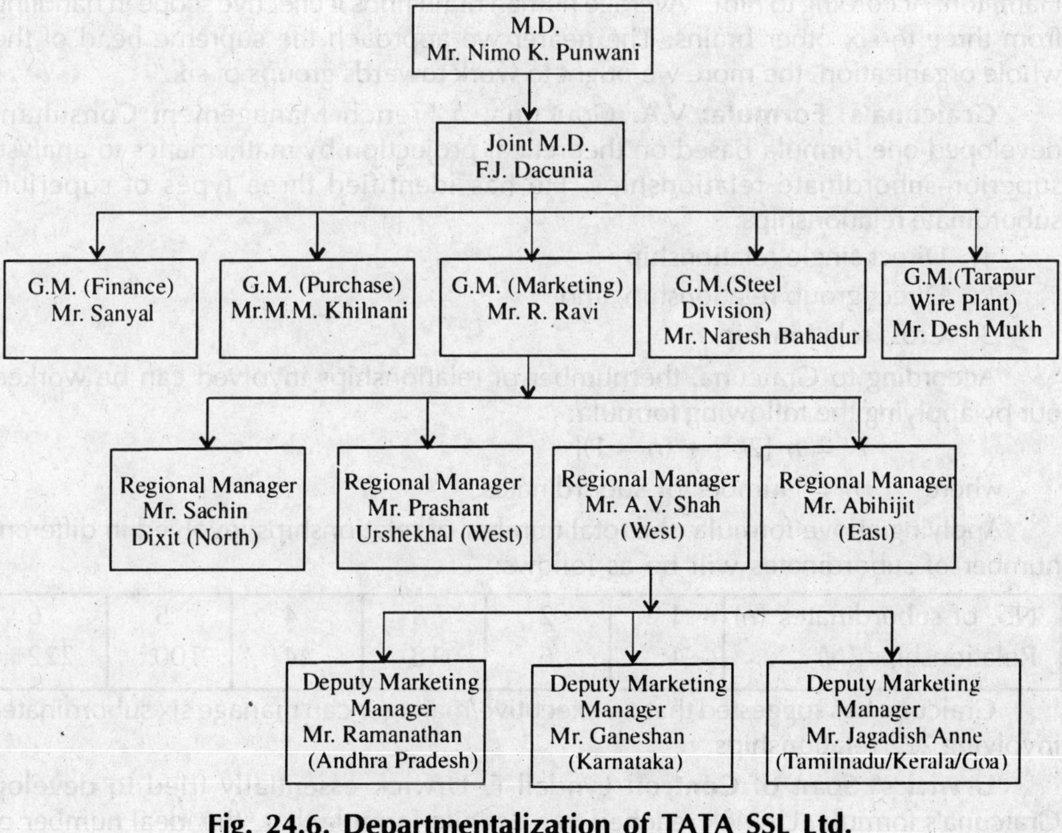

M.D.
Mr. Nimo K. Punwani
Joint M.D.
F.J. Dacunia
G.M. (Finance)
Mr. Sanyal
G.M. (Purchase)
Mr.M.M. Khilnani
G.M. (Marketing)
Mr. R. Ravi
G.M.(Steel Division)
Mr. Naresh Bahadur
G.M.(Tarapur Wire Plant)
Mr. Desh Mukh
Regional Manager
Mr. Sachin Dixit (North)
Regional Manager
Mr. Prashant Urshekhal (West)
Regional Manager
Mr. A.V. Shah (West)
Regional Manager
Mr. Abihijit (East)
Deputy Marketing Manager
Mr. Ramanathan (Andhra Pradesh)
Deputy Marketing Manager
Mr. Ganeshan (Karnataka)
Deputy Marketing Manager
Mr. Jagadish Anne (Tamilnadu/Kerala/Goa)

Fig. 24.6. Departmentalization of TATA SSL Ltd.

24.3.3 SPAN OF CONTROL

The term '**Span of Control**' is also known as **'span of management'** or **'span of authority'.** In simple words, span of control refers to the number of subordinates/individuals a manager can effectively supervise. Knowing span of control is necessary because managers/executives have limited both time and ability.

How many subordinates can a manager efficiently and effectively direct or supervise? This is because the number of subordinates should neither be too large nor too small. When the span becomes too large, subordinate performance suffers because managers no longer have the time to provide the necessary direction and support. At the same time, too small span suffers from problems like increased levels of management, complexity in the vertical communication, encouraging overly tight supervision, and discouraging subordinate/employee autonomy.

Now, a basic question arises: What should be ideal size of span of control? Experts differ on it. While some experts consider four as ideal span at higher levels, others view it ranging from eight to twelve at the lower levels. Such a variation is because of the fact that the nature of jobs and capacity of individuals vary from one organisation to another. Nonetheless, some of the approaches in determining ideal span of control are given as follows:

Hamilton's Thesis: The first known work on this topic is done by late General Sir Hamilton. According to him, "Average human brain finds it effective scope in handling from three to six other brains. The nearer we approach the supreme head of the whole organisation, the more we ought to work towards groups of six."

Graicuna's[5] Formula: V.A. Graicuna, a French Management Consultant developed one formula based on theoretical projection by mathematics to analyse superior–subordinate relationships. He has identified three types of superior-subordinate relationships:

1. Direct single relationship
2. Direct group relationship, and
3. Cross relationship

According to Graicuna, the number of relationships involved can be worked out by applying the following formula:

$$N = n\ [2^{n-1} + (n - 1)]$$

where n = Number of subordinates.

Applying above formula, the total number of relationships involved in different number of subordinates will be as follows:

No. of subordinates (n)	1	2	3	4	5	6
Relationships (N)	1	6	18	44	100	222

Graicuna has suggested that an executive/manager can manage six subordinates involving 222 relationships.

Urwick's[6] Span of Control: Lyndall F. Urwick essentially tried to develop Graicuna's formula. Urwick reached to a definite formula that "the ideal number of subordinates for all superior authorities was to be four" and "at the lowest level of organisation, where, what is delegated is the responsibility for the performance of specific tasks and not for the supervision of others, the number may be eight to twelve". He also maintained that span of control is not a rigid rule but a general guidance.

What should be the ideal number of subordinates under the control of an executive or manager depends on a number of factors[7]. Some of the more important of these factors are listed below:

- Nature of work.
- Ability of the manager.
- Efficiency of the organisation.
- Time available for supervision.
- Ability of the subordinates.
- Degree of decentralization.
- Communication Techniques.
- Staff assistance.

24.3.4 DELEGATION OF AUTHORITY

Before we discuss delegation of authority, let us first explain what authority does mean. In simple words, authority refers to the rights inherent in a managerial position to give orders and expect the orders to be obeyed. To facilitate coordination, organisations give each managerial position a place in the chain of command, and each manager is also given a degree of authority in order to meet his or her responsibilities. An unbroken line of authority that extends from the top of the organisation to the lowest echelon is called the **chain of command**. It answers questions for employees such as "who do I go to if I have a problem?" and "Who am I responsible to?"

No one person in an enterprise can do all the tasks necessary for accomplishment of goals. Also, as we just mentioned, there is always a limit to the number of persons a manager can effectively supervise. Then, the managerial success lies in his ability to multiply himself or herself through people or subordinates. The only way to do so is through delegation of authority. Thus, delegation of authority is the sharing of power or authority with another for the performance of certain tasks and duties. In brief, to delegate means to grant or confer.

Delegation of authority can be defined as the entrustment of a part of the work, or responsibility and authority to another, and the creation of accountability for performance. Responsibility is the work assigned to a position. Authority is the sum of powers and rights entrusted to make possible the performance of the work delegated. Accountability is the obligation to carry out responsibility and exercise authority in terms of performance standards established. It is the obligation of an individual to render an account of the fulfilment of his responsibilities to the boss to whom he reports.

Delegation of authority bears a unique dual characteristic. A manager–superior delegates authority to his subordinates. However, the superior at the same time still retains authority. In this context, George O. Terry's Observation seems worth mentioning, *"it is something like imparting knowledge. You share with others who then possess the knowledge, but you still retain the knowledge too*"[8].

Some people view delegation of authority and work assignment synonymous. However, there is a difference between the two. Delegation constitutes a master agent relationship while work assignment constitutes master servant relationship. An employee's work assignment may be reflected in his job description whereas delegated duties may not form the part of the employee's normal course of duties.

Now, it is clear from the above discussion that delegation of authority involves the following three elements:

1. Entrustment of work to another for performance.
2. Grant of power, right or authority to be exercised to perform the work.
3. Creation of an obligation on the part of the person accepting delegation.

As these elements are self explanatory, hence not discussed in details.

Research studies report that a moderate degree of delegation of authority is exercised in the business organisations in India[9]. It is further reported that degree of delegation of authority is higher in the public sector organisations than in the private sector ones[10].

Ideas to Use While Delegating Authority

Proper delegation creates a team spirit and helps one accomplish much more than if one tries to work alone. Here are some important tips that make delegation more effective:

- Pick people who can accept responsibility. Surround yourself with the best.
- Try to match the person to the task. Try to delegate assignments that will capitalize on the person's talents.
- Remember that the person performing the task may not do it as well as you do it. Do not be tempted to take over the project or task. Weigh the time you might lose at first against the time you will save in the long run.
- Build the person's confidence by assigning low-risk projects at first.
- Let delegatees put their own spin on the assignment. Their way may be better. Be sure to listen to their ideas.
- When communicating a task, use words that are easily understood. **A good idea**: Dictate the instructions on a cassette or write them out so that person can recheck the message.
- Keep tabs on what you delegate. As the deadline nears, check to make sure that everything is on target.

Give a due date for assignment and explain how this assignment relates to other priorities.

24.3.5 CENTRALISATION AND DECENTRALISATION

Delegation of authority is closely related to the concepts of centralisation and decentralisation of authority. The term centralisation refers to the degree to which decision making is concentrated at a single point in the organisation. In other words, centralisation is the reservation or withholding of authority by individual managers within themselves. Top management makes the organisation's key decisions with little or no input from lower-level personnel. Say, control and decision-making reside at the top levels of management.

In contrast, decentralisation is the systematic effort to delegate authority to the lower levels of organisation. The lower-level personnel provide input or are actually given the discretion to make decision. Thus, the essence of decentralisation is the transference of authority from a higher level to a lower level. Decentralisation, thus, respects individual employees for their inherent worth and constitution.

According to Henry Fayol[11], 'everything that goes to increase the importance of the subordinates' role is decentralisation, everything which goes to reduce it is centralisation'. However, both absolute centralisation and decentralisation are not tenable. While absolute centralisation is untenable because it would mean the subordinates have no duties, power or authority, absolute decentralisation is also not possible because managers cannot delegate all their power or authority.

The degree of centralisation and decentralisation is shown in Fig. 24.7.

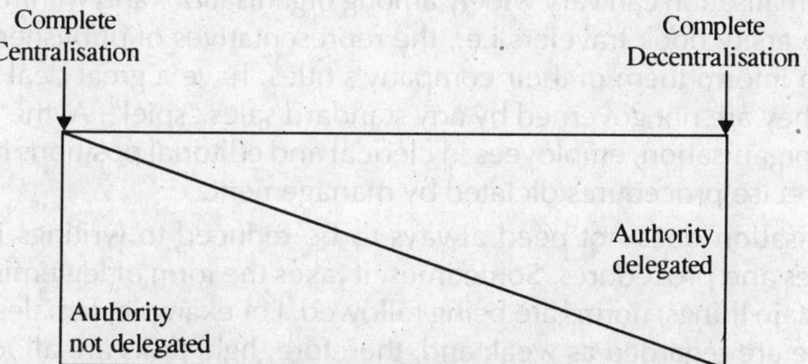

Fig. 24.7: Degree of Centralisation and Decentralisation

Delegation of Authority differs from Decentralisation

Although decentralisation is a correlate of delegation of authority, there are some differences between the two. The important ones are:

1. While delegation is a process of systematic transfer of authority, decentralisation is the end result of planned delegation.
2. Delegation is between a superior and a subordinate while decentralisation is company-wide delegation as between top management and divisions or departments.
3. In delegation, delegatee exercises the operational control while the top management itself exercises the overall control in case of decentralisation.
4. In delegation, authority transfers from one individual to another but decentralisaion refers to the systematic delegation of authority to all units in a company-wide context.

24.3.6 FORMALISATION

Organisations, irrespective of their forms of structures and ways of distributing authority, need and tend to be organised. **Formalisation** refers to the degree to which jobs within the organisation are standardized. It helps the job incumbant know what is to be done, when it is to be done, and how he or she should do it. Formalisation is done through written policies, rules and regulations. **Policies** are guidelines how an activity can be performed or a goal accomplished. For instance, most organisations have policies on recruitment, training, and promotion of employees. On the other hand, **rules** prescribe codes of conduct that need to be strictly enforced. "Nobody can come to office late more than two times during a month", may be an example of rules followed in an organisation. In simple words, rules make people understand what they can do and cannot do. **Procedures** prescribe how the jobs or tasks are to be done. They indicate the steps to be taken to complete the job. Procedures, for instance, will specify to a new operator what various tasks he needs to do in assembling various components of a car.

Formalisation helps managers **"manage by exceptions".** Managers do not need waste their time and energy paying attention to the daily routine aspects of the workplace. Instead, managers need to concentrate on the exceptional cases. The degree of formalisation can vary widely among organisations and within organisations. College/University book travelers i.e., the representatives of publishers who call on Professors to inform them of their company's titles, have a great deal of freedom in their jobs. They are not governed by any standard sales "spiel". At the other extreme in the same organisation, employees in clerical and editorial positions have to adhere to a set of precise procedures dictated by management.

Formalisation does not need always to be reduced to writings in the form of policies, rules and procedures. Sometimes, it takes the form of legitimised process as well. For certain things, norms are being followed. For example, females are by almost every culture are regarded as weak and, therefore, light tasks are allocated to them. Similarly, though the British Constitution is not in the written form, still its practices are passed on from generation to generation and it is being followed.

24.4 TYPOLOGY OF STRUCTURES

Organisation structures take different forms. Following are the broad types of structural forms:

1. Functional and Divisional Structures
2. Vertical and Horizontal Structures
3. Mechanistic and Organic Structures
4. The Matrix Structure

These are discussed one by one.

Functional and Divisional Structures: The oldest and commonly used structure is functional. In functional structure, organisation is departmentalized on the basis of functions performed by it. In case of divisional structure, organisation is departmentalized on the basis of product, customer, or region. These we have already discussed under the section 19.3.2 **Departmentalisation.**

Vertical and Horizontal Structure: Both absolute centralization and decentralisation are neither desirable nor possible. Hence, the writers and organisations began to explore ways to modify the two structures. The essence of modified structure lies in the modifications to the classical principles of delegation of authority and standard of control. Accordingly, organisations having a series of narrow spans of control were termed as **vertical structures**. On the contrary, structures incorporating wide spans and limited layers of control at horizontal levels were called **horizontal structures**. Both the structures have their advantages and disadvantages. For example, vertical structure (tall structure) calls for control and close supervision over the subordinates. Similarly, in case of horizontal structure, it may not be possible to keep close control over subordinates but it provides for decentralization, individual initiative and self-control. Nonetheless, vertical or tall structures are less favourably viewed in modern organisation analysis.

Mechanistic and Organic Structures: Two contrasting types of organisational structure were recommended by Burns and Stalker[12] in their study of twenty industrial firms in England. The structure suitable to stable conditions was termed as **mechanistic structure** while the one considered appropriate to changing conditions was called **organic structure.** The differences between these two types of structures are presented in Table 24.1.

Table 24.1: Distinction between Mechanistic and Organic Structures

Mechanistic Structure	Organic Structure
1. Tasks are divided into separate specialized jobs.	1. Tasks may not be highly specialized, and employees may perform a variety of tasks to accomplish the group's task.
2. Tasks are clearly and rigidly defined.	2. Tasks are not elaborately specified, they may be adjusted and redefined through employee interactions.
3. Strict hierarchy of authority and control with many rules.	3. Informal hierarchy of authority and control with few rules.
4. Knowledge and control of tasks are centralized, and tasks are directed from the top of the organisation.	4. Knowledge and control of tasks are located anywhere in the organisation.
5. Communication is vertical through the formal hierarchy.	5. Communication is horizontal; employees talk to whomever they need to communicate with.

The Matrix Structure: The matrix organisation structure was proposed by Dairs and Lawrence[13] for Aero Space Programme of the United States. In this structure, attempts were made to combine the advantages of product and functional departmentalization to achieve the organisational goals. In other words, this dual structure simultaneously organises part of organisation along product lines and part of the organisation along functional lines to gain the advantages of both. Such a simultaneous overlapping of these two functions is a **matrix organisational structure**. This is illustrated in Fig. 24.8.

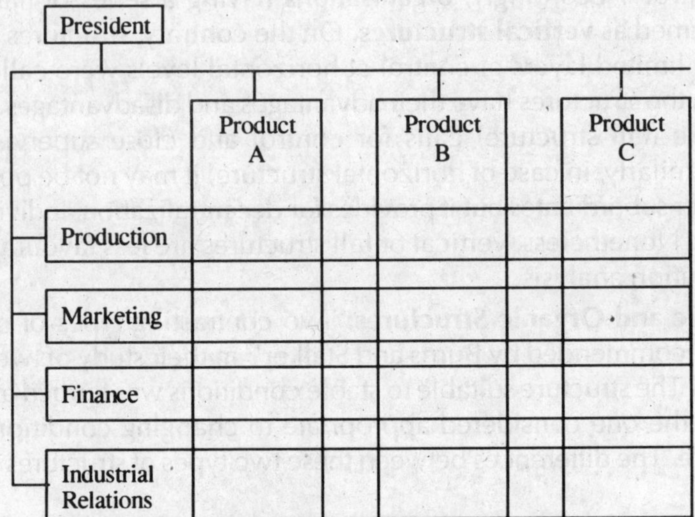

Fig. 24.8: Matrix Organisational Structure

In a matrix organisation, each department reports simultaneously to both product managers and functional managers. The product managers and functional managers have equal authority within the organisation, and employees report to both of them. Let it be clarified with an example. An employee of the legal department may be assigned to assist with the development of a specific product and assume the responsibility for all the legal activities associated with the development, production, and distribution of the product. Thus, this employee would report to both the product manager and the supervisor of the legal department. The major drawback of the matrix organisational structure is that the principle of unity of command is sacrificed as the single employee is subjected to dual authority, that of the functional heads and the project/product managers.

Having gone through different types of organisation structure, some questions arise in our mind: Why are various organisations structured differently? What are the forces that determine the structure that is chosen? In the following pages, we present the major forces that have been identified as determinants of an organisation's structure.

24.5 WHY DO STRUCTURES DIFFER ?

The following four factors determine the type of structure an organisation chooses:

Strategy

An organisation's structure serves as a means to help management achieve its objectives. As objectives themselves are derived from the organisation's overall strategy, strategy and structure, therefore, need to be closely linked. More specifically, structure should follow strategy. In other words, any change in organisational structure necessitates changes in its structure as well to accommodate and support the strategic change[14].

There are three strategy dimensions- innovation, cost minimization, and limitation. A brief description of these follows:

Innovation Strategy: A strategy that introduces and emphasizes the introduction of major new products and services is called **innovation strategy**.

Cost Minimisation Strategy: This is a strategy that emphasizes tight control over costs, avoidance of unnecessary innovation or marketing expenses, and cuts in prices.

Imitation Strategy: This type of strategy seeks to move into new products or new markets only after their viability has already been proven. It introduces successful innovations only.

Structural options vary alongwith strategic dimensions. Robbins[15] has matched the two as follows:

Table 24.2: The Strategy-Structure Matches

Strategy	Structural Options
Innovation	**Organic:** A loose structure, low levels of specialization, formalization, and decentralization.
Cost Minimization	**Mechanistic:** Tight control, extensive work specialization, high levels of formalization, and centralization.
Imitation	**Mechanistic and Organic:** Mix of loose with tight properties, tight controls over current activities and looser controls for new undertakings.

Organisation Size

The organisational size is measured in terms of number of employees, scale of operations, size of investment, etc. There is considerable research evidence to support the notion that there exists a relationship between organisation's size and its structure.[16] When an organisation is small, interaction is confined to a relatively small group, communication is simpler, less information is required for decision-making, and there is less need for formal structure. On the other hand, larger organisations tend to have more specialization, more departmentalization, more vertical levels, and more rules and regulations than do small organisations[17]. However, the relationship is not linear. In fact, size affects structure at a decreasing rate. Take an example of an organisation already employing 2000 employees and, thus, is already fairly mechanistic. Now, adding 300 employees to it have not much impact. Yes, if 300 employees are added to 800 employees of another organisation, it is likely to result in a shift toward a more mechanistic type of structure.

Technology

'Technology' is the buzzword of the time. What does technology mean? In simple words, technology refers to a process converting inputs into outputs. This very concept of technology applies to every organisation – be it an business/industrial organisation or educational institution. The Maruti Limited, for example, predominantly uses an assembly line process to make its cars. On the other hand, the Department of Business Administration in the Assam Central University uses a host of instruction technology such as the ever popular formal lecture method, the case analysis method, the quiz method, so on and so forth.

The relationship between technology and structure has been studied mainly based on the type of technology. Viewed from this angle, technologies have been classified into two types: routine and non-routine activities. It is found that routine tasks are associated with taller and more departmentalized structures. The relationship between technology[18] and structure is found stronger. Studies consistently show routineness to be associated with the presence of rule manuals, job descriptions, and other formalized documentation

Environment

Environment is a composition of all that exists around. An organisation's environment is composed of those institutions or forces that exist outside the organisation. The organisation interacts continuously with its environment. In the process, it is affected by the environment and also affects the environment. Such an interaction affects organisational processes including its structure.

Environment is usually classified as static and dynamic. Expectedly, static environments create either no or significantly less uncertainty for the organisation than do dynamic ones. Accordingly, the more dynamic and uncertain the environment, the greater the need for flexibility. This will call for an organic structure to adapt to the environmental dynamism. Conversely, in case of stable environment, the mechanistic type of structure will be the better choice[19].

24.6 LIFE CYCLE VS. STRUCTURE OF ORGANISATION

Like human beings, organisations do also progress through a life cycle. The various stages involved in life cycle are sequential in nature and follow a natural progression. Quinn and Cameron[20] have proposed four major stages to describe an organisation's life cycle. These stages are shown in Fig. 24.9.

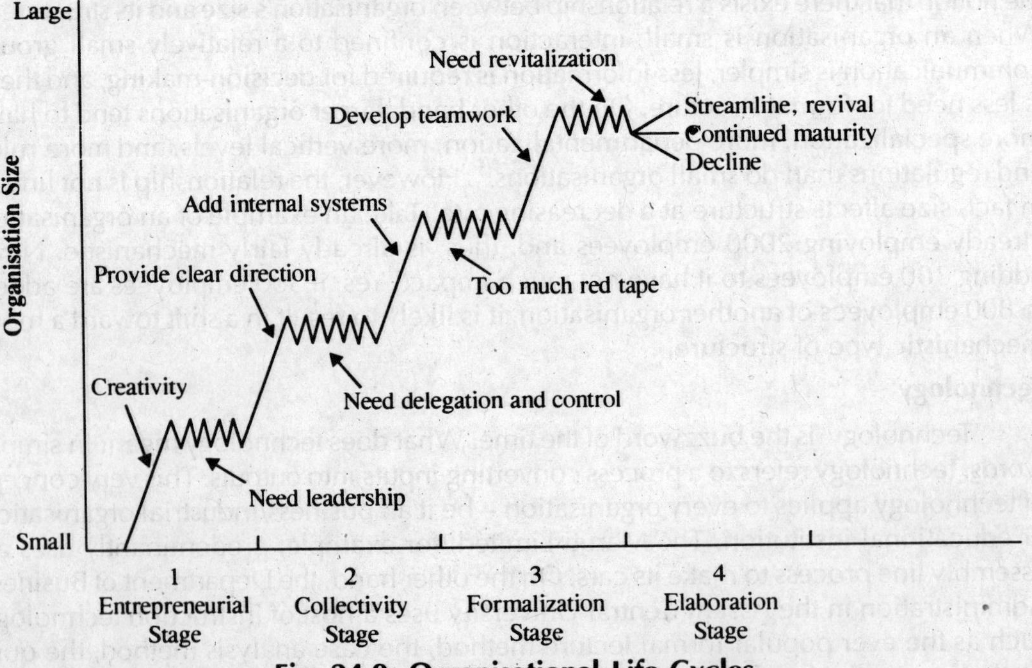

Fig. 24.9: Organisational Life Cycles

Source: Adapted from Robert E. Quinn and Kim Cameron, "Organisational Life Cycles and Some Criteria of Effectiveness: Some Preliminary Evidence," **Management Science**, vol. 29(1983), pp. 33-51.

It is seen that each stage is associated with a typical organisational structure. A brief description of these follows:

1. **Entrepreneurial Stage:** Every organisation starts with the entrepreneurial stage. The entrepreneur devotes his/her whole energy in producing and marketing the product. At this stage, the size of the organisation is small. This stage is also known as 'one-man show'. He/she being the owner of the organisation, controls it. The organisation at this stage adopts organic structure. The organisation requires to introduce management techniques to move to the next stage.

2. **Collectivity Stage:** Having with the managerial direction and control, organisation tends to take formal shape. Departmentalization starts based on division of labour following a hierarchy of authority. A strong leadership motivates employees to contribute their maximum mite for accomplishing the organisational goals. This makes the structure a highly organic one. Now, the organisation needs delegation of authority to move from stage 2 to stage 3, *i.e.*, formalization stage.

3. **Formalization Stage:** This is the middle stage of an organisation. In this stage, the bureaucratic characteristics emerge in the organisation. Now, policies, procedures, and rules are finalised to formalize the whole organisation. It is clarified who will report to whom. These help managers exercise control over system and coordinate the organisational activities effectively. When bureaucratization and formalization assume excessive proportions, these need to be curbed to advance to the next stage, namely, elaboration stage.

4. **Elaboration Stage:** The elaboration stage is marked by extensive control systems, rules, and procedures. Innovation is formally institutionalized and assigned to the research and development (R & d) department of the organisation. Individual employees often focus on maintaining the organisational activities. In order not to allow organisation to decline or die, this stage needs periodically to be revitalized. For introducing revitalizing changes, the old top managers are often replaced by new managers with fresh ideas.

The organisation that fails to revitalize itself treads to decline and ultimately dies.

Before we close this chapter, the last mention about organisation structure and its employee behaviour seems pertinent.

24.7 ORGANISATIONAL STRUCTURE AND EMPLOYEE BEHAVIOUR

Remember, we opened this chapter by implying that organisation structure affects employee behaviour. Now, in this last section, we are trying to assess just what those effects might be. Recall, we mentioned in chapter 4 that individuals differ in many respects like personality, perception, attitudes, and so on. Therefore, while attempting at assessing effects of organizational structure on employee, one needs to take individual differences into consideration. To illustrate this point, we are considering employee preferences for work specialization, span of control, and centralization. These are discussed in seriatim.

Work Specialization: Whether work specialization contributes to employee productivity, accumulated evidences indicate both in affirmative and negative. It starts affecting productivity adversely when doing repetitive and narrow tasks tend to overtake the economies of specialization. Added to it is individuals' less tolerance of overly specialized jobs. Yes, there may be segment of the work force that prefers the routine and repetitiveness of highly specialized jobs. For such people, high work specialization serves as a source of job satisfaction. Nonetheless, negative behavioural outcomes from high specialization are most likely to surface in professional jobs occupied by individuals with high need for achievement.

Span of Control: Though research fails to establish any conclusive relationship between span of control and employee performance, it can intuitively be argued that large spans of control lead to higher employee performance. This is because large spans provide more distant supervision and also more opportunity for personal initiative. However, it is difficult to state that any particular span of control is best for producing high satisfaction and, in turn, high performance among the subordinates. Here again, the reason is individual differences. While some people like to be left alone, others prefer to have the security of the boss readily available at all times. Nonetheless, there is some evidence indicating that a manager's job satisfaction increases alongwith the number of subordinates he or she supervises increases.

Centralization: There are fairly strong evidences establishing link between job satisfaction and centralization. In case of less centralized *i.e.*, decentralized organisations, decision-making practices become participative and participative decision making is positively related to job satisfaction. The reason being employees realize themselves as meaningful entities in the organisations particularly those with low self-esteem. However, individual differences surface here too.

SUMMARY

This summary is organized by the 'learning objectives' given on page no. 399:

- *Organisation structure indicates the manner in which an organisation divides its group members into different and specific tasks and establishes coordination among members through a hierarchy and authority structure. The need for organisation structure is felt for division of labour among members and coordination of what has been divided.*
- *An organisational structure consists of elements such as division of labour, departmentalization, span of control, delegation of authority, centralization, decentralization and formalization.*
- *The main types of organisational structure are functional and divisional structures, vertical and horizontal structures, mechanical and organic structures, and matrix structure.*
- *Factors like technology, strategy, organisation size, and environment decide the type of structure an organisation chooses for it.*
- *An organisation's structure is associated with the stage of its life cycle.*
- *How an organisation structure affects employee behaviour depends on individual differences. While some may like to work in a mechanistic structure, others may prefer to work in an organic one.*

REVIEW QUESTIONS

1. Define organisation structure. Why is it needed? Explain with example.
2. "Organisation structure refers to the differentiation and integration of activities and authority, roles and relationships." Explain.
3. What are the various bases of departmentalization? How will you decide departmentalization for a large manufacturing concern?
4. Distinguish between delegation and decentralization.
5. What do you mean by span of management? As a manager, will you prefer to a narrow or wide span? Give your reasons.
6. "Absolute decentralization is as hypothetical as absolute centralization." Explain.
7. A steel producing corporation decides to diversify its activities and undertake production of automobiles. The chief executive seeks your advice on whether to group the activities primarily by product or by function. What advice would you tender and why?
8. You, as a manager, have been requested to design the organisation structure of Punjab National Bank having a large number of branch offices. What will you recommend? Give justification.
9. How does technology affect organisation structure? Bring out effect of technology on behaviour of organisation members.
10. Identify and describe the manner organisation structure affects individual behaviour.
11. "Organisation structure varies alongwith stages of organisation life cycle". Discuss.
12. Write short notes:
    (*a*) Departmentalization
    (*b*) Span of Control
    (*c*) Delegation of Authority
    (*d*) Mechanistic and Organic Structure
    (*e*) Matrix Structure

REFERENCES

1. J. Child: Organisational Structure, Environment and Performance: The Role of Strategic Choice, **Sociology,** Vol. 6, 1972, pp. 1-22.
2. James A. Stoner: **Management,** Printice-Hall of India Private Limited, New Delhi, 1984, p. 262.
3. Stephen P. Robbins: **Essentials of Organisational Behaviour**, Printice-Hall of India Private Limited, New Delhi, 1997 (Fifth Edition), p. 185.
4. Arthur H. Walker and J.W. Lorsch: Organisational Choice: Product versus Function, **Harvard Business Review,** November-December 1968.
5. V.A. Graicuna: Relationship in Organisation, **Bulletin of the International Management Institute,** International Labour Office, Geneva, 1933.
6. Lyndall F. Urwick: The Span of Control-Some Facts Fables, **Advanced Management**, November 1956, pp. 5-19.
7. J. Stieglitz: Optimizing Span of Control, **Management Record**, September 1962, pp. 25-29.
8. George O. Terry: **Principles of Management,** Richard D. Irwin, Homewood Ill, 1978, p. 336.

9. D.N. Elhance and R.D. Agarwal: **Delegation of Authority,** Progressive Publishers, Bombay, 1975, p. 138.
10. A.S. Choudhry and L.M. Prasad: Delegation of Authority, **Integrated Management,** February 1978; pp. 21-26.
11. Henry Fayol: **General and Industrial Management**, Pitman, London, 1964, p. 3.
12. Tora Burns and G.M. Stalker: **The Management of Innovation**, Tavistock Institute, London, 1961.
13. Stanley M. Dairs and Paul Lowrence: **Matrix**, Addison Wesley, Reading, Massachusetts, 1977.
14. T.L. Amburgey and T. Dacin: As the Left Foot Follows Right: The Dynamics of Strategic and Structural Change, **Academy of Management Journal,** December 1994, pp. 1427-52.
15. Stephen P. Robbins: ***op. cit.,*** 1997. pp. 199-200.
16. Richard H. Hall: **Organisation: Structure and Process,** Printice-Hall, Englewood, Cliffs, N.J., 1972, p. 112.
17. D.S. Pugh et al: The Context of Organisational Structure **Administrative Science Quarterly,** March 1969, p. 98.
18. C.C. Miller, W.H. Glick, Y. Wang, and G.P. Huber: Understanding Technology Structure Relationships: Theory, Development and Meta-Analytic Theory Testing, **Academy of Management Journal,** June 1991, pp. 370-99.
19. Paul R. Lawrence and Jay W. Lorsch: Organisation and Environment, **Harvard Business School**, Boston, 1967, p. 23.
20. Robert, E.Quinn and Kim Cameron: Organisational Life cycles and Some Shifting Criteria of Effectiveness: Some Preliminary Evidence, **Management Science**, Vol. 29, 1983, pp. 33-51.

Case 24.1 : A Simple Structure of FNF Strips Company

FNF Strips Company is a small family owned organisation in the business of manufacturing ferrous and non-ferrous strips, and is situated in Andhra Pradesh. The owner was also the chairman and managing director of the company and below him there were six functional directors who were related to him (one son, one son-in-law, wife, two nephews and the son of a family friend) and also owned shares in the company.

The total strength of FNF Strips was about 150 and most of the employees were employed as "temporary" workers (although they had been with the company for the last eight years or so) in the manufacturing unit. These people had been handpicked by the owner in the earlier days of the company, when the owner used to look after the factory. The structure in the factory was the only part of the organisation which was somewhat elaborated, and in recent years an "outsider" was appointed as the Vice-President to manage it (the Factory Manager and two of the shop managers were also the owner's relatives). The owner, however, had continued to maintain control on the factory operations; he would visit the factory every day, give instructions to supervisors and workers, sometimes even overruling the directions given by factory executives. The technical investment decisions were mostly based on the owner's subjective judgement, than on any objective process of planning and market survey. Once, for instance, he ordered a costly high capacity plant from West Germany, which was too sophisticated for the volumes required by the company. Its operations became viable only after three years, during which the company built up a large inventory of unsold stocks and huge debt.

The main office of the organisation was a rented flat next to the owner's residence. Apart from the owner, and the functional directors, there were just about five or six other employees housed in this office. These included two typists (one of whom also worked in the owner's residence after office hours) and a "marketing officer" (whose tasks also included errands like receiving guests, arranging for taxis, purchase of raw materials and stationary, etc.). This lack of role boundaries could also be seen among the functional directors, who would often look after each others jobs, though in all cases, the final consent had to come from the owner.

QUESTION

1. Go through the structure and analyse it.

25

ORGANISATIONAL THEORY

"Efforts to explain why events occur as they do better understanding."

*– **Anonymous***

Learning Objectives

After studying this chapter, you should be able to:

- **Define** organisation theory.
- **Classify** and **discuss** various types of organisational theories.
- **Understand** various approaches of organisational theory and their relevance for organisational design.

The previous two chapters have discussed, in detail, organisation and its structure. This chapter accordingly moves to the next level of analysis and deals with organisational theory. This chapter especially tries to answer the questions: What is an organisational theory? What are the various types of organisational theories? And, What is their relevance for organisations?

Let us begin with defining organisational theory.

25.1 DEFINITION OF ORGANISATIONAL THEORY

It may be comforting to know we are not the first to contemplate questions about what organisational theory is. Instances indicate that organisational theory issues were addressed even in the Bible[1]. The word 'theory' is derived from the Greek word **Qewpix** meaning theoria. It means looking at, viewing, or contemplation. Thus, theory means a systematic grouping of interrelated happenings having relationships between two or more dependent and independent variables. Let us first consider here some of the important definitions of organisational theory.

Tosi[2] defined organistion theory as "a set of interrelated constructs (concepts), definitions, and propositions that present a systematic view of behaviour of individuals, groups, and sub-groups interacting in some relatively patterned sequence of activity, the intent of which is goal-directed."

Pugh[3] opined organisation theory "as the study of the structure, functioning and performance of organisations and the behaviour of groups and individuals working therein."

According to Tyson and Jackson[4], "Organisation theory is like a guide for decisions, a set of explanations and statements, based on research and experience, which describe different kinds of working relationships and their consequences".

Having gone through above definitions, now it is not difficult to deduce what we mean by the term **organisational theory**. It is the study of structure, functioning, and performance of organisations and behaviour of individuals working therein. In brief, organisational theory prescribes how best to organise people and tasks to effectively accomplish organisational goals.

25.2 TYPES OF ORGANISATIONAL THEORY

Theory is the general belief or truth based on the past and present observations and a prescription for the future. As observations about the same happening are likely to vary among the observers, so their prescriptions as well, so to call theories. This holds true of organisational theory also. Various organisational theories propounded so far have been classified into the following five types :

1. Classical Organisation Theory
2. Neo-classical Approach
3. Systems Approach
4. Modern Organisation Theory
5. Contingency Approach

Now, these are discussed in seriatim.

25.2.1 CLASSICAL ORGANISATIONAL THEORY

The term 'classical' means something traditionally accepted or long established. The evolution of organisation theory is traced back to the second half of the nineteenth century when industry and urbanisation started expanding considerably. Following are the important theories propounded during that period:

Taylor's Scientific Management

Frederick Winslow Taylor, who was a mechanical engineer by background, introduced an alternative to the prevailing system of management by initiative and incentives based on his work experiences in Midvale and Bethlehem Steel Companies in Pennsylvania. After years of conducting experiments with workers, he strongly believed that workers' output was only about one-third of what was possible. He set out to correct the situation by applying the scientific method to jobs to replace methods based on **trial and error** and **rule of thumb.** Taylor published his views on scientific management in 1911[5]. He proposed **four principles of scientific management :**

1. The replacement of rule-of-thumb methods for determining each element of a worker's job with scientific determination,
2. The scientific selection and training of workers,
3. The co-operation of management and labour to accomplish work objectives, in accordance with the scientific method, and
4. A more equal division of responsibility between management and workers, with the former doing the planning and supervising, and the latter doing the execution.

Taylor developed a number of techniques to facilitate scientific management. Following are the important techniques which, taken together constituted the mechanism of the Taylor's new approach:

1. Time study to analyse and measure the time taken in doing the various elements of a job, and to set standards for both work and time for a day.
2. Motion study to eliminate wasteful motions and decide on the best way of doing the job.
3. Standardization of tools, equipments and machinery and working conditions.
4. Differential piece rate of wages for efficient and inefficient workers.
5. Functional foremanship involving different specialist formen supervising machine, speed, group work, repairs, etc.

The biggest strength of the Taytor's scientific management was conservation and proper use of every ounce of workers' energy. His time and motion techniques are important tools to organise the task in the **"one best way"** in which it should be done. This forms a part of what today we call the issue of 'work design'.

Nonetheless, scientific management is not free from limitations. One of its shortcomings is assuming workers inherently lazy and, thus, requiring strict supervision and exercise of authority by managers. It only believes monetary rewards as the best motivators. No importance is attached to social and psychological aspects of work environment.

Fayol's Administrative Management

As mentioned above, Taylor focussed on increasing the productive efficiency of the lowest level in the organisation-shop-level management. At about the same time, Henry Fayol, director of a coal mining company in France, made a systematic analysis of the process of management. His approach to the study of management is also known as the **Process** or **Functional Approach**. In Fayol's view, every business organisation consists of six inter-dependent operations viz., technical, commercial, financial, security, accounting and administrative or managerial operations. He analysed the nature of managerial activities and skill requirements which did not receive due attention from thinkers. According to him, management involves application of certain skills which can be acquired by persons on the basis of systematic instructions and training. He emphasizes that once such skill are acquired, these could be applied to all types of institutions including, church, schools, political, industrial organisations and so on.

Fayol proposed fourteen principles of management[6] which, he argued, were universally applicable. These are:

1. **Division of Work:** This principle is the same as Adam Smith's **"division of labour"**. It believes that specialization increases output by making employees more efficient.
2. **Authority:** Managers must be able to give orders. Authority gives them this right. Along with authority, however, goes responsibility. Wherever authority is exercised, responsibility arises.
3. **Discipline:** Employees must obey and respect the rules that govern the organization. Good discipline is the result of effective leadership, a clear understanding between management and workers regarding the organization's rules, and the judicious use of penalties for infractions of the rules.

4. **Unity of Command:** Every employee should receive orders from only one superior.
5. **Unity of Direction:** Each group of organizational activities that have the same objective should be directed by one manager using one plan.
6. **Subordination of Individual Interests to the General Interest:** The interests of any one employee or group of employees should not take precedence over the interests of the organization as a whole.
7. **Remuneration:** Workers must be paid a fair wage for their services.
8. **Centralization:** This term refers to the degree to which subordinates are involved in decision making. Whether decision making is centralized (to management) or decentralized (to subordinates) is a question of proper proportion. The task is to find the optimum degree of centralization for each situation.
9. **Scalar Chain:** The line of authority from top management to the lowest ranks represents the scalar chain. Communications should follow this chain. However, if following the chain creates delays, cross-communications can be allowed, if agreed to by all parties and superiors are kept informed.
10. **Order:** People and materials should be in the right place at the right time.
11. **Equity:** Managers should be kind and fair to their subordinates.
12. **Stability of Tenure of Personnel:** High employee turnover is inefficient. Management should provide orderly personnel planning and ensure that replacements are available to fill vacancies.
13. **Initiative:** Employees who are allowed to originate and carry out plans will exert high levels of effort.
14. ***Esprit de Corps*:** Promoting team spirit will build harmony and unity within the organization.

Max Weber's Ideal Bureaucracy

Max Weber, the German Sociologist, is regarded as the father of the concept of bureaucracy. Based on sound reasons, Weber developed a structural model[7], which he called **'ideal-type'** and argued that it was the most efficient means for achieving organisational ends. According to him, an ideal structure of bureaucracy should have the following characteristics in it:

(*i*) Division of labour,
(*ii*) A clear authority hierarchy
(*iii*) Formal selection procedures,
(*iv*) Expert training
(*v*) Detailed rules and regulations, and
(*vi*) Impersonal relationships

Weber's work was primarily a theory of organisation structure. It has become so popular that most of today's large organisations are based on his bureaucratic structure. Weber was so convinced of the utility of his bureaucratic principles that he felt the sins of bureaucracy were the sins of failing to follow its principles.

25.2.2 NEO-CLASSICAL APPROACH

We have discussed earlier the classical theories concerned with the efficiency and productivity of workers (F.W. Taylor) and the managerial effectiveness (Henry Fayol). These theories regarded human factor as mechanistic one. They gave little importance to workers as human beings, their attitudes, feelings and needs. By the 1930s and 1940s, informal relationships at work were seen to have a significant influence on work output. It was against this background that some theorists started recognizing the social nature of organizations. These theorists viewed organisations as made up of both tasks and people. In other words, neo-classical theorists represented a human counterpoint to the classical theorists' machine view. Among the neo-classical organisational theories, the two most important ones are by Elton Mayo and Douglas McGregor.

Elton Mayo and the Hawthorne Studies

Recognizing labourers as human beings, frequently referred to the **human-relations approach to management**, was started by Elton Mayo with a set of experiments undertaken at Western Electric Company's Hawthorne plant in Cicero, Illinois, between 1924 and 1927. The Hawthorne studies were initially started by the Western Electric Industrial engineers to examine the effect of illumination on workers' productivity. Having undertaken experiments with varying intensities of lighting, the engineers reached to the conclusion that illumination intensity and workers' productivity are not clearly related. In order to explain the behaviour witnessed by the electric engineers, the Harvard psychologist Elton Mayo was associated in the subsequent experiments that lasted till 1932. The numerous experiments conducted encompassed the redesign of jobs, changes in the length of the work day and workweek, introduction of rest periods, individual versus group wage plans, and effect of a group piecework incentive[8] pay system on group productivity [9]. The findings were as follows :

1. Physical environment at the work place do not have any impact in influencing workers productivity.
2. Workers' positive attitudes and sense of work-team influence workers efficiency and productivity.
3. Workers' satisfaction derived from the fulfilment of their social, economic and psychological needs contributes to their morale and efficiency.
4. Compared to monetary rewards, non-monetary ones like job security, recognition by the authority, and freedom of expression motivate workers more.

Douglas McGregor and Theory X and Theory Y

One of the most frequently mentioned neo-classical organisation theory is Douglas McGregor's **participation theory**. Douglas McGregor formulated two distinct sets of assumptions about human beings based on the participation of workers. One basically negative–**Theory X**–and the other basically positive **Theory Y[10].** McGregor concluded that while dealing with the employees, a manager tends to mould his or her behaviour toward subordinates according to these assumptions. **Theory X presumes** that :

1. Employees are fundamentally lazy and inherently dislike work and, whenever possible, will try to avoid it.
2. Since employees dislike, therefore, they need to be coerced, controlled, or threatened with punishment to achieve the organisational goals.
3. Employees avoid making decision whenever possible and prefer to be directed by the managers.
4. Most of them place job security above all and work mainly to ensure it. Hence, they are not interested in achievements.

In contrast to these negative views about human beings, his theory Y is based on altogether different assumptions. **Theory Y presumes** that people by nature:

1. Work hard towards objectives to which they are committed.
2. Learn to accept and seek responsibility.
3. Exercise self-direction and self-control their own behaviour.
4. Wish their organisation to succeed.

Finally, **McGregor advocates that managers should follow Theory Y assumptions.**

McGregor's Theory X and Theory Y are discussed, in more details, earlier in the Chapter 9.

25.2.3 SYSTEMS APPROACH

What is a system? In simple words, a system is a set of interdependent parts forming an organised unit or entity. Thus, a system can be thought an organised whole. Kast and Rosenzweig[11] have defined a system as "an organised, unitary whole composed of two or more independent parts, components, or subsystems and delineated by identifiable boundaries from its environmental supersystem". Thus, a system is a set of objects characterised by relationship among them which act as an entity. The behaviour of an entity is a unitary function of the behaviours of the individual parts. These parts, known as subsystems, interact with each other. Subsystems being interrelated as well as interdependent, any changes in one subsystem lead to changes in others.

The system approach has the following features :

1. System is a set or group of interrelated and interdependent but separate identifiable elements or parts.
2. All the elements must be arranged in an orderly manner.
3. A proper communication system must be there to facilitate interaction between the elements.
4. This interaction should lead to achieve a common goal set by the organisation.

Now, let us look at how system approach works or functions. In an enterprise, the various elements or parts are viewed as engaged in procuring and transforming inputs into outputs. Various parts of the enterprise such as employees, money, machine and managers are engaged in transforming inputs like material, information and energy into outputs in the form of products, goods, and services. The output is, then, presented, or say, sold to the environment. Thus, sale of output provides feedback, called energy, about the system function. Energy, thus, facilitates to repeat this system process or cycle again and again.

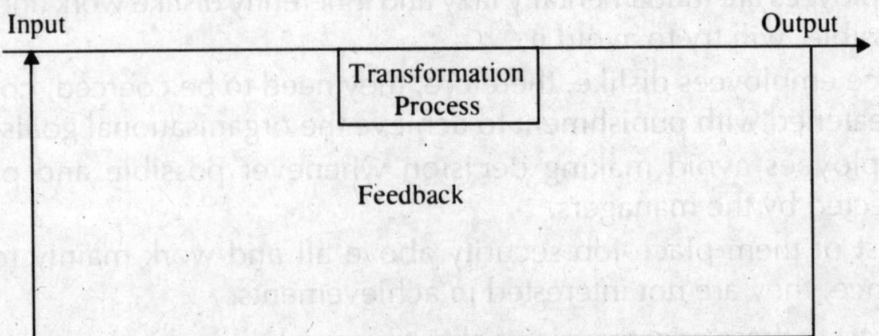

Fig. 25.1: System Approach Functioning in a Cyclic Manner

The system approach is applicable to all types of organisations be these business organisations or educational institutions. Here is an example to clarify how system approach functions in an educational institution, namely, **Assam Central University, Silchar.**

> We can regard Assam University as a system and its various departments and divisions as subsystems. Further, aspects like teaching, research and administration within its all departments could be regarded as sub-subsystems.
>
> Now, see how system and subsystems work together to achieve the goal. The University receives inputs in the form of students, teachers, officials, grants, books, etc. It then processes students with transformed knowledge and skill. The students so transformed as MBAs, for example, are delivered to the environment. The teachers in the Department also generate knowledge and disseminate the same through their publications. The University constantly obtains feedback on its output and services rendered through various bodies like the Academic Council, Executive Council, etc. These bodies have members representing the various sections of society who act as watch-dogs for activities undertaken by the University. This cycle of activities goes on and on. This is how best the Assam University has been organising its employees and tasks to effectively accomplish its goal, *i.e.*, to produce its post-graduates in its as many as 24 departments.

Remember, one system could be regarded as subsystem for another system. For example, the Assam University could be regarded as a subsystem of the University Grants Commission as a system which itself could be regarded as a subsystem of the Ministry of Education which also could be considered as a subsystem within the Government of India as a system.

Thus, this illustrative case of the Assam Central University explains how system approach works for fulfilling the organisational goals.

25.2.4 MODERN ORGANISATION THEORY

Modern organisation theory has been evolved on the pattern of **General System Theory** (GST) of Bertalanffy[12]. As GST is an integration of several levels of systems[13], so is modern organisation theory also. Modern organisation theory is an integrative theory and combines the valuable concepts of classical and neo-classical theories. It is an amorphous aggregation of various parts and systems of an organisation that enables us to understand organisations in a better manner. The integrative nature of the theory, according to Sharma[14], attempts to answer the following questions:

1. What are various parts of the system?
2. What is the nature of their interdependency?
3. What are the linking processes among the parts?
4. What are the goals of the system?

Folllowing are the main features that distinguish modern organisation theory from other theories:

1. This theory treats the organisation as an open system. This is where modern theory differs from classical theory which treats organisation as closed system.
2. According to modern theory, the process of interaction between various parts or sub-systems is dynamic not static in nature. In order to maintain equilibrium, organisation frequently interacts with the changing environment.
3. It provides a unified focus to organisational efforts. It takes an integrated view of a phenomenon taking into all factors affecting the phenomenon.
4. Modern theory is based on multilevel and multidimensional approach. It consists of both micro and macro approaches to understand an organisation.
5. The theory is based on multiple variables. This suggests that an event may be the product of not a single factor but of many factors which, in turn, may be interrelated and interdependent.

25.2.5 CONTINGENCY APPROACH

Early management contributors such as F.W. Taylor, Henry Fayol, and Wax Weber propounded principles of management and organisation and also assumed the same to be universally applicable. However, later research found exceptions to many of their principles. For example, to improve productivity, supporters of scientific management may prescribe work simplification and additional incentives, the behavioural scientist may recommend job enrichment and democratic participation of employees in the decision-making process. Thus, it becomes clear that no universal principles to be applied in all cases or situations. Against this background, one view held is that there is no one best way to manage organisations. In fact, there are many ways to perform various managerial functions.

The best approach to manage organisations is **contingency approach or situational approach.** This approach considers all factors or circumstances within a situation. In short, contingency approach focuses on the following two aspects:

1. It emphasizes attention on specific situational factors that influence the appropriateness of one managerial strategy over another.
2. It highlights the importance of developing skills for managers in situational analysis.

Thus, contingency approach compels managers to be aware of the complexity prevalent in different situations and suggests to take a dynamic view while determining what best strategy would work in every situation.

However, the biggest criticism lebeled against this theory is its heavy theoretical complexity. Even a simple problem needs to be analysed on a number of counts, each of which having innumerable dimensions. This makes its empirical testing very difficult. Nonetheless, these do not undermine intituitive logical background of the contingency theory.

SUMMARY

This summary is organized by the 'learning objectives' given on page No. 420 :

- *Organisation theory is how best to organise people and tasks to accomplish organisational goals.*
- *Various organisational theories developed over the years are broadly classified into five types, namely, classical, neo-classical, system, modern, and contingency approach.*
- *Classical organisation theories regarded human factor as mechanistic one, while neo-classic ones were based on social nature recognization of organisations. System approach recognizes the various sub-systems together function in a unitary manner as an entity.*
- *Modern organisation theory is an integration of various parts and systems of an organisation that helps us understand organisations in a better manner. Lastly, contingency approach emphasizes that there is no universal approach or principle to be applied in all situations. It focuses attention on specific situational factors that influence the appropriateness of one managerial strategy over another.*

REVIEW QUESTIONS

1. Define organisation theory. What are the important elements of Classical Organisation Theory?
2. Discuss the relationship between scientific management and administrative management approaches of classical theory.
3. What is the main contribution of Henry Fayol to the theory of organisation?
4. Examine critically assumptions underlying Classical Organisation Theory.
5. What are the various elements of neo-classical organisation theory?
6. Bring out similarities and differences between classical and neo-classical theories of organisation.
7. Discuss the contribution of Hawthorne Experiments to organisation theory.
8. What is the system approach to organisation? Can you explain it with an imaginery example?
9. Discuss, in detail, modern theory of organisation. How does it differ from system approach of organisation?
10. What do you mean by contingency approach of organisation theory? What are its advantages and disadvantages?

REFERENCES

1. Cited in Stephen P. Robbins: **Organisation Theory** (Structure, Design and Application), Printice-Hall of India Private Limited, New Delhi, 1998, pp. 32-33.
2. Henry L. Tosi: **Theories of Organisation**, St. Clair Press, Chicago, 1975, p. 7.
3. D.S. Pugh (ed): **Organisation Theory**, Modern Management Readings, Penguin, 1971, p. 10.
4. Shaun Tyson and Tony Jackson: **The Essence of Organisational Behaviour,** Printice-Hall of India Private Limited, New Delhi, 1997, p. 135.
5. Frederick Winslow Taylor: **The Principles of Scientific Management**, Harper & Row, New York, 1911.
6. Henry Fayol: **General and Industrial Administration**, translated by Costance Storrs, Sir Issac Pitman & Sons Ltd., London, 1949.
7. Max Weber: **The Theory of Social and Economic Organisation,** translated by A.M. Henderson and Talcott Parsons, Oxford University Press, New York, 1947.
8. Elton Mayo: **The Human Problems of Industrial Civilization,** Macmillan, New York, 1933.
9. Fritz J. Roethlisberger and William J. Dickson: **Management and the Worker**, Harvard University Press, Cambridge, 1939.
10. Douglas McGregor: ***op. cit.,*** 1960.
11. F.E. Kast and J.E. Rosenzweig: **Organisation and Management**, McGraw-Hill, New York, 1979.
12. L. Von Bertalanffy: **Problem of Life,** Watts and Company, London, 1952.
13. K.E. Boulding: General Systems Theory: The Skeleton of Science, **Management Science**, April 1956.
14. R.A. Sharma: ***op. cit.,*** 1998, p. 147.

26

ORGANISATIONAL CLIMATE (OC)

"Organisations have a set of attributes induced from the way they deal with people and environment."
– John P. Campbell

Learning Objectives

After studying this chapter, you should be able to:

- **Define** the term 'Organisational Climate.'
- **Distinguish** between organisational culture and organisational climate.
- **Appreciate** the need for and significance of organisational climate.
- **Delineate** and **discuss** the various dimensions of organisational climate.
- **Discuss** the major determinants of organisational climate.

26.1 INTRODUCTION

Along with organisational structure and culture just discussed in the two preceding chapters, organisational climate (OC) is yet another organisational element that also affects employee behavior, i.e. OB and, in turn, organisational performance. In a sense, there is much similarity between natural climate and organisational climate. How? Like natural climate, there are certain elements prevalent in an organisation that form its climate. Organisational climate varies from organisation to organisation and from time to time in case of the same organisation. Organisational climate may have positive or negative effects on employee behaviour and, in turn, organisational performance. Recognizing the effect of organisational climate on organisational performance, increasing interest is shown in understanding and application of organisational climate. This is against this backdrop; the present chapter is devoted to discuss the major aspects of organisational climate in relation to employee behaviour. Let us begin with explaining the concept of organisational climate.

26.2 CONCEPT OF ORGANISATIONAL CLIMATE

Before defining organisational climate, it would be pertinent to first define the term 'climate' itself. Climate, in its natural sense, is meant as the average conditions of weather prevalent in a place or region over a period of time as exhibited by temperature, wind velocity, and precipitation. Thus, depending on weather conditions, climate is classified into various types such as cold climate, hot climate, and humid climate. Different types of climates are suitable for different things like food-grain, vegetable, and fruit cultivation.

Now that we have understood what climate means, we can now profitably define organisational climate. As a matter of fact, we all intuitively understand what the terms 'organisational climate' mean, but there is still no generally accepted meaning of it among the organisational thinkers though there are areas of agreement. There is no gainsaying that, like natural climate, organisational climate is also formed by its different properties or constituents. Different words like atmosphere, culture, environment, and milieu are often used interchangeably to describe it. In fact, a number of studies have tried to measure organisational culture in the operational sense of climate. Hence, a clear- cut specification of the properties of organisational climate is not very specific and simple. As such, different thinkers have listed different properties involved in forming organisational climate and accordingly defined it differently. Therefore, there is no common definition of organisational climate but variety of definitions. Nonetheless, it seems pertinent to give some formal definitions of organisational climate.

G.A. Forehand and B.V.H. Gilmer have tried to conceptualize organisational climate considering its potential elements or properties. According to them, "Organisational climate consists of a set of characteristic properties that describe the organisation and that (a) distinguishes one organisation from other organisationa, (b) are relatively enduring over time, and (c) influence the behaviour of people working in it."[1]

John P. Campbell et. al. defined organisational climate as a "set of attributes specific to a particular organisation that may be induced from the way that organisation deals with its members and its environment. For the individual members, i.e., employees working in the organisation, climate takes the form of a set of attitudes and expectancies which describe the organisation in terms of both static characteristics such as degree of autonomy and behaviour outcome and also outcome contingencies."[2]

According to Renato Taguiri, "Organisational climate is a relatively enduring quality of the internal environment that is experienced by the members, influences their behaviour, and can be described in terms of values of particular set of characteristics of the organisation."[3]

One common element present in above definition is the prevalence of some characteristics or properties in an organisation that constitute its climate. Based on these, organisational climate can now be defined as a set of measurable properties of the work environment, that are perceived by the people who work and live in it, and that influence their motivation and behaviour. Climate characteristics that have been determined to significantly impact an organisation's bottom line include flexibility, responsibility, standards, rewards, clarity, and team commitment.

26.3 ORGANISATIONAL CLIMATE *VIS-A-VIS* ORGANISATIONAL CULTURE

There has been a debate among the organisational thinkers on whether organisational climate and organisational culture are synonymous or not. While some consider the two terms as synonymous and use these interchangeably, others consider the two terms conveying two different meanings. Many authors including Schein, have drawn sharp line of demarcation between the constructs of organisational climate and culture[4]. Rousseau differentiated between these two constructs on the basis of climate being the descriptive beliefs and perceptions individuals hold of the organisation, whereas culture is the shared values, beliefs, and expectations that develop from social interactions within the organisation. The boundaries between organisational climate and culture can appear to be artificial, arbitrary, and even largely unnecessary[5].

Taguiri's systemic model offers an interesting means for integrating these two constructs; he presented culture as one of four components of organisational climate, along with ecology, milieu, and organisation or structure[6]. Within his construct of organisational culture, he included assumptions, values, norms, beliefs, ways of thinking, behaviour patterns, and artifacts. This definition seems to the organisational hierarchy parallel closely many of the prominent authorities in the field. However, his construct of organisational climate tends to be more encompassing than that of many of his peers. Within the sub-component of ecology, he included buildings and facilities, technology, and pedagogical interventions. Within milieu, Tagiuri subsumed the race, ethnicity, socio-economic levels, and gender of organisational members and participants, their motivation and skills, and the organisation's leadership. His organisation or structure construct includes communication and decision-making patterns within the organisation, the organisational hierarchy and formal structures, and the level of bureaucratization. Of course, this definition of organisational climate is quite comprehensive and, therefore, can blur the core definition of organisational climate. Nonetheless, this serves as a good reminder of the interrelatedness of all these factors with organisational climate and culture. It also illustrates the broad range of organisational issues that must be taken into consideration when planning of organisational improvement especially of large-scale improvement.

26.4 WHY ORGANISATIONAL CLIMATE ?

There is no gainsaying that good or healthy climate, in its natural sense, facilitates performance whatsoever it may be. Similarly, there is research evidence to believe that sound or healthy organisational climate contributes to improve organisational performance in different ways. Research on motivation over the past 40 years has shown that the climate in the workplace, i.e., organisational climate has a significant impact on employee behaviour and organisational performance. Organisational climate that energizes workers to produce their best can improve profit as much as 30 per cent - by increasing revenues, lowering costs, and improving customer loyalty. And these positive effects of organisational climate have been proven time and time again[7]. Just contrary is also true. Bad or poor organisational climate deters and distorts organisational performance. Good organisational climate affects employees' attitude, job satisfaction, and performance in different ways. Following are the four major ways by which organisational climate affects organisational performance:

1. Organisational climate serves as facilitator to organisational performance. The organisational properties govern employee behaviour by prescribing what types of behaviour will be rewarded and what will be punished. Thus, an organisation can influence and motivate people to behave in desired manners that suit to organisation.

2. Organisational variables enable people to evaluate self and others to improve their behaviour. The evaluation mechanism involves both physiological and psychological variables that help improve employee behaviour and, in turn, performance.

3. Variables included in organisational climate serve as stimuli to employees' activities. As stimuli, organisational variables arouse employees' level of activation in their works. This, in turn, improves employees' performance.

4. Organisational factors shape and improve employees' perception towards organisation and their jobs. As explained earlier in the chapter 'perception', perception affects attitude, satisfaction, and performance in a lockstep manner. Better the perception, more and better the performance and vice versa.

It seems pertinent to cite some research findings on impact of organisational climate on employees' behaviour and performance to support our above statements.

N. Frederiksen conducted one laboratory experiment on 260 middle level managers to see the relationship between organisational climate and employee performance[8]. He summarized his research findings as follows:

1. It appears that the amount of administrative work in the stimulated job is more predictable in a climate that encourages innovation, i.e., individual autonomy than in one that encourages standard procedures, i.e., bureaucratic system.
2. Higher productivity can be expected of people with skills and attitudes that are associated with independence of thought and action and the ability to be productive in free and innovative climate.
3. Performance is expected to be more predictable for employees who worked in a consistent climate than those who have to work in an inconsistent organisational climate.
4. An inconsistent or uncertain organisational climate was having negative impact on employees' attitude and performance.

Frederiksen finally concluded that different organisational climates have different effects on employee's performance.

George H. Litwin and R. Stringer conducted yet another laboratory experiment to verify differences in impact of different organisational climates[9]. Salient findings of the experiment were reported as follows:

1. Experiment found broadly three types of organisational climates: authoritarian - structured, democratic friendly, and achieving business.
2. Employees in authoritarian - structured organisation produced goods of highest quality because of rigid specifications put by organisational orders and rules and regulations.
3. Employees in democratic friendly organisational climate expressed maximum satisfaction with their jobs.
4. Employees produced the most in terms of money volume, number of products, and cost-saving innovations in an achieving organisational climate.

The above two are the illustrative research studies that establish relationship between organisational climate and employee performance. There are yet another research studies that also confirm that a good / healthy organisational climate has positive effect on employee attitude, behaviour, and, in turn, performance.

26.5 DIMENSIONS OF ORGANISATIONAL CLIMATE

Having understood the meaning and relevance of organisational climate in organisational performance, it becomes desirable to know what the dimensions of organisational climate are, or say, what are the properties of organisational climate. That organisational climate varies from organisation to organisation also indicates that the properties of organisational climate are likely to vary from organisation to organisation. This has led to a problem of absence of general set of properties of organisational climate across organisations. Different organisational thinkers have listed different sets of properties of organisational climate. Following are some of these:

In their attempt to identify the constituents of organisational climate, B. Schneider and C.J. Bartlett have listed six factors that determine the climate in an organisation[10]. These are : (i) Managerial Support, (ii) Managerial Structure, (iii) Concern for New Employees, (iv) Inter - Agency Conflict, (v) Agent Dependence, and (vi) General Satisfaction.

Based on information received from managers, Renato Taguiri has identified five factors in organisational climate[11]:

1. Practices relating to providing a sense of direction or purpose to employees' jobs - setting of objectives, planning and feedback.
2. Opportunities for exercising individual initiative.
3. Working with a superior who is highly competent and competitive.
4. Working with co-operative and pleasant people.
5. Being with a profit - minded and sales - oriented organisation.

Based on their research study, G. H. Litwin and R. Stringer list the six factors that influence organisational climate of an organisaiton[12]. These are: (i) Organization structure, (ii) Individual autonomy, (iii) Rewards, (iv) Risk-taking, (v) Warmth and support, and (vi) Tolerance and control.

In view of above mentioned diverse set of the properties of organisational climate, it is very difficult to generalize what constitutes organisational climate. Nonetheless, some broad generalization about the constituents of organisational climate can be drawn from the above classifications. Accordingly, the general set of factors of organisational climate, also called dimensions of organisational climate can be listed as follows:

1. Individual Autonomy: This refers to feelings of autonomy of being one's own boss. In other words, this refers to the degree to which an employee is free to manage himself / herself, enjoys the power of making decisions by self, and always not accountable to higher level officer or manager.

2. Position Structure: This refers to the degree to which an employee has to follow rules, regulations, and procedures laid down in the organisation relating to a job. This also means the degree to which an employee needs to be under the direct supervision of some senior or superior official or manager.

3. Reward System: This refers to the degree to which an employee is rewarded for his/her better performance by the organisation and the employee is sure and certain that he/she will get reward for his/her performance. The organisation which orients its employees to perform better and duly reward them for the same is likely to have a good organisational climate.

4. Support System: This refers to the extent to which an employee gets support and stimulation from the organisation to perform his / her job. An organisation which extends required support and encouragement to its employees to perform their jobs is likely to have a considerate, warm, and supportive climate

5. Progress and Development: This refers to the extent to which an organisation creates and fosters conditions for progress and development of its employees. Organization also allows employees to apply new ideas and application methods to develop themselves.

6. Conflict: This refers to the extent to which inter-personal disagreements, conflicts, and confrontations exist among the employees in the organisation and organisation's willingness to tolerate and resolve these conflicts. An organisation evincing higher level of tolerance and resolution of employee conflicts, organisational climate is likely to be more compromising and adjusting.

7. Control: This refers to the extent to which employees' behaviour is regulated and monitored to enable to behave in desired manners. In practice, this can be done through two mechanisms. *One,* bureaucratic mechanism, i.e., control systems are well defined and prescribed. *Two,* self-regulation mechanism in which an employee without any prescribed system controls his behaviour or actions by himself or herself. These two types of control systems are also called as *"tightness"* versus *"looseness."*

8. Risk Taking: This refers to the extent to which an employee is free to try out his/her new ideas and be ready to share the responsibility for not trying out the same. This dimension of organisational climate is akin to *"cautious"* versus *"venturesome"* nature of an organisation.

Before we move on to the next topic on "Determinants of Organisational Climate", it seems pertinent to make a distinction between dimensions and determinants of organisational climate. To put simply, while dimensions are the components of organisational climate, determinants are the causes of it. One may also say, determinants are those which influence and dimensions are those which are influenced.

Let us have an exercise on dimensions of organisational climate. Go through the following exercise in which the left column lists the dimensions of organisational climate and right column shows their major focus. Apply your knowledge to match each dimension with its corresponding focus.

Dimensions	Focus
1. Individual Autonomy	A. The extent of freedom to apply one's new and creative ideas.
2. Position Structure	B. The degree of checks exercised on the actions / behaviour of employees in the organisation.
3. Reward System	C. The extent of benefits and incentives offered to employees to enable them to perform more and better.
4. Support System	D. The extent of collusions and disagreements to thwart and blockade other's efforts.
5. Progress and Development	E. The extent of direct supervision and prescription of formal rules and regulations applicable to employees while at work.
6. Conflict	F. The degree of freedom from accountability and answerable to others.
7. Control	G. The nature and extent of social support received from others at workplace.
8. Risk Taking	H. The scope and possibilities of one's growth and progress in the organisation.

Answers: 1F, 2E, 3C, 4G, 5D, 6H, 7A, 8B

26.6 DETERMINANTS OF ORGANISATIONAL CLIMATE

Having discussed the dimensions of organisational climate, an obvious question arises is what determines the climate of an organisation. No doubt, organisational climate usually refers to the internal properties of an organisation; there are also host of internal and external factors that determine the nature of organisational climate. Accordingly, one of the basic premises of organisational behaviour is that outside environmental forces also bear their impact on events within an organisation. For example, change in economic policies of the Government is likely to influence the internal matters like compensation, reward, and retention policies of an organisation. Nonetheless, we shall focus on the following major internal determinants of organisational climate:

1. Economic Health
2. Organisational Policies and Procedures
3. Organisational Size
4. Organisational Structure
5. Leadership Styles
6. Managerial Values and Ethos

These are now discussed in that order.

Economic Health

Just as several factors affect the dimensions of human health, so does happen in case of an organisation also. Economic health or soundness of an organisation influences, among other things, the type of organisational budgets will be prepared. You may say, a tight budget is prepared when economic condition of the organisation is weak. In such situation, organisation will be very cautious in undertaking its activities. On the country, during the period of prosperity, a loose budget will be prepared and organisation will tend to be risk-taking, i..e., venturesome. This suggests that the various dimensions of organisational climate such as reward, control, risk-taking, progress and development etc. are going to be influenced by economic condition or health of the organisation.

Organisational Policies and Procedures

More often than not, organisations formulate certain policies and procedures that regulate and monitor their activities and, in turn, facilitate their performance. There is evidence to believe that such policies and procedures do also influence certain dimensions of organisational climate. Let it be exemplified with some instances. Suppose, an educational institution like the National Institute of Financial Management (NIFM) evolves a policy that the faculty will not be asked to leave even after superannuation age if it is worthy of contributing to the Institute, it would, then, foster an organisational climate, i.e., climate that is supportive and humanistic. Similarly, if the NIFM formulates the policy to give incentive to its faculty @ Rs. 500 per point earned above 450 points in an academic year subject to a maximum of Rs. 1,50,000/ only, then it would influence its reward dimension of organisational climate characterized as *'High Reward Orientation'*.

Organisational Size

Research evidence is available to believe that size of an organisation influences, among other things, climate and of an organisation[13]. As regards effects of size of organisation on dimensions of organisational climate, a smaller-sized organisation fosters climate of creativity and / or innovation and it also suits to participative style of management or leadership. As against this, a relatively larger-sized organisation facilitates authoritative style of management and leadership which encourages vertical type of delegation of authority. Thus, smaller size of organisation influences employees' autonomy or freedom, whereas larger size of organisation influences monitoring and control dimensions of organisational climate.

Organisational Structure

Organisational structure is an abstract in the sense that it is not visible in the same way as mechanical structure. Nonetheless, it affects organisational climate in different ways. For example, a bureaucratic organisational structure will influence organisational climate quite differently from non-bureaucratic structure like System 4 organisation. What is meant by System 4 organisation? According to Rensis Likert, organisations can be classified into 4 groups, namely, Exploitative authoritative, Benevolent authoritative, Consultative, and Participative. But, here the problem is how to decide under which system an organisation falls. It depends on the manner an organisation perceives its different processes such as leadership, motivation, communication, and decision-making processes. Then, these processes are evaluated and rated by the employees of the organisation. Rating is based on employees' answers to the questions relating to these processes. Following are some illustrative questions that employees ask and answer:

1. How much the superiors rely on their subordinates?
2. How do superiors know the problems the subordinates face on their jobs?
3. Who do actually take organisational decisions?
4. Who do generally resist the organisational proposals?

Now, based on the answers given to the questions, an organisation can be classified as System 1 or 2 or 3 or 4. For example, a bureaucratic structure can be rated as System 1 or 2. Needless to mention, the organisational climate of System 1 or 2 organisation will be different from that of System 4 organisation.

Leadership Style

You have already read much about leadership and its styles in the chapter 21 on 'Leadership.' Organisational history is replete with the crucial role leadership plays in an organisation. Leadership styles influence various dimensions of organisational climate. In fact, the impact of leadership on organisation is so profound and pervasive that one may wonder whether the organisational climate is a product of the philosophies and practices of leaders. It is due to such profound impact of leadership on organisation, some people view that an organisation is the effect for which leadership is the cause.

You know that different leaders use different leadership styles and different leadership styles influence the dimensions of organisational climate differently. Leadership styles and their influence on the dimensions of organisational climate is summarized in the following Table 26.1.

Table 26.1 : Leadership Styles *vis-à-vis* Organisational Climate

Leadership Styles	*Dimensions of Organisational Climate*
Authoritative Leadership	
• Always follows order	• High position structure
• Criticizes violation of orders and rules and regulations	• High control
• Exercises authority and control	• Low individual autonomy
• Avoids involvement with employees	• Low warmth and support
Democratic Leadership	
• Involves employees in organisational matters	• High warmth and support
• Gives general positive rewards	• High reward orientation
• Creates friendly relationships	• Low conflict
• Gives individual and organisational support	• High progressiveness and development
Free-Reign Style	
• Maintains informality	• High individual autonomy
• Allows employees to work the way they like	• High risk-bearing
• Stresses free working in the organisation	• High individual autonomy

Managerial Values and Ethos

Managers run and manage the show in an organisation. Managers possess values, i.e. an enduring belief that a specific mode of conduct is personally and socially preferable to other alternative modes of conduct. Both character and values form managerial ethos. Examples of some of the contemporary values that the managers possess are autonomy, equity, security, opportunity, and work value. Research evidence suggests that managerial values and ethos do also influence organisational climate[14]. How? This is because values shape decisions and actions of the managers. For example, the enlightened managers believe that many employees prefer to work freely and they are given much latitude to work freely as long as the use of this freedom does not violate basic norms of the organisation. Such managers, thus, foster individual autonomy dimension of the organisational climate. Most of the managers also value that employees should get reward in proportion to their efforts made for the organisation and, thus, subscribe the value of fairness. The terms "hire and fire" was the perception of managers till yesterday. Now, managers also show concern for the security of employees' jobs[15]. Modern managers also exhibit concern for the career growth of their employees and, therefore, create opportunities for them. Last but not the least, work value of managers also influences the climate of an organisation. Work value means the worth a person ascribes to the opportunity of work. There can be different facets of work value. For example, one may view work as an opportunity to: (i) accept challenges, (b) serve society, (iii) earn money, (iv) enjoy status and respect, and be independent, i. e., one's own boss[16].

SUMMARY

This summary is organized by the 'learning objectives' given on page no. 430 :

- Organisational climate is a set of relatively enduring properties of the work environment that are perceived by the employees and that influence their behaviour and, in turn, organisational performance.
- Organisational climate differs from organisational culture in the sense that the former refers to descriptive beliefs and perceptions individuals hold of the organisation, whereas the latter is the sharedness of values and beliefs among the organisational members. In this sense, organisational culture is a sub-component of organisational climate.
- The need for and significance of organisational climate are imbued with multiplicity of justifications that it serves as facilitator, stimulator, evaluator, and perception shaper which, in turn, improve employee behaviour and performance.
- Dimensions of organisational climate refer to its components that are influenced. The examples of dimensions of organisational climate are individual autonomy, position structure, reward system, support system, progress and development, etc.
- Determinants of organisational climate mean the factors that influence its dimensions. Economic condition, organisational policies, organisational size, organisational structure, leadership styles, and managerial values and ethos are the common examples of the determinants of organisational climate.

REFERENCES

1. G.A. Forehand and B.V. Gulmer: Environmental Variation in Studies of Organization Behaviour, **Psychological Bulletin**, No. 62, 1964, pp.361-382.
2. John P. Campbell et al: **Managerial Behaviour, Performance, and Effectiveness**, McGraw - Hill, New York, 1970, p.390.
3. Renato Tagiuri: The Concept of Organisational Climate, In: Renato Tagiuri and George H. Litwin (Eds.): **Organisational Climate,** Division of Research, Graduate School of Business Administration, Harvard University, Boston, 1968.
4. E. H. Schein: **Organisational Culture and Leadership**, Jossey-Bass, San Francisco, 1992.
5. D. M. Rousseau: Assessing Organisational Culture: The Case for Multiple Methods,, In: B. Schneider (Ed.): **Organisational Climate and Culture**, Jossey-Bass, San Francisco, 1990, pp. 153-192.
6. R. G. Owens: **Organisational Behaviour in Education: Adaptive Leadership and School Reform**, Allyn & Bacon, Boston, 2004.
7. htt://www.dirigoconsulting.com
8. N. Frederiksen: Some Effects of Organisational Climates on Administrative Performance: **Research Memorandum**, 1966. Quoted in John P. Campbell et al, 1970, op. cit. p.401.
9. G. H. Litwin and R.Stringer: The Influence of Organisational Climate on Human Motivation, Paper presented in Organisational Climate, **Foundation for Research on Human Behaviour**, Michigan, March 1966, Quoted in John. P.Campbell et al, 1970, op. cit, 1970, p.391.
10. B. Schneider and C.J. Bartlett: Individual Differences and Organisational Climate, **Personnel Psychology**, No. 21, 1968, pp.323 - 334.
11. Renato Taguiri: **Comments on Organisational Climate**, quoted in John P. Campbell et al, op. cit., 1970, p.392.
12. G. H. Litwin and R. Stringer: *op. cit*, 1970, p.391.
13. Baldev R. Sharma: **Organisational Climate and Employer-Employee Relations in India**, International Management Institute, New Delhi, 1986.
14. R. C. Dangwal and Arun Sacher: Influence of Managerial Values on Organisational Climate: A Study of Selected Pharmaceutical Companies, **NICE Journal of Business**, Volume 2, Number 2, 2007, pp. 25-38.
15. S. N. Biswas: Perception of Organisational Climate and Effectiveness, **Indian Journal of Industrial Relations**, Vol. 28, No. 1, January 1993.
16. T. V. Rao and S. N. Chattopadhyay: A Study of the Perceptions of Organisational Climate by the Employees of Small Industries, **Indian Journal of Industrial Relations**, Volume 10, No. 1, 1974.

Case 26.1 : Developing Achieving Climate at Excel Industries*

Ever since Excel Industries was started in the 1940s, headquartered in Mumbai, western India, its mission was to develop indigenous technology to produce world - class chemicals, a mission that reflected the patriotic urges of the founding family. By the 1990s, Excel had plants in five locations and was producing highly sophisticated chemicals for industrial and agricultural applications. It had developed in house over a hundred alternative processes for manufacturing chemicals, all without any foreign technology, collaboration, or agreement, and, in fact, had supplied technology not only to Indian companies but also to foreign companies. It had won several awards for export performance, excellent plant management, and fair business practices. In 1990, Excel re-committed itself for the next 50 years to technological excellence and contribution to the development of the country, industry, and rural society through what the Japanese call rental, or 'togetherness', and extended its vision to develop responsible, creative, and productive persons to serve society. In this 50 - year vision of excellence, Excel committed itself to the dignity and capability of every human being and to creating an environment where everyone was motivated to realize her/his full potential. The stress was on teamwork, academic learning environment, and maternal concern for the stakeholders.

`Excel worked hard to make its vision a reality. Group brainstorming was widely used in problem solving for generating fresh ideas, and for this purpose temporary inter-functional teams were formed. A blackboard was installed in every office to instill a learning culture, and was used widely for presentations or explanations. No need was seen for a suggestion scheme, as it was expected that employees would feel free to discuss their ideas with higher-ups. If an idea was accepted, the proposer became a member of the team formed to implement the idea. To facilitate informal interactions, employees, including the CEO, lunched together in the company canteen. Formal designations and status symbols were discouraged. Socialisation of new members involved not only exposure to technical subjects, but also to talks by seniors on the history and culture of the organisation, innovativeness, and teamwork. Right from the start, young recruits were assigned to teams ad tasks that might not be related to their past experience and training.

No one was sacked at Excel. There was planned job rotation. The Excel Institute of Technology, Environment, and Management provided in-house training, although employees were also sent for outside courses. There were even courses on yoga and meditation, and the company funded the higher education (including doctorates) of staff members. The gap between the emoluments of top and bottom-level employees was kept modest. Before a formal promotion, the employee was tried out for a while in the new job. Excel frequently induced innovation through overloading. Employees

---

***Source:** Udai Pareek: **Understanding Organisational Behaviour** (Second Edition), , Oxford University Press, New Delhi, 2007, p. 660.

were challenged with targets like halving the cost or doubling the production.

Regarding R&D, Excel's philosophy was of exploring the possibilities of impossibilities - by taking up only those projects that were difficult and challenging. Excel's R&S was geared to providing it with the first-mover advantage in new, high-quality products. Most of the R&D work was done in teams and their work was reviewed by task forces. A forum called 'Innovation 1992' was formed for teams to present their innovative ideas. It was fairly commonplace to appoint groups to brainstorm on alternative uses of the technologies developed at Excel, including some 'failures'.

By 1992, Excel had become one of the top five Indian private sector chemicals companies in size. It was the most profitable of the top 10.

Case 26.2 : Organisational Climate at NIIT**

NIIT was founded in 1981 by two IIT, Delhi graduates, Rajendra S Pawar and Vijay K Thadani with a vision of meeting basic requirements for IT talent in a world moving into an information based economy. They had anticipations about the unpreparedness of Indian society to cope with the forthcoming information age and adopted the mission "bringing people and computers together, successfully". Initially, NIIT delivered IT training to a broad spectrum of people - from students seeking a career in computers to IT professionals requiring advanced skills; form managers giving their careers in edge, to school children using computers as a learning tool. NIIT's innovative offerings demonstrated the company's ability to constantly renew itself to anticipate future technology trends. From a computer training institute, NIIT has emerged as a global IT solutions corporation offering knowledge solutions along with developing software solutions. Headquartered in New Delhi, NIIT operates through 100% subsidiaries in the US, Asia Pacific, Europe, and Japan and has operations in about 40 countries.

Its mission keeps pace with the developments in the field of IT and is evolved through organisation wide discussions which helps develop commitment among employees. The organisation operates with the help of task teams designed for specific customer requirements for a specific period to carry out the work. Team culture and openness are emphasized a great deal. NIIT's corporate culture focuses on values such as quality, creativity, and customer satisfaction. The quality culture of NIIT has been the result of the sustained efforts of its management - perpetuated through induction, socialization, reinforcement, innovation, and concern for internal and external customers. The quality culture is ingrained at NIIT in such a way that the priority is to prevent mistakes rather than rectify them. Also, quality efforts are backed by results, which are rewarded.

****Source:** Mirza S. Saiyadain (Ed.): **Organisational Behaviour**, Tata McGraw-Hill Publishing Company Limited, Delhi, 2003, p.p. 255-256.

Employees are treated as intellectual capital and are looked after well. The happy and committed employees ensure customer satisfaction and this has got them wide acceptance across the globe. It has got well designed mechanisms for monitoring the quality for its products, services and or software processes. Most of NIIT's businesses have ISO 9000 certification. The work culture at NIIT has gone through all the stages of culture development like symbols, behaviour, organisational values, attitudes, and shared assumptions, and probably this is the reason it has been able to sustain it.

27

ORIGANISATIONAL CULTURE

"In any organisation, there are the ropes to skip and the ropes to know."

– R. Ritti and G. Frank Louser

Learning Objectives

After studying this chapter, you should be able to:

- **Define** organisational culture and **list** its characteristics.
- **Discuss** the various types of cultures.
- **Outline** the functions performed by culture.
- **List** the factors that create, sustain, and change a culture.
- **Describe** how employees learn an organisation's culture.
- **Discuss** theory Z Culture.

You have already studied in Chapter 5, the individual personality and its impact on behaviour. Just as individuals have personalities, so too do organisations. The organisational personalities are called **organisational cultures**. Just what organisational culture is, how it is created and maintained, how it is learnt, and how it affects the employees' behaviour at work are the main foci of the present chapter.

Let us first understand what organisational culture is.

27.1 DEFINITION OF ORGANISATIONAL CULTURE

Culture is something which is created and resides in the minds of the people. Culture is, therefore, interpreted and defined differently by different people. For example, Ott[1] reviewed 58 books and journal's articles, and identified as many as 73 key words/phrases used by different authors to define organisational culture. The meanings attributed to organisational culture range from behavioural to cognitive, from explicitly stated to tacitly followed, from being consciously enacted to being unconsciously felt and so on. That an appreciation of some important definitions may profitably contribute more to our understanding of organisational culture, a few important definitions are, therefore, produced here.

Edgar Schein[2], who is the most closely associated with the study of organisational culture, defines it as "A pattern of basic assumptions invented, discovered, or developed by a given group as it learns to cope with its problems of external adoption and internal integration that has worked well enough to be considered valuable and, therefore, to be taught to new members as the correct way to perceive, think, and feel, in relation to those problems."

Turnstall[3] defined organisational culture as "A general constellation of beliefs, morals, value systems, behavioural norms, and ways of doing business that are unique to each corporation".

Recently, Joanne Martin[4] while emphasizing differing perspectives of cultures in organisations, defined it as:

"As individuals come into contact with organisations, they come into contact with dress norms, stories people tell about what goes on, the organisation's formal rules and procedures, its formal codes of behaviour, rituals, tasks, pay systems, jargon, and jokes only understood by insiders, and so on. These elements are some of the manifestations of organisational culture".

One central theme flowing from above definitions is a system of **shared meaning**. This system of shared meaning is a set of key characteristics that the organisation values.

Thus, organisational culture can be defined as a pervasive underlying set of beliefs, assumptions, values, shared feelings and perceptions, which influence the actions and decisions taken by the organisations. The same distinguishes one organisation from another.

Organisational culture is marked by a number of **characteristics.** Following are the most readily agreed upon ones[5] :

1. **Observed Behavioural Regularities:** When people in the organisations interact with one another, they generally use common language, terminology, and other rituals that relate to deference and demeanor.

2. **Norms:** Standards of behaviour are set to guide the organisational members how much work to do. This, in many organisations, is expressed as **"Do not do too much, do not do too little."**

3. **Dominant Values:** Organisations advocate some major values and expect the same to be imbibed by its organisational participants. A few examples of such popular values are high product quality, regularity, and efficiency.

4. **Philosophy:** Organisations set forth certain beliefs about how employees and/or customers are to be treated.

5. **Rules:** There are guidelines prescribed how the new participants of the organisations have to adopt so as to be accepted the full-fledged members of their group in the organisation.

6. **Organisational Climate:** This is an overall "feeling" that is conveyed by the physical layout, the way organisational participants interact with one another, and the mode organisational members conduct themselves with outside persons.

Each of these characteristics exists on a continuum from low to high. There is empirical research support for most of them, such as the important role that dominant values play in organisational culture. **Here is a real-world illustration.**

In the **Reliance Group,** one of the much talked about and practised principles is the value of time. There are also countless stories of how people (ranging from departmental managers to (Late) Dhirubhai Ambani himself) took quick decisions to meet a crisis, how people show their concern about doing things, and doing them in shortest possible time. Not surprisingly, the Reliance Group completed their Patalganga project in a record time of 15 months. Even their collaborators, El Du Pont de Nemours found this achievement unbelievable and unparalleled[6].

As stated earlier, an organisational culture is a common perception held by the members of the organisation. However, all members may not do so to the same degree. As a result, there can be more than one type of culture. The next section discusses the same, *i.e.*, types of cultures.

27.2 TYPES OF CULTURES

The more prominent types of cultures are discussed here include :

1. **Dominant Culture and Subculture:** A **dominant culture** is marked by a set of core values that are shared by a majority of the organisational members. In fact, when we talk about an organisation's culture, we refer to its dominant culture. The dominant culture gives a macro view of organisation's personality. For example, most of the employees at the Reliance Group seem to share a concern for the value of the time. This creates a dominant culture in the organisation that helps guide the day-to-day behaviour of employees.

A **subculture** expresses a set of values that are shared by the members of a division or department. Subcultures typically are a result of problems or experiences that are shared by members of a particular department or unit. These subcultures can form vertically or horizontally[7]. When one product division of a coglomerate has a culture unique from that of other divisions of the organisation, a vertical subculture exists. When a specific set of functional specialists, such as accountants, have a set of common shared understandings, a horizontal subculture is formed. It is important to mention that a particular department will include the core values of the dominant culture plus values distinct to the members of the particular department.

2. **Strong and Weak Cultures:** Based on intensity of sharedness, organisational cultures are of two types: **strong** and **weak**. A strong culture is characterised by the organisation's core values being intensely held and widely shared. So to say, more intensely the core values are shared, the stronger the culture is. The degree of sharedness depends on two factors: **orientation** and **rewards.** In order for people to share the same cultural values, orientation programmes are organised to tell the new comers about the organisation's philosophy and method of operation. Orientation may be done through both words-of-mouth and day-to-day work habits and examples. Rewards do also affect sharedness. For example, promoting employees those who hold the core values helps others as well better understand the core values. This, in turn, results in lower employee turnover. When core values are not shared with high degree of intensity, it forms **weak culture.** Weak culture is usually characterised by high turnover of employees.

27.3 FUNCTIONS OF CULTURE

We have just alluded how organisational culture affects the employee turnover. In other words, we mentioned about organisational culture's impact on employee behaviour. What other functions organisational culture performs are more carefully reviewed in this section.

As a matter of fact, culture performs several functions in an organisation. Based on review of studies[8,9] on organisational culture, the major functions performed by culture are:

1. Culture provides shared patterns of cognitive perceptions or understanding about the values or beliefs held by the organisation. This enables the organisational members how to think and behave as expected of them.
2. It also provides shared patterns of feelings to the organisational members to make them know what they are expected to value and feel.
3. It provides a boundary that creates distinctions between one organisation and other. Such boundary-defining helps identify members and non-members of the organisation.
4. Culture facilitates the generation of commitment to something larger than one's individual self-interest.
5. It enhances social stability by holding the organisational members together by providing them appropriate standards for which the member should stand for.
6. It serves as a control mechanism that guides and shapes the attitudes and behaviour of organisational members. It helps organisational members stick to the confirmity to the prescribed and expected mode of behaviour.
7. Culture finally, ensures that everyone is pointed in the same direction.

Culture exists in every organisation. Now, the question arises is whether it is good or bad. It is clear from the functions just outlined that culture is valuable for both the organisation and the employee. Culture is valuable for the organisation because it enhances organisational commitment of the employees. It guides employees how things are done and what is important for them. These clearly are benefits to employees. But, it does not mean that culture is free from dysfunctional aspects.

Sometimes, culture is marked by dysfunctional aspects as well especially when the shared values do not agree with those that will further the organisation's effectiveness. Such a situation mostly occurs when the organisational environment is quite dynamic. This is so because the organisation's embeded culture may not remain appropriate any more in the changed environment of the organisation. Behaviour remains consistent in the stable environment. Given the culture's inability to respond to changes in the environment becomes organisation's liability. Liability, be it in any form, requires to be discharged. Hence, the embeded culture needs to be changed or modified to suit to the changed environment of the organisation. Change in culture is discussed little later in this chapter.

27.4 CREATING, SUSTAINING, AND CHANGING A CULTURE

As mentioned ealier, culture is sharedness of understanding values among the organisational members. Culture once established may fade away also. The established culture needs to be changed to respond to the environmental changes. Then, it is against this background, certain obvious questions arise: How is culture created ? What forces sustain culture? and How does culture change? This section answers these questions one by one.

Creating a Culture

Beliefs and values have their base on the past happenings. It implies that the ultimate source of an organisation's culture is its founders[10]. The founders start their organisation with a vision of what their organisation should be. Then, the vision is imposed on all organisational members. The members imbibe the vision through interaction and their own experience. Thomas Watson of IBM is a good example. Watson's views on research and development, product innovation, employee dress attire, and compensation policies still influence practices at IBM, though he died long back in 1956.

J.R.D. Tata is another example who typifies this type of culture creation. His supportive-consultive role, his belief on professionalism, and assumption that only honesty and fair dealings will pay have made the vast Tata empire what it is today.

Luthans[11] has outlined a distinct process involved in the creation of a culture. The process, according to him, involves the following steps :

1. A single person (founder) has an idea or vision for an enterprise.
2. The founder brings in some people and creates a core group that shares a common vision with the founder. All in the core group accept the idea or vision and work for it.
3. The founding core group begins to act in concert to create an organisation by raising funds, obtaining patents, incorporating, locating space, building, and so on.

Sustaining a Culture

Culture once established may fade away also. Hence, once a culture is created, it needs to be sustained through reinforcement practices of human resources. Three such practices particularly important in sustaining a culture are selection practices, the actions of top management, and socialization methods. Let's take a closer look at each of these.

Selection: The first step involved in sustaining culture is the careful selection of entry level candidates. The basic purpose of selection process is to appoint right people for right jobs. For this, the trained recruiters interview candidates and attempt to screen out candidates those whose personal styles and values do not make a fit with the organisation's culture. Thus, by identifying the suitable candidates who can culturally match the organisational culture, selection helps sustain culture considerably. **Let's illustrate it with a real-world illustration.**

> In **Procter and Gamble (P&G),** applicants for entry-level positions undergo an exhaustive application and screening process. The interviewers who will identify the candidates who will best fit in at P & G, are trained extensively via lectures, videotapes, films, and role plays. The candidates are thoroughly interviewed to adjudge their suitability to fit in organisation's culture. P & G values rationality and seeks applicants also who think rationally. All these practices count for success at P & G.

Top Management: Subordinates emulate their superiors. Hence, the actions of top management such as what the managers say and how they behave have a major impact on the employees working at lower levels. As a matter of fact, this filters down in the entire organisation and becomes a common feature or culture of organisation. Managerial actions like degree of freedom granted to the subordinates, prescriptions for the employee uniform, pay off in terms of pay raises, promotions, and other rewards also help create a common history *i.e.,* culture in the organisation.

Socialisation: Socialisation can be conceptualised as acquisition of work skills and abilities, adoption of appropriate role behaviours and adjustment to the norms and values of the work group[12]. In simple words, socialisation is the process of adaptation. New organisational members coming from different moods and mores are likely to disturb the common customs and beliefs already established in the organisation. Therefore, the new employees need to be indoctrinated to adapt the organisational culture. This adaptation process is called **socialisation.** Socialisation process involves three phases:

- Pre-arrival
- Encounter
- Metamorphosis

A brief description of these follows:

Pre-arrival refers to all the learning that occurs before a new member joins the organisation.

Encounter is the stage of induction which the new recruit joins the firm and put on the job. The role playing starts here. The recruit starts comparing expectations, the image, which he had formed during pre-arrival stage with reality. If expectation and reality concur, the encounter is smooth. But seldom it concurs. When the two differ, stress and frustration set in. What follows thereafter is a mental process of adjustment. In this adjustment, the individual tries to replace his/her own values and norms with those of the organisation at least in vital areas, if not in all. In the other extreme, the recruit simply cannot reconcile to those values and norms of the organisation and get illusioned and quit the job.

Metamorphosis is the completion stage of changes and consolidation of changed behaviour (defreeze). In this stage, the employees master the skills required for their new roles, and make the adjustment to the organisation's norms and values. This is, of course, a voluntary process and a conscious decision which enables them to become compatible with the group and organisation. This signals the completion of socialisation process.

Changing a Culture

The ever fast changing business environment has made everything euphemeral in nature. So is organisational culture also. As organisations do not remain the same over a period of time, so is the case of culture as well. Culture established in one type of environment may not remain effective in changed environment. If it is so, the organisation must either adapt to new conditions of environment or it may not survive. Hence, the need for change in organisational culture.

However, changing culture is as much important is not so simple. Changing a strong culture is particularly difficult because the cultural values and assumptions have taken deep roots and employees become so committed to them. Yes, it is easier to change the culture when it is weak.

Deal and Kennedy[13] identified five situations which facilitate change in the culture:

Figure 27.1 delineates how culture is created and sustained through various forces.

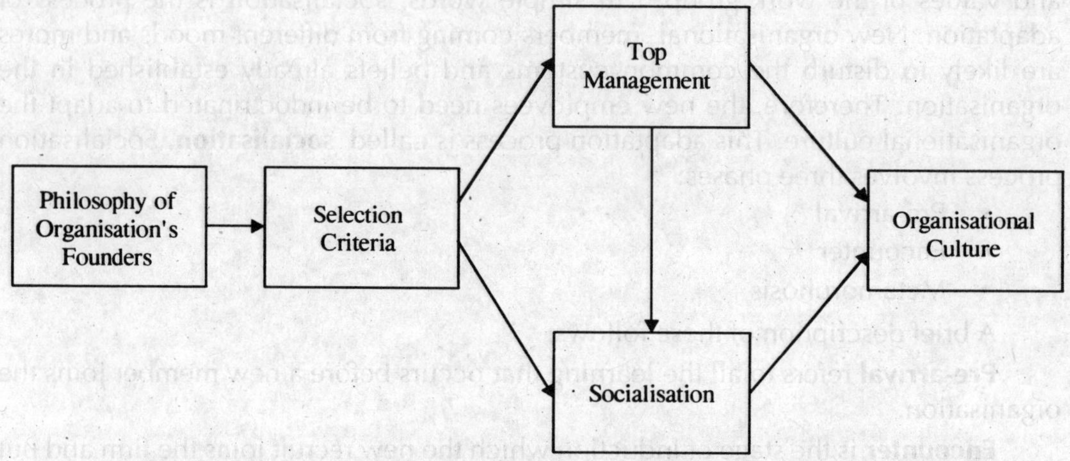

Fig. 27.1: How Organisational Cultures Form and Sustain

1. When the environment is going rapid changes, and the company has always been highly value-driven.
2. When the industry is highly competitive and the environment changes quickly.
3. When the company is mediocre, or worse.
4. When the company is truly at the threshold of becoming a large corporation.
5. When the company is growing very rapidly.

Among other major factors that create the right conditions for change in culture include:

A Dramatic Crisis: At times, there can be some shocks that undermine the *status quo* of culture and question its relevance in a new crisis. The examples of such crises might be a surprising financial setback, the loss of a major customer, or a dramatic technological breakthrough by a competitor which can change the market structure. For example, once the **Maruti car** was introduced in the Indian market, it shock up the otherwise sedate passenger car market, and forced other companies to take a more productive stance. Similarly, the economic reforms initiated during the 1990's, as well as the opening up of the global market, forced many companies to attempt changing their cultural orientation.

Change in Leadership: Changing top leadership can also have a major impact on organisational culture. New leadership at the organisational apex heralds signals of change. It will not be less than correct to say that the top leadership is the personification of the culture. This is because the top leadership sets the norms, values and formal reward system for achieving organisational goals. Many Indian companies like MMTC, SAIL and ACC, saw major changes occuring after new Chief Executive Officers (COEs) took over.

27.5 HOW IS CULTURE LEARNT ?

Since the term organisational culture refers to the underlying beliefs and values that are shared by organisation members, culture can't be dictated by the top management. Instead, organisational culture is transmitted to employees in a number of forms. The most potent ones are stories, rituals, symbols, and language.

Stories

The stories, be these true or false, told to the organisational members can have a profound impact on organisational culture. Most stories are narratives based on true events about the organisation's founders, rule breaking, rags-to-riches successes, reductions in the work force, relocation of employees, reactions to past mistakes, and organisational coping. Some stories are considered legends because the events are historic. However, there also may be stories embellished with fictional details. Stories are useful because they preserve the primary values of the organisation by anchoring the present in the past. The popular practice of story telling by the grand-parents to their grand children in our own society also aims at inculcating old values and beliefs in the new generation so as the same can be preserved for all the times.

Here is a real world case.

During the days, when Henry Ford II was chairman of the Ford Motor Co., one would have been hard-pressed to find a manager who had not heard the story about Mr. Ford's reminding his executives, when they got too argumentative, that "**It's is my name that is on the building**". The message was clear. Henry Ford II ran the company!

Rituals

Rituals also are a means for transmitting culture. Activities such as award ceremonies, weekly Friday picnic, and annual general meetings are some examples of rituals. These rituals reinforce the key values of the organisation, what goals are important, which people are important and which are expendable. The annual convocation function organised by the Tezpur Central University is an example of ritual performed in an educational institution.

Many organisational researchers[15] have even considered some of the established management methods and techniques as cultural rituals. Managers employ techniques such as PERT/CPM, complex modelling and simulation, dissemination of regular updates on projects, brainstorming sessions, etc. The work is still performed in the same manner as it was being done earlier.

Symbols

A symbol is something that represents something else. Physical symbols in organisations are often used to represent and support organisational culture. Examples of symbols include the size of offices, the elegance of office furnishings, executive perks, and the presence of reserved parking spaces for certain employees. The value of these symbols is that they communicate important cultural values. Symbols become more powerful facilitator of culture if symbols are consistent with the stories that are narrated to the organisational members.

Languages

As language is a means of universal communication, most organisations tend to develop their own language in the forms of jargon, phrases, acronym, slogans, etc. By learning this language, the members attest to their acceptance of the culture and, in so doing, help preserve the organisational culture.

Organisations use a specific slogan, metaphor, or saying to convey special meaning to employees. Metaphors are often quite meaningful and convey an entire sermon in only a short sentence. Slogans can be readily picked up and repeated by employees as well as customers of the company. "**IBM means service**" is an example of slogan that symbolizes what the company stands for to both employees and the society.

Organisations also develop unique terms to describe their key personnel, products, equipments, and so on. For example, IBM has developed a term "**a one performer**" to identify an employee with IBM's top performance rating. New employees frequently come to hear such terms and over time, these terms become part of their language.

Organisational Culture at NIIT

Go through the following caselet of NIIT. It will help you understand how the various manifestations like shared values, beliefs, and assumptions create informal organisational culture.

NIIT was founded in 1981 by two IIT, Delhi graduates, Rajendra S. Pawar and Vijay K. Thadani with a vision of meeting basic requirements for IT talent in a world moving into an information based economy. They had anticipations about the unpreparedness of Indian society to cope with the forthcoming information age and adopted the mission "**bringing people and computers together, successfully**." Initially, NIIT delivered IT training to a broad spectrum of people-from students seeking a career in computers to IT professionals requiring advanced skills; from managers giving their careers an edge, to school children using computers as a learning tool. NIIT's innovative offerings demonstrated the company's ability to constantly renew itself to anticipate future technology trends. From a computer training institute, NIIT has emerged as a global IT solutions corporation offering knowledge solutions along with developing software solutions. Headquartered in New Delhi, India, NIIT operates through 100% subsidiaries in the US, Asia Pacific, Europe, and Japan and has operations in about 40 countries.

Its mission keeps pace with the development in the field of IT and is evolved through organisation-wide discussions which helps develop commitment among employees. The organisation operates with the help of task teams designed for specific customer requirements for a specific period to carry out the work. Team culture and openness are emphasised a great deal. NIIT's corporate culture focuses on values such as quality, creativity, and customer satisfaction. The quality culture of NIIT has been result of the sustained efforts of its management-perpetuated through induction socialisation, reinforcement, innovation, and concern for internal and external customers. the quality culture is ingrained at NIIT in such a way that the priority is to prevent mistakes rather than ractify them. Also, quality efforts are backed by results, which are rewarded.

Employees are treated as intellectual capital and looked after well. The happy and committed employees ensure customer satisfaction and this has got them wide acceptance across the globe. It has got well designed mechanisms for monitoring the quality for its products, services and/or software processes. Most of NIIT's businesses have ISO 9000 certification. **The work culture at NIIT has gone through all the stages of culture development like symbols, behaviour, organisational values, attitudes, and shared assumptions, and probably this is the reason it has been able to sustain it**.

Source: Adapted from Mirza S. Saiyadain (Ed.): **Organisational Behaviour**, Tata McGraw-Hill Publishing Company Limited, New Delhi, 2003, pp. 255-256.

27.6 THEORY Z CULTURE

The remarkable economic success of Japanese firms influenced the U.S. organisations to imitate some selected Japanese practices, if not all. In consequence, some of the major American organisations such as IBM, Kodak, and Procter & Gamble attempted to adopt the Japanese management styles in their organisations. The American adaptation of the Japanese style of management is known as the "**Theory Z Organisational Culture**".[16]

The overriding feature of a type Z organisation is a feeling of cooperation and collaboration between managers and employees. In case of theory Z management culture, the employees feel a sense of equality and identity and also involvement as the partners of the organisation. Employees have a better and greater understanding about one another's point of view which serves a seedbed for shared norms and values in the organisation. In summary, in the type Z organisations, employment is effectively a lifetime commitment. Consequently, employee turnover is low and employees progress through a well defined order of career positions over the period. Decision-making is done by consensus. There is a shared sense of collective responsibility for the success of a decision. The sense of collective responsibility increases productivity.

The basic distinction among type A, *i.e.*, the typical American corporation, type J, *i.e.*, the Japanese organisation, and type Z, *i.e.*, an organisation patterned after the Japanese hierarchical clan is illustrated in the following Table 27.1.

Table 27.1: Comparison of Three Organisational Cultures

Type A (American)	**Type J (Japanese)**	**Type Z (Modified American)**
Short-term employment	Lifetime employment	Long-term employment
Individual decision making	Consensual decision making	Consensual decision making
Individual responsibility	Collective responsibility	Individual responsibility
Rapid evaluation and promotion	Slow evaluation and promotion	Slow evaluation and promotion
Explicit, formalized control	Implicit, informal control	Implicit, informal control with explicit, formalized measures
Specialized career path	Nonspecialized career path	Moderately specialized career path
Segmented concern	Holistic concern	Holistic concern, including family

SUMMARY

This summary is organized by the 'learning objectives' given on page no. 444 :

- Organisational culture is a set of the beliefs, norms, and behaviour that are shared by the employees.
- Organisational culture may not be shared by all the employees to the same degree. A dominant culture is a set of core values that is shared by a majority of the organisation's members. A subculture, on the other hand, is a set of values shared by a small percentage of the organisation's members. Depending upon the sharedness and intensity of values and belief, organisations may have strong culture and weak culture.
- Organisational culture performs functions like giving members a sense of identity and increasing their commitment, providing shared pattern of feelings, facilitating generation of commitment to larger organisational interests, and serving as a control mechanism for shaping the employees' behaviour.
- Creation of culture is based on the vision of the founding fathers of the organisation. Culture so established is sustained and maintained through the practices such as selection, top management practices, and socialisation process. Socialisation process involves three phases, namely, pre-arrival, encounter, and metamorphosis. Culture needs to be changed in order to remain competitive and even survive in a changed environment. A dramatic crisis and change in leadership are the two major factors that make culture prone to change.
- Culture is learnt through stories, rituals, symbols, and language.
- Theory Z culture is a modified version of the Japanese management practices adapted by the American organisations.

REVIEW QUESTIONS

1. What is meant by organisational culture? Define it and also give some examples of its characteristics.
2. How does a strong culture differ from weak culture ?
3. Discuss the functions performed by organisational culture.
4. How is organisational culture created and sustained?
5. How do organisations go about maintaining their cultures? What steps are involved in it? Describe them.
6. How is culture learnt? In your answer, give example wherever relevant.
7. What is Theory Z Culture? What are its salient characteristics?
8. How does a dominant culture differ from a subculture?
9. Identify a set of characteristics that describe your University's culture. Compare them with several of your classfellows. How closely do they agree?

REFERENCES

1. J.S. Ott: **The Organisational Culture,** Perspective, Dorsey Press, Chicago, 1989.
2. E.H. Schein: **Organisational Culture and Leadership**, Jossey-Boss, San Francisco, 1985 p. 9.
3. W.B. Turnstall: Cultural Transition at AT & T, **Sloan Management Review,** 25, 1983 pp 1-12.
4. Joanne Martin: **Cultures in Organisations**, Oxford University Press, New York, 1992, p. 3.
5. Fred Luthans: ***op. cit.,*** 1985 (Seventh Edition), pp. 497-98.
6. Madhukar Shukla : ***op. cit.,*** 1996, p. 151.
7. Stephen P. Robbins: **Organisational Theory** (Structure, Design and Applications), Printice-Hall of India Private Limited, New Delhi, 1998, p. 441.
8. J.S. Ott: ***op. cit.***, 1989.
9. Stephen P. Robbins: ***op. cit.,*** 1998, p. 601
10. E.H. Schein: The Role of the Founder in Creating Organisational Culture, **Organisational Dynamics**, Summer 1983, pp. 13-28.
11. Fred Luthans: ***op. cit.***, 1995, p. 504.
12. Daniel, C. Feldman: The Multiple Socialisation of the Organisation Members, **Academy of Management Review**, April 1981.
13. T.E. Deal and A.A. Kennedy: **Corporate Cultures: The Rites and Rituals of Corporate Life,**, Addison-Wesley, Reading (Mass), 1982.
14. Cited by Stephen P. Robbins: ***op. cit.,*** 1998, p. 610.
15. T.E. Deal and A.A. Kennedy: ***op. cit.***, 1982
16. William G. Ouchi: **Theory Z,** Addison-Wesley, Reading, Mass, 1981.

Case 27.1: The New Procter & Gamble (P & G)

For years the culture at P & G had supported steady growth and profits. In recent years, however, the company found itself under a great deal of pressure from the external competitive environment. For example, Kimberly-Clark had cut deeply into P & G's disposable-diaper market, one of the company's most lucrative market niches. At the same time, Lever Brothers was making inroads into P & G's share of the soap and detergent market. On the newproduct development front, things were no better. The company was having disappointing results with its Pringles potato chips and was suffering financial losses on its Coldsnap Homemade Ice Cream Mix, Wondra hand cream, and Rely Tampons. These setbacks were reflected on the company's bottom line as pretax earnings fell for the first time in over thirty years. At the same time, the firm was having union problems. Its Kansas City plant voted to unionize, and the company went through a long fight with worker representatives in its efforts to change work practices and inprove efficiency.

These developments led P & G to make changes in its organisational culture. Some of these were the following:

1. The work team concept, in which production and maintenance workers called "technicians" are required to master and use a second skill, was extended throughout P & G's operations.

2. The lifetime-job tradition that once made P & G workers the envy of their blue collar counterparts elsewhere gave way to layoffs.
3. The corporate paternalism of the past yielded to some hard practicalities as executives and workers alike were put on notice that plants that didn't measure up on productivity, cost, and quality would be shut down.
4. A determined management vigorously resisted attempts by organized labour to dictate how P & G's operations should be run.

In addition to the above, P & G trimmed its work force by 5 percent on the plant floor and 4 percent company-wide. This was accomplished through reduced hiring, early retirement, and, in some cases, layoffs. Changing conditions had led P & G to change its culture.

QUESTIONS

1. How has the environment affected P & G's culture ?
2. If you were hired as a consultant by P & G's Board, what recommendations would you make to improve the company's cultural effectiveness ?

28

ORGANISATIONAL CHANGE AND DEVELOPMENT (OD)

"To improve is to change, to be perfect is to change often." – ***Winston Churchill***

"Change when you are still strong and when change appears unnecessary - do not wait for the day when you have no option but to change." – ***Jamshed J. Irani***

Learning Objectives

After studying this chapter, you should be able to:

- **Appreciate** why organisations must change.
- **Define** and **discuss** planned change.
- **Understand** the process of resistence to change and means of overcoming resistance.
- **Define** organisation development (OD) and **highlight** its characteristics.
- **Discuss** various OD models in use.
- **Explain** the major organisation development interventions.
- **Know** about the factors that influence choice of an intervention in an OD programme.

INTRODUCTION

We are aware of the axiom that the only certainty in the world is that there will be 'change'. **"The old order changeth, yielding place to new."** If we compare closely, we find that in many respects an organisation is akin to a living organism. Just like animate, organisations do not remain the same over a period of time. As a matter of fact, either through a planned efforts or through a process of adapting to changes in internal and external circumstances, organisations change. Just as any animate needs to keep harmony with the ever changing environment for its survival, so does an organisation need to respond to the barrage of changes taking place in its environment. Why? Because of the Darwin theory of *"the survival of the fittest."*

Taking note of this, the present chapter focuses on why organisational changes occur, the nature of change process, planned change, resistance to change, the strategies for coping with the organisational change, and the key aspects of organisation development (OD).

28.1 WHY ORGANISATIONAL CHANGES ?

We began with comparing organisations with animate like human beings. Why organisations change can be better understood by understanding why individuals change. Individuals experience two types of changes. **One,** they try to adjust and adopt to the changes occuring in the external environment such as offer of a new job, sickness, competition or loss of property. **Second**, even if nothing changes in the external environment, still individuals automatically keep changing (adulthood, oldage, family responsibilities, etc.)

Like human beings, organisations are also open systems[1]. Therefore, the same reasons also apply to organisational changes. So to say, organisations change both because of situational fluctuations in the environmental demands as well as because it is in their nature to grow and develop. Nokia presents a classical example of this.

Changing Nokia : From Start to Today

Nokia is a classical example of how companies survive and remain competitive by adapting to environmental changes. The Finish conglomerate started in 1865 as a pulp and paper company in a mill town near Helsinki. The company bought into the rubber business 30 years later and into cable wiring in the 1920s. Many Finns still associate Nokia with the rubber shoe boots they wore as children in the 1960s. Nokia invested in electronics and was soon making televisions and computer monitors. In the 1980s, Nokia executives sensed an emerging market for mobile telecommunications and took enormous risks by investing in that environmental shift. Today, people around the world know of Nokia for its sleek cellular telephones. It were mainly changing environmental factors that helped Nokia executives anticipate opportunities and change the organisation to realize these opportunities.

Source: N. Bennister : Nokia : From Start to Finnish, **The Age** (Mebourne), October 26, 1999.

A short list of some of the changes which affected almost all organisations in the past few decades is given here:

- Technological innovations have multiplied, products and knowhow are fast becoming obsolete.
- Basic resources have progressively become more expensive.
- Competition has sharply increased.
- Communication and computers have reduced the time needed to make decisions.
- Environmental and consumer interest groups have become highly influential.
- The drive for social equity has gained momentum.
- The economic inter-dependence among countries has become more apparent.

All the reasons for organisational change can be classified into two categories : external reasons and internal reasons.

External Reasons

An umpteen number of changes in the external environment may cause change in the organisation. Here, we are mentioning some of the most common and obvious external reasons of organisational change :

All the reasons for organisational change can be classified into two categories : external reasons and internal reasons.

1. **Government Rules and Regulations:** One can catalogue a long list of the Government's changing rules and regulations necessitating changes in organisations. For example, the recent slashing of grants by the University Grants Commission (UGC) to the Universities have forced them to strengthen their revenue–generating functions, such as training programmes, consultancy, offering self-financing courses, etc. Likewise, the Government's policy to privatise the power sector encouraged by Jayprakash and the DLF to diversify into the power sector.

2. **Competition:** The present time is the survival of the fittest. Organisations need to come up the challanges posed by the competitors to sustain and survive. In 1993, Mudra Communication decided to reorganise itself to counter the threats from its competitors Lintas and HTA[2].

3. **Technological Advances:** Technology has become the buzzword of the time. Rapid changes in technology has posed a question before the organisation — either run or ruin. The revolutionary change in communication technology *i.e.*, communication satellite, cable networking, dish antenna, etc. compelled the Doordarshan to restructure itself by segmenting its services to different categories of viewers and become more competitive.

4. **Changes in People Requirements:** Customers dictate organisations what they actually require. With changing requirements of customers, the five-star-hotels have, of late, started to offer new services, such as business centres, conference hall facilities, secretarial services, etc.

Internal Reasons

Though there may be a host of internal factors that may also cause change in organisations, some of the illustrative ones are listed here:

1. **Change in Leadership:** We have already discussed in the previous chapter that leadership changes culture and values in the organisations. V. Krishnamurty of SAIL, Tapan Mitra of INDAL, Ratan Tata of Tata Sons are the examples how the change in leadership led to internal changes in these organisations.

2. **Introducing New Technology:** Introduction of new technology in an organisation is bound to have consequences for other functions as well. For example, the computerisation of the Examination Division of the Assam University affected other aspects as well, such as reporting relationships, span of control, coordination mechanism and so on.

3. **The Domino Effect:** The source of change is change itself. The domino effect means one change triggers off a series of related changes. For example, establishing a new department *e.g.* the Department of Business Administration may cause the creation of teaching and non-teaching positions, budgeting allocation, building construction etc. Ignoring domino effect leads to the problems of coordination and control.

4. For Meeting Crises: Just like human life, some unforeseen happenings, say, crisis in the organisation makes continuation of the *status quo* unthinkable and difficult. Sudden death of a CEO, the resignation of the executives holding key positions, loss of major suppliers, a drastic cutback in budget, and civil disturbances are the examples of unforeseen crises. These make the organisational condition unstable and this unstability becomes the stimulus for thorough self-assessment and reform to change the organisation to overcome the crisis before it.

5. Organisational Life-Cycle: As human beings pass through certain sequential stages of life-cycle, so do the organisations also. As an organisation grows from tiny sized to giant sized or from young to mature stage, according to Larry Greiner[3], it passes through five stages. Each stage creates new demands for adjustment for the organisation, and so, acts as a potent sources of organisational change. Each stage culminates in a crisis (which Greiner calls 'revolution'), which the organisation must overcome before graduating to the next stage.

Greiner's five stages of organisational life are shown in the following figure 28.1

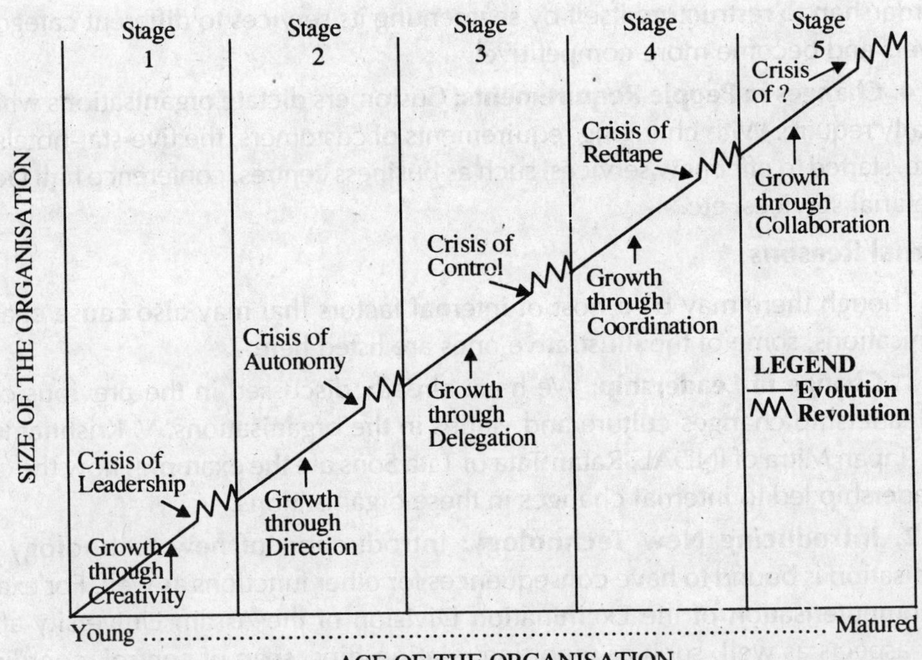

Fig. 28.1: Five Stages of Organisational Growth

That change in any part of the organisation can have impact on the total organisation is illustrated by Newstrom and Davis by comparing an organisation to an air filled ballon. When a finger (representing an external force) is, pressed at a point on the balloon (representing organisation), the contour of the ballon visibly changes; it becomes intended at the point of finger contact. If we look minutely we find that the shape of the entire balloon has changed; it has stretched slightly. This is how they have concluded that change in any part of organisation, in a manner of 'Domino Effect, affects the whole organisation.

Types of Changes

Organisational changes are of two types :

1. Reactive changes, and
2. Proactive changes

A brief description of these follows :

Reactive Changes: Reactive changes occur when forces compel organisation to implement change without delay. In other words, when demands made by the forces are complied in a passive manner, such a change is called reactive change.

Proactive Changes: Proactive changes occur when some factors make realize organisation think over and finally decide that implementation of a particular change is necessary. Then, the change is introduced in a planned manner.

The difference between reactive and proactive changes can be made on the basis of behavioural angle.

1. Reactive change involves a reflexive behaviour whereas proactive change involves purposive behaviour.
2. Reactive change covers a limited part of the system but proactive change coordinates the various parts of the system as a whole.
3. While reactive changes respond to immediate symptoms, proactive changes address to underlying forces creating symptoms.

An example will help you distinguish the two changes in more clear manner.

> Remember, you respond reflexively to a sudden intense light by blinking your eyes or by pupillory contraction. Undoubtedly, your's this is an automatic and instant response to a force (intense light) without giving any thought. But, your purposive response to the same force would involve devising a plan either to shield the eyes or removing the light. Obviously, your's this action would involve coordination of central nervous system and psychomotor capacities.
>
> In this chapter we are concerned about the proactive changes, also called planned changes. The same is discussed, in more detail, in the following section.

28.2 PLANNED CHANGE

You have just studied that proactive changes are effected in a planned manner after assessing the underlying forces in the system. When changes are effected after working out when and how they will be carried out, planned changes occur. For initiating planned change, the manager needs to constantly watch the changes taking place in the external and internal environment of the business so that corrective measures are taken accordingly and the changes could be effected successfully.

Changes can be introduced successfully only when there are conducive factors in existence in the system. Kurt Lewin[4] developed a useful technique, namely, the **Force Field Analysis,** for diagnosing whether or not the given system is conducive for introducing change. Lewin's analysis is discussed subsequently.

Force Field Analysis

Lewin's model of change is derived from the laws of physics, which state that the position of an object and its direction are determined by the forces operating on it. In his model, Lewin used three terms-driving forces, restraining forces, and quasi-static equilibrium to explain human behaviour at any given point of time. He contends that a person's behaviour is the product of two opposing forces: One force pushes toward preserving the *status* quo (**restraining force**), and another force (**driving force**) pushes for change. When the two opposing forces are approximately equal in opposite direction, (**quasi-static equilibrium**), current behaviour is occured. For changing behaviour, the forces maintaining *status quo* must be overcome. This can be accomplished by increasing the driving forces, reducing the restraining forces or by converting a restraining force into driving force.

Let us explain the two types of forces and the concept of equilibrium with an example. Consider that you have been studying your management course under the semester system and want to switchover to trimester system. This change or switchover might involve two types of forces. There will be some forces that will appreciate the need for switching over to the trimester system. Some of these forces will be :

1. The students will go through the broader coverage of the subject in terms of the number of more papers under the trimester system.

2. The trimester system will increase their chances for getting exmployment.

3. This will not give leisurely–pleasurely going attitude to the students which will prove beneficial for their work life.

These forces are called "*driving forces*" of change.

There will also be some forces that will operate against change. Some of these forces will be :

1. Given the time constraint, the trimester system will be characterised by the 'touch and go' style of teaching and learning.

2. The students will not get indepth knowledge in the subject and will become simply 'jack of all and master of none'.

3. This will adversely affect atleast one's prospects of progress on the job.

If the above two sets of forces are equal in strength , the system will be in the state of equilibrium and the change will not occur. Yes, if the driving forces are stronger than the restraining forces, then the system will be changing to find a new equilibrium and, in turn, change will occur. If, however, the restraining forces are stronger than the driving forces, then it indicates that the time is not propitious for changes to be introduced. In such case, efforts need to be made to reduce the restraining forces and increase the driving forces to introduce the required change.

Now, here is an exercise for you to apply Kurt Lewin's Force Field Analysis.

This exercise is meant to diagnose the situation described below, identify forces for and against change, and recommend strategies to reduce resistance to change. Follow the following steps:

Step 1 : Students will form groups of four or five people and every group will read the following situation.

(Jogiroad Paper Mill (A Unit of HPC), in Assam is earning a profit of five percent and wants to increase it to eight percent. The mill might want to bridge the gap between the existing and desired percentage of profit by increasing productivity through new technology, *i.e.* by mechanizing the labour – intensive tedious work.)

Step 2 : Using Lewin's force field analysis model (see Exhibit 28.1), identify the forces that seem to support the change and the forces that likely oppose the change to eight percent profit. The students should try to consider all possible sources of support and resistance as per the situation.

Step 3 : For each restraining force, or say, source of resistance, identify one or more strategies that would most effectively manage change. Recall from the textbook that the change management strategies included communication, training, employee involvement, negotiation, and coercion.

Exhibit 28.1 : Force Field Analysis Model

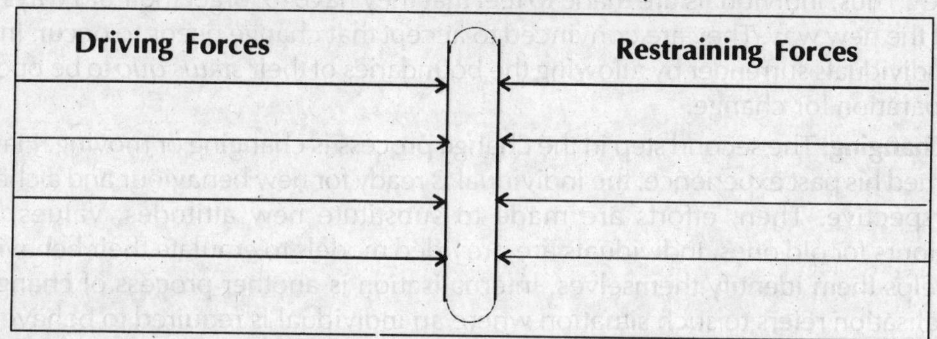

Step 4: The class will discuss each group's results.

Here is an example of Kurt Lewin's Force-Field Analysis.

Assume that the management of Jagiroad Paper Mill (A Unit of HPC) wants to reduce its excessive turnover of 25% to 8%. The management generates the Force-Field Analysis to correct the situation as follows:

Current Situation (25%)	**Desired Condition (8%)**
Driving Forces	*Restraining Forces*
1. The Security of "having a job."	1. Low starting wages
2. The HPC Headquarter is eager to reduce turnover at Jagiroad Paper Mill.	2. No wage increase allowed until one year on the job.
3. The new General Manager of the Mill wants turnover reduced.	3. Old equipment is hard to operate and maintain.
4. There are few large employers in the area.	4. Supervisors manage by fear, intimidation, and criticism.
5. Etc.	5. Personnel office hires a large number of 'transients'
	6. Working conditions are dirty and dangerous
	7. Morale is low; attitudes toward the company are negative
	8. Etc.

Lewin's Change Model

Lewin's change model is a three-step process **unfreezing, changing and refreezing.** A discussion of each of these steps follows.

Unfreezing: No change occurs in a vacuum of no prior perspective. To the extent the new perspective differs from the old one, the old one then implies doubting of its own existence. This necessitates unlearning of old things in order to learn new things. The same is called **unfreezing.**

Unfreezing involves encouraging individuals to discard old behaviours by shaking up the equilibrium state that maintains *status quo*. Unfreezing is accomplished by linking rewards with willingness to change and punishment with unwillingness to change[5]. Thus, individuals are made to feel that they have to forget their old ways and accept the new way. They are convinced to accept that change needs to occur. In this way, individuals surrender by allowing the boundaries of their *status quo* to be opened in preparation for change.

Changing: The second step in the change process is changing or moving. Having unlearned his past experience, the individual is ready for new behaviour and a change in perspective. Then, efforts are made to substitute new attitudes, values, and behaviours for old ones. Individuals are provided models to emulate their behaviour. This helps them identify themselves. Internalisation is another process of changing. Internalisation refers to such situation where an individual is required to behave in a new manner in order to operate effectively in such given situation. What happens that he or she behaves time and again in the same way and that particular behaviour becomes his usual or routine behaviour. Thus, this implies the trial and error learning of a new behaviour.

Refreezing: Refreezing is the final step in the change process. In this step, new attitudes, values, and behaviours are established as the new *status quo*. For this, the new ways of operating are cemented in and reinforced. The managers need to ensure the organisational compatibility so that the new behaviour is repeated again and again. In the absence of organisational compatibility, the new behaviour is likely to extinguish.

In most of training programmes for business executives, what happens that during the training period, the executives learn an umpteen number of new behaviours. Some of the behaviours, they accept also. But, when they again go back to their organisations, they soon forget the new behaviour because of want of appropriate atmosphere in the organisation to display their newly learned behaviour[6]. Therefore, this calls for reinforcement of new behaviour to make it one's usual or *status quo* behaviour.

28.2.1 RESISTANCE TO CHANGE

Although change is inevitable, people tend to resist it in a rational response based on self-interest. Resistance to change is not always bad or harmful. In some cases, resistance is positive also. Resistance to change can also be a source of functional conflict. For example, resistance to a change in product line can stimulate a healthy debate over the merits of the idea and, thus, result in a better decision. However, it also hinders adaptation and progress.

Some evidences of resistance to change are very overt such as wildcat strikes, work stoppage, turnover, and protests about a proposed change. Resistance to change, may also be very subtle and indirect, such as dissatisfaction, grievances, requests for transfers, absenteeism, and conflict among the members of a work team. The reasons of resistance to change can be divided, for analytical purposes, into two broad categories : individual and organisational resistance to change. This is shown in the following Table 22.1. In the real world, these reasons often overlap.

Table 28.1: Reasons of Resistance to Change

Driving Forces for Change →	← Forces Resisting Change
Internal Force →	← **Individual Resistance**
1. New technology	1. Fear of the unknown
2. Changing work values	2. New learning
3. Creation of new knowledge	3. Disruptions of stable friendships
4. Product obsolescence	4. Distrust of management
5. Desire for leisure and alternative work schedules	
Environmental Forces →	← **Organisational Resistance**
1. Competition	1. Threat to the power structure
2. Changes in consumer demands	2. Inertia of organizational structure
3. Resource availability	3. System relationships
4. Social and political change	4 Sunk costs and vested interests
5. International changes	

Individual Resistance

Individuals resist change for a variety of reasons. Here are the four reasons why individuals may resist change :

1. **Fear of the Unknown:** Changes often bring with it ambiguity and uncertainty. If, for example, the introduction of a new computer system requires that the employees learn some specific statistical techniques, some may fear they will be unable to do so. They may, therefore, develop a negative attitude toward the introduction of new computer system.

2. **New Learning:** For doing new task, one requires to learn a new language, develop a new technology, or adjust to a totally new culture. No doubt, learning new ideas can be exciting, most people report that excitement comes only after the learning is occured, not before.

3. **Disruption of Stable Friendship:** Almost all organisational changes disrupt the previous stable friendship. This, in turn, results in uncomfortable feelings of social isolation and loneliness. This may serve as a source of indirect resistance to change.

4. **Distrust of Management:** There are well-documented findings available from the history of labour relations that managers exploited labourers. That's why employees

often suspect the reason for change and try to oppose the same.

Organisational Resistance

The organisational structure itself also resists change. The four reasons of organisational resistance to change have been summarized as follows:

1. **Threats to the Power Structure:** Most changes have the capacity to disrupt the organisations's power structure. Introduction of decentralised decision making is example of change that is often seen as threats to the power of supervisors and middle level managers but a welcome by lower-level employees.

2. **Structural Inertia:** Organisational structures have several mechanisms designed to produce stability. Accordingly, job assignments, selection and training of new employees, and performance reward systems are designed to maintain stability, thereby resist to change. Whenever an organisation is confronted with change, this structural inertia acts as a counterbalance to sustain stability[7].

3. **System Relationships:** As mentioned earlier, any change has domino effect. Change in one subsystem affects changes in other subsystems also. For example, a change in the accounting department may influence the methods of reporting and recordkeeping of every other department. Hence, the other departments may resist to such change.

4. **Sunk Costs and Vested Interest:** Sunk costs are investments in fixed assets, such as land and building and machinery. Vested interests are the personal commitments of individuals to programmes, policies, or other people. As individuals find it difficult to abondon, so the organisations to recoup the sunk cost. The same becomes a source of organisational resistance to change.

We have discussed several reasons or sources of resistance to change. It is well accepted that unless the present conditions create enough discomfort, there is no motive for change. Therefore, the challange before managers, *i.e.*, change agents is to assess how much emotional people feel regarding the change issues for managing resistance to change.

28.2.2 MANAGING RESISTANCE TO CHANGE

Organizational change is inevitable. Therefore, managers should be sensitive to the barriers or resistance to changes so that it can be overcome. In a sense, resistance to change is simply a form of feedback that can be used very productively to manage the change process. This, of course, is easier said than done. However several useful approaches have been developed and suggested to manage the organisational change. The six key ones are reviewed here briefly.

1. **Education and Communication:** If reason of resistance to change is misunderstanding about the change, it can be reduced by providing employees with details why change is needed. Employees can be educated about the change through one-on-one discussions, memos, group presentations, or reports. New information is a powerful force for change in ambiguous situations. For example, new employee orientations are particularly effective in changing the behaviour of new employees, because they wouldn't have known how to behave otherwise. Studies on the introduction of computers in the workplace indicate that providing employees with

opportunities for hands-on practice helps alleviate fears about the new technology. Employees who have experience with computers display more positive attitudes and greater efficiency[8,9].

2. **Participation:** Research evidence lends support to the fact that individuals find it difficult to resist a change decision in which they participated. Hence, before a change is introduced, particularly those oppose the change can be brought into the decision process. In a classical study, workers in a garment factory were introduced to change in three different ways. One group was simply told about the new procedure, one group was introduced to the change by a trained worker, and one group was allowed to help plan the implementation of the new production. The results were dramatic. The third group, those who participated in the change, adopted the new methods very quickly, was more productive and experienced no turnover[10]. However, against these advantages are negatives as well.

3. **Facilitation and Support:** Another strategy for managing resistance to change is providing support and empathy to those employees who have trouble dealing with the change. Counselling and therapy, skill training, or a short paid leave may be examples of support extended to the employees. However, like education and participation, this strategy also suffers from the drawbacks, such as it is time-consuming and expensive also.

4. **Negotiation:** Negotiation particularly with a group of powerful individuals resisting to change is yet another strategy to deal with potential resistance to change. For this, a specific reward package can be negotiated with the powerful individuals to meet their individual needs. Yes, one cannot ignore its potentially high costs. In addition, once a few powerful individuals are made so ready avoid resistance to change, it may so happen that they are being blackmailed by the change agents to resolve even rather crucial matters in their favour.

5. **Manipulation and Co-optation:** In brief, manipulation implies covert attempts to influence. Examples of manipulations are twisting the facts to make them more attractive, withholding information not pleasant to the receivers, and spreading rumors to make employees ready accept a change. As regards cooptation, it includes both manipulation and cooptation. The leaders of a resistance group are invited not to reach to a better decision, but to get their endorsement.

Though both manipulation and cooptation are less expensive and simple ways to seek support of the adversaries. However, against these advantages are the negatives: possibility for the tacits being backfired if the target comes to know that they are being tricked or misused.

6. **Coercion:** Last on the list of suggested tactics is coercion. The organisation, as a last resort, can apply direct threats on the resisters to make them ready accept the proposed change. Threats of transfer, loss of promotion, negative performance evaluation, a poor report on performance, and dissatisfactory recommendation are the examples of coercion. Coercion is labelled with advantages and disadvantages similar to those labelled with manipulation and cooptation.

Table 28.2 Methods for Dealing with Resistance to Change

Strategy	Example	When used	Problems
Communication	Customer complaint letters are shown to employees	When employees don't feel an urgency for change or don't know how the change will affect them.	Time-consuming and potentially costly.
Training	Employees learn how to work in teams as the company adopts a team-based structure.	When employees need to break old routines and adopt new role patterns.	Time-consuming and potentially costly.
Employee Involvement	Company forms a task force to recommend new customer service practices.	When the change effort needs more employees commitment, some employees need to save face, and/or employee ideas would improve decisions about the change strategy.	Very time-consuming. May also lead to conflict and poor decisions if employees interests are incompatible with organization needs.
Stress Management	Employees attend sessions to discuss their worries about the change.	When communication, training, and involvement do not sufficiently ease employee worries.	Time-consuming and potentially expensive. Some methods may not reduce stress for all employees.
Negotiation	Employees agree to replace strict job categories with multiskilling in return for increased job security.	When emloyees will clearly lose something of value from the change and would not otherwise support the new conditions. Also necessary when the company must change quickly.	May be expensive, particularly if other employees want to negotiate their support. Also tends to produce compliance, but not commitment to the change.
Coercion	Comapny president tells managers to get on board and accept the change or leave.	When other strategies are ineffective and the company needs to change quickly.	Can lead to more subtle forms of resistance, as well as long term antagonism with the change agent.

Sources : **Adapted from J.P. Kotter and L.A. Schiesinger, "Choosing Strategies for Change"**, Harvard Business Review **57 (1979), pp. 106-14; P.R. Lawrence, "How to Deal with Resistance to change?" Harvard Business Review (May-June 1954), p.p. 49-57.**

Before we leave this section, a small mention about what facilitates successful implementation of organisational change.

We mentioned earlier that the major challange before the managers is how to manage change successfully. This implies that for managing change successfully, the change strategy needs to include and manage all the three stages (*i.e.*, unfreezing, changing, refreezing) of the change process. This facilitates the achievement of organisational changes in a consistent manner. This is corroborated by Greiner's study[11] also in which he found that successful changes appeared to follow a relatively consistent pattern while there was inconsistency of pattern among the unsuccessful changes. Greiner identified the following **eight stages** through which organisations achieve successful implementation of change :

1. Internal or external pressures create a need for change, which is shared in the organisation, but particularly felt by the top management.
2. An outsider, either a new executive or a consultant, who has reputation for creating change, enters the organisation.
3. This change agent encourages the organisation to re-examine its past practices and present problems.
4. The top team assumes a direct and highly involved role in conducting this examination.
5. The change agent, with the help of the top team, involves different levels in this diagnosis.
6. The change agent provides people at different levels with new ideas and methods for developing solutions for the organisational problems.
7. The initial solutions are tested/implemented at a small scale, and, if found successful, applied at a large scale.
8. As the change efforts spread, they get absorbed permanently as the organisation's way of life.

To sum up, organisational change is both inevitable and desirable. Also, it is people's involvement that makes change successful. Then, the moot question is how to involve people in the change process? Research findings lend support to the view that change introduced at a sudden is often resisted and rejected. On the other hand, evidences corraborate that a gradual change often tends to succeed. Jacque Passino, a consultant in Change Management Practices at Anderson Consulting also holds the similar views. While giving a fillip to the Indian change management practices, Passino opines, **"There's this story about the frog ; if you put a frog in a pot of boiling water, it will jump out. If you put a frog in a pot and heat the water gently, it will not jump out, but die. Companies also are like that."**[12]

Go through the following caslet of the India's biggest organization in the banking sector. It will help you understand the effective planning and implementation of change in an organisation.

The State Bank of India is the largest bank in India. The old Imperial Bank was nationalized in 1955 to promote rural development, broad base entrepreneurship, and provide finance to the public sector. The State Bank grew phenomenally after its rationalization, and by 1970 it had increased the number of its offices from about 400 to over 2100 (in the early eighties it had some 6000 offices and over 100000 employees). In 1969, several other banks were nationalized, and from having a monopoly over public sector of business. Huge size, bureaucratic structure, the lack of expert staff support to the branch manager lost near the bottom of the managerial hierarchy, and having to compete compelled the State Bank of India to reorganize its structure with the help of outside consultants. The objective was to devise a structure that could facilitate the pursuit of profitability and growth but keeping in mind the bank's social responsibility.

'A SWOT analysis was performed to identify the strengths and weaknesses of the organization and it was agreed that organization change should be implemented to improve the bank's competitive position, facilitate decentralization (with accountability for performance), develop resilience and challenge taking capacity in the organization, and bring about greater clarity in the staff about the bank's tasks, thus, facilitating the development of managers. Several "Principles" of reorganizatgion were articulated, such as greater emphasis on catering of different market segments, increasing performance orientation by adopting performance budgeting and review of performance, bringing about greater unity of command over the branch managers, and the separation of operations from planning and staff function.

'A participative process was used to usher in the changes. The following major changes were made:

- Accounting was now done on market segment basis and managers of market segment division were appointed to report to each branch manager. these included the commercial and institutional banking, small industries and small business, agricultural banking, personal banking divisions.
- Annual budgeting was introduced with monthly performance reporting and review from branch level upwards.
- A unified chain of command was introduced starting from managers of divisions reporting to branch manager, who in turn reported to the regional chief, who, in turn, reported to the regional manager (operations) at the local head office, who in turn reported to the chief general manager of the local head office, who in turn reported to the managing director at the central office. A regional manager controlled about 75 branches and a general manager (operations) controlled 5-6 regional managers. There were 12 local head offices.
- Specialized staff and functional support at local head offices was provided under a general manager (planning) Development managers who were specialists in each market segment, planning manager, a personnel manager, and specialists like the organization and methods officer, and other service functionaries reported to this general manager. At the central office, the managing director was assisted by depurty managing directors (in charge of operations, development and planning, personnel and services and associate banks) and these were assisted, in their functional areas, by specialists in their fields.
- Overall corporate coordination was provided by the Central Management Committee consisting of the chairman, managing director, and deputy managing directors. Similarly, at each local head office, there was a "Circle"

management committee consisting of the chief general manager, general manager (planning), general manager (operations), and chief regional managers as invitees, and a "Circle" Coordination Committee of the same officials. At each branch, there was a Branch Management Committee consisting of the branch manager, managers of sectoral divisions, and account manager.'

Adapted from Pradip N. Khandwalla : **Innovative Corporate Turnarounds**, Sage Publications, New Delhi, 1992.

Organizations operate in an envrionment which consists of economic and non-economic factors. When the operating environment of an organization becomes unfavourable, the organization needs to change to what P.N. Khandwalla has called "domauin reshuffling", i.e. favourable environment. Organisational history bears evidences that such domain reshuffling enables the organizations to survive and thrive. Below are presented some of such cases that demonstrate how Third World organizations managed change successfully.

'Organisational sickness is frequent in the third world. A common response to sickness in the West is for sick oragnizations to exit from depressed domains and enter buoyant domains. but in many Third World countries, there are legal and other restrictions on choosing what domains or business the organization can operate in. And yet, there are many examples, some ingenious ones, of how sick Third World organizations have successfully sought to get into more buoyant environments and/or out of unfavourable environments:

- Gambia Produce and Marketing Board owned by the Government of Gambia, Africa, was originally set up to trade in oilseeds, cotton, rice, etc. It also operated oil mills and river transportation facilities, and traded in fertilizer, lime, soap, etc. The company began to make losses. As part of its turnaround effort, it withdrew from the loss-making import of rice and fertilizers and from dealing in other loss-making products.
- Richardson and Cruddas, India, a producer of structurals and various machineries, began to make losses in the mid-seventies. As part of its turnaround strategy, it sought to get out of the highly competitive and loss-making low-valued structurals business, reversed its proposed expansion of structurals making capacity, and moved more aggressively into high-valued structurals. It also doubled sales of scrap, moved aggressive into foreign markets, capitalizing in part on Indian aid to other countries, and pressured various government bodies for others.
- Jamica Railway Corporation, operating in Jamaica, West Indies, was a loss-making railway. It sought to make its environment more buoyant by helping to reopen a port, and by organizing luxury and educational tours and excursion trips. It also aggressive sought to carry greater passenger traffic and bulk cargo, such as petroleum products.
- Sylvania and Laxman, an Indian producer of lamps and bulbs, began to loose money in the mid-seventies. It aggressively penetrated the hitherto neglected rural market as part of its turnaround strategy.

- Standard Motors, an Indian producer of cars and a loss-making unit, moved away from producing vehicles that used petrol, and into vehicles, using the much cheaper diesel, the latter being a growth segment of the automobile industry.
- Enfield, an Indian producer of two-wheelers and agro-engines, sought to diversify into the high growth chemicals and electronics industries. Based in south India, Enfield had hitherto neglected North Indian markets. Enfield aggressively sought to penetrate these markets.
- State Timber Corporation, owned by the Government of Sri Lanka, a producer of timber, sought forward vertical integration into such buoyant product markets as teak paneling, doors and window frames, and charcoal.
- Tinplate, India contracted with its holding company, Tata Steel , a giant steel maket, to galvanize the latter's steel sheet.
- Air India embarked on a major image revamping exercise to turn into a truly international airline from being mainly an ethnic airline catering mostly to Indian passengers. It aggressively sought to tap the first class and business class travelers businesses, and also sought new routes.
- Bharat Heavy Plate and Vessels, a Government of India owned producer of sophisticated heat exchangers, pressure vessels, and cryogenic equipment, and loss-making since its inception did an ABC analysis of its orders, and found that small orders contributed the bulk of its losses. Accordingly it decided not to take small orders. It sought to expand business in the lucrative area of system selling (as opposed to marketing pieces of equipment).
- Bharat Heavy Electricals, a producer of electric equipment, another Government of India undertaking, made losses in the early seventies. As part of its revival strategy, it set up an export division, and sought and landed foreign turnkey projects. It began to emphasize the marketing of energy systems rather than of just electrical equipment.'

Adapted from P.N. Khandwalla : **Innovative Corporate Turnarounds**, Sage Publications, New Delhi, 1992, p. 163.

So far, we have discussed the dynamics of change that occur in organisations. Closely related to organisational change is another concept of organisational development , abbreviated as OD. Hence, any discussion on organisational change will perhaps remain incomplete without a discussion on OD.

28.3 ORGANISATIONAL DEVELOPMENT (OD)

As with other concepts and approaches in behavioural sciences discussed earlier also in this text, it is difficult to pin point the exact and precise beginning of the concept of OD. As per the organisational history, the emergence of the field of OD in behavioural sciences is traced back during the 1940s and 1950s when OD practitioners focussed their attention almost exclusively on interpersonal, dyadic, and small group dynamics[13]. At that time, the field of ED was equated with T-groups, also called '*Laboratory Training*' which later became popular as 'Sensitivity Training'.In the 1960s, the field of OD was approached by developing a new and integrated approach that is now known as 'Organisational Development (OD)'[14]. Henceforth, OD is used for organisational development. Later French and Bell[15], who are considered to have done the most seminal work on the historical development of OD, felt that "organisational development has emerged from applied behavioural science and social psychology and from subsequent efforts to apply laboratory training and survey feed-back insight into total systems".

Thus, it becomes clear that the two historical roots for OD are laboratory training and survey feedback. These will be discussed, in details, later in this chapter under 'OD Interventions'.

28.3.1 MEANING OF OD

Essentially, OD tries to understand how to understand and how to manage planned change in organisations. The same has been defined differently by different thinkers.

According to Koontz et. al. [16]:

"OD is a systematic, integrated and planned approach to improve the effectiveness of the enterprise. It is designed to solve problems that adversely affect the operational efficiency at all levels."

Burke[17] had offered a more simple definition :

"Organisation development is a planned process of change in an organisation's culture through the utilization of behavioural science technology, reasearch, and theory".

French and Bell[18] had given this classic definition :

"Organisation development is a long-range effort to improve an organisation's problem-solving and renewal processes, particularly through a more effective and collaborative management of organisation culture–with special emphasis on the culture of formal work teams–with the assistance of a change agent, or catalyst, and the use of the theory and technology of applied behaviour sicence, including action research."

Thus, OD can be defined as the process of planned change and improvement of organisations through the application of knowledge of the behavioural sciences, such as psychology, sociology, cultural anthropology, and other related fields of study.

28.3.2 CHARACTERISTICS OF OD

The salient characteristics of OD implied in its definitions are gleaned as follows:

First, OD is a systematic approach to planned change. It is a structured cycle of diagnosing organisational problems and opportunities and then applying expertise to them.

Second, OD is grounded in solid research and theory. It involves the application of our knowledge of behavioural science to the challanges that the organisations face.

Third, OD recognizes the reciprocal relationship between individuals and organisations. It acknowledges that for organisations to change, individuals must change.

Fourth, OD is goal-oriented. It is a process that seeks to improve both individual and organisational well-being and effectiveness.

Fifth, OD is designed to solve problems.

28.3.3 OBJECTIVES OF OD

The main objectives of OD are to:

1. Improve organisational performance as measured by profitability, market share, innovativeness, etc.
2. Make organisation better adaptive to its environment.
3. Make the members willing face organisational problems and contribute creative solutions to the organisational problems.
4. Improve internal behaviour patterns such as interpersonal relations, intergroup relations, level of trust and support among the role players.
5. Understand one's own self and others, openness and meaningful communication and involvement in planning for organisational development.

28.3.4 OD MODELS

Four models of OD are quite popular in organisational behaviour. They are: Kurt Lewin's **Unfreezing, changing and refreezing model;** Greiner's **Equential model;** Leavitt's **System model and Action Research.** These are discussed one by one.

Lewin' Model: Lewin's model is based on the premises that before actually introducing a change, organisation needs to be prepared for change, motivated to change and stabilised and integrated the change into behaviours of organisation. Accordingly, Lewin's change model includes three-steps in its process: unfreezing changing and refreezing[19]. These have already been discussed under 28.2 **Planned Change.** Hence, the same has been avoided here for the sake of repitition.

Greiner's Model: According to this model, change occurs in terms of certain sequential stages[20]. The external stimulus pressurises the management of organisation to initiate change process. The management in response to stimulus is motivated to take actions to introduce change in organisation. Following the actions, the various change stages occur in a subsequential manner such as diagnosis of the problem, invention of a new solution, experimentation with new solution and reinforcement from positive results. Greiner's these OD sequential stages are shown in Fig. 28.2.

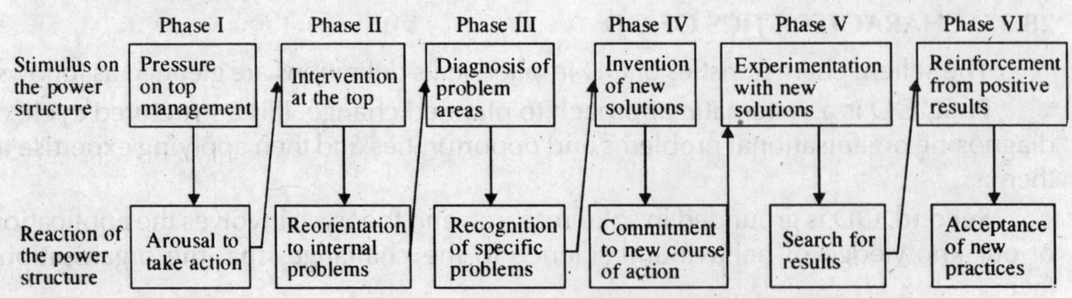

Fig. 28.2: O.D. Sequential Stages

Leavitt's Model: Leavitt's[21] OD model is founded on the interactive nature of the various sub-systems in a change process. In an organisational system, there are four interacting sub-systems-task, structure, people and technology. Due to their interacting nature, change in anyone of the sub-systems tends to have consequences for the other sub-systems also. Change in anyone of the subsystems can be worked out depending upon the situation. How the various sub-systems interact with each other in a change process is shown in the following Fig. 28.3.

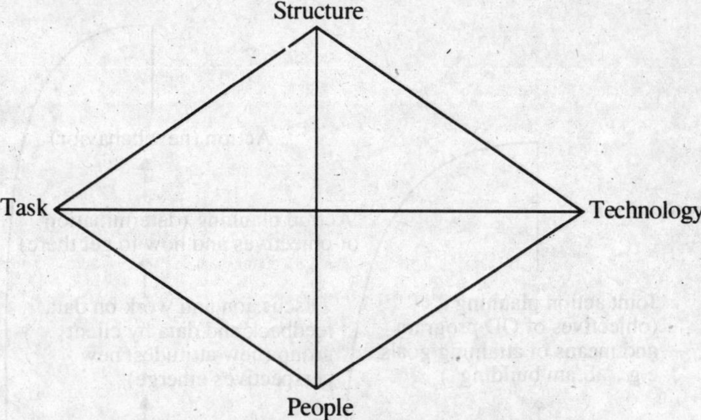

Fig. 28.3: Interacting of Sub-systems

Action Research Model of OD : Action research is an OD model advocated by Kurt Lewin, H.A. Shepard and W. French[22] to implement change in organisation. It is based on the premise that problem solving process, or say, change process begins with awareness or diagnosis of the problem that causes tension in the system. And, action research guides action to solve the problem with an objective to improve the organisational performance. W.L. French and C.M. Bell[23] have defined action research as follows :

"Action research is the process of systematically collecting research data about an ongoing system relative to some objective, goal, or need of that system; feeding these data back into the system; taking actions by altering selected varaiables within the system based both on the data and on hypothesis; and evaluating the results of actions by collecting more data".

Thus, action research is a cyclical process of identifying system problems, gathering data, taking corrective actions, assessing progress, making ongoing judgements, and learning from experience.

Action research is usually carried out by an outside consultant also called change agent. There are several steps involved in action research process. These are problem identification and diagnosis, planning for change, developing interventions, and evaluation of progress (as shown in Figure 28.4).

The action research model (see figure 28.4) is self-explanatory and needs no elaboration. It is well indicated by the model that action research is research inextricably linked to action ; it is research with a purpose, that is to guide present and future action to achieve organisational development on a continuous basis.

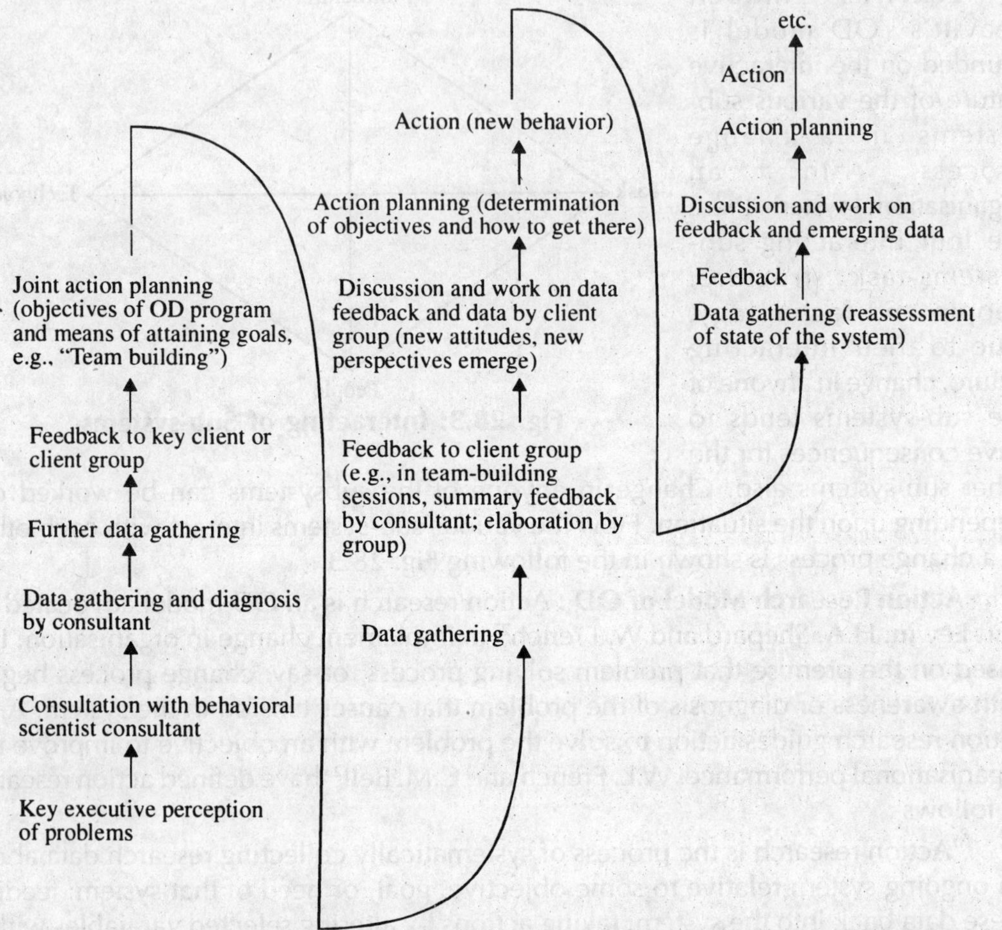

Fig. 28.4 : An Action Model for OD

Adapted from **California Management Review,** XII, No. 2, p. 26, Figure 1.

Evolution and Types of Action Research

As per available literature, the origin of action research can be traced to two independent sources. **One**, John Collier[24], who was a man of behavioural science. Collier was Commissioner of Indian Affairs from 1933 to 1945 and his role was to diagnose problems and recommend remedial programmes for improving race relations. Collier found that effecting changes in ethnic relations was extremely difficult and required joint efforts on the part of the scientist (researcher), the administration (practitioner), and the layman (client).

The **other** source of action research is behavioural scientist Kurt Lewin who was profoundly interested in applying behavioural knowledge to help solve social problems. In the mid-1940s and early 1950s, Lewin applied action research principles to improving inter-group relations and to changing eating habits[25]. Lewin succinctly stated the issue : "No action without research and no research without action." Lewin's Action Research Model was further developed by French and Shepard.

Four varieties of action research are identified as follows :

1. **Diagnostic Action Research :** In this research, a scientist (researcher) enters a problem situation, diagnoses it, and makes recommendations for remedial treatment to the client.

2. **Participant Action Research :** It is the type of action research in which people who are to take action are involved in the entire research and action process from the beginning. Such participation increases the likelihood of carrying out the actions once decided upon and also keeps the recommended actions feasible.

3. **Empirical Action Research :** This type of research is also called record-based research. In this research, the actor-researcher maintains a systematic, extensive record of what he or she did and what effects it had.

4. **Experimental Action Research :** It is a controlled research on the relative effectiveness of various action techniques. There is often more than one possible way of trying to accomplish something. The problem is to find which one among the available possible ways is the best. This is research on action in the strictest sense of both words.

28.3.5 OD INTERVENTIONS

How to bring about OD? The answer is through OD interventions. Interventions are the set of structural activities in which selected organisational units, be individual or their groups, engage with a task or a sequence of tasks. Goals are related directly or indirectly to organisational improvement. For this, an umpteen number of alternative OD intervention methods exist. One way of classifying these methods, for the convenience of readers, is by the target of change. In practice, the target of change may be the individuals, their groups within the organisation, or organisation itself. OD interventions aimed at these three targets are now discussed in seriatim.

Individual – Focussed Interventions

OD interventions that are targeted toward individuals include skill training, job redesign, role negotiation, and career planning.

Sensitivity Training:

Sesitivity training also known as T-Groups (for training groups) or laboratory training or encounter groups is a method by which small face-to-face interaction experiences are used to give people insight into themselves (e.g., who they are, the way others respond to them). The concept of sensitivity training has evolved from the group dynamics concept of Kurt Lewin. The main objective of sensitivity training is to help individuals understand how they communicate, how their behaviour affects others and how they are perceived by others. Developed in the 1940s, sensititivity training was among the first organisational development techniques used in organisations, such as Standard Oil and Union Carbide and State Teachers College (USA). The rationale behind sensitivity training is that people are usually not completely open and honest with each other, a condition that often thwarts insights into oneself and others. But, when people are placed in special situations within which open, honest communication is allowed and duly encouraged, personal insights may be gained to a large extent.

To do this, a small group (usually about eight to fifteen in number) is formed and left to themselves without any structured agenda to interact with each other as they sit in a circled manner. The group is asked to sit for several days to interact among themselves. An expert trainer (referred to as the 'facilitator') guides the group to maintain the right direction of interaction[26]. Usually, in the beginning there are awkward and utter silences, nervous laughter and not much conversation among the members to understand each others. The members will be goofing off, for instance what happened the cricket match India vs Australia they witnessed last week. Here comes the role of facilitator to get the ball rolling. To do this, the facilitator will frustrate the group members by not getting involved at all in the desired interaction. The group members begin to feel angry at the facilitator and turn to the required interaction. They become more and more free and frank in their interactions with their regular sittings. The members are encouraged to continue discussing the theme freely and honestly and do not hide their feelings as is often done on job. If you think, for example, some other member heavily depends on you, this is the time and forum to tell so.

Different people hold different views about the effectiveness of sensitivity training. Some hold the view that measuring insights into one's personality/feelings is difficult and elusive. even if interpersonal skills improve, according to them, people will not always be able to successfully use that improved skills in interpersonal relations when they go back to their jobs. However, there are some others who hold the view that getting valid into one's personality is possible through intensive lab sessions especially for those who are interested to receiving feedback from others. according to Sekaran, sensitivity training have helped aggressive people become moderate and friendly, timid people to become more assertive, and outwardly brusque managers to change their behaviour to exhibit more empathy. She views sensitivity training as symbiotic.

Skill Training: Skill training refers to increasing the job knowledge, skills, and abilities that are necessary to do a job effectively. Skill training is imparted either in formal classroom setting or on the job. The need for imparting skill training is aroused due to the rapid changes that organisations face. The job knowledge, therefore, needs to be continuously updated to keep pace with rapid change. The objective of training is to enable a worker to be more effective on the job. For example, while new workers can be trained to achieve levels of output attained by experienced older workers, existing workers can be retained to improve their output at par.

Job Redesign: As an OD intervention, job redesign alters jobs to improve the fit between individual skills and the demands of the job. We have already discussed job redesign in Chapter 10. Examples of job redesign interventions include job enlargement, job enrichment, job simplification, and job rotation. These job redesign methods are used as OD techniques for realigning task demands and individual capabilities, or for redesigning jobs to fit new techniques or organisation structures better.

Role Negotiation: Sometimes, group members have differing expectations of one another within the working relationship. Role negotiation is a simple technique whereby individuals meet and clarify their psychological contract. In doing this, the expectations of each party are clarified and negotiated. The outcome of role negotiation is improved understanding between the members.

Career Planning: Career planning refers to matching an individual's career aspirations with the opportunities available in the organisation. In other words, it involves activities offered by the organisation to individuals to identify strength, weaknesses, specific goals that they would like to occupy. Career planning activities benefit both individuals and organisations. Counselling sessions are held to help employees identify their skills and deficiencies in their skills. The organisation then can plan its training and development programmes based on this information to improve individual's skills required for assuming higher responsibilities. Such a process may help the organisation identify and also nurture the talented employees for potential promotion.

Management Development Training: Management development encompasses a host of techniques designed to enhance a manager's skills on the job. Training for management development generally focuses on four types of learning: verbal information, intellectual skills, attitudes, and development. One way to achieve development is through the use of action learning, *i.e.*, an integration of classroom learning with on-the-job experiences. Action learning enables managers to know about themselves through the challanges of their camrades. Simulation, business games, role playing, and case studies are other techniques that provide active learning for the participants.

Organisation and Group-Focused Interventions

OD intervention methods aimed at changing the organisation itself or changing the work-groups within the organisation include survey feedback, management by objectives, quality of work life, team building, and process consultation. These are discussed briefly :

Survey Feedback

Like sensitivity training, orginally influenced by the Lewin's 'Force Field Analysis', survey feedback has also been one of the popular OD technique used in organisations. Over the years, survey feedback as an OD technique has been most closely associated with the Institute for Social Research (ISR) of the University of Machigan as the ISR developed a comprehensive questionnaire for conducting survey of different aspects of an organisation. Today, this OD technique of survey feedback has become the basis for the 360 – degree feedback technique of performance appraisal by providing information to individuals from their superior, peers, and subordinates. The main objective of survey feedback technique is to make the employees understand the current strengths and weaknesses of their organisation.

The survey feedback process is often conducted by either the organisation's top management or a consultant to management. The survey can help the management diagnose and solve the organisational problem by providing important insights and information about employees beliefs and attitudes. This technique follows the three steps as summarised in figure 28.5

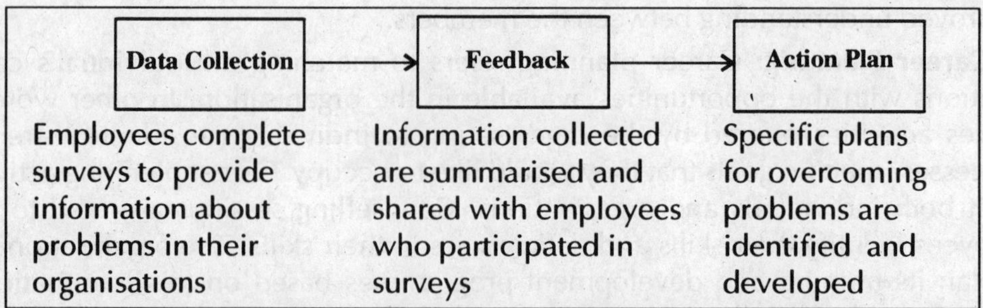

Fig. 28.5 : The Survey Feedback Process

Data Collection : The **first step** in survey feedback is data collection about matters of general concern to employees, such as organisational climate, leadership styles, and job satisfaction. This can be done either by administering a structured questionnaire or by conducting extensive interviews, or both. To ensure that the data/information collected be unbiased as much as possible, this process is usually conducted by the outside consultant.

The **second step** calls for reporting the information obtained back to the employees who have participated in the filling up of questionnaires. The feedback may be given either orally by conducting group discussions or problem solving sessions or in a written form of summary of findings. Whatever be the form of feedback adopted, it should be constructive and suggestive so that the identified weaknesses are overcome through follow-up actions. In no case, feedback should be threatening and hurting to the employees emotions.

In the final and **third step**, i.e. action plan, follow-up action plans are formulated based on feedback generated. Action plans can be prepared either by the employees themselves to overcome the problems or as is more commonly done, in the form of developing some OD interventions by the consultant.

Survey feedback is a widely used OD technique because of the advantages it offers. To name a few, it is efficient, allows to collect a great deal of information relatively quickly, and it is very flexible also and can be tailored to the needs of different organisations facing various types of problems. Yes, the technique can be no better than the quality of the questionnaire used. The maximum benefits to be derived depend on the support and sanction to it from the top management. If these conditions are met, the survey feedback can be a very effective OD technique.

Management by Objectives (MBO)

MBO is not essentially on OD technique in its strict sense like other OD techniques that have been discussed so far. Rather, it is a motivational tool that helps in improving organisational performance. Experiences demonstrate that compared to a general goal, setting specific goal benefits more-both the employees and the organisation. Cutting costs and cutting costs by 5 per cent are the examples of general and specific goals respectively. This is in consonance with an old saying : "**It's usually easier to get somewhere if you know where you are going.**" Peter Drucker had this experience while consulting in General Electric during the early 1950s that setting clear and specific goals benefit more. Drucker promoted this idea in the form of a technique popularly known as MBO. MBO is a programme that encompasses specific goals participatively set by the managers and the employees/subordinates to be achieved within a specific time period, with regular feedback on goal progress. Thus, MBO directly advocates specific goals and feedback.

The MBO process, as depicted in Figure 28.6, consists of three basic steps :

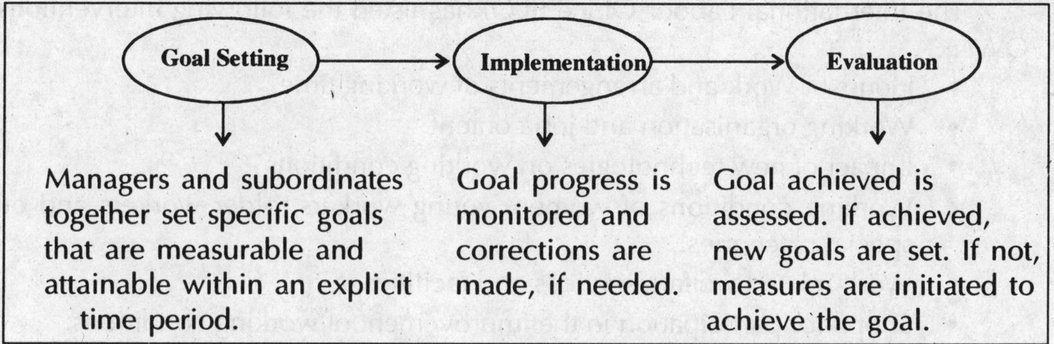

Fig. 28.6 : The MBO Process

1. **Goal Setting :** The MBO process starts with setting goals together by the employees and The goals should be set mutually, not be imposed on subordinates by their managers. The goals set should be measurable and achievable within an explicit time period. The goals that cannot be measured or goals without any specific time limit, are useless. Once the specific goals with a time period are set, both the subordinates and managers have to jointly develop specific action plan to attain the set goals.
2. **Implementation :** Once goals are set and action plans also developed, the next step calls for implementation of action plan and regular assessment of its progress. Implementation considers the questions such as : Is the action plan working? Are the goals being approximated ? What are the problems, if any, being faced while attempting to attain the goals? If the plan is failing, necessary midcourse measures will be initiated to correct the plan, or even the goal itself.
3. **Evaluation:** Having the plan implementated and monitored, the final and third step is evaluation of the plan. The goal of the plan attained is assessed and evaluated. The issues considered in evaluation step include : Was the organisation's goal achieved? If yes, what should be the new goal for further improvement of the organisation ? If not, what measures should be initiated to achieve the goal ? Thus, MBO becomes a continuous process.

   MBO serves as a potentially effective source of planning and implementing change for organisational development. The pre-requisites for the success of an MBO plan include setting goals participatively, top management's commitment, everyone's involvement in the process, realistic expectations regarding results, etc.

Quality of Work Life (QWL): Like other behavioural terms, there have been divergent views as to what really QWL is. According to one view,[27] QWL consists of a whole parcel of terms and notions all of which really belong to an umbrella of QWL. QWL as an umbrella concept encompasses literally dozens of specific interventions that have a common goal of humanizing the workplace. Davis and Newstrom[28] have percieved a wide range of QWL activities as open communication, equitable reward systems, a concern for employee-job security and participation in job design.

The International Labour Office (ILO) has listed the following interventions of QWL:

- Hours of Work and arrangements of working time.
- Working organisation and job content.
- Impact of new technologies on working conditions
- Working conditions of women, young workers, older workers and other special categories.
- Work-related welfare services and facilities.
- Shopfloor participation in the improvement of working conditions.

Any comprehensive list of QWL programmes would encompass job redesign, participative management, and involving unions, education, training and legislative measures[29]. The overriding purpose of these interventions is to change the climate at work so that a better quality of work life is created.

In view of QWL's tremendous effects on organisational behaviour, it is dealt with separately later in the penultimate Chapter 30.

Team Building

Team building as an OD intervention is based on the concept of synergy building for improving organisational performance. The main objective of team building is to get members of a work group to diagnose and recognise their problem, know how they work together and then ponder and plan how their performance may be improved. As work groups are considered the basic building blocks of organisations, hence there is a need for giving more emphasis on changing groups instead of individuals.

How to go about team building, *i.e.*, creating effective work teams. It involved a process as shown in Figure 28.7.

Team building starts when the members of a work group admit that they have a problem and gather relevant data/information to have more and better insight into the problem. The problem can be identified from any source like sensitivity training sessions, attitude surveys, performance data, etc. These data are then shared among members to identify the group's current strengths and weaknesses. Based on this, a list of desired goals, or say, changes is prepared, along with action plans to implement the desired change. In other words, action plans are developed to solve group's problems as diagnosed in the beginning. The action plan is then implemented and subsequently evaluated to see if the problem is solved or not. If the problem is solved, the team building process is over and the team may disband and stop meeting. If problem is not solved, the process should restart to see the problem is solved.

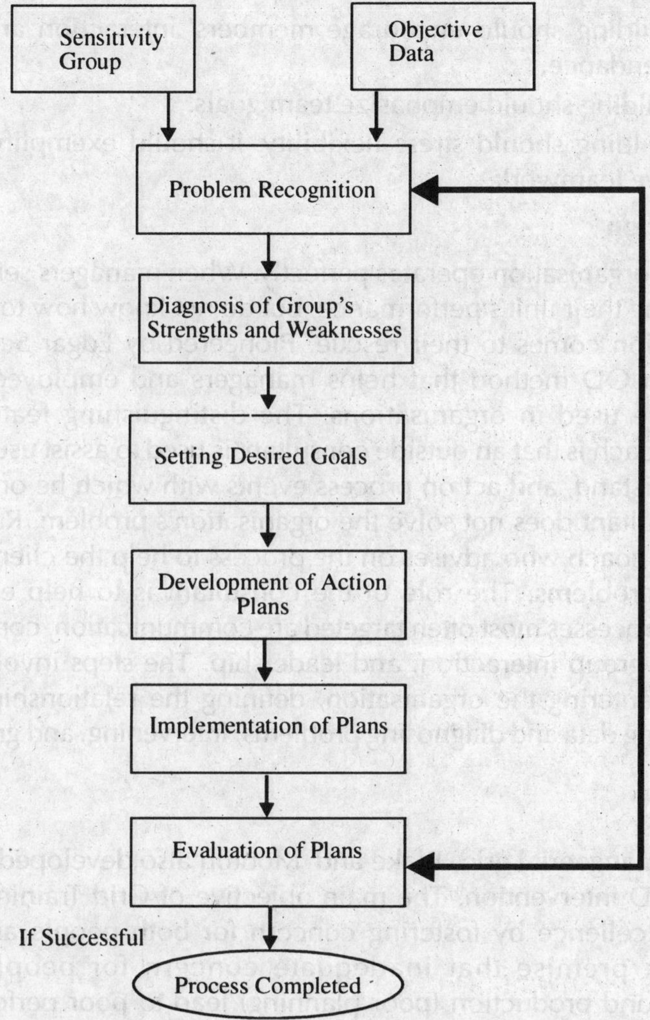

Fig. 28.7 : Steps in Team Building Process

What benefits does team building offer to its members and organisation? The benefits offered by work team, as already discussed in chapter 11, are also offered by team building. The very essence of benefits of team building lie in what Baltasar Grasaifi's views : "*The path to greatness is along with others*". In aggregate, team building had a positive impact on the employees' productivity, attitudes like motivation, job satisfaction, loyalty, absenteeism, turnover, etc. It also helps improve group process. According to a recent meta-analysis that examined the effects of OD interventions from 126 studies found that team building was the most effective technique of changing employee stasifaction and other attitudes.

What makes team building effective? Researchers have identified the following four areas in team building as critical to its success as an OD intervention :

1. Team building should develop effective communication between the members.
2. Team building should encourage members' interaction and also mutual interdependance.
3. Team building should emphasize team goals.
4. Team building should stress flexibility. It should exemplify effective and ineffective teamwork.

Process Consultation

In reality, no organisation operates perfectly. When managers sense that there is room for improving their unit's performance, but do not know how to improve it, the process consultation comes to their rescue. Pioneered by Edgar Schein[30], process consultation is an OD method that helps managers and employees improve the processes that are used in organisations. The distinguishing feature of process consultation approach is that an outside consultant is used to assist usually a manager to perceive, understand, and act on process events with which he or she must deal. The process consultant does not solve the organisation's problem. Rather, he or she acts as a guide or coach who advises on the process to help the clients or managers solve their own problems. The role of the consultant is to help employees help themselves. The processes most often targeted are communication, conflict resolution, decision making, group interaction, and leadership. The steps involved in process consultation are entering the organisation, defining the relationship, choosing an approach, gathering data and diagnosing problems, intervening, and gradually leaving the organisation.

Grid Training

Along with mangaerial grid, Blake and Mouton also developed 'Grid Training' as an effective OD intervention. The main objective of Grid Training is to achieve organisational excellence by fostering concern for both people and production. Working on the premise that inadequate concern for people (ineffective communication) and production (poor planning) lead to poor performance, Blake and Mouton[31] developed a multi-step training to cultivate these skills and, in turn, improve organisational performance. This multi-step training takes anywhere between three and five years for improving organisational performance to reach its defined level of excellence.

The multi-step training begins with holding a grid seminar in which selected key managers who have been previously trained in appropriate training and skills, help the managers assess their own management styles, their concern for people and production. Recall, these dimensions of leadership are already discussed in Chapter 16 under 'Managerial Grid'. Hence, these are not repeated here. Once managers' positions along the grid is determined, training is imparted to improve concern over people (communication skills) and concern over production (planning skills) so as to reach the ideal, 9,9 state which Blake and Mouton term as 'Team Management.' In the second step, managers try to create and develop teams and learn the culture the team shares. This step is followed by exploring group dynamics in terms of competition and cooperation among the team members. This training consists of organisation - wide team training aimed at helping people interact more effectively with each other. The next step is envisioning the level of excellence for the organisation and work out the strategy to reach this defined level of excellence. The final step is to evaluate the organisational performance. Based on the performance evaluation, the problem areas are identified and the future course of action is charted out for further improvement in organisational performance.

Some skeptics argue three points regarding the effectiveness of grid training, **First**, being too many changes involved in the implementation of grid training, it becomes difficult to specifically tell which change results in improved organisational performance. **Second**, because grid graining is designed to be used in general in all organisations, it may not be suitable to meet the special development needs of a particular organisation. **Third**, contrary to some situations in which effective leadership requires more of one of concern for people and production than the other, grid training always assumes that having concern for both people and production is the best management/ leadership style. Regardless of these critics, grid training has been found as an effective OD intervention in implementing planned change and, in turn, improving organisational performance.

Action Research

Action Research as an OD Model has already been discussed earlier. The same is not discussed here again for the sake of repetition.

Transactional Analysis

In common parlance, transaction means give and take taking place between the two persons or parties like a business transaction. Likewise, there is social transaction also when one person responds to another. In fact, these social transactions serve as connective tissues to hold the various sub-parts of organisation together. The study of these social transaction is called 'Transactional Analysis (TA)'. Eric Berne[32] developed TA for the first time in 1950 to study the psychotherapy of his patients. While observing his patients, Berne found that often it was as if different types of people were inside each patient. He also observed that there are different types of selves transmitted into a patient in different ways. Based on these observations, the application of TA, later on, was extended to ordinary social transactions also by Berne, Harris and Jongerward[33]. Now, TA has become a useful technique to study human relationship. TA can succinctly be defined as a study of social transactions or interactions between people to improve communication and human relationships. These, in turn, improve organisational performance. Hence, TA has also been used as an OD intervention. A detailed discussion on TA follows subsequently.

How one behaves with or responds to others depends on two cognitive elements. **One**, how much one is aware of self, *i.e.*, 'levels of self awareness'. **Two**, what is one's psychological position at the time of his/her transaction with others, *i.e.* 'ego states.' Now, these are discussed, in detail, one by one.

Levels of Self Awareness: 'Self' is the core of one's interaction with others. And, self is composed of two types of constructs. First one are those known to the person concern and are shared by other participants. Second are those hidden to the person but known to others. These constructs form the dyadic relationship between people. The two behavioural scientists, namely, Joseph Luft and Harrignton Ingham[34] have developed a diagramatic window presentation popularly known as '**Johari Windows**' to look at what one knows about self and also what one does not. Here, the term 'Johari' means nothing but is a combination of the first few letters of their names.

The '**Johari Window**' looks like the following :

	Knows others	Does not know others
Knows self	(1) Open self	(2) Hidden Self
Does not know self	(3) Blind Self	(4) Undiscovered

Figure 28.8 : Johari Window

A brief description of these follows.

1. **The Open Self :** As the term 'open' implies, the person knows his/her feelings and is open to share the same with others. One's openness and straight forwardness in behaviour makes know his/her feelings and motives. This promotes camaraderies among people in an organisation.

2. **Hidden Self :** In this situation, the person is known to oneself but does not know others. This is characterized by one's nature to hide things from others and this happens right from childhood and becomes a nature with the advancement in age.

3. **Blind Self :** This is opposite to hidden self. An individual is known to others but not to oneself. In other words, what is happening to an individual is known to others but the individual does not know it. What happens sometimes is that people speak unconsciously in a certain way, *i.e.*, with a tone of voice, a look on their face, a gesture. These are not known to them but others are well aware of these. People's such behaviour affects others how they perceive the people and then behave accordingly[35].

4. **Undiscovered Self :** This refers to the situation when neither the person nor others know about him/her. Expectedly, such situation creates vagueness in understanding between the people and affects inter-personal relationship accordingly.

Ego States: People all the times rest in certain psychological positions, called 'ego states'.According to Eric Berne, there are three types of ego states, namely, parent ego state, adult ego state, and child ego state. It is important to mention that ego states have no relationship with the chronological age of the individual. One can be at any ego state at any age. So to say, an old person may have child ego state and a child also may have a parent ego state. An individual reacts with another from any one these three ego states; *i.e.* psychological positions. These three ego states are discussed now.

Parent Ego State : The parent ego state is characterised by behavioural pattern like protective, nurturing, instructive, etc. People with parent ego exhibit facial and verbal clues like wagging fingers to show displeasure, referring to rules, policies, procedures, and standards in their interaction with others. There are two types of parent ego states : instructive and critical. a comment like "The leave rule is known to you, Tridib. Follow it in future" is an example of instructive parent ego state.

Adult Ego State : The characteristics of a person acting with adult ego state are like rational logical, factual, reasoning, unemotional, etc. By controlling emotional expressions and updating factual validity in behaviour, one can gradually block his child and parent ego states respectively and act with adult ego only based on his factual and rational experience.

Child Ego State : This ego state reflects the emotions people develop in response to their childhood experiences. The behavioural characteristics of child ego state are dependent, creative, rebellions, etc. People acting with child ego state show physical and verbal clues like temper tantrumps giggling, coyness, attention seeking, etc. People with child ego state expect quick approval from others and desire immediate rewards for their actions.

Three conclusions about ego states stand out :

1. Interactions that take place between people generally are a mixture of reactions with parent, adult and child ego states.

2. None of the three ego states is absolutely positive or negative. Rather, each ego state is characterised by both positive and negative features.

3. Compared to group conversations the ego states are more apparent in two-person transactions.

Life Positions. Research in behavioural sciences indicates that the dominant attitude of people toward self and others affects their interaction or behaviour with others. Such attitude is developed from experiences in the very childhood itself and tends to remain in the very childhood itself and tends to remain with the person for life time unless some major experiences occur to change it. Hence, it is called 'life position'. Of course, one life position tends to dominate a person's interaction/transaction with others, nonetheless other life positions may also occur from time to time in specific transactions. It means, though a life position dominates a person, it is not the only life position that ever exists.

What is the basis for formation of a life position? Psychologists report that the formation of life positions stems from a combination of two view points. **First**, how does a person view himself/herself? **Second**, how does he/she views others? The combination of these views fall into four categories called four possible life positions:

1. I am O.K. you are O.K.
2. I am O.K. you are not O.K.
3. I am not O.K. you are O.K.
4. I am not O.K. you are not O.K.

These are also shown in Figure 22.9.

Attitude toward self	Negative	Positive
Positive	I am O.K. — You are not O.K.	I am O.K. – You are O.K.
Negative	I am not O.K. — You are not O.K.	I am not O.K. You are O.K.

Attitude towards others

Fig. 28.9 : Four Life Positions

Among the four life positions as depicted in Figure 22.9, "I am O.K. — You are O.K." is the most desirable one as it involves positive view towards self and others. In other words, it shows healthy acceptance of self, on the one hand, and respect for others, on the other. Such view is based on rationality and adult ego. In the organisational context, it is likely to lead to constructive communication and functional conflict and, thus, in turn, help managers take rational decisions.

As regards the other three life positions, these are, in one respect or other, less psychologically mature and rational. These do not have either importance of self or respect for others or both. Hence, the need for changing these positions to "I am OK— You are O.K." life position. This can be learned through experiences and interventions.

In this lies the hopes and scope for better and improved inter-personal relationships and transactions in the organisations and in the society as a whole.

Stroking. It is believed that the term 'stroking' has orginated from the studies dealing with the baby needs for physical affection required for their proper psychological development. Just like babies, the grown-up people, i.e. adults and parents, do also seek affection, and for that matter, stroking. Hence, stroking has become one of the important aspects of Transactional Analysis. What is meant by stroking is any act of recognition for another. Speaking alternatively, it is any act of recognition such as physical, verbal and non-verbal contact between people. While patting on the back and a firm handshake are the examples of physical strokes, words like "well done" is the example of verbal one. Behavioural studies[36] have established a positive relationship between stroking and employee well—being on the job.

Depending on the impact of strokes, these may be of three types, viz., positive, negative, and mixed. **Positive** strokes make the recipient feel good, *i.e.*, a sense of 'I'm OK.' When the supervisor tells : "Manoj, you have an impressive sales record during the last month", it's an example of positive stroke. As against this, the stroke that hurts the recipient making him/her feel less good or OK about himself/herself is a **negative** one. An example of negative stroke is this supervisor's comment : "Ravi, your sales record is very poor given your long experience". In case of **mixed** strokes the stroke makes the recipeint feel both good as well as bad. Supervisor's comment like : "Pradip, you did a nice job, but not a great job," is the example of mixed strokes. Obviously, among all the three strokes, the positive stroke, also called adult-to-adult communication is the most desirable as it results in the positive impact on the recipient.

28.3.6 FACTORS INFLUENCING CHOICE OF AN OD INTERVENTION

How to select a particular OD intervention to fit the best in the situation? Selection of an OD intervention is usually influenced by the following three factors:

1. Applicability
2. Feasibility
3. Acceptability

Applicability

Applicability means the potential of a given intervention to yield desired results. This is possible when an intervention is capable enough to address the real problem and holds good promise of solving it. One way to ascertain applicability of an intervention is to examine the likely positive and negative consequences associated with it. What follows from above is the need for evaluating one's client system with great care and concern before actually introducing any intervention.

Feasibility

Feasibility means the suitability of an intervention to suit to the client system. In other words, one needs to evaluate whether an intervention can actually be effectively introduced in a given type of client system.

Acceptability

Whatever applicability and feasibility an intervention carries has no use unless it is acceptable to the client system. It means an intervention needs to be accepted by its client system to yield desired results. Experience shows that an intervention is likely to be less acceptable unless sufficient preparatory work has been done before introducing it.

Some Salient Issues in OD

1. The OD effort should begin at the top of the organisation *i.e.,* management level and then should permeate down to the lowest level of organisation.
2. Whoever be the client, be a particular target group or the total organisation, it has its implications for OD effort.
3. The identification of change to be introduced depends on the nature and type of problem the organisation is facing. Diagnostic studies help identify the needed change in the organisation.
4. The consultant helps the client understand how to better help oneself.
5. The OD techniques can be implemented at individual level, and the organisational level depending upon where the change is to be brought.
6. No one OD technique is apporpriate for different types of problems. Hence, the intervention techniques appropriate to problems at hand should be applied.
7. Both relevance and value of OD effort depend on its outcome. Therefore, OD efforts need to be evaluated on an objective basis.

SUMMARY

This summary is organized by the 'learning objectives' given on page no. 457:

- *Organisations need to change to sustain, survive, and thrive in the market.*
- *A change resulting from a deliberate decision to alter the organisation is called 'planned change'. Planned change involves an analysis of, what is called 'Force Field Analysis', driving and restraining forces in existence in the organisation. The most talked about change model is 'Lewin's Change Model' consisting of three steps, namely, unfreezing, changing, and refreezing.*
- *Change is often resisted by both individuals for the reasons like fear of the unknown, new learning, distrust on management and disruption of stable relationship) and organisation (due to the reasons like threats to the power structure, sunk costs, and vested interest). Resistance to change can be overcome through communication, participation, facilitations, support, negotiation, manipulation, and co-operation.*
- *Organisation development (OD) is a process of system wide change at various levels designed to make organisation more effective.*
- *The main OD models in use include Lewin's model, Greiner' model, Leavitt's model, and action research model.*
- *Sensitivity training, job redesign, career planning, management development training, survey feedback, management by objectives (MBO), quality of work life (QWL), team building, process consultation, transactional analysis, etc. have been the major OD interventions.*
- *The factors that influence the choice of an OD intervention are applicability, feasibility, and acceptability.*

REVIEW QUESTIONS

1. What is meant by organisational change? What are the major external and internal forces for change in organisations?
2. Why is organisational change often resisted by individuals and groups within the organisation? How can such resistance be prevented or overcome?
3. "Resistance to change is a normal part of the process of change." Discuss. What techniques would you use in overcoming such resistance?
4. What are the steps involved in the change process? Discuss.
5. What is OD? How is it undertaken by organisations?
6. Discuss Lewin's model of O.D.
7. Discuss the major OD interventions. In your opinion, which OD intervention is most effective and why?
8. If you were in charge of designing the ideal management development programme, what topics would you include? Why?
9. Distinguish between:
   (*a*) Individual change and organisational change
   (*b*) Reactive change and proactive change

10. Write notes on:
(*a*) Sensitivity Training
(*b*) Job Redesign
(*c*) Quality of Work Life
(*d*) Team Building
(*e*) Management by Objectives
(*f*) Force Field Analysis

REFERENCES

1. G. Saxena: Organisational Change, **Management Review,** 1, 1985, pp. 9-16.
2. Madhukar Shukla: ***op. cit.*** 1996, p. 192.
3. Larry E. Greiner: Evolution and Revolution as Organisations Grow, **Harvard Business Review,** July-August, 1972, pp. 37-46.
4. Kurt Lewin: **Field Theory in Social Science,** Harper and Row, New York, 1951.
5. E.H. Schein: Management Development as a Process of Influence, In : D.R. Hampton (Ed.), **Behavioural Concept in Management,** Dickinson Publishing Co., Inc., Belmont, California, 1968.
6. R. A. Sharma: ***op. cit.***, 1998, p. 287.
7. Stephen P. Robbins: ***op. cit.,*** 1999, pp. 634-635.
8. L. Livingstone, M.A. White, and D.L. Nelson: **The Effects of Delayed Implementation on Employee Attitudes toward Computer Innovations,** Oklahoma State University, Working Paper, 1992.
9. A. Rafacli : Employee Attitudes towards Working with computers, **Journal of Occupational Behaviour**, april 1996, pp. 89-106.
10. L. Coch and J.P. French : Overcoming, Resistance to Change, **Human Relations**, Vo. I, 1948, pp. 512-532.
11. L.E. Greiner : Patterns of Organisation Change, **Harvard Business Review**, May-June 1967, pp. 199-130.
12. **The Economic Times**, 10-16 September, 1999, p.3.
13. Kurt Lewin : Frontiers in Group Dynamics: Concept, Method and Reality in Social Science, Social Equilibria and Social Change, **Human Relations**, June 1947, pp. 5-41.
14. Robert R. Blake and Jane S. Mouton : **Building a Dynamic Organisation through Grid Organisation Development**, Addison Wesley, Reading, Mass, 1969, p. 16.
15. Wendell L. French and Cecil H. Bell : **Organisation Development : Behavioural Science, Interventions for Organisation Improvement**, Princtice-Hall, Englewood Cliffs, NJ, 1978, p.14.
16. H. Koontz; C.O. Donnell and H. Weihrich : **Management**, McGraw-Hill, Kogakusha Ltd., Tokyo, 1972.
17. W. Warner Burke : **Organisation Development : A Normative View,** Addison– Wesley, Reading , Mass, 1987.
18. Wendell L. French and Cecil H. Bell : ***op. cit.***, 1978.
19. Kurt Lewin : ***op. cit.***, 1947, pp. 5-41.
20. Larry E. Greiner : Patterns of Organisation Change, In : Dalton, Lawrence and Greiner (Eds.) : **Organisational Change and Development,** Richard D. Irwin, Homewood Ill, 1970.
21. Harol J. Leavitt : **New Perspectives in Organisation Research**, John Wiley & Sons, New York, 1964.

22. Kurt Lewin : **Field Theory in Social Science**, Harper and Row, 1951. H.A. Shephard : An Action Research Model, In : **An Action Research Programme for Organisation Improvement**, University of Machigan, Ann Arbor, MI, 1960; W. french : Organisation Development : Objectives, Assumptions and Strategies, **California Management Review**, 1969, 12, pp.23-34.
23. W.L. French and C.H. Bell : **Organisation Development**, Printice- Hall, Englewood Cliffs, N.J. 1978.
24. John Collier : United States Indian Administration as a Laboratory of Ethnic Relations, **Social Research**, 12, May 1945, pp. 275-276.
25. Kurt Lewin : ***op. cit.***,1969, 12, pp.23-34.
26. J. Campbell and M. Dunnette : Effectiveness of T-Group Experiences in Managerial Training and Development, **Psychological Bulletin**, No. 70, 1968, pp. 73-103.
27. Sangeeta Jain : **Quality of Work Life**, Deep Publication, New Delhi, 1991, p. 17.
28. Keith Davis and John Newstron: ***op. cit.***, 1998, p. 387.
29. J.P. singh : Improving Quality of working Life in the Indian Context, **Productivity**, 22(4), 1982, pp. 13-20.
30. Edgar H. Schein : **Process Consultation : Its Role in Organisation Development**, Addison-Wesely, Reading, Mass, 1988.
31. R.R. Blake and J.S. Mouton : **The Managerial Grid**, Gulf Publishing, Houston, 1964.
32. Eric Berne : **Transactional Analysis in Psychotherapy**, Grove Press. New York, 1961.
33. Eric Berne : **Games People Play**, Grove Press, New York, 1964; Thomas A. Harris : **I'm OK—You're OK : A Practical Guide to Transactional Analysis**, Harper & Row Publishers, New York, 1969; Dorothy Jongeward and Philip Seyer : **Chosing Success : Transactional Analysis on the Job**, John Wiley, New York, 1978.
34. Joseph Luft : **Of Human Interaction**, Mayfield : Publishing, New York, 1969.
35. Dorothy Jongeward and Philip Seyer : ***op. cit.***, 1978, p. 5.
36. Dorothy Jongeward and Philip Seyer : ***Ibid***, 1978, p. 130.

Case 28.1 : MR. KAMAL NAYAN*

Mr. Kamal Nayan joined as Office Manager, Industrial Products Limited, Bombay, after coming back from U.S. A. from where he got his M.B.A. degree with specialisation in personnel management. He was young and energetic and believed in results. Before proceeding to U.S.A. he had several years of experience in India in different capacities. When Mr. Nayan joined Industrial Products Limited, its office time was 10.30 A. M. to 5.30 P.M. He felt that the timing should be changed to 10.00 A.M. to 5.00 P.M. because he knew that office personnel in U.S.A. did not work after 5.00 P.M. He thought this to be true for India also and to ensure more availability of effective time for office, he changed it to 10.00 A.M. to 5.00 P.M. He announced the change officially.

No one reacted initially but after two days Mr. Nayan received a written memorandum by all office personnel that old office timing be restored. Mr. Nayan did not yield to this demand. However, he was convinced that the first step was to build co-operative spirit among his employees through informal get-together.

---

* Adapted from: Stephen P. Robbins: **Organisation Theory: Structure, Design and Applications,** Printice-Hall of India Private Limited, New Delhi, 1998, pp. 600-503.

Therefore, he prepared a scheme of having monthly dinner party of all members of the office. In the party, all members were to bring their home-made dishes. Their wives and children were to be encouraged to attend the monthly dinner party. The scheme was announced through placing it on the information bulletin of the company. The notice also invited suggestions from the members for making the scheme successful. Two weeks elapsed and no suggestion came. On one occasion when the day was nearing for the first dinner meeting, he overheard the following conversation between two of his office members:

First employee: "So, what are you bringing for the party? As for myself, I will bring Bhelpuri."

Second employee: "I will bring Chana." (Both laughed)

Mr. Nayan felt that nobody was seemed to be concerned in his scheme.

QUESTIONS

1. What were the reasons for not supporting the actions of Mr. Kamal Nayan by his employees?
2. Advise Mr. Kamal Nayan how he should proceed in the matter.

Case 28.2 : OD Effort in BHEL, Bhopal*

Organisation Development adopted in this company is through six phases:

1. Phase I: September 1976 to December 1977

Problem identification workshop for senior executives was held and the issues identified were:

(*i*) Site problems due to failure of our equipment.

(*ii*) Fall in labour productivity due to withdrawal of the incentive scheme

(*iii*) Communication gap between Management and Employees. Action Steps were to hold training programmes :

- (*a*) To update engineering knowledge of engineers:
- (*b*) To improve quality and to develop quality awareness among various levels of our employees.
- (*c*) To acquaint and familiarise customer's operative and maintenance staff with our products, their manufacture, their maintenance problem, etc.

2. Phase II: January 1978 To March 1980

15 interactions of various levels of our employees with an outside Consultant was brought by a second type of diagnostic interventions.

The problems identified were:

(*i*) Communication gap between employees and management.

(*ii*) Lack of human concern and recognition.

(*iii*) Faulty personnel policies and dysfunctional role of personnel department.

(*iv*) Poor and work decision-making characterised by adhocism.

---

* V.K. Jain: OD Effort in BHEL, In: T.V. Rao and D.F. Pereira (Eds.): **Recent Experiences in Human Resources Development,** Oxford and IBH, New Delhi, 1986, pp. 183-192.

Lack of team work and cooperation and interpersonal and interdepartmental conflict were also seen as major hurdles to effective functioning of the organisation.

3. This led to the Following Action Steps Rather Than Training Interventions

(*i*) Management Employee Communication Meetings for bridging the communication gap and developing better understanding.

(*ii*) Behavioural science oriented programmes for heads of divisions and supervisors for creating awareness and social skills for effective interpersonal relationships.

(*iii*) Programme for personnel executives to change the attitude and their perceived dysfunctional role.

(*iv*) Change of cadre programme for all promotees.

(*v*) Development of faculty resources in the training department to cope with the increasing emphasis on training in behavioural science-oriented programmes.

4. Perceived Benefits of the Effort

As a result of intensive training and multi-dimensional interventions, a vague sense of change for the better was experienced.

It was at this time that decision to conduct a survey to find out the effectiveness of the OD effort so far was conceived and implemented through a questionnaire.

5. Phase III: April 1980 to Date

The survey revealed the following strengths and weaknesses of the organisation:

(*i*) Employees perceived a positive change in the organisation.

(*ii*) Employees have high sense of belonging and commitment to the unit.

Weaknesses perceived were:

(*i*) Poor decision-making

(*ii*) Lack of appreciation and recognition

(*iii*) Lack of opportunities for growth and development

(*iv*) Lack of team work

(*v*) "Affiliation & Control" being the dominant motivational climate prevailing in the organisation.

This phase was initiated by sharing the findings of the survey, initially the HODs and later with all levels of employees through MEÇOM. The purpose was to focus their attention on the negative and positive aspects of the organisational health and thus create an awareness at all levels.

The major interventions during the second phase were:

(*a*) Five Team Building Programmes

(*b*) Six workshops for the Top Management group to review the OD effort

(*c*) Appointment of task forces

(*d*) OD effort in Departments

(*e*) Development of Internal Resource Persons (IRPs)

(*f*) Achievement Motivation Programme

Encouraging OD effort had made distinct progress in the areas of:

(*i*) Openness in interpersonal relations at senior levels.

(*ii*) Bridging the communication gap by direct interaction of all levels with the top management.

(*iii*) Mutual trust and confidence.

(*iv*) Faith in the management's sense of fairness and justice.

(*v*) Team work, cooperation and understanding.

(*vi*) Lot of improvement in welfare amenities like schools, roads, housing facilities etc.

(*vii*) Customer satisfaction-improvement in sequential supplies, supply of shortages/spares.

(*viii*) General discipline and punctuality.

6. Phase IV: April 1984 onwards

On the basis of the finding of the April, 1984 workshop the following actions seems to be emerging for the current year.

(*i*) Intensifying diversification activities etc.

(*ii*) Development of IRPs

(*iii*) Feedback survey

The new feedback survey at the organisational level will comprise three aspects:

(*i*) To measure the changes during the last four years and assess future directions.

(*ii*) Certain new dimensions will also be added in the proposed new feedback survey.

(*iii*) In view of the recent changes and also to percolate the OD awareness down the line, it is felt necessary to conduct programme for HODs.

In addition to the above activities, a number of new activities will emerge on the basis of findings of proposed feedback survey, which will cover cultural, managerial and administrative aspects. A set of new interventions will be designed accordingly.

29

ORGANISATIONAL EFFECTIVENESS (OE)

"Efficiency is doing things right, and effectiveness is doing the right things."

– Peter Drucker

Learning Objectives

After studying this chapter, you should be able to:

- **Define** OE
- **Discuss** various approaches to OE.
- **Mention** factors that determine OE.

So far we have tried to understand why people behave as they behave at work. Nonetheless, the basic purpose to study OB has been understanding how people should be handled effectively for the successful attainment of organisational goals. This is because proper handling of people and organisational resources helps managers make organisations more effective. This chapter is, therefore, devoted to address to various aspects of organisational effectiveness (OE) such as, what OE actually means, what are various approaches and factors involved in OE.

Let us begin with understanding meaning of OE.

29.1 OE DEFINED

Organisational effectiveness (OE), being a relative term, is conceptualised by different students of organisations differently. As such, no unanimity is found in their approaches. The diverse approaches are not only judgemental but open to questions also. The various terms, such as, efficiency, productivity, profitability, and growth are often used interchangeably to denote OE.

Organisations as social systems have no one goal but multiple goals to attain. Take the examples of Universities, or prisons which pursue several goals. The University must simultaneously teach and create valid knowledge through research; the prison must keep criminals out of circulations but also provide opportunities for rehabilitation. Then, the question is, the effectiveness of the organisation to be judged by its performance on one function, on both separately, or on some complex integration of several goals or functions?

That judging OE is beset by certain problems is well illustrated by the example of effectiveness of your own Department of Business Administration.

> How do you determine if your Department is doing well, *i.e.,* effective? If its all students get jobs upon completion of their MBA, does that tell us the Department is effective? Or should we look at the percentage increase or decrease in fresh applications year after year, a statistical report of the number of books, magzines and research journals checked out from the library by students during the previous semesters, a survey asking seniors what they thought of their department experience, the number of research publications by faculty members to their credits, awards won by the students, or the average salary of former students during five years after their MBA.

Indisputedly, all above mentioned criteria need to be taken into consideration while assessing the effectiveness of the Department.

Acknowledging that every organisation has multiple goals or functions and also exists within organisation an environment that provides unpredictable inputs; an organisation's effectiveness can be defined as its capacity to survive, adapt, maintain itself, and grow, regardless of the particular function it fulfils[1].

Organisations are social systems. Several parties have their stakes in organisations. Hence, they do not exist in isolation. Therefore, how they do pursue their goals has a great deal to do with well being of various parties holding stake in them. Given such case, it seems, therefore, pertinent to conceptualise the term 'organisational effectiveness' in such a way that the term encompasses a multiple criteria to cover all. Viewed from this angle, OE can be defined as organisation as a social system, given certain resources and means, fulfils its objectives without incapacitating its means and resources and without placing undue strain upon its members. This conception of OE subsumes the following:

1. Organisational productivity;
2. Organisational flexibility
3. Absence of organisational conflicts.

Thus, OE is reflected in how the organisation is equipped to:

1. Move toward its goals, and
2. Survive in the face of external and internal variability through creative adaptation strategies.

What next is discussed is the diverse approaches that the study of OE has taken so far.

29.2 APPROACHES TO OE

The various approaches used to conceptualise the term OE are grouped into four categories:

1. Goal-Attainment Approach
2. Systems Approach
3. Strategic-Constituencies Approach
4. Competing Values Approach.

These are discussed one by one.

Goal-Attainment Approach

Organisations are created to achieve one or more goals. Hence, it should not come as no surprise then to find that goal attainment is one of the most widely used criteria of effectiveness. Organisations consider goals or ends to which they are created to achieve. Profit maximization, high productivity, employees' high morale, providing efficient service, etc. may be examples of goal attainment criteria. In goal-attainment approach, achieving set goals is the bottom line that counts.

Katz and Kahn[2] explicate organisational effectiveness as the maximization of profit or return to the organisation by all means. While studying organisational effectiveness, Likert[3] has identified three variables that help assess attainment of goals. These three variables are: independent variables (such as leadership style, organisation structure, technology, etc.), intervening variables (like perceptions, attitudes, values, motivational forces, etc.), and dependent variables (such as production, sales, employee turnover, etc.).

The goal attainment approach of organisational effectiveness assumes that:

1. Organisations must have ultimate goals.
2. Goals must be identified and defined to be understood.
3. Goals must be few enough to be manageable.
4. There must be general agreement on these goals.
5. Goals must be measurable.

However, goal-attainment approach is fraught with some limitations also. These limitations make its exclusive use highly questionable. The main limitations are:

1. While operationalizing goal-attainment approach, one is confronted with a problem like whose goals?
2. Organisation's official goals do not always reflect the organisation's actual goals. This is because official goals at times are influenced by some factors like social desirability.
3. An organisation's short-term goals differ from its long-term goals.
4. Sometimes organisation's multiple goals compete with each other and sometimes are even incompatible. The achievement of "high product quality" and "low unit cost", for example, may be directly at odds with each other.

These limitations, while certainly damning, should not be construed as a blanket indictment of goals. Organisations are deliberate goal-seeking entities. The real problem lies in how to identify and measure the attainment of goals. If managers are willing to confront the complexities inherent in goal-attainment approach, they can obtain reasonably valid information for assessing an organisation's effectiveness.

Systems Approach

It has already been said that assessing organisational effectiveness on the basis of attainment of multiple goals does not seem appropriate. The reason being some of multiple goals may be in conflict with each other. It may so happen that in regard to some goals, its performance may be highly encouraging and it may be a dismal failure in regard to others[4]. Hence, we can never say that an organisation is wholly effective or ineffective in terms of its multiple goals. As goals focus on outputs, hence, an organisation should also be judged on its ability to acquire inputs, process these inputs, channel the outputs, and maintain stability and balance. Another way to look at OE, therefore, is through a systems approach[5]. Some behavioural scientists[6] call it as **"input-throughput-output approach".**

Bennis[7] has clearly explained OE based on systems approach involving the following criteria:

1. **Adaptability:** The ability to solve problems and to react with flexibility to changing environmental demands.
2. **A Sense of Identity:** Knowledge and insight on the part of the orgnaisation of what it is, what its goals are, and what it is to do. How outsiders do perceive the organisational goals?
3. **Capacity to Test Reality:** The ability to search out, accurately perceive, and correctly interpret the real properties of the environment, particularly those which have relevance for the functioning of the organisation.
4. **Integration:** It is integration among the sub-parts of the total organisation, such that the parts are not working at cross-purposes.

Argyris[8] and McGregor[9] have argued in a similar vein for the integration of personal and organisational goals and for them integration criterion in the systems approach is central.

It is important to mention that in the systems approach, end goals are not ignored at all. However, they remain only one element in the whole system. Systems approach emphasizes criteria that will increase the longterm survival of the organisation such as the organisation's ability to acquire resources (inputs), maintain itself internally as a social organism, and interact successfully with its external environment. Thus, what follows from above that the systems approach focuses not so much on specific ends *i.e.*, goals as on the means needed for the attainment of those set ends or goals.

The systems approach to OE assumes that:

1. Organisations are made up of interrelated sub-parts. Pertormance ot one part affects the performance of other parts as well.
2. Effectiveness requires both awareness and successful interactions with environmental constituents.
3. Survival requires a steady replenishment of resources consumed by the organisation. Failure to replenish will result in the organisation's decline and, ultimately, death.

Like goal-attainment approach, systems approach to OE also suffers from certain limitations. The two telling shortcomings of the systems approach relate to measurement and the issue of whether means really matter.

1. **Problem of Measurement:** While measuring specific goals may be easy, it is difficult to measure process variables such as "flexibility of response to environmental changes' or 'clarity of internal communication'. There has not been any accurate and convincing criterion to measure the process variables in quantity or intensity. Therefore, whatever measures are used are open to question.

2. **Problem of Means:** Another problem of systems approach is how much valid it is to attach significance to means to end for assessing OE. This is because if ends are achieved, means may become importanceless. We know, in case of sports, it is often said that **"it's whether you win or lose that counts, not how you play the game".** One can argue that the same holds true for organisations also.

Strategic-Constituencies Approach

One closely related approach to systems approach is the strategic-constituencies approach. This approach proposes that an effective organisation is one that satisfies the demands of those constituencies in its environment from whom it requires support for its continued survival[10]. this approach differs from the systems approach in the sense that it did not concern with all of the organisation's environment, but seeks to appease only those constituencies in the environment who can threaten the organisation's survival. Let it be clarified with an example.

> The Government Universities, be the State or Central, will consider their effectiveness in terms of acquiring students but need not be concerned with potential employers of their graduate students. Why? Because the survival of these Universities is not influenced by whether their graduates get jobs. On the contrary, the private management institutions which charge considerably more than what their government counterparts do, spend a great deal of time and money in trying to get placement for their students. This is because when parents spend two lacs or more rupees to get their son or daughter a mangement diploma, they expect it to lead to a job. If this does not occur, it will be increasingly difficult for the private management institutes to get freshmen applications in the subsequent years.

Table 29.1 identifies a list of strategic constituencies a business firm might confront and the typical organisational effectiveness criteria each constituency is to use.

Table 29.1 Typical OE Criteria of Selected Strategic Constituencies

Constituency	**Typical of Criteria**
Owners	Return on investment; growth in earnings.
Employees	Compensation; fringe benefits; satisfaction with working conditions
Customers	Satisfaction with price, quality, service.
Suppliers	Satisfaction with payments; future sales potential
Creditors	Ability to pay indebtedness.
Unions	Competitive wages and benefits; satisfactory working conditions; willingness to bargain fairly.
Local community	Involvement of organization's members in local officials affairs, lack of damage to the community's environment.
Government	Compliance with laws; avoidance of penalities agencies and reprimands.

Adapted from: Stephen P. Robbins: **Organisation Theory: Structure, Design and Applications,** Printice-Hall of India Private Limited, New Delhi, 1998, p. 66.

The organisation's effectiveness would be assessed on how much able organisation is to satisfy goals of various constituencies.

As with the previous approaches, this one too is not free from problems. The noteworthy ones are :

1. The task of separating the strategic constituencies from the larger environment of a business is easy to say but difficult to do so in practice. This is because, given the fast changing business environment what was strategic to the organisation till the other day, may not be so to-day. The converse of this example may also hold true.

2. That what expectations various constituencies hold for a business organisation is also difficult to identify in the absence of required information in this regard. There has so far been no reliable technique how to tap information accurately on what constituencies actually expect of organisation.

Given above problems, the strategic-constituencies approach cannot be rejected in toto. If organisation has to survive, then it is incumbent upon managers to understand just who it is, in terms of constituencies, that survival is contingent upon. Knowing whose support is needed to make organisation survive, management can accordingly modify its order of goals as necessary to satisfy expectations of various strategic constituencies.

Competing-Values Approach

OE assessed on the basis of one single criterion in terms of goals or systems or constituencies, as discussed in the preceding three approaches, does not give a comprehensive understanding of OE. Hence, there is a need to integrate all of key variables in the domain of organisational effectiveness. Such an integrative approach is offered by the **Competing-values approach[11].**

The basic theme underlying the **competing-values approach** is that the criteria you actually value and also use in assessing an organisation's effectiveness be it, for example, return on investment, or market share of your product, or new product development depends on who you are and the interest you represent in the orgnaisation. Different stakeholders such as stockholders, unions, suppliers, management, employees, or public represent different interests in the organisations. It should come as no surprise then to find that all above mentioned stake-holders look at the same organisation but evaluate its effectiveness entirely differently. You can conveniently relate this fact by thinking about how you the students of MBA differently evaluate your teacher who teaches you Management Concepts and Organisational Behaviour.

In your semester of thirty students, your evaluations of the above course teacher is expected to differ markedly. Expectedly, some of you will find and see the teacher as one of the best you have in your Department of Business Administration. The converse may also be true. Some others may evaluate the same teacher as one of the worst in the Department. Why? Because it is based on the individual student's varied standards of what a good teacher is, who creates the different rating. Remember, the teacher's behaviour is the constant. Thus, the differential rating probably tells us more about how the students value their same teacher than it tells us about the teacher's effectiveness.

Let us further look at how competing values operate. Robbins[12] has listed three basic sets of values, namely, flexibility versus control, people versus organisation, and means versus ends. A brief description of each of these follows:

Flexibility versus Control: Flexibility and control are two incompatible dimensions of organisational structure. While the former values innovation, adaptation, and change, control favours stability, order, and predictability.

People versus Organisation: Whether people in organisation should be valued more or organisation itself. This is because people-organisation dichotomy is another set of essentially incompatible dimensions. People concern values realisation for the feelings and needs of the people within the organisation. In contrast, concern for productivity and task accomplishment appraises concern for organisation.

Means versus Ends: The third set of values relates to organisational means versus ends. Means stress internal forces and the long term, whereas ends value final outcomes and the short term. This dichotomy is very similar to goal attainment and systems approaches respectively as discussed earlier. Goal attainment focuses on ends, and system emphasizes means.

The abovementioned three sets of values are depicted as a three-dimentional diagram in Fig. 29.1.

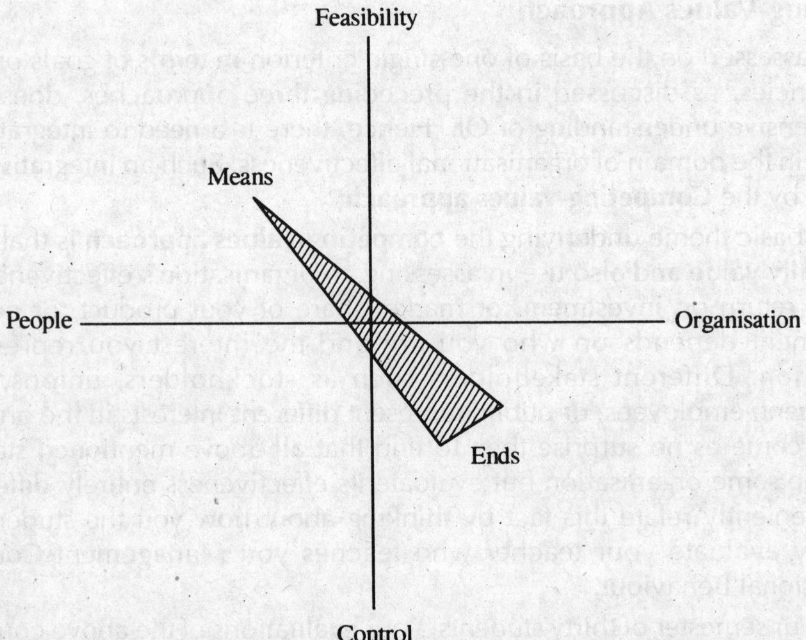

Fig. 29.1: A Three-Dimensional Model of Organisational Effectiveness.

The competing-values approach is conceived upon the following assumptions:

1. The concept of OE is subjective. The evaluator values goals as per his or her interests and preferences.
2. It assumes that the evaluator's diverse preferences can be combined in such a way as to create a set of competing-values. Each set defines a different model of OE.

A Comparison of Four OE Approaches

We have presented four different approaches as useful ones in their own ways. Now, we are answering under which conditions each approach is preferred. Look at Table 29.2. It will help you identify what each approach uses to define effectiveness and under which conditions each approach is most useful.

TAble 29.2: Comparing the Four Approaches of OE

Approach	Definition	When Useful
Goal attainment	**An organisation is effective to the extent that ...**	**The approach is preferred when ...**
Systems	it accomplishes its started goals.	goals are clear, time bound, and measureable.
	it acquires needed resources.	a clear connection exists between inputs and outputs.
Strategic constituencies	all strategic constituencies are at léast minimally satisfied.	constituencies have powerful influence on the organization, and the organization must respond to demands.
Competing values	the emphasis of the organization in the four major areas matches constituent preferences.	the organization is unclear about its own emphases, or changes in criteria over time are of interest

Adapted from Kim S. Cameron, "The Effectiveness of Ineffectiveness," in B.M. Staw and L.L. Cummings, **eds., Research in Organisational Behaviour,** Vol. 6.

29.3 FACTORS INFLUENCING OE

Knowing only criteria or approaches for OE may not serve a practising manager's purpose. It is also equally important for a manager to identify the underlying factors in organisational effectiveness. Individually, each factor matters in affecting organisational effectiveness. But, what actually matters more is each factor's relationship to the entire organisation. Viewed from this angle, Likert[13] has classified all factors into three groups. These are:

1. Causal Factors
2. Intervening Factors
3. End-Result Factors

We will discuss them one by one.

Causal Factors: These are the factors that cause or influence development within an organisation. Likert states that causal variables are independent variables that determine the course of development within an organisation and the results achieved by the organisation. The causal variables can be changed by the organisation and its management. Examples of causal variables are organisational structure, managerial policies, leadership styles, and skillls.

Intervening Factors: Intervening factors are those which get their reflection in the internal state of organisation. Causal variables cause intervening variables or factors.

Intervening factors are reflected as the loyalties, attitudes, motivations, performance goals, communication and so on. Intervening factors can be devided into two broad types : **one** attitudinal, and the **second,** behavioural. These factors help in building and developing the organisation.

End.-Result Factors: These are the dependent factors caused by causal and intervening factors. These are often in terms of the factors which managers use to measure effectiveness of organisation. Production, sales, earnings, etc., are examples of end-result factors.

The interrelationship among these three factors is juxtaposed in the following Table. 29.3.

Table 29.3: Interrelationship among Three Factors

Causal Variable		Intervening Variables		End-result Variable
Leadership strategies, skills, and styles Management's decisions Organisational philosophy, objective, policies and structure Technology, etc.	⇒	Commitment to objective, motivation and morale of members Skills in leadership, communications, conflict-resolution, decision-making problem-solving, etc.	⇒	Production costs Sales Earnings Management, union relations Turnover, etc.

SUMMARY

This summary is oragnized by the 'learning objectives' given on page No. 496

- *OE defined as the degree to which an organisation attains its short (ends) and long-term (means) goals, the selection of which reflects strategic constituencies, the self-interest of the evaluator, and the life stage of the organisation.*
- *Four approaches: goal attainment, systems, strategic constituencies, and competing values have been adopted to assess organisational effectiveness. Each, in its own way, is a useful model to assess OE.*
- *All factors underlying in effectiveness of organisations are classified into three groups, namely, causal factors, intervening factors, and end-result factors. These influence OE in a well-knit interdependency manner among them.*

REVIEW QUESTIONS

1. Define OE. Why is OE relevant in the study of organisational behaviour?
2. What are the different approaches which have been developed to study OE? Do you agree with the view that it is difficult for organisation to be effective?
3. Give three examples of OE criteria that are consistent with the goal-attainment approach.
4. Compare the strategic-constituencies and competing-values approaches. How are they similar? How are they different?

5. Select your own Department of Business Administration as a case. How would you assess its effectiveness using the goal-attainment, systems, and strategic constituencies?
6. "Goals are a viable standard against which OE can be measured". Build an argument to support this statement. Then build an argument to refute this statement.
7. "Measuring effectiveness is a critical but problematic issue in the study of organisation". Discuss.
8. Discuss various factors underlying in OE.

REFERENCES

1. Edgar H. Schein: ***op. cit.,*** 1997, p. 231.
2. D. Katz and R.L. Kahn: **The Social Psychology of Organisations,** John Wiley & Sons, Inc., New York, 1978.
3. R. Likert: **New Patterns of Management,** McGraw-Hill, New York, 1961.
4. Edgar H. Schein : ***op. cit.,*** 1997, pp. 232-233.
5. Ephraim Yuchtman and Stanley E. Seashore: A Systems Resource Approach to Organisational Effectiveness, **American Sociological Review**, December 1967, pp. 891-903.
6. Uma Sekaran: ***op. cit.***, 1998, pp. 247-252.
7. W.G. Bennis: Toward a Truly Scientific Management: The Concept of Organisational Health, **General Systems Yearbook**, 1962, 7, pp. 269-282.
8. C. Argyris: **Integrating the Individual and the Organisation**, Wiley, New York, 1964.
9. Douglas M. McGregor: ***op. cit.,*** 1960.
10. Jeffrey Pfeffer and Gerald Salancik: **The External Control of Organisations**, Harper & Row, New York, 1978.
11. Robert E. Quinn and John Rohrbaugh: A Competing Values Approach to Organisational Effectiveness, **Public Productivity Review**, No. 5, 1981, pp. 122-140.
12. Stephen P. Robbins: ***op. cit.***, 1998, pp. 69-70.
13. Rensis Likert: **The Human Organisation**, McGraw-Hill, New York, 1967, pp. 26-29.

Case 29.1: Which is Effective? Ford or General Motors*?

In the U.S. automobile industry, Ford Motor Co., and General Motors have been giants for more than sixty years. By the late 1920s, they had each become large and inflexible bureaucracies, and they stayed that way until quite recently.

To understand the Ford structure, you have to go back to its founder, Henry Ford. Henry became famous for introducing mass production techniques to the auto industry. But he was a man who feared change and loved control. He stubbornly refused to alter the Model T, even when it was a decade old, and proudly claimed that customers could have "any colour car they want, as long as it was black." By the late 1940s, even though Ford Motor Co. had become a massive manufacturing organization, old Henry refused to delegate authority and still tried to make every decision in the company, just as he had done back in its infancy. This historical

* **Adapted from: Stephen P. Robbins: Organisation Theory: Structure, Design and Applications, Printice-Hall of India Private Limited, New Delhi, 1998, pp. 600-503.**

precedent carried on with later generations of managers. Ford Motor Co. came into the 1980s with a culture built on top-down directives and suppression of any ideas that hadn't originated at the top.

When Alfred Sloan put GM together in the 1920s, he believed in decentralized authority with centralized control. He created separate divisions for Chevrolet, Pontiac, Oldsmobile, Buick, and Cadillac-and each was given a specific market segment within which to compete. Division managers were relatively autonomous but headquarters controlled operations through an extensive reporting system and through its power to allocate financial resources. No one person ran GM. Important decisions required approval by half-a-dozen or more committees and another half-dozen executives. The system worked at culling out poorly reasoned or risky decision options.

By the early 1980s, GM and Ford held very different positions in the automobile industry. GM was on a roll. It controlled 48 per cent of the U.S. market and was generating record-breaking profits. Ford, on the other hand, had less than a 16 per cent market share. Ford was also losing money-a whopping $3.26 billion between 1980 and 1982 alone. But the companies embarked on different roads during the 1980s and, by the end of the decade, had arrived at very different destinations. GM's market share had fallen to 35 percent, whereas Ford saw its share increased to 22 percent.

More startling was the fact that Ford's earnings had now surpassed GM's, even though its sales were only about two-thirds of the General's. To better understand how this came about, we need to look at the problems each faced entering the 1980s, the strategy they decided to pursue, and the specific actions they took.

Ford's problems in 1980 were many. Its cars were nondescript. A number of its products had reputations for shoddiness. The Japanese were rapidly expanding sales in the United States. And, very importantly, Ford's volume was significantly below GMs. This meant each Ford car had to shoulder a larger percentage of fixed costs than did GM products and resulted in significantly greater per-car profits for GM. Ford executives realized they had to take some drastic actions if the company was to survive. What they did was introduce a broad-based cost-cutting effort, initiate a massive program to change Ford's culture, put renewed emphasis on listening to and working with the people who made Ford products, and change the corporate strategy to become the styling leader among the U.S. "Big Three".

Ford became more efficient by cutting layers of management, getting employees more involved in the production process, and cutting defects by focusing people's attention on improving product quality. Managers and nonmanagers alike took part in a major program to increase their level of participation, commitment, and creativity. Management training particularly emphasized the need to replace the company's autocratic management style with one of participation. Encouraging its design staff to emulate the successes of European stylists, impressively restyled cars began coming off the assembly line in late 1985. The Taurus and Sable, the sporty Probe, and the new models of the Lincoln Continental and Ford Thunderbird became immediate hits with consumers. Meanwhile, by 1987 the company had succeeded in reducing its breakeven point by 40 percent and cutting labour-hours per car down to where the same number of cars could be produced as in 1979 but with 120,000 fewer employees.

General Motors entered the 1980s in a much stronger position than Ford. But GM pursued another strategy which proved, over time, to be flawed.

Like Ford, GM had high costs and a bloated organization. It, too, had a tradition-bound culture and an internal system that stifled innovation and was slow in reacting to a changing environment. Yet GM had high profits, huge cash reserves, and a pervasive belief that it could do no wrong. So, ironically, GM was a prisoner of its past successes. Its management was cocky and unable to be self-critical.

GM's management assumed that gas prices would rise and fuel shortages would prevail throughout the 1980s, so smaller cars would be highly sought. Aware of the increased competition from Japanese and European manufacturers, GM decided to use its vast financial resources to spend its U.S. and foreign competitors into the ground. For example, it would spend $50 billion between 1980 and 1987 on capital investment-enough to have bought Toyota and Nissan and have a few spare billions left over. GM bought and installed robots, lasers, and computers designed to step up efficiency, boost quality, and make product and engineering changes faster than the old system could. Rather than focus on product styling, it would generate huge economies of scale by building its cars out of common parts. High technology and high volume would enable GM to make cars more cheaply than anyone.

Unfortunately for GM, things didn't work out the way management planned. Fuel prices dropped and, with it, the demand for small cars. Consumers sought large cars, which were being produced in large quantities by Ford and Chrysler. GM spent enough money on capital investment to buy several of its major Japanese competitors, yet the company *lost* market share. The new hightech factories were hardly more efficient than the old ones. GM found out the hard way that new technology pays off only when combined with changes in the way work is organized on the factory floor. Moreover, the heavy vertical integration at GM whereby company subsidiaries produced two-thirds of the parts that went into its cars meant that GM couldn't take advantage of competition among outside suppliers. Ford and Chrysler, using competitive bidding, could buy parts at a significantly cheaper price than GM. The net result was that between 1981 and 1987, GM's breakeven point *rose* to 30 percent.

GM executives, particularly in the middle-management ranks, resisted any changes. People tended to say, "Hey, we came through this recession and that recession, we survived the oil shocks, we turned a $760-million loss a few years ago into a $4-billion profit. Why would anybody want to come in here and tell us to do anything differently *now*?" Complacency ruled. Attempts to reorganize the car divisions only led to look-alike products. For example, in 1987, it was almost impossible to tell the difference between a $10,000 Oldsmobile Calais and a $26,000 Cadillac Seville¾and consumers responded by snubbing GM products. In spite of all of GM's efforts between 1980 and 1988 to expand market share and become more competitive, the company lost a significant percent of its market share and took forty-one labour-hours to assemble a midsize car while Ford did it in only twenty-five hours.

By late 1987, GM's executives seemed to have gotten the mesage. No longer were they pursuing the strategy of expanding market share. Rather, like Ford, they were concentrating on producing more stylish and differentiated cars, and beginning to restructure the company so as to be able to produce fewer cars more efficiently. Plans were being made to close at least four of its twenty-six North American auto assembly plants and slash at least 100,000 jobs from its 600,000-person work force. And this approach seemed to be paying off. In the last half of 1988, GM's profits increased smartly.

QUESTIONS

1. Assess both companies's effectiveness in terms of their "environment-structure" fit.
2. Contrast these two organisations' approaches to assess effectiveness.
3. Using competing values, assess why Ford is widely considered more effective than GM. How could GM have used the competing-values approach in the early 1980s to recognize that it had problems?

30

QUALITY OF WORKING LIFE (QWL)

"Quality is fitness for purpose." – ***Juran***

"Happy places to work are all alike; each unhappy place is unhappy in its own way." – ***Tolstoycker***

Learning Objectives

After studying this chapter, you should be able to:

- **Define** QWL.
- **Trace** out the evolution and development of the concept of QWL.
- **Know** what constitute QWL.
- **Delineate** QWL in the Indian context.

We began with stating, in Chapter 1, OB is the study of human behaviour at work. We discussed, in the subsequent chapters, umpteen number of factors that explain why people behave as they behave at work. Conditions prevalent at the work place is yet another factor that also influences human behaviour at work.The types of working conditions available at the work place determine the quality or otherwise of working life which, in turn, influences human behaviour at work. This is precisely the reason why QWL has, of late, assumed increasing interest and importance in the study of OB. The present chapter, therefore, deals with the major aspects of QWL such as its meaning and definition, evolution and development, its constituents, and QWL in the Indian context.

30.1 WHAT IS QWL ?

What is meant by QWL? There have been divergent views as to what really QWL is. Let the important ones be reproduced here for your information and knowledge.

The American Society of Training and Development established a task force on the QWL way back in 1979. This task force defined QWL as "a process of work organisations which enables its members at all levels to actively participate in shaping the organisations' environment, methods and outcomes. This value based process is aimed towards meeting the twin goals of enhanced effectiveness of organisation and improved quality of life at work for employees".[1]

Cohen and Rosenthal[2] define QWL as an "internationally designed effort to bring about increased labour management cooperation to jointly solve the problem of improving organisational performance and employee satisfaction."

Nadler and Lawler[3] summarized six potential definitions of QWL as given in Table 30.1.

Table 30.1: Definitions of QWL

First definition (1969–1972)	QWL = Variable
Second definition (1969–1975)	QWL = Approach
Third definition (1972–1975)	QWL = Methods
Fourth definition (1975–1980)	QWL = Movement
Fifth definition (1979–1982)	QWL = Best Approach
Sixth definition	QWL = Nothing

Source: David A. Nadler and Edward E. Lawler: Quality of Work Life: Persepectives and Directions, **Organisational Dynamics,** Winter 1983, p. 26.

Nadler and Lawler provide a concise definition of QWL as "a way of thinking about people, work and organisations. Its distinctive elements are: (*i*) a concern about the impact of work on people as well as on organisational effectiveness; and (*ii*) the idea of participation in organisational problem-solving and decision-making".

Beinum defines QWL "based on a general approach and an organisational approach. The general approach includes all those factors affecting the physical, social, economic, psychological and cultural well-being of workers, while the organisational approach refers to the design and operation of organisations in accordance with the value of democratic society".

According to Luthans[5], "the overriding purpose of QWL is to change the climate at work so that the human-technological-organisational interface leads to a better quality of work life."

Sangeetá Jain[6] viewed QWL as consisting of a "whole parcel of terms and notions all of which really belong under the Quality of Working Life Umbrella. They include industrial effectiveness, human resource development, organisational effectiveness, work restructure, job enrichment, socio-technical systems, working humanization, group-work concepts, labour management, co-operation, working together, workers involvements, workers participation, and co-operative work structures."

Having gone through above definitions of QWL, now QWL can easily be, defined as an approach concerned with the overall climate of work and the impact that the work has on people as well as on organisational effectiveness. Direct participation of employees in problem solving and decision making in areas related to their work helps upgrade the quality of life at work.

30.2 EVOLUTION AND DEVELOPMENT OF THE CONCEPT OF QWL

Like other concepts, evolution of QWL is also traced back to various phases in history. One such tracing is done by Walton[7] by turning the pages of history of the last century. He reports that, in early 20th century, legislation was enacted to protect employees from job-injury and to eliminate hazardous working conditions, on the one hand, and inauguration of unionization movement, on the other. Emphasis was given to work related conditions such as job-security, due process at the work place and economic gains for the worker. This was followed by propounding different theories by psychologists proposing a positive relationship between morale and productivity. They also tried to prove with research findings that harmonious human relations foster both morale and productivity. They also proposed reforms to acquire equal employment opportunities and job enrichment schemes.

It was against above background that finally, in the 1970s, the idea of QWL was conceived. QWL was quite broader in sense and scope than these earlier stray developments mentioned above. Human values, needs and aspirations were at the heart of the concept of QWL.

The theories of motivation and leadership propounded by the behavioural scientists also served as seed-bed for the development of the concept of QWL. To quote, Maslow[8] depicted in his well known theory, 'Need Hierarchy Theory of Motivation', the complexity of human nature with regard to needs and their satisfaction. He says that no sooner the lower-order needs are satisfied, people start seeking satisfaction for higher-order needs of their need-hierarchy. Herzberg[9], in his two factor theory, maintained that it is 'hygiene factors' that motivates employees to improve their performance. Hygiene factors, in a way, refer to better working conditions. While lying assumptions for his 'Theory Y', McGregor[10] also views that under proper conditions *i.e.,* under better work environment, people have tendency to exploit their potential to a larger extent.

Thus, it becomes clear that the basic concept underlying the QWL is what has come by now to be recognized as 'humanisation of work."[11] It gave genesis to the need for developing an overall work environment that stimulates the creative abilities of the workers, generates co-operation, and interest in self-growth. As a matter of fact, with growing awareness of work force, the realisation and application of 'humanization of work' is on increasing. Truthfully speaking, it is this wide-spread realisation of humanisation of work that has made QWL a buzzword of the time. There is no looking back but to realize more and more how to make work environment more and more humane. The proliferation of the concept of QWL especially in the Indian context is discussed later in the chapter under 30.4 **QWL in the Indian Context.**

Let us turn our focus on what constitutes QWL.

30.3 CONSTITUENTS OF QWL

Like the concept of QWL, there have been divergent views as to what really constitute QWL. The most important views on constituents of QWL are discussed hereunder.

Walton[12] lists eight conceptual categories *i.e.,* constituents that together make up the quality of working life. These are briefly discussed below :

1. **Adequate and Fair Compensation:** In brief, it refers to a just and fair balance between worker's effort and reward out of it. In other words, it means whether compensation helps in maintaining a socially desirable standard of life and whether compensation bears an appropriate relationship to the pay received for other work. In India, for example, labour legistations like Payment of Wages Act, 1936 and Minimum Wages Act, 1948 ensure adequate and fair compensation to the employees.

2. **Safe and Healthy Working Conditions:** Factors like reasonable hours of work, zero-risk physical conditions of work and age restrictions on both upper and lower side create safe and healthy working conditions. In India, once again, the Factories Act, 1948 enshrines minimum standards of protection from machine and other hazards such as noise, pollution, fume, gases, etc. at the place of work with a view to ensure safe and healthy working conditions.

3. **Opportunity to Use and Develop Human Capacities:** One way to improve QWL is let the job allow sufficient autonomy and control, use of wider range of skills and abilities, provide immediate feedback to the worker to take corrective measures, and provide opportunity to plan and implement by workerself.

4. **Opportunity to Continued Growth and Security:** Here the focus is on career opportunities not on job itself. Opportunities available for growth of employees also contribute to improving QWL.

5. **Social Integration in the Work Organisation:** QWL is also aimed at generating sense of belonging to organisation in which one works, on the one hand, and developing of self-respect, on the other. Equal opportunities in employment irrespective of race, caste, creed, religion and sex are enshrined in Article 16 of the Indian Constitution.

6. **Constitutionalisation in the Work Organisation:** The constitutional guarantees such as right to personal privacy, free speech, equitable treatment, and governance by the "**Rule of Law**" are necessary to uphold to improve QWL.

7. **Work and the Total Life Space:** The demands of the work like late hours, frequent travel, quick transfers, etc. occurring on regular basis depress the employee, his or her family, and ultimately QWL.

8. **The Social Relevance of Work Life:** The discharge of social responsibility of business organisation also contributes to QWL. On the contrary, lack of organisation's concern for social causes like waste disposal, low quality product, overaggresive marketing, etc impinge upon self-esteem of workers.

Nadler and Lawler list determinants of QWL as participative problem-solving, work restructuring, innovative reward systems and improving the work environment.

Davis and Newstrom[13] identify QWL constituents as open communications, equitable reward systems, a concern for employee-job security, and participation in job designs. They suggest that emphasis should be given to employee skill development, the reduction of occupational stress and the development of more co-operative man-management relations.

While deliberating on QWL, the International Labour Office (ILO)[14] enumerates the following areas as determinants of QWL:

- Hours of work and arrangements of working time.
- Work Organisation and job content.
- Impact of new technologies on working conditions.
- Working conditions of women, young workers, older workers and other special categories.
- Work-related welfare services and facilities.
- Shopfloor participation in the improvement of working conditions.

Added to above constituents are Herrick and Maccoby's[15] identified four basic principles which result in humanisation of work. A brief description of these principles follows:

1. **The Principle of Security:** One of the preconditions of humanisation of work is that work should be free from anxiety, fear, and the loss of future employment. Such a safe and secured working conditions help foster skills and ideas.

2. **The Principle of Equity:** This implies fair reward for effort made by the working. Profit sharing between the owner and workers is one such example of following the principle of equity. This also reflects humanisation of work.

3. **The Principle of Individuation:** Individuation refers to freedom and autonomy to workers so as to encourage them to develop themselves to their utmost competence.

4. **The Principle of Democracy:** Akin to the principle of individuation, the principle of democracy implies right to personal privacy, freedom of speech, and equitable treatment. Ongoing participative management in business organisations symbolises the principle of democracy.

Knowledge about what constitutes QWL sets a stage to delineate the QWL scenario in the Indian Context. What is next discussed is the same.

30.4 QWL IN THE INDIAN CONTEXT

It will not be less than correct to mention that, of late, QWL in India has emerged as a movement. It is the V.V. Giri National Institute of Labour which took an active lead in familiarising the concept of QWL in India. Following are the major factors that led to the QWL movement in our country:

1. Available evidences[16] indicate that the changing profile of the Indian worker from an illiterate, rural, low caste individuals to educated, urban and essentially belonging to upper strata of caste structure has made him/her more concern for own hopes and aspirations. The blue coller worker, for example, seems more committed one duly moulded to fit in the emergent social structure of the day[17].

2. That worker is not just like other factors of production such as, machinery, land, and capital but a human being with feelings and emotions, has made organisations behave with workers accordingly. The establishment of a separate Ministry of Human Resources Development by the Government of India is a testimony to such realisation. However, the Indian worker is so far deprived of such a position is reported by Sen Gupta[18]. Indian worker's wish has yet to be duly recognized and rewarded accordingly.

3. In India, around 10 per cent of workers in organised sector are unionised. The past records relating to labour unions lend enough evidence that the unionised work force has been much vocal for demands of one type or other. These usually relate to their better working conditions.

4. That human behaviour is highly unpredictable and complex underlines the need for the study of organisational behaviour. QWL is one of the newer concepts experimenting how to make effective utilization of human resources.

QWL in India seems in practice in a variety of operational systems like workers participation, job enrichment, quality circles, etc. Here, an attempt has been made to give an overview of these in terms of their broad coverage and experiences of Indian organisations with them.

Workers Participation

Workers participation is also known as **industrial democracy.** The concept of participation means sharing, in an appropriate way, the decision-making powers with the lower levels in the organisations. The basic objective of workers participation is to make workers realize a sense of their importance, pride, freedom, and opportunity for self-expression, a feeling of belongingness that help create cordial industrial relations and congenical industrial peace[19].

The emergence of workers participation in India is dated back to 1920 when under the influence of Mahatma Gandhi, the workers and employers in Ahmedabad Textile industry agreed to settle disputes by mutual participation. The spirit of workers participation is very much enshrined in the Constitution of India. To be specific, Article 43-A of the Constitution very clearly directs the State "to take steps by suitable legislation or in any other way, to secure the participation of workers in the management of undertakings, establishments and other organisations engaged in any industry." The enactment of Industrial Disputes Act, 1947 gave further reinforcement to the workers participation in management.

In 1957, a study group consisting of representatives of employers, workers and government under the chairmanship of Mr. Vishnu Sahai was formed. The group recommended launching of the Joint Management Council (JMC) in public sector undertakings on a voluntary basis[20]. In 1970, as an extension of JMC, the Government also suggested workers directors on the Boards of Directors in some public and private sector industries. As a result, workers directors were appointed on the Boards of various nationalised banks in 1973[21]. In October 1975, some scattered attempts were made to introduce workers' participation in industry at shop floor and plant levels in all manufacturing and mining units employing 500 or more workers. Having participation, the Government of India in 1983 introduced a comprehensive scheme of workers' participation in central public sector undertakings. Though the scheme has left the private sector from its purview, it is also encouraged to implement the scheme, *i.e.*, workers' participation in management.

It is difficult to narrate workers' participation practices in individual organisations for the want of space. Suffice will be to mention that the concept of workers' participation in management has become wide spread in industrial organisations. Truly speaking, it has become an industrial philosophy of the time to effectively utilize human resources and accomplish the set goals.

Job Enrichment

Job enrichment refers to the process of making jobs more interesting, satisfying and challenging by adding new contents to jobs. Job enrichment is done through job redesign. In India, job redesign is based on experiments relating to socio-technical system made by Emery[22]. Among the job redesign studies conducted in the Indian context, one of the most significant and oft quoted study was conducted in Dynamo Corporation Limited by Professor Nitish De[23]. The study diagnosed that the fragmented work sytem, where every one was concerned with his own trade resulted in lack of emotional or rational commitment to the product, extensive forced idle time because of interdependence of tasks, and having done the same jobs for years workers felt bored with the task and lacked a sense of challange. The overall productivity was at 26.8 per cent.

Saiyadain[24] has reviewed the different experiments done by various researchers on different professional samples with a view to summarize the role of job enrichment in influencing workers' productivity.

Quality Circle

The concept of quality circle (QC) originated in the Japanese soil in 1949 with the establishment of the Japanese Union of Scientists and Engineers as a concern for statistical quality control. What is QC? QC is defined as a "small group of five to ten workers voluntarily performing quality control activities within the workshop to which they belong[25] Ohmae[26] has given a comprehensive definition of QC. According to him, "quality circle is a group of about 10 relatively autonomous workers from the same division of a company who volunteer to meet for an hour or so, once or twice a month. After work (actually they are paid over-time), they discuss ways to improve the quality of their products, the production process in their part of the plant and the working environment. The long-term objective is to build a sense of responsibility for improving quality but the immediate goal is to exchange ideas in a place uninhibited by barriers of age, sex or company rank."

QC is marked by the following characteristics:

1. It is a group effort and not an individual effort.
2. The participating members are volunteers.
3. Their efforts are directed to improve quality within their shops or places of work.
4. They meet frequently, often at company cost.
5. They represent a cross-section of age, sex and positions in the organisation.
6. Their concern is to find ways and means to improve quality of their output.

QC are formed to achieve the following main objectives:

1. To improve and develop an organisation:
2. To develop respect for human-relations and induce job satisfaction: and
3. To deploy human capabilities to the fullest extent and draw out their infinite potential.

Let us have a cursory look at QCs in India.

Bharat Heavy Electricals Limited (BHEL) is considered the pioneer of QC in India. It started five QCs in various shops in January 1981, in its Ramachandrapuram unit. Subsequently, it spread to other shops also[27]. The specific objectives set for QC in the BHEL are[28]:

1. Reduce human error and enhance quality.
2. Inspire more effective team work.
3. Promote job involvement.
4. Increase employee motivation.

5. Build an attitude of problem prevention.
6. Improve company communication.
7. Develop harmonious manager/worker relationship.
8. Promote personal and leadership development.

For achieving above objectives, the BHEL performed the following functions of QC:

1. Preparation of quality control manuals.
2. Preparation of quality plans for various products.
3. Formulation of annual quality improvement plans.
4. Conduct quality audit.
5. Quality training and education.
6. Creation of quality awareness.

Following the BHEL, an umpleen number of other organisations have started QC. Prominent among them are Kirloskar Oil Engines Ltd., J.K. Jute Mills, Bharat Forge Co. Ltd., Sri Ram Fibres Ltd., Hindustan Aeronautics Ltd., TELCO, Jyoti Ltd., Lucas-TVs, Hindustan Machine Tools Ltd., Crompton Greaves, Bajaj Auto, and Durgapur Steel Plant, etc. So much so, the Government has set up Quality Circle Forum in 1982. It has two pruposes: **one,** to provide the Indian organisations a forum to share their experiences on QC, and **two,** to disseminate QC information to all those concerned. For achieving the latter objective, a quarterly journal, named '**Quarlity Circle India**' is started.

Before we close the discussion on QWL, one last mention about how to improve QWL in India. Following are some suggestions that can help, to a large extent, improve quality of working life in India:

1. The employers should:

(*a*) Provide physical amenities at the work place, health and safety, and welfare provisions.
(*b*) Involve workers in decision-making on all matters.
(*c*) Initiate suitable forms of work design.
(*d*) Formalize QWL experience for future use.
(*e*) Re-examine policies of work.
(*f*) Develop an appreciation of changing environment.

2. The unions and workers should:

(*a*) Educate and make workers aware of QWL.
(*b*) Identify areas of collaboration with management.
(*c*) Identify ways and means to satisfy workers needs through non-monetary alternatives.
(*d*) Encourage workers to participate in QWL activities.
(*e*) Organise labour in the unorganised sector and specially make them aware of QWL.

3. The Professional Organisations should:

(*a*) Organise workshops and seminars to bring about greater awareness of QWL.

(*b*) Initiate specific research projects in this field.

(*c*) Provide professional assistance to organisations to help generate internal competence.

(*d*) Develop state-of-art profiles on QWL.

(*e*) Develop a network for collection, storage and dissemination of information on QWL.

4. The Government should:

(*a*) Legislate standards and norms in newer areas.

(*b*) Change in policy to provide greater autonomy to experiment with QWL.

(*c*) Execute actions to ensure implementation of legislated facilities.

(*d*) Encourage and adopt appropriate technology.

(*e*) Find projects on QWL.

(*f*) Modify the structure and scope of education in the country.

Now, the preceding description can be summed up as such that the basic spade-work for QWL is almost ready in India. But, what is still left is to develop the political will to make the concept of QWL a reality to actually improve the life of an average worker in India. Sooner it is done, better will be QWL.

SUMMARY

This summary is organized by the 'learning objectives' given on page no. 509.

- *QWL refers to overall climate of work and its impact on people as well as on organisational effectiveness.*
- *QWL related activities are several but revolve around participative problem solving, work restructuring, quality circles, reward systems, and work environment. In India only lip service has been paid to such a vital area of concern.*
- *QWL in India can be improved through a variety of instrumentalities like education and training, employee communication, union participation, research projects, and appreciation of changing environment.*

REVIEW QUESTIONS

1. What do you mean by QWL? Why is QWL required?

2. "India has given only lip service to QWL". How will you explain it?

3. What makes QWL? Discuss.

4. Take an example of your own University and describe the constituents of its QWL. Suggest how can the QWL be improved in your University?

5. What is the basic philosophy behind quality circles? What are its objectives?

REFERENCES

1. D. Skrovan: A Brief Report from the ASTD. Quality of Working Life Task Force, **Training and Development Journal**, 1980, 34(3) p. 29.
2. R. Cohen and E. Rosenthal: Should Unions Participate in Quality of Working Life Activities?, **Quality of Working Life-The Canadian Scene**, 1980, 1(4), pp. 7-12.
3. David A. Nadler and Edward E. Lawler: Quality of Work Life: Perspectives and Directions, **Organisational Dynamics**, Winter, 1983, pp. 20-30.
4. Hans Van Beinum: Coming to Terms with QWL, **Management in Government**, 16(2), July-September, 1984, pp. 133-139.
5. Fred Luthans, ***op. cit.***, 1995, Seventh Edition, p. 182.
6. Sangeeta Jain: ***op. cit.***, 1991, p. 17.
7. Richard E. Walton: Quality of Working Life: What is it? **Sloan Management Review,** Vol. 15, No. 1, Fall, 1973, pp. 11-21.
8. Abraham H. Maslow: **Motivation and Personality,** Harper and Row, New York, 1954.
9. Frederick Herzberg: One More Time: How Do you Motivate Employees, **Harvard Business Review**, Jan. - Feb. 1968, pp. 53-64.
10. Douglas McGregor: ***op. cit.***, 1960.
11. Mirza S. Saiyadain: **Human Resources Management,** Tata McGraw-Hill Publishing Company Limited, New Delhi, Eighth Reprint, 1997, pp. 311-312.
12. Richard E. Walton: Criteria for Quality of Working Life, In: L.E. Davis and A.B. Cherms (Eds.) **The Quality of Working Life**, (Vol. I), Free Presss, New York, 1975.
13. Keith Davis and John W. Newstrom: ***op. cit.,*** 1989, p. 387.
14. ILO: Recommendations from the National Seminar on Improving Quality of Working Life, **Productivity**, Vol. 22, No. 4, 1982, pp. 79-83.
15. N.Q. Herrick and M. Maccoby: Humanising Work: A Priority Goal of the 1970s. In: L.E. Davis and B. Cherms (Eds.): **The Quality of Working Life,** Volume 1, Free Press, New York, 1975.
16. B.R. Sharma: Labour Force Commitment: Some Implications for Industrial Relations, **Management and Labour Studies**, Vol. 4, No. 1, 1978, pp. 7-17.
17. M.L. Monga: The Industrial Worker, Emerging Realities about this commitment to the Factory System: **NLI Bulletin**, Vol. 4, No. 12, 1978, pp. 464-467.
18. C. Sen Gupta: Industrial Man in India Reconsidered, **Economic and Political Weekly**, 1982, Vol. 17, No. 22, 1982, pp. M52-M56.
19. K.C. Alexander: **Participative Management: The Indian Experience,** Shri Ram Centre for Industrial Relations and Human Resources, New Delhi, 1972.
20. N.R. Seth: **The Joint Management Councils: Problems and Prospects**, Shri Ram Centre for Industrial Relations and Human Resources, New Delhi, 1972.
21. V.K. Agarwal: Workers' Participation in Management, **Indian Labour Journal,** Vol. 22, No. 7, 1981, pp. 945-949.
22. F. Emery: **Characteristics of Socio-Technical Systems**, Tavistock Institute, London, 1959.
23. Nitish De: Training Strategy for Changes in Attitudes: Micro Level Experiences, **Economic Times**, 26 February, 1978.
24. Mirza S. Saiyadain: ***op. cit.***, 1997, pp. 325-326.
25. K. Ishikawa: Quality Control in Japan, In: N. Sasaki and D. Hutchins (Eds.) **The Japanese Approach to Product Quality,** Pergamon Press, New York, 1984.

26. K. Ohmae: Quality Control Circles: What Makes them Work? **The Asian Wall Street Journal**, March 31, 1982.

27. B.R. Dey: **Quality Circles: An Human Resources Approach to the Management of Industrial Relations,** Tata Management Training Centre, Pune, 1984.

28. M.G. Korgaonkar: **Quality Circles at BHEL-A Case,** Indian Institute of Management, Ahmedabad, 1986.

Case 30.1: QWL in Bhilai Steel Plant

Non-statutory welfare programmes in the Bhilai Steel Plant (BSP) initially emerged because of its geographic location. Housing was the main problem. Though BSP undertook extensive construction programmes, it also provided loans to its employees to construct their own houses. Medical and educational facilities followed, BSP now has a 520-bed hospital with the most modern facilities. Persons suffering from cancer or requiring artificial limbs are sent to other hospitals with an escort and the expenses are reimbursed. BSP spends Rs. 3 crores annually on this operation. There are 40,000 children receiving free education with 1800 teachers on the roll. Car, scooter, and cycle loans are easily available with long term interest-free payment plans. BSP also supports the Bhilai Mahila Samaj, a voluntary all-women organisation which stitches uniforms and manufactures soap-all of which are bought by the 110 Bhilai Cooperatives. It has also initiated a village adoption scheme.

BSP's most significant programme was the establishment of the Steel Employees Welfare Association (SEWA) in 1973 to promote social and welfare activities, to foster fellow feelings among employees, to create a social security fund, and to render financial assistance to nominees in the event of the death of a member, irrespective of the cause or place of death (SEWA, 1975). These activities are over and above those provided by statutory welfare. Contributions come from over 50,000 employees (Rs. 125 per month per member). By the end of April 1976, SEWA had settled 151 cases and paid out Rs. 8,48,750. A member's contribution is refunded to him consequent upon his retirement/resignation/termination/transfer to another establishment; and in the termination on medical grounds, his contribution is doubled irrespective of the period of membership.

QUESTION

1. Analyse the case and also suggest how to use SEWA to improve QWL in BSP.

31

INTERNATIONAL ORGANISATIONAL BEHAVIOUR

"The Americans working with people of other cultures may find that their own values are not universally accepted." – ***Jennifer Hanson and Wanda Fox***

Learning Objectives

After studying this chapter, you should be able to:

- **Describe** individual behaviour in international organisation.
- **Discuss** group behaviour in the context of international organisation.
- **List** the characteristics of an international organisation exhibits.
- **Outline** the dynamics of organisational change usually experienced in an international organisation.

We have so far discussed organisational behaviour in the context of national organisations. International business organisations once thought to be fiction only have become, of late, a fact. An international business organisation is one which expands its business activities beyond the national borders. It may include any type of business activity that crosses national border. However, most companies go international initially by focusing on either exporting, licensing , or franchising[1]. Exporting means selling abroad, either directly to target customers or indirectly by retaining foreign sales agents and distributors. As regards international licensing, it is an agreement whereby a firm (the licensor) grants a foreign firm the right to use intangible (intellectual) property such as patents, copyrights, manufacturing processes, or trade names for a specific period of time, usually in return for a royalty[2]. Franchising is an option in which a parent company grants another company/firm the right to do business in a prescribed manner. Franchising differs from the licensing in the sense that it usually requires the franchisee to follow much stricter guidelines in running the business than does licensing. Further, licensing tends to be confined to manufacturers, whereas franchising is more popular with service firms such as restaurants, hotels, and rental services.

Sometimes, companies in order to take full advantage of opportunities offered by foreign markets, make a direct, and substantial investment of their own funds in another company through foreign direct investment (FDI).

There are similarities and dissimilarities in certain respects between national and international organisations. As regards dissimilarities, it is mainly cultural variations across the nations that distinguishes organisational behaviour in international organisation from national organisation. Given the varying cultural background across the nations, human behaviour at work in them is, therefore, inevitable to vary. The same underlines the need for understanding organisational behaviour in an international context.

This chapter is, therefore, devoted to deal with the international organisational behaviour. The major aspects of OB such as individual behaviour, interpersonal processes, and characteristics of an international organisation are the subject matters of this chapter.

31.1 CULTURAL DIFFERENCES AND SIMILARITIES

Before we delve into human behaviour in the context of international organisations, a brief focus as study scaffolding on differences and similarities in human behaviour across cultures seems pertinent. Such a delineation is required mainly for two reasons. **First**, in many cases, both culture and national boundaries do not necessarily coincide. For example, some areas of India (*e.g.* Jammu & Kashmir) are very much like Switzerland. Within India too, there are profound cultural differences among southern, northern and eastern India.

One recent review of literature[3] on differences and similarities in human behaviour across cultures listed the following five salient features :

1. Human behaviour at work varies across cultures given the varying organisational context.
2. Culture is a major cause for variation in human behaviour across organisations.
3. While behaviour varies across cultures, organisations reveal a tendency to become more and more similar.
4. The behaviour of the same manager varies from culture to culture.
5. Diversity in culture turns out to be an important ingredient in achieving synergy required for effective organisational performance.

31.2 INDIVIDUAL BEHAVIOUR IN INTERNATIONAL ORGANISATION

As we just stated under 25.1, the first two features clearly indicate that human/ individual behaviour across cultures. Then, the question arises : What causes variations in individual behaviour across cultures? It is mainly varying individual differences, managerial behaviour motivation and rewards in operation across cultures cause variations in individual behaviour from culture to culture. A mention of these is in turn.

Individual Differences :

No two persons are alike. Individuals differ from each other owing to their varying characteristics that ultimately form an individual's individuality. That is precisely the reason why each individual is considered as an island in himself or herself. The behaviour of individual is determined by the characteristics of individuals. One researcher[4] in his massive study of 1,60,000 workers in 60 countries has identified certain important dimensions of individuals, as shown in figure 31.1, along which individual behaviour varies.

Individualism/Collectivisim :

Individualism is a state of mind in which a person considers his/her interest first, on a priority basis. The examples of individualistic culture abound in the United

States, Great Britain, Canada, and Australia. On the contrary, collectivitism refers to the situation in which group interest comes first.

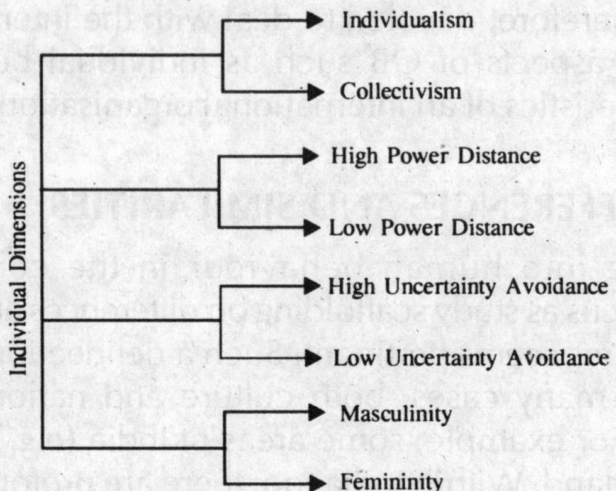

Figure 31.1 : Variations in Individual Dimensions

India, Singapore, Japan, and Hong Kong represent the cultures in which collectivitism prevail in greater degree.

Power Distance

This refers to the situation in which organisational members consider the existence of different levels of power in operation. In a high-power-distance, also known as autocratic culture, the top managers make decisions which are followed by the subordinates without questions. This is also known as 'military culture'. Pakistan, Brazil, France and Mexico represent cultures characterised by high-power distance. On the other hand, low-power-distance reflect the situation in which employees follow the boss's orders/command only when they consider the order as right. The United States, Australia, Germany, and New Zealand are examples of cultures with a low power-distance.

Uncertainty Avoidance

Feelings to accept or avoid uncertainty varies among individuals. While some individuals become ready to accept uncertainty and, in turn, risk to thrive in the challenging and exciting situations, there are others who simply avoid uncertainty and want certainty in future courses of actions. Employees in the United states and Australia, for examples, represent the two cases respectively.

Masculinity/Femininity

Work force structure dominated by either sex has its bearing on employee behaviour at work. A cross-country examination reveals that societies characterised by masculinity define male-female roles more rigidly than do the feminine societies. India is an example of highly masculine, Sweden that of highly feminine, for example.

Managerial Behaviour

As individual differences influence individual behaviour, so does managerial behaviour affect employee behaviour. It is mainly the managerial belief about the role of authority and place of power in the organisation, that affects employee behaviour at work. In practice, the managerial beliefs vary across cultures. For example, the Japanese managers believe that the very purpose of having an organisation structure is to make every employee know who his or her boss/superior is. But, the German manager believe that the purpose of organisation structure is to effectively coordinate the group behaviour and effort. While Indian managers believe in value-based management for getting things done from employees, the German managers just ignore value system and accept by passing one's superior to get things done.

Motivation

Variations in motivation across cultures also affect employee behaviour at work. For example Abrahim Maslow's need hierarchy theory of motivation does not apply in similar manner across cultures. While security needs are considered as most important in Japan, Sweden weighs social needs as more important for employees to work more. Similarly the Indian managers believe their performance and success are determined solely by God. But on the contrary, U.S. Managers attach high importance to hard work to lead to high performance and success.[5]

31.3 GROUP BEHAVIOUR

A group is an association of two or more persons interacting with one another in such a manner that each person influences and is influenced by each other person. Groups are thus, made up of individuals coming from different cultures. As we just noted that individual behaviour varies across cultures, so does group behaviour also. There are four key areas in which group behaviour varies. These are group dynamics leadership power and conflicts and communication. These are discussed subsequently.

Group Dynamics

Group formation based on members belonging to diverse cultural backgrounds may create several situations, at least at the initial stage, for managers to effectively manage the group. Possibility for existence of distrust among group members, stereotyping and communication problems are some of the probable situations managers will have to face while getting work done from group members. Given such situation managers need to appreciate and recognize that a culturally diverse group will hardly function smoothly especially at its initial stage. Managers, therefore, need to help the group become cohesive and cooperative in its functioning.

Leadership

We have already noted in Chapter 16 that, according to Hersey and Blanchard[6], leadership effectiveness depends upon the situation in which leadership is exercised. Along with other factors, cultural factors contribute to constitute a situation. A cross-cultural comparison indicates that, like managerial behaviour, as we just noted, leadership styles are also dictated by the cultural factors in a situation. For example, in a culture characterised by high power distance, leaders adopt autocratic style of leadership as employees expect the leaders to make decisions, exercise control, and solve problems. On the contrary, in a culture with low power distance, employees expect the leader to give them greater say in the matters relating to employees. So to say, such a situation requires the leader to adopt the participative style of leadership involving employees' participation in the decision making process.

Like leadership styles, leadership roles also vary from culture to culture. Leaders in India, for example, function only within the clear confines of their legitimate powers.

But, in a different cultural setting like Japan, leaders are expected to facilitate group performance than merely act as supervisory mechanism

Power and Conflict

Power is the strength. Organisations run with legitimate power and, therefore, there is always a craze for hoarding power as much as one can. As where there are utensils, they will collide. Similarly, where there are people they will disagree or conflict. Conflict among organisational members is inevitable and just a part of running business. Conflict, unless it is dysfunctional, goes unnoticed and unconcerned.

However, depending upon the nature of culture, conflict and power may vary from culture to culture. For example, power and conflict are more pronounced in India and Great Britain. Japan, on the other hand, presents the other extreme of dimension. Not only the attempts to increase one's power are foiled, but more focus is given on promoting group harmony group cohesiveness, mutual trusteeship and alike in the Japanese culture.

Communication

As already discussed in Chapter 20, communication, *i.e.,* transference and understanding of message, binds organisational members together. Hence, communication becomes an important aspect of interpersonal processes and, in turn, group behaviour in the organisation. Like the two other aspects just noted, variations in language and coordination issues across cultures also affect communication in the international organisations. Let us explain how.

Language

Undisputably language varies from country to country and, in turn, culture to culture. Not only that, the same language — both in verbal and nonverbal terms — can mean different things in different cultures? To quote, the name of a soap powder 'dainty' in English meant 'horse' in African, 'hazy' in Persian, and 'crazy' in Korean languages. Similarly, non-verbal communication can also convey a quite different meanings across cultures scattered in the globe. For example, while the 'green' colour conveys disease in jungle-covered countries, the same suggests cosmetics in France and Sweden. So is true of body language as well. The American sign of OK is an obscenity in Spain, for example.

Coordination

Closely related to communication is the coordination issue. As noted earlier, it is communication mainly that binds and coordinates people together working in different cultures. While communicating with one's counterpart across cultures distantly scattered in the globe, a manager needs to contend not only with the differences in language, but a time difference also, which might be in some cases for several hours. When an Indian manager, for example, needs to talk on the telephone, his/her Russian counterpart in Moscow (Russia) may be home asleep. This, then, creates coordination problem between the two. Clearly the solution lies in evolving innovative methods for coordinating organisational activities across the cultures scattered in the globe.

31.4 ORGANISATION CHARACTERISTICS

In the last Part Four of the book, we have already described how organisation characteristics, in the context of international organisation, affect human behaviour at work. In this section, we consider some of the internation extensions and implications that parallel these topics. We specifically examine cross-cultural influences on environment, technology, organisational structure and organisation design in the context of international organisation.

Environment

Environment refers to everything our surrounding. The number of components included in an environment around make it complex and frequent changes therein make it dynamic. Cultural variations affect the organisational environment which, in turn, affect human behaviour in organisations. For example, the economies of Japan and Sweden are fairly stable mainly because of their stable environment. But, France presents a contrasting case with its much more dynamic environment. Environments across cultures also vary widely in terms of their complexity, *i.e.*, the number of the components in an environment. As such, managers are subject to face an array of varying cultural norms and values. To mention, India has an extremely complex environment with a mosaic of age-old caste system.

The interplay between cultural variation and environmental complexity and dynamism in case of an international organisation is depicted structurally in figure 31.2.

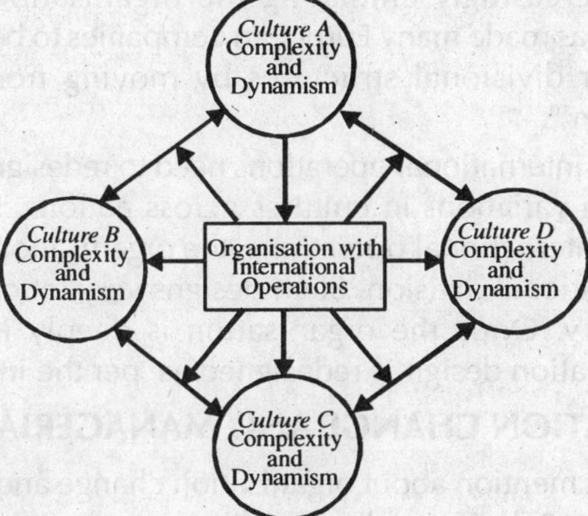

Figure 31.2: Interplay Between Cultures and Environments Technology

Technology

By definition, technology means the ideas, skills, knowledge, methods, machinery, and equipment required to convert resources into useful goods and services. In fact, an economy is the effect for which technology is the cause. It is technology that differentiates Europe from Asia. Technological variations are of two types : variations in available technology and variations in attitude towards technology. Many underdeveloped countries lack in technology, for example, lack of power, telephones, and similar other facilities. Obviously, managers working in such countries have to face many frustrations. Here is a real case to support our above point.

> A few years ago, some Brazilian officials convinced a US Company to build a high-tech plant in their country. Midway through construction, however, the Government of Brazil decided it would not allow the company to import some accurate measuring instruments it needed to produce its products. The new plant was abandoned before it ever opened[8].

Attitudes towards technology also vary across cultures. Some societies accept technology without much hesitation, while others resist for technology for one apprehension or other. Both types of examples abound in the globe. For example, while most of the western countries have a generally favourable attitude toward technology, the Asian countries (with exception of Japan), however, do not.

Organisation Structure and Design

As might be expected, like environment and technology, organisation structure and design of companies also vary across cultures. For example, one recent study compared the structures of fifty-five U.S. and fifty-one Japanese manufacturing plants. The results of the study revealed that the Japanese plants had less specialisation, more formal centralisation and taller hierarchies than their U.S. counterparts. The U.S. plants were more affected by their technology as compared to the Japanese ones'.

In contrast, another study unfolded that successful organisation structure are emulated by others as well even across cultures. To quote, a good number of European companies are increasingly emulating the organisation structure of their U.S. counterparts. This has made many European companies to become more decentralised and also to go for divisional structures by moving from functional to product departmentalization[10].

Firms going to international operations need to redesign their organisation design to better cope with variations in cultures across nations. Having being achieved a moderate level of international operations, the organisation design is shaped so as to establish an international division. Such designs very much abound in India in case of banking industry. Once the organisation is deeply involved in international operations, organisation design is redesigned as per the international matrix.

31.5 ORGANISATION CHANGE AND MANAGERIAL CAREER

Now , one last mention about organisation change and managerial career before we close this chapter. These are discussed in turn.

Organisation Change

We have already discussed, in detail, the theoretical perspective of organisation change and development in Chapter 22. Here, we shall be confined to the international aspects of change. Accordingly, we consider mainly two points for discussion at this context. **One** is how international environments dictate organisation change. Alternatively speaking, how international environments force the organisationto succumb to change. Given the environmental compelexities and dynamism, as noted earlier, international organisations are more susceptible to change than their domestic counteroparts. The reasons are not difficult to seek.

Second, just as attitude toward technology varies from culture to culture, so do change also. While change is considered and accepted as a normal part of organisational life in one culture, it is resisted in other. thus, what follows from this that the techniques for managing change worked successfully in one culture may not work at all and may even trigger negative responses if used indiscriminately in other different culture[11].personal Numerous cases of this kind abound across the cultures and even across organisations within the same culture.

Managerial Careers

Understanding careers across cultures is assuming increasing importance for managers. This is so because international assignments sometimes involve some implications as well. For example, a manager who is transferred from New Delhi to Finland to London may experience a certain amount of trauma and stress[12].

The managers should also understand that the norms and standards related to career paths widely vary across cultures. For example, the U.S. culture supports personal ambition. In other words, the US culture supports and appreciates those persons who are ambitious, want to excel and succeed, and always strive for advancement and improvement. But, the same is considered unseemely in the Japanese culture. Instead, the Japanese culture supports the organisational concern and priorities above personal ones.

Just as norms and standards to career paths vary from culture to culture, so do sex considerations also. Cases of widespread sex discrimination abound in the world. In Japan and Finland, for example, women are quite restricted in their opportunities and career advancement. Generally, the Japanese women are expected to become wives and mothers. So is the case of the Indian women as well. Though change has set in, but it is still indiscernible. In Finland, on the contrary, women have a strong heritage to work outside the home. Notwithstanding, women still lag for behind their men counterparts in the matters of income and opportunities for advancement[13].

SUMMARY

This summary is organized by the 'learning objectives' given on page no. 520.

- *Both similarities and differences in human behaviour exist across cultures. The pattern of individual differences, managerial behaviour, and motivation vary from culture to culture.*
- *Just like individual behaviour, group behaviour related to group dynamics, leadership, power and conflict, and communication also vary across cultures.*
- *Organisation characteristics such as environment, technology, and organisation structure and design widely vary from organisation to organisation in the international context.*
- *Organisation change, both in terms of forces for and techniques of it, also widely varies across cultures. Finally, an understanding of how career-paths when receiving international assignments, becomes an important consideration for managers in the context of international organisations.*

REVIEW QUESTIONS

1. Identify both similarities and differences in human behaviour in case of international organisation.
2. What stereotypes exist about the motivational pattern of workers from different cultures?
3. Supposing, you had just been appointed leader of a group of employees from another culture, what would you do first to be more effective?
4. If you were offered a temporary assignment abroad, would you like to accept it? Why or why not?
5. Suppose, you work for a firm that recently transferred in a manager from quite different culture/country. This is the manager's first international exposure. What might you do to help this manager adjust in the new environment/culture.
6. Write short notes on the following :
   (*a*) Similarities and differences across cultures;
   (*b*) Individual behaviour across cultures;
   (*c*) Interpersonal processes across cultures;
   (*d*) Organisation charactreristics across cultures;
   (*e*) Career paths across cultures.

REFERENCES

1. Gary Dessler : **Human Resource Management**, Printice Hall of India Private Limited, New Delhi, 1999, p. 671.
2. John Daniels and Lee Radebaugh : **International Business**, Addison - Wesley, Reading, M.A. 1994, p. 544.
3. Simcha Ronen and Oded Shenkar : Clustering Countries on Attitudinal Dimensions : A Review and Synthesis, **Academy of Management Review**, July 1985, pp. 435-454.
4. Greet Hofstede : **Culture's Consequences : International Differences in Work Related Values**, Sage Publications, Beverly Hills, Calif, 1980.
5. Nancy J. Adler : **International Dimensions of Organisatonal Behaviour**,. Kent, Boston, 1991.
6. Paul Hersey and Kenneth Blanchard : **Management of Organisational Behaviour** : Utilizing Human Resources, Printice Hall, Englehood, Cliff, N.J. 1977, p.p. 170-177.
7. David A. Ricks : **Big Business Builders : Mistakes in Multinational Marketing**, Dow Jones – Irwin, Homewood Ill, 1983.
8. Andrew Kupfer : How to Be a Global Manager, **Fortune**, March 14, 1998, pp. 52-58.
9. James R. Lancolin et. al. : Organisational Structures in Japanese and U.S. Manufacturing, **Administrative Science Quarterly**, September 1986, pp. 338-364.
10. Karkland : Europe's New Managers, **Fortunes**, July 20, 1987, pp. 95-98.
11. Alfred M. Jaeget : Organisation Development and National Culture : Where's the Fit? **Academy of Management Review**, January 1986, pp. 178-190.
12. P.M. Pestonjee : Executive Stress : Should it be Avoided? **Vikalpa**, Vol. 12, No. 1, 1987, pp. 20-30.
13. Kaisa Kauppinen – Toropainen et. al. : Sex Segregation of Work in Finland and the Quality of Women's Work, **Journal of Organisational Behaviour**, Vol. 9, 1988, pp. 15-27.

Case 31.1: British Airways Bounces Back

British Airways has made one of the most stunning turnarounds of any business in history. Much of the credit for that turnaround goes to people—the individuals who manage the firm and operating employees who carry out mundane jobs ranging from handling baggage to preparing meals in flight.

When Margaret Thatcher became prime minister of Great Britain in 1979, many of the country's largest businesses were owned and operated by the government. One of her first agenda items was to privatize (sell to private owners and investors) most of these businesses.

But no one wanted British airways. The firm had a huge, unproductive work force, suffered frin lax management, and was incurring annual losses approaching $1 billion. service had slipped badly; many joked that the acronym BA stood for "Bloody Awful".

Thatcher asked John King, a leading British industrialist, to step in and restore British Airways' image, competitiveness, and effectiveness. One of King's first major decisions was to cut the work force. Within a few months of taking over, he cut the payroll from 59,000 to 36,000 employees. To help ease the pain of such a cutback, he offered a generous severance package to all employees who left voluntarily.

Then King made major changes on the firm's board of directors. Membership on the board had been largely symbolic, and directors really knew little about running a business. King convinved most of the current directors to leave and replaced them with experienced executives. He also changed advertising agencies and even moved the firm's insurance coverage to a different carrier.

King also recognized that he needed to direct a lot of attention to the remaining British Airways employees, many of whom felt bitter and insecure. Some of the changes in this area also were largely symbolic. For example, King bought all employees new uniforms (some uniforms had not been changed in over Twenty years), adopted a new corporate slogan, and repainted all British Airways aircraft.

King had known all along that his job was not to run the "new" airline. Instead, his charge was to manage its transformation. Thus, while all these changes were going on, he was also looking for a new CEO to take over when the transformation and privatization were complete. Colin Marshall was selected to take over in early 1983 and received immediate opportunities to make his own assessments of the changes taking place.

Marshall recognized that employees needed more than just new uniforms, so he initiated a series of training seminars for them. The seminars were designed to change their attitudes about the company and to motivate them to provide better customer service. These seminars were a big success, and a whole new culture began to emerge.

British Airways was privatized in February 1987. A key part of the initial stock packages was to allow employees to participate in ownership. Around 74 percent of them took advantage of this opportunity. Many noted that as owners they would be even more dedicated to improving service and profits.

Since then, the foundation laid by King and Marshall has paid enormous dividends. British Airways has become the largest airline in the world and also one of the most profitable. And customers rate its service as the best in the industry. The current state of affairs is a far cry from the days of "Bloody Awful," and much of the credit goes to a large group of people working together for a common cause.

QUESTIONS

1. Identify as many behavioural concepts and processes in this case as you can.
2. Do you think King and Marshall made any serious mistakes?
3. What perils or threats does British Airways face in the future?

GLOSSARY

The purpose of the glossary is to present definitions of some of the important terms that are often used in the very wide range of subject areas covered in the book.

Absence : The failure of employees to report for regularly for scheduled work.

Ability : This is an individual's skill and capacity to perform a job.

Accountability : A concept whereby persons are held responsible for their own performance and the performance of their subordinates.

Achievement Motivation : One's drive to overcome challenges and obstacles in the pursuit of goal.

Action Research : A cyclical process of identifying system problems, gathering data, taking corrective action, assessing progress, making on going adjustments, and learning from experience.

Affect: It is a generic term that covers a broad range of feelings that people experience.

Affective Events Theory (AET): A psychological model that proposes that organizational events are proximal causes that produce affective reactions or responses.

Altruism: People having concern for others' welfare without concern for one's own self-interest.

Ambivert : One who is neither extrovert (much talking) nor introvert (less talking) but in between the two.

Applied Research : A research or study conducted to find a solution to a particular problem.

Assessment : The process of making a judgement, against evidence of an individual's competence.

Assessment Centre : A process in which employees are evaluated through a series of exercises to determine their promotability.

Attitudes : Individual's general affective, cognitive, and intentional responses toward objects, other people, themselves, or social issues.

Authority : One's legitimate right to influence others/subordinates.

Autocratic Style : A style of leadership in which the leader uses strong, directive, controlling actions to enforce the rules, regulations, activities, and relationships in the work environment.

Autonomy : The degree to which a job provides substantial freedom, independence, and discretion to a person in scheduling and carrying out his or her work.

Bias : A personal preference or inclination that undermines impartial judgement.

Brainstorming : An idea–generating process that encourages alternatives while withholding criticism.

Bureaucracy : An ideal type of organisational structure proposed by Max Weber with characteristics like having a hierarchy of authority, a system of rules and procedures and division of labour.

Burnout : The overall feeling of exhaustion a person feels when simultaneously experiencing too much pressure and too few sources of satisfaction.

Business Environment : The composite of social, economic, political, technological, market and other conditions external to any given business organisation that are likely to have their dent in overall performance of the business.

Career Path : A sequence of job experiences that an employee moves along during his or her career.

Career Planning : The process of planning one's life work, involves evaluating abilities and interests, considering alternative career opportunities, establishing career goals, and planning practical development.

Career Plateau : A point in an individual's career in which the probability of moving further up the hierarchy is low.

Career Management : A lifelong process of learning about self, jobs and organisations; setting personal goals; developing strategies for developing the goals; and revising goals based on work and life experiences.

Case Study : An intensive and thorough analysis of an organisational problem.

Centralization : The concentration of decision making authority at the top of the organisational hierarchy.

Civic Virtue: It is a manifestation of employee's concern in participating in the life of organization like organizational functions and meetings.

Classical Conditioning : An approach to learning through modifying behaviour so that a conditioned stimulus is paired with an unconditioned stimulus and elicits an unconditioned response. This approach of learning is associated with Ivan P. Pavlov, the Russian psychologist and his experiments with dogs.

Cognitive Dissonance: Inconsistency held in attitudes that causes tension or conflict for the person.

Cognitive Dissonance : The anxiety a person experiences when two sets of knowledge or perception are contradictory or incongruent. It also occurs when a person behaves or responds in a way inconsistant with his or her attitude.

Cognitive Theory : A learning process that involves conscious and active behaviour.

Cohesiveness : Degree to which employees stick together, rely on each other, and desire to remain members of a group.

Command Group : It is a relatively permanent, formal group with functional reporting relationships,

Competition : Group interaction that occurs when the goals of the groups are incompatible and interactions are important to goal attainment of each group.

Commitment : One's profound feelings of identification with and strong attachment to the organisation.

Communication : A process that involves transfer of information and also understanding from one person to another person.

Conflict : An interaction or disagreement between the groups that occurs when one group perceives that its attempts to attain set goals are frustrated by another group.

Controlling : The process of monitoring actual organisational activities so as to keep them headed toward the set goal and correcting flaws or deviations, if any.

Counselling : A personal function concerned with giving practical help to employees on personal problems that usually have emotional content.

Creativity : A process involving one's ability to develop something new and novel by conceiving the idea and articulating the new knowledge.

Critical Incident Technique : A method of performance evaluation that involves interviewing employees to ask them to define the most important (critical) incidents of their effective and ineffective performance on the particular job.

Cultural Shock : An employee's feeling of confusion, insecurity, and anxiety caused in a strange new work environment.

Custodial Model : Managerial view that security needs are dominant among employees.

Data : The facts that are unanalysed and uninterpreted.

Decentralization : The delegation of power and authority from higher to lower levels in an organisation. This is done by creating smaller units in the organisation.

Decision Making : A process through a problem is identified, solution objectives are defined, a predecision is made, alternatives are generated and evaluated and finally an alternative considered to be the best, is chosen, implemented, and followed up.

Delegation of Authority : The process of assigning duties to subordinates who are allowed to act within the authority granted to them. The person assigning duty and granting authority retains responsibility for that person's exercise of authority.

Delphi Technique : A method of improving group decision using the opinions of experts, which are solicited by mail and then compiled. The expert consensus of opinions is used to make a decision. The experts in this technique never meet face-to-face.

Demotion : The reassignment of an employee to a lower job.

Departmentalization : The manner in which divided tasks are combined into work groups for smoothening coordination activity. The methods commonly used for making work groups are business function, process, product or service, customer, and geography.

Discipline : An organisational condition when employees conduct themselves in accordance with the organisation's rules and standards of acceptable behaviour.

Distress : The adverse psychological, physical, behavioural and organisational consequences that may arise as a result of stressful events.

Division of Labour : The process in which the work of the organisation is separated into different jobs to be done by different people having different types of skills.

Domino Effect : It is a change that triggers of a series of related changes.

Dysfunctional Conflict : An unhealthy, distractive disagreement between two or more people.

Ego States: Psychological positions as parent, adult, and child that form basis for and influence one's behaviour or transaction with others.

Emotion: This is primary motivating force and a process which arouses, sustains, and directs activity.

Emotional Competence: This refers to an individual's underlying emotional characteristic that enables him/her in dealing with others effectively.

Emotional Episode: This refers to a series of emotional precedents to the present feeling toward something or somebody.

Emotional Intelligence: This is the ability to monitor the feelings of the self and others, discriminate among them and use this information to guide one's thinking and action.

Emotional Literacy: This is becoming aware of one's as well as other people's emotions.

Empathy : It is a person's ability to understand and be sensitive to the feelings, thoughts, and situations of others. Popularly called *"putting one's feet in others shoes."*

Empowerment : A process that provides greater autonomy to employees through information sharing and exercising control over factors affecting job performance.

Encounter : The second stage of socialisation process in which the new comer learns the tasks associated with the job, classifies roles and establishes new relationships at work.

Environment : One's surrounding composed of work, colleagues and supervisors, workshops, amenities and facilities.

E.R.G. Theory : An alternative to Abrahim Maslow's need hierarchy theory proposed by Clayton Alderfer, which proposes that when one need is frustrated, people simply concentrate on others. According to Alderfer, there are three basic human needs – existence, relatedness, and growth.

Esteem Needs : These refer to two slightly different types of human needs : (*i*) the need for a positive self-image and self-respect and (*ii*) the need to be respected by others.

Espoused Value : What members of an organisation say they value.

Ethic : It is the way the values are acted out as what is good and bad, desirable and undesirable.

Eustress : A positive form of stress that can motivate, stimulate, and often, reward a person.

Expectancy : The beliefs that people hold regarding the extent to which their efforts will influence their performance.

Expectancy Theory : The theory that asserts that motivation is based on people's beliefs about the probability that effort will lead to performance (expectancy), multiplied by the probability that performance will lead to reward (instrumentality), multiplied by the perceived value of the reward (valence).

Extinction : The attempt to weaken a behaviour by withholding positive consequences that were previously provided for a desirable behaviour.

Feedback : Information from the job itself, management, or other employees that tells workers how well they are performing.

Flextime : An alternative work schedule that allows employees to determine their starting and stopping times, provided that they work a set number of hours per day or week.

Followership : The process of being guided and directed by a leader in the work environment.

Formal Groups : Groups that are created by the organisation intentionally designed to direct its members towards some organisational goal. These are usually included in the organisation chart.

Free-rein Leaders : Leaders who avoid power and responsibility and leave it to employees to make decisions.

Frustration : Result of a drive or motivation being blocked to prevent one from reaching a desired goal.

Functional Conflict : Any conflict or disagreement between two or more people, that has healthy, positive, constructive and non-divisive results.

Functional Job Analysis : A method of job analysis that includes the Department of Labour's procedure to describe what a worker does, catalogue into three general functions: data, people, and things.

General Adaptation syndrome : A model of the stress experience, consisting of three stages : alarm reaction, resistance, and exhaustion.

Goal : A set of desirable objectives that invididuals or organisations aim to achieve within set periods of time.

Goal Compatibility : The extent to which the goals of more than one group can be achieved at the same time.

Goal Setting : The process of determining specific levels of performance for workers to attain.

Graphic Rating Scale : A method of rating individual performance whereby the rater checks or circles the point on the scale that best represents the performance level of the employee.

Grievance : A complaint by an employee concerning a possible violation of the labour contract, law, or past practice of the employer.

Grievance Procedure : The steps followed for handling contractual disputes arising out of a collective bargaining agreement.

Group : A collection of two or more interacting individuals who maintain stable patterns of relationships, share common goals, and perceive themselves as being a group.

Group Cohesion : The "interpersonal glue" that makes members of a group stick together.

Group Dynamics : Social process by which people interact face-to-face in small groups.

Group Structure : The pattern of interrelationships between the individuals constituting a group, the guidelines of group behaviour that make group functioning orderly and predictable.

Halo Effect : In performance appraisal, the tendency to let the rater's assessment of an employee on one trait influence his or her evaluation of that employee on other specific traits also.

Hawthorne Effect : A concept that mere attention to workers tends to change the way the group of workers operates in a work environment.

Hawthorne Studies : A series of experiments conducted by Elton Mayo and his associates at the Hawthorne Plant of Western Electric near Chicago between 1920s and 1930s. The overall conclusion of the studies was that individual and social processes are too important to ignore.

Heredity : It refers to qualities determined at conception through biological mechanism.

Hierarchy of Needs : A five-level classification of human needs, in order of merit or importance, developed by the psychologist Abraham Maslow, are : (1) physiological, (2) security, (3) social, (4) self-esteem, and (5) self-actualisation.

Hot-Stove Rule : Suggested by Douglas McGregor, a rule of discipline to touching a hot-stove, in that a warning is given, the response is immediate, enforcement is consistent, and the rule is applied impersonally to all.

Human Resource Information System (HRIS) : A system frequently computerised, for collecting, storing, maintaining, retrieving, and validating data concerning an organisation's personnel.

Hygiene Factors : A work condition related to dissatisfaction caused by discomfort or pain.

Impression Management : The process by which individuals try to control the impressions others have of them.

Incentives : Payments made to employees in addition to basic pay as an encouragement to increase the quantity or quality of output.

Individual Difference : The way in which factors such as skills, abilities, personalities, perceptions, attitudes, values, and ethics differ from one individual to another.

Individualism : A cultural orientation in which people belong to loose social frameworks and their primary concern is for themselves and their families.

Industrial Democracy : Government-mandated worker participation at various levels of the organisation with regard to decisions that affect workers.

Industrial Relations : Relations between trade unions and employers, or between an employer and unions representing employees. Also the relations between management, government and employees in an industrial environment.

Industrial Revolution : Phenomenon that peaked in the United States in the late nineteenth century and marked the move from an agrarian to an industrial society, from the use of hand-powered tools to mechanised tools, and from small local workshops to large factories.

Informal Groups : Groups formed by the members of an organisation. They include the relatively permanent friendship group and the interest group, which may be less long-lived.

Informal Leadership : Unofficial leadership accorded to a person by other members of the organisation.

Information Technology : Use of computers, software, and telecommunications for a wide variety of productivity and communication applications.

Inputs : An individual's contribution to the organisation, such as experience, effort, and loyalty.

Interactional Justice: A high degree of courtesy, dignity, and inter-personal sensitivity shown by organization toward its employees.

Interventions : Structured activities designed to help individuals or groups improve their work experience.

Interview : A face-to-face interaction between two persons for a specific purpose.

Investiture Socialisation : A socialisation process that ratifies the usefulness of the characteristics that the person brings to the new job.

Involvement : A person's willingness to go beyond the standard demands of his or her job as an organisational "citizen".

Jargon : A specialized or technical language of a trade, field, profession, or social group.

Job : A set of specified work and task activities that engage an individual in an organisation.

Job Analysis : A systematic investigation into the tasks, duties, and responsibilities of a job.

Job Classification : A method of grouping or grading jobs based on skills, training, qualifications and levels of responsibility needed to perform a task. It is also called 'Job Grading'.

Job Description : A written statement of what the jobholder does, how it is done and why it is done. The description is a product of job analysis.

Job Design : The process of deciding on the tasks and responsibilities to be included in a job and deciding on the methods to be used to carry out the tasks specified.

Job Dissatisfaction : The displeasure or negative attitude of an employee toward his or her job.

Job Enlargement : Increasing the scope of a job or number of tasks performed in order to overcome the boredom of over specialized work, on the one hand, and increase employee satisfaction, on the other.

Job Enrichment : Designing or redesigning jobs by incorporating more responsibilities, challenges, and motivational factors into them. It is also called "vertical enlargement".

Job Evaluation : The determination of the relative worth of each job in the organisation.

The technique forms the basis for establishing pay differentials.

Job Hopping : Moving to different organisations in search of job rather than making adjustments within the present organisation.

Job Involvement : Degree to which employees immerse themselves in their jobs, invest time and energy in them, and view work as a central part of their over all lives.

Job Redesign : An organisation development (OD) method that alters jobs to improve the fit between individual skills and the demands of the job.

Job Rotation : The process of transferring an employee from one job to another at a similar level in an organisation so as to give him or her wider experience.

Job Satisfaction : A positive or pleasureable emotional state resulting from the appraisal of one's job or job experiences.

Job Sharing : An alternative work pattern in which there is more than one person occupying a single job.

Job Specification : The minimum skills, education, and experience necessary for an individual to perform a job.

Job Stress : The physical or psychological response by an individual caused by an external action, situation, or event in the work place.

Kaizen : This is a Japanese term that implies that all employees should constantly drive themselves to be seeking ways to improve everything around them in an organisation.

Laissez Faire : A leadership style in which the leader fails to accept the responsibilities of the position.

Lateral Communication : Communication that takes place across chains of command. It is also known as "cross-communication".

Leader : An advocator for initiating change and new approaches for problem solving.

Leadership : The process of guiding and directing the behaviour of others to work enthusiastically toward achieving set objectives.

Leadership Styles : The various patterns of behaviour that leader exhibits during the process of guiding and influencing others to behave in a desired manner.

Leadership Substitutes : Individual, task, and organisational characteristics that tend to negate the leader's ability to affect subordinate satisfaction and performance.

Leading : The process of enabling members of organisation to work together in a fashion consistent with the goals of the organisation.

Learning : A relatively permanent change in behaviour or potential behaviour as a result of experience.

Legitimate Power : Power that is granted by virtue of one's position in the organisation.

Life Change : Any meaningful change in a person's personal or work situation.

Life Position: A dominant way of relating to others that tends to remain with the person for long-time or even life-long unless some major experience occurs to change it.

Life Stressors : Events that take place outside the organisation and cause stress in organisational settings, generally termed as 'life change'.

Life Trauma : Any single upheaval in one's life that disrupts his or her attitude, emotions, or behaviours.

Locus of Control : An individual's generalized belief about internal control (self control) versus external control (control by the situation or by others).

Machiavellianism : A personality characteristic indicating one's willingness to do whatever it takes to get one's way.

Management : The process of efficiently getting activities completed with and through other people.

Management by Crisis : A management style which focuses on problems as and when these arise.

Management by Objectives (MBO) : Process of jointly setting objectives, creating action plans, conducting periodic reviews, and engaging in annual performance evaluations to facilitate desired performance.

Management Development : A stystematic process by which persons acquire the skills, knowledge, and abilities to lead and manage organisations effectively.

Management Games : The simulation of conditions faced by real organisations, used primarily for educational purposes (also called 'Business Games').

Management Information System (MIS) : A formal, usually computerized, structure for providing management with information, often through an MIS department.

Manager : A person who plans, organises, leads and controls other individuals in the process of pursuing organisational goals in an effective manner.

Managerial Grid : A grid designed by Blake and Mouton on scale of 9 points, to understanding a manager's concern for production and concern for people. The preferred style is said to be 9.9 – this refers to a style with high concern for both people and production.

Maslow's Hierarchy of Needs : A motivational theory developed by Abrahim Maslow in which human needs are arranged in a five-tiered hierarchy of importance, from physiological needs at the bottom, to security needs, social needs, esteem needs, and at the top, self-actualisation needs.

Matrix Organisation : An organisational structure which is a combination of the functional and product types of organisation.

McClelland's Three Needs Theory : A motivational theory based on the need for achievement, the need for affiliation, and the need for power.

Mechanistic Organisations : Organisations characterised by the use of hierarchy, centralised direction, certainty of task assignments, and strict definition of roles.

Mentor : More experienced employees helping younger ones grow and advance by providing advice, support, and encouragement.

Merit Rating : A technique for assessing an employee's performance and personal qualities. It is usually applied to administrative staff assessment.

Message : Thoughts and feelings that the communicator is attempting to elicit in the receiver.

Metamorphosis Stage : The socialization stage whereby the new member must work out any problems discovered during the encounter stage.

Mission : The unique reason for an organisation's existence that makes it different from all others.

Modeling : Learning through the experience of others. It is also referred to as vicarious learning.

Morale : A collective feeling to work together persistently and consistently in pursuit of a common purpose.

Motivating Potential Score (MPS) : Index that reflects the degree to which a job is perceived by an employee to be meaningful, foster responsibility, and provide knowledge of work results.

Motivation : The set of processes that arouse, direct, and maintain human behaviour toward attaining some goal.

Motivational Factors : Conditions intrinsic to work such as achievement and motivation that tend to motivate workers when they exist, but their absence rarely is dissatisfying.

Motive : One's urge to achieve his or her goal.

Moving : The second step in Lewin's change model, in which new attitudes, values, and behaviours are substituted for old ones.

Multinational Organisations : Those organisations that do business in more than one country.

Need : A deficiency experienced by an individual.

Need for Achievement : A manifest (easily perceived) need that concerns individuals' issues of excellence, competition, challenging goals, persistence, and overcoming difficulties.

Need for Affiliation : A manifest (easily perceived) need that concerns an individual's need to establish and maintain warm, close, intimate relationships with other people.

Need for Power : A manifest (easily perceived) need that concerns an individual's need to make an impact on others, influence others, change people or events, and make a difference in life.

Nepotism : Favouritism or patronage to relatives in hiring or promotional processes.

Network : Group of people who develop and maintain contact to exchange information informally, usually about a shared interest.

Networking : The linking of groups of computers, either intraorganisationally or interorganisationally, so that they can communicate with each other and share common data bases and resources.

Nominal Group : Group structure that combines individual input group discussion, and independent decision making.

Nominal Group Technique (NGT) : A method of improving group decision making whereby group members follow a generate - discussion - vote cycle until they reach an appropriate decision.

Non-Verbal Communication : The transmission of message without the use of words (*e.g.* by gestures, the use of space).

Norms : Generally agreed- on informal rules that guide group members' behaviour.

Objectives : The targeted goals of an organisation to which efforts and resources are channelled.

Occupation : A group of jobs similar as to the type of tasks and training involved.

Operant Conditioning : Modifying behaviour through the use of positive or negative consequences following specific behaviours. It is generally associated with the work of skinner.

Oral Communication : The most prevalent form of organisational communication whereby the message is encoded into audible sounds.

Organic Structure : A type of organisation design characterized by flexible tasks and roles, open communications, and decentralized decision making.

Organisation : A group of people working together to attain common goals.

Organisation Chart : A diagram of an organisation's structure, showing the functions, departments, reporting relationships, and positions of the organisation and how they are related.

Organisation Structure : A system of linking of jobs and departments within an organisation.

Organisational Behaviour : The study and application of knowledge about how people – as individuals and groups – act within organisations.

Organisational Change : Alterations in the operations of organisations that are either planned or unplanned, and are a result of either internal or external influences.

Organisational Citizenship Behaviour (OCB): Employee behaviour that goes beyond that which is formally prescribed by the organization, but that behaviour does contribute to the overall organizational effectiveness. OCB is also called *'extra-role behaviour.'*

Organisational Climate: A set of elements or properties that describe an organization, are distinct to an organization, are relatively enduring, and influence people behaviour constitute organizational climate.

Organisational Conflict : Disagreement between two parties in an organisation based on the perception of one party that another party has negatively affected, or is about to negatively affect, something that the first party cares about.

Organisational Culture : A common perception held by the organisation's members : which actions are considered acceptable and which are considered unacceptable.

Organisational Design : The process of constructing and adjusting an organisation's structure to achieve its goals.

Organisational Development : A process of systemwide change at various levels (group, intergroup and total organisation) designed to make organisation more adaptive.

Organisational Socialisation : Continuous process of transmitting key elements of an organisation's culture to its members/employees.

Organisational Stressors : Factors at the work place that can cause stress, task demands, physical demands, role demands, and interpersonal demands.

Orientation : The activities involved in introducing new employees to the organisation, work and division/unit.

Outputs : Transformed inputs that are returned to the external environment as products or services.

Participative Management : A way of decision making in which employees are allowed the opportunity to participate in decisions.

Path Goal Leadership : A theory of leadership suggesting that subordinates will be motivated by a leader only to the extent they perceive this individual (leader) as helping them to attain valued goals.

Perception : A process through which we select, organize, and interpret information gathered by our senses in order to understand the world around us.

Performance : Effective and efficient work, which also considers personnel data such as measures of accidents, turnover, absence, and tardiness.

Personality : The unique and relatively stable patterns of behaviour, thoughts, and emotions shown by individuals.

Planned Change : A change resulting from a deliberate decision to alter the organisation.

Planning : The process of establishing objectives and suitable courses of action before actually taking action.

Porter-Lawler Model : This model suggests that performance may lead to various intrinsic and extrinsic rewards. When an individual perceives the rewards as equitable, the rewards lead to satisfaction.

Positive Re-inforcement : The process by which people learn to perform behaviours that lead to the presentation of desired outcomes.

Power : The capacity to change the behaviour or attitudes of others in a desired manner.

Proactive : Anticipating events, initiating change, and taking control of one's destiny.

Problem Solving : A special kind of decision making in which the issue is unique and requires development and evaluation of alternatives without the aid of a programmed decision rule.

Productivity : A measure of performance of a worker or an operations system relative to resource utilization; or output divided by input.

Promotion : The reassignment of an employee to a higher-level job within an organisation.

Psychoanalysis : Sigmund Freud's method for delving into the unconscious mind to understand better a person's motives and needs.

Punishment : The attempt to eliminate or weaken undesirable behaviour by either bestowing negative consequences or withholding positive consequences.

Quality : The total set of features and characteristics of a product or service that determines its ability to satisfy stated or implied needs.

Quality Assurance : An activity that confirms whether or not a product or service meets the specifications promised by the supplier or expected by the customer.

Quality Circle : Periodic meeting of labour and management personnel to solve quality control and productivity problems.

Quality Control : The activity, process or study of ensuring that the output of production processes confirms with a pre-determined standard.

Quality of Work Life (QWL) : The extent to which the members of an organisation meet their personal needs through their work in the organisation.

Quality Team : A team that is part of an organisation's structure and is empowered to act on its decisions regarding product and service quality.

Questionnaire : A collection of written questions about the respondents' attitudes, opinions, perceptions, and/or demographic characteristics.

Quick Fixes : Managerial use of fads that address symptoms while ignoring underlying problems.

Quorum : A minimum number of persons required to be in attendance at a meeting in order to transact business.

Reactive : A manner of responding to events, adapting to change, and tempering its consequences.

Red Circle Job : A job whose current pay exceeds the maximum for that pay grade.

Redundancy : The loss of job on the grounds that it is no longer required or available at a place of employment.

Reference Group : A group of those persons whose norms a person imbibes and accepts.

Refreezing : The third and final step in Lewin's change model, which involves the establishment of new attitudes, values, and behaviours as the new *status quo.*

Reinforcement : The attempt to develop or strengthen desirable behaviour by either bestowing positive consequences or withholding negative consequences.

Reinforcement Theory : A learning theory that suggests that the behaviour is a function of its consequences. It is generally associated with the work of skinner.

Research : An activity related to the acquisition of knowledge or information with an objective to gain greater understanding of a phenomenon and directed towards the solution or elucidation of a problem.

Research Design : The set of procedures used to test the predicted relationships among natural phenomena.

Resistance to Change : The tendency for employees to be unwilling to go alongwith organisational changes, either because of individual fears of the unknown, or organisational impediments (such as structural intertia).

Retrenchment : A mode of downsizing an organisation when the organisation faces an environment of decline.

Risky Shift : An act of a group becoming more willing to take chances when its members are dealing with the resources of others and cannot be held individually responsible.

Role : The typical behaviour that characterizes a person in a specific social context.

Role Ambiguity : A situation that occurs when it is unclear or unknown what behaviour is expected of a role occupant.

Role Conflict : A situation that arises when others have different perceptions or expectations of a person's role. The four types of role conflict are interrole, intrarole, intrasender, and person-role.

Role Models : Leaders who serve as example for their followers.

Role Perception : The individual's understanding of the behaviour needed to accomplish a task or perform a job.

Role Playing : A training technique in which a trainee is asked to assume a specified role and act out a situation which involves that role.

Rules : Standing plans that detail specific actions to be taken in a given situation.

Rumour : Information with little basis in fact, often communicated through informal channels (like *grapevine*).

Scalar Chain : A concept in which authority is delegated in a clear and straight line from top to the bottom in an organisation.

Scientific Management : A systematic investigation and approach to management designed to find the most efficient means of production and employee productivity. The concept is developed by F.W. Taylor.

Script Analysis: A plan that indicates how the person will live and die.

Selective Perception : The process of selecting information that supports our individual viewpoints while discounting information that threatens our viewpoints.

Self-Actualisation : The need to discover who we are and to develop ourselves to the fullest possible.

Self-Efficancy : A Person's belief that he or she has the ability, motivation, and resources to complete a task successfully.

Sensitivity Training : An OD intervention that seeks to enhance employees' understanding of their own behaviour and its impact on others. Such changes, it is believed, will reduce the interpersonal conflicts that interfere with organisational effectiveness.

Seven 'S' : These include strategy, structure, system, staff, style, skills and super ordinate goals of an organisation.

Simulation : A form of off-the-job training which simulates, or replicates, as closely as possible, the actual work environment and the actual problems and issues the trainee faces on the job.

Situational Leadership Theory : A theory suggesting that the most effective style of leadership depends on the extent to which followers require guidance, direction and emotional support.

Social Cues : Positive or negative bias of information that employees receive from their social surroundings and that act to influence how they react to a communication.

Social Loafing: The tendencies for individuals to exert fewer efforts when working collectively than when working individually.

Socialisation : A continuous process of adapting of values and norms of an organisation by its members.

Social Facilitation : The tendency for the presence of others sometimes to enhance an individual's performance and at other times to impair it.

Social Learning : Belief that employees gain substantial information about how to perform and act by observing and imitating role models around them. This is also called *vicarious learning.*

Social Loafing : Employees lessening of output when they think their contribution to a group cannot be measured.

Social Responsibility : An organisation's obligation to protect and contribute to the social environment in which it functions.

Span of Control : The number of subordinates in an organisation who are supervised by managers.

Stress : The pattern of emotional states and physiological reactions occurring in response to demands from within or outside organisations.

Stressors : Various factors in the external environment that trigger the stress response.

Stroking: This is performing any act of recognition for another person.

Structure : The manner in which an organisation's work is designed at the micro level, as well as how departments, divisions, and overall organisation are designed at the macro level.

Substitute for Leadership : Characteristics of the task, employees, or organisation that may reduce the need for leadership behaviours.

Succession Planning : An executive inventory report indicating what individuals are ready to move into higher positions in the company.

Survey Feedback : A widely used method of intervention whereby employee attitudes are solicited using a questionnaire.

Synergy : A concept which suggests that the investment of additional resources produces a return which is proportionately greater than the sum of the resources invested (This is often known as the 2 + 2 = 5 effect).

Task : An organisation's mission, purpose, or goal carried out for a distinct purpose.

Team : A group whose members have complementary skills and are committed to a common purpose or set of performance goals for which they hold themselves mutually accountable.

Team Building : An OD technique designed to improve the effectiveness of a work group.

Technology : The mechanical and intellectual processes that transform inputs into outputs.

Theory : An explanation of how and why people think, feel, and act as they do in the organisation.

Theory X : A set of assumptions of how to manage individuals who are motivated by lower-order needs.

Theory Y : A set of assumptions of how to manage individuals who are motivated by higher-order needs.

Theory Z : A model that adopts the elements of Japanese management systems to the U.S. culture and emphasizes cooperation and consensus decision processes.

Total Quality Management (TQM) : This is a cost effective system for integrating the continuous quality improvement efforts of people at all levels in an organisation to deliver products and services which ensure customer satisfaction.

Trade Union : An association of employees with the objectives of regulating wages and conditions of work for its members by negotiating with employers.

Training : The process of systematically teaching employees to acquire and improve job related skills and knowledge.

Trait : Physical, intellectual, or personality characteristics that differentiate between leaders and non-leaders, or between successful and unsuccessful leaders.

Trait Theory : The personality theory that states that in order to understand individuals, we must break down behaviour patterns into a series of observable traits.

Transactional Analysuis (TA) : This is a study of social transactions between people meant to improve communication and human relationships between them.

Transfer : The reassignment of an employee to a job with pay, status, and responsibilities similar to those of a former job.

Transformational Leadership : The process of leading to initiate bold strategic changes rather than maintaining *status que*.

Uncertainty Avoidance : The extent to which a culture tolerates ambiguity and uncertainty.

Unfreezing : The first step in Lewin's change model, which involves encouraging individuals to discard old behaviours by shaking up the equilibrium state so that new ones can be learned.

Union : An organisation of workers, acting collectively, seeking to protect and promote their mutual interests through collective bargaining.

Unplanned Change : Change that is imposed on the organisation and is often unforeseen.

Upward Communication : Flows of communication from lower to higher levels in an organisation.

Valence : The value a person places on the rewards he or she expects to receive from an organisation. It is a concept of Expectancy Theory.

Validity : The extent to which a test actually measures what it purports to measures.

Value Auction: A value inventory generated to facilitate the participants to add to and/or appropriate their values.

Values : Basic convictions about what is right or wrong, good or bad, desirable or not.

Value Judgement : The degree to which a message reinforces or challenges the receiver's basic personal beliefs.

Value Theory : A theory devised by Locke, suggesting that job satisfaction depends primarily on the match between the outcomes individuals value in their jobs and their perceptions about the availability of such outcomes.

Verbal Communication : The transmission of messages using words, either written or spoken.

Vicarious Learning : Learning through the experiences of others. It is also referred to as modeling.

Virtual Team: The team that works across space, time, and organizational boundaries with links strengthened by webs of communication technologies.

Vision : Challenging and crystallized long-range portrait of what the organisation and its members can and should be – a possible (and desirable) image of the future.

Whistle-Blowing : Calling attention to organisational actions that are inconsistent with established organisational norms or policies.

Work : A mental or physical activity that has productive results.

Work Group Inertia : Forces operating within work groups, such as norms, that discourage organisational change.

Work Ethic : Employee attitude of viewing work as a central life interest and desirable goal in life.

Written Communication : A form of communication in organisations in the form of letters, memos, reports, manuals, and forms.

BIBLIOGRAPHY

Ahmed Nazimuddin and S.S. Jha : Job Stress : Strain and Social Support, *Indian Journal of Training and development,* May-June, 1989.

Ahmed Salma : Talent Retention : A Challange, *Personnel Today,* Vol.18 No.2, July - September, 1997.

Alder A. : *Understanding Human Nature,* Greenberg, New York, 1927.

Alder Ralph and Markus Milne : *Communication Skills and Attitudes, Chartered Accountants Journal of New Zealand,* December 1994.

Alderfer C.P. : A New Theory of Human Needs, *Organisational Behaviour and Human Performance,* No. 4, 1969.

–: *Existence, Relatedness, and Growth : Human Needs in Organisational Settings,* The Free Press, New York, 1972.

Argenti J. : *Corporate Collapse : The Causes and Symptoms,* Mc Graw Hill, New York, 1976.

Argyris Chris : Double Loop Learning in Organisations, *Harvard Business Review,* Sept - Oct. 1977

–: Teaching Smart People How to Learn, *Harvard Business Review.* May-June, 1991.

–: Good Communication That Blocks Learning, *Harvard Business Review,* July - August 1994.

Asch S.E. : *Social Psychology,* Printice Hall, Englewood Cliffs, 1952.

Axley Stephen R. The Practical Qualities of Effective Leaders, *Industrial Management,* Sept-Oct. 1990.

Axline Larry L. TQM : A Look in the Mirror, *Management Review,* July, 1991.

Austin Nancy and Tom Peters : A Passion for Excellence, *Fortune,* May 13, 1985.

Barnard Chester I. : *Functions of the Executive,* 30th Anniversary Edition, Harvard University Press, Cambridge, 1938.

Bartlett Christopher and Sumantra Ghosal : Changing the Role of Top Management : Bey and Systems to People, *Harvard Business Review,* May-June , 1995.

Bass Barnard M. : *Leadership and Performance beyond Expectations,* Free Press, New York 1985. : From Transactional to Transformational Leadership : Learning to Share the Vision, *Organisational Dynamics,* Winter 1990.

Bass Barnard M. and Ralph Mell Stogdill : *Bass and Stogdill's Handbook of Leadership,* The Free Press, New York, 1990.

Benjamin Maynard H. The Power of Information, Association Management, 47, 1995.

Bennis Warren : How to be the Leader They'll Follow, *Working Women* 15 March 1990. : Managing the Dream Leadership in the 21st Century,Training, 27, May, 1990. : On Becoming a Leader : On Becoming a Leader, Austin Press and Erwin, Illinois, 1995.

Bhandarker A. and P. Singh : Managerial Stress : A Case Study in Cydical Perspective, *Abhigyan.* Autumn, 1998.

Bhattacharya S.K. : *Achieving Managerial Excellence,* Macmillan, New Delhi, 1989

Blake Robert R. and Jane S. Mouton : *The Managerial Grid III,* 3rd Ed. Gulf Publication, Texas, Houston, 1984.

Bottoms David : Facing Change or Changing Face, *Industry Week,* May 1, 1995

Brown Andrew D. : Transformational Leadership in Tracking Technical Change, *Journal of General Management,* Summer 1994.
Brown Stephen W. : Managers Are Not Necessarily Leaders, *Marketing News,* October 23, 1989.
Brown Thomas L. : Leaders for the 90s : What Key Traits Are Called For, *Industry Week,* March 5, 1990.
Burns T. and G.M. Stalker : *The Management of Innovation,* Tavistock, London, 1961.
Business Today, Managing Tomorrow, April 22-May 6, 1992.
Cameron K.S. and David Whetten : Perception of Organisational Effectiveness Over Organisational Life-Cycle, *Administrative Science Quarterly,* December, 13 1981.
Chattopadhyay G.P. : Covert Group Dynamics, Organisational Insights and Diagnosis, In. G.P. Chattopadhyay, Z.H. Gangjee, M.L. Hunt and W.G. Lawrence (Eds.) : *When the Twain Meet,* A.H. Wheeler & Co. New Delhi, 1986.
Chaudhury S. : Corporate Strategy : Concept and Its Relevance in Indian Context, *Vikalpa,* 4, 1979.
Child J. : Predicting and Understanding Organisation Structure, *Administrative Science Quarterly,* 18, 1973.
Chopra B.S.K.S. : *Cases in Corporate Planning,* The Times Research Foundation, June, 1989.
Chopra K.K. : Leadership in Management, In : Sunil Kumar (Ed.) : *Managerial Effectiveness,* Excell Books, New Delhi 1998.
Chowdhry K. and S. Kakar : *Understanding Organisational Behaviour,* Tata McGraw-Hill, New Delhi, 1971.
Chris Lee : Can Leadership Be Taught ? Training, July 1989.
Clark K. B. : What Strategy Can Do For Teachnology, *Harvard Business Review,* Nov.-Dec. 1989.
Cohen William A. : *The Art of aLeader,* Printice Hall, Englewood Cliffs, 1990.
Coleman James C. : *Psychology and Effective Behaviour,* foreman & Co., Scott, U.S.A., 1969.
Conner Daryl R. : *Managing at the Speed of Change,* Villard Books,New York, 1995.
Crocker O.L., S. Charerey and I.S.L. Chin : *Quality Circles : A Guide to Participation and Productivity,* Methuen Publications, New York, 1984.
Cummings T. : Self-Regulating Work Groupas : A Socio-Technical Synthesis, *Academy of Management Review,* 3, 1978.
Davis Keieth : *Human Behaviour at Work,* Tata Mc Graw Hill, New Delhi, 1978.
Davis S.M. : *Managing Corporate Culture,* Ballinger, Cambridge, Mass, 1984.
De Nitish : Training Strategy for Change in Attitude; Micro-Level Experiences, *Economic Times,* 26 February 1976.
De N.R. : *India : In New Forms of Work Organisations,* International Labour Organisation, Geneva, 1979.
Deshpande R. and A. Parasuraman : Linking Corporate Culture to strategic Planning, *Business Horizons,* May-June, 1986.
Dhameja Nand (Ed.) : *Case Studies in Administrative Environment and Decision Making,* Indian Institute of Public Administration, New Delhi 1995.
Dhuru J. : *Project Management in Government and Joint Sector Organisation* (Unpublished doctoral dissertation) Indian Institute of Management, Ahmedabad, 1987.

Drucker Peter F. : *The Practice of Management,* Harper & Row Publishers, New York, 1954.

—: *Management, Tasks, Responsibilities, Practices,* Harper & Row Publishers, New York, 1974.

—: *Managing in Turbulent Times,* Harper & Row Publishers, New York, 1985.

—: Effective Executive, Harper & Row Publishers, New York, 1985.

—: *Innovation and Entrepreneurship,* Pan Books, London, 1986.

—: *Management Challanges for the 21st Century,* Butterworth Heinemanm, New Delhi, 1999.

Duck Jeanie Daniel : Managing Change : The Art of Balancing, *Harvard Business Review,* November-December, 1993.

Duncun Robert B. : What is the Right Organisation Structure ? *Organisational Dynamics,* Winter, 1979.

Dwivedi R.S. : The Relative Importance of Personality Traits among Indian Managers, *Indian Management,* April 1970.

Earl P. : *The Corporate Imagination,* ME Sharp, Inc, New York, 1984.

Easton George S. : The 1993 State of U.S. Total Quality Management, *California Management Review,* Spring 1993.

Elhance D.N. and R.D. Agarwal : *Delegation of Authority,* Progressive Press, Bombay, 1975.

Etzioni Amitai : Modern Organisation, Printice Hall of India Private Limited , New Delhi, 1972.

Emory William C. : *Business Research Methods,* Illinois Richard D. Irwin, Homewood, 1976.

Erikson E.R. : Growth and Crisis of the Healthy Personality, In : C. Cluckholm, N.A. Murray and D. Schneider (Eds.) : *Personality in Nature, Society and Culture,* Knopf, New York, 1953.

Erikson E.H. : *Identity* : *Youth and Crisis,* W.W. Norton, New York, 1968.

Etizioni Amitai : *Complex Organisations,* Holt, Rinehart & Winston, New York, 1961.

Etizioni D. : Moderating Effect of Social Support on the Stress-Burnout Relationship, *Journal of Applied Psychology,* 1984.

Evans M.G. : The Effect of Supervisory Behaviour on the Path-Goal Relationship, *Organisational Behaviour and Human Performance,* 1970.

Farrell D. And J.C. Petersen : Patterns of Political Behaviour in Organisations, *Academy of Management Review,* July, 1982.

Fayol Henry : *General and Industrial Management,* Pitman, London, 1964.

Fazio R.H. and M.P. Zanna : On the Predictive Validity of Attitudes : The Roles of Direct Experience and Confidence, *Journal of Personality,* Vol. No. 46, 1978.

Feldman Daniel C. : The Multiple Socialisation of the Organisation Members, *Academy of Management Review,* April, 1981.

Feldman Daniel C. and H.J. Arnold : *Managing Industrial and Group Behaviour in Organisations,* Mc Graw-Hill, New York, 1983.

Fiedler Fred : *A Theory of Leadership Effectiveness, Mc Graw- Hill, New York, 1967.*

Field R.H.G. : A Critique of Vroom-Yetton Contingency Model of Leader Behaviour, *Academy of Management Review,* 1979.

Fleishman E.A. : Evaluating Physical Abilities Required by Jobs, *Personnel Administrator,* June 1979.

Ford Robert N. : *Motivation Through the Work Itself,* American Management Association, 1969.

Fox William M. : Anonymity and Other Keys to Successful Problem-Solving Meeting, *National Productivity Review,* Spring, 1989.

Frederick William C., James E. Post and Keith Davis : *Business and Society,* McGraw-Hill Book Company, New York, 1992.

French W. : Organisation Development : Objectives, Assumptions, and Strategies, *California Management Review,* 1962.

French W.L. and C.H. Bell : *Organisation Development,* Printice Hall, Englewood Cliffs N.J. 1978.

French J.R.P. and B. Raven : The Basis of Social Power, In : D. Cartwright (Ed.) : *Studies in Social Power,* Institute of Social Research, Machigan University, Ann Arbor 1959.

Friedman M. and R. H. Roseman : *Type A Behaviour and Your Heart,* Fawcett Publications, Greenwich C.T., 1974.

Freund Ray J. : Leadership Training for Long– Term Results, *Management Review,* July 1991.

Galbraith J. : *Organisation Design*, Addison - Wesley, Reading (Mass) 1977.

Gandz J. and Murray V. : The Experience of Workplace Politics, *Academy of Management Journal,* Volume 23, 1980.

Ganguli H.C. : Role of Status and Money as Motivation Among Middle Management Personnel, *Indian Journal of Industrial Relations,* October, 1974.

Gardner William M. : Lessons in Organisational Dramatury : The Art of Impression Management, *Organisationsal Dynamics,* Summer, 1992.

Gellermen S.W. : *Management by Motivation,* American Management Association, New York 1968.: *Motivation and Productivicty*, American Management Association, New York, 1963.

Gerwin D. : Relationship between Structure and Technology at Organisation and Job Levels, *Journal of Management Studies,* Vol. 16, 1979.

Ghosh P.K. and Munerikar : In Search of Personality Characteristics of Managers, *Industrial Journal of Applied Psychology,* January 1974.

—: Similarities and Differences in Personality Characteristics of Indian Managers, *Indian Journal of Applied Psychology,* April 1975.

Giacalone Robert A. : Image Control : The Strategies of Impression Management, *Personnel,* May, 1989.

Gibson Virgina M. : Stress in Work Place,H.R. Focus, January 1993.

Gold K. A. : Managing for Success : A Comparison of Private and Public Sectors, *Public Administration Review,* Vol. 10, 1985.

Gordon Thomas : *Leader Effectiveness Training,* Bantam, 1980.

Graicuna V.A. : Relationship in Organisation, *Bulletin of the International Management Institute,* International Labour Office, Geneva, 1933.

Gray B. And S.S. Ariss : Politics and Strategic Change Across Organisational Life Cycles, *Academy of Management Review,* vol.10 1985.

Gray D.H. : Uses and Misuses of Strategic Planning, *Harvard Business Review,* Jan.-Feb., 1986.

Greiner Larry E. : Patterns of Organisation Change, *Harvard Business Review,* May-June ,1967.: Evaluation and Revolution as Organisations Grow, *Harvard Business Review,* July-August, 1972.

—: Senior Executives as Strategic Actors, *New Management,* Vol.1, 1983.

Grigaliunas B.S. and F. Herzberg : Relevancy in the Test of Motivation – Hygiene Theory, *Journal of Applied Psychology,* 1971.

Grove Andrew S. : Taking the Hype out of Leadership, *Fortune,* March 28, 1988.

Grover Mary Seth : Letting Both Sides Win, *Forbes,* September 30, 1991.

Gulick Luther and L. Urwick (Eds.) : *Papers on the Science of Administration,* Institute of Public Administration, New York, 1937.

Gupta I. : Leadersip Styles, *Business India,* April, 1980.

Hackman J.R. : Power and Centrality in Allocation of Resources in Colleges and Universities, *Administrative Science Quarterly,* Vol. 30, 1985.

Hackman J.R. and G.R.Oldham : Development of Job Diagnostic Survey, *Journal of Applied Psychology,* Vol. 60, 1975.

Hage J. : An Axiomatic Theory of Organisations, *Administrative Science Quarterly,* Vol. 10, 1965.

Hall R.H. : Professionalisation and Bureaucratisation, *American Sociological Review,* Vol. 34, 1968.

Hammer M. : Reengineering Work : Don't Automate, Obliterate, *Harvard Business Review,* July- August, 1990.

Harari O. and L. Mukai : A New Decade Demands a New Breed of Manager, *Management Review,* Vol. 79, 1990.

Harris T. : I. M. *OK– You're OK; A Practical Guide to Transactional Analysis,* Harper & Row Publishers, New York, 1969.

Harvery B.H., J.P. Rogers and J.A. Schultz : Sick Pay vs Well Pay : An Analysis of the Impact of Rewarding Employees for Being on the Job, *Public Personnel Management Journal,* Summer, 1983.

Harvery E. : Technology and Structure in Organisations, *American Sociological Review,* Vol 33, 1968.

Hedberg B.L.T. : How Organisations Learn and Unlearn, In : P.C. Nystrom and W.H. Starbuck (Eds.) : *Handbook of Organisation Design,* Oxford University Press, New York, 1981.

Henderson George : *Cultural Diversity in the Workplace : Issues and Strategies,* Greenwood Publishing Group Inc., 1994.

Herbert T.T. : *Dimensions of Organisational Behaviour,* The Macmillan Co., New York, 1976.

Herrick N.Q. and M. Caccoby : Humanising Work : A Priority Goal of the 1970s, In : L. E. Davis and B. Cherms (Eds.) : *The Quality of Working Life, Volume I,* Free Press, New York, 1975.

Harsey Paul : The Situational Leader, Centre for Leadership Studies, Escondido, Calif, 1984.

Hersey Paul and John E. Stinson : *Perspectives on Leader Effectiveness,* Ohio University Press, Columbus, Ohio, 1980.

Hersey Paul and Kenneth H. Blanchard : Cultural Changes : Their Influence on Organisational Structure and Management Behaviour, *Training and Development Journal,* October, 1970.

—: So You Want to Know Your Leadership Style, *Training and Development Journal,* February 1974.

—: What is Missing in MBO ? *Management Review,* October 1974.

—: Life Cycle Theory of Leadership *Training and Development Journal,* May, 1969.

Paul Hersey, Kenneth H. Blanchard and Dewey E. Johnson : *Management of Organisational Behaviour (Utilizing Human Resources),* Printice-Hall of India Private Limited, New Delhi, 2000.

Herzberg Fredrick : *Work and Nature of Man,* World Publishing Company, Cleveland, Ohio, 1966.

—: One More Time : How Do You Motivate Employees? *Harvard Business Review,* January - February, 1968.

Herzberd Fredrick, B. Mausner and B. Snyderman : *The Motivateion to Work,* John Wiley, New York, 1959.

Hodgetts R.M. : *Modern Human Relations,* Dryden Press, Hinsdale, 1980.

Homans G.C. : *The Human Group,* Harwart Brace and World, New York, 1950.

—: Social Behaviour as Exchange, *American Journal of Sociology,* No. 63, 1958.

—: *Social Behaviour : Its Elementary Forms,* Harcourt Brace and Jovanovick, New York, 1961.

House Robert J. : A Path Goal Theory of Leader Effectiveness, *Administrative Science Quarterly,* 1971.

House Robert J. and Terence R. Mitchell : Path Goal Theory of Leadership, *Journal of Contemporary Business,* Autum, 1974.

Hunt J.G. and L.L. Larson (Eds.) : *Contingency Approaches to Leadership,* Southern University Press, Carbondale III, 1974.

Hunt J.G. : Personal Factors Associated with Leadership : A Survery of the Literature, *Journal of Psychology,* January, 1982.

Hussein Raef T. Understanding and Managing Informal Groups, *Management Decision,* November 8, 1990.

Ingram Larry C. : *The Study of Organisations,* Greenwood Publishing Group Inc., Westport.,

Isenberyg D. J. : How Senior managers Think ? *Harvard Business Review,* Nov.-Dec. 1984.

Ishikawa K. : Quality Control in Japan , In : N. Sasaki and D. Hutchins (Eds.) : *The Japanese Approach of Product Quality,* Pergamon Press, New York, 1984.

Ivancevich John M. and Michael T. Matteson : *Organisational behaviour and Management ,* Homewood III, Irwin, 1993.

Jaggi B.L. : Management Leadership Styles in Indian Work Organisations, *Indian Manager,* April-June, 1978.

Jain Sangeeta : *Quality of Work Life,* Deep & Deep Publications, New Delhi 1991.

James Art and Dennis Kratz : *Effective Listening Skill,* Burr Ridge, III, Irwin, 1994.

Janis I.L. : *Victims of Group Think,* Houghton Mifflin, Boston, 1982.

Janis I.L. : Group Think, *Psychology Today,* November, 1971.

Jauch Lawrence R. and Sally A. Caltrin : *The Managerial Experience : Cases and Exercise,* The Dryden Press, Texas, 1993.

Anthony Jay : *Management and Machivaelli,* Holt, Rineheart & Winston , New York, 1967.

Jessup Hartan R. : New Roles in Team Leadership, *Training and Development Journal,* November, 1990.

Johnson Dewey E. : *Concepts of Air Force Leadership,* Air Force ROTC, Washington, D.C. 1970.

Jung C. *Psychological Types,* Routledge and Kepan paul, London, 1923.

Kahn R. L : Productivity and Job Satisfaction, *Personnel Psychology,* Vol. 13, No. 3, 1960.

Kakar S. : Authority Relations in Indian Organisations, *Management International Review,* Vol. 1. 1972.

Kalra H.K. : *Leadership Styles of Executives in indian Enterprises,* Unpublished Research Report, Punjab Agricultural University, Ludhiana, 1980.

Kanter R. : Power Failure in Management Circuits, *Harvard Business Review,* July-August, 1979.

Keller L. M., T.J. Bouchard , R. D. Arvey, N.L. Segal and R.V. Dawis : Work Values : Genetic and Environmental Influences, *Journal of Applied Psychology* , February, 1992.

Kelly J. : *Organisational Behaviour,* Homewood, Irwin, 1974.

Kelman H.C. : Compliance, Identification and Internationalisation : Three Processes of Attitude Change, *Journal of Conflict Resolution,* March, 1958.

Kerlinger F.N. : *Foundations of Behavioural Research,* Surjeet Publications, Delhi, 1978.

Khandwalla P.N. : *Organisational Design for Excellence,* Tata McGraw Hill, New Delhi, 1992.

Khanka S.S. : Coping With Stress : Self-Management Approach, *The Chartered Accountant,* October, 1999.

King A.S. : Expectation Effects and Organisational Change, *Administrative Science Quarterly,* Vol. 19, 1974.

Kolasa Blair J. : *Introduction to Behavioural Sciences for Business,* Wiley Eastern Limited, New Delhi, 1991.

Kolb D.M. and J. M. Bartinek (Eds.) : *Hidden Conflicts in Organisations,* Sage Publications, Newbury Park, CA. 1992.

Korgaonkar M.G. : *Quality Circles at BHEL, A Case,* Indian Institute of Management, Ahmedabad, 1986.

Kotter John P. : What Leaders Really Do ?, *Harvard Business Review,* May-June, 1990.

—: *A Force for Change : How Leadership Differs from Management,* The Free Press, New York, 1990.

Kotter John P. and J. L. Heskett : *Corporate Culture and Performance,* The Free Press, New York, 1992.

Kotter John P. and L. A. Schlesinger : Choosing Strategies for Change, *Harvard Business Review,* March-April 1979.

Krishnamurthy V. : Management of Organisational Change – The BHEL Experience, *Vikalp,* Vol. 2 No. 2, April, 1977.

Katz Daniel and Robert L. Kahn : *The Social Psychology of Organisations,* Wiley Eastern, New Delhi, 1970.

Kumar U. and K.K. Singh : Interpersonal Construct System of Indian Managers : A Determinant of Organisational Behaviour, *Management International Review,* Vo. 18, 1978.

Kushel Gerald : *Reaching the Peak Performance Zone : How to Motivate Yourself and Others to Excel,* AMACOM, New York, 1994.

Lahiri D.K. : Motivatiom of Managers : What Indian Managers Want from Their Job, *ASCI Journal of Management,* September, 1973.

Lahiri D.K. and S. Srivastava : Determinants of Satisfaction in Middle Management, *Applied Psychology,* No. 3, 1967.

Lala R.M. : *The Creation of Wealth,* IBH Publishing Company, Bombay, 1981.

Lawler E.E. : *The Ultimate Advantage : Creating the High-Involvement Organisation,* San Francisco, Jossey-Bass, 1992.

Lawrence P.R. and J. W. Lorsch : *Organisation and Environment,* Harvard University Press, Boston, 1967.

Leads Dorothy : Eight Steps to Better Body Language, *Real Estate Today,* June, 1994.

Lee Chris : Followership : The Essence of Leadership, *Training,* January, 1991.

Lee J.A. : Leader Power and Managing Change, *Academy of Management Review* Vol. 2, 1977.

Lele R.D. : Stress and Tension : Medical View, *B.MA. Review,* Vol. 4, No. 6, November-December 1993.

Lewin Kurt : Frontiers in Group Dynamics, *Human Relations,* No.1, 1947.

—: *Field Theory in Social Science,* Harper and Brothers, New York, 1951.

LewinKurt, R. Lippett and R. White : Leader Behaviour and Member Reaction in Three Social Climates, *Group Dynamics : Research and Theory,* Peterson & Company, Evanston III, 1960.

Likert Rensis : *New patterns of Management,* McGraw-Hill, New York, 1961.

—: *The Human Organisation,* McGraw-Hill, New York, 1967.

—: A Technique for Measurement of Attitudes, *Archives of Psychology,* No. 140, 1952.

Likert Rensis and J.B. Likert : *New Ways of Managing conflict,* Mc Graw-Hill, New York, 1976.

Locke E. A. : The Naturé and Cause of Job Satisfaction, In : M. Dunnette (Ed.) : *Handbook of Industrial and Organisational Psychology,* Rand Mc Nally,Chicago, 1976.

—: Toward a Theory of Task Motivation and Incentives, *Organisational Behaviour and Organisational Performance,* May, 1968.

—: *The Essence of Leadership : The Four Keys to Leading Effectively,* The Free Press, New York, 1992.

Loeb Marshall : Where Leaders Come From, *Fortune,* September, 1994.

Luthans Fred : *Organisational Behaviour,* Mc Graw-Hill, New York, 1995.

Luthans Fred and R. Kreitner : *Organisational Behaviour Modification and Beyond,* Scott, Foresman, Glenview, 1985.

Maccoby Michael : How to Be a Quality Leaber, *Research Technology Management,* September-October, 1990.

Maddi S. R. : *Personality Theories : A Comparative Analysis,* Dorsey, Homewood II, 1980.

Maheshwari B.L. : *Decision Styles and Organisational Effectiveness,* Vikas Publishing House, New Delhi, 1980.

—: *MBO : Concepts, Methods on the Experiences,* Tata Mc Graw-Hill Publishing Company Limited, New Delhi, 1980.

Maslow Abraham H. :A Theory of Human Motivation, *Psychological Review,* Vol. 50, March-April, 1943.

—: *Motivation and Personality,* Harper & Row Publishers, New York, 1954.:

—: *New Knowledge in Human Values,* Harper & Row Publishers, New York, 1959.

Mayo Elton : *The Human Problems of an Industrialised Civilization,* Harvard University Press, Cambridge, Mass, 1933.

McClelland David C. : *Personality,* Rineheart & Winston, New York, 1951.

—: Towards a Theory of Motive Acquisition, *American Psychologist,* Vol. 20, 1965. *Achievement Motivation* Can be Learned, *Harvard Business Review,* Vol. 43, 1965.

—: The Achieving Society, Van Nostrand Co., Princeton, 1961.

Mc Clelland David C. and D. H. Burnham : Power is The Great Motivator, *Harvard Business Review* , March-April, 1976.

McGregor Douglas : *The Human Side of Enterprise,* McGraw-Hill Book Company, New York, 1960.

—: *Professional Manager,* McGraw-Hill Book Company, New York, 1967.

Menon, S.A. : Personality, Executive Training and Organisation, *Indian Journal of Industrial Relations,* July, 1974.

Miller D. : Common Syndromes of Business Failure, *Business* Horizons, November, 1977.

Miller Sandra A. : Controlling How Others See You is Good Business, *The C P A Journal,* October, 1994.

Mintzberg H. : Planning on the Left Side and Managing on the Right, *Harvard Business Review,* July-August, 1976.

—: *Power In and Around Organisations,* Printice Hall, Englewood, New Jersey, 1983.

Monga M.L. : The Industrial Worker, Emerging Realities about His Commitment to the Factory System, *NLI Bulletin,* Vol. 4, No. 12, 1978.

Murray H.A. : *Explorations in Personality : ACritical and Experimental Study of Fifty Men of College Age,* Oxford University Press, New York, 1938.

Nadler D.A. : Managing Organisational Change : An Integrated Perspective, *Journal of Applied Behavioural Science,* Vol. 17, 1981,

Nadler D.A. and M.L. Tushman : Beyond the Charismatic Leader : Leadership and Organisational Change, *California Management Review,* Winter, 1990.

Narain Laxmi : Managerial Motivation in Public Enterprises, *Lok Udyog,* December, 1971.

Narayanan V. K. and L. Fahey : The Micro Politics of Strategy Formulation, *Academey of Management Review,* Vol. 7, 1982.

Nedd A. N. B. : The Simultaneous Effect of Several Variables on Attitudes Toward Change, *Administrative Science Quarterly,* 1971.

Nelson Bob : *1001 Ways to Reward Employees,* Workman Publishing, New York, 1994.

Nelson Robert B. : *Empowering Employees Through Delegation,* Irwin, Burr Ridge, III, 1993.

Newcomb T. : Intrafamily Relationship in Attitude, *Sociometry,* Vol. 1, 1937.

Newman D. : *Organisational Design,* Edward Arnold, London, 1973.

Newstrom J.W. and Keith Davis : *Organisational Behaviour : Human Behaviour at Work,* Tata McGraw-Hill Publishing Company Limited, New Delhi, 1998.

Nichols Ralph G. : Listening is Good Business, *Management of Personnel Quarterly,* Winter 1962.

Norman R.D. : The Interrelationships between Work and Nonwork Domain, *Administrative Science Quarterly,* 1980.

Odiorne George S. : *Management by Objectives,* Pitman Publishing Corporation New York, 1965.

Ohmae K. : Quality Control Circles : What Makes Them Work, *The Asian Wall Street Journal,* March 31, 1982.

Ohmae K. : How Japanese Managers Manage; In : A .A. Thompson, Jr. A.J. Strickland III and W.E. Fulmer (Eds.) : *Readings in Strategic Management,* Business Publicátions, Plano (Texas), 1987.

Osborn Alex F. : *Applied Imagination,* Charles Scribner's Sons, New York, 1953.

Ott J.S. : *The Organisational Culture,* Perspectives, Dorsey Press, San Francisco, 1985.

Ouchi William G. : *Theory Z,* Addison-Wesley, Reading, Mass, 1981.

Ouchi William G. and J.B. Dowling : Defining Span of Control, *Administrative Science Quarterly,* Vol. 19, 1974.

Owens H. : The Business of Business is Learning, *Newsletter of Mithya,* Summer 1990.

Panchanathan N. : Effects of Stress : Reduction on the Creative Personality of Execuives Through Counselling, *Sankalpa,* Vol. VI, No. 1, January-June, 1998.

Panchanathan N. and V. Shanmuga Ganeshan : The Effect of Psychological Stress on Academic Achievement, *Journal of Community Guidance and Research,* Vol. 9, No.2 1992.

Pareek Udai : *Organisational Behaviour Processes,* Rawat Publications, New Delhi, 1996.

—: The Concept and the Process of Organisation Development, *The Indian Journal of Social Work,* July 1975.

—: *Managing Conflict and Collaboration,* Oxford & IBH Publishing Co., New Delhi, 1982.

Paterson T.T. : *Management Theory,* Business Publications, London, 1969.

Patil V. and Munerkar :The Profile of Indian Executives Using MMPI, *Indian Journal of Applied Psychology,* January, 1976.

Perrow Charles : The Analysis of Goals in a Complex Organisation, *American Sociological Review,* December 1961.

Pestonjee P. M. : Executive Stress : Should It be Avoided ? *Vikalpa,* Vol. 12, No. 1, 1987.

—: *Stress and Coping : The Indian Experience,* Sage Publications, New Delhi, (2nd Edition), 1999.

Pestonjee P.M. and G. Basu : Study of Job Mot:vation of Indian Executives, *Indian Journal of Industrial Relations,* July, 1972.

Peters T. J. : *Thriving on Chaas ;* Tata McGraw-Hill, New Delhi, 1987.

Peter Tom J. and Nancy Austin : *A Passion for Excellence – The Leadership Difference,* Random House, New York, 1985.

Peter Tom J. and Robert Waterman : *In Search of Excellence,* Harper & Row, New York, 1982.

Pitman Ben : How Do I Motivate and Lead My People, *Journal of Systems Management,* March, 1991.

Poddar C.K. : Retention of Employees - HR Manager's Challange, *The Hindu,* Jan. 10, 1996.

Pondy L. R. : Organisational Conflict : Concept and Models, *Administrative Science Quarterly,* Vol. 12, 1967.

Porter L.W. and E.E. Lawler : *Managerial Attitude and Performance,* Richard D. Irwin, Homewood Ill, 1968.

Prasad L.M. : Formal and Informal Communication in India, *ISTD Review,* May June, 1976.: An Assessment of Upward Communication in a Public Sector Organisation *Lok Udyog,* July 1976.

Pugh D.S. : The Measurement of Organisation Structure : Does Context Determine Form? *Organisational Dynamics,* Spring, 1973.

Pugh D.S., D.J. Hickson, C.R. Hinings and C. Turner : The Context of Organisation Structure, *Administrative Science Quarterly,* Vol. 14, 1969.

Quick J.C. and J.D. Quick : Organisational Stress and Preventive Management, McGraw- Hill, New York, 1984.

Quickel Stephen W. : Forget Managers :What We Need Are Leaders, *Business Month,* January, 1989.

Quinn James Brain : Managing Innovation : Controlled Chaos, *Harvard Business Review,* May-June ,1985.

Quinn James Brain : Managing Strategic Change, *Sloan Management Review,* Vol. 21, 180.

Quinn Robert E. and John Rohrbaugh : A Competing Values Approach to Organisational Effectiveness, *Public Productivity Review,* No. 5, 1981.

Quinn Robert E. and Kim Cameron: Organisational Life Cycles and Some Shifting Criteria of Effectiveness : Some Preliminary Evidence, *Management Science,* Vol. 29, 1983.

Ramaswamy N. : Is Stress a Distress ? *Indian Management,* November, 1989.

Ramnarayan S., T.V. Rao and Kuldeep Singh (Eds.) : *Organisation Development* (Interventions and Strategy), Response Books (A Division of Sage Publications), New Delhi, 1998.

Rangaswamy G. and D. Helmick : A Comparative Study of Indian and American Executives' Leadership Styles, *Indian Administrative and Management Review,* July-September 1976.

Rao T.V. HRD, Audit, Response Books, New Delhi, 1999.

Rao T.V. and D.F. Pereira : *Recent Experiences in Human Resources Development,* Oxford and IBH, New Delhi ,1986.

Reddin William J. : *Managerial Effectiveness,* McGraw-Hill Book Company, New York, 1970.

Reynolds G.S. *A Premier of Operant Conditioning,* Foresman, Glenview, Ill, Scott, 1975.

Robbins Stephen P. : *The Administrative Process,* Printice-Hall of India, New Delhi, 1994.

—: *Organisational Behaviour,* Printice-Hall of India, New Delhi, 2000.

: *Organisation Theory : Structure, Design and Applications,* Printice-Hall of India, New Delhi, 3rd Edition, 1998.

Roethlisberger F.J. : *Management and Morale,*Harvard University Press, Cambridge, Mass, 1941.

Roethlisberger F. J. and William J. Dickson : *Management* and the Worker, Harvard University Press, Cambridge, 1939.

Rokeach M. : *The Nature of Human Values,* Free Press, New York, 1973,

Rosenberg M. J. : A Structural Theory of Attitude Dynamics, *Public Opinion Quarteryly,* No. 24, 1960.

Ruch Floyd L. : *Personality and Life,* Scatt Foreman, 1963.

SainiDebi S. and Sami A. Khan : *Human Resource Management* (Perspectives for the New Era), Response Books, New Delhi 2000.

Saxena G. : Organisational Change, *Management Review,* Vol. 1, 1985.

Schein Edgar H. : *Organisational Psychology,* Printice-Hall of India, New Delhi, 1987. : *Organisational Culture and Leadership,* Jossey-Bass, San Francisco, California, 1985.

Sekaran Uma : *Organisational Behaviour : Text and Cases,* Tata McGraw Hill Publishing Company Limited, New Delhi, 1989.: The Path to the Quality of Life, *Prajnan,* 1986.

Sekhar R.C. : *Ethical Choices in Business,* Response Books, New Delhi, 1997.

Senge P.M. : The Leader's New Work : Building Learning Organisation, *Sloan Management Review,* Vol. 31, 1990.

—: How to Build a Learning Organisation ? *World Executive's Digest,* May 1992.

Selye Hans : *The Stress of Life,* McGraw Hill Book Company, New York, 1976.

Shepherd Clovis R. : *Small Groups,* Chandler, San Francisco, 1984.

Shetty Y.K. : Managerial Power and Organisational Effectiveness : A Contingency Analysis, *Journal of Management Studies,* Vol. 15, 1978.

Shukla Madhukar : *Understanding Organisations* (Organisational Theory and Practice in India), Printice Hall of India, New Delhi, 1996.

—: *Competing through Knowledge* (Building a Learning Organisation), Response Books, New Delhi, 1997.

Simon Herbert A. : On the Concept of Organisational Goal, *Administrative Science Quarterly,* June 1964 : *Administrative Behaviour,* Free Press, New York, 1966.

Singh Anup K., Rajen K. Gupta and Abad Ahmad : *Designing and Developing Organisations for Tomorrow,* Response Books, New Delhi, 2001.

Singh Pritam : *Occupational Values and Styles of Indian Managers,* Wiley Eastern, New Delhi, 1979 : Chief Executive.

—: Role and profile, *Indian Management,* March 1985.

Singh Pritam and A. Bhandarkar : *Corporate Success and Transformational Leadership,* Wiley Eastern, New Delhi, 1990.

Singh Pritam and K. Parthasarthy : Conflict Management Strategy – A scenario of Avoidance, *Abhigyan,* Auteem 1985.

Sinha J.B. : The Automation Leadership : A Style of Effective Management, *Indian Journal of Industrial Relations,* 1976.

Stogdill R.M. : *Handbook of Leadership,* Free Press, New York, 1974.

Stogdill R.M. and Alvin E. Coons (Eds.) : *Leader Behaviour* : Its *Description and Measurement,* Ohio State University, Ohio, 1957.

Tannenbaum R. and S.A. Davis : Values, Man and Organisations, *Industrial Management Review,* Vol. 10, 1969.

Tannenbaum R. and Warrent H. Schmidt : How to Choose a Leadership Pattern, *Harvard Business Review,* May-June ,1973.

Taylor Frederic W. : *The Principles of Scientific Management,* Harper & Brothers, New York, 1911.

Terry George R. : *Principles of management,* Richard D. Irwin, Homewood III, 1988.
Thompson J.D. : *Organisations in Action,* McGraw-Hill, New York, 1967.
Tichy Noel : *Transformational Leader,* John Wiley and Sons, New York, 1990.
Tichy Noel and D.D. Ulrich : The Leadership Challange : A Call for the Transformational Leader, *Sloan Management Review,* Vol. 26, 1984.
Torbert W. : Learning from Experience, Columbia University, New York, 1973.
Trice Harrison M. and Janice M. Boyer : Studying Organisational Cultures Through Rites and Ceremonials, *Academy of Management Review,* Vol. 9, No. 4, 1984.
Turnstall W.B. : Cultural Transition at AT & T, *Sloan Management Review,* Vol. 25, 1983.
Tushman M.L. : A Political Approach to Organisation : A Review and Rationale, *Academy of Management Review,* No. 2, 1977.
Umiker William : Powerful Communication Skills : The Key to Prevention and Resolution of Personnel Problems, *Health Care Supervisor,* March, 1993.
Urwick Lyndall F. : *The Theory of Organisation,* American Management Association, New York, 1952.
—: The Word Organisation, *Academy of Management Review,* January, 1976.
Varma Madhurendra : *Managing More Effectively,* Response Books, New Delhi, 2001.
Venkata Ratnam C.S. : *Globalisation and Labour - Relations Management,* Response Books, New Delhi, 2001.
Virmani B.R. : *Managing People in Organisations,* Response Books, New Delhi, 2001.
Vroom Victor H. : Can Leaders Learn to Lead, *Organisational Dynamics,* Winter, 1976.
Vroom Victor H. and Arthur G. Jago : *The New Leadership : Managing Participation in Organisations,* Printice Hall, Englewood Cliffs, New Jersey, 1988.
Vroom Victor H. and Philip Yetton : *Leadership and Decision Making,* University of Pittsburgh Press, Pittsburgh, Penn, 1973.
Walton R.E. and J.M. Dutton : The Management of Interdepartmental Conflict : A Model under View, *Administrative Science Quarterly,* Vol. 14, 1969.
Wayne Sandy J. and Robert C. Liden : Effects of Impression Management on Performance Ratings : A Longitudinal Study, *Academy of Management Journal,* Vol. 38 No. 1, 1995.
Weber Max : *The Theory of Social and Economic Organisation,* Free Press, New York, 1947.
White R.W. : Motivation Revisited : The Concept of Competence, *Psychological Review,* Vol. 66, 1959.
Wrapp E.H. : Good Managers Don't Make Policy Decisions, *Harvard Business Review,* September-October, 1967.
Wrong D.H. : *Power : Its Forms, Bases and Uses,* Harper & Row, New York, 1980.
Zaleznik R. : Power and Politics in Organisational Life, *Harvard Business Review,* May-June, 1970.
Zalkind S.S. and T.W. Costello : Perception : Some Recent Research and Implications for Administration, *Administrative Science Quarterly,* 1962.
Z and D.E. and R.E. Sorensen : Theory of Change and Effective Use of Management Science, *Administrative Science Quarterly,* Vol. 20, 1975.
Zigon Jack : Making Performance Appraisals Work for Teams, *Training,* June, 1994.